*Training Research and Education*

# TRAINING RESEARCH AND EDUCATION

## Robert Glaser, Editor

### With Chapters by

Glenn L. Bryan
John B. Carroll
Launor F. Carter
Meredith P. Crawford
James Deese
Philip H. DuBois
Paul M. Fitts
Edwin A. Fleishman
Norman Frederiksen
Robert M. Gagné

Thomas F. Gilbert
Murray Glanzer
Robert Glaser
Arthur A. Lumsdaine
Robert B. Miller
Alfred F. Smode
Robert M. W. Travers
Theodore R. Vallance
Clark L. Wilson

SCIENCE EDITIONS®
John Wiley & Sons, Inc., New York

Publication as a Science Editions paperback authorized by Columbia University Press.

First Science Editions printing 1965

Science Editions Trademark Reg. U.S. Pat. Off.

PRINTED IN THE UNITED STATES OF AMERICA

# PREFACE

One of the essential obligations of a society at peace is the education of its members. It is also true that an essential mission of a military establishment during peacetime is the training of its personnel. Both education and training have a common basis in the findings of psychological research. This book examines training research accomplished by experimental psychologists, and considers its implications for education in general.

One of the major trends in psychology over the past 15 years has been the increasing employment of scientists for research and development on psychological problems of interest to the military services. In 1948, the Directory of the American Psychological Association indicated that there were 98 psychologists working for the Departments of Defense, Army, Air Force, or Navy; this represented about 2% of the 5,000 members of the APA at that time. In 1957, a minimum estimate of 729 psychologists were listed as working for agencies of the military departments; this represented almost 5% of the 15,000 members of the APA during that year. In relation to the number of positions in universities and colleges, this figure meant that there was one full-time psychologist in military work for every 6.5 academic psychologists. This trend was further extended by a contract research and development program to universities, colleges, and research organizations amounting to approximately $5,000,000.[1]

A good portion of the work performed by the individuals involved in this effort has been devoted to research and development in problems of training and the underlying phenomena of learning that are involved. The results of this endeavor are obviously relevant not only to specialized military problems, but to civilian education and to the science of learning. A unique aspect of this activity is the fact that an increasing number of persons trained in experimental psychology have been turning their attention to the problems of training and education. In the light of the expressed concern of the United States with education, this meeting of science and education is of great interest.—The purpose of this volume is to present a representative account of the training research that has been carried out and to examine its implications for psychological research and for training and education.

[1]Melton, A. W. "Military psychology in the United States of America." *Amer. Psychol.*, 1957, *12*, 740-746.

In 1959, Dr. Denzel D. Smith, then director of the Psychological Sciences Division of the Office of Naval Research,[2] and I discussed the problem of collecting and integrating the results of investigations in training research that existed in widely scattered publications which were issued as government report series, contractor reports, and professional journal articles. It seemed to us that some stock should be taken of gains and losses and of promising paths and avoidable detours. We finally decided that one way to accomplish this was to assemble the leading men in the field and have them report on their research findings and experiences. As a result of this decision, a contract was awarded by the Office of Naval Research to the University of Pittsburgh for the purpose of accomplishing this, and I agreed to take on the job of prevailing upon the time of a number of very busy research psychologists. A working conference was arranged which met at the University of Pittsburgh in February 1960. In preparation for this conference, each of the participants prepared a chapter for a book in an assigned area of interest. Before the meeting, the chapters were distributed to the other conference members and in particular to one member who prepared a detailed critique.

At the conference, over three days and nights, authors presented a summary of their chapters, the chapters were then critiqued, and the group as a whole discussed them. Discussion was intense and incisive. Interest was high enough so that a special late night meeting was called to discuss a persistent concern which arose in the course of discussion, that of the problem of a task taxonomy for the behavioral specification of training objectives (and this theme reappears in many of the chapters). Armed now with his colleagues' commentary, each author went back home to edit and revise his writing. When all the completed chapters were returned to me, I prepared an additional chapter to serve as a general integration. This book, then, is the product of this endeavor.

As editor, my major debt is to the chapter authors, many of whom graciously put up with my attempts at editing for some continuity of style and for flow of content. They were reinforcing to work with and I found their ideas quite stimulating.

My debt to Dr. Denzel D. Smith is very large, since it was his encouragement that helped generate the volume and support for the conference. For participation during the conference and his advice during the course of preparing the book, I wish to express my sincere appreciation. Appreciation is due to those who assisted in planning and carrying out the conference, Dr. David J. Klaus, who served as conference coordinator,

---

[2]Now Deputy Head, Office of Institutional Programs, National Science Foundation.

and Kaye Hamilton, the conference secretary. Special acknowledgment is made to Margaret Fullick for her invaluable assistance in all the details of reading and editing the manuscript.

I am indebted to the Department of Psychology of the University of Pittsburgh, in particular to Dr. Robert A. Patton for his encouragement and helpful arrangements in carrying out this project. My appreciation is also due to Dr. John C. Flanagan, whose devotion to the application of psychological research at the American Institute for Research has done much to stimulate my interest in training and educational research problems.

I am also grateful to Mary Ann Malinchak for her assistance in the preparation of the manuscript and to Gil Dannels for the drawings and graphs that are included.

Robert Glaser

January, 1962
Pittsburgh

# TABLE OF CONTENTS

*Training Research and Education*

Chapter 1 | Psychology and
Instructional Technology

Robert Glaser[1], University of Pittsburgh

The process of training and education is concerned with techniques and procedures for guiding and modifying human behavior. A student comes to school with a past history that manifests itself in the ways in which he performs at the time of entrance. It is the task of the teacher and the school environment to enable the student to leave a school term with new or modified ways of behaving, so that he can now read a book and answer questions about it, translate a foreign language, repair a piece of electronic equipment, diagnose a disease, do research on atomic structure, or produce a work of art. The purpose of an educational system, with its teachers, textbooks, audio-visual aids, teaching machines, and so forth, is to create the conditions that will cause this new or modified student behavior to occur. The practical task is to perform certain operations, generally referred to as "educational methods" or "instructional techniques," that result in definable changes in accordance with specified instructional objectives.

It is the thesis of this book that the process of behavioral modification called training and education should be built upon the findings and consequent technological implications brought about by research in psychological science, just as in other fields where there is a continuum of effort from basic science to practical endeavors. This continuum ranges from fundamental exploratory research, to applied research, to technological development, through the specification of work-a-day methods of practice. By and large, movement along this continuum from psychological knowledge to educational practice has not taken place. Basic psychological research has been carried on and teaching practices have been de-

---

[1]Dr. Glaser also serves as Research Adviser for Training and Education at the American Institute for Research.

veloped in the presence of a hiatus between the two endeavors. The borders of this hiatus define a "no-man's land" of educational research. It is an area in which relatively few have been trained to tread. The desired objective in this area is the application of what is known about the science of behavior to educational psychology and educational practice, and as a corollary, the feedback of practical problems to scientific research.

The point being made is that, for the most part, educational psychology to date has not fruitfully interacted with its basic science counterpart, the science of learning. Experimental psychologists and educational psychologists are trained in different academic worlds and in different universes of discourse. As a result, educational psychology and the teaching practices it generates have not been closely nurtured by their mother science. Often, old-fashioned practices, long de-emphasized, are still applied and the potential of new developments is often not recognized. However, signs of the times indicate that the interaction of science and technology is important and essential. In recent years, more experimental and learning-theory oriented psychologists have been working on education and training problems. The number of psychologists employed by the government and by private organizations to work on education and training has increased manyfold. The approaches these individuals have made to problems and their records of success and failure in the application of the methods and knowledge of their science have important implications for education in general.

In the universities, educators and experimental psychologists are talking to each other more than ever before, and joint appointments are being encouraged. Increased research support is beginning to be available for joint research ventures. A number of schools and colleges are in the midst of experimenting with radical curriculum changes—not so much as to subject matter content, but with respect to teaching methods. Professional articles have encouraged this *rapprochement* between the "science of learning and the art of teaching." It is this *Zeitgeist* that has produced the chapters in this book. These chapters report contributions which range along the continuum of effort from basic research to research applications. They represent the work and thinking of psychologists who have been concerned in various ways with the interaction between psychology, particularly the science of learning, and educational practice.

Few will disagree with the proposition that the science of learning is fundamental to instructional technology. However, it is true that these two endeavors have different goals. Basic science espouses a philosophy of ignorance, emphasizing how little is really known and the necessity for discovery. In contrast, applied science and technology concentrate on how much is known and how this can be incorporated into practical procedures. The progress of basic science does not insure systematic and fruitful interplay between basic knowledge, applied research, and subsequent technology. Unless someone works at it, there seems little reason to expect direct transfer of laboratory findings and direct application of theoretical formulations to training and educational practice. The analogy used by Estes (1960) is useful here, that is, the relationship between the science of learning and education is more like that of physiology to medicine than like medicine to the patient. Expectations of a more direct relationship will be and have been a source of disappointment. Psychology can supply findings which offer leads for applied research in school learning, and this can lead to a body of teaching practices—but there must be active research and development concerned with implementing this transition from scientific knowledge to practical technology.

As such a technology comes into being, the artful and creative potential of each teacher can be enhanced. Outstanding performance in teaching and training, as in any profession, is achieved by those who, in addition to a firm grounding in a communicable technology, possess a high degree of creativity and inspiration. At the same time, however, the highest achievements in any profession are likely to be realized only when they build upon a well-developed technology. The underlying concept involved in developing this instructional technology is that the processes of teaching and learning can be made an explicit subject matter for scientific study. The work reported in this book represents only a beginning of the sort of effort that is needed to implement the consequences of this point of view and to develop the technology of instructional methods that it can generate. By way of introduction, this first chapter considers the following: the distinction between training and education, components of the instructional process, and the plan and content of the book.

## TRAINING AND EDUCATION

Since the contents of this book have been, in large part, the outgrowth of *training* research sponsored by the military, and since it is suggested that much of this effort is quite valuable for civilian *education*, it is desirable to discuss the words "training" and "education." Much controversy has centered about the meanings of and differences between the operational consequences of these two words. In American education much has been made of the distinction between vocational *training* and a general *education*; in higher education, between professional *training* and a liberal arts *education*. Since the basic concern in both training and education is the modification and development of student behavior, the distinction between these two words is best examined in terms of the instructional operations utilized to modify this behavior. The position can be taken that training and education can be so defined that they both constitute a part of the instructional process. The training component can refer to the aspect of the process which is concerned with teaching students to perform similar or uniform behaviors such as teaching them to add, to read, and so forth. However, over-laying this training component is the fact that students display individual differences, and that some will add more quickly while others will read with more expression, etc., as a result of outside variables over which the instructional system has little control. On this basis of individual differences, it is the responsibility of the system to guide the student's behavior in accordance with individual talents. This developing of individual differences can be referred to as the educational component. The teaching process can then be considered to consist of both base-line training *and* education which capitalizes on individual differences.

Although there is much disagreement on the matter, when one examines the common usage of the two words, the distinction between training and education is usually made in two ways. (*a*) The specificity of the behavioral end-products. When the end-products of learning can be specified in terms of particular instances of student performance, then instructional procedures can be designed to directly train or build in these behaviors. When the end-product behaviors cannot be specified precisely because they are too complex or because the behaviors that result in successful accomplishment in many instances are not known, then the individual is expected to transfer his learning to the performance of the behavior which was found difficult to analyze. Obviously, schools do not train for every instance of behavior that will occur in the future, but they rightly expect that individuals will generalize or transfer their behavior to similar and novel instances. A distinction between training and education being made here is the amount of transfer involved and the precision with which the behavioral end-products are specified. If the end-products of the learning process can be rather precisely specified, as, for example, learning to use a slide rule, then it can be said that the student is being trained to use a slide rule. On the other hand, if the behavioral end-products are complex and present knowledge of the behavior makes them difficult to specify, then the individual is educated by providing a foundation of behavior which represents approximations to the behavior it is wished that the student will eventually perform, e.g., being a creative scientist. (*b*) Minimizing vs. maximizing individual differences. A second distinction between training and education has been referred to above. This is related to the fact that training with reference to specific behaviors implies a certain uniformity. Individuals are taught to perform similar behaviors, and they learn to do so within the limits of the variability introduced by individual differences. Education, on the other hand, attempts to maximize individual differences by teaching in such a manner that each individual eventually behaves in a way singular to him on the basis of the groundwork of a basic education. As a result, individuals learn to create, invent, and solve problems in non-uniform ways. Civilian education and military training involve problems of both education and training.

One resolution of the training-education distinction is the following. Training and education are two aspects of the teaching process. The two terms refer to two classes of teaching processes that are not mutually exclusive. Certain dimensions which form the continuum along which the distinctions fall are specificity of behavioral goal, and uniformity vs. individual development. Although one may wish to distinguish between "training" and "education" in terms of behavioral goals and the methods of attaining them, the technological practices required to carry out either are built upon principles for modifying, developing and guiding behavior that are generated from behavioral research. In the various definitions of the two verbs "to train" and "to educate," the underlying similarity is "to develop or form by systematic instruction." The term "instruction" seems to be a word which can refer to the general operations with which both training and education are concerned. In this sense this book is about research in instruction and "instructional technology."

## COMPONENTS OF THE INSTRUCTIONAL PROCESS

The chapters in this book are organized around a general (and simplified) conception of an instructional system. The system is analyzed into the following components: (*a*) Instructional Goals—the System Objectives, (*b*) Entering Behavior—the System Input, (*c*) Instructional Procedures—the System Operator, (*d*) Performance Assessment—the Output Monitor, and (*e*) Research and Development Logistics. The structure of the system is diagrammed in Figure 1.1.

The development of the system is initiated with the specification of the goals of instruction. These goals constitute the objective to be

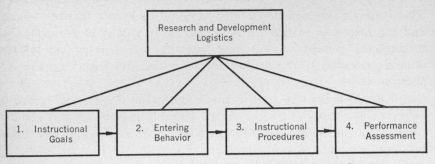

FIGURE 1.1.  The Component Phases of an Instructional System

accomplished and the purpose for which the system is to be designed. The main input into the system, upon which it is designed to operate, consists of the entering behavior of the student. This consists of the initial repertoire, aptitudes, and prior educational background with which the instructional process begins. The next phase constitutes the actual instructional procedures and experiences which are employed to guide and modify behavior. The final phase in an instructional situation is some sort of "quality control," that is, assessment of the extent to which the end-of-course behavior has been achieved by the student in the light of the kind of performance required by the specified instructional goals. These phases are the main flow of the instructional system, but it has many feedback loops and subsidiary inputs. The information obtained in each phase supplies data which are useful for monitoring and correcting the output of the preceding phase; for example, measurement of the kind of performance achieved can provide information for redesign of instructional procedures, and information on instructional procedures can interact with the characteristics of the entering behavior. Feeding in to all phases are the results of research and development. The implementation of these results and the fruitful interplay between research and development, on the one hand, and the operating aspects of the system, on the other, involve important logistical considerations. With this overview of the instructional system in mind, each of the components will now be considered in more detail.

## Instructional Goals and Terminal Repertoire

A first step in the designing of an instructional system is the specification of the purpose and objectives to be achieved. In an instructional system, the "end-product" is the behavior of the student.

This behavior involves the subject material presented to the student and the responses to this material that he is taught to perform; the instructional process is concerned basically with the subject matter stimuli presented to the learner and with the responses he makes in their presence.

A distinction must be made between instructional goals and terminal behavior. The goals of education are desirably long range and involve complex human behaviors and aspirations. Specification of these goals involves philosophical and ethical considerations for which the educator must share responsibility as a member of society. However, in this book, discussion is limited to considerations of instructional technology, i.e., the procedures for behavioral modification through systematic instruction when certain objectives are specified (although technique and objectives, the means and the ends, are intimately related). Primary concern is with the methods by which instructional objectives need to be developed and described in order to assure their attainment in an instructional system, rather than the establishment by the community and the educational society of the nature of educational goals.

In contrast to the broad question of educational goals, "terminal behavior" is defined as the performance that the student should display at the end of a specific instructional situation. There can be minimum levels set for attainment and maximum levels left for individual initiative. When a minimum achievement level is established, it is the task of the instructional system to get most individuals to that point. In military and industrial training, minimum levels are required for the optimal functioning of complex man-machine systems, and the instructional situation must be arranged to accomplish this. In civilian education, minimum levels are required for entrance into a higher and more complex educational level. Within all of this, however, the instructional system does not preclude the "realization of individual talent and potential" and the development and exercise of creativity, inventiveness and artistry. Certainly the instructional situation must be arranged to permit these abilities to grow. Nevertheless, it seems possible that, as a result of systematic study, the terminal behaviors which foster or indicate that this growth is taking place can be identified. Such student performance should be specified, clearly recognized, and actively developed by an appropriate instructional situation. If eventual creativity in a subject matter is an instructional objective, then the terminal behaviors which are related to this comprise the specific behaviors to be elicited in an instructional situation.

Terminal behavior, then, is the end-product objective of a particular instructional situation, and the procedures of instructional technology should result in definable changes in student behavior which approximate this end-product. In order to be appropriately developed, the responses of the learner should be operationally specified in so far as possible. In the learning laboratory, when the psychologist studies the development and control of behavior, the task to be learned is carefully analyzed and described. Perhaps one of the indications of the lack of interaction between experimental psychology and instructional practice is to be seen in the fact that the educational literature indicates a concern with such terms as "readiness," "understanding," the "whole child," and so forth. Certainly these are important words and need to be analyzed because the behaviors they refer to are amenable to experimental attack and manipulation only when they are behaviorally defined in stimulus and response terms, i.e., specific subject matter situations and observable student performance. This has been a necessity in the work of experimental psychologists in developing laws of learning; increasingly, larger and larger units of behavior such as concept formation and problem solving are being studied and analyzed in such terms. In contrast, there has been a general reticence among educators to submit student responses to analysis in stimulus-response terms.

It is an interesting commentary that when experimental psychologists have turned their attention to training research in the military, they have been concerned with the lack of explicit specification of the behavior under consideration and have attempted to develop techniques of "task analysis" for behaviorally specifying performance objectives. When confronted with this endeavor, the psychologist had to face up to the fact that a definitive terminology for behavioral description was not available nor foreseeably forthcoming from the science of psychology in the immediate future. Much concern has been expressed over this basic lack, and, at present, the development of a taxonomical scheme for specifying the properties of the task to be learned and the objectives of instruction is an urgent problem (Melton, 1959; Bloom, 1956).

## Initial or Entering Behavior

The behavior brought to the instructional situation is the raw material input from which the end-product will be shaped. These initial behaviors need to be assessed and made explicit so that they can be used as the basis on which to guide student performance. The objective of instruction is to take the student from this initial repertoire to the terminal repertoire. Assessment of entering behavior usually is made with aptitude and achievement tests which are used for student selection, placement, and guidance. Such tests are used as predictors of performance that occurs during or at the end of an established course of study. In most cases, tests are employed to weed out individuals who are likely to be unable to attain the specified terminal behavior under the instructional conditions and time allowed in a particular training establishment. It is also possible to determine the best combination of instructional objectives, entering behavior requirements, and instructional procedures in order to achieve overall organizational goals with maximum utility (Cronbach & Gleser, 1957). These aspects interact so that test selection standards and the time, cost, and characteristics of instruction can be varied to permit optimal functioning of the system. In the military services, for example, the tasks assigned to the various personnel that contribute to the accomplishment of a particular mission may be reorganized so that either more or less rigid selection and training standards are required. This can permit the more intensive training of specialists on particular job aspects while certain portions of their former jobs can be assigned to individuals who have less time available for training. In civilian life, the shortage in certain professions might benefit from such an arrangement. In education at the high school and college levels, advanced placement programs and the use of college professors in high school courses are further indications of the result of consideration of the interaction between entering behavior and other components of an instructional system. It is not impossible to envision different colleges that require two, three, four, or five years of attendance that all bring their students to a somewhat similar level of terminal behavior. Such schools would require different initial repertoires for their entering classes, as assessed by various tests of achievement and motivation, and they would have different long-range educational goals.

*Instructional Procedures*

In a particular instructional situation, instruction begins with the student's entering repertoire and ends with the terminal repertoire with which the student leaves the situation. During the interval between these two points, instructional manipulations and learning experiences take place in the course of which the student emits responses which guide him toward the terminal behavior. The behavior elicited from the student by the teacher for this purpose can be called auxiliary behavior. The instructional process is concerned with the utilization of auxiliary behavior in order to approximate the desired educational objectives. This process is facilitated by determining, for various stages of learning, the subject matter stimuli, e.g., words, paragraphs, symbols, formuli, etc., to which the student must respond and the kind of response required to each of these, e.g., solving problems, writing, building something, etc. These activities must be specified in terms of observable behavior so that appropriate feedback can be obtained by the teacher for use in further instruction. While the precise specification of behavior may be limited by an inadequate descriptive taxonomy and by a lack of psychological knowledge in analyzing complex behaviors, it seems possible to outline to some extent such things as behavior development through reinforcement, readiness, the guidance of learning, transfer, practice, understanding and reasoning, and motivation, in terms which permit instructional control and which also permit research on the instructional guidance of complex behavior. Since the heart of the instructional process is the actual procedures and techniques used in shaping and modifying behavior, and since this is also a main concern of the science of learning, a brief examination of some points of contact between the two is relevant here.

At the start, the point of view should be expressed that the application of current *theories* of learning will be less fruitful at the present time than the application of current *findings*. To illustrate, almost all psychologists of learning, regardless of their stand on some form of reinforcement theory, would agree with the empirical statement of the role or reinforcement in the acquisition of behavior. Vigorous disagreement, however, shows up in theoretical interpretations of the empirical findings. Most of the recent work on teaching machines and programmed learning is an example of the application of findings about the effects of reinforcement. The empirical facts have been known for some time but only recently quite seriously applied in the development of instructional devices.

*The Guidance of Learning.* As has been indicated, guidance during the instructional process is concerned with the way in which student responses are employed in the course of auxiliary behavior leading to terminal behavior. Several notions can be considered here. First, *the transfer of stimulus control over a response.* At the beginning of a learning sequence, subject matter stimuli are used to evoke responses that are already in the initial repertoire that the student brings to the teaching situation. Instruction takes place when the student proceeds to perform stimulus-response combinations that are different than these. What happens in the course of auxiliary behavior is the gradual transfer of responses to new stimuli and the bringing of new or extended responses under new stimulus control. The gradual transfer of behavior to new stimuli is what happens, for example, in teaching spelling. The word which the student reads is first shown in its entirety, then the student supplies the missing parts until he can write the whole word in the absence of contextual stimuli and in the presence of spoken or pictorial stimuli. The notion behind this response transfer has general application to educational technology, and the specifics of the process are a matter for investigation (Taber & Glaser, 1961).

A second notion is *response prompting.* When the initial repertoire is specified, the instructional procedure can utilize only these available responses. The instructional task is to get the student to emit small increments in response which move in the direction of the terminal behavior. It is sometimes thought that the successive approximation procedure employed in a Skinner box is a useful paradigm here. The analogy is useful up to a point. In a Skinner box, one often waits for certain behaviors to occur which are in the direction of the terminal behavior and then reinforces these responses. In the classroom it is more efficient to supply a variety of stimulus materials which prompt out appropriate behavior that can then be appropriately reinforced. The use of prompting to enable students to emit new or low strength responses with a minimum of errors appears to be an important consideration in the development of instructional procedures. The occurrence of a response is made probable when the presentation of instructional stimuli is designed so that each learning step makes the correct response in the next step more likely. The probability of such success is increased by the use of prompting stimuli based upon what is known about the student's initial response repertoire at a point in learning. The characteristics and uses of response prompts and cues are interesting areas for research and analysis.

Related to response prompting is *the withdrawal of cues* in the course of auxiliary behavior so that the student eventually responds to the form of the stimuli desired in the performance of the terminal repertoire. In the course of an instructional procedure, response prompts are gradually eliminated in so far as required so that the student learns to perform in the presence of minimal or covert cues and in the absence of seeming external prodding. Teaching machine programs refer to this withdrawal process as stimulus fading or vanishing (Skinner, 1960). Research is required in various subject matters on specifics of this process such as the rate, repetitiveness, sequencing, etc.

A third parameter of response guidance in instructional procedures is *the form of the response* emitted by the student. There has been much pseudo-controversy on this aspect in research on teaching machines. In his early work on self-instructional scoring devices, Pressey employed multiple-choice responses. In his recent work, Skinner has emphasized the role of constructed responses. Psychological experimenters, however, alert for a controversial variable, have rushed to test the effectiveness of these two "points of view." In reality, the basic assumptions of both Pressey and Skinner do not make one kind of responding more correct than the other. It is again a function of where the student is to go, the desired terminal behavior. In the development of instructional procedures, however, the form and encoding of the responses can be an important matter. For example, multiple-choice responding is much easier to evaluate objectively, write-in responses permit more subjective evaluation, and covert responses leave little data for analysis. However, the mode of response needs to be considered in relation to the task to be learned (Evans, 1960; Coulson & Silberman, 1960; Holland, 1960). Future research must investigate the relationship between particular forms of response and stated educational goals. To be considered in this research is the effectiveness of response modes at various educational levels and with various aptitude patterns.

*Readiness.* Involved in instruction are behaviors imposed on subject matter learning such as paying attention, learning to learn, readiness, etc. These extra-subject matter behaviors also require explicit definition before they can be manipulated by specified instructional procedures. An illustration of this point is the contrast between the concept of readiness employed in education and the notion of "learning to learn" as studied by Harlow (1949). Readiness is generally considered to be some function of maturation and previous learning, but has been rather ill-defined as specific responses that can be brought under the control of instructional procedures. Learning to learn, on the other hand, is concerned with intertrial improvement in the course of learning and has been brought more fully under experimental control than readiness. As a result, "learning to learn" defines a learning principle that is more ready for inclusion in an educational technology than "readiness." This distinction is discussed by Estes (1960).

*Reinforcement.* There seems little doubt at the present time that a significant aspect of educational technology will be the management of reinforcing operations. As has been indicated, this should continue to be so despite the on-going development of learning theories to explain the process of acquisition. The central role of reinforcement in the acquisition of behavior is a long-standing empirical fact. Notwithstanding the various interpretations in terms of "law of effect" and "contiguity," the operations employed in the course of manipulating the acquisition of a response are similar for the study of both types of explanatory theories. The concept of reinforcement states that behavior is acquired as a result of a contingent relationship between the response of an organism and a consequent event. Or, put another way, reinforcing operations are those which lead to acquisition when appropriately correlated with response occurrences. In general, "In its factual sense, reinforcement refers to any of a wide variety of conditions which may be introduced into the learning situation to increase the probability that a given response will reappear in the same situation" (Kimble, 1961 p. 137). Both basic and applied research in learning are concerned not so much with what reinforcement is but with how it operates. What both endeavors can supply is a description of the variables which determine the effectiveness of certain reinforcing operations for achieving desired terminal responses.

Work in the science of learning has pointed up certain facts about reinforcement which seem to be firmly enough established so that they can be utilized in the applied investigations which lead to the development of an instructional technology. One of the facts about operations that are reinforcing is that there is an event that takes place as a consequence of the occurrence of a response. It seems obvious, then, that a principle in the design of instructional procedures should be the establishment of such a reinforcing contingency. This contingency is influenced by several factors in the learning situation. For example, it is necessary that a sufficient number of reinforced response evocations occur in order that the response is strengthened, i.e., its probability of occurrence is high in appropriate situations. A further well-established finding concerning response acquisition is that the contingency between a response and a reinforcing event must be an immediate one. Delay of reinforcement may result in little or no learning. In instructional devices, this known fact about the delay of reinforcement has been taken most seriously in the development of teaching machines and programmed instruction. In school learning, one major reinforcing event for the student is "knowledge of results," that is, knowledge about whether or not the response he performs is a result considered correct. In programmed learning techniques, such confirmation is immediately forthcoming upon the completion of the student's response. The need to implement this fact of learning in educational technology is emphasized by the frequent delay of reinforcement that occurs in many classroom procedures.

Another finding in the study of reinforcement is the effect of the intermittency or scheduling of reinforcement contingencies. Essentially this refers to the fact that reinforcing events occur with different frequencies and in different patterns in the course of learning sequences. While a great deal of activity has concentrated on this aspect of reinforcement, it has had little applied development in educational procedures. It has been indicated (Skinner, 1938; Keller & Schoenfeld, 1950; Ferster & Skinner, 1957) that with an optimal schedule of intermittent reinforcement, higher and more stable rates of responding can be attained than with continuous reinforcement. Estes and his students have shown that the responses of individuals seem to be highly correlated with the overall proportion of reinforcement to non-reinforcement in a learning task. Estes (1960, p. 760) states this finding in this way ". . . the probability of the response will approach the probability of reinforcement. Thus we might expect that . . . if it were the case that 90% of English nouns encountered by a student formed their plurals with 's' and 10% with 'n', we could expect that the student would form the plural of a newly encountered noun with 's' about 90% of the time." The effects of intermittent reinforcement probably vary with the kind of task being learned. The implication, however, for instructional procedures is that the effect of this factor is influential and requires applied research for appropriate practical implementation.

*Interference and Transfer.* As a general premise, it can be stated that interference in learning which results in forgetting and a decreased rate of acquisition is a function of competition between the response under consideration and other responses which have been learned prior to or subsequent to it. The results of experimental study in learning have indicated a number of variables to be considered in this connection. Transfer comes about as a result of stimulus components in several learning situations which are similiar to one another so that the response is generalized among these situations. The education of a student involves, to a great extent, two aspects: (*a*) learning to respond to similar elements in stimulus situations, i.e., to generalize so that all words of a certain class are called nouns, and (*b*) learning to make differential responses to different stimulus situations, i.e., to form discriminations such as differentiating between nouns and verbs. Much instructional procedure involves teaching students to generalize within stimulus classes and to discriminate between class instances. Interference in instruction often comes about in the course of this generalization-discrimination process, and research suggests that this can be overcome by practice sequences in which many response instances are presented which progressively narrow down the discriminations to be made. Such "discrimination sequences" can be used to teach the student different responses to two stimulus situations which in the course of instruction might be confused. The sequence is set up so that the student responds correctly to the appropriate stimulus and also identifies situations in which a particular response is inappropriate. In so far as possible, the student is not permitted to perform an inappropriate response in the presence of a particular stimulus. Such a discrimination series should minimize interference resulting from the similarity of stimulus elements.

Interference may result from the introduction of emotional responses which are incompatible with the response to be learned. The results of learning experiments point up situations in which such emotional behavior is produced. In extinction, a response is permitted to occur in a situation where there are no contingent reinforcing events. As a result, the response attains a low strength and can be replaced by a response which is more frequently reinforced. In the course of extinction, it is noted that emotional or frustration behavior occurs. It has also been found that after a history of continuous reinforcement, the omission of a reinforcement is frustrating and similarly results in certain emotional behaviors which may be incompatible with learning the appropriate response. In the development of instructional methodology it seems desirable to minimize the possibility of the occurrence of such behaviors. A way of implementing this might be to provide a history of intermittent reinforcement and thus subsequent omission of a reinforcing event would be much less frustrating.

In training and education there has been much concern about transfer of training. The behavior of interest in this respect is the ability to utilize one's learning in stimulus situations which differ to some extent from those in which learning occurred. Interference in the application of learning to these new situations often arises. The existence of positive or negative transfer can be presumed to be a function of the generalization-discrimination sequences that occur in learning. The notions of generalization and discrimination indicate that the search for transferable elements is less useful for the development of an instructional technology than is the study of the production of transfer as a result of practice with graded sets of experiences containing a variety of instances with varying stimulus characteristics. This will be further elaborated in the section on reasoning and understanding.

A pervasive body of research in the psychology of learning is the work on interference in verbal learning that is characterized by the investigations of Underwood (1960) and others. Here the effect of a host of factors on the learning of a restricted class of verbal behavior has been studied. These factors include such variables as meaningfulness, task similarity, active recitation versus passive study, affective characteristics of the material, whole versus part learning, and such dependent variables as spread of effect and incidental learning. The relationship of these factors to classroom learning may be difficult to see in a direct manner, but as Underwood (1959) has pointed out, it should be possible to determine their relevance to instructional technology through classroom experimentation.

*Practice and Review.* It is established that review and repetition are necessary in the process of acquisition and for the maintenance of previous learning. The conditions of practice over the course of learning trials are indicated by many of the aspects of learning discussed above. The general implication for instructional procedures is that these procedures must incorporate the appropriate amount of review and repetition necessary to maintain previous learning and to maintain already learned concepts which need to be strengthened and utilized in further learning. Sufficient practice is necessary so that early material is mastered before or while new material is introduced. Practice should incorporate the conditions which facilitate learning. However, for many subject matters, the effects of particular characteristics of practice and review upon response strength and retention are not known and must be determined by empirical classroom investigation.

The distribution of practice has been a very frequent variable in experimental study, and at the present time, many experimental psychologists would agree that learning appears to be most effective, i.e., acquisition is faster and performance levels are higher, when practice is spaced, that is, divided into a number of daily trials (Estes, 1960). This would suggest that instructional techniques should be studied in which practice is interspersed with other aspects of instruction.

*Reasoning and Understanding.* When prescriptions for definitive instructional programs are presented, a frequent statement made by teachers goes something like this: "Yes, the student seems to be learning, but does he really understand?" The reply to this question refers to the observable terminal behavior desired by the teacher. The reply goes something like this: "Tell me what kind of behaviors (perhaps test performance) you would like the student to display so that you know he is understanding and reasoning." With such terminal responses specified, it is then the task of instructional technology to determine what combination of learning experiences (including teachers, devices, and self-study) result in this behavior.

The terminal behaviors defined as understanding, concept formation and concept utilization, and reasoning seem to be brought about by continuous variations of the stimulus context in which the student responds. This stimulus variation can be set up in the instructional process so that the student gradually receives new information, learns to make finer discriminations and appropriate generalizations, and learns to apply his responses to a wide variety of situations. This has the effect of enriching the student's breadth of learning and is an operational way of defining the development of understanding. Instructional sequences can provide a series of well-organized examples by which the student is led to develop abstractions and complicated concepts. As pointed out by Skinner (1959, p. 65), "An important goal is to 'enrich the student's understanding' by inducing him to permute and recombine the elements of his repertoire." At the extreme of these stimulus and response variations, the goal of instruction is really not concerned with the student's response to any one situation. This is only an example of an abstraction. The educational objective is that the student acquire not a uniform and explicit set of responses about the concept, but rather acquire a repertoire which is applicable in a variety of situations so that he can use the concept to solve problems, describe it to others, modify it for certain purposes, build a model of it, and so forth. Such terminal behavior can be defined as reasoning with or understanding a concept. Appropriately designed instructional sequences including various kinds of learning experiences can provide this stimulus and response variation which contributes to the growth of understanding.

*Motivation.* When one measures the usefulness of a learning concept in terms of the extent to which it generates applications for instructional research and practice, the concept of motivation does not fare well. The theoretical and experimental concerns with this concept do not present readily translatable findings. In fact, many leading theorists have avoided the word in their conceptual thinking in the attempt to account for learning phenomena in more operational terms. In view of the state of the concept of motivation, one is tempted to say that motivation includes those events and operations that make a particular response-event contingency reinforcing. Such a statement is, in large part, an expression of ignorance of a variety of factors in the learning situation which need to be identified. Motivation, as studied, has been related to drives which are produced by certain experiences in an organism's history. In the laboratory, the operation of deprivation, e.g., of food and water, has been employed to make certain events reinforcing. It taxes one's ingenuity, however, to see how deprivation can be employed in instructional practice unless it can be conceived as withholding reinforcement. Furthermore, much research is required to investigate the nature and use of secondary reinforcers such as school grades, being correct, approval, and status.

Sometimes the word motivation is used to imply certain behaviors that are the outcomes of instruction, for example, when a student continues to study after the usual classroom hours, when he works on special projects on his own, or when he uses the library to look up topics related to his school subjects. When a student does these things he is often referred to as being "well motivated." When motivation is used in this way it is best to state such terminal objectives in behavioral terms and then introduce instructional practices that produce these behaviors. The judicious use of reinforcement is motivating in this sense. When a student receives frequent reinforcement in the course of learning, he often appears to become very interested in the subject matter and his constant success in handling it makes him act in a way that one would call "motivated." It is of course presumptuous to attempt to talk in any definitive way about the problem of student motivation. Much research needs to be considered such as the effects of anxiety as studied by Spence (1956), the effects of "social conditions," e.g., cooperation and competition, the generalization of motivating effects from one motivating condition to another (Kendler, 1945; Braun, Wedekind, & Smudski, 1957), and the experimental work on curiosity and exploratory drive (Glanzer, 1958). For technological purposes, it seems practical at the present time to define the terminal behaviors which fall into a class called "showing motivation." The task then is to manipulate the instructional situation in a way so that these behaviors can be produced with some degree of consistency.

## Performance Assessment

During a course of instruction and at its end, the performance of the student needs to be measured. Such measurement provides information about the extent to which auxiliary and terminal behaviors have been attained. This information can be used to decide upon the course of subsequent instruction and to determine the extent to which certain standards of proficiency have been reached. In an instructional system there are two primary uses made of the results of performance assessment. One is to provide information about a *student's present behavior;* measurement for this purpose is primarily designed to discriminate between individuals. The second use is to provide information about the *instructional techniques* which produced that behavior; measurement for this purpose is designed to discriminate between instructional methods.

The assessment of performance is desirable in several phases of an instructional system. Measurements of behavior are frequently made, as has been indicated, in assessing the entering repertoire of the student. These measures take the form of aptitude tests or tests of "job knowledge" or "educational placement." However, by placing the performance assessment phase after the instructional procedures in the simplified diagram of an instructional system given in Figure 1.1 the intention is to emphasize the assessment of terminal behavior. As instruction proceeds and particular units of instruction are completed, performance assessment is employed as a kind of quality control in order to determine whether the student has reached or surpassed terminal performance standards that have been established.

Underlying the concept of performance assessment is the assumption of a continuum of subject-matter skills, ranging from low proficiency to high proficiency. A student's performance at a given subject-matter task falls at some point along this continuum, as measured by the behavior he displays during testing. The standard against which an individual's performance can be compared consists of the behaviors which define the points along the underlying skill continuum. Performance levels can be established at any point in the course of instruction where it is necessary to obtain information about the adequacy of a student's performance. The specific behaviors implied by each level of proficiency can be identified and used to describe the specific subject content skills that a student is capable of performing as he achieves a particular level. In this sense, performance measures can be "content-referenced" in terms of specific task accomplishments falling along a continuum of proficiency.

In contrast to content-referenced measures where the performance of an individual is compared with specific subject-matter skills, performance assessment information is frequently expressed in terms of "norms" where a student's performance is compared with or relative to the performance of other individuals. In much of current practice, an individual's *relative* standing along the underlying proficiency dimension is the primary information required and reference need not be made to subject-matter content. Educational achievement examinations, for example, are often used primarily to order students in a class in terms of "grades on a curve." When such "norm-referenced measures" are used, a student's proficiency is evaluated in terms of a comparison between his performance and performance of other members of the group, e.g., in terms of a percentile score. Measures of this kind provide little information about the degree of student achievement in terms of what behaviors he can actually perform. Norm-referenced measures supply information that one student is more or less proficient than another student but do not provide information about how proficient either of them are with respect to the specified terminal behavior of instruction. The distinction made here between content-referenced and norm-referenced measures of the outcomes of instruction is similar to that made by Flanagan (1951) and Ebel (1960). They have suggested that most achievement measures used in education are norm-referenced and thus do not provide the degree of information, *both* order (relative standing) and content, made available by the use of content-referenced measures. In the kind of instructional system being outlined in this chapter, content-referenced scores could supply appropriate information about the adequacy with which a particular instructional situation produces its specified instructional objectives.

## Research and Development Logistics

Superimposed upon the functioning of an instructional system is the entire research and development endeavor. It has been indicated that the outcomes of exploratory research should be subjected to further study and applied research with an eye toward the development of techniques for incorporation in instructional practice. There are two aspects involved in accomplishing this. One is research designed to further basic knowledge in the science of learning, and the other is research and development designed to implement and evaluate new and changing practices in instructional procedures. This latter effort involves implementation and logistical considerations in working with existing educational systems. The chapters in this book discuss both of these aspects, research at various points along the basic-applied continuum, and problems and procedures involved in translating research findings into instructional practice.

### THE PLAN AND CONTENT OF THE BOOK

The purpose of this book is to provide an account of representative research and thinking that has gone on in the context of training research and to examine the implications for education in general. The chapters are arranged so that they follow closely the structure of an instructional system as outlined in this introductory first chapter. The second chapter is concerned with instructional goals and the specification of terminal behavior; later chapters consider the measurement of entering repertoires, research on basic aspects of the learning of skills, the measurement of terminal proficiency, and examples and problems in the implementation and conduct of research in training and education.

*Analysis of Instructional Objectives.* Chapter 2 considers the specification of terminal behavior objectives and is concerned with the development of a schema and techniques for describing and classifying the behavior that the instructional situation should produce in the student. A main criterion underlying the utility of such a scheme for classifying behavior is that it can facilitate the instructional process by identifying the learning properties of a particular class of behavior. The eventual attainment of such a taxonomy would be analogous to a state of affairs in a science where a class name for certain events identifies the laws involved in the occurrence of these events. In chemistry, for example, the use of class names like "acid" and "alkali" identify classes with certain properties that follow certain principles of chemistry. In psychology and education, at the present time, class names like "problem solving," "concept formation" and "thinking" refer to less definitive underlying functional relationships.

*Individual Differences and the Design of Instruction.* In the context of the design of studies in training, Chapter 3 considers the relationship between the testing of initial behavior and learning. A contrast between testing and training is apparent when it is pointed out that in the field of psychological testing there are many practical, technological books, while books on the theory of testing are few. On the other hand, in the field of learning, theoretical books are common, whereas there are few practical books on the technology of training which represent an elaboration of these theories. A further aspect of the relationship between the testing of entering behavior and instruction is that measures of intelligence and general aptitude, often defined as the ability to learn, generally have essentially zero correlations with measures of learning progress. That is, learning ability, or the gain in proficiency from initial behavior to some specified terminal behavior, are often reported to be unrelated to performance on psychological tests. Chapter 3 reports work which investigates procedures of determining the relationship between individual differences and measures of change in an instructional situation.

Chapter 4 describes a program of research on the development of selection tests that are useful for minimizing the number of training failures in certain intensive courses of instruction and which are also useful for providing knowledge about factors contributing to success in training. The general model this chapter describes for studying the prediction of success in training is of special interest when considering an overall instructional system. The model takes account of aptitude and motivation as well as instructional variables. It attempts to suggest the nature of these variables and the way in which they affect the degree of learning. Two main classes of variables are considered: instructional variables such as the adequacy of instructional presentation and the time allowed for learning; and individual variables such as general intelligence, time required for learning, and the amount of time the individual applies himself. Formal relationships between functioning of a specific aptitude test and success in learning are postulated and examined.

*Skill Training.* The next three chapters describe various research approaches basic to the learning and training of perceptual-motor skills. Under the sponsorship of the military services, much research and thinking have gone on in this area. The impetus for this undoubtedly has been the programs of training research concerned with pilot training, the training of gunnery crews, etc. Perceptual motor skills are important aspects of many man-machine tasks in the military, and have been emphasized more in this context than in civilian education. Chapter 5 gives an account of a procedure employing experimental learning situations and the methods of factor analysis for analyzing and classifying the component tasks in complex skills. A set of descriptive categories are set up to describe psychomotor skills. Progressive and systematic changes in these reference categories are identified as practice in a task continues and increased proficiency is attained. Information from the laboratory tasks studied is then related to instructional technology since it seems possible to use this information about progressive changes in skill components in the design of instructional procedures. As it is known that certain task components become important at given points in the development of proficiency, training can be implemented on these particular components at the appropriate time.

Chapter 6 is a consideration of skilled performance in a general sense which includes motor skills. The concern of present-day training researchers in the specification of the behavior that is the object of instruction is again emphasized here, and a preliminary taxonomical schema for skilled performance is presented. General categories for describing skilled activity are discussed in detail and include the degree of gross body movement involved, the extent of external pacing, the stimulus-response relationships, the characteristics of the feedback information, the physical equipment aspects of the situation, and the overall complexity of the activity involved. In addition to laboratory studies, an account is given of the utility of field investigation of the training of skilled performance. Differences between proficiency development in real-life tasks are compared with laboratory tasks. On the basis of research findings, probable phases in the learning of skills are hypothesized and the implication for training considered.

Chapter 7 is a discussion of stress in the context of training research on psychomotor performance. The elusive concept of stress is defined operationally in terms of a class of stimulus events which produce certain common response properties in individuals. In general, with respect to psychomotor skills, stressful conditions are characterized by reports of discomfort, generalized motor arousal such as tremor, increase in the force applied by muscles, shorter latency of movement, increased variability of precision, etc. The effects of stressful conditions can be either inhibiting or facilitating, depending upon the nature of the task being performed. By analyzing how the characteristics of tasks (using the analysis of psychomotor tasks presented in Chapter 5), interact with effects of stress, predictions are made of how task performance is effected. This is a useful notion for training in that it might point to a way of identifying those tasks which are most or least vulnerable to stress effects and can suggest investigations of instructional procedures which could minimize the inhibitory effects.

*Simulators and Instructional Aids.* Chapters 8 and 9 provide detailed analysis and review of instructional aids such as simulators, training aids, and other instructional devices, e.g., teaching machines. Chapter 8 offers a discussion of simulation in the perspective of its purposes and its appropriate use in the course of instruction. A simulator first of all attempts to represent a real situation in which certain learned tasks are to be carried out. A well-designed simulator must provide opportunity for controlled variation of the situation it simulates. In this way it can provide a rich variety of standardized environments and present a more efficient instructional situation than the real-life environment. A distinction is made between a simulator which trains for a very specific purpose and a training device which may have a more general purpose. With such specificity, simulators are optimally used in late stages of training where the consolidation of skill and maintenance of proficiency is required. In the early phases of instruction, learning may not be well-served by attempting to approximate reality. The point is made that it is not equipment that is being simulated, but it is rather a task or behavior; a preliminary attempt is made to classify simulators in terms of the characteristics of the task categories they are designed to represent and to train.

Chapter 9 is a review of the variables and issues involved in research on instructional devices. This chapter departs from the usual classification of instructional media in terms of the kind of device used, such as films, recordings, teaching machines, etc. Descriptive categories based on stimulus and response features of the instructional technique are employed instead. This permits some generalizability of research results and allows similarities and differences in various research studies to show up. The categories used include: student response as a factor in instruction, e.g., the effectiveness of overt response, the form of response, response feedback; guidance and cueing, e.g., prompting and "vanishing" procedures, the effects of demonstration; stimulus characteristics of certain media, e.g., cues provided by animation, pictorial representation and auditory inputs; verbal factors in instruction, e.g., readability, the degree of verbalization; and factors in the organization and content of instructional sequences. For research in instruction, instructional media offer the advantage of reproducible instructional sequences into which a specific variable for study can be incorporated and which remains constant from experiment to experiment. This is certainly not the case with teaching procedures which are not so "packaged."

*The Training of Technicians.* Because of its great importance in military operations, a large portion of the effort in military training research has gone into research designed to improve the training of electronics technicians. A review of this work is presented in Chapter 10. In this work there are many parallels between the problems of military training and education in general. In formal school training, the chapter considers the problem of a core curriculum to fit a man for his future job. The problem involved centers around the decision of whether to provide a general education in electronics principles or more specialized training; the experimental question is that of what kind of generalized training can provide maximum transfer to various types of later job requirements. A common core is suggested which is strikingly similar to the requirements of efficient civilian technical education. Further training problems considered are the continuation of school training with on-the-job training, the transition from school training to job performance, and the implementation of feedback information from the job situation to the schools so that evaluation is provided of the adequacy of instruction for job requirements. Research on the challenging problem-solving task of electronics maintenance (trouble shooting) is described, and a formal analysis of the diagnostic trouble-shooting process is presented. This process is related to diagnostic problem solving in other fields such as medicine and clinical psychology and to psychological research in problem-solving behavior.

*Proficiency Measurement.* The assessment of the performance produced by the instructional process is the topic of Chapters 11 and 12. With the awareness that the predominant emphasis in test development has been on selection and the prediction of future criteria, these chapters concentrate on achievement testing and proficiency measurement. Chapter 11 is concerned with the need for evaluating the outcomes of instruction and the effects of instructional procedures. A major question to be answered is, "Does education produce the objectives it sets for itself?" Appropriate measurement procedures can be developed to answer this only if these objectives are defined in behaviorally explicit terms. A test is defined as a stimulus situation constructed to elicit the kind of behavior it is desired to assess. On the basis of this definition, classes of test procedures are described: soliciting opinions, administering attitude scales, measuring knowledge, eliciting related behavior, eliciting "what would I do" behavior, eliciting lifelike behavior, and observing real-life behavior. A number of examples are given to show the variety of training evaluation problems which can be attacked by tests of the sort which elicit lifelike behavior.

Chapter 12 gives an account of on-the-job measures of performance and the assessment of the criterion behavior which is the object of prediction by selection tests. Three kinds of measures are described: operational performance measures including product measures, measures of specific behavior elements, gross performance measures, inferred performance, and malperformance measures; work samples, considering the reproducibility of the task, the degree of intellectual involvement, and measurement technique employed; and finally, rating procedures. The chapter emphasizes the development of measures that identify specific aspects of the task involved. Appropriate specificity provides both the trainer and the trainee with information that permits them to improve their performance. Gross measures may be useful for the validation of selection tests, but are of little value for instructional feedback. The relative utility of various kinds of specific measures and their characteristics are discussed.

*Training for Multi-Man Systems.* The next two chapters turn to the problem of instruction for group interaction, i.e., the training of teams and of large-scale multi-man systems. Chapter 13 reports a program of research on team training and reviews field investigations of team operation and experimental laboratory studies on the functioning of teams and small groups. The implications of these investigations for team training are then discussed. Several problems are considered: the problem of the definition of a team as an entity for study, the emphasis of most laboratory study on team structure rather than on the instructional procedure required to increase team proficiency, and the problem of assessing team proficiency for the purposes of training evaluation. Critical problems in team performance center around the supervision and monitoring of the output of the team members and of the feedback received by each member in the course of his performance. It is indicated that research on team training procedures should investigate the reinforcement feedback conditions supplied to each team member as a function of the team organization. Once these conditions are identified, the reinforcement contingencies that influence learning can be studied in a way similar to the way they are studied in investigations of individual learning.

Chapter 14 reports the efforts of one of the largest training research and development efforts ever carried out, involving country-wide air-defense exercises. The factors involved in implementing and evaluating such a large training enterprise are described. Two points stand out in this chapter. One is the repeated emphasis on the feedback of information in learning. It appears that the greatest potential for improving performance, particularly the decision-making process involved, lies in the post-exercise portion of training, and an important need is for careful development and improvement of the post-exercise period. The second point is that in the complex learning of large-scale systems such as military exercises and simulated business games, it is difficult to identify the behavior that contributes to the success of the enterprise. As a result it is a complex task to pinpoint exactly what is being learned and what should be learned in the course of a simulated training exercise. This is a realistic problem and analytical research is required to identify the variables which influence system improvement and which suggest appropriate instructional procedures.

*New Developments in Training Research.* Chapter 15 is a compilation of new developments in training research. It reviews the field with broad coverage and includes the work reported in the preceding chapters. The chapter provides a detailed reference source for selected training research publications. Developments are presented under four major topics: ways of determining the requirements for training, ways of providing learning experiences, ways of measuring progress and outcomes of training, and ways of providing knowledge of results. The results of this compilation were presented to the training research scientists participating in the University of Pittsburgh Working Conference on Training Research, and they were asked to judge the present and future importance of the new developments described. The consensus is reported in this chapter.

*The Coordination of Research and Practice.* The final three chapters are concerned with the implementation of research, the acceptance of psychological research into educational practice, and an outline for research endeavors. Chapter 16 gives an account of the operation of a large training research enterprise that generates many of its problems from on-going training programs and coordinates its efforts with them. A model is presented which analyzes a research and development operation in relation to the educational system which it supports. The functional units in the model consist of a problem-posing agency, a research and development facility, logistical support, personnel and materiel, and an implementing agency. The generation of research requirements and the importance of a commitment to the implementation of useful outcomes in training systems are discussed. Additional issues considered include the relationship between requirements for development and requirements for research, the role of the scientist in the solution of practical problems, the extent of analysis required before undertaking a research and development job, and the appropriate administrative position for supporting a training research agency.

Chapter 17 presents a historical and cultural analysis of the reasons why the results of research on learning and educational psychology have had little impact upon bringing about change in educational practice. A number of propositions are carefully documented and discussed: (*a*) While it is often the assumption of educational research that teachers will change if they are shown how their teaching can be more efficient, it is probably true that teacher behavior is the aspect of an instructional system that is least amenable to manipulation. (*b*) Feedback from the results of evaluating student achievement reinforces teacher behavior if the results are pleasant; if the results are punishing, the information is frequently rejected. (*c*) There is a scientific lag between current thinking in psychology and current thinking among educators with respect to psychology. (*d*) Educational "research" is often an activity that is not what experimental psychologists define as "research." (*e*) The present outlook is not greatly encouraging, since the number of experimental psychologists also interested in education is not very great, and individuals working in educational settings are not those necessarily trained in psychological research. In this light, conditions are suggested which are likely to contribute to the impact of scientific knowlege on training and educational procedures.

The final chapter outlines a plan for a coordinated enterprise which involves the activities of individuals doing research and individuals developing the results of research for educational practice. The development of such interaction is the main theme of this book. The chapter proposes a situation in which individuals engaging in basic exploratory research, applied research, and technological development interact with one another and desire to see certain common ends accomplished. Several entities in this enterprise are described: an exploratory research endeavor; a fundamental development entity which pursues exploratory leads and continues the line of continuity from theoretical research to educational practice; a specific development activity which develops prototype models made possible by new principles and findings; a design and proving activity in which operating characteristics are investigated in non-laboratory conditions; and a training and follow-through function in which individuals are trained in the use of the new techniques and participate in their implementation, evaluation, and improvement.

The development of instructional practice on the basis of experimental research is of great importance to present-day society and is of rapidly expanding interest to behavioral scientists and educators. Psychological research in training and education can be of tremendous value for the understanding and improvement of educational methods. It is the purpose of this book to collect together accounts of representative activities by psychologists who have turned their attention to research problems in education that have grown out of the pressures of training in the military services. It is hoped that readers of this volume will come to recognize the importance of the interaction between scientific research in psychology and technical developments in educational practice and will also be stimulated to consider and work on some of the challenging problems for future pyschological research.

## REFERENCES

Bloom, B. S. (Ed.) *Taxonomy of educational objectives*. New York: Longmans, Green, 1956.

Braun, H. W., Wedekind, C. E., & Smudski, J. F. The effect of an irrelevant drive on maze learning in the rat. *J. exp. Psychol.*, 1957, *54*, 148-152.

Coulson, J. E. & Silberman, H. F. Results of an initial experiment in automated teaching. In A. A. Lumsdaine & R. Glaser (Eds.) *Teaching machines and programmed learning*. Washington, D.C.: National Education Association, 1960. Pp. 452-468.

Cronbach, L. J. & Gleser, Goldine C. *Psychological tests and personnel decisions*. Urbana: University of Illinois Press, 1957.

Ebel, R. L. Content standard test scores. Paper presented at the APA Division 5 Symposium on Standard Scores for Aptitude and Achievement Tests, Chicago, September 7, 1960.

Estes, W. K. Learning. In *Encyclopedia of educational research*. (3rd ed.) New York: McMillan, 1960. Pp. 752-767.

Evans, J. L. An investigation of "teaching machine" variables using learning programs in symbolic logic. Doctoral dissertation, University of Pittsburgh, 1960.

Ferster, C. B. & Skinner, B. F. *Schedules of reinforcement*. New York: Appleton-Century-Crofts, 1957.

Flanagan, J. C. Units, scores, and norms. In E. F. Lindquist (Ed.), *Educational measurement*. Washington, D.C.: American Council on Education, 1951.

Glanzer, M. Curiosity, exploratory drive, and stimulus satiation. *Psychol. Bull.*, 1958, *55*, 302-315.

Harlow, H. F. The formation of learning sets. *Psychol. Rev.*, 1949, *56*, 51-65.

Holland, J. G. Design and use of a teaching machine program. Paper read at Amer. Psychol. Ass., Chicago, September 1960.

Keller, F. S. & Schoenfeld, W. N. *Principles of psychology.* New York: Appleton-Century-Crofts, 1950.

Kendler, H. H. Drive interaction: I. Learning as a function of the simultaneous presence of the hunger and thirst drives. *J. exp. Psychol.,* 1945, *35,* 96-107.

Kimble, G. A. *Hilgard and Marquis' conditioning and learning.* New York: Appleton-Century-Crofts, 1961.

Lumsdaine, A. A. & Glaser, R. (Eds.) *Teaching machines and programmed learning.* Washington, D.C. National Education Association, 1960.

Melton, A. W. The science of learning and the technology of educational methods. In K. W. Spence, A. W. Melton, & B. J. Underwood, A symposium: Can the laws of learning be applied in the classroom? *Harvard educ. Rev.,* 1959, *29,* 84-106.

Skinner, B. F. The programming of verbal knowledge. In E. Galanter (Ed.), *Automatic teaching: The state of the art.* New York: Wiley, 1959. Pp. 63-68.

Skinner, B. F. Teaching machines. In A. A. Lumsdaine & R. Glaser (Eds.), *Teaching machines and programmed learning.* Washington, D.C.: National Education Association, 1960. Pp. 137-158.

Spence, K. W. *Behavior theory and conditioning.* New Haven: Yale University Press, 1956.

Taber, J. I. & Glaser, R. *An exploratory evaluation of a discriminative transfer learning program using literal prompts.* University of Pittsburgh, Cooperative Research Project 691 (9417), March 1961.

Underwood, B. J. Verbal learning in the educative process. In K. W. Spence, A. W. Melton, & B. J. Underwood, A symposium: Can the laws of learning be applied in the classroom? *Harvard educ. Rev.,* 1959, *29,* 107-117.

Underwood, B. J. & Schulz, R. W. *Meaningfulness and verbal learning.* New York: Lippincott, 1960.

Chapter *2*  | *Analysis and Specification of Behavior for Training*

*Robert B. Miller, International Business Machines*

The brief history of task analysis procedures has seen several points of view as to what kinds of information should properly constitute task descriptions for training purposes. According to one point of view, given the title Equipment Task Analysis (Miller & Folley, 1951), it is sufficient to describe in procedural detail the quantitative and qualitative characteristics of signal inputs to the operator, and the respective control activations to be made to these inputs in order to meet system performance specifications. It is also necessary to specify the order in which these signal-response units are to be performed. Task description limited to this content is objective and can be accomplished without any background in the behavioral sciences, largely by following formats. It is likely to be suitable as a detailed performance criterion of the position-tasks, and in many respects provide the specification for a comprehensive performance test.

A second school of thought holds that although it is necessary to specify physical performance requirements, they are not sufficient for personnel purposes, including good training design. It is believed that in addition to a physical description of displays, controls and their respective activations, a psychological description is at least desirable if not essential. For example, recall the cliché that the physical stimulus is related to, but not necessarily identical with, the psychological stimulus. Whereas it may be argued that making psychological inferences should be the proper role of the training designer, not the task analyst, it is nevertheless the latter who is most steeped, firsthand, in task information. His purview should better reveal "likely human errors" and performance contexts which make for behavioral difficulties. It should also give him more freedom in perceiving where procedural alternatives exist in the task setting, and which alternative will be optimum from both the operator's standpoint and that of the system in which he acts. Accordingly, this chapter is slanted from the second viewpoint, and emphasizes it rather than the mechanics of stating performance specifications as such. Furthermore, this viewpoint is better adapted to tasks in which control manipulations are symbolic rather than physical, hence apposite to education as well as training.

In the matter of terminology, the term "operator" refers to any person performing any kind of task with an objective goal and outcome. In this chapter he may be a maintenance mechanic, pilot, or a scientist performing an experiment. "Input" is a convenient shorthand for external stimulus events that have bearing on task performance, and "output" is overt work response connected with the task objective. These terms seem to have convenient, shorthand generality; they are not intended to convey any aura of quasi-engineering precision or elegance. "Task" is a partially defined term: any group of activities performed at about the same time or in close sequence, and sharing a common work objective. A position or job is the sum-total of tasks a single person may be responsible for.

## The Subject Matter of Task Analysis and Performance Requirements

For purposes of this chapter, training is defined as the planned sequences of experience leading to proficiency in specified patterns of stimulus-response relationships. Training design may therefore be measured by three major criteria: (*a*) validity, or the extent to which training experiences are relevant as measured by transfer to the job situation; (*b*) completeness, or the extent to which additional on-the-job experiences are not required for reaching job proficiency criteria; and (*c*) efficiency, the relative cost in time, dollars and talent of the training.

The specification of job performance requirements is aimed directly towards validity and completeness of training, indirectly at efficiency in training. Stated in its broadest and simplest terms, a good job or task description is one which specifies what criterion responses should be made to what task stimuli and under what ranges of conditions. This statement is the conceptual heart of any sound procedure for behavior description. To the extent that the terms and the organization of the description refer to principles of learning and transfer of training in the scientific and empirical literature, the task description aids the design of efficient training.

It should be emphasized that task description is an instrument, not an end in itself. Questions to be asked in developing this instrument must include: what are the available sources for task description, how to sample from the practically infinite details and variables with which any phenomenon can potentially be described, how to classify the phenomena, what levels of detail to use, how to structure and organize the information, how to relate psychological knowledge systematically to task information and how to use the information. The answers to the last question should help answer many of the former questions. Note that all these questions deal with validity, completeness or efficiency in task description as an instrument. This chapter is concerned with responding to or amplifying these questions.

## History

Taylor, Gilbreth and their followers a generation ago initiated interest in looking at job behaviors in order to make decisions about the design of task procedures, work-place layout and tools. Gilbreth formalized a procedure for identifying and setting down descriptions of task operations. Adaptations of this procedure permitted the analysis of micromotions in one-hundredth second intervals. These analyses led not only to ideas for improvements, but also to quite precise, analytical measurements of improved performance. Although the usefulness of the method was somewhat restricted to highly routinized and standardized activities, it was an important step toward what later became human engineering as an art and as a branch of study.

After World War II, the Critical Incident Technique as developed and used by John C. Flanagan and his associates for design of selection tests was found to have by-products for training (1954). Data collected from supervisors and peers established priorities in importance for on-the-job activities which were deemed critical to the job. Such data, however, were not complete enough to frame a total pattern of training requirements, and, since they assumed an operator and observer, could not be used to anticipate training requirements for newly designed systems. The Critical Incident Technique may be a valuable adjunct to other methods in that it focusses attention on job behavior as such (as opposed to judgments about what a man "should know in order to do the job"), and on judgments as to what behavior makes for success or lack of it where the latter is indicative of human "errors."

In the early 1950's, the Air Force recognized the need for training personnel to parallel the later stages of development of new equipment. The purpose was to reduce the lag in time (sometimes amounting to several years) between availability of the equipment and trained personnel to operate and maintain it. Support was given to study contracts for developing procedures for anticipating maintenance and operator job requirements from pre-production data about equipment under development. Concepts and procedures were developed and formalized under the general term of "task analysis."

In the years that followed, and up to the present date, considerable controversy has been expended on formats and symbols for entering behavioral information. But whereas much effort has been expended in criticism of these clerical factors, relatively little creative energy has been directed towards the more fundamental problems of what can, and what cannot, be expected of task information, or how to mate the problems of training design with those of behavioral description and analysis, or of the inherent logical problems of any classification structure and operational validity. It seems fair to say that in task analysis the format has largely been confused with the concept. Perhaps this has come about partly because practitioners (and their critics) have often treated behavioral and task description as an end in itself. A moment's reflection should show that task analysis is useful as a means of aiding the training designer, and that the structure and terms used in communicating the analysis are most useful when they are compatible with whatever mode of conceptualization and decision is (or should be) used in training design.

The perception and description of job requirements in behavioral terms has not been necessary in every training philosophy. This point should be underscored. There is a belief and practice widely extant that formal training teaches a man *about* his job, and that he can learn his job only while serving on the job; formal training "helps him learn his job." In this case, training is equated with education. On the other hand, the philosophy that seeks to maximize the acquisition of actual on-the-job skills and knowledges in formal training demands behavioral information about the job to be taught. This latter philosophy is gaining wider acceptance, especially where cost of training in time, dollars and operational expediency shape policy towards efficiency.

## Training as an Engineering Art

Training is to the behavioral sciences what engineering is to the physical sciences. These application arts may be guided by scientific generalizations, laboratory data and conceptual models, but no specific application is prescribed by "scientific" data and principles. A particular application is an invention—or a copy from some other invention. And an invention is a synthesis of information, often of various kinds. Thus, the selection and organization of a training stimulus pattern for a given response or response sequence is, in some degree, an act of invention, or at least a decision-making choice from some number of options.

If the development of the form and content of training were reduced to a mathematical model of all the variables essential to the design of the teaching enterprise, and if the values of all parameters were known, obviously the information essential to the design of training could be precisely specified in kind and structure. In the absence of such a design model (and its absence implies the need for decision-making and inventive processes), the gathering, classifying and organizing of input information to training design must, of necessity, be heuristic rather than precise. This point of view has significant bearing on procedures and indexing schemes for task information.

Training, like the psychology of child-raising, has many fads and local prejudices depending on subject matter. When a man is taught to drive, the instructor usually comes straight to the point and gives him practice in the various tasks of driving. The man is not given the physics of traction, or of internal combustion engines. But when he is taught to become a ham radio operator, he virtually learns how to design and build the equipment which the task requires only that he operate. Training in many areas of human endeavor includes much of what seem, from objective standards, initiatory and tribal rituals. Thus an actual description of performance requirements may often seem meager and trivial when compared with the ritualistic forms of training which are provided the trainee. Science may guide the art of training by helping to differentiate the irrelevant and ritualistic from the essential.

## Major Classes of Training Decisions

Information about the requirements for training is useful if it aids in making decisions in the design of training. A review of the nature of these decisions should help specify what information is needed.

*What are the criterion performance requirements?*—In other words, what responses are required to what stimulus ranges and patterns in the tasks which make up the job? When this information is stated so that the stimuli can be controlled and representatively sampled, and the output responses categorized and measured, one can specify when training has been completed to the point of job proficiency. This task criterion information should (but does not necessarily) point out the priorities of relevance in the content of training.

*What sources of stimuli and what response controls to represent?*— What are the physical objects and situations to be represented actually or symbolically, or both, in teaching the skill; and what are the objects to be manipulated actually or symbolically in learning and performing the skill? In a perceptual-motor task, either discrete or continuous, these are the displays and controls.

*What stimuli to sample?*—It is practically impossible to represent in training all the combinations and permutations of cues and stimulus conditions that the job incumbent will encounter in operational performances of the tasks on which he is being trained. From what universes of cues and conditions should samples of stimuli for training be drawn and organized into patterns for exercise material or for job "knowledges." The stimuli will usually need to include environmental conditions, "noisy" messages, or messages with gaps and misleading errors, if total training for job proficiency is the objective.

*On what behaviors should there be concentrated effort?*—Assuming that it is unrealistic for the student graduate to be able to cope successfully at once with any and all potential job situations, what priorities should be established in training, and how should they be established?

*By what means to encode capability in the student?*—Should all elements of the task or tasks be proceduralized and taught the student by repetitive rehearsal so that they can be performed "automatically" on signal? Should they be taught and performed from a set of self-instructions or rules? Or should the content be taught as conceptually associated principles, apperceptions and strategies from which the student deduces what responses to make when confronted with particular job situations? And under what conditions should various of these alternatives be combined?

*What training media to use, and how?*—These decisions deal with the mode of practice offered the student in acquisition of job knowledges and skills.

*How to sequence training?*—This is the pattern of what will follow what from the student's first day to his graduation and the acknowledgement of his job proficiency.

*Requirements of Behavior and Performance Information*

The last two topics cited above are not germane to this chapter, the concept of encoding capability is on the borderline of training technique. The objective of task requirements information (in the context of training) is to provide essential data for answering the first four questions and possibly the fifth. But the concepts and formats for setting down task information should serve the training specialist in additional ways. They should be a guide to the collection of information and, as a guide, be a good compromise between standardization and flexibility. They should remind him of what kinds of information to get.

Furthermore, the way the information is set down should assist him in holding in mind what he should take into account in making training design decisions such as are summarized above. These data should combat prejudices and ritualistic practices as to training content by enabling him to perceive what is relevant and non-relevant. Thus the organization and encoding of performance requirements is important to the training designer. If his memory is sufficient, and if he has no need for communication or cooperation with other training officers in the project, obviously there is no particular need to write down task information. But where a number of specialists are to work from a common reference, that reference is likely to be a written document. Task information is not only a communal guide to training decisions, but a set of operational stipulations for the training enterprise.

## The Parts of Tasks

The archetype image of a "task" which frequently springs to mind is that of a man feeding a punch-press, a pilot manipulating a joystick in a landing maneuver, a mechanic unfastening a cover-plate. Such examples rarely convey the behavioral richness and operational contexts of real life any more than the statement "tracking the right half of a roadway" connotes what one has to do in driving an automobile. This section examines some of the parts which, in degree, are characteristic of nearly every task when viewed in job context. (Another report [Miller, 1956b], has used the following topic titles as a first step to "part-task training," and elsewhere as a very preliminary cut at a task classification scheme.) For lack of a better term, these parts of tasks can be called "task functions."

### Nomenclature and Locations of Work Objects and Symbols

The ability to recognize work objects by appearance and name, and conversely to conceptualize their appearance or function by name, is a necessity in following instructions. The instruction may be given by another, read from a text, map or chart, or it may be recalled self-instruction. The displays and controls of the work space are examples; features of the environment which serve as cues or which must be operated in (clouds to the pilot, wet roads to the driver) are other examples. Even where it is practicable to reduce all elements of a maintenance task to written and pictured procedures which a "schoolboy" could perform, the schoolboy would nevertheless have to learn to identify by name, appearance and location considerable numbers of work objects before he could successfully carry out the instructions. Much on-the-job learning is complicated because the incumbent is trying to learn operations with an imperfectly mastered vocabulary of terms and their references. He is in the situation of trying to make associations between nonsense syllables. Conceptualization is poor, hence recall is poor.

On the other hand, task learning may be unnecessarily complicated because the learner has not distinguished between those work objects, or features of them, which provide relevant displays (discriminanda) and controls (manipulanda) as opposed to those which are irrelevant to his duties. Information irrelevant to task performance may sometimes be excused as providing mnemonic benefits; task irrelevance more likely will act as "learning noise" in acquisition and transfer of skill. In summary, it is important to determine the manipulanda and discriminanda which are task-relevant, their nomenclature and their identifying features, for purposes of task description. The means by which they are taught is, of course, a matter of training design.

## Scanning, Search and Detection of Task Relevant Cues

Scanning and search imply the active inspection of data and data sources for information that requires some form of action that may be overt as in a manipulation, or covert as in decision making. The radar operator, the reconnaissance observer, the mechanic reading a diagram while troubleshooting, the foot soldier on patrol, an inspector, a typist abstracting from a message—all these perform this function. In some cases a principal component is vigilance; it may be detecting the onset of a critical signal through perceptual noise; it may be looking for the exception from a standard; or the search may be a cue that fills in or supports a concept, hypothesis or stage in strategy. Scanning and search for, and of, response feedback is also an important ingredient in effective performance on the job, and of course, a requirement for efficient on-the-job learning and maintenance of proficiency.

Except where the task function of search and detection is obviously central to the task, such as in vigilance and inspection activities, relatively little attention seems given to it in formal training, except as incidental to other exercise material. And because of the usual antiseptic conditions of task stimuli provided in training, there is likely to be little contained in the exercise material. Yet virtually every task has some element of scan and search, even those tasks which are considered routine. Perhaps this is why immediately after graduation, the novice on the job seems so literally disoriented.

Scanning and searching are likely to be particularly difficult habits to maintain when these are activities that must be time-shared with other ongoing activities which, because they are ongoing, may be more compelling to the operator's attention. The constriction of the perceptual field, and (by definition) constriction of the field which is being actively scanned, may lead to errors ranging from nuisance value to mission failure and loss of human life. Tolman has given this phenomenon the eloquent titles of "strip maps" and "tunnel perception." Search was recognized by Gilbreth as a type of therblig in the tasks studied for time and motion analysis.

## Identification of Cue Patterns

The detection of a task cue and its identification may often seem to be part of the same act, and in many cases there is little pragmatic value in differentiating these functions. But the maintenance mechanic may detect an out-of-tolerance condition and fail to associate it with some peripheral symptom and thus fail to diagnose a fault quickly. The reconnaissance specialist may detect an "unusual" stimulus without identifying its nature. Identification is an objective way of referring to one kind of "interpretation."

Identification may interact with scanning behavior. In many cases the proper identification of a condition or object requires the delay of a consummatory response until more information comes in. The operator must, after detecting the first cue, refrain from judgment until he has searched for additional cues and additional sources of cues. This is often the case in identifying a machine malfunction. It may be the only basis by which he can read through perceptual noise, since the "message" is likely to have far more redundancy than its component signals taken separately. The act of identification may, in important operations, require verification. Because verification tends to delay the consummatory behavior, whatever it may be, it is a habit difficult to teach and readily disinhibited in the Pavlovian sense, and not likely to be learned by the student after a few of even very dramatic feedback occasions.

The task should be examined so as to bring out how best to maximize the redundancy available to the operator. An example is that of teaching the typist to scan a major portion of a sentence at a time, rather than single words or a fixed number of words at a time. As the Gestalt people point out, pattern seems easier to perceive, generalize and remember than elements of patterns—obviously because patterns usually have more redundancy than the sum of the components taken separately.

Training in scanning and identification of job-relevant stimuli should therefore include practice in identifying sources of such stimuli in an optimum sequential fashion, in grouping signals, in recognizing in- vs. out-of-tolerance indications, and in reading signals through perceptual noise of various kinds. The qualitative and quantitative characteristics of the perceptual noise likely to be encountered in task operations should be carefully ascertained for some degree of simulation during training. External noise may be environmentally produced, or occur as a function of task performance. Internal noise to adequate perception and identification may come about through selective attention (preoccupation), false hypothesis on the part of the operator, motivational stress or physiological disturbance. An attempt should be made to anticipate the operational conditions, both external and internal, that may produce inaccuracies and inadequacies in perception.

A special type of identification is that which requires a one-to-one decoding by the operator such as translating telegraphic code, or of typing or keypunching from source information. In such cases, accuracy and output rates and ratios required for criterion performance should be ascertained and specified. Samples should be obtained (or predicted) of worst case conditions of unusualness of message and of the various disturbances and delays that may occur in the input messages. These disturbances require flexibility on the part of the operator in "reading ahead," and in monitoring his own output. These skills are not likely to be acquired in classroom exercises from clear and legible inputs. Training, by the way, should include practice in what the operator should do when, in the course of transcribing messages, he detects that he has made an error.

## Short-Term Recall

Short-term recall is the retention of information which is peculiar to a particular occasion on which a task is performed, and which is essential to performing one or a series of task-relevant responses. The pilot who bears a number of instrument readings in mind while deciding what is wrong; the waiter who memorizes a series of orders from diners; the words of text perceived "at a glance" by the typist who types them as a group; the briefed and observed information which, in combination, leads to a tactical decision by a platoon commander: these are examples of short-term recall. Few tasks, except those which are repetitive and routine in the most strict sense, are free of short-term recall requirements, and few classes of behavior more conspicuously differentiate the novice on a job from the "old professional." Whether superior short-term retention of task information comes about through acquired associative mnemonics, "familiarization," "meaningfulness," or the development of implicit "patterns"—or by some other hypothetical phenomenon—is beside the point here. Direct practice of the task insofar as it requires short-term recall peculiar to that task is essential to the development of increased capability.

Short-term recall may be likened to a buffering capability where information is temporarily stored until used. To the extent that the limited channel capacity of the human is used up by active rehearsal of short-term information, there is less channel capacity available for other information processing. Such processing may consist of problem solving with that information, or storage of additional short-term information. A more simple-minded way of saying this is that the more information a person can bear in mind at the same time, the more complex the problem he can solve, or the more extensive the series of responses he can execute, or the more flexibility he has in sequencing and monitoring his responses of execution. There is likely to be a close linkage between ability at short-term recall and ability to recognize or identify the "meaning" of a complex arrangement of disparate cues.

Effective short-term recall is almost certainly an important determiner of rate of that learning which involves the recallable subject matter. This suggests that considerable emphasis be placed early in learning on nomenclature and identification of work objects, cues and responses. Older writers would call this phase of learning "familiarization." The attempt here is to treat it as a learning mechanism rather than an explanatory phenomenon. In any event, it is clearly desirable to specify, for analytical purposes, what seem extraordinary short-term recall requirements in tasks and positions under study so that provision can be made to insure adequate practice in training.

## Long-Term Recall of Procedures

Whereas short-term recall refers to memory of events peculiar to any specific cycle of task performance, long-term recall refers to memory of stimulus-response relationships applicable to virtually any occasion on which the task is performed. In this context, the paradigm is "when X, do Y." In computer language, it is the "computer program." Examples of long-term recall include: conceptualization and verbalization of task procedures, cause-effect relationships, precautions, logical procedures, rules, policies.

In general, the derivation of long-term recall requirements is determined in a straightforward manner, e.g., what self-instructions describe a check-out procedure, or a loading procedure, or procedures for cleaning a rifle. Long-term recall requirements sometimes impose performance difficulties which should be noted. The following are examples:

*When S-R's are not in routine sequences.* When the performance of the order of steps in sequence is conditional on a variety of factors, recall is likely to be more difficult than where one step is a direct mnemonic for the next step.

*When precautions should be taken.* Precautions are necessary when human or machine failure or error may produce hazard or relatively irreversible results, and where the error may have appreciable likelihood of occurring. Human errors may occur through error or failure in scanning and detecting, identifying, short-term or long-term recall, decision making, manipulation, or in combinations of these factors. Precautions obviously should be built into habit systems through training rather than added as afterthought warnings.

*When a procedure is rarely performed.* A major liability in requiring the human monitor to take over an automatic function is that, through lack of practice, his skill grows rusty. Response to emergencies, which usually requires rapid thinking and action, has the same liability. Attention may need to be given to special mnemonics and redundant habit systems to help guarantee recall (Craig & Miller, 1957). Thus one can require sufficient practice to make the perceptual-motor relationship practically automatic—that is, performed without mediating self-instructions between external stimulus and overt response. A habit system redundant to automatized response would be verbalization of the procedure. Another habit system, redundant to the other two, would be conceptualization of what the display-control arrangement does with respect to the mechanism or the environment.

For example, how to make an emergency engine shutdown to a fire warning signal should be known so well that the pilot "could do it in his sleep." In other words, the series of S-R's is automatized. In addition, however, the pilot should have a verbal memory of each step in the procedure, so that if his motor memory falters, his verbal memory (which may also be motor but should involve different muscles) acts as a crutch. In other words, he should be able to verbalize the procedures without making the control movements, and in the absence of the display and control objects. His visualization of what the fire is doing in the engine and what mechanical or electrical action is brought to bear by manipulating respective controls will act as a mnemonic for his verbalization of the procedures. In order to train for habit redundancy, the task analyst must obtain the information essential in shaping the redundant habits. But increments in reliability of performance are likely to be obtained rather expensively through the burden of teaching redundant habits. For this reason, the information going into the redundant habits should be considered discriminately where training time and dollars are important.

It should be remembered that, at least in adults, performance of acts during initial stages of learning is largely by self-instruction, that is, verbalization of the stimulus-response relationship. This verbalization or conceptualization mediates the external stimulus and overt response —provides an associative link between them. But with continued repetitive practice (which probably needs to have some proper balance between massing and spacing) those mediating processes tend spontaneously to drop out and the overt response is made "automatically" to the task stimulus. The advantage to the behavioral economy is enormous. Response automatization frees the naturally limited channels of conceptualization and verbalization for other activities such as scanning ahead (thus permitting anticipatory action), or for more extensive monitoring of the task scene, or for scrutiny of response feedback, or for improvisation and decision making.

It is therefore desirable that the task analyst make estimates of the rate and variety of display-control interactions required of the operator as well as the varieties of symbolic information which the operator must process at about the same time. From these estimates, at least qualitative statements can be made as to the habits which need to be automatized in order to meet task requirements with respect to rate of output. Mediational activities, besides using up channel capacity, also take time. On the other hand, automatized behavior is likely to be stupid, relatively inflexible to changing conditions. The generalization gradient is likely to be restricted. Therefore practice of automatized responses should probably be made to a wider range of task-representative stimuli than might be required if the performance were conceptually mediated. Concepts and verbalizations tend to have broader generalization, speaking practically, not theoretically, than motor habits as such. These trade-offs need to be considered.

## Decision Making

"Problem-solving situation" is here defined by the behavioral processes rather than the external nature of task conditions. The reason for this non-objective definition, for purposes limited to this chapter, will become apparent in the text.

In the design of human behavior mechanisms, as in the design of computing machinery, a large memory storage may be traded off against computational complexity and speed. One can memorize the multiplication table, say, of all two place numbers, or can learn how to compute them through arithmetic operations of serial addition. An intermediate course is to memorize the multiplication table of one-place numbers and multiply larger numbers by a combination of this memory and use of computation rules. Observe that some memorization (program storage) of the computing procedure is required. Depending on the associations that need to be acquired in order to perform the task—and also on individual differences in verbal "intelligence"—there will be cases in which training will be more efficient if the trainee memorizes the table of specific stimulus-response pairs of "When X, then Y," or "When X plus Y, then Z," and so forth. In other cases, memorization and/or conceptualization of the logical rules for converting task data into problem solutions may be more efficient in reaching a training objective. The factors here would be the relative number of items in the table to be memorized and applied.

There are performance tradeoffs as well as training tradeoffs between solution by "table look-up" versus solution by computation. It can be expected that the table look-up will produce answers more rapidly than computational procedure. It will be done with less "channel capacity" —that is, the association between "11 times 12" and "132" may be so immediate and direct that one can "think about other things" while summoning the answer. Thus if solutions must be found while the operator must time-share his attention, there may be no alternative to memorization of the table as opposed to computation. But there are also disadvantages to "learning by principle." If the "principle" or logical procedure for solving a problem is forgotten, it will be impossible for the operator to produce any answers at all to that entire class of problems. He will not even have neighboring values from which to make interpolations or extrapolations. Unless he has learned and can recall a "superordinate" set of principles from which to deduce the necessary operating principles, he cannot reconstruct a forgotten rule or concept. Even if the logical procedures and concepts are remembered, errors may occur in short-term recall during the logical operations. He may improperly sequence the logical operations with disastrous results.

The major advantage in learning by concept, principle or generalized procedure is that the operator can solve problems which contain terms he has not previously encountered. The operator who has memorized the square roots of all two-place numbers is totally lost in providing a square root for a three-place number, whereas the computational procedure can generate an answer to any member of the problem type. Thus in problem-solving tasks where there are large numbers of alternative situations and response alternatives, there may be no practicable option but to teach by general procedure or principle. The demand on intelligence is likely to be greater where problem-solving operations are required, thus restricting selection of personnel. Untalented people have to be taught by direct memorization of answers to questions arising in task operations. This does not rule out the possibility that a simplified or superior training technique cannot be found whereby the principle can be more easily learned and applied.

It is likely that any set of non-routine activities can be associated with many different kinds and orders of "principles" and concepts. Some orders are likely to be much better than others. For example, in electronic troubleshooting, theoretically, and in some cases practically, what has been called a procedural cookbook can be prepared to apply to any symptom or pattern of symptoms. All steps for localizing any trouble from its symptom are laid out, and can be either memorized or sought in a manual. An opposite extreme is to teach in detail the theory of operation of the machine and let the maintenance mechanic discriminate what information is relevant to troubleshooting in general, or a particular problem of the moment, and deduce procedures and strategies for localizing the trouble from peripheral symptom to replaceable part. The retention, discriminations and deductive capabilities thus taxed rarely produce effective results on the job. Various middle courses may be pursued in laying out and teaching task requirements. For example, one may abstract data flow from test point to test point in the equipment, describe sequencing and timing of signals, and teach a set of strategy rules that will optimize the selection of test points that provide most information per next check in converging on the trouble. An example of such a rule is the so-called "half-split" principle. Tests are made at successive check points where each test splits in half the probability that the trouble will be found on one side or the other of the check points chosen. This strategy may be expanded to include the variable of time to make the respective checks. Although the rule may be clear, its application may still require discriminations and compromises, and in some cases may be inadequate. Nevertheless, a generalizable procedure is provided the student. The procedure furthermore provides a mesh for distinguishing relevant from irrelevant information to the problem-solving process: this is likely to be significant both for the training and the operational economy.

Consider now the less deductive and somewhat more constructive types of decision making where there is no single "right" answer. Examples are the platoon leader thinking out a defensive strategy in enemy territory, or the business executive attempting to plan a profit-making course of action for his company. These people may be provided with a large store of information, gained through trial-and-error exposure to symbolic and real-life situations, from which they "intuit" decisions. Or task and operations analysts may determine what variables of input information are important to the selection of response options, what the priorities and interactions of these variables may be, how to search for data pertinent to these variables, and finally develop some principles or rules for selecting or combining response options into a decision, or a series of decisions. In current terms, the analyst generates a "model" for the decision type. In some cases the model may look deceptively like an equation. The utility of such a model for training is apparent. It provides an associative reference whereby the student can relate, interpret and recall experiences in dealing with specific problems. He may test and modify his own concept of the model. The task analyst should search for exceptions to the model, so that training may inculcate a balance between standardization and flexibility in following, changing and even rejecting the model in real-life situations.

The fatuous charge is often made that some students and operators perform on an "intuitive" basis better than other operators who use procedures and procedural principles. The analogue is the rejection of selection tests because sometimes a good man is rejected and a poor man accepted, that is, the fallacy of generalization from the dramatic instance. The training objective (unless compounded with a selection objective) is to get the best mean performance from the entire group to be trained, and to do this most efficiently.

The relatively large number of paragraphs given here to decision making seems justified on the basis that training for the decision-making functions of tasks and jobs is often accomplished poorly and naively. This is in opposition to training in perceptual-motor skills and in message identification and translation types of performance. In the formulation of behavioral models for decision making in job-tasks, it seems necessary for the task analyst to take responsibility. Presumably the source information for constructing such models is directly available to him, and only indirectly available to the training officer. Admittedly, this role requires the task analyst to combine the knowledges of operations analyst, psychologist and training specialist. But that is a general thesis of this chapter. Whereas some examples of format for task analysis have outlined "decision trees," the problems cited are of a deductive rather than constructive nature. In the former, one variable can be handled at a time (sequential binary choices), and the information is of a "yes-no" type. Where it is applicable, the decision-tree structure is an excellent tool for description and training purposes.

## Motor Response

Whereas it makes sense to think of part-task training centering around various of the task functions thus far described, it is of course meaningless to think of teaching motor behavior without stimulus considerations. There are, however, features of motor activity as they relate to manipulation of controls that justify some mention in the interests of performance efficiency and accuracy.

The task analyst should perceive problems involving the differentiation and coordination of body members and muscle groups. These problems tend to be more apparent in tracking tasks, less apparent in tasks that require discrete S-R's, whether in conjunction with a tracking task (such as turning on headlamps while driving a car) or otherwise (such as playing the piano). Thus, where practicable, pre-positioning of the body member on the next control to be activated is good procedure. There are procedures for best using the body's center of balance and body members as levers for mechanical advantage. Precision in small movements may be obtained by using the frictional resistance of the moving body member sliding against a solid, or pivoted on a solid base. The task analyst may perceive and describe groups of motor movements that make a good pattern of motion from the standpoint of bilateral symmetry, sequence of flexion and extension, or sequence of tension and relaxation. By describing these, he may suggest both training content and training procedure.

But of perhaps most significance in examination of motor behavior is the spotting of "error-likely" situations. Some of these may be hazards arising from reflex activity or preoccupation, e.g., the exposed high voltage terminal adjacent to an adjustment point. Others may generate operational error such as: negative transfer producing incorrect control activation; improper anticipatory movements that result in the omission of a last step in a procedure; violation of "population stereotypes" in control movement. Still other motor problems arise from physical constraints on movement.

One might take a human engineering check list and wherever violations of good practice are uncovered, note a special training situation. The perceptive task analyst may spot motor performance problems that are specific to a particular task context and which do not appear in the human engineering check list. Determination or estimate of likely human errors suggests special considerations in training for programming and response evaluation. Where an error tendency may occur rarely, but be catastrophic when it does occur, it is obviously desirable to give elimination of this tendency more emphasis than it should get if "frequency of operational occurrence" is the basis for selecting exercise material.

### THE COLLECTION AND ORGANIZATION OF TASK INFORMATION

*Sources of Task Information*

The proper first source of task information should be the statement of system performance requirements in which the task or position is embedded. This statement, if complete, should provide both the context of operations in which the task is to be performed, and some quantitative time limits within which various functions must occur. Human engineering information should be a prime source of data based on considerations during system development. Specific performance data from human engineering research may be available. The rationales for the psychological factors in the system design could, under ideal conditions, provide a major portion of the behavioral analysis.

In systems under development, engineering blueprints and design statements have had practical value in projecting task requirements. Much better are studies based on mock-ups and simulators which permit direct observation by the analyst, even though simulation is incomplete. If handbooks of instructions are available, they are valuable insofar as the instructions are valid; however, this is not always the case, and the analyst may have to test their validity as best he can by having the instructions followed in simulated task situations.

Where the system is already developed so that the tasks are actually performed in operational context, direct observation is an additional and important source of task data. The analyst should be warned that not even the best performers of the task behave in an optimum fashion; he should be alert to using his psychological and operational background in hypothesizing improvements in procedure, even though this may take him into "human engineering" activities.

Task information may be supplemented by interviews in which "critical incidents" are reported by operators and their supervisors. These incidents are accounts of outstanding and ineffective behaviors experienced or observed in performing the task. And since tasks are rarely unique, information can be obtained about the class characteristics of similar tasks as taught and performed in present and past systems.

## Organization of Task Information

Organization of task information should proceed from the general to the particular, and from the more critical to the less critical. In their simplest terms, the functional requirements of a task, or of a position, can be stated in the following set of terms: (*a*) the kinds and amount of output required, with tolerance limits for rate and accuracy described with respect to each important variable in the output, (*b*) the input variables, conditions and situations, and (*c*) the work objects which the operator is to use in transforming task inputs to task outputs.

Requirements, stated in these qualitative and quantitative terms, will be recognized as criteria. Meaningful criteria are relationships between input and output conditions; it is meaningless to state criteria solely in output terms unless the input context is tacitly assumed. For practical purposes, tacit assumptions dealing with criteria should be explicit. Rarely can all of the task requirements be identified with the quantitative precision implied above. It is likely to be worth the effort to do so. For example, the rate and accuracy of a typist lend themselves readily to objective test. "Neatness" of copy may not, when considered as a single attribute. But neatness can be reduced to amount and proportion of respective margins, number of strikeovers, discernible differences in darkness of characters, number of discernible erasures, number and size of dirtmarks per page, page edges crimped or bent. As specifics are increased, counting becomes easier.

There may still remain aspects of performance which are unmeasurable in ways that are both objective and meaningful: the "good will" of the customer to the salesman, initiative, care of tools and equipment. It is somewhat easier to measure such factors when people are performing than to stipulate them precisely for tasks in advance of actual performances. Comparable measurements can be made only of events or products that are standardized with respect to each other. Thus one act of invention is not likely to be equivalent to another. To the extent that patterns of behavior are unique to the occasion, or to the individual, they are not measurable in the hard-boiled sense. And there are kinds of performance which, to the extent that they are reduced to a behavior formula, cease to retain the important part of their character; cooperation, initiative, improvisation and invention are examples. Task variables which are intrinsically resistant to direct measurement, either in procedure or outcome, can be called the "heuristic variables" of the task. Heuristic variables may sometimes be important, and therefore should be recognized by the task analyst, and indicated as selection and training "requirements." Extreme caution should be used in citing heuristic variables since they confess an inadequacy of description by the analyst which is likely to be compounded by an equivalent inadequacy in training technique. Instances of the required behaviors and the contexts in which they occur should be specified. (As in the case of neatness, attempts to measure the factors and operations connoted by the heuristic variable may be successful in reducing the stimulus and response ambiguity of the variable.)

There are many cases in which it is desirable to identify training requirements before there is someone actually performing the tasks. The following comments are intended to cover such circumstances. The terms may suggest a man-machine task, and, whereas this is the reference, applications can be extended to any circumstances where input-output relationships through the human link can be specified.

## Determining the Operational Consequences of Position-Task Performance

Rarely does a task constitute an end in itself. The same may be said for a job-position. In order to determine what is relevant and irrelevant in task and position performance and to establish priorities, some consequence boundaries should be established. In man-machine situations, these can be called system outputs, and when stated as quantitative input and output relationships of variables (with respect to the system entity) they are system criteria. The term "system" is, of course, relative, and may mean any pattern of objects and humans that, according to some plan or set of procedures, is required to perform a specifiable mission. Whereas a pilot's tasks are performed in connection with an aircraft and its missions, a secretary's tasks are performed in a "system" which includes her manager and his departmental organization.

It is advisable, and usually imperative to establish the operational criteria of the team complex of which the operator is a member, whether the complex consists of the man and the machine he uses, or a man working with other men with or without a machine environment. Determine the criterion variables and their quantitative limits of acceptability. Even unreliable and incomplete data are better than a total lack of data.

The position taken here is that ultimate system criteria are established by authoritative decree or natural law. Natural law determines whether the pilot and his equipment recover from a maneuver, or survive running out of fuel on a runway approach. Authoritative decree covers a range of outputs such as acceptable bombing error, number of words typed per minute and error rate per 100 words, proportion of targets detected and identified per raid or simulated raid, proportion of tactical missions accomplished according to a strategic plan, mean time to localize malfunctions in a machine. The procedures whereby authoritative decrees are made or should be made is a subject outside the scope of this chapter.

*Identifying the Kinds and Amount of Input Conditions with which the System Must Cope*

In earlier reports (Craig & Miller, 1957; Miller, 1953; Miller, 1956a), analysis of input conditions has been given the general term "program analysis." Because of computer language, this use of the word "program" would be ambiguous in a system context, although the analogy is somewhat apt: one asks for what problems a computer is "programmed." Input analysis consists of identifying the stimuli which enter the system and confront the operator, or may be available to the operator. These include the rates, frequencies, peaks of work signals; disturbances and "noise" in connection with work signals; environmental conditions. The pilot has to cope with static on his radio receiver and with turbulent weather; the typist may have to cope with the buzz of conversation of her idle associates and the handwriting of her manager.

Contingencies form a special class of inputs that should be examined carefully and thoroughly. These contingencies fall into three general classes:

*Environmental and input contingencies:* Examples of these are overloading of inputs such that backlogs pile up. Does the operator have the responsibility for monitoring inputs and for establishing priorities in the sequence with which they are handled? Does work flow in from a number of channels, such that a number of activities should be (from a system's viewpoint) performed at the same time? Do work inputs occasionally fail to arrive when expected, and what are the operator's responsibilities under these circumstances? Icy roads and fog to the driver, landing light failure to the pilot, the incomplete but critical message from the absent manager to his secretary, power failure in the operating room to the surgeon—these are dramatic instances. Less dramatic ones may still prove overwhelming challenges to the partially "trained."

*Equipment malfunction:* These contingencies are generally most serious in tasks performed in "real time" such as a blowout of a tire while the car is in motion, or a skipping space key when a report is due in twenty minutes. It is also important when machine errors are largely irreversible such as on-line operations in data processing where the error goes into internal storage and may be compounded into many other errors. Obviously the operator should know at least how to detect a malfunctioning state of the equipment, and perhaps recognize its nature and how to correct the state of affairs, or at least ameliorate it. In any event, the range of these conditions should be identified so that responsibilities may be established.

*Human error:* "Whatever can be done will sometimes be done wrong," is ungrammatical but realistic advice in task analysis. By what means will the operator's errors be identified? If and when identified, how can they be corrected, or the operational consequences mitigated? What are the operator's responsibilities in response to these questions? Study may profitably be given to ascertaining the most error-likely situations and the relative gravity of their operational consequences.

Finding the full range of conditions, including contingencies, under which tasks must be performed is likely to be more difficult than ascertaining criterion work outputs, but equally rewarding in adequate provisions for training. In general, task analyses have been skimpy in consideration of work inputs. Unfortunately, some knowledge of the variables which affect human performance is necessary in selecting, from the universe of physical stimuli in the actual or potential work situation, those variables which are psychologically significant.

*Preparing a Flow Diagram of Tasks in a Typical Job Cycle*

A job cycle is a sequence of activities from some starting condition to the return of that starting condition. The aircraft mission is an example. The typist being handed a draft manuscript and returning the completed report (possibly after several stages of revision) is another. The flow diagram shows the sequence of these activities. It should also show, perhaps in block diagram form, what additional activities may have to be performed at about the same time as the primary activities.

The time sequence provides an excellent thread for continuity and completeness of task identification, and ultimately of task description. Inserting actual time units such as seconds, minutes, or hours on the baseline may be postponed to later stages and forms of description. From this chart a general picture of time-shared activities (those performed at about the same time) may emerge. Refinements of this chart may suggest points of human overload either because of too stringent time limits, or because of the complexity of the decisions required by the operator.

*Preparing a Step-by-Step Statement of the Position Elements in Each Task*

The previous step will have provided a listing of tasks by title. The task title should be followed by a description of the various input conditions and contingencies which constitute work context. The same should be done where they apply to individual steps in the task. In addition, there should be opportunity for comments about such possibilities as error-likely conditions, or special difficulties expected in performance. Now follows a detailed behavioral description to each step, and the display-control components of each step for procedural tasks that are performed as a standard routine. The essential elements in a task step consist of (*a*) the signal or stimulus that initiates the step plus its display source, (*b*) the control and the control activation required, and (*c*) the feedback information to the operator of response adequacy. In many cases, this feedback, in whole or part, is the stimulus for the next step. In some cases there may be immediate (proximal) feedback and a remote (distal) feedback available as a system output. These various stages of feedback should be identified.

Summary statements, either adjacent to the task title or in the neighborhood of the appropriate task step, should identify classes of behaviors that might be lost in the detail of step-by-step description. These statements should take into account the factors of perception (scanning, detecting, identifying patterns of cues), short-term recall, long-term recall, decision making and motor performance. Where the step-by-step description is, for some reason, impractical or undesirable, the entire task may be summarized by a description of the work objects (displays and controls), a text description of the activity, and some estimates of the training problems as they may center around the various factors cited immediately above.

## Describing Decision-Making Tasks

Decision making, for purposes of this chapter, is defined not by an external situation but by the symbolic processes that intervene between the presentation of stimulus information and the implicit or symbolic selection of a response. In earlier discussion it has been seen that at least some tasks which seem to require conceptual and inferential processes can be reduced to sets of procedures. At least some kinds of diagnosis are examples. As a yardstick, if a machine can be programmed to do the task, however inefficient the data-handling processes, the task *can* be proceduralized; but for a machine, generalization must be codified and proceduralized.

The following steps are proposed for analyzing the decision-making task requirements for training purposes:

1. Identify the task in general terms.
2. State the criterion or criteria of response adequacy: what is to be maximized or minimized by the outcome of the decision. If there are multiple criteria, establish some kind of priority structure; if necessary, determine the operational conditions under which the priority structure is modified.
3. Determine the classes of response option, the response alternatives, and whether they are mutually exclusive or interrelated with respect to their effect on the criteria. If possible, provide some model as to their interrelationships.
4. Determine the stimulus situation which should identify the need for this class of decision.
5. Determine the sources of input information and the nature of the information relevant to choosing from among response alternatives.
6. Work out the strategy or tactical rules for proceeding from available information to the selection and combination of response alternatives. When

this is done formally, the result may be a game model. But qualitative principles of strategy are better than none.

Troubleshooting electronic equipment is one task that has lent itself to this type of task analysis. The business-gaming situation which is becoming popular with the availability of high-speed computers to evaluate responses is another. In the latter case, the classes of response option available to the person playing the game are far more restricted than in real life, and this could lead to narrow-gauge decision making if the student's training were limited to these choices.

It is at this point that training and education merge—the point where the range of response options and strategy rules are selected on the basis of high probability of successful relationship with criteria in the past. The act of invention frequently consists in perceiving the applicability of quite new and unconventional orders of response alternatives. In this respect, real life differs from games of chance where rules strictly define response alternatives. A man attempting to survive in the jungle, or on Wall Street or Madison Avenue has many more alternatives than can be programmed. It may be possible to conceive of strategies for *developing* alternatives even in these circumstances.

In any event, a systematic approach may be taken to the training of decision making in virtually any task by recognizing the half dozen variables cited above, organizing the information obtained and teaching by means of these variables and their interrelationships. In heuristic training (education) alternative response possibilities may be expanded in range and detail, but with training time and technique held constant, the broader the range of alternatives and strategy rules that are learned, the more unreliable the association between any one of them and a single real-life situation. This is the tradeoff between intensive and extensive teaching.

The objective in training for decision making is not only to put information about strategy rules, response alternatives and criterion priorities into cold memory storage. This is necessary but not sufficient. It also is necessary that the operator be able to handle these varieties of information in his head at the same time, and process them. This activity is related to the short-term recall behavior described in an earlier section. It is therefore necessary for the task analyst to obtain or postulate a (graded) series of realistic decision-making situations relevant to the task on which training is to be given. The designer of training is not likely to have realistic exercise material at his fingertips.

It is, however, the responsibility of the designer of training to select or invent symbols and modes of presentation of the subject matter that will enable the student most readily to conceptualize the decision-making situation and task. He may do this through images, associative trains, associative clusters and other mnemonics and associative redundancies. The training specialist may assist the student in regularizing the sequence of steps he takes in tackling a problem so that some portions of his decision-making process become "automatized." This automatization of implicit activities will give him increased effective channel capacity. Except for "decision-making trees"[1] the exploration of teaching decision making through display techniques is yet to be started.

This concludes discussion on the description and organization of task information. Formats with column headings and ruled lines are abundantly available from various sources (Miller, 1953; Miller, 1956a; Miller & Folley, 1951) and have been deliberately excluded from this text. Their appearance of simplicity is misleading with respect to the concepts that should underlie the information that is set down in describing and analyzing the task. It has been seen that the behavioral picture of a task reveals itself through a series of layers and facets not readily captured by an optical mesh of precut dimensions. Task analysis is itself a heuristic exercise, and the reasons will be amplified in the next section.

## THE CODING OF TASK INFORMATION

In what terms shall task information be set down? What shall be the level of detail? This is like answering the question, "What do I put on a map that I have to draw?" or "How shall I tell the motorist how to get from here to the Courthouse?" The answer depends partly on what the motorist already knows about the community. The first answer may be: "Turn right at Main, then go to Mayfair, then left to the Common." If the motorist can already find these choice-points, the description is adequate. If not, then the description must include many more choice-points and identifying signals. But information irrelevant to choice-points is generally irrelevant to the task and apt to be confusing (ex-

[1] A decision-making tree is a verbalized procedure applicable in proceeding from choice-point to choice-point. The choice takes the left-hand branch if in the problem the reading at the choice is equivalent to "no," and the right-hand branch if the signal found at the choice-point is "yes."

cept for some cases when signals are provided for reassurance after making a choice).

It is unfortunate that psychologists lack a behavioral taxonomy which is related to the generalization characteristics of task performances. Such a taxonomy would enable the task analyst and training designer to find a common ground in the psychological research literature. There is a fair research literature on perception of PPI radar returns, but how do these findings apply to reconnaissance by direct viewing of terrain? The question is, by what concepts and rubrics can the factors in any task and task context be analyzed so that the findings about that task can be related to the next task that is encountered?

Ideally, a classification structure for tasks would be closely related to methodology and decision structure for the design of training. It is unrealistic to expect, or to want, the design of training ever to come entirely out of a handbook. This would eliminate the incentive to creative adventure and invention in teaching which should probably continue pushing forward as new tasks and positions are created by the culture. On the other hand, the guidance of sound handbooks for training, should they emerge in the future, would tend to insure that, even in the hands of the uninspired training officer, training design will not be downright bad in terms of irrelevance and inefficiency.

The concept of a task taxonomy based on transfer of training, and other operations denoting equivalence of knowledge about a set of tasks, is beginning to be heard. Fleishman (see Chapter 5) initiated a program of experimental study on the problem, taking into account the important consideration that different degrees or stages of training are marked by somewhat different behavioral characteristics in performing the same objective task. Cotterman at Wright Air Development Center has published a preliminary report on the problem (1959). The work of Guilford in problem-solving tasks, although based on the individual differences approach, should have at least indirect relevance to this problem (1956). A considerable amount of groping should be expected before even the objectives of the mammoth factorial studies necessary for this study can be clarified. And orthodox experimental designs may be impractical so that new methodologies may have to be devised in order to make the job realizable.

The accomplishment of a task taxonomy would put precision into task description by providing the analyst with a glossary of terms and reference operations for looking at tasks and their behavioral ingredients. Meanwhile, task description for training design is somewhat of a cut-and-try matter. The more elegant term is "heuristic." At present the task analyst can be most useful if he has a broad background in experimental psychology and training technique, considerable private insights into the psychological literature, and considerable imagination about behavioral processes in real-life contexts. He can be of help to himself and others by finding ways of *organizing* the complex of information he can obtain about performance requirements and behavioral processes much as road maps may be organized from general to detailed. And because he may not at the time realize the importance of what he leaves out in description, he should err on the side of voluminousness rather than scantiness.

## From Task Analysis to Training Design

Performance requirements and behavioral analysis of tasks establish the functional objectives and criteria for training and its general content. The analysis may suggest efficient methods for acquiring specific proficiencies, but it will not prescribe them. The task analyst may have contributed some "human engineering" effort to the design or modification of the procedures by which the operator performs his task, but the training specialist may add his own insights to the task information he is given. The analyst will also have given to the designer of training representative samples of the stimulus contexts with which and in which the job tasks will probably have to be accomplished.

The designer has the problem of blocking out which tasks and task-functions will be taught at one time and to what degree of skill, and of sequencing the training material so that one knowledge and skill is built upon another as the student progresses. The designer and his associates decide what training functions will be given to text, diagrams, training aids, mockups, procedural trainers and "simulations," and how these are to be integrated. They also "program" the practice situations, select the input stimuli and establish what kind of feedback will be given the student and when. Furthermore, they organize the knowledge content and work out methods of presentation for ready grasp and reliable recall and application by the student.

In this design effort, the training specialist may work from a systematic set of design principles, from conventional practice or from private insights and intuitions. Other chapters in this book may suggest what fund of procedural knowledge of learning and the design of teaching is available.

## IMPLICATIONS FOR GENERAL EDUCATION

Thus far the terms used (such as input, output) and the examples cited (pilots, stenographers, mechanics) have suggested the limited task domain of man as a *physical* controller. The discussion on problem solving and decision making made these processes antecedent to symbolic and overt response "outputs." The general term for the human in the task situation has been "operator." The concern with validity, completeness and efficiency in teaching, and the avoidance of irrelevance to task performance goals suggest a crass point of view diametrically opposed to most points of view in education. Two oversimplified goals can be assumed for education: (*a*) to increase the capacity to experience and contemplate the external and internal worlds, and (*b*) to increase the capacity to operate ("do" things) in the external world. In some views about the balanced individual, these two goals are somewhat reciprocal. The substance of this chapter seems relevant at least to the latter goal of providing the student with coping skills in his professional and economic environments.

Information in every professional field is expanding explosively; and even within each professional field there are proliferating languages, terminologies and reference schema. A piece of new information may come to be symbolized, hence interpretable, in many different ways. On what bases shall educational content be selected or rejected, especially in the professional training fields and in the "operative" subjects such as arithmetic, mathematics, logic, science, law, business? And how shall information to be poured into the student be codified for his own association and retrieval purposes? Machines can now put information into vast numbers of pigeon-holes, but the manner of getting the information out is precisely equivalent to the indexing operations used for putting the information into the machine. But the human being has generalization and inter-associative capabilities far exceeding practical, and perhaps theoretical, limits of machines. Nevertheless, within a couple of generations it can be expected that humans will be using machines intimately for retrieving pigeon-holed information as adjuncts to their human memory systems. What indexing concepts can be developed compatible both with the present and this future expectation?

It is proposed that some increased attention be given by educators to the operational and psychological factors of the real world in which the profession or coping skill is to be applied. Reference operations, including those of problem solving and decision making, may thus be generated for the semantic and pragmatic relationships of information at various levels of abstraction. This suggestion does not limit education to the teaching of "applied" material as the unimaginative may conclude. Nor does it necessarily mean the "project method" of teaching which many misguided followers of John Dewey have employed. The work-a-day world, the psychological world and the academic world meet in the arena of decision-making and problem-solving structure where the outcome is, or symbolizes, a control action as well as a value judgment. Information processing that does not lead to a control action reference is clearly no more than some redefinition of the source information. Redefinitions are important to clarification in thought and knowledge but are ultimately circular.

To be more specific, it is proposed that at least some educators inquire into the nature of decisions that are or should be made by graduates from their area of subject specialization. What are the conditions which signal the need for a decision to be made, or a problem to be solved? What are the information variables? What search strategies should be employed to obtain further essential information in representative situations? What are the classes of response options, or how can they be established? What are the consequences of various response alternatives both in terms of operational outcome and ethical or professional value? What logical and procedural strategies may be used in arriving at decisions in work situations? The sojourns into the world of practiced application which are required of educators in order for them to find answers to these questions may be salutary both to the educators and the world of practice which they study. The general concepts and rubrics of task analysis discussed above should provide guidance for the examination of professional-type situations as well as those from which the examples were drawn, with the provision that no format should tyrannize observation or thought. But besides noting passively what *is* done, the inquirer should have some courage in recognizing the inadequacies of common practice. He may have to adopt, at least loosely, some of the concepts and practices of systems analysis and operations research in reformulating decision structures for the real-world tasks he examines. However, to assert that formal education is intended solely to teach a man how to learn his job seems to beg the entire question and evade responsibility; unfortunately it has that mote of truth which can blind the eye. The hard-headed questioner of this philosophy might in return ask "Where and in what curriculum is this specifically undertaken?"

The teaching technology to be opened up by automated teaching (see Chapter 9 by Lumsdaine) will provide opportunity and challenge for reassessment of the content and structure of what is taught. In the frame-by-frame program of the material to be taught, it is simple enough to set down the stimulus material in itself; it can be taken from an ordinary textbook. But to set down the material in terms of the meaningful question to be asked about the content on the single frame is usually a difficult enterprise; it calls for continual assessment of the relationship of the subject matter to reference concepts, decisions and operations. No teacher can approach the preparation of a teaching machine "program tape" without asking the searching question of "What are the skills and knowledges for which this subject matter is essential?" Teaching machines will demand a continuously active role of the student, as opposed to his present passive role in listening to lecture and reading text. The responses demanded by teaching machine procedures will pose again to the teacher the question, "What are the criteria for the kind of responses I want to get from the student who studies this subject matter?"

One leg of this answer may stand on something like task and performance analysis, and it may be an excellent platform from which to stride. The striding leg, however, will not rest on a platform. This is the leg which moves the student, and all the rest of us, into improvisation, invention, and the exercise of judgment and wisdom. Task analysis may modestly suggest, but obviously not circumscribe, the information essential to performing the activities connoted by these terms. But the proposition consistently offered in these pages is that task analysis is in any case a heuristic and never a definitive effort. When applied to tasks demanding invention it is more heuristic. And the inventiveness required in making the task analysis may be greater than that required by the task analysed. In this light, the educator will maintain his own unique and personal prerogatives.

## REFERENCES

Cotterman, T. E. *Task classification: An approach to partially ordering information on human learning.* Wright Air Development Center, January 1959. WADC TN-58-374.

Craig, R. C. & Miller, R. B. *Training for emergency performance. I. General description of a human factors approach.* Pittsburgh: American Institute for Research, March 1957.

Flanagan, J. C. The critical incident technique. *Psychol. Bull.*, 1954, *51*, 327-358.

Guilford, J. P. The structure of intellect. *Psychol. Bull.*, 1956, *53*, 267-293.

Miller, R. B. *A method for man-machine task analysis.* Wright Air Development Center, June 1953. WADC TR 53-137.

Miller, R. B. *Some working concepts of systems analysis.* Pittsburgh: American Institute for Research, February 1954.

Miller, R. B. *A suggested guide to position-task description.* Lowry AFB, Armament Systems Personnel Research Laboratory, Air Force Personnel and Training Research Center, April 1956. ASPRL-TM-56-16. (a)

Miller, R. B. *Task and part-task trainers and training.* Wright Air Development Center, October 1956. WADC TR 56-41. (b)

Miller, R. B. & Folley, J. D., Jr. *A study of methods for determining skill, knowledge and ability requirements for maintenance of newly developed equipment.* Pittsburgh: American Institute for Research, June 1951.

Miller, R. B., Folley, J. D., Jr., & Smith, P. R. *Systematic troubleshooting and the half-split technique.* Chanute AFB, Human Resources Research Center, July 1953. HRRC TR 53-21.

Miller, R. B. & Van Cott, H. P. *The determination of knowledge content for complex man-machine jobs.* Pittsburgh: American Institute for Research, December 1955.

Wright Air Development Center, *Uses of task analysis in deriving training and training equipment requirements.* Wright Air Development Center, Training Psychology Branch, Aerospace Laboratory, 1960. WADC TR 60-593.

Chapter 3

# The Design of
# Correlational Studies in Training[1]

*Philip H. DuBois, Washington University*

In the scientific analysis of learning one may elect to study very small changes in behavior, such as the acquisition of a single integral act, which, for all intents and purposes, is merely present or absent. Attention may be focussed on the circumstances and conditions, both within the organism and external to it, which are related to the acquisition of this act. As an aid in the description of what is happening and as a source of hypotheses, a mathematical model of the associations between the act on the one hand and antecedent and concomitant circumstances on the other may be developed. Certainly psychology has great need for the scientist who studies the behavior of the organism in the smallest observable units and who relates learning in its simplest forms to basic biological processes. Psychologies in the mode of 19th century chemistry, such as the element-seeking psychologies of Wundt and Watson, are by no means as obsolete as one might think. Researchers interested in the basic phenomena of learning must necessarily deal with small units, and there is a strong tendency to think of small units as elements.

When training is discussed, however, the tendency is to emphasize an alternative approach. Instead of the acquisition of single acts, the interest is in the development of complex skills composed, perhaps, of many elements and integrated into far more than the simple sum of such elements. Instead of relating change in behavior to precisely describable external conditions, the concern is with relating changes in proficiency to broad and general characteristics of the learner and to major events in the learner's environment. If knowledge of practical

[1]This paper was prepared in part under Contract Nonr 816(02) between Washington University and the Office of Naval Research.

value in training programs is to be developed, a comprehensive view of this problem must be taken. To some extent one can be analytical, but there is important work still to be done at a level descriptive of the general contours of the area. In years to come, perhaps, the psychologist interested in training may develop interest in fundamental units and the minutiae of learning phenomena.

In the literature related to two of the main branches of personnel psychology—testing and training—there is a curious contrast. In the field of individual differences and psychological tests, practical books are many, theoretical books are few. In the general field of learning, theoretical books are common, practical books on the psychology of training are few (at least if books on formal classroom instruction are disregarded). In the field of individual differences an art with numerous applications has developed; in the field of learning, theories have been elaborated, but relatively few attempts have been made to apply them.

Perhaps the learning theorist should be relieved of any responsibility for developing generalizations that might be applied to the administration of training programs. The psychologists with interests in training people in complex skills might develop a field of research complete with hypotheses and methods of investigation, and yielding an organized body of generalizations. In time, such a psychology of training might have findings to interest the learning theorist; but the test of its success would be whether or not it could develop a coherent body of knowledge applicable to a large area of potential psychological endeavor.

Up to the present time certain of the findings in the study of complex skills have been contradictory. Intelligence has been defined as the ability to learn, yet most of the correlations between measures of intelligence and changes resulting from training are reported to be essentially zero. One talks of the ability to learn, and yet gain in proficiency in one task is often reported to be unrelated to gains in other tasks. It is widely believed that new knowledge must be built on old, and yet many a study has come to the conclusion that those who know the most at the beginning of training profit least from instruction. Psychological knowledge of training is fragmentary. In selection research a "training criterion" is often employed, but almost invariably the criterion is merely an achievement measure at the end of a training course. In this measure, initial proficiency and gain are mixed together, and there is usually no attempt to separate them. The criterion is a measure of the results of training only if the assumption is made that all members of the group start at an identical level of proficiency. This is seldom, if ever, the case.

Sometimes there is overlapping of the format and the content of predictors on the one hand and achievement measures on the other, so that correlations are spuriously high. In the training situation psychological tests are often diagnostic rather than prognostic, since relatively little forecasting of change is involved. Few deductions about the nature of learning can be made from current prediction studies which use a training criterion. In the complex learning situation relatively little is known about the relationships between specific aptitudes, interests and personality characteristics on the one hand and gain in proficiency in specific areas of knowledge and skill on the other. Relatively little is known about the effect of motivating conditions, rewards and reinforcement, and methods of instruction on gain; still less is known about the interaction of within-learner characteristics with extra-learner conditions. Most psychologists who are teachers probably share the belief that even the best instruction is inefficient, but few have more than very general ideas on how an applied science of teaching might be effectively developed.

There are conditions confronting the teaching profession that make the development of a science of training important. First of all, urgency comes from the fact that at last it is generally recognized that knowledge, especially scientific knowledge, is a prime national asset, essential to national survival. Increasing numbers of scientists, social scientists and engineers must be trained.

Secondly, there seems to be recognition of the need to make training more efficient. The limit of the number of years that a professional knower is required to spend in formal training as opposed to the number of years he may expect to spend in his profession may be approaching. The less useful parts of the curriculum need to be eliminated and the ability to train oneself after the completion of formal training needs to be developed.

In the third place, a still larger proportion of the population must be dealt with, especially at the higher levels of formal education, continuing a trend that extends back in this country for many decades. Perhaps the continued democratization of educational opportunities and the need for more efficient adjustment of the learner to the learning situation will force the development of a systematic body of knowledge in the counseling and guidance field.

Finally, the curve of human knowledge, the curve of discoveries and inventions, continues to rise. Education is a chief means of transmitting the custody of accumulated knowledge from generation to generation.

While specialization is the classical method of dealing with the flood of knowledge, prudence would dictate a multiple program involving also greater efficiency in learning and the development of more philosophers, integrators of knowledge and men with interests centered between specialties rather than within specialties.

## RELATIONSHIPS BETWEEN THE STUDY OF INDIVIDUAL DIFFERENCES AND LEARNING RESEARCH

To many investigators in the field of learning, individual differences among the organisms that are the subjects in their studies are chiefly a nuisance. Groups of subjects, rather than single individuals, are used only to permit averaging of results. In this way learning curves are smoother than curves obtained by observing single individuals, and a generalization is established that tends to be applicable to a whole population. The mean of scores obtained from a number of individuals can be shown to have a much smaller proportion of random error than the score of a single individual, and may also be taken as more representative of a parameter. When consistent results can be obtained, many experimentalists prefer research using only one subject at a time. However, in the field of learning, only a limited range of problems can be attacked in this fashion.

While the psychological study of individual differences has its primary applications in personnel placement, it has another important field of potential application in the study of training. If characteristics that vary from individual to individual are ignored, investigations of learning are limited to the study of a relatively narrow range of topics, chiefly the effect of variations of internal drives and of external stimuli, including rewards and reinforcement, on changes in behavior.

In the study of the acquisition of simple acts by relatively simple organisms, this limitation may not be particularly serious. The study of individual differences among simple organisms has not been a major preoccupation of contemporary psychologists. However, in the study of complex human skills it appears likely that a major portion of the variance of interest to psychologists is directly or indirectly related to individual differences in prior skill, aptitudes, interests and personality characteristics. The impact of individual differences is such that human variation must be taken into account in the study of most of the problems of interest to educators and others concerned with human learning. These problems include the identification of the individuals who may be trained, the determination of areas of training appropriate to each individual, and the interaction of incentives and training methods with personal characteristics of trainees. In general, the level of initial skill is of interest chiefly as a variable to be controlled, but it is obviously a most important source of variability in the learning situation as a whole.

What happens in human learning is that a complex organism is modified through experience so that its future behavior will be different from its past behavior. Of course, with almost any organism, behavior changes constantly, but in what we call learning the changes are systematic and tend to enable the organism to meet more adequately specified phases of the environment. The phenomena of interest are nearly coextensive with human behavior, relatively little of which remains fixed and unaltered from one time to another.

As in all psychological studies, the concept of the variable is indispensable in establishing a framework for the study of learning. In the simplest type of a psychological study the concern is with the relationship between two variables: an independent variable generally under the control of the experimenter and a dependent variable with which changes in the independent variable are correlated. In an experiment, the variables may be conditions or behaviors which change from time to time for the same individual; in studies of individual differences a variable is a measurable characteristic, such as an aptitude or degree of skill on the job, of a number of individuals. It is apparent that in any training situation involving groups of trainees there are many variables that need to be considered, some of them relatively permanent traits of individuals and others characteristic of situations and temporarily associated with individuals. The problem of research design is to manipulate these variables so that a dependable and important generalization may be discovered.

In psychology there seem to be two basic research designs, which for want of better terms might be designated as Design I and Design II. In Design I there is a single independent variable, a single dependent variable and $n'$ control variables, $n'$ taking any integral value from zero to indefinitely large. In Design II there are n independent variables, a single dependent variable and, again, any number of control variables from none to many. Although Design I is often considered the classic paradigm for psychological research, it is apparent that it is really a special case of Design II.

The basic problem is to find correlates, if possible antecedent and necessary correlates, of changes in the dependent variable. Since behavior transpires in an interlocking network of many variables, a principal task of the researcher is to minimize the effects of certain variables. There are the control variables in which, at the moment, he is interested only in a negative way. During a particular experiment he wants to study only the relationship between independent variables and the dependent variable, ruling out from consideration effects of the controls. At another time and in another study he may be much interested in the control variables which then may become independent variables in their own right. From study to study independent and control variables are completely interchangeable.

Various ingenious techniques are available for handling control variables, which in general are related to the experimental variables but have to be modified so that they become more or less unrelated. One method of handling a control variable is by eliminating it entirely, as when vision is controlled in a rat study by using only blinded rats as subjects. A second method is by matching on one or more control variables. This is particularly useful when subjects are divided into groups according to various degrees (including presence-absence) of the independent variable. Another technique is balancing, sometimes utilized when neither elimination nor precise matching is feasible. In balancing, matching is on average values of a control variable rather than on individual values. The fourth technique is to assign different cases to different groups and different treatments by lot, in order to minimize the effect of more or less unknown and unmeasurable extraneous variables.

These four techniques may be considered devices to reduce to zero the correlation between a control variable and an independent variable. However, with elimination, the correlation becomes indeterminate and with randomization the correlation is of the magnitude expected by chance. With balancing, linear correlation becomes zero, and with perfect matching there is no correlation whatsoever, either linear or non-linear. In these four methods a given individual is placed in a category established with reference to the experimental variable. The methods seem to be particularly appropriate when an independent variable is categorical or exists in relatively few degrees. In learning research these methods of treating control variables appear to be highly appropriate when the independent variable is method.

Along with elimination, matching, balancing and randomizing as methods of handling extraneous variance, there is the method of statistical adjustment. This has a purpose similar to the other methods but is accomplished somewhat differently. A function is fitted by least squares between a control variable and an experimental variable. Then the part of the score predictable from the control variable is subtracted from the experimental variable. This type of adjustment is common to both analysis of variance and correlational analysis. The function fitted is generally a straight line, but, especially in analysis of variance, a non-linear function may be used. Some of the uses of this technique will be explored later.

In the case of human learning, it appears that information on individual differences among the trainees may be of great utility in influencing its course. At one time older individuals were not regarded as good learners; today the entire adult education movement is predicated upon the established fact that older individuals can and do learn. While the area has not been fully explored, enough has so far been discovered that it is realized that learning in older people may have considerable utility not only to themselves but to society. In order to plan for the appropriate use of the years of longer life which are resulting from modern medicine and better nutrition and housing, a great deal must be known about the characteristics of the adult learner: what he can learn most readily, how potentially good learners may be identified, and optimal training methods. It seems likely that retirement programs integrated with training programs appropriate to individual capacities can make later years more pleasant for the individual and, to some extent at least, less of a burden to society as a whole. Correlations of age with intelligence and aptitude scores are typically curvilinear when considered over the life span. However, when age is treated in a restricted range the regression may be linear. Provided the relationship between age and other variables is tested for linearity and appropriate steps are taken when non-linearity appears, no particular difficulty should be encountered in handling age along with other measures of individual differences.

In the past century there has also been a notable change in attitudes toward the education of women. Here again further research would seem to be in order although the general contours are now reasonably apparent. As learners in the higher branches of knowledge, the chief difference between men and women seems to depend on differences in interests rather than in aptitudes. It is possible that sex differences in favor of men in mechanical and mathematical skills and in favor of women in verbal skills are basically the result of their somewhat separate cultures rather than direct physiological differences. It has gradually been realized during the last century that women as such have no particular limitations as far as formal education is concerned. Much of this was discovered simply by admitting women to more and more courses of training, courses which originally had been closed to them. Perhaps, in the long run, this is the most satisfactory way of studying the question. However, in working with specific problems in the area of the relationship of individual differences to learning, we may often wish to use sex either as an independent or a control variable. While sex is a categorical variable, it may be coded arbitrarily and treated as scaled. When sex is correlated with other variables the sign of the correlation coefficient is arbitrary and must always be interpreted.

If Design II is considered as the typical research design in human learning, allowing Design I as a special instance, all psychological knowledge of individual differences can be incorporated into learning research. Any measure of aptitude, interest, achievement or personality characteristics can be used as an independent variable (or predictor) or as a control variable. When the interest is chiefly in methods, variables reflecting individual differences will generally be used as controls; when the interest is in identifying the best learners irrespective of method, measures of individual differences will be used as predictors. In some studies one may be sensitive to the interaction of individual differences with method and hence will be looking for the methods most appropriate to certain categories of individuals. For the development of a comprehensive psychology of training, investigations that take human variability into account are indispensable.

## THE DIMENSIONALITY PROBLEM

In psychological research on learning, insufficient attention has been given to the dimensionality of the variables. Any time numbers are used to represent varying degrees of a "characteristic," it is implied that the characteristic is measurable along a single dimension. Human behavior is so complex, however, that it is questionable whether it is ever measured along a pure dimension. Some measurements better represent a single unitary dimension than others. When the experimentalist uses time or errors as a criterion of performance, he assumes he is working with a unidimensional scale. It is obvious that for different cases and for the same case at different times, his measurements come from the same general domain, but generally no test for unidimensionality is applied. In fact under most laboratory conditions, a test for unidimensionality would be impossible to develop. Measurements are global, rather than the sum of somewhat discrete parts. Consequently correlational methods of testing for unidimensionality do not apply. However, it is plausible to believe that a scale, such as time, taken from the physical sciences can be taken to represent a single dimension of behavior, at least reasonably well.

It is in measuring complex skills and in determining the correlates of the learning of complex skills that the problem of dimensionality definitely emerges. There is probably no important aspect of human behavior that can be measured in terms of time, distance, weight or temperature. For investigating socially important human learning, some attention must be given to finding measurements in which different numbers represent different degrees of some underlying unitary trait.

## Unifactor Measures

One test for dimension, applicable when the total measurement is the sum of a number of part scores (as with items), is whether or not the intercorrelations of the parts or items can be explained as arising from a single common factor. The criteria for a single common factor underlying a matrix of correlations are well-known: hierarchy, perfect column to column to column correlations, tetrad differences of zero, and proportionality of elements. All of these are indications, some more acceptable mathematically than others, of a matrix of unitary rank. A group of variables can be tested for rank 1 by extracting a single factor by one of several different methods and noting whether any significant variability remains in the component variables residualized with respect to the posited general factor.

The special case in which all the intercorrelations are identical (and represented by $r$) may be of interest. In this special case all the intercorrelations are completely explained in terms of a single underlying factor and the correlation between the composite variable and the underlying general factor is

$$r_{xg} = \frac{n\sqrt{r}}{\sqrt{n + (n^2 - n)r}} \tag{1}$$

in which $n$ is the number of components. Apparently high intercorrelations are not needed when the number of components is large. For example, if all intercorrelations are .16 and there are 20 components, the correlation of the total score with the general factor is approximately .90. Incidentally, Formula (1) is merely the square root of the familiar Spearman-Brown prophecy formula, which gives the proportion of the non-error variance in a composite variable of uniform intercorrelations.

## The Guttman Scale

Since scaling in the Guttman fashion has been advocated as a model way to develop a unifactor scale, it may be of interest to examine the factor composition of a theoretically perfect Guttman scale. It may be stated categorically that the shape of the distribution of the composite variable has no important bearing on the outcome of our demonstration. Arbitrarily, a $C$-distribution has been chosen as indicated in Table 3.1. Here is perfect reproducibility of all item scores from knowledge of the total score. Intercorrelations of the 10 items are shown in Table 3.2. It will be noted at once that the tetrad criterion is satisfied perfectly as long as all four elements come from one side of the diagonal or the other. It is not satisfied when elements from both sides of the diagonal are involved in a single tetrad.

TABLE 3.1

Score Roster for 100 Cases ($C$-Distribution) of a
Perfect Guttman Scale. Artificial Data

| Individuals Numbered | Total Score | Item Scores | | | | | | | | | |
|---|---|---|---|---|---|---|---|---|---|---|---|
| | | 1 | 2 | 3 | 4 | 5 | 6 | 7 | 8 | 9 | 10 |
| 1 | 0 | 0 | 0 | 0 | 0 | 0 | 0 | 0 | 0 | 0 | 0 |
| 2-4 | 1 | + | 0 | 0 | 0 | 0 | 0 | 0 | 0 | 0 | 0 |
| 5-11 | 2 | + | + | 0 | 0 | 0 | 0 | 0 | 0 | 0 | 0 |
| 12-22 | 3 | + | + | + | 0 | 0 | 0 | 0 | 0 | 0 | 0 |
| 23-40 | 4 | + | + | + | + | 0 | 0 | 0 | 0 | 0 | 0 |
| 41-60 | 5 | + | + | + | + | + | 0 | 0 | 0 | 0 | 0 |
| 61-78 | 6 | + | + | + | + | + | + | 0 | 0 | 0 | 0 |
| 79-89 | 7 | + | + | + | + | + | + | + | 0 | 0 | 0 |
| 90-96 | 8 | + | + | + | + | + | + | + | + | 0 | 0 |
| 97-99 | 9 | + | + | + | + | + | + | + | + | + | 0 |
| 100 | 10 | + | + | + | + | + | + | + | + | + | + |

TABLE 3.2

Intercorrelations of 10 Items of a Perfect Guttman Scale.
Artificial Data. $N = 100$ ($C$-Distribution)

| | 1 | 2 | 3 | 4 | 5 | 6 | 7 | 8 | 9 | 10 |
|---|---|---|---|---|---|---|---|---|---|---|
| 1 | | .492 | .286 | .189 | .123 | .082 | .053 | .035 | .020 | .010 |
| 2 | .492 | | .580 | .384 | .250 | .167 | .108 | .072 | .042 | .021 |
| 3 | .286 | .580 | | .662 | .431 | .287 | .187 | .124 | .072 | .035 |
| 4 | .189 | .384 | .662 | | .650 | .434 | .282 | .187 | .108 | .053 |
| 5 | .123 | .250 | .431 | .650 | | .667 | .434 | .287 | .167 | .082 |
| 6 | .082 | .167 | .287 | .434 | .667 | | .650 | .430 | .250 | .123 |
| 7 | .053 | .108 | .187 | .282 | .434 | .650 | | .662 | .384 | .189 |
| 8 | .035 | .072 | .124 | .187 | .287 | .430 | .662 | | .580 | .286 |
| 9 | .020 | .042 | .072 | .108 | .167 | .250 | .384 | .580 | | .492 |
| 10 | .010 | .021 | .035 | .053 | .082 | .123 | .189 | .286 | .492 | |

Actually what is exhibited here is a perfect example of another Guttman discovery, the simplex. Each coefficient can be shown to be the ratio of what Guttman calls the saturations of the two variables entering into the correlation. The matrix, as might be expected, represents increasing degrees of "saturation" or complexity. However, in the Spearman-Thurstone sense, the sum variable is not factorially pure. Recently (DuBois, 1960), it was shown that the rank of a perfect simplex is $n/2$, when $n$ is the number of constituent variables and when any fraction resulting from the division is disregarded. In the case of Table 3.2, the rank of the correlation matrix is 5, and five additive factors are required to explain the intercorrelations. It is apparent that the requirement that item scores be perfectly reproducible from total score is not sufficient to generate a single factor score.

## Homogeneous Scaling

Another technique, developed by Loevinger, Gleser and DuBois (1953), also needs attention. In the homogeneous scale, items are added to a composite as they increase the saturation defined as the ratio of the sum of the covariances to the total variance. At any stage an item may be eliminated from the composite if such elimination would increase the saturation. Too high a saturation reduces the number of discriminations a test will make, but with usual types of test material this limitation does not appear to be of practical importance. In the technique of homogeneous scaling, the nucleus is generally a cluster of three items which, necessarily, define a single factor. The routine is such that the factor composition of the developing scale tends to extend the unitary factor of the original nucleus, even though the formulae used do not appear to turn on factor composition per se.

The item intercorrelations of several published homogeneous scales have been examined empirically by a conventional factor technique. In each case it was found that after the extraction of a single common factor there was no systematic variance remaining that could be considered the basis for a second factor. In other words, while the matrices were not perfect examples of rank 1, they seemed to be of rank 1 within sampling error. Certainly homogeneous scaling is worthy of further exploration in connection with the development of variables of interest in the study of learning.

## Testing Variables for Unidimensionality

Whenever the intercorrelations of the components make up a composite variable, there is a simple test for unidimensionality. By a Spearman formula for the correlation of a test with a factor central to a group of tests

$$r_{ig} = \sqrt{\frac{(\Sigma r_{ij})^2 - \Sigma r_{ij}^2}{2\,(\Sigma\Sigma r_{jk} - \Sigma r_{ij})}} \qquad , i \neq j \neq k \qquad (2)$$

the loadings in a posited central factor can be found, and this factor may be then partialed from the matrix. If the resulting partial covariances are zero within sampling error, the matrix can be taken to have a rank of 1. Also the sum of the values obtained by Formula (2) divided by the sum of the complete matrix, including unity in each diagonal sum, will be a reasonable approximation of the correlation of the composite with the factor central to it. It is an approximation because all variances of the component variables have been converted to unity, thus changing to some degree the correlation from that which would have been obtained by using unadjusted scores. Any existing variable, for which intercorrelations of components are available, can be so examined. It would appear that much psychological research would be improved with more attention to the unidimensionality of our measurements.

## THE PROBLEM OF REPEATED MEASUREMENTS[2]

As indicated earlier, training situations in education, in industry and the armed services require, generally speaking, the development of complex skills. Such a skill is complex either because it represents a large collection of relatively separate and simple dimensional activities or because it is an integration or hierarchy of part-skills rather than merely their sum. (See Chapter 5 by Fleishman.) In either case the total skill to be acquired is typically much more extensive than can be measured at any one time. This is in marked contrast to the usual laboratory study of learning in which total skill is periodically assessed. For example, as a laboratory animal learns a maze, its skill on the entire task is considered to be measured at each trial and the resultant learning curve is plotted as a series of assessments on a more or less constant task.

A further difference is that the investigator in education, industry and the armed services must often deal with the training situation as it exists, since it may be impractical to introduce major alterations. This is especially true if alterations would result in a marked decrease in the

[2]This section prepared in collaboration with Dr. Edward R. Jones of McDonnell Aircraft Co., St. Louis, Missouri.

quality of the end product or would induce safety problems. Learning situations analyzed by orthodox psychological methods are characteristically those involving situations under the complete control of the investigator and utilizing equipment that is relatively inexpensive to operate. Such situations rarely have the potential of requiring activity that may be hazardous to the individual or to society.

In the practical training situation there are usually no identical trials which can be evaluated as to merit by a single criterion. A salient characteristic is that the nature of the task changes from trial to trial, either by design or as a result of conditions inherent in the situation. The variation from trial to trial may be necessary to allow adequate coverage of the wide range of material composing the task, or to allow for progression both in terms of difficulty level and curriculum content. One may therefore inquire into the possibility of developing scientific methodology for dealing with the intact and complex learning situations encountered by the applied psychologist.

There are two scientific approaches to the study of the acquisition of skills. In the first the psychologist is interested in the outcome of learning, ignoring the shape of the learning curve. Characteristic of this approach is the control group method in which two or more equated groups of subjects are treated differentially. If the groups have equivalent ability and skill at the beginning of the study, the relative utility of different methods of training can be evaluated by methods well-known in experimental psychology. In most studies of complex learning situations, this approach has been favored since relatively few evaluation devices are needed. In fact, a single device for measuring proficiency is often considered sufficient.

In the second approach, emphasis is placed on the course of learning. Studies of this type are more difficult to design when the total training situation is larger than the feasible measurement situation. Points along the learning curve can be established only by sampling, in the sense that a limited performance is to be taken as representative of the total performance at that particular time. In order to establish the learning curve for such a skill, a number of equivalent tests are necessary, each of which samples the critical elements of the tasks and thus is directly representative of the total skill.

Studies involving the comparison of training devices or training techniques should result in more usable and more basic information on the nature of the tasks involved if information on the course of the learning process is available. In certain academic situations it is fairly easy to secure this type of information. For example, alternate forms of reading proficiency tests and foreign language achievement tests are available in considerable numbers. It is also relatively simple to construct equivalent forms for spelling, arithmetic, and other basic skills. Characteristically, however, the skills involved in the academic situation are collections of relatively homogeneous part-skills rather than a complicated integration or hierarchy of skills. That is reflected in the fact that, generally speaking, the greater the number of items passed on a proficiency test, the higher the level of skill can be assumed to be.

To investigate conditions which influence the acquisition of complex skills, a fixed requirement is to have some means of measuring the level of the skill at specified times during the learning process. The alternatives are: (a) the use of a standard testing situation repeatedly; and (b) the use of equivalent testing situations. One objection to the repeated use of a single standard testing situation is that learning occurring during the testing situation may obscure the effects of other training periods. A second objection is that a single testing situation may be biased and unrepresentative of the total task especially since the task content will probably change from trial to trial.

The use of equivalent testing situations is more promising, but, at the same time, entails a number of technical difficulties. One method of constructing equivalent testing situations is to secure random samples of the totality of part-tasks constituting or representative of the total task. The assumption is that the total task can be broken into a large number of discrete bits and that performance on a random sample of these bits will be adequately representative of the total task. This is a reasonably good assumption, for example, when used as a basis for measuring foreign language vocabulary, but its application to a complex military or industrial skill, where the sub-tasks are probably hierarchical, is highly questionable.

A second method is to establish the difficulty value of a number of part-skills or part-tasks and then select stratified samples of these skills or tasks to use as equivalent measuring devices. This method has been found to be useful in constructing alternate forms of spelling tests, yet again, it is of doubtful utility in the complex skills of interest to the applied psychologist. Like the first method, it assumes that a complex skill can be broken down into a number of relatively discrete parts. Statistically, it takes variances of part-skills into account but omits consideration of covariances or interrelationships.

The third and preferred method is to employ the conceptual framework of modern psychometric theory and construct equivalent but non-identical testing situations. Two testing situations may be considered equivalent if: (*a*) the total variances are equal; (*b*) the covariances of items within tests are representative of the covariances of items between tests; and (*c*) tests means are equal in an experimental population used for standardization. If these three criteria are met, equivalent test situations can be used to measure changes brought about by learning. Within this conceptual framework, the plot of a learning curve of a complex skill is limited to *n* points when *n* is the number of equivalent testing forms which are available. The construction of these forms then becomes a necessary prerequisite to any investigation of the course of learning. A method proposed by Berkeley (1954) would seem to be of value in the development of equivalent or comparable forms of tests composed of heterogeneous items which are applicable in the complex learning situation. The method used for selecting the items was derived from that presented by Loevinger, Gleser and DuBois (1953) for maximizing test saturation. Berkeley was able to obtain, using his method, score distributions for two forms of a test which yielded equal means and variances. The covariances of the two forms with two external measures were equal.

In the practical situation, as in the development of a curriculum, it is suggested that training situations and testing situations be intermixed. For example, in a series of a dozen training periods in a flight simulator, several equivalent testing flights might be included. As a preliminary step, and to reduce the need for statistical manipulations, material for these testing flights should be prejudged by a panel of experts and then tried out on an experimental population. Materials should be judged for: (*a*) pertinence to the total skill; and (*b*) equivalence of the different forms. Increment in performance through learning in the testing situations should be compensated for by presenting items in different orders to different subjects. Statistical analysis of the results will then provide the basis for the construction of the equivalent forms. Such equivalent tasks should prove of great value in determining optimum conditions of learning and in other studies of complex learning.

## THE QUESTION OF UNITS AND THE USE OF RESIDUALS

The psychologist working with animal learning in the laboratory is not greatly bothered by the question of units on his scales, many of which he borrows directly from the physicist. He tends to use ratio scales, with a true zero point and demonstrated equality of units. He applies these measures, including numbers of errors and numbers of responses, to relatively simple forms of behavior, generally without encountering contradictions in their use. It is unfortunate that a similar solution is not available for studies of training with complex human behavior. In studies of complex skills, the measures that are of interest are primarily conventional psychometric devices, such as tests of intelligence, aptitude, interest, personality and attainment. Occasionally the researcher develops a device of his own, especially when appropriate achievement measures are not available for a skill he is studying. It would appear that any of the accepted psychometric devices would qualify as ordinal scales, that is, they measure along a single dimension and place in order the individuals measured. It is doubtful whether any of these devices constitute true interval scales, that is, scales demonstrating equality of units throughout their length. While there is reason to believe that it may eventually be possible to develop psychometric devices that constitute interval scales, the appraisal at the present time would seem to be that they are a little more than ordinal and a little less than interval. It is common psychological practice to compute means, standard deviations, variances and correlation coefficients with psychometric test data. Empirically, these methods justify themselves in terms of enabling us to summarize data readily, to make inferences about parameters and to make predictions useful in individual instances. However, all these statistical operations involve additive steps, and strictly speaking, are not appropriate unless one is dealing with interval scales. This point was elaborated some time ago by Stevens (1951).

What seems to be the case is that all psychometric devices are sufficiently close to measuring in equal units that statistics based on summation work reasonably well as long as the operation is basically some form of addition. If the units in different parts of a scale are not perfectly equal, the departure from a true interval scale may have only minor effect when a mean or variance is computed or when several variables are added together as in multiple correlation. On the other hand, unevenness in scale may be accentuated when the numerical operation is subtraction, as in the computation of a difference score (such as the score at a second point in time less the score at a first point in time) to indicate change. Such a crude difference score has often been used in studies of training, but it may be the idiosyncrasies of the metric that have led to three anomalous results:

1. In studies of training, crude gain, defined as final score less initial score, is always (or practically always) negatively correlated with initial score. It can be shown that for the correlation of crude gain and initial score to be positive the following inequality must hold $r_{12} \sigma_2 > \sigma_1$ in which the subscripts 1 and 2 represent initial and final score respectively. In practice the standard deviation of the final score is seldom greater than the standard deviation of the initial score. Possibly this may indicate that the units high in psychometric devices are not wide enough as compared with the units in median position. Or, stated somewhat differently, measurements may not have sufficient "top."

2. In the second place, crude gain has been notoriously difficult to predict. Scaling difficulties may be one reason for this.

3. Finally, crude gain scores in different tasks seem relatively unrelated, contrary to what might be logically expected. Again, the difficulty may be one of scaling.

For several years, in conferences and in print, the use of the regressed score, or residual, has been advocated as a measure of change in a learning situation and it has been used in a number of studies.[3] The next few paragraphs follow earlier presentations closely (DuBois & Manning, 1960).

Consider two points in time at which there are adequate and reliable measures of some aspect of behavior. The first measure in $z$-score form is $z$, and $z_2$ is the second measure. $z_2$ can be divided into two uncorrelated portions: $\hat{z}_2$ which is perfectly correlated with $z_1$, and a residual score, $z_{2.1}$, which is uncorrelated with $z_1$. Thus, $z_{2.1} = z_2 - r_{12} z_1$. The use of a residual score to define change has several advantages:

1. The residual can be defined precisely and meaningfully.

2. The residual in $z$-form is completely independent of units of measurement and hence is applicable even if initial score and final score are in different metrics.

3. The residual is independent of and completely uncorrelated with initial status. Hence when it is correlated with outside variables, the correlation is with gain defined as independent of initial status, rather than a mixed function, an unknown part of which is initial status.

---

[3]Executed under Contract 816(02) between the Office of Naval Research and Washington University.

4. By the use of a residual score the question as to whether those who know most at the start of the study learn more than the others cannot be answered. However, there is no restriction on investigations of outside correlates of learning.

5. The residual score as a measure of learning fits perfectly into correlational statistics in terms of variances. The variance of the final score is divisible into two uncorrelated portions: a part associated with and a part independent of initial status. The independent part can in turn be analyzed to find proportions associated with outside predictors of learning. These analyses should help in understanding what goes on during the learning process.

6. It is perfectly feasible statistically to use residuals of any order as measures of learning, thus dissociating gain from any number of variables known to be associated with final status.

It is not to be supposed that the residual score, $z_{2.1}$, is a pure measure of change. Its usefulness depends upon the degree to which $z_1$ validly and reliably measures initial status and the degree to which $z_2$ validly and reliably measures final status. If non-pertinent variance is introduced into one of the measures but not the other, $r_{12}$ will be reduced and $z_{2.1}$ will be too large. Its correlations with outside variables will be affected. Since initial and final status tend to be positively correlated, the reliability of $z_{2.1}$ tends to be somewhat lower than the reliabilities of its constituent parts. It is therefore obvious that care must be taken to develop measurements which reflect both initial and final status adequately and with a minimum of extraneous variance.

### CORRELATIONAL ANALYSIS AND THE ANALYSIS OF VARIANCE AND COVARIANCE

The popularization of the work of Sir Ronald A. Fisher among psychologists a quarter of a century ago appears to have resulted in something resembling a bifurcation in quantitative psychology, with the experimentalists using analysis of variance models and those psychologists working with tests emphasizing regression and correlational analysis. Certainly many of the points that were introduced or emphasized by Fisher were important. First of all, it is important to be concerned with estimating parameters, rather than merely summarizing findings within a particular sample. However, in training and educational research there generally are relatively large numbers of cases, reasonably well selected, so that the descriptive statistics are relatively good estimates of parameters.

Secondly, in laboratory studies and to some extent in field studies of learning, important variables may be nominal scales. Instructional method almost always is nominal, whereas measures of individual differences, important in studies of learning, are on the ordinal-interval scales described earlier. Only the Fisher techniques give an adequate means of handling a number of nominal scales simultaneously as independent and control variables.

Another advantage of the Fisher techniques is that they lend themselves somewhat more readily to the investigation of curvilinear relationships than does correlational analysis. In instances when variables are on interval scales (or nearly so) and when relationships are more or less linear, it is practically a matter of taste as to whether one should use correlational analysis or the analysis of covariance. The reasons for preferring to work with a complete matrix of correlations, whenever it is possible to do so, include the following:

1. The overall pattern of variables is clear-cut and easy to follow. One variable is the criterion, and there can be any number of independent variables (or predictors) and any number of control variables, which may be partialed out of the predictors, the criterion, or both.

2. A simple notation is available, so that through a long series of manipulations each coefficient can be precisely identified as to its meaning and as to the variables concerned.

3. In addition to the usual tests of significance, measures of the degree of relationships are readily available, either in terms of proportions of variances, in terms of correlation coefficients, or in terms of regression.

4. Correlational analysis is closely allied to techniques for determining dimensionality, such as factor analysis, which has important potential applications in the study of training.

In reviewing below some of the applications of correlational analysis to training research, cognizance is taken of the fact that in most research studies the statistical design may be stated in alternate notation and terminology. Attention is invited, however, to the flexibility and simplicity of the correlation-regression model. Several types of correlation were reviewed as part of a simple system (DuBois, 1957), based on pivotal condensation, which conceptualizes statistical manipulations involving an indefinite number of structured variables.

## Multiple Partial Correlation

Multiple partial correlation is a special type of correlation that might have some application in training research. In it the criterion and all predictors are first residualized with respect to an identical set of control variables. The multiple is then computed between the residualized criterion and an indefinite number of predictors. As in the case with any multiple, $R$'s may be interpreted as the proportion of the criterion variance predictable from specified sources. It is useful when the logic of a study demands widespread statistical control before determining the proportion of the variance of a residual criterion predictable from a team of residual predictors.

## Part Correlation

A statistic more directly applicable to training research would seem to be part correlation, sometimes called semi-partial $r$. Raymond Franzen (1928) gave the formula for a first order part correlation as follows:

$$r_{(2.1)3} = \frac{r_{23} - r_{12}r_{13}}{\sqrt{1 - r_{12}^2}} \qquad (3)$$

and suggested that the formula be used to determine the correlation of an outside variable, 3, with gain in a function defined as final status less that portion predictable from initial status. It follows from the formula that there is no need for computing gain scores for individuals. An analysis of the matrix of the intercorrelations of three variables yields all pertinent information.

Formula (3) above may be written in terms of notation involving the variances and covariances of $z$-scores as follows:

$$r_{(2.1)3} = \frac{C_{23.1}}{\sqrt{V_{2.1}}} \qquad (4)$$

Two points may be mentioned. While $C_{23.1}$ is a partial covariance, it is numerically equal, when all variables are in $z$-form, to either of two part covariances, $C_{2(3.1)}$ or $C_{3(2.1)}$. It is the latter that must be divided by two standard deviations, the partial standard deviation of Variable 2 less the portion predictable from Variable 1, namely $\sqrt{V_{2.1}}$ or $\sigma_{2.1}$ and the standard deviation of Variable 3. Variable 3 is, however, a zero order $z$-score, and hence its standard deviation of unity can be dropped from the formula.

A major question is why partial correlation should not be used instead of part correlation to study the relation of gain to some outside variable. The reason is simple. A partial $r$ would be a biased estimate of the relationship under investigation. A glance at Formula (3) shows that it would become $r_{(2.1)(3.1)}$ or, more conventionally, $r_{23.1}$, merely by dividing the expression by the partial standard deviation, $\sigma_{3.1}$, or $\sqrt{1-r_{13}^2}$. Since this first order partial standard deviation is less than unity (except when $r_{13}=0$), it is readily seen that partialling out initial score both from the final score and from the predictor would inflate the $r$. In all cases the summarization demanded by the logic of the situation should be performed, and in this case there is no reason to residualize the predictor.

## Multiple Part Correlation

There are two main varieties of multiple part correlation. One of them is the correlation between an unmodified criterion and a set of predictors, all residualized with respect to the same control variable or variables. A specific example is $R_{0(1.4,\ 2.4,\ 3.4)}$ in which the three predictors (1, 2 and 3) are residualized with respect to Variable 4 and the multiple correlation is found with the criterion, Variable 0. No applications of this type of multiple part correlation in training research have been found. On the other hand, another type of multiple part correlation, in which a residualized criterion is related to a number of unmodified predictors, seems to be of considerable potential utility. This is exemplified by the notation, $R_{(2.1)(3,\ 4,\ 5...)}$, in which Variable 2, which might be the final attainment score, is residualized with respect to Variable 1, initial standing, and the multiple correlation obtained with Variables 3, 4, 5... weighted, as in any multiple, so as to maximize the relationship.

In this type of multiple part correlation it is possible to use a criterion of any order, that is to say, before finding the multiple, variance associated with any number of control variables may be subtracted out of the final score. The square of this multiple $R$ tells the proportion of the gain predictable from stated sources of variances. As in any multiple, the relative importance of the various predictors can be readily determined. Computation of multiple part $R$ proceeds rapidly. The simplest method is to residualize the criterion, restore the variance of the residualized criterion to unity, and proceed in the normal fashion to compute the multiple by reduction of criterion variance.

## Intercorrelations of Gain Scores

The correlation between two sets of residual scores, $z_{2.1}$ and $z_{4.3}$, may be found from the formula:

$$r_{(2.1)(4.3)} = \frac{r_{24} - r_{12}r_{14} - r_{23}r_{34} + r_{12}r_{13}r_{34}}{\sqrt{1-r_{12}^2}\ \sqrt{1-r_{34}^2}} \tag{5}$$

This formula is given by Franzen (1928) and is appropriate for finding the intercorrelations of changes in different characteristics. For slightly greater convenience in computation, Formula (5) may be written:

$$r_{(2.1)(4.3)} = \frac{C_{24.1} - r_{34}C_{23.1}}{\sqrt{V_{2.1}}\ \sqrt{V_{4.3}}} = \frac{C_{24.3} - r_{12}C_{14.3}}{\sqrt{V_{2.1}}\ \sqrt{V_{4.3}}} \qquad (6)$$

Formula (6) is written in the notation of DuBois (1957), with $V$ to indicate a variance and $C$ a covariance. Secondary subscripts indicate variables eliminated in forming partial variances and covariances.

If we wish to determine consistency of learning in different areas, Formula (5) is the proper one to use. It seems likely that the lack of consistency of gain scores in different areas pointed out some years ago by Woodrow (1940) was a statistical artifact caused by his using crude gain instead of regressed scores (or residual gain) as a measure of change in function.

## Special Types of Correlation

Probably in training research there is application for designing a correlation coefficient to fit the logic of the particular question to be investigated. First of all, measurable variables should be sorted into three categories: the criterion, the predictors, and the control variables. Next it must be decided whether the control variables are to be generally or partially applied. In general, it would seem that initial status, as a control, should be applied only as a negative component of the gain measure. Similarly, in investigating the influences of method, measures of personal characteristics might be used as controls only in connection with the predictor.

The notation $r_{(2.1)(3.456)}$ represents a situation in which final status (Variable 2) is residualized with respect to initial status (Variable 1) and the gain score related to method (Variable 3) residualized with respect to three measures of individual differences (Variable 4, 5, 6). In order to compute this coefficient, method on some sort of a scale is necessary. However, it would appear that a dichotomy would be sufficient, since point measures fit neatly into the Pearson system. While this type of correlation does not seem to have been christened and formulas do not appear to have been presented, it is simple to work with. The required residuals are merely expressed in regression equation format and the appropriate multiplication and summations are performed to obtain the statement of the required covariance. This covariance will be a function of certain covariances and betas. When it is divided by two partial standard deviations, the required correlation is found. The interpretation of $r_{(2.1)\ (3.456)}$ is clear. It states the degree of relationship between a defined change in behavior and a predictor of that change when certain stated sources of variance are statistically eliminated from consideration. Tests of significance are similar to those used with partial correlation.

## Factor Analysis

In research on training, factor analysis would seem to have application in describing what is learned and in analyzing conditions determining the gain. It seems appropriate to insist that a factor system to be maximally useful should be a logical extension of multivariate correlation, the chief difference being that in factor analysis one may deal with variables unencumbered with error and unique variance. Common factors are thus definable as abstractions of aspects of observed variables. (See Chapter 5 by Fleishman.)

## RESEARCH IN ON-GOING SITUATIONS

The chief advantage of the use of statistical controls, whether in correlational analysis or in the analysis of covariance, is their convenience in psychological research in on-going situations. It appears likely that if investigations should be restricted to training situations in which extensive experimental controls are possible, much needed research could not be accomplished in the foreseeable future. A psychological study on almost any topic needs confirmation by repeating it in a somewhat altered context, and this is particularly true when reliance is on statistical controls. Nevertheless it would appear that dependable and generalizable knowledge may be developed in situations in which investigations are incidental to the learning activity.

In the psychology of training that seems to be developing, attention must be given to many of the factors that influence gain, including prior skills and knowledge; aptitudes and capacities of the learner; goals, motivation and the readiness to learn; training methods and equipment; and the effects of reinforcement. Perhaps in the current generation, experiments in education should become usual rather than exceptional as various types of training are conducted. A research point of view, careful measurement, and the use of the best research designs available, should greatly increase knowledge of training principles.

## REFERENCES

Berkeley, M. H. A method for developing equivalent forms of tests of complex functions. *Educ. psychol. Measmt*, 1954, *14*, 518-528.

DuBois, P. H. *Multivariate correlational analysis*. New York: Harper, 1957.

DuBois, P. H. An analysis of Guttman's simplex. *Psychometrika*, 1960, *25*, 173-182.

DuBois, P. H. & Manning, W. H. *Methods of research in technical training*. St. Louis: Washington University, May 1957, Revised Edition, January 1960. ONR Technical Report No. 3.

Franzen, R. A comment on partial correlation. *J. educ. Psychol.*, 1928, *19*, 194-197.

Loevinger, J., Gleser, G. C., & DuBois, P. H. Maximizing the discriminating power of a multiple score test. *Psychometrika*, 1953, *18*, 309-317.

Stevens, S. S. *Handbook of experimental psychology*. New York: Wiley, 1951.

Woodrow, H. Interrelations of measures of learning. *J. Psychol.*, 1940, *10*, 49-73.

Chapter 4

# The Prediction of Success In Intensive Foreign Language Training

John B. Carroll, Harvard University

The advent of World War II brought the military services, and perhaps even the general public, to recognize the desirability of having available, certainly in wartime, considerable numbers of personnel equipped to speak foreign languages of military or political importance. In most cases, this meant that it was necessary to train the requisite personnel almost from scratch, since insufficient numbers had been trained in schools and colleges in critical languages. The "Army" method of intensive language training was developed, largely under the guidance of linguistic scientists, and for the first time in its history, the nation found itself alerted to the possible falsity of the widespread belief that Americans have no aptitude for languages. These "intensive" language learning methods have the drawback of requiring rather large amounts of time. In the program now in effect at the Army Language School (ALS) at the Presidio of Monterey in California, for example, the student devotes almost his entire attention to mastering a foreign language during an eight month, or, in the case of difficult languages, a twelve month period. The length of the training period is similarly long in programs operated by the Air Force, the Navy, the Foreign Service Institute of the Department of State, and other government departments and agencies. No way has been found to reduce the length of the training program beyond a certain point and still produce a satisfactory and useful product. Because of the inevitable expense of these training programs, it is widely accepted that all efforts should be made to minimize the number of training failures both by appropriate screening procedures and by the provision of the best possible instruction. (Training failures are sometimes very numerous. Williams and Leavitt [1947] report an attrition rate of 80% in the Japanese language program in which they did their study.)

Over the past few years the author has been engaged in a program of research on the measurement of aptitude for foreign language learning.[1] Investigations have been made in a variety of settings—in schools, colleges, and universities, in military and governmental training programs, and at the elementary school level as well as at the adolescent and adult level. This chapter is intended to report the major findings that are applicable to the screening of personnel for military and governmental programs for intensive or semi-intensive foreign language training.

A word should be said, however, about research in foreign language training methods. The word can be brief, however, because the amount of psychological research on language training methods in military settings has been pitifully small. One brief attempt was made to carry out a program of such research, but this had to do with the teaching of English to foreigners. A series of instructional materials were developed, but the program was terminated before these could be properly evaluated. One or two research papers on fundamental questions in language training were published (e.g., Kopstein & Roshal, 1954), but they could not begin to answer all the interesting and pertinent questions that could be raised about the psychology of language training. Elsewhere, the psychological research literature in this area has been reviewed (Carroll, 1962), but very little of this research has been done in the setting of a modern, intensive language training program emphasizing the attainment of fluent speaking and reading comprehension of the foreign language. Much research remains to be done; some of the funds appropriated under Title VI of the National Defense Education Act of 1958 have become available for psychological research on methods of language teaching. Up to now, the major need has been for methods that are better organized from a linguistic point of view— texts, tapes, and films that present language sounds, patterns and structure in a clear and well-ordered way, based on adequate linguistic re-

[1]This research was supported chiefly by grants to Harvard University from the Carnegie Corporation of New York. That Corporation, however, is not to be held responsible for opinions expressed here, which are solely the responsibility of the author. Thanks are due to all who were associated with this project, particularly to Dr. Stanley M. Sapon of Ohio State University who spent two years (1953-1955) with the author in developing and studying foreign language aptitude measures. The author is indebted to Robert Gardner for helpful comments regarding a preliminary version of this chapter.

search. Even with the best linguistic research, however, there still remain questions which one would hope psychological research could answer, such as: How much will use of the native language help or hinder learning? How long or how often should a given item be practiced? How can the teaching of grammar be organized to give the student maximum flexibility in varying language patterns?

The theme here, however, is selection, and at the outset two propositions should be mentioned, the truth of which this chapter will attempt to demonstrate, and which if accepted will serve to accent the needs which prompted the program of research reported. These propositions are (a) that facility in learning to speak and understand a foreign language is a fairly specialized talent (or group of talents),[2] relatively independent of those traits ordinarily included under "intelligence" and (b) that a relatively small fraction of the general population seems to have enough of this talent to be worth subjecting to the rigorous, intensive, expensive training programs in foreign languages operated by military and governmental organizations, or by such private organizations as missionary societies, businesses, and industries engaged in overseas operations. This latter proposition is not meant to imply that the American population is abnormally low in foreign language aptitude, for, in any case, there are no comparative data from non-American populations. Further, it should not be taken to suggest that only a relatively small number of American school children or college students ought to study foreign languages. The question of whether a student of lower than average aptitude should study foreign languages for purposes of general and liberal education depends upon a number of important considerations which do not bear upon the selection of students for intensive foreign language courses of the type described here. The proposition applies only to situations where the organization sponsoring a language training course has a legitimate reason for exercising selectivity.

[2] In speaking of "talent" and "abilities," the conveniences of ordinary language are being indulged in; from a strictly operational behavioristic point of view the references would have to be to correspondences observed between behavior on tests and behavior in training programs, with possibly some inferences about "prior learning," "learning sets," etc. It still remains to be investigated to what extent the behavior measured on the aptitude tests which were developed can be modified by training and whether such learning would transfer to real language learning situations.

The proposition that foreign language aptitude is relatively specialized can be introduced by pointing out the well-known fact that intelligence tests have been largely unsuccessful in screening individuals for language training. To be sure, certain cutting points may be introduced to eliminate those of limited intellectual ability, but there are apparently wide variations in the language learning ability of those who are above the cutting point. The screening procedure used by the U. S. Air Force before the advent of valid aptitude tests may be cited. As described by Frith (1953), this involved the use of a so-called "trial course" in a foreign language, either in Russian or in Chinese; success in the trial course, of one to three weeks' duration, was required before the individual was selected for longer, intensive language training. Requirements for entrance into the trial course were: (*a*) an Armed Force Qualification Test (AFQT) score of 70 or better; (*b*) a Technician Specialty Aptitude Index of eight or better;[3] (*c*) a high school diploma or the equivalent; and (*d*) a desire to study the language. Despite the imposition of requirements with an intellectual component, success in the trial course varied widely. In fact—and this supports the second proposition—the proportion of those selected for further, intensive training was relatively small, sometimes as low as 25%. In two trial courses in Chinese in which the language aptitude tests which were developed were tried out, the figures were 41% and 44%, based only on those who did not *voluntarily* withdraw from the course before its completion. The figures were 30% and 38% when based on the total input. These low percentages were not the result of small quotas and undue selectivity; they were the result of experience which showed that it was necessary to enter large numbers of personnel into the trial course in order to obtain candidates with what appeared to be the requisite aptitude. In fact, in the tryouts of aptitude tests, the test results agreed well with the appraisals of the instructors who ran the trial course; in two such trial courses the multiple correlations were .76 and .84 respectively. Furthermore, the evidence avail-

---

[3]The following explanation of these scores was furnished by Dr. Francis D. Harding of the Personnel Laboratory, Wright Air Development Center (Air Research and Development Command), Lackland Air Force Base, Texas: "The scores on the AFQT represent percentile scores in a sample equivalent to the World War II mobilization population. The Technician Specialty Index of eight converts to about a 75 percentile score. The Technician Specialty Index, now known as the General Aptitude Index, is really a measure of general ability."

able suggests that both the aptitude tests and the instructors' appraisals in the trial course were valid for predicting success in further training.

Later in the chapter the details of the experiments alluded to above will be reported but it seems now sufficiently well established that there was need for better selective devices than intelligence tests, trial courses, and the like.

## PREVIOUS RESEARCH

If intelligence tests were not adequate for screening candidates for language training, why was there no resort to previously published language aptitude tests? The reasons for this are complex, and must be presented in the light of a brief history of language aptitude testing.

Apparently the first efforts to develop aptitude tests for foreign language study were made in the second and third decades of this century. This work was summarized in a publication edited by Henmon (1929). The tests were generally of two sorts: (a) tests of ability and achievement in the English language—vocabulary, grammar, spelling, etc., and (b) work-sample testing involving short "lessons" or problems in the language to be studied or in an artificial language. In every case, however, the tests were of the paper-and-pencil variety and emphasized ability to deal with the intellectual, cognitive aspects of language study, that is, in the main, with the learning of a written language. In the 1920's and 1930's, for various reasons which will not be developed here, the main objective of foreign language study in the schools was to teach the student to read, or perhaps it would be stated better to say—to translate a foreign language. Some of the tests developed during this period, e.g., the Iowa Foreign Language Aptitude Examination (Stoddard & VanderBeke, 1925), the Symonds Foreign Language Prognosis Test (Symonds, 1930), the Luria-Orleans Modern Language Prognosis Test (Luria & Orleans, 1928), and the George Washington University Language Aptitude Test (Hunt, Wallace, Doran, Buynitzky, & Schwarz, 1929) were reasonably effective in predicting success in language learning under these conditions. However, they tended to have high correlations with intelligence tests; indeed, one part of the American Council on Education Psychological Examination is an artificial language test presenting vocabulary and grammar rules in an artificial language which the student must apply in completing the test. They presented an essentially intellectual task which the student could solve by an analytical procedure quite similar to that which was demanded by the kind of foreign language teaching which tended to be prevalent at the time. But since success in these courses could generally be predicted about as well by intelligence tests as by the special prognostic tests, the latter were not widely used. Another characteristic of these tests which undoubtedly affected their validity (either increasing or decreasing it, depending on the nature of the criterion) was that they assumed or tested certain specific prior learnings, such as the knowledge of grammatical terminology, and recognition of morphological processes like prefixing and suffixing.

During World War II, selection of men for training in intensive language courses was based mainly on amount of education. The Army developed a work-sample language aptitude test, but did so too late for wide use during the war. It was pressed into service, however, as one part of a battery of tests for aiding in the selection of candidates for the U. S. Military Academy at West Point (for this reason the test appears sometimes in the literature with the designation WPAT or WPQ). This test is still in use for that purpose; data on its validity in one West Point class that was studied will be given below. Even so, the test was not designed with the requirements of modern intensive language training in mind and continued the tradition of posing linguistic puzzles in an artificial language that could be solved analytically.

There were sporadic attempts to investigate the prediction of language learning success in intensive language learning contexts. Bottke and Milligan (1945) suggested several types of test items which might bear on aural and oral abilities, but they did not publish results of any kind. Williams and Leavitt (1947) investigated the usefulness of a series of tests in predicting success or failure in an intensive course in spoken and written Japanese, conducted by the U. S. Marine Corps during World War II. The tests included the U. S. Navy Officer Qualification Test (with three parts: Verbal Opposites, Mechanical Comprehension, and Arithmetical Reasoning); the U. S. Army Language Aptitude Test WPQ-1; the American Council on Education Psychological Examination for college freshmen (with separate scores on the Language and Quantitative subtests); Anderson's Adult Placement Test (parts 1, 2, 3, only); the Shipley-Hartford Retreat Scale; the National Defense Research Council (NDRC) Personal Inventory Form; a "specially devised Symbol Digit Test in which the symbols were Japanese-like nonsense characters"; a "specially devised Figure Recognition Test of visual memory of geometric forms"; the AGCT (Army General Classification Test); and the Army Mechanical Aptitude Test.

Critical ratios greater than 3.0 between means of 27 passers and 48 failers were obtained only for the ACE Language Score, the Army Language Aptitude Test, the Verbal Opposites test of the Navy Officer Qualification Test, and the Vocabulary section of the Shipley-Hartford Retreat Scale—all verbal tests. Computations from data presented by these authors yield biserial $r$'s of .71 for the ACE language score and .70 for the Army Language Aptitude Test. Williams and Leavitt were evidently working in a situation where verbal intelligence was a good predictor of success in intensive foreign language training. It would be possible to organize and teach a course in such a way that verbal intelligence would be at a premium, and it is conceivable that this was true for the Marine Corps course. The studies to be reported here, however, demonstrate that verbal intelligence will not always be a good predictor. This will be seen in the fact that the Cooperative Vocabulary Test is only a moderately good predictor in Tables 4.1 and 4.10.

The first large-scale study of foreign language aptitude after World War II was conducted by Dorcus, Mount and Jones (1952) under a contract with the Department of the Army. Working at the Army Language School in California, they investigated two sets of variables as possible predictors of language success. The first set of variables comprised data already available for 279 cases from files of the school, including scores on the AGCT, three subtests of the Seashore Musical Aptitude Test (Tonal Memory, Timbre, and Pitch), and the Army Language Aptitude Test WPQ-1. Of these variables, only the last yielded any significant correlation with language grades, and then chiefly with grades in the first two weeks of the course. The second set of variables, applied to 152 new cases, included a series of ten novel, specially-constructed tests of abilities in the verbal, auditory, perceptual, and memory domains; six of these were presented by means of magnetic tape. The new variables failed to produce any impressive gain in predictive power over the Army Language Aptitude Test WPQ-1; in fact, in most cases they themselves had non-significant validity coefficients.

In appraising this study, one can hardly criticize the criterion variables, on which much labor was expended. Measures of both spoken and written proficiency for six languages taught at the ALS were constructed, and grades were obtained for both initial and final phases of the course. The authors argue, in fact, that the high correlations of early and final course examinations "indicate that important factors do exist for the prediction of language proficiency . . . on the assumption that insufficient learning has occurred in the first few weeks of training to account for the relationship to the final examination score" (Dorcus, et al., 1952, p. 3).

It may be suggested that the Dorcus, Mount and Jones study failed to achieve satisfactorily high predictive validities for the new tests because these tests just missed measuring certain abilities that were crucial in language learning. The tasks sampled were not sufficiently close, in behavioral structure, to the tasks actually involved in learning a new language. For example, language learning does not involve memory span for *digits* (as was measured in one of the tests), though it might well involve memory span for *speech sounds*; likewise, there is nothing in language learning which resembles the "Difficult Reading" task (e.g., stating how many English words are found in the following sequence: wo Uld HaRd;ly bef At Alev entho Ugh hew As by hiMse;lf and).

The wide variations in the success achieved by various projects seeking to predict progress in learning foreign languages further indicated that there was an acute need not only for tests which would reliably predict success in different kinds of foreign language courses, but also for better knowledge of the factors making for success. Tests would be useful not only in selection, but also in guidance, placement, and research. Knowledge about factors making for success might eventually make it possible to improve teaching procedures so as to overcome some of the commoner student difficulties. Idealistically, one would like to see instruction improved to the point where the need for aptitude tests will be eliminated, but that day does not seem to be very near at hand. In any case, valid language aptitude tests would be highly useful for providing controls in experimentation on language teaching methods. It appeared, then, that an urgent practical problem was to be faced, as well as an interesting scientific puzzle.

## Test Development

In embarking on the research it seemed that there was a place for broad-scale empiricism, guided when possible by theory, and where that was impossible, by hunches. Random experimentation in prediction studies is to be deplored, to be sure (Travers, 1954; Travers, 1956) and it was seldom the case, in these studies, that a predictor variable was investigated simply because it was available. The primary consideration in selecting and devising the tests of the initial trial batteries was to include a variety of tests each of which promised to measure some aspect of the complex of traits deemed requisite for success in the criterion performance.

The first battery which was tried out contained 20 separate tests and included additional predictor variables that were obtained in several of the samples used for the tryouts. In assembling the tests, one of the guiding principles was to include tests of several of the established "factors" or dimensions of the domain of verbal abilities. It seemed reasonable (Carroll, 1953) to suppose that some of the dimensions of individual differences observable through tests of ability with the English language might also manifest themselves in learning a second language. The factors of verbal ability thus included were: (*a*) the verbal knowledge factor V; (*b*) the word-fluency factor *W* (which can be regarded as mainly involving knowledge of orthographic habits); (*c*) the fluency-of-expression factor *FE*; (*d*) the associative memory factor *M*; and (*e*) the naming factor *Na*. (The designations given by French [1951] are also used here.) In the case of each of these factors, it was hypothesized that the behaviors measured by the corresponding tests had certain elements in common with behaviors involved in foreign language learning. These hypotheses are, of course, incapable of direct confirmation, although they would tend to gain support if one were to obtain consistently significant positive validity coefficients for the corresponding tests.

Other tests were developed and included in the initial tryout battery because they were believed to measure certain specific abilities required in second language learning. One was essentially a "grammatical analogies" test in which the terms of the analogy were relations between a given linguistic form, a word or phrase, and the sentence in which it is placed; thus, in the following sample item

The man went into the HOUSE.

The *church* next to the *bowling alley* will be built in a new *location* next *year*.
　　A　　　　　　B　　C　　　　　　　　　　　D　　　　E

the examinee has to find which lettered element in the second sentence has the same relation to its sentence as "house" has to its sentence. The test therefore appears to measure "grammatical sensitivity," that is, the ability to recognize the grammatical function of words in sentences ("Words in Sentences" is the name for this test), and it does this without at the same time requiring the examinee to know the meaning of such grammatical terms as noun, adjective, predicate, preposition and the like. It was thought very likely that some kind of sentence-analysis would be involved in foreign language learning, regardless of whether the emphasis was on speech or writing.

Still another test included in the battery to fit a particular hypothesis was a test of Phonetic Discrimination which was developed by Dr. Stanley M. Sapon. One of the first tasks which the learner of a foreign language has to master is to recognize the differences among the sounds of the foreign language; often these sounds appear to be so similar to the native speaker of English as to be almost indistinguishable, that is, while they are phonemically distinct in the foreign language, they are not so in English. It was therefore believed that a test of the ability to perceive phonetic distinctions would be a useful item in an aptitude battery. In the initial form of the test, a series of triads of sounds in various languages were presented by tape recording; in each triad, two of the sounds were alike and the third was different, the subject being instructed to identify the odd member. This test, incidentally, tended to be too easy and to have low reliability; a later form used the more conventional multiple-choice type of item, but this was still unreliable. What is more, the validity coefficients were consistently low in comparison to those of other tests, and the conclusion was reached that phonetic discrimination ability is not crucial in foreign language learning. Most normal people have enough discrimination ability to serve them in learning a foreign language, and in any case, it is more a matter of *learning* the discrimination over a period of time than any fundamental lack of auditory discrimination which can readily be tested in an aptitude battery.

One other consideration in the assembly of the initial tryout battery was the desirability of including some "work-sample" tests. The use of work-sample tests in aptitude batteries has sometimes been criticized, either on account of the low level of theoretical sophistication that they imply, or on account of the high specificity which they seem to involve. It is claimed that the too frequent use of work-sample tests may imply that one needs a different work-sample test for every conceivable kind of task for which one might want to predict an individual's success. These arguments do not apply in the present case, and they also mistake the potential value of the work-sample test. To be sure, it is perhaps regrettable that a special language prognosis test is needed to supplement other kinds of tests in the psychometrician's kit, but as long as it is—presumably because of the specific nature of language aptitude—there is no reason to exclude a work-sample test if such a test is found to have adequate validity. (On work-sample tests, see Chapter 12 by Wilson.) Furthermore, a work-sample test is seldom as specific as has been claimed. As a sample of the kinds of tasks to be learned, it may very well require the same abilities that are required in a broad class of criterion tasks. The abilities may appear to be specific to this class of criterion tasks only because nobody has invented a way of tapping them in other connections.

Several kinds of work-sample tests were devised in the course of this project. One of the simplest was adapted from a test developed some years before for research on verbal abilities (Carroll, 1941). This was an artificial language test in which the examinee has to learn the names for a simple foreign language number system, after which he is required to write down three-digit numbers from dictation. The examinee must not only learn the number system; he also has to be able to attend to and respond to a complex auditory signal, i.e., the artificial language numbers as read from a tape recording. The behavior can be regarded as highly similar to that of understanding a foreign language when spoken rapidly.

Another work-sample test, tried out in the initial battery, was one in which an attempt was made to simulate modern oral language learning as closely as possible. This test, described by Sapon (1955), was perhaps one of the first fully "automated" language teaching sequences; it presented the lesson material in easy steps by a tape recording synchronized with a film strip. There was no use of English beyond initial directions, and the lesson material was arranged so as to make possible inductive learning of the vocabulary and grammar of "Tem-Tem," the artificial language constructed for this test.

Still another work-sample test was devised to simulate *traditional* language instruction of the grammar-translation type designed with solely the reading objective in mind. The test was designed to outdo the Army's West Point Aptitude Test by being based more squarely on linguistic principles. It, too, was administered by tape, but traditional grammar lessons were read and explained to the examinee, with proper attention to the pronunciation of words in the artificial language, "Perdašeb," contrived for the purpose of the test.

Work samples such as these have the drawbacks of complexity and of excessive time requirements. Both the Tem-Tem and Perdašeb tests required nearly a half-hour of testing time apiece, and the former required the use of a colored strip-film in a suitable projector. They could not be used in the final test battery which resulted from the project, but they were valuable in the research program for helping to delineate the nature of language aptitude.

The project was conceived of, in short, as an opportunity to try out different kinds of tests and modify hypotheses until more was known about factors involved in language aptitude. At a rather early stage in the project, two correlation matrices were subjected to factor-analysis study (Carroll, 1958). It is probably more appropriate to defer discussion of these results and their implications for the nature of foreign language aptitude until after presenting results of the several validation studies that were conducted. The following sections provide an overview of these results. In general, only results pertinent to intensive language training will be included. Validation studies performed in connection with regular academic courses will be presented elsewhere. Results for two service academies, the U. S. Military Academy at West Point and the U. S. Air Force Academy in Colorado, will be included here because their courses may be described as semi-intensive.

## TEST VALIDITY IN INTENSIVE LANGUAGE COURSES

The paramount concern in any research on aptitude is the validity of the test. This and several following sections will provide an overview of those phases of the research program which were designed to identify the most promising tests of language aptitude and to investigate the conditions under which they were valid.

At the outset, it was desirable to try out a large number of tests in a situation where criterion measurements would not be long in becoming available. The tests were tried out first in connection with one of the "trial courses" conducted by the U. S. Air Force to screen personnel for further language study. In February 1954, a battery of 20 tests, totalling about four hours of testing time, was administered to 111 men who had been previously screened by the requirements listed above (Frith, 1953) and who had volunteered to try for the chance of being selected for an eight-months' course in Mandarin Chinese at the Institute of Far Eastern Languages (IFEL), Yale University. The list of tests is given in Table 4.1. (All of the tests mentioned here are briefly described in the Appendix at the end of the chapter.) Immediately after the completion of testing on Monday, the men started intensive study of spoken Mandarin Chinese under experienced instructors, and lessons continued through Friday. Of the 111 men tested, 31 voluntarily withdrew from the program, 10 of them immediately

Table 4.1

Validity Coefficients and Related Data for Experimental Language Aptitude Tests Administered to Two Air Force Trial Course Groups

Entries are correlations or beta-weights with normalized academic grade criterion.

| Test | Tested Feb. 1954 (N=80) r | Tested June 1954 (N=88) r | Selected Multiple R's with Beta Coefficients | | |
|---|---|---|---|---|---|
| | | | Feb. (a) | June (a) | June (b) |
| Artificial Language Part I | .33 | .45 | | | |
| Artificial Language Part II | .46 | .52 | .33 | .23 | .27 |
| Artificial Language Part III | .45 | .46 | | | |
| Turse Spelling | .40 | .47 | | | |
| Turse Phonetic Association | .53 | .62 | .35 | .16 | |
| Spelling Clues | — | .53 | | -.04 | |
| Turse Word Discrimination | .30 | — | | | |
| Letter—Star | .24 | — | | | |
| Word Squares | .19 | — | | | |
| Disarranged Letters | .33 | .48 | | | |
| Rhyming | .32 | .51 | | | |
| Phrase Completion | .24 | — | | | |
| Cooperative Vocabulary Form Z | .36 | .42 | | | |
| Artificial Language Numbers | .45 | — | | | |
| Number Learning | — | .53 | | .27 | .29 |
| Words in Sentences | .51 | .52 | .23 | .06 | |
| Phonetic Discrimination P-120-A | .22 | — | | | |
| Phonetic Discrimination P-123-A | — | .27 | | | |
| Disarranged Words | .45 | — | | | |
| Paired Associates | .50 | .55 | .23 | .14 | .19 |
| Word Elements | .42 | — | | | |
| Anagrams | .18 | — | | | |
| Picture Naming | .06 | — | | | |
| Verbal Enumeration: Number Attempted | .00 | — | | | |
| Verbal Enumeration: Number Wrong (Refl.) | .21 | — | | | |
| Same—Opposites: Number Attempted | .24 | — | | | |
| Same—Opposites: Number Wrong (Refl.) | .26 | — | | | |
| Devanagari Script | — | .37 | | -.05 | |
| Perdašeb (Total) | — | .56 | | .14 | |
| Phonetic Script (Total) | — | .68 | | .27 | .40 |
| r Required at 5% level | .22 | .21 | | | |
| r Required at 1% level | .29 | .28 | | | |
| r Required at 0.1% level | .37 | .36 | | | |
| Multiple R for the variables which have beta's listed in the column above | | | .75 | .84 | .82 |

after the first day; 47 were failed, and 33 were finally selected for study at IFEL. The 31 cases of voluntary withdrawal were excluded from further analysis (there was no significant contingency between voluntary withdrawal and test scores), and validity coefficients were based on the remaining 80 cases.

Two criterion measurements were employed: the academic grades (transformed to approximate normality) assigned by the instructors to both cases selected and not selected for further study, and selection or non-selection. Selection or non-selection was highly correlated with the academic grades, but not perfectly, since those responsible for selection paid some attention to judged character and temperament. As shown in Table 4.1, a large number of test variables showed highly significant correlations with the criterion measurements; at the same time, there were a number of tests which manifestly did not have statistically significant validities. There were no striking or systematic differences between validities for the two criteria. When the academic grade criterion was employed, it was found possible to obtain a multiple correlation of .77, shrunken by Wherry's formula, from just six tests by a test selection computation. Four tests—Test 2 (Artificial Language Learning, Part II), Test 5 (Turse Phonetic Association), Test 14 (Words in Sentences) and Test 17 (Paired Associates)—yielded a multiple $R$ of .75. An interesting aspect of the results was that the beta-weights were of the same general order of magnitude: .33, .35, .23 and .23, respectively. Not only did this first validation run produce startlingly high validity coefficients, it also yielded a set of tests with high validities and relatively low intercorrelations, a situation idealized by the textbooks but seldom found in practice. The validities were so high that under the selection conditions which actually obtained, the trial course results and the prediction test results agreed on the classification of 66 out of 80 cases, or 82.5%.

These results obviously begged for replication and cross-validation. A battery of tests was administered to another group under the same conditions in June 1954; 103 men were tested, of whom 15 voluntarily withdrew before completion of the trial course, 44 were failed, and 34 were selected. This second group was highly comparable to the first in test scores, criterion academic grades, and percentage selected. The battery of tests administered to this group contained a few new ones which had been constructed in the light of previous results, and some of the tests previously found invalid were now omitted. The results are to be found in Table 4.1. Using the regression equation developed on the basis of the best combinations of the tests in the February results, a correlation of .77 was obtained between predicted scores and actual (normalized) academic grades, as compared with a multiple $R$ of .75 obtained for the original sample. If anything, this was negative shrinkage. When certain of the newer tests were utilized in the prediction formula, a correlation of .84 was achieved. In comparison with validity coefficients commonly obtained for aptitude tests and in view of the possibility of some unreliability in the criterion, these figures represented an unusual degree of success in the prediction of learning ability.

It should be noted, however, that the criterion itself had many elements of a test situation; in fact, the trial-course was conceived of by the instructors as a week-long test and men were almost mercilessly dropped at the first real sign of weakness. Furthermore, the tasks used in the training program were highly similar to some of the tasks used in the test itself. For example, one of the first things the students had to learn was to recognize the correspondences between a series of Chinese phonemes, including the famous "tones," and their representations in the phonemic transcription used in the course, e.g., to know how to pronounce syllables marked thus: mā, má, mǎ, mà. This was very similar to the task posed in the Phonetic Script Test which had been introduced as a part of the aptitude test battery. Another task which had to be mastered was that of constructing simple Chinese sentences conforming to one of several "sentence-types" with characteristic placement of subject, verb, object, etc. This required that the individual be able to recognize subjects, verbs, objects, etc., and this was tested quite directly by the Words in Sentences task. Similar statements could be made for many of the other tests which yielded high validity coefficients.

It was therefore of interest to investigate the test validities with reference to a less immediate criterion—grades received by the selected cases at IFEL. Grades after five weeks of training were available for 65 cases from the two groups. These grades could be predicted with a correlation of .34 from a regression equation based on the tests, and .54 from the academic grades which had been assigned at the end of the trial course. On the basis of the high degree of selection which had taken place, it may be estimated that the test battery would probably have had a validity of more than .52 if all persons in the trial course had been allowed to study at IFEL. This figure, though not at all as high as the validity obtained for the prediction of trial course grades, would still represent a highly useful degree of prediction. The tests do not appear to be quite as valid as the trial course itself, but the former have many economic advantages in comparison to the relatively expensive trial course.

Further data were compiled by Air Force psychologists on the subsequent use of the aptitude tests in the prediction of success in trial courses. As will be explained below, on the basis of the first year's studies of test validity in a number of situations, five tests were selected to compose a semi-final battery; tentatively, the battery was known as the Psi-Lambda Foreign Language Aptitude Battery (Psi-Lambda being an abbreviation of psycholinguistic). This battery was made available to the Air Force for further predictive studies. One of these studies concerned the prediction of success in a trial course in Russian. A multiple $R$ of .64 was obtained for four of the tests (Phonetic Script I, Words in Sentences, Spelling Clues, and Paired Associates) with four classes comprising 95 cases; cross-validation of the resulting weighted composite on the next six classes, comprising 151 cases, yielded a correlation of .70 (Harding, 1956a).

Results were not quite so good in the Air Force studies of the trial course in Chinese (actually, this was precisely the same course as the one that had been used in the previous studies at IFEL, but the Air Force studies concerned groups subsequently entering training with possibly different selective biases); the multiple correlation on 135 airmen was only .45 (Harding, 1956b). The composite which had been developed from the Russian sample correlated only .39 with the criterion—which in this case was simply acceptance or non-acceptance into the longer course. Harding suggested that possibly a different combination of abilities was required to study Chinese.

A further experiment conducted by Harding (Harding, 1958; Harding & McWilliams, 1957) compared the use of a four-week trial course with use of the aptitude tests in predicting final grades of students in a six-months' intensive course in Russian. The validity coefficients obtained for a language aptitude composite score, .44 and .42 ($N = 42$), were comparable to those obtained for trial course grades, .39 and .53 ($N = 62$ and 52), respectively for two samples. The estimated validities which the tests would have had if all examinees had been allowed to go into training were .72 and .64 for two samples. Harding (1958, p. 122) further concluded that aptitude tests are more efficient than trial courses because applicants can be more readily screened by this means. He writes that, "This finding is at variance with a commonly held opinion that a trial performance in a language is the best predictor of subsequent performance." This finding is also somewhat at variance with the IFEL results cited above, showing that trial course grades predict later grades (after five weeks) somewhat better than aptitude tests. A conservative plan for the selection of language trainees would utilize language aptitude tests to screen the input into a trial course; under these conditions, very few members of the trial course would be withdrawn for incompetence and hence the trial course would represent very little wasted effort. This, in fact, is the plan now being used by the Air Force.

Further validity coefficients as such will not be recited here. (The almost endless replication necessary in prediction studies makes aptitude testing in some ways one of the less interesting fields of applied psychology.) The remainder of this section will be used to introduce evidence on collateral questions such as the non-specificity of language aptitude to type of language, the nature of language aptitude, the role of background variables such as age and sex, etc.

Two series of tests were conducted at ALS and at the Foreign Service Institute. Both these institutions offer intensive training in a variety of languages, in courses of up to 12 months in duration. Data from ALS bear on *the question of the non-specificity of language aptitude to type of language*, since enough cases were available to warrant separate validity computations for several groups of languages, but not for individual languages. The languages involved could have been grouped in several ways, but it was decided to group them in a cross-classification of language family and use of Roman characters in the writing system since it could be argued that validity might depend on these factors. Table 4.2 shows a series of validity coefficients against final grades, oral and written work being weighted equally, for five subtests of the Psi-Lambda Foreign Language Aptitude Battery and for a weighted composite which had been developed on the basis of results from the Chinese trial course. It may be seen that while the validity coefficients in two successive samples vary somewhat, there is little evidence of a consistent pattern in these variables. For example, while the validity of the test is at its lowest in predicting success in the "character languages" (Japanese, Chinese, Korean) in one sample, it is not as low in the second sample. These data support the hypothesis of the non-specificity of language aptitude, a hypothesis which is supported by many other tabulations of research data which have been made. This is to say that high, as well as low, validity has been recorded for many different kinds of languages.

Table 4.2

Validities of Part and Total Scores for the
Psi-Lambda Foreign Language Aptitude Battery

Two Groups Tested at ALS by Language Group, Final Grades Used as Criterion
Group I, $N=211$; Group II, $N=374$

| Languages | Group | N | Psi-Lambda Test Parts | | | | | Total |
|---|---|---|---|---|---|---|---|---|
| | | | I Number Learning | II Phonetic Script | III Spelling Clues | IV Words in Sentences | V Paired Associates | |
| Indo-European, | I | 83 | .47 | .36 | .41 | .52 | .36 | .58 |
| A* | II | 163 | .33 | .51 | .38 | .44 | .41 | .54 |
| Indo-European, | I | 47 | .54 | .44 | .28 | .46 | .46 | .57 |
| B* | II | 92 | .32 | .29 | .18 | .47 | .18 | .35 |
| Non-Indo- | I | 77 | .15 | .29 | .14 | .28 | .17 | .27 |
| European, B* | II | 104 | .39 | .42 | .26 | .38 | .33 | .45 |
| All languages | I | 211 | .34 | .32 | .28 | .41 | .30 | .45 |
| | II | 374 | .36 | .42 | .30 | .43 | .33 | .49 |

*Indo-European, A are Indo-European languages using the Roman alphabet:
Czech, French, German, Polish, Romanian; Indo-European, B use other alpha-
bets: Bulgarian, Greek, Russian. Non-Indo-European, B are non-Indo-European
languages not using the Roman alphabet: Chinese, Japanese, and Korean. The
data given for "all languages" include a few cases studying Hungarian, a non-
Indo-European language using the Roman alphabet.

Table 4.3

Comparative Validities of Part Scores and Total Scores for the
Psi-Lambda Foreign Language Test, Against Grades in Oral and Written Work,
Together with Associated Inter-Correlation Data

Two Groups Tested at ALS, Group I ($N=211$), Group II ($N=374$)

| Group | | Grade Intercorrelations | | | | Psi-Lambda Test | | | | | |
|---|---|---|---|---|---|---|---|---|---|---|---|
| | | Oral | | Written | | Parts* | | | | | |
| | | 3rd week | 7th week | 3rd week | 7th week | I | II | III | IV | V | Composite Score |
| Oral, | I | 1.00 | .85 | .68 | .67 | .23 | .41 | .23 | .33 | .26 | .40 |
| Third week | II | 1.00 | .83 | .71 | .68 | .27 | .43 | .35 | .34 | .27 | .44 |
| Oral, | I | .85 | 1.00 | .72 | .77 | .32 | .43 | .31 | .41 | .29 | .49 |
| Seventh week | II | .83 | 1.00 | .71 | .76 | .33 | .46 | .39 | .37 | .25 | .48 |
| Written, | I | .68 | .72 | 1.00 | .81 | .34 | .34 | .23 | .31 | .26 | .40 |
| Third week | II | .71 | .71 | 1.00 | .78 | .33 | .47 | .36 | .42 | .30 | .51 |
| Written, | I | .67 | .77 | .81 | 1.00 | .40 | .35 | .27 | .42 | .28 | .48 |
| Seventh week | II | .68 | .76 | .78 | 1.00 | .34 | .46 | .41 | .42 | .27 | 52 |
| Final Grades | I | .45 | .59 | .46 | .48 | .34 | .32 | .28 | .41 | .30 | .47 |
| | II | .59 | .62 | .52 | .54 | .36 | .42 | .30 | .43 | .33 | .51 |

*Test names are shown in Table 4.2

The data from ALS also bear on *the question of the differential predictability of oral and written work.* However, it should first be pointed out that grades in oral and written work at the school are highly correlated; the correlation between oral and written work grades at the seventh week of training was .82 in one sample of 251 cases that had been tested for aptitude at the outset of training. Table 4.3 shows the comparative validities of five tests and the weighted composite score. The differences between the correlations are relatively small. Possibly the difference for Phonetic Script is of theoretical as well as statistical significance, because it is a test involving sounds and the learning of symbols to represent sounds; this is probably an ability which is required to a greater extent in oral aspects of language learning than in written aspects. In interpreting this result, however, one should consider the fact that the high correlation between oral and written grades is probably a function of the way languages are taught at ALS and in similar programs. Both the oral and the written aspects are taught simultaneously or at least in close succession; the common element is therefore the language itself, its structure and its lexicon. Students must make approximately equal progress in oral and written work if they are to maintain their standings. Only in courses in which the reading objective or the speech objective is stressed nearly to the exclusion of the other objectives will there be a possibility of a low correlation between the separate kinds of evaluation; at the same time it may be expected that the aptitude test will best predict whichever criterion, oral or written, is stressed in the instruction. (Data bearing on this can be adduced from civilian academic settings, but will not be introduced here.)

Two sets of data are available from experimental testings at the Foreign Service Institute (FSI), Department of State. One interesting result pertained to *the nature of the criteria.* Thus far, little has been said about the criterion variables used in the studies reported; chiefly they have been grades assigned by instructors on a combination of subjective and objective bases. No efforts have been made to ascertain their reliability, but reliability must be quite high in view of the high validity coefficients they often engender. In the FSI testing, end-of-course criterion ratings were obtained on two bases: (*a*) "actual overall accomplishment," and (*b*) "estimated" aptitude and facility in language learning. The instructors were asked to give ratings on a hypothetical scale with 50 as the mean and 10 as the standard deviation; actually, they tended to spread their ratings somewhat more widely than this around a mean in the neighborhood of 54 to 59. The courses were in 12 different languages and were six months in length.

In the first testing, which took place before the condensed battery took shape and thus involved a considerable number of tests, further evidence on the relative validity of the tests was obtained, as shown in Table 4.4. The Foreign Language Aptitude Index, computed from

Table 4.4

Validity Coefficients for Language Aptitude Tests
for 68 Persons at the FSI

| Test | Criteria (End-of-course Ratings by Instructors) | |
| --- | --- | --- |
| | Actual Overall Accomplishment | Estimated Ability |
| Number Learning | .48 | .51 |
| Phonetic Script, first 30 items | .68 | .68 |
| Phonetic Script, last 30 items | .60 | .61 |
| Phonetic Script, total | .67 | .67 |
| Words in Sentences (Number attempted in 12½ minutes) | .37 | .41 |
| Words in Sentences (Number right in 20 minutes) | .62 | .67 |
| Artificial Language Learning (Total) | .60 | .64 |
| Spelling Clues | .58 | .62 |
| Oriental Script | .26 | .31 |
| Disarranged Letters | .50 | .54 |
| Paired Associates | .50 | .52 |
| Devanagari Script | .64 | .62 |
| Foreign Language Aptitude Index (weighted composite of Paired Associates, Number Learning, and Phonetic Script Total) | .69 | .70 |

an integral-weight combination of five test scores, and developed in one of the Air Force trial course samples, had a correlation of .69 with the "actual accomplishment" criterion and .70 with the "estimated ability" criterion. While this difference is obviously not significant, it suggests that instructors in intensive language courses are not only able to make accurate judgments of accomplishment but also make allowances for factors which may attenuate the criterion, such as motivation, vicissitudes of personal life, etc. More use could be made of a criterion in which instructors are asked to estimate the ability demonstrated in a learning situation.

A question might be raised about the role of motivation to do well on the test. In the Air Force testings described earlier, it was distinctly the case that the examinees were under the impression that the test batteries would have a role in determining their selection for the course. This condition probably did not hold for the first FSI group, since most of the persons tested had already been selected for training. An attempt was made, therefore, to study *the effect of test anxiety* by administering, after the completion of the test battery, the Test Anxiety questionnaire developed by Sarason and Mandler (1952) who generally have found low but significant negative correlations between anxiety and performance on intelligence tests. Questions 3 to 13 on Sarason and Mandler's questionnaire ask about various feelings and attitudes which may be taken to reveal test anxiety; they concern mainly intelligence tests. A further question (number 14) was added, asking specifically how anxious the examinee felt during the aptitude tests he had just taken. Table 4.5 shows the correlations between these questionnaire results, the lan-

Table 4.5

Correlations between Test Anxiety Questions,
Language Aptitude Index, and Criterion Scores

$N = 68$ FSI Language Trainees

|  | Mean | $\sigma$ | 1 | 2 | 3 | 4 | 5 |
|---|---|---|---|---|---|---|---|
| 1. Total Test Anxiety Score items 3-13 (possible range, 11 to 99) | 31.6 | 15.0 | | .35 | −.14 | −.20 | −.22 |
| 2. Question 14 (anxiety about this test, range 1 to 9) | 2.3 | 1.7 | .35 | | −.19 | −.10 | −.05 |
| 3. Language Aptitude Index (T-score scale) | 60.3 | 10.3 | −.14 | −.19 | | .69 | .70 |
| 4. Criterion: Actual Accomplishment | 59.0 | 14.8 | −.20 | −.10 | .69 | | .96 |
| 5. Criterion: Estimated Ability | 58.0 | 15.0 | −.22 | −.05 | .70 | .96 | |

guage aptitude index, and the two criterion variables. General test anxiety had low negative correlations with test scores and with the criterion. The multiple correlation of total test anxiety and the language aptitude index as predictors of the "estimated ability" criterion is .71, a non-significant increase over the language aptitude index zero-order correlation of .70. The question asking whether the examinee felt any anxiety in taking the language aptitude test showed little relation to either test scores or criteria; the mean score, 2.3 on a scale from 1 to

Table 4.6

Intercorrelations, Means, and Standard Deviations for Psi-Lambda Foreign Language Aptitude Battery Subtests, Foreign Language Aptitude Index, Age, Prognostic Interview Ratings, and Criterion Ratings after Language Training

$N = 83$ Trainees at the FSI

|  | Predictor Variables | | | | | | | | Criteria | |
|---|---|---|---|---|---|---|---|---|---|---|
|  | 1 | 2 | 3 | 4 | 5 | 6 | 7 | 8 | 9 | 10 |
| 1. Number Learning |  | .58 | .57 | .59 | .53 | .79 | -.27 | .40 | .60 | .60 |
| 2. Phonetic Script | .58 |  | .69 | .62 | .38 | .78 | -.23 | .52 | .69 | .75 |
| 3. Spelling Clues | .57 | .69 |  | .62 | .46 | .82 | -.28 | .36 | .57 | .64 |
| 4. Words in Sentences | .59 | .62 | .62 |  | .51 | .87 | -.22 | .29 | .68 | .72 |
| 5. Paired Associates | .53 | .38 | .46 | .51 |  | .74 | -.29 | .14 | .46 | .52 |
| 6. Foreign Language Aptitude Index | .79 | .78 | .82 | .86 | .74 |  | -.32 | .40 | .74 | .80 |
| 7. Age | -.27 | -.23 | -.28 | -.22 | -.29 | -.32 |  | -.00 | -.21 | -.18 |
| 8. Prognostic Interview Rating (reflected) | .40 | .52 | .36 | .29 | .14 | .40 | -.00 |  | .55 | .54 |
| 9. Criterion: Accomplishment | .60 | .69 | .57 | .68 | .46 | .74 | -.21 | .55 |  | .91 |
| 10. Criterion: Estimated Ability | .60 | .75 | .64 | .72 | .52 | .80 | -.18 | .54 | .91 |  |
| Mean | 53.96 | 56.58 | 53.34 | 52.12 | 51.15 | 54.37 | 34.23 | 2.10* | 56.47 | 54.00 |
| σ | 10.94 | 9.32 | 10.75 | 11.09 | 11.16 | 12.00 | 4.99 | 1.21 | 17.27 | 17.22 |

* For unreflected interview ratings, mean is 2.90. Original ratings were on basis of 1 = highest, 5 = lowest.

9, showed that there was very little test anxiety in any case. Anxiety, as measured, apparently did not affect the validity of the test, and it can hardly be said that the test is a measure of anxiety, despite the fact that the language aptitude score was correlated to the extent of $-.19$, not significant at the 5% level, with the self-appraisal of anxiety on the test.

A second group of 83 trainees, 77 men and six women, at the FSI was tested at the outset of training. No statements were made to the group with regard to whether the tests would be used in further selection. In advance of the testing, each examinee was also given an individual 15-minute "diagnostic interview" by the chairman of the language department in which he was to study. A number of questions on background, previous experience, and motivation were asked, but the ratings of probable language aptitude, on a five-point scale, were based chiefly on responses to informal mimicry tests in which candidates had to imitate short spoken phrases in a foreign language as accurately as possible. At the end of the six- or eight-month intensive courses into which the examinees were placed, the instructors made criterion ratings similar to those made for the earlier group. The results (means, standard deviations, and correlations of all variables, including age of subjects) are shown in Table 4.6. The scores on the five subtests of the Psi-Lambda Foreign Language Aptitude Battery are in terms of a $T$-score scale which had been developed from a preliminary standardization sample of 912 cases from a variety of sources.

For a multiple regression analysis of the five subtests as predictors of the two criterion variables, the zero-order correlations, beta-weights, and multiple correlations are as follows:

| Test | Criterion 1 (Accomplishment) | | Criterion 2 (Estimated Ability) | |
|---|---|---|---|---|
| | $r$ | $\beta$ | $r$ | $\beta$ |
| Number Learning | .60 | .16 | .60 | .07 |
| Phonetic Script | .69 | .38 | .75 | .43 |
| Spelling Clues | .57 | $-.01$ | .64 | .04 |
| Words in Sentences | .68 | .33 | .72 | .32 |
| Paired Associates | .46 | .07 | .52 | .13 |
| Multiple $R$ | .78 | | .83 | |

The validity coefficients obtained in this sample are among the highest that have been attained with any sample. Yet, the criterion was performance on a long, intensive course rather than simply a short trial course. It should be commented that the group was quite heterogeneous, in that it included prospective foreign service officers and civilian employees of various government agencies as well as Air Force enlisted men. Unfortunately, it was impractical to administer a measure of verbal intelligence to this group, but there was probably a considerable range of intelligence represented.

The beta-weights tended to confirm the previous findings that the various subtests had important independent contributions to validity. Some of the beta-weights, of course, were close to zero, but experience has indicated that these weights are subject to considerable sampling fluctuation and may also be responsive to differences in types of courses and criteria used. It has seemed safest to leave all five subtests in the final battery in order to attain maximal overall validity in the long run and to provide prospective users with the possibility of performing their own studies of the differential validity of the subtests.

Another question answerable from the data presented in Table 4.6 is that of the relative usefulness of the language aptitude test, the prognostic interview ratings, and age. The zero-order correlations and beta-weights bearing on this question are as follows:

| Predictor | Criterion 1 (Accomplishment) | | Criterion 2 (Estimated Ability) | |
|---|---|---|---|---|
| | $r$ | $\beta$ | $r$ | $\beta$ |
| Foreign Language Aptitude Index | .74 | .62 | .80 | .71 |
| Interview Rating | .55 | .30 | .54 | .26 |
| Age | −.21 | −.01 | −.18 | .05 |
| Multiple $R$ | .79 | | .84 | |

It is evident that while the interview rating contributes a useful amount, significant at the .1% level in each case, over and above the language aptitude index, its validity comes nowhere near surpassing that of the test score. This is true despite the fact that the interview rating may contain a spurious overlap with the criterion ratings in that many of the interview ratings were made by the same individuals who later awarded the criterion ratings. In many situations, of course, use of a prognostic interview would be impractical, either because of the large numbers of cases to be handled or because of the unavailability of qualified, linguistically-trained interviewers at the site of testing. Nevertheless, the results do indicate that interviewing which includes a mimicry test may be of some help in selecting language trainees. One interesting facet of the results is that the prognostic interview rating correlates most highly with the Phonetic Script Test, suggesting that there is much in common between what is measured by this test and the informal mimicry exercises given in the prognostic interview. This matter will be discussed in the section on the nature of language aptitude. Among the samples studied, this group is unusual in that its mean age is 34.23, $\sigma= 4.99$. Age shows a slightly negative linear correlation with success in language learning, but since the age variable does not contribute to prediction over and above the aptitude test, it may be assumed that the aptitude test measures whatever in the age variable is relevant for language training success. These results tend to deny the popular notion that older individuals cannot learn foreign languages readily.

There were two notable examples of situations where the language aptitude tests showed very poor or even negligible validity. One of these was at the National Security Agency (NSA) of the Department of the Army, but here the criterion was very poorly defined, or perhaps it was irrelevant to what the language aptitude tests were supposed to measure. It was pointed out that the criterion grades at NSA represented the extent to which the students were able to learn to use foreign language skills in cryptanalysis and related matters. Many of these already had prior training in foreign languages. In any case, 62 persons were given a large battery of tests at the outset of certain training courses, and at the end of the courses, typically six months in duration, test scores were correlated with course grades. Scores on several other tests were available for 37 of these cases. A small portion of the results is given in Table 4.7. Of chief interest is the fact that none of the validity coefficients approaches significance.

The correlations between selected language aptitude tests and other tests merit attention. It may be noted that the Words in Sentences Test appears to have a consistently high correlation with intelligence tests. Its correlation, .87, with the Language Inference part of the Iowa Foreign Language Aptitude Test is quite high; this is a part in which it is required that the examinee infer, from context and from knowledge of cognates, the meanings of Esperanto words like *luno, urbo*. The possibility that these two tests are strongly affected by previous language training experiences should be investigated. Other tests, such as the Phonetic Script Test and the Paired Associates Tests, are not highly correlated with subtests in the Iowa test, although there are a few moderate correlations; these tests, at least, seem to be rather dissimilar to previous language aptitude tests.

Table 4.7

Intercorrelations Between Language Aptitude Tests,
Intellectual Ability Tests, and Course Grades

$N = 37$ cases at the NSA

| Test | Coop. Vocab. | Words in Sentences | Phonetic Script | Disarranged Letters | Paired Assoc. | Course Grade (Criterion) | Mean | σ |
|---|---|---|---|---|---|---|---|---|
| ACE Quantitative | .22 | .47 | .16 | .51 | .21 | .14 | 50.97 | 9.55 |
| ACE Linguistic | .56 | .58 | .35 | .27 | .37 | .25 | 99.92 | 9.74 |
| ACE Total | .46 | .62 | .30 | .46 | .34 | .22 | 150.97 | 16.38 |
| Iowa FL Apt.: Lang. Inference | .13 | .87 | .30 | -.11 | .18 | .08 | 27.00 | 4.42 |
| Iowa FL Apt.: Lang. Construction | -.09 | .51 | .26 | .50 | .41 | .20 | 80.24 | 12.55 |
| Iowa FL Apt.: Grammar | -.20 | .56 | .13 | .11 | .41 | .13 | 67.73 | 8.78 |
| Iowa FL Apt.: Total | -.11 | .51 | .25 | .07 | .43 | .17 | 174.70 | 22.36 |
| Coop. Read. Comp.: Vocabulary | .74 | .30 | .27 | .33 | -.06 | .15 | 74.95 | 5.64 |
| Coop. Read. Comp.: Speed | .57 | .52 | .15 | .46 | .28 | .07 | 77.65 | 13.43 |
| Coop. Read. Comp.: Level | .53 | .42 | .14 | .44 | .15 | .15 | 72.27 | 10.62 |
| Course Grade ($N=62$) | .12 | .12 | .12 | .03 | .14 | 1.00 | 5.48 | 1.24 |
| Mean | 78.38 | 46.46 | 52.57 | 23.97 | 19.76 | 5.86 | | |
| σ | 6.18 | 7.03 | 7.19 | 6.32 | 4.62 | 1.32 | | |

The other situation in which the attempt to predict language learning grades was largely unsuccessful was at a university specializing in the intensive teaching of Russian to U. S. Air Force personnel. Two classes were given the same experimental battery that had also been given to the Air Force "trial course" group. Class II had just begun Russian language training, while Class I was being tested at the beginning of its second term of Russian language study. The examinees were all enlisted Air Force personnel who had been preselected like the members of the Chinese trial course group, and they had also been screened by a similar trial course, but in Russian. The criterion scores consisted of oral and written grades for the first five marking periods from October to March for Class I, and for the first two marking periods for Class II. Table 4.8 shows selected data from this study; data are given only for tests which are identical or similar to tests which were later chosen for the final battery. Actually, the only test which yielded validity coefficients significantly different from zero at the 1% level was the Turse Phonetic Association Test, which seems to measure much the same trait or traits as Spelling Clues and Phonetic Script in the final form of the battery, and even these results were not consistent for the two classes.

Table 4.8

Selected Validity Coefficients for Air Force Russian
Language Trainees, with Intercorrelations of Oral and
Written Criteria in the Several Marking Periods

| Variable | Class 1 ($N=46$) Average Grades | | | | Class 2 ($N=30$) Average Grades | |
| --- | --- | --- | --- | --- | --- | --- |
| | Oral | | Written | | Oral | Written |
| | 1, 2 | 3, 4, 5 | 1, 2 | 3, 4, 5 | 1, 2 | 1, 2 |
| *Tests:* | | | | | | |
| Turse Phonetic Association (cf. Spelling Clues) | .43* | .22 | .13 | .40* | .02 | −.13 |
| Artific. Lang. Numbers (cf. Number Learning) | .02 | .05 | −.24 | −.17 | −.02 | −.16 |
| Words in Sentences | .12 | .06 | .03 | .01 | .05 | −.03 |
| Paired Associates | .15 | .07 | .10 | −.01 | −.08 | −.22 |
| *Grades:* | | | | | | |
| Oral, Period 1, 2 | 1.00 | .74 | .68 | .69 | 1.00 | .09 |
| Oral, Period 3, 4, 5 | .74 | 1.00 | .60 | .70 | — | — |
| Written, Period 1, 2 | .68 | .60 | 1.00 | .68 | .09 | 1.00 |
| Written, Period 3, 4, 5 | .69 | .70 | .68 | 1.00 | — | — |

*Significant at the 1% level.

A number of hypotheses to account for the low validity coefficients may be considered, including the restriction in range due to the prior selection by a trial course, poor motivation due to the groups' already having been selected, and inadequacy of the criteria. Analysis shows that restriction in range can account for only a slight amount of the decrement in validity. No data are at hand concerning the effects of poor motivation. The inadequacy of the criterion is probably the most reasonable explanation; the negligible correlation between oral and written grades in Class II leads one to cast considerable doubt on the criterion at least for that class. Associated with the criterion should be considered such matters as the quality of the teaching, the quality of the text materials, and the reliability of grading.

The fact that the tests do not always predict a given set of criterion ratings does not mean necessarily that the tests are invalid. The data collected tend to show that the tests assembled in the battery are, generally speaking, highly valid, and it can be inferred that they measure some complex of traits which make for success in language learning. Individuals who score low on the tests will sometimes do well in a classroom, but it is hypothesized that such an individual will have to work harder than a high-scoring student, or that such a student must have a more than ordinarily patient teacher. Later in this chapter a theoretical discussion will be presented of the conditions under which aptitude test scores show high correlations with criterion measures.

### Use of the Tests in the Diagnosis of Learning Difficulties

If the tests do indeed provide measures of several somewhat independent abilities involved in language learning, it follows that the subtest scores ought to contain information which would be useful for the diagnosis and prediction of specific learning difficulties. An opportunity to investigate this in the context of an intensive language training course was presented by the so-called Five-University Summer Program in Middle Eastern Languages. In 1958 and 1959, groups of students in this program were tested at the beginning of the summer, and the scores were compared with the results of graphic rating scales filled out by instructors at the end of the eight-week intensive courses in Arabic, Turkish, Persian, or Modern Hebrew. The rating forms called for assessments of highly specific aspects of language learning behavior. In the first summer, when they were handed out near the end of the course, instructors complained that they had not been observing individual students closely enough to make accurate ratings in every case; in the second sum-

mer, therefore, they were distributed to instructors well
the end of the course.

The correlations (one from each year) of each rating scale w
part of the Modern Language Aptitude Test (MLAT), the comm
version of the Psi-Lambda Test (Carroll & Sapon, 1958), are shown
Table 4.9. Correlations are also shown for three questions which the
students answered on a questionnaire filled out at the outset of the
course. Despite the small number of cases, the correlations for the two
years show a reasonably consistent pattern; the correlations for 1959
tend to be somewhat higher. From the standpoint of overall validity
against final course grades, the results presented here are promising. The
correlations of total test with final grade are .40 and .58 respectively,
for the two summers. Validities against mean diagnostic rating are even
higher, .55 and .69, respectively; this result is reminiscent of that obtained at the FSI wherein ratings of "estimated ability" were predicted
slightly better than ratings of actual performance.

The tests also appear to have some degree of diagnostic significance.
Each diagnostic rating is related to a particular test or combination of
tests. Thus, ability to hear phonemic distinctions seems to be related
more consistently to the Phonetic Script Test than to any other. Ability
to produce phonemes accurately and to mimic basic sentences seems most
closely related to Spelling Clues. Memorizing vocabulary is most closely
associated with the Number Learning and the Paired Associates Tests
which are, in fact, memory tests. It had been thought that ratings of
ability to understand grammar and to speak grammatically would have
closest relationships with the Words in Sentences Test, and while there
is indeed a consistent relationship, they are also predicted reasonably
well by the Phonetic Script Test, or even by the Number Learning Test.
Some ratings are about equally well predicted by all subtests. Of course,
it is hard to know whether to take the ratings themselves at face value,
since there is no way of guaranteeing that an instructor would be able
to separate the several aspects of behavior even conceptually. Nevertheless, the results shown here suggest that a careful diagnostic study
of test scores can be worthwile in predicting later learning difficulties.

The last three rows of the table show that: (*a*) whether or not a
person likes foreign language study is not related significantly either
to aptitude or to achievement; (*b*) the subject's statement of whether
he has found foreign languages easy or hard is moderately well related
to certain aspects of aptitude (most consistently to the Number Learning, Phonetic Script, and Words in Sentences Tests) and also to

Table 4.9

Correlations Pertinent to the Use of Language Aptitude Tests
for Differential Diagnosis; Results from Testing in the Five-University
Summer Program in Mideast Languages*

| Variables | Number Learning | | Phonetic Script | | Spelling Clues | | Words in Sentences | | Paired Associates | | Mean Total | | Total course grade | |
|---|---|---|---|---|---|---|---|---|---|---|---|---|---|---|
| Total course grade | .41 | .58 | .26 | .49 | .31 | .42 | .42 | .41 | -.07 | .59 | .40 | .58 | 1.0 | |
| Instructors' ratings on ability to: | | | | | | | | | | | | | | |
| Hear phonemic distinctions | .40 | .51 | .56 | .58 | .32 | .58 | .51 | .39 | .25 | .43 | .59 | .59 | .64 | .81 |
| Produce phonemes accurately | .37 | .49 | .38 | .59 | .48 | .52 | .34 | .35 | .05 | .45 | .45 | .56 | .63 | .72 |
| Mimic basic sentences | .22 | .30 | .13 | .49 | .46 | .41 | .13 | .21 | .29 | .39 | .36 | .41 | .39 | .66 |
| Memorize vocabulary | .61 | .64 | .54 | .58 | .31 | .43 | .56 | .51 | .14 | .75 | .63 | .68 | .71 | .78 |
| Understand grammar | .47 | .51 | .52 | .56 | .21 | .42 | .50 | .45 | .03 | .58 | .50 | .58 | .75 | .85 |
| Speak grammatically | .57 | .59 | .55 | .60 | .37 | .47 | .62 | .56 | .15 | .57 | .67 | .66 | .67 | .85 |
| Comprehend spoken language | .47 | .56 | .48 | .49 | .43 | .50 | .43 | .46 | -.02 | .48 | .51 | .60 | .76 | .75 |
| Comprehend written language | .28 | .67 | .41 | .55 | .00 | .38 | .45 | .52 | .12 | .68 | .38 | .65 | .39 | .88 |
| Mean of above ratings | .48 | .65 | .46 | .61 | .39 | .53 | .50 | .51 | .07 | .64 | .55 | .69 | .82 | .90 |
| Student responses to questionnaire: | | | | | | | | | | | | | | |
| Liking for foreign languages | .24 | .19 | .16 | .26 | -.01 | .16 | .10 | .31 | -.27 | .34 | .04 | .29 | .12 | .16 |
| Judged ease of foreign languages | .57 | .42 | .57 | .35 | -.05 | .11 | .63 | .45 | .03 | .50 | .52 | .42 | .41 | .31 |
| "Academic compulsiveness" | .24 | -.06 | .24 | -.27 | -.04 | -.37 | .14 | -.37 | .21 | -.11 | .21 | -.29 | -.17 | -.05 |

*Two values in each cell are presented; the first is for $N = 32$ students in the 1958 program, the second is for $N = 30$ students in the 1959 program. Approximate significance levels: $r = .36$ for 5% level; $r = .48$ for 1% level.

achievement as measured by the final grade in the course; (c) there is relatively little significance in the question about "academic compulsiveness," i.e., self-classification into Type A or Type B students as described below.

## VALIDITY OF LANGUAGE APTITUDE TESTS
### AT THE SERVICE ACADEMIES

Although this chapter is concerned chiefly with the prediction of success in intensive "full-time" language learning, it has been indicated that it is not irrelevant to consider results obtained at the two service academies, the U. S. Military Academy at West Point, and the U. S. Air Force Academy in Colorado. The fact is that, at least at West Point, the cadet spends somewhat more time on language learning in his first two years than is the case at many colleges. Further, the language instruction at both academies tends to emphasize speaking and understanding rather than reading and writing.

A large test battery was administered in 1954 to a total of 619 "plebes," cadets in their freshman year, approximately four months after foreign language training had begun. These cadets had been assigned to study the language of their choice as far as possible within the quota set up for each language: 114 in French, 110 in German, 54 in Portuguese, 107 in Russian, and 234 in Spanish. The tests were the same as those also administered to the Air Force Chinese trial course group and the Air Force Russian language training groups, except that because of time limitations only half of the tests could be given to any one cadet. In addition, a questionnaire was administered to yield data on background, previous foreign language contacts, and motivational factors. Further, two scores were available on the West Point Aptitude Test (WPAT) given prior to entrance, the Total Score and the Language Aptitude Score.

The criterion data consist of first-term grade averages, on a percentage scale, collected nearly concurrently with the testing, and also the language average for the complete two years of language study, on the West Point grading scale of 0.0 to 3.0. In addition, academic standings at the end of the first two years were collected for English and mathematics as well as the Cumulative Order of Merit, which reflects both academic and certain non-academic kinds of performances at West Point. The first-term language grades were adjusted in such a way as to eliminate the effect of prior training in the respective languages.

## Table 4.10

### Correlations of Experimental Language Aptitude Tests with the West Point Aptitude Test and with Grades in Foreign Languages and Other Subjects at the U. S. Military Academy

| Test or Variable | N | West Point Aptitude Test | | Foreign Lang. Grades | | Two-Yr. Averages in: | | Cum. Order of Merit (refl.) |
|---|---|---|---|---|---|---|---|---|
| | | Lang. Score | Total Score | First Two-Yr. Term Aver. | | Eng. | Math | |
| Artificial Lg. Learning I | 242 | .16 | .22 | .17 | .16 | .22 | .16 | .23 |
| Artificial Lg. Learning II | 242 | .17 | .15 | .14 | .14 | .20 | .11 | .18 |
| Artificial Lg. Learning III | 242 | .10 | .23 | .14 | .11 | .19 | .16 | .20 |
| Turse: Spelling | 242 | .07 | .24 | .24 | .30 | .41 | .12 | .22 |
| Turse: Phonetic Association | 242 | .13 | .30 | .39 | .40 | .45 | .13 | .26 |
| Turse: Word Discrimination | 242 | .18 | .36 | .26 | .30 | .54 | .10 | .24 |
| Letter—Star Test | 297 | .06 | .13 | .17 | .24 | .22 | .16 | .24 |
| Word Squares | 297 | .02 | .01 | .01 | .02 | .00 | .10 | .12 |
| Disarranged Letters | 297 | .13 | .22 | .17 | .26 | .36 | .10 | .23 |
| Rhyming | 297 | .16 | .29 | .26 | .31 | .41 | .13 | .26 |
| Phrase Completion | 297 | .17 | .22 | .11 | .13 | .33 | .04 | .16 |
| Coop. Vocabulary | 297 | .16 | .35 | .21 | .22 | .42 | .08 | .21 |
| Artificial Language Numbers | 277 | .25 | .31 | .28 | .30 | .26 | .25 | .32 |
| Words in Sentences | 277 | .26 | .27 | .18 | .25 | .35 | .28 | .36 |
| Phonetic Discrimination P-120 | 277 | .08 | .06 | .10 | .07 | .02 | .02 | .06 |
| Disarranged Words | 291 | .31 | .37 | .27 | .30 | .40 | .14 | .27 |
| Paired Associates | 291 | .24 | .21 | .20 | .20 | .25 | .12 | .19 |
| Word Elements | 291 | .31 | .34 | .30 | .30 | .36 | .26 | .33 |
| Anagrams | 291 | .17 | .11 | .14 | .13 | .21 | .07 | .12 |
| Picture Naming | 291 | −.02 | −.06 | .12 | .11 | .12 | .06 | .08 |
| Verbal Enumeration: No. attempted | 291 | .09 | .10 | .08 | .07 | .04 | .04 | .05 |
| Verbal Enumeration: Wrong (Refl.) | 291 | .06 | .03 | .01 | .10 | .14 | −.02 | .06 |
| Same—Opp.: No. attempted | 291 | .20 | .15 | .13 | .20 | .18 | .17 | .20 |
| Same—Opp.: Wrong (Refl.) | 291 | .07 | .04 | .02 | .05 | .12 | −.01 | .03 |
| WPAT: Language Score | 611* | 1.00 | .60 | .31 | .33 | .32 | .24 | .31 |
| WPAT: Total | 611* | .60 | 1.00 | .32 | .36 | .46 | .45 | .49 |
| Foreign Language Grade: 1st Term | 611* | .31 | .32 | 1.00 | .82 | .44 | .41 | .54 |
| Foreign Language Grade: 2-yr. Aver. | 611* | .33 | .36 | .82 | 1.00 | .54 | .47 | .65 |
| English Grade: 2-yr. Aver. | 611* | .32 | .46 | .44 | .54 | 1.00 | .39 | .59 |
| Mathematics Grade: 2-yr. Aver. | 611* | .24 | .45 | .41 | .47 | .39 | 1.00 | .92 |
| Cumulative Order of Merit (Refl.) | 611* | .31 | .49 | .54 | .65 | .59 | .92 | 1.00 |
| Composite Language Apt. Score A** | — | .32 | .40 | .38 | .42 | .48 | .29 | .42 |
| Composite Language Apt. Score B** | — | .59 | .53 | .42 | .46 | .51 | .32 | .45 |

*Correlations in these rows were computed by averaging (via Fisher's z-transformation) correlations obtained for four separate but overlapping subgroups.
**Composite A contains (with unit weights for standard scores) Artificial Language Numbers, Turse Phonetic Association, Words in Sentences, and Paired Associates. Composite B contains the preceding four tests plus the WPAT Language Score.

The results are presented in Table 4.10. The five language groups were pooled since analysis of data for separate language had not shown consistent differential patterns. The following observations may be made about the results:

1.  None of the experimental series of tests correlates even moderately well with the Language Score of the West Point Aptitude Test; the highest correlation is .31 and though it is significant at the 1% level, it is not such as to suggest any substantial degree of overlap with that test. The correlations of the experimental tests with the Total Score of the WPAT are somewhat higher, but only for those tests with a considerable verbal component such as the Cooperative Vocabulary Test or the Word Discrimination subtest of the Turse Stenographic Aptitude Test.

2.  The correlations of the experimental tests with West Point foreign language grades are generally low, but several tests have validities high enough to be of predictive value, namely, the Phonetic Association subtest of the Turse Test, the Rhyming Test, and the Artificial Language Numbers Test. The first of these tests had a validity coefficient of .40 which is higher than that of the WPAT Total Score, .36, against the two-year grade criterion. This test battery, of course, was the first battery to be constructed and reported on. It did not contain several tests, notably, the Phonetic Script Test, which later proved to have an important role in the final prediction battery. Nevertheless, if a composite is formed from the four tests most closely approximating the final battery (Turse Phonetic Association, Artificial Language Numbers, Words in Sentences, and Paired Associates), the correlations with first-term language grades and the two-year average will approximate .38 and .42 respectively. These correlations are increased to .42 and .46 if the WPAT Language Score is added to the composite. (These composites are formed by assigning unit weights to standard scores.)

3.  Some of the tests are also fairly good predictors of English grades, particularly those involving a clear verbal component. There is only one test, Artificial Language Numbers, which tends to have a higher correlation with language grades than with English grades.

4.  The language aptitude tests are distinctly poor predictors of mathematics grades, as they should be.

It is quite likely that there are extraneous factors at West Point which serve to depress the validities of the language aptitude tests. Because of the strictly regulated study time available to the student, success in a foreign language class may easily be affected by the amount of study time which the student feels he has left over from other courses such as mathematics, which may loom larger to him as a factor determining his career at West Point and which thus demand more of his attention. It is possibly partly for this reason that the WPAT Total Score is a better predictor of language grades than the language score itself, because the Total Score predicts success in other courses besides foreign language courses.

Data on the validity of the Psi-Lambda Foreign Language Aptitude Battery for the Class of 1959 at the U. S. Air Force Academy are presented in Table 4.11.[4] The validity coefficients are similar in magnitude to those obtained at the U. S. Military Academy. The relatively small degree of correlation can probably not be accounted for in terms of restriction of range, since the Air Force sample shows a mean $T$-score close to the mean of a preliminary standardized group known to be quite heterogeneous.

Table 4.11

Validity Coefficients for Psi-Lambda Foreign Language Aptitude Battery (Total Weighted Score) at U. S. Air Force Academy

| Language | $N$ | $r$ with First Semester Grades | $r$ with End-of-Year Grades | Mean Psi-Lambda ($T$-score scale) |
|---|---|---|---|---|
| German | 19 | .53 | .53 | 50.0 |
| Russian | 35 | .30 | .24 | 54.8 |
| French | 56 | .23 | .30 | 49.0 |
| Spanish | 91 | .30 | .32 | 47.5 |
| All languages | 201 | .30 | .34 | 49.2 |

## A MODEL FOR STUDYING THE PREDICTION OF SUCCESS IN COMPLEX LEARNING TASKS

Up to the present point in this chapter, a very simple model for studying the prediction of success in foreign language training has been assumed. The model assumes that success is a direct function of measured aptitude, plus errors which may exist in the tests or in the criterion; thus, for a given individual, $c + e_c = f(a) + e_a$, where $c$ is the true score for the criterion, $a$ is the true score for aptitude, and $e_a$ and $e_c$ are symbols for errors in $c$ and $a$. Aptitude, $a$, may be regarded as a composite of true scores for various aspects of aptitude. The validity coefficient, i.e., the

---

[4] Furnished through the courtesy of Lt. Col. William F. Long, Director of Admissions.

correlation between aptitude test scores and a criterion measurement, is regarded as an indication of the extent to which errors have been minimized.

Obviously this model is oversimplified, if not downright wrong. It might be approximately correct under certain conditions, as where students are equally well motivated to learn, and are given only as much opportunity to learn as is actually needed by the more apt students. The model also assumes that there is only one kind of aptitude which is relevant to task success no matter how the learning task is organized. Travers (1954) has suggested a model which involves both motivation and aptitude; he believes these factors should be combined by a multiplicative function. McBee and Duke (1960) have presented evidence for an additive function, however. It would seem desirable to develop a model which would take account of not only aptitude and motivation, but also the relevant instructional variables. The analysis to be presented here is stated in general terms so that it is not restricted to the case of foreign language learning.

Consider a complex learning task as composed of a series of subtasks, which may be learned with varying degrees of perfection depending upon a number of circumstances. The model attempts to suggest the nature of these circumstances and the manner in which they affect the degree of learning. The degree of learning is measured in terms of the amount of success achieved in the total learning task after a fixed amount of elapsed time, e.g., after a specified number of weeks or months of a course, or after a specified number of instructional hours. The independent variables needed in the model fall into two categories, variables associated with the conduct of instruction and variables associated with the individual.

*Instructional Variables.*

$p_j = adequacy\ of\ presentation\ of\ task\ j$ (on a scale from 0 to 1). This is a measure of how clearly the task is presented and explained, and how appropriately it is placed in the sequence of graded tasks to be learned. Efforts to "program" instruction for teaching machines and the like are essentially efforts to maximize $p_j$ for every task; good textbooks and good teachers also seek to maximize $p_j$'s.

$o_j = the\ time\ allowed,\ "opportunity,"\ for\ learning\ task\ j$. Opportunity is presumed equal for all individuals; at least $\sum_j o_j$ is constant for all individuals over a group of tasks collected into a course of instruction.

*Individual Difference Variables.*

$g_i =$ *that characteristic, general intelligence or verbal intelligence, which determines the extent to which the individual will be able to understand directions and explanations or to infer such directions and explanations from the total content of the instruction even when they are lacking.* This variable is measured on the standard score scale (mean $= 0$, $\sigma = 1$) and is assumed to interact with $p_j$ in such a way that $u_{ij} = f_1(g_i, p_j)$, that is, the individual's understanding of the task requirements or his cognitive orientation to the means of meeting them is a function of his general intelligence, $g_i$, and the adequacy with which the task is presented. The $f_1$ function is tentatively defined so that $u_{ij} = f_1[p_j/A(g_i)]$, where $A(g_i)$ is the normal curve area above the value of $g_i$, but also such that $u_{ij} = 1$ for all $p_j > A(g_i)$.

$a_{ij} =$ *the time which would be needed by individual i to learn task j to a specified criterion of learning,* on the assumption that $u_{ij} = 1$ (i.e., that the task is presented well enough for him to understand the task in the light of his $g_i$). This variable represents "aptitude," and is assumed to be a relatively invariant characteristic of the individual, not subject to easy modification by learning. It is assumed further that there may be a net of functional relationships among the values of $a_{ij}$ for a given individual over different values of $j$; these functional relationships may be represented by "factors" (as in factor analysis), and it is possible that a very small number of factors may account for the relationships to a given degree of precision. It should be noted that low values of $a$ denote "high" aptitude, i.e., the individual needs little time for learning.

$m_{ij} =$ *the maximum amount of time individual i would apply himself to the learning of task j.* This may in turn be a function of the amount of difficulty the individual perceives in the task, his "motivation," and other variables, but these subsidiary variables will not be directly represented in this model.

The attempt can now be made to postulate a functional relationship between a criterion of success in learning and the above variables. This relationship will still be very much oversimplified but it will help to study the separate effects of the several variables on the correlation between aptitude and the criterion. First, it will be useful to define several derived variables. As stated above, if $u_{ij} = 1$, it can be assumed that the time needed by an individual to learn a task is $a_{ij}$. But if $u_{ij} < 1$, he can still learn the task, but this will require more time. If $p_j$ takes any value from 0 to 1, the time actually needed by individual $i$ to learn a criterion is

$$a'_{ij} = a_{ij}/u_{ij}.$$

Obviously, as $p_j$ approaches zero, $a'_{ij}$ approaches infinity.

In the course of learning a task, whether he ever reaches the criterion of mastery or not, the time the individual spends will be a function of $a'_{ij}$, $m_{ij}$, and $o_j$. In fact, the time he spends will be the smallest of these values, since it is assumed that the individual will stop work as soon as he either ($a$) learns the task to the specified criterion of mastery, ($b$) spends an amount of time denoted by $m_{ij}$, or ($c$) is precluded from completing his learning because of the expiration of time as denoted by $o_j$, whichever of these events occurs earliest. In this way, $t_{ij}$ can be defined as the total amount of time spent by individual $i$ in learning task $j$, or, $t_{ij} = Sm\ (a'_{ij}, m_{ij}, o_j)$, where the symbol $Sm$ denotes the function "smallest of the values listed."

Finally, it can be assumed that the efficiency, $c_{ij}$, with which task $j$ is learned by individual $i$ is a direct function of the ratio of the time spent to the time needed; that is, $c_{ij} = t_{ij}/a'_{ij}$. The final criterion of success in a series of tasks ($j = 1, 2, \ldots, n$) could then be represented as equal to $\sum_j c_{ij}$.

It is now of interest to study the relations between $c_{ij}$ and $a_{ij}$ (and other variables) under varying conditions of $p_j$ and $o_j$, the instructional variables, assuming normal distributions of $g_i$ and $a_{ij}$ and also assuming that $g_i$ and $a_{ij}$ are independent. For this purpose it is assumed that only one task is being studied, i.e., $j$ is a constant, and will therefore not appear as a subscript in what follows. The method adopted is to construct synthetic, hypothetical data and then to compute various statistics from these data under varying assumed conditions of instruction and "motivation" as represented by the variable which has been designated $m_{ij}$. The number of possible combinations of initial conditions from which one might start is of course infinite; it has been necessary to choose several such combinations arbitrarily, but the results will nevertheless suggest the trends which may be expected under a variety of conditions. In constructing hypothetical data, a basic sample of 100 cases was established; it was assumed that $a_i$ and $m_i$ were distributed normally with a population mean $= 5.0$ and variance $= 1.0$, also that $g_i$ was distributed normally and independently of $a_i$ and $m_i$ with a population mean $= 0.0$ and variance $= 1.0$; from these assumptions sample values were developed by random sampling techniques. The sample values of $a$, $g$, and $m$ had means, variances, and intercorrelations well within 95% confidence bands around their expected values. A program was written for the IBM 704 electronic data processing machine to compute means and $\sigma$'s of $c_i$ for various combinations of $o$ and $p$. The results of two runs are displayed as Case 1 and Case 2 in Figure 4.1.

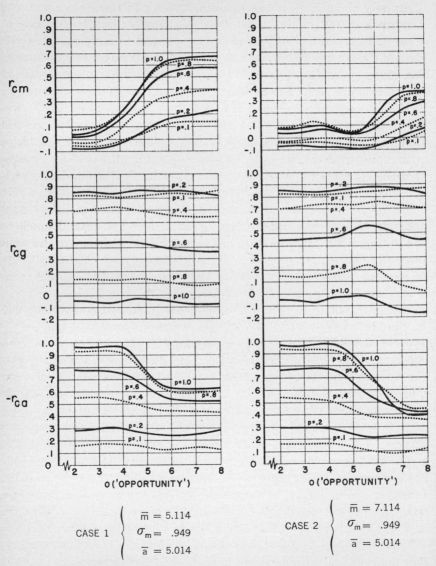

$$\text{CASE 1} \quad \left\{ \begin{array}{l} \overline{m} = 5.114 \\ \sigma_m = .949 \\ \overline{a} = 5.014 \end{array} \right. \qquad \text{CASE 2} \quad \left\{ \begin{array}{l} \overline{m} = 7.114 \\ \sigma_m = .949 \\ \overline{a} = 5.014 \end{array} \right.$$

FIGURE 4.1   Computed Values of $r_{ca}$, $r_{cm}$, and $r_{cg}$ for Various Values of $o$ and $p$, for Two Levels of $m$ (Hypothetical Data)

Case 1 is for a hypothetical group whose values of $m_i$, in the population, are distributed with the same mean and variance as their values of $a_i$, as indicated above. If $m$ is regarded as a measure of motivation, it may be said that Case 1 refers to a group with relatively poor motivation; only about 50% of the group are willing to spend the amount of time in learning the task that they need. In computing the data for Case 2, however, a constant of two was added to each $m_i$. Thus, the data of Case 2 can be regarded as referring to a highly motivated group; for, given adequate opportunity and adequate instruction, nearly all individuals are posited to be willing to spend enough time to learn.

If $o_j$ is varied, the amount of opportunity (measured in time) given for learning is varied; the less opportunity given, it may be expected that the less apt students will have less and less chance to catch up with more apt students. As $o_j$ decreases, therefore, it would be expected that the correlation between aptitude ($-a_i$, that is, the amount of time needed, measured in reverse) and success increase, and this is seen to be true in both Case 1 and Case 2 in Figure 4.1. The relation between aptitude validity and opportunity to learn does not depend much on the average level of motivation in the range studied here. At the same time, the relation between success and degree of individual motivation is, as would be expected, generally higher in Case 1, that is, the group with a lower average level of motivation.

If $p_j$ is varied, the quality of instructional presentation is varied; that is, the clarity with which the subject matter is presented and/or the appropriateness of the grading or ordering of material is varied. ($p$ is conceived to be independent of $o$, e.g., material might be presented very clearly, but little time is given the student to assimilate it.) Since a low quality of instruction is in this model conceived to cause the learner to require more time to assimilate the material, depending upon his general intelligence, $g_i$, variations in $p$ will affect the relations between success, on the one hand, and aptitude, $a$, general intelligence, $g$, and motivation, $m$, on the other. As $p$ decreases from the optimum, aptitude has less relation to the criterion and general intelligence has much more. Likewise, the influence of individual differences in motivation is attenuated. (In the model, $p$ is conceived to be independent of $m$, although in practice, it is possible that low $p$ lowers student motivation.)

This model has been designed chiefly to illustrate the possible effects that instructional variables may have on the functioning of an aptitude test. Some of its assumptions are over-generous, e.g., the assumption that general intelligence is uncorrelated with aptitude and that it operates only in orienting individuals to understand tasks. Nevertheless, it can be used to interpret some of the results presented in this chapter.

It will be recalled that the highest degree of relationship between aptitude and achievement was demonstrated for the two U. S. Air Force trial courses. It is assumed that in this course the value of $o_j$ was relatively low, probably near the point where the relationship between $c_{ij}$ and $a_{ij}$ would be at a maximum. It is entirely credible that $o_j$ was relatively low because of the extreme brevity of the course and the fact that the instructors were almost ruthless in eliminating trainees. At the same time, $m_{ij}$ for all tasks was sufficiently high so that $a_i$ could have its full effect; the high value of $m_{ij}$ can be inferred from the fact that the candidates were trying for a much-prized opportunity to study a foreign language in a civilian setting and thus escape some of the routines of military service. Finally, one may judge that $p_j$, the adequacy of presentation, was uniformly high. The instruction was highly systematized and the instructors had had much experience in administering the trial course.

Very similar conditions obtained in the FSI language courses, another situation in which language aptitude test validities were extremely high. To be sure, the course was much longer than the four-day trial course, but in view of the large amount of material to be learned, it is probably the case that $o_j$ for each subtask was relatively small. Further, the courses themselves had been under development for some time and were carefully planned; motivation was probably high in the sense that students were usually willing to put as much time as necessary into the task of learning.

The course conducted by the U. S. Marine Corps during World War II and studied by Williams and Leavitt (1947) is possibly an instance of a situation where both $o_j$ and $p_j$ were quite small. The former condition (small $o_j$) is judged from the fact that the course is described as exceedingly rigorous—"requiring acquisition of a speaking and reading mastery of Japanese in six months," according to Williams and Leavitt, and yielding an attrition rate of something like 80%. The latter condition (small $p_j$) is judged from the fact that as far as can be known, the course in Japanese conducted by the U. S. Marine Corps during the war years was not much influenced by the methodological notions which were being developed by linguistic scientists working with the Army. It is quite likely that the learning content was presented by means of fairly traditional grammar-translation methods which put a premium on the students' ability to understand the learning task itself. If this analysis is correct, it is not surprising that the best predictors of success were measures of verbal intelligence (including the Army Language Aptitude Test, which is chiefly a measure of verbal intelligence).

The very moderately satisfactory validities obtained at the U. S. Military Academy may be interpreted by assuming that $o_j$ (opportunity) was in general much greater (longer) than in the very intensive courses of the U. S. Air Force and the FSI, for the service academy courses resemble, if anything, language courses in civilian universities. This allowed $m_{ij}$ to play a somewhat larger role than it usually plays in intensive courses. As a matter of fact, an attempt was made to measure a variety of academic motivation at West Point. In a questionnaire given at the time the tests were given, each student was asked to classify himself into one or the other of the following categories:

"A. The type of student who in every subject works for the highest level of accomplishment he can achieve, regardless of whether he thinks the subject valuable for him. Even when the going gets rough, or even when the learning seems unproductive, this student maintains a high level of effort.

"B. The student who works hardest only on the subjects that interest him or that he thinks valuable to him in some way. This type of student is satisfied to get average or even below-average grades in subjects which do not interest him particularly."

The inclusion of this question was prompted by the then-recent finding of Frederiksen and Melville (1954) that interest tests predicted grades in engineering school better for "non-compulsive" students than for "compulsive" students; in contrast to the indirect measures of compulsiveness used by Frederiksen and Melville, the attempt was made here to get at this by a direct question. It seemed that if interest tests predicted grades better for "non-compulsive" (Type B) students, aptitude tests would predict better for "compulsive" (Type A) students, who would at least be highly motivated in the sense of being more willing to spend the amount of time needed to master the material. Table 4.12 presents the comparative validity coefficients for A and B type students, for the four tests which are most similar to the tests in the final battery, as well as for the WPAT Language and Total Score. Although the differences are not statistically significant beyond the 5% level, the results tend to contradict the hypothesis, since the correlations are uniformly higher for Type B students for all tests listed except WPAT Total. Perhaps the characteristic of Type B students is not that they work on what interests them most but that they work chiefly on what they find easy, i.e., have highest aptitude for; this would ac-

Table 4.12

Comparative Validity Coefficients for Selected Tests,
"Type A" (Compulsive) vs. "Type B" (Non-Compulsive) Students
at the U. S. Military Academy

| Test | Criteria (Language Grades) | | | | | | | |
|---|---|---|---|---|---|---|---|---|
| | First-Term Grades Adjusted for Previous Training | | | | Two-Year Cumulative Grades | | | |
| | Type A | | Type B | | Type A | | Type B | |
| | r | N | r | N | r | N | r | N |
| Artificial Language Numbers | .28 | 158 | .28 | 119 | .24 | 158 | .40 | 119 |
| Turse Phonetic Association | .35 | 137 | .48 | 105 | .40 | 137 | .45 | 105 |
| Words in Sentences | .14 | 158 | .19 | 119 | .19 | 158 | .30 | 119 |
| Paired Associates | .19 | 151 | .20 | 137 | .20 | 151 | .19 | 137 |
| WPAT Language Score | .26 | 305 | .25 | 249 | .30 | 305 | .35 | 249 |
| WPAT Total | .35 | 305 | .29 | 249 | .38 | 305 | .34 | 249 |

count for the higher validities of aptitude tests in this group. This interpretation would suggest that in applying the model, $m_i$ should in some circumstances be made to depend to some extent on $a_i$.

## THE NATURE OF FOREIGN LANGUAGE APTITUDE

Having identified situations in which aptitude, $a_{ij}$, can be shown to exist as a variable (or complex of variables), there remains the task of describing the nature of foreign language aptitude as it can best be discerned by inspection of the language aptitude tests and consideration of results, including factor analytic results (Carroll, 1958). Accordingly, language aptitude can be considered under the following four headings:

*Phonetic Coding.* One of the most important abilities required in learning a foreign language is *the ability to "code" auditory phonetic material* in such a way that this material can be recognized, identified, and remembered over something longer than a few seconds. The "coding" is presumably a cognitive process which cannot be directly observed, but something of this sort may be inferred from the following case report: A woman who had received a low score on the Phonetic Script Test was presented with two spoken nonsense syllables /θeǰ; θaeǰ/, and then ten seconds of mental arithmetic to do, after which she was asked to repeat the two syllables. She could not do this, although this task was known to be relatively easy for most people. Further, the woman could herself repeat the syllables accurately when allowed to do it immediately after original presentation. Thus, this ability is not the ability to make an echoic response to phonetic material, but the ability somehow to "code" or represent it in imagery so that it can be recognized or reproduced after an intervening period filled with other activity. This ability, it would seem, is measured chiefly by the Phonetic Script Test, in which the individual has to learn how a series of speech sounds are represented by alphabetic characters; in order to do this, however, the sounds themselves have to be "coded" or "stored" long enough to be compared with other sounds, and the individual has to build up a considerable repertoire of responses. This ability may also be drawn upon, however, by paired-associates tests utilizing nonsense syllables or paralogs. To a slight extent, also, it may be involved in the Artificial Language Numbers Test, although in this test the individual has considerable opportunity to consolidate his learning of the nonsense materials. It is also measured by the Spelling Clues Test insofar as this represents phonetic-orthographic habits which the individual has learned.

In learning a foreign language, a person low in this ability will have trouble not only in remembering phonetic material, words, forms, etc., but also in mimicking speech sounds. Apparently the process of making an echoic response involves some degree of "phonetic coding," or perhaps it would be better to say phonemic coding because the individual will impose upon his repetition of a heard utterance whatever system of phonemes he has acquired most strongly.

*Grammatical Sensitivity.* A second important variable in language aptitude is *the ability to handle "grammar,"* i.e., the forms of language and their arrangements in natural utterances. This implies that the individual is sensitive to the functions of words in a variety of contexts. This may be a learned trait, but it is conceivable that variations in this ability may be observed even when the individual has no formal training in grammar. It is postulated that this trait is particularly well measured by the Words in Sentences subtest of the Modern Language Aptitude Battery.

*Rote Memory for Foreign Language Materials.* A third important variable is that of *rote memorization ability for foreign language materials.* This ability is to be regarded as independent of and different from the phonetic coding variable described above; it has to do with the capacity to learn a large number of these associations in a relatively short time. Though a certain degree of phonetic coding ability is necessary, perhaps prerequisite, those who have requisite phonetic ability may still not be able to hear and remember the relationships. It is postulated that the Paired Associates Test measures this ability fairly accurately; it is also tapped by the Number Learning Test.

*Inductive Language Learning Ability.* A fourth variable is what may be called *"inductive language learning ability."* This is the ability to infer linguistic forms, rules, and patterns from new linguistic content itself with a minimum of supervision or guidance. It is not measured to any appreciable degree by the tests of the present final MLAT battery, but it had turned up in certain earlier studies (Carroll, 1958).

The above four factors do not include what is ordinarily called the verbal or verbal knowledge factor, which according to the results of the studies reported is not very important in predicting success. Vocabulary tests do not serve as particularly good predictors, at least in situations where other tests serve well, since the first stages of learning language do not require one to acquire a large vocabulary. On the other hand, the present Spelling Clues Test functions in part as a vocabulary test.

Travers (1954) has attempted to classify aptitude variables into the following categories:

1. Measurement of the extent to which the individual has already acquired the responses required in training.
2. Measurement of the extent to which prerequisite responses have been learned.
3. Measurement of the extent to which "related" responses which facilitate learning have been acquired.
4. Measurement of the ability to make the discriminations necessary to profit from learning.
5. Measurement of motivational variables (anxiety, exploratory drive, etc.).

While it is evident that Travers has tried to stick closely to a kind of parsimonious model which stresses stimulus and response, this framework is not completely satisfactory for schematizing the variables that have been postulated in foreign language aptitude. A sixth category is therefore proposed:

6. Measurement of the extent to which the individual can perform tasks with a behavioral structure characteristic of those required to be learned in the training.

Space will not permit a full explication of what is meant by "behavioral structure"; what is implied is that one cannot describe a task solely in terms of stimuli or in terms of responses, as Travers attempts to do; rather, the tasks must be described in terms of an interaction of stimulus, response, and time variables.

Of the four chief elements which have been postulated in language learning, only one, grammatical sensitivity, could be reasonably regarded as falling under Travers' categories, and even in this case it is debatable whether it might better fall under his category 2, 3, or 4, if not in the new category 6. Further research will be needed to help decide this issue. In the meantime, the remainder are rather clearly to be considered under category 6. For example, phonetic coding is represented by tasks in which it is necessary for the examinee to identify a particular kind of (phonetic) stimulus, associate it with another stimulus which constitutes its symbol or "code" (either overtly or covertly), and demonstrate mastery of this association even after interference from other intervening tasks. Rote memorization involves a somewhat similar behavioral structure, except that the stimulus itself may not involve associations, and characteristically there are a considerable number of associations to be learned in a given time. Inductive language learning, finally, is a matter of how rapidly the subject can utilize a range of contrasting stimulus materials in order to arrive at certain rules of procedure in his future behavior.

## APPENDIX

### Descriptions of Tests

*Anagrams.* The task is to write as many words as possible using the letters in the word "occupation"; four minutes.

*Artificial Language Learning.* This test uses "Tem-Tem," a specially constructed artificial language. From simultaneous presentation of still pictures projected on a screen and spoken Tem-Tem equivalents recorded on tape, S (the Subject) inductively learns to understand Tem-Tem sentences. His learning is then tested by asking him to select pictures corresponding to spoken sentences. The test contains three parts, each representing a lesson with an associated test of 10 items. Total time required: 26 minutes.

*Artificial Language Numbers.* By tape recording, S is taught a simple artificial system of number expression utilizing nonsense syllables. He is then asked to write down the Arabic numeral equivalents of a list of two- and three-digit numbers in the artificial system, spoken at a fairly rapid pace on the tape. This test utilized only the digits 0, 1, 2, and 3. Total time: 11.5 minutes.

*Cooperative Vocabulary Test (Form Z).* A non-speeded, wide-range vocabulary test of the conventional multiple-choice type, constructed by Davis and Davis and published in 1949 by the Cooperative Test Division of the Educational Testing Service. A time limit of 19 minutes was used; a scaled score is computed by procedures prescribed in the test manual.

*Devanagari Script.* By means of a tape recording lasting about 15 minutes, and a printed worksheet, S is taught the sounds of seven symbols (four consonants and three vowels) in the Devanagari script, the system of writing used in Sanskrit and other languages of India. The test consists of 24 items, in each of which S must indicate which of two trisyllabic words in Devanagari script (the "neither" response also being offered) is spoken on the tape.

*Disarranged Letters.* Words are given with letters disarranged, e.g., uckd (=duck). The task is to write the word correctly. For each group of items a class name is given; "Birds," "Furniture," etc. Speeded; 42 items, four minutes.

*Disarranged Words.* S is required to rearrange segments of two words (always an adjective and a noun, respectively) into meaningful order, indicating his solution by marking the number of the last syllable in the second word. Sample:

| 1 | 2 | 3 | 4 | 5 | |
|------|------|------|--------|-----|-------------|
| ing | able | dark | notice | en | (Answer: 1) |

Score is number right. 40 items, six minutes

*Letter-Star Test.* S is presented with patterns of letters and asterisks such as * Y * S, and is to invent a meaningful phrase fitting this pattern by substituting a word for each symbol, with the restriction that words substituted for capital letters must begin with the letter indicated. Score is the number of items completed in five minutes; 50 items.

*Number Learning.* A slightly harder version of Artificial Language Numbers utilizing the digits 0, 1, 2, 3, and 4. Total time: ten minutes. Constitutes Part 1 of the Psi-Lambda Foreign Language Aptitude Battery.

*Oriental Script.* Similar to Devanagari Script except that this test is based on the system of writing used in classical Mongolian. 50 items; the tape takes 15 minutes.

*Paired Associates.* Examinee studies a list of 24 "Turkish-English" vocabulary equivalents for two minutes; in the next two minutes, he practices recalling the English meanings, and in the final four minutes he completes from memory a multiple-choice test of the presented vocabulary. Constitutes Part 5 of the Psi-Lambda Foreign Language Aptitude Battery.

*Perdašeb.* "Perdašeb" is an artificial language constructed specially for this test (designed by S. M. Sapon), which is an attempt to duplicate, in miniature, the learning situation in the typical "grammar-translation" foreign language course. The student is taught the grammer of Perdašeb in a series of taped lessons, during which he follows material in the test booklet as in a textbook. He then checks the accuracy of translations from English to Perdašeb and from Perdašeb to English. 26 items; 38 minutes.

*Phonetic Discrimination I, Test P-120.* Designed to measure the ability to discriminate between minimally different speech sounds in various foreign languages. Each item consists of three spoken quasi-words presented auditorily on a tape; two of these are precisely the same, while the third differs in its medial sound. S is to indicate which of the three stimuli is different. 50 items.

*Phonetic Discrimination II.* Similar to Phonetic Discrimination I except that the items follow a multiple-choice pattern: a syllable is heard, after which S is to identify which of four syllables heard subsequently is the same as the first. 25 items.

*Phonetic Script.* S learns a series of phonetic symbols for some of the phonemes of English by listening to pronunciations recorded on magnetic tape and following syllables printed in phonetic symbols on the test paper; after every five items for the first 30 items S goes back and gets a test on the material just learned. After the 30-item learning period, there is a 30-item test in which S must indicate, for each item, which of four phonemically-printed syllables is pronounced on the tape. All the phonemes used in the test are in English, and no fine phonetic discrimination is required. 60 items; 15 minutes. (The first 30 items may be separately scored, and constitute Part 2 of the Psi-Lambda Foreign Language Aptitude Battery.)

*Phrase Completion.* S is given a number of incomplete sentences or phrases, such as "But it's all ----," which are to be completed with the first word that comes to mind. Scoring based on community of response, high score for most frequent responses. 24 items; no time limit.

*Picture Naming.* S writes the first letters of the names of a series of common objects as pictured. Highly speeded: 147 items, two minutes.

*Rhyming.* Subjects are to give as many rhymes as possible to each of four words (low, case, speak, lose), one minute allowed per word.

*Same-Opposites (F-S version).* A multiple-choice test similar to an ordinary vocabulary test, except that in each item S must find either a synonym or an antonym of the given word depending on whether it is marked with an asterisk. S presumably must shift set rapidly and often. Scored for both accuracy and speed. 100 items; four minutes.

*Spelling Clues.* An adaptation of the Turse Phonetic Association Test to objective scoring. S chooses which of five words has the same meaning as the word represented in abbreviated form. Sample: kataklzm = 1. mountain lion; 2. disaster; 3. sheep; 4. chemical reagent; 5. population. Highly speeded: 50 items, five to eight minutes. Constitutes Part 3 of Psi-Lambda Foreign Language Aptitude Test.

*Turse Phonetic Association.* This is Test 3 of the Turse Shorthand Aptitude Test published by the World Book Company. S must spell out correctly, in writing, a word which is printed in abbreviated form "approximately as it is pronounced." Sample: *tox* = "talks." 60 items; five minutes.

*Turse Spelling.* This is Test 2 of the Turse Shorthand Aptitude Test published by the World Book Company. S is asked to identify which, if any, of three alternative spellings of a word is correct. 45 items; four minutes.

*Turse Word Discrimination.* This is Test 5 of the Turse Shorthand Aptitude Test published by the World Book Company. Choose, from among words likely to be confused, the word that fits correctly in a sentence. Sample: The (leak lick lack lake) of water made irrigation necessary. Speeded: 30 items, five minutes.

*Verbal Enumeration (F-S version).* This test was designed by S. M. Sapon to measure a postulated "flexibility of set" factor which might be relevant in switching rapidly from one language to another. Use is made of Thurstone's verbal enumeration test format, in which S marks all words in a column which are names of things in the category given by the column heading. In this version, however, columns contain many words falling in classifications used in preceding columns, and S must presumably avoid carrying over the set established in the preceding columns. Scored for both speed and accuracy. 18 columns of 40 words each.

*Word Elements.* S is required to select, inductively, examples of Latin and Greek roots and affixes found in English words and to give their meanings in a multiple-choice test. 30 items, 11 minutes.

*Words in Sentences.* Designed to measure ability to understand the function of words and phrases in sentence structure, without calling upon knowledge of grammatical terminology. Each item consists of a key sentence with a word or phrase printed in capital letters, followed by one or more sentences with words and phrases underlined and numbered. S is directed to pick the word or phrase in the second sentence or sentence group which does the same thing in that sentence as the capitalized word does in the key sentence. Sample:

He spoke VERY well of you.

*Suddenly the* music became *quite loud.*
    1      2                3      4

30 items; 16 minutes (allowing most to finish). Constitutes Part 4 of the Psi-Lambda Foreign Language Aptitude Battery.

*Word Squares.* For 15 seconds S views a word square composed of sets of homophones, such as "cent," "scent," "sent," after which he selects which of a number of word squares is exactly the same as the one he has viewed. This is done solely from memory. The test contains three such word squares.

## REFERENCES

Bottke, K. G. & Milligan, E. E. Test of aural and oral aptitude for foreign language study. *Modern Language J.*, 1945, *29*, 705-709.

Carroll, J. B. A factor analysis of verbal abilities. *Psychometrika*, 1941, *6*, 279-307.

Carroll, J. B. Some principles of language testing. *Georgetown Univ. monogr. series in languages and linguistics*, 1953, No. 4, 6-10.

Carroll, J. B. A factor analysis of two foreign language aptitude batteries. *J. gen. Psychol.*, 1958, *59*, 3-19.

Carroll, J. B. Research on teaching foreign languages. In N. L. Gage (Ed.), *Handbook of research on teaching.* 1962. (In press)

Carroll, J. B. & Sapon, S. M. *Modern Language Aptitude Test, Form A.* Test Booklet, Practice Exercise Sheet, Answer Sheet, Answer Keys, Manual, Tape. New York: The Psychological Corporation, 1958, 1959.

Dorcus, R. M., Mount, G. E., & Jones, Margaret H. *Construction and validation of foreign language aptitude tests.* Los Angeles: Department of Psychology, University of California, 1952. (Personnel Research Branch Research Report 993, The Adjutant General's Office, Department of the Army, Contract DA-49-083 OSA-75 PR 3576.)

Frederiksen, N. & Melville, S. D. Differential predictability in the use of test scores. *Educ. psychol. Measmt*, 1954, *14*, 647-656.

French, J. W. *The description of aptitude and achievement tests in terms of rotated factors.* Chicago: University of Chicago Press, 1951. Psychometr. Monogr., No. 5)

Frith, J. R. Selection for language training by a trial course. *Georgetown Univ. monogr. series in languages and linguistics*, 1953, No. 4, 10-15.

Harding, F. D., Jr. *Language aptitude tests as predictors of success in a trial Russian course.* Lackland AFB, Personnel Laboratory, Air Force Personnel and Training Research Center, 1956. Technical Memorandum PL-TM-56-5. (a)

Harding, F. D., Jr. *Language aptitude tests as predictors of success in a trial Mandarin Chinese course.* Lackland AFB, Personnel Laboratory, Air Force Personnel and Training Research Center, 1956. Technical Memorandum PL-TM-56-8. (b)

Harding, F. D., Jr. Tests as selectors of language students. *Modern Language J.*, 1958, *42*, 120-122.

Harding, F. D., Jr. & McWilliams, J. T. *Language aptitude tests as predictors of success in a six-month Russian course.* Lackland AFB, Personnel Laboratory, Air Force Personnel and Training Research Center, 1957. AFPTRC-TN-57-86.

Henmon, V. A. C., Bohan, J. E. & Brigham, C. C. *Prognosis tests in the modern foreign languages.* New York: Macmillan, 1929.

Hunt, Thelma, Wallace, F. C., Doran, S., Buynitzky, K. C. & Schwarz, R. E. *George Washington University Language Aptitude Test.* Washington: Center for Psychological Services, 1929.

Kopstein, F. F. & Roshal, S. M. Learning foreign vocabulary from pictures vs. words. *Amer. Psychologist*, 1954, *9*, 407-408.

Luria, M. A. & Orleans, J. S. *Luria-Orleans Modern Language Prognosis Test.* Yonkers: World Book Co., 1928, 1930.

McBee, G. & Duke, R. L. Relationship between intelligence, scholastic motivation, and academic achievement. *Psychol. Rep.*, 1960, *6*, 3-8.

Sapon, S. M. A work-sample test for foreign language prognosis. *J. Psychol.*, 1955, *39*, 97-104.

Sarason, S. B. & Mandler, G. Some correlates of test anxiety. *J. abnorm. soc. Psychol.*, 1952, *47*, 810-817.

Stoddard, G. D. & VanderBeke, G. E. *Iowa Placement Examinations,* Series FAI, Revised, A. Iowa City Extension Division, State University of Iowa, 1925.

Symonds, P. M. *Foreign language prognosis test.* New York: Teachers College, Bureau of Publications, 1930.

Travers, R. M. W. *An inquiry into the problem of predicting achievement.* Lackland AFB, Personnel Research Laboratory, Air Force Personnel and Training Research Center, 1954. AFPTRC-TR-54-93.

Travers, R. M. W. Personnel selection and classification research as a laboratory science. *Educ. psychol. Measmt,* 1956, *16*, 195-208.

Williams, S. B. & Leavitt, H. J. Prediction of success in learning Japanese. *J. appl. Psychol.*, 1947, *31*, 164-168.

Chapter 5 | *The Description and Prediction of Perceptual-Motor Skill Learning*

*Edwin A. Fleishman, Yale University*

This chapter describes one approach to the understanding of skilled performances. Essentially, these studies use the facts of individual differences to probe into the requirements of tasks to be learned. Investigators interested in learning and training have seldom been interested in individual difference variables in this context. As has been pointed out by DuBois in Chapter 3, interest has traditionally centered on variations in training treatments, with individual differences regarded as troublesome error variance. Yet, one has to be impressed with the large differences in learning due to individual differences when these are compared with the effects usually obtained from different treatments and methods. Besides, the interaction of treatment effects and individual difference variables (e.g., abilities) would seem to be of major theoretical and practical significance. (See Cronbach, 1957; Ferguson, 1954; Ferguson, 1956.)

In the approach to be described, ability variables (inferred from individual difference measurements) are considered to be parameters of the learning function. In these experiments we have dealt mainly with perceptual-motor tasks, but the approach is relevant to other areas. The hope is that this approach will eventually assist our understanding of the dimensions of perceptual-motor performance and that this information may be useful in predicting later proficiency as well as in the structuring of training. It is also felt that these studies provide one approach to the classification of tasks to be learned.

This chapter summarizes some research concerned with the isolation of ability variables predictive of high proficiency levels in perceptual-motor skill learning. This program was originally carried out in laboratory research, but more recently the studies have been extended to more "operational type" tasks and even to some actual operational training programs. In one of the most recent studies an attempt was made to manipulate a training program which was structured in terms of a previous analysis of ability requirements. In another study an attempt was made to predict retention of a complex perceptual-motor skill at different intervals up to 24 months after original training was completed. The original research will be summarized first and then these studies will be brought up to date. Portions of the earlier work have been summarized elsewhere, but there is some value in including this in the present training context. Furthermore, these studies illustrate the research strategy involved, and the problems and issues encountered in this type of approach.

The research to be described was started at the Air Force Personnel and Training Research Center Program. One phase of the research was an attempt to understand the structure of human perceptual-motor abilities. The focus in this phase was on the identification and definition of abilities contributing to individual differences in a wide variety of perceptual-motor tasks. In a sense, these studies represent an attempt to develop a way of classifying tasks in terms of the abilities required to perform them. The second phase was the attempt to relate the ability dimensions identified to progress in learning more complex skills, and especially to performance at eventual high proficiency levels in such skills. More recently, these studies have been extended to problems of retention and problems of training. The present review is presented essentially in chronological order although the several phases have overlapped considerably through the history of this program.

## IDENTIFICATION OF PERCEPTUAL-MOTOR ABILITIES

First, a distinction between the terms ability and skill should be clarified. As the term is used here, *ability* refers to a more general trait of the individual which has been inferred from certain response consistencies on certain kinds of tasks. These are fairly stable traits, which, in the adult, will not change very much unless the individual is subjected to some unusual environmental change. Many of these abilities are, of course, themselves a product of learning, but at a given stage of life they may be considered analogous to the "wiring diagram" that the individual brings with him to a specific task. These abilities are related to performances in a variety of human tasks. The fact that spatial visualization is importantly related to performance on such diverse tasks as aerial navigation and dentistry make this ability somehow more basic. The term *skill* refers to the level of performance on a specific task or related group of tasks. As the term skill is used here, it is task oriented. In talking about proficiency in flying an airplane or in trouble shooting a circuit, a specific skill is being talked about. Thus, when in speaking of acquiring the skill of operating a turret lathe, what is meant is that a person has acquired the sequences of responses required of this specific task. Much of this is not new, but it is helpful to keep this kind of distinction in mind.

One objective of the studies carried out has been to describe certain skills in terms of these more general ability components. The primary approach in these studies has been to score the performance of the same individuals on a large variety of especially designed psychomotor performance tasks in the laboratory. For the most part, in any particular study, these tasks are constructed with a view to certain definite hypotheses about the organization of abilities contributing to performance on these tasks. It then remains to verify or modify these hypotheses through analysis of the correlation patterns obtained among these tasks. Specifically, the techniques of factor analysis are applied to the intercorrelations in order to delineate more precisely the possible common abilities underlying these performances. The purpose here is to define the fewest independent ability categories which might be most useful and meaningful in describing performance in the widest variety of tasks.

No attempt will be made here to describe individual studies, except to provide a rough outline of the sequence. The more important ability factors identified from all studies will be summarized at the end of this section. In 1953, the writer presented a review of previous factor analysis studies of psychomotor abilities (Fleishman, 1953). Although the number of previous studies was few, and the range of tasks investigated small, there was considerable agreement on the factors identified. The first study in this series (Fleishman, 1954a) was an attempt to reproduce in a single study tasks representative of all the psychomotor ability factors previously identified. Forty different tests were administered to 400 basic airmen. In order to facilitate testing there were four models of each of the psychomotor tests. Because of the space requirements, six moving-van type trailers, each divided into three compartments, were used to supplement the available experimental rooms.

In general, this study confirmed the hypothesized factors, but there were some exceptions and some new discoveries. Other studies included analyses of fine manipulative performances, e.g., finger and manual dexterity, etc. (Fleishman & Hempel, 1954a) and gross physical proficiency, e.g., pushups, ·chins, etc. (Hempel & Fleishman, 1955). One study focused on positioning movements, reaching, moving controls to specified positions, etc., and "static reactions," e.g., hand steadiness (Fleishman, 1958a). The former concerns movements in which the terminal accuracy of the response is critical, and the latter involves primarily maintenance of limb positions (Brown & Jenkins, 1947). The most important series of studies (Fleishman, 1958b; Fleishman & Hempel, 1956) concerned "movement reactions," where the skill involved coordinated responses, or smooth responses, or precisely controlled movements, or continuously adjustive reactions.

Thus far, more than 200 different tasks have been investigated. These tasks have been administered to thousands of subjects in a series of interlocking studies. From the patterns of correlations obtained, it has been possible to account for performance on this wide range of tasks in terms of a relatively small number of abilities. In subsequent studies, the definitions of these abilities and their distinctions from one another are becoming more clearly delineated. Furthermore, as a result of these studies it should be possible to specify the best tests to measure each of the abilities identified.

Some interesting discoveries have been made. For example, results show that there is no such thing as general physical proficiency or general psychomotor skill or general manual dexterity. Rather, each of these areas breaks up into a limited number of unitary abilities. It has been found that feet coordination, foot-hand coordination, and two-hand coordination seem to depend on the same underlying ability. Another finding is that a person with a fast reaction time to a light signal is apt to have a fast reaction time to other stimuli.

## Psychomotor Ability Components

A description of some of the more important ability factors identified is presented in this section.

*Control Precision.* This factor is common to tasks which require fine, highly controlled, but not overcontrolled muscular adjustments, primarily where larger muscle groups are involved (Fleishman, 1958b; Fleishman & Hempel, 1956; Parker & Fleishman, 1959a; Parker & Fleishman, 1959b). This ability extends to arm-hand as well as to leg movements. It is highly important in the operation of equipment where careful positioning of controls by the hands or feet is required. It is most critical where such adjustments must be rapid but precise. This ability is measured by the Complex Coordination and Rudder Control Tests previously described, but the Rotary Pursuit device is a more sure measure of it. In earlier studies, this factor also has been called Psychomotor Coordination and Fine Control Sensitivity. The present term has emerged and the generality and limits of the ability have been sharpened through successive studies.

*Multilimb Coordination.* This is the ability to coordinate the movements of a number of limbs simultaneously, and is best measured by devices involving multiple controls (Fleishman, 1958b; Fleishman & Hempel, 1956; Parker & Fleishman, 1959a; Parker & Fleishman, 1959b). The factor has been found general to tasks requiring coordination of the two feet (e.g., the Rudder Control Test), two hands (the Two Hand Pursuit and Two Hand Coordination Tests), and hands and feet (the Plane Control and Complex Coordination Tests). Thus far, a pure measure of this factor has not been developed since it is difficult to partial out the Control Precision factor from such tasks. The tests mentioned, however, are most heavily "loaded" with this factor.

*Response Orientation.* This ability factor has been found general to visual discrimination reaction psychomotor tasks involving rapid directional discrimination and orientation of movement patterns (Fleishman, 1957a; Fleishman, 1957b; Fleishman, 1958b; Fleishman & Hempel, 1956; Parker & Fleishman, 1959a; Parker & Fleishman, 1959b). It appears to involve the ability to make the correct movement in relation to the correct stimulus especially under highly speeded conditions. In other words, "given this stimulus, which way should I move?" Thus, where the first ability represents skill in controlling movements and the second ability component above represents skill in coordinating movements, this factor appears to emphasize the selection of the appropriate response which is independent of either precision or coordination. This factor may be measured by such tasks as discrimination reaction time tasks or other tasks involving rapid differential reactions to different stimuli which appear in rapid sequence. The Discrimination Reaction Time Test (Melton, 1947) and the Direction Control Test (Fleishman, 1954b) used in Air Force research are among the best measures of this factor. In a sense, this ability is a kind of motor-spatial ability. The purest measures of this factor do not involve any spatial components in the stimulus aspects but only spatial components in the response aspect. For example, the most pure test recently developed presents the subject with two colors of light appearing in the same little window and two kinds of sound. The lights may be red or green and the sound may be a bell or a buzzer. These stimuli come on at approximately four second intervals and the subject may have to respond to a green light, a red light, a bell or a buzzer in some random sequence. If it is a red light, he pushes a right lever with the hand forward. If it is a buzzer, he depresses a pedal with his right foot. If it is a bell, he depresses a pedal with his left foot. The score is the cumulative reaction time over 40 such reactions.

*Reaction Time.* This represents simply the speed with which the individual is able to respond to a stimulus when it appears (Fleishman, 1954a; Fleishman, 1958b; Fleishman & Hempel, 1955; Parker & Fleishman, 1959a; Parker & Fleishman, 1959b). There are consistent indications that individual differences in this ability are independent of whether the stimulus is auditory or visual and are also independent of the type of response which is required. However, once the stimulus situation or the response situation is complicated to involve alternate choices, reaction time is not the primary factor that is measured. There is considerable evidence, however, that reaction time does contribute to individual differences in more complex tasks, especially at high levels of proficiency in such tasks. Consequently, although initially this is not a critical ability, it appears that measures of the effects of certain factors on reaction time have considerable implications in generalizing to more complex tasks. The most pure measures of reaction time appear to be obtained when the subject is required to keep his finger on a button rather than to have him move his hand a number of inches to the button when the stimulus appears.

*Speed of Arm Movement.* This represents simply the speed with which an individual can make a gross, discreet arm movement where accuracy is not the requirement (Fleishman, 1958b; Fleishman & Hempel, 1954b; Fleishman & Hempel, 1955; Parker & Fleishman, 1959a; Parker & Fleishman, 1959b). There is ample evidence that this factor is independent of the reaction time factor. It is measured by tasks in which the subject must tap, alternately and as rapidly as possible, two metal plates with a stylus when these metal plates are placed more than six inches apart. This factor has also been measured by tasks which require the subject to move his arm past sets of photoelectric cells as rapidly as possible using scalloped kinds of arm movements. Research has shown that this factor contributes variance in more complex kinds of tasks, but primarily at high levels of proficiency achieved after continued practice on such tasks.

*Rate Control.* This ability involves the making of continuous anticipatory motor adjustments relative to changes in speed and direction of a continuously moving target or object (Fleishman, 1958b; Fleishman & Hempel, 1955; Fleishman & Hempel, 1956). A common feature of all of the tasks which measure this factor is the element of pursuit which seems to be involved. Compensatory as well as following pursuit tasks load on this factor. In addition, tasks involving responses to changes in rate such as controlling the movement of a steel ball through certain kinds of tortuous alley mazes by appropriate control movements are loaded on this factor. Research has been conducted to discover whether emphasis on this factor is in judging the rate of the stimulus as distinguished from skill in judging or in estimating the rate of one's response. Thus, in one study an apparatus test was used in which a target line moved through a slot. The subject was required to press a button when it was anticipated that the target would come in coincidence with a set of reference lines. Thus, the response required was a simple button pressing response ruling out the fact that rate was involved in the response. This task did not load on the rate control factor, suggesting that emphasis is, in fact, on the response aspect.

In a further study, not yet published, a motion picture test of rate judgment was used. Here, the subject was required to extrapolate the course of a plane moving across the screen in front of the subject. Several tests of this type were used. The subject's response was simply to make a mark on an IBM answer sheet. Hence, again emphasis was on judging the rate of the stimulus and not on the response. The results showed that these motion picture tests did not load on the rate control factor which was common only to apparatus tests requiring an actual response in relation to the changing direction and speed of the stimulus object. As indicated earlier, it has been found that either compensatory or following pursuit tasks give an indication of this ability.

*Manual Dexterity.* This ability involves skillful, well-directed arm-hand movements in manipulating fairly large objects under speed conditions (Fleishman, 1953; Fleishman, 1954a; Fleishman & Hempel, 1954a; Hempel & Fleishman, 1955; Parker & Fleishman, 1959a; Parker & Fleishman, 1959b). This ability appears to support performance on tasks requiring tool manipulation, the assembly of large components, and the wrapping of packages. The Minnesota Rate of Manipulation Test which is commercially available is the most frequently used measure of this ability. However, improved measures of manual dexterity involving manipulation of larger blocks are under development.

*Finger Dexterity.* This is the ability to make skillful, controlled manipulations of tiny objects involving primarily the fingers (Fleishman, 1953; Fleishman, 1954a; Fleishman & Hempel, 1954a; Hempel & Fleishman, 1955; Parker & Fleishman, 1959a; Parker & Fleishman,

1959b). It has been found important in small parts assembly tasks, in wiring electrical circuits, in watchmaking, and in similar tasks involving, primarily, skillful finger manipulations. Measures of this ability which load highly on this factor are the O'Conner Finger Dexterity Test and the Purdue Peg Board.

*Arm-Hand Steadiness.* This is the ability to make precise arm-hand positioning movements where strength and speed are minimized; the critical feature, as the name implies, is the steadiness with which such movements can be made (Fleishman, 1953; Fleishman, 1954a; Fleishman, 1958a; Fleishman, 1958b; Fleishman & Hempel, 1955; Hempel & Fleishman, 1955; Parker & Fleishman, 1959a; Parker & Fleishman, 1959b). This factor is measured by tasks which involve moving a stylus at arm's length through a slot without touching the sides, back, or bottom of the slot, as well as by tasks which require holding a stylus as steadily as possible in a small hole without hitting the sides. It has been found that the best measures of this ability allow the recording of the most minute tremors on the part of the subject. This ability has been found to extend to tasks involving needle threading, rifle marksmanship, and the stacking of small components one on top of the other.

*Wrist-Finger Speed.* This ability has been called "tapping" in many previous studies through the years (e.g., Greene, 1943; Fleishman, 1953). It has been used in a variety of different studies, primarily because printed tests can be used which are quick and easy to administer. However, our research shows that this factor is highly restricted in scope and does not extend to many tasks in which apparatus is used (Fleishman, 1954a; Fleishman & Hempel, 1954a). It has been found that the factor is best measured by printed tests requiring rapid tapping of the pencil in relatively large areas. As a matter of fact, it has been found that loadings on this factor decrease as the size of the circle or square to be dotted in decreases. In other words, as visual alignment and control become more involved in the task, tapping or wrist-finger speed seems less involved. The name "wrist-finger speed" has been adopted rather than "tapping" because it appears that pendular as well as rotary arm movements may be involved in this ability.

*Aiming.* This ability appears to be measured by printed tests which provide the subject with very small circles to be dotted in where there are a large number of circles and the test is highly speeded (Fleishman, 1953; Fleishman, 1954a; Hempel & Fleishman, 1955). The subject typically goes from circle to circle, placing one dot in each circle as rapidly as possible. This factor has not been found to extend to apparatus tests and hence the naming of this factor as "aiming," or as other investigators have called it, "eye-hand coordination," seems much too broad. It appears to represent a highly restricted type of ability; generalizations based on performance measures of this type must be considered highly tentative. As the counterpart of the tapping factor, it has been found that as the size of the circles to be dotted in increases, loadings on this factor drop systematically.

## Abilities in the Physical Proficiency Area

Before closing the discussion of motor abilities which have been identified, some mention should be made of another area of motor performance. This is the area commonly thought of as involving physical proficiency or more gross kinds of motor activities. There is much interest today in the general area of physical fitness and the measure of capacities in this area. Factor analyses of tasks in this area indicate that there is no general "athletic" ability, but that abilities in this area may be described in terms of some more basic components (Hempel & Fleishman, 1955). While it is not known what interest there is in relating these to general training problems, no comprehensive review of psychomotor abilities should exclude these areas. From the correlations among performances of tasks in this area, the following factors seem to emerge. The first general area appears to involve, mainly, strength. Thus far, strength of limbs and strength of trunk appear as separate factors. Strength of limbs can be measured by such tasks as chinning. Trunk strength appears to be measurable in the task of push-ups as well as in certain "dynamometer" tests. A second large area appears to involve flexibility or suppleness of muscle groups. Factors of limb flexibility and trunk flexibility have been identified. Such tasks as sit-ups involve trunk flexibility while limb flexibility can be measured in such tasks as kicking height or leg bends. The critical feature here is the capacity of the muscle groups involved to resist distortion and to recover from this distortion. A third area has been called energy mobilization or "explosive ability." This appears at first to be related to strength, and studies are underway to throw light on this relationship. For the present, however, it may be said that energy mobilization is exhibited in performances where exerting a maximum of energy at a given moment is critical. Examples of tasks which measure this ability are throwing a medicine ball as far as possible, putting a shot as far as possible, broad jumping, etc.

Balance abilities appear independent of these abilities already cited. Balance appears to be measured in such tasks as walking a rail, standing on one foot, etc. Two additional factors, gross body coordination and endurance, emerge from research in this area. Gross body coordination appears independent of multilimb coordination, since apparatus tests involving multiple limb coordination do not correlate with athletic skill. Gross body coordination seems to emphasize the use of the entire body. The area of endurance has not been explored in detail mainly because of the methodological problems involved in testing people continuously over lengthy periods of time.

Present evidence indicates that abilities in this general area of physical proficiency are somewhat independent of the kinds of psychomotor abilities outlined above.

## PREDICTING PROFICIENCY AT DIFFERENT STAGES OF LEARNING

It is a fairly common observation that people differ considerably in the skill they achieve in complex tasks, even after extensive training. Moreover, it is found that prolonged practice or experience with such tasks may actually increase individual differences. An oftenmade assumption is that the variability between people observed early in learning is highly related to that observed at later levels of performance. An example of this assumption in practice is that test batteries are more often validated against more immediate training criteria in place of more ultimate performance criteria. It is assumed that the aptitudes contributing to individual differences in the training situation are the same as those contributing to eventual higher proficiency levels.

The second research phase to be discussed concerns the use of these ability constructs (see above) in describing proficiency at different stages of learning more complex skills. What is the contribution of these more general ability components, which people bring with them to a new task, as proficiency in those skills is increased? Thus, ability patterns at early and advanced stages of practice can be compared with a view to establishing the kinds of abilities most predictive of higher proficiency levels in such skills.

In one approach, the typical design of these studies consisted in giving samples of 200-300 subjects extended practice on a criterion laboratory task. In addition, the same subjects received a carefully selected, comprehensive battery of printed and apparatus reference tests. Correlations among scores taken from different segments of the practice period on the criterion task and from the reference tests are then subjected to factor analysis study. The loadings of the various stages of practice of the criterion task on the factors defined by the reference tests specify the changes in the factor pattern of this task as practice continues.

In general, these studies indicated that the particular combinations of abilities contributing to performance on such tasks may change as practice continues and proficiency increases. It was also shown that these changes are progressive and systematic through the practice period until a point later in practice where they become stabilized. In other words, the combination of abilities contributing to individual differences later in training may be quite different from those contributing early in training.

A typical example is illustrated in one of the earlier studies in which the Complex Coordination Test was used as the practiced criterion task (Fleishman & Hempel, 1954b). Basically this task requires the subject to manipulate stick and rudder controls in a coordinated fashion in response to patterns of visual cues. Practice on this task was distributed over a two-day period. Table 5.1 represents the matrix of rotated factor loadings derived from the intercorrelations among eight segments of practice on this task and the indicated reference variables. The factors are identified from the reference tests as Psychomotor Coordination,[1] Speed of Arm Movement, Spatial Relations, Perceptual Speed, Visualization, Mechanical Experience, Numerical Facility, and Psychomotor Speed. Factor I is common only to the practice stages of the criterion task itself and is not defined by any of the external reference tests.

It can be seen that the loadings of the Complex Coordination Test on these factors show progressive changes through practice. The factors of Spatial Relations and Visualization drop out after the early trials, while the factor called Speed of Arm Movement assumes increasing importance. At the same time the factor common only to the task itself increases from an insignificant contribution to a point where it is the main factor sampled by the task. The Psychomotor Coordination factor contributes at a fairly stable level throughout the practice period. In addition to the changes noted, it was also observed that the task was most complex in terms of number of factors measured early in practice, but that the task became less complex factorially as practice continued. In addition, the increase in importance of the "within task" factor further suggested that the predictability of advanced performance levels from external measures may become increasingly difficult to accomplish.

---

[1]Since these studies the Psychomotor Coordination factor has been split into two factors, Multiple Limb Coordination and Control Precision (see above).

Table 5.1

Rotated Factor Loadings of Test Variables and Stages
of Practice on the Complex Coordination Task
(From Fleishman & Hempel, 1954b)

| Variable | I | II | III | IV | V | VI | VII | VIII | IX | X | h² |
|---|---|---|---|---|---|---|---|---|---|---|---|
| 1. Practice Stage 1, Complex Coordination | .24 | .48 | .10 | .39 | .20 | .38 | .28 | .03 | .22 | .02 | .76 |
| 2. Practice Stage 2, Complex Coordination | .45 | .62 | .26 | .24 | .26 | .17 | .21 | .04 | .15 | -.15 | .90 |
| 3. Practice Stage 3, Complex Coordination | .41 | .60 | .33 | .29 | .27 | .16 | .19 | .03 | .18 | .01 | .88 |
| 4. Practice Stage 4, Complex Coordination | .62 | .45 | .38 | .20 | .25 | .06 | .25 | .00 | .18 | -.03 | .93 |
| 5. Practice Stage 5, Complex Coordination | .65 | .46 | .40 | .11 | .16 | .13 | .22 | .00 | .15 | .01 | .92 |
| 6. Practice Stage 6, Complex Coordination | .63 | .47 | .43 | .02 | .15 | .12 | .20 | .06 | .09 | -.01 | .89 |
| 7. Practice Stage 7, Complex Coordination | .60 | .48 | .40 | .12 | .13 | .13 | .16 | .06 | .17 | .21 | .90 |
| 8. Practice Stage 8, Complex Coordination | .62 | .47 | .37 | .10 | .22 | .10 | .18 | .04 | .08 | .17 | .88 |
| 9. Numerical Operations II | .07 | .07 | .05 | .21 | .25 | .03 | .16 | .66 | .09 | -.05 | .59 |
| 10. Dial and Table Reading | .07 | .13 | .03 | .26 | .32 | .30 | .30 | .60 | .21 | .00 | .79 |
| 11. Mechanical Principles | .17 | .06 | -.14 | .15 | .24 | .41 | .49 | .14 | .20 | -.02 | .60 |
| 12. General Mechanics | -.03 | .05 | .00 | .26 | .14 | .06 | .62 | .08 | .16 | .13 | .52 |
| 13. Speed of Identification | .12 | .01 | .10 | .35 | .47 | .29 | .08 | .21 | .37 | -.09 | .65 |
| 14. Pattern Comprehension | .07 | .04 | .10 | .33 | .23 | .60 | .19 | .18 | .21 | -.11 | .60 |
| 15. Visual Pursuit | .15 | .20 | .09 | .16 | .50 | .24 | .02 | .04 | .11 | -.06 | .42 |
| 16. Decoding | .17 | -.03 | .01 | .59 | .22 | .36 | .06 | .35 | .10 | .11 | .71 |
| 17. Instrument Comprehension | .02 | .09 | .20 | .46 | .35 | .20 | .16 | .24 | -.12 | .03 | .52 |
| 18. Spatial Orientation I and II | .10 | .07 | .04 | .35 | .45 | .32 | .09 | .12 | .27 | .26 | .61 |
| 19. Speed of Marking | .10 | .09 | .20 | .23 | .26 | .24 | -.03 | .26 | .50 | .00 | .56 |
| 20. Log Book Accuracy | .03 | .05 | .27 | .04 | .27 | .12 | .07 | .31 | .55 | -.05 | .58 |
| 21. Rotary Pursuit | .03 | .48 | .34 | .12 | .21 | .18 | .18 | .06 | .10 | .17 | .51 |
| 22. Plane Control | .07 | .25 | .33 | .29 | .04 | .09 | .29 | -.10 | .07 | -.09 | .38 |
| 23. Discrimination Reaction Time | .08 | .12 | .25 | .52 | .22 | .23 | .13 | .24 | .12 | -.18 | .58 |
| 24. Nut and Bolt | .03 | .08 | .14 | .12 | .29 | .17 | .32 | -.07 | .03 | .03 | .26 |
| 25. Reaction Time | .06 | .08 | .54 | .08 | .03 | -.11 | -.03 | .03 | .07 | .01 | .33 |
| 26. Rate of Movement | .03 | .17 | .48 | -.01 | .04 | .28 | -.03 | .12 | .07 | -.05 | .36 |
| $\Sigma a^2/k$ | .10 | .10 | .08 | .08 | .07 | .06 | .06 | .05 | .05 | .01 | |

*Factors are identified as follows: I. Complex Coordination Test Specific; II. Psychomotor Coordination; III. Rate of Movement; IV. Spatial Relations; V. Perceptual Speed; VI. Visualization; VII. Mechanical Experience; VIII. Numerical Facility; IX. Psychomotor Speed; X. Residual.

In order to check the generality of some of these findings, a parallel study was carried out (Fleishman & Hempel, 1955) using the Discrimination Reaction Time Apparatus as the practice criterion task and a somewhat different set of reference tests hypothesized to measure aptitudes involved in this task. This task differs from the Complex Coordination Task in several important ways. The task requires the subject to respond as quickly as possible with one of four switches in response to the spatial arrangement of a set of red and green lights. Unlike the Complex Coordination device which is self-paced, this task is paced. The subject receives a series of stimulus settings and three seconds to respond before a new setting is presented.

Figure 5.1 pictures the results obtained. The size of the labeled areas represent the per cent of variance contributed by each factor at each stage of practice on the Discrimination Reaction Time Task. Each stage of practice represents the cumulated time of reaction for a block of 20 settings. It can be seen that the main factor originally measured by the task, Spatial Relations, decreases in importance through the practice period (from a 36% contribution initially to 11% later). At the same time two other factors, Reaction Time and Rate of Arm Movement, not sampled at all initially, increase in importance. In fact, their combined contribution at advanced levels (over 30%) is greater than that contributed by the main factor originally measured by the task. It is also noted that, again, there are fairly consistent increases in the contribution of a factor common only to the practiced task itself.

To illustrate these changes in another way, the group of subjects was stratified into ability levels based on scores achieved on selected tests and then the performance curves of these sub-groups on the practice task were plotted. When the group was stratified on the basis of scores on the Word Knowledge Test (representing a measure of the Verbal Fluency factor) the learning curves tended to converge through practice. This is in direct contrast to the curves stratified on the Visual Reaction Time and Rotary Aiming Tests (representing the Reaction Time and Speed of Arm Movement factors, respectively). In these latter cases the curves tend to diverge as practice continues. It is obvious that individual differences at later stages of learning this task depend on different abilities than at early stages of learning.

In general, the results with this task confirmed the results with the previous task. However, the Discrimination Reaction Time Task did not become less complex in terms of the number of factors measured. In

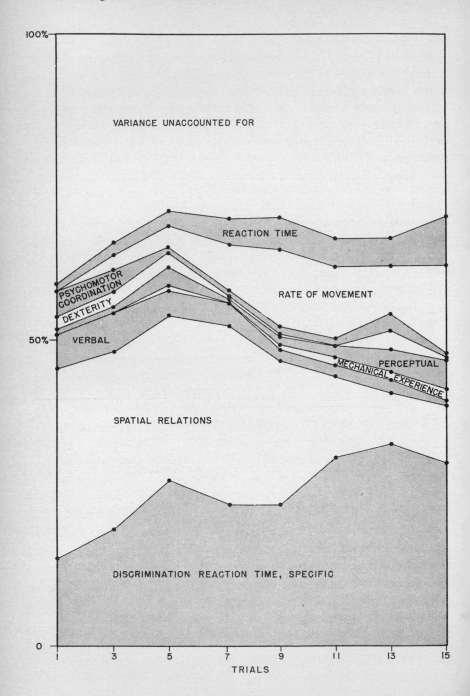

addition, although a "within-task" factor appeared, the increase in this factor was not as marked.

Another task investigated (Fleishman, 1960) in this manner was the Rotary Pursuit Task. This task was chosen for several reasons. First, it represents a different kind of performance from the previous tasks; second, previous analyses had indicated that initially it was a relatively pure measure factorially; and third, it is one of the most commonly used devices in motor skills learning research and knowledge about what it measures would be useful. Figure 5.2 shows the performance curve of

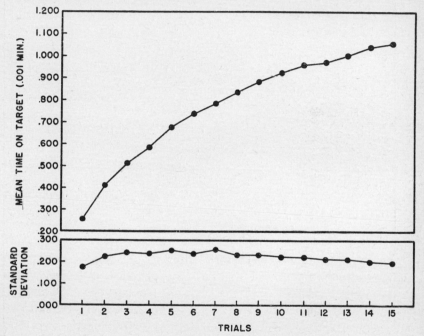

FIGURE 5.2. Acquisition Curve of Performance on the Rotary Pursuit Practice Task (From Fleishman, 1960)

our group of subjects. Basically, the task requires the subject to keep a stylus in contact with a small metal target set in a rapidly revolving "phonograph-like" disc. Score is time on target during each of a series of test periods.

FIGURE 5.1. Percentages of variance represented by loadings on each factor at different stages of practice on the Discrimination Reaction Time Task (percentage of variance is represented by the size of the shaded areas for each factor). (From Fleishman & Hempel, 1955.)

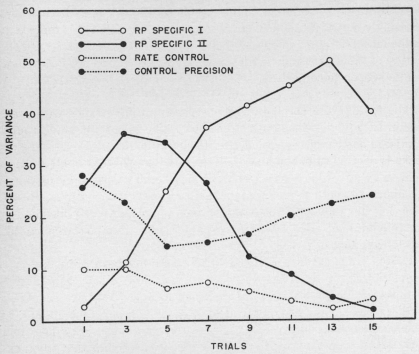

FIGURE 5.3. Contribution of Ability Factors at Different Stages of Rotary Pursuit Learning (From Fleishman, 1960)

Figure 5.3 summarizes the factor loadings of the trial scores on this task. Again these factors were defined from reference tests given to the same subjects. Actually, eight factors were identified in this analysis but only those found represented at some stage of Rotary Pursuit performance are plotted here. A major finding is that again there is a "within-task" factor increasing progressively and then leveling off in a negatively accelerated fashion. In addition, there is a similar factor decreasing in importance with practice. Neither of these two factors is defined by any of the reference variables. The Control Precision factor contributes variance throughout performance on the Rotary Pursuit Task. The Rate Control factor contributes slightly early but drops out with practice. This is consistent with the nature of the Rotary Pursuit Task; the target course does seem harder to anticipate at the beginning of the task.

So it seems that here is a task in which the major common factor contributes variance at a fairly stable level throughout practice on the task. However, as before, a factor specific to the task itself creasingly important. It is assumed for the moment that this re individual differences in specific habits acquired on the task itself nature of the decreasing "within-task" factor which had not been four before is open to conjecture. Whether it represents some kind of "learning set" for example is unknown.

The finding of a specific factor increasing in importance with practice in each of these separate studies has some important implications. If a large portion of the variance at advanced proficiency levels on such tasks is specific to habits and skills acquired on the task itself and not defined by any other test variables, it may be necessary to be pessimistic about predicting advanced levels from external measures. Before adopting this view, other classes of variables, not previously included in our reference batteries, have been explored in an attempt to reduce this specific variance or to better understand its nature.

Evidence against any specificity hypothesis has been presented in a correlation study by Adams (1954). It was found that a combination of measures, including those taken from advanced practice scores on certain psychomotor tests, provided better predictions of advanced proficiency on a criterion psychomotor task than did a measure taken from early practice on the task itself. Moreover, it was found that when extended practice is given on two psychomotor tasks, the correlation between scores taken at the end of practice may be higher than the correlation between the same tasks early in practice. This raised a further question of whether the "within-task" factors found at advanced proficiency levels in the separate analyses have anything in common with each other; in other terms, are these "within-task" factors really confined to each individual task or is there something in common between these different tasks which is found only at advanced levels of proficiency on these tasks.

To get a partial answer to this problem, an analysis was made of extended practice given to the same subjects on seven different psychomotor tasks (Fleishman, 1957a). Considerably longer practice was given on one of the tasks, the Complex Coordination Task, and this was again considered the criterion task in the present study. Two separate factor analyses were carried out, each one of which involved the same 18 variables. These are listed in Table 5.2. In each analysis the first eight variables were the reference tests. Variables 9—12 represented scores taken at four stages of practice on the criterion task. The only difference between the two analyses was the particular scores included

## Table 5.2

Comparison of Factor Patterns of Performance Measures Taken at Early Versus Late Levels of Proficiency in Several Experimental Tasks
(From Fleishman, 1957a)

| | I SAM | | II Vz | | III PS | | IV ME | | V SR | | VI RO | | VII | | VIII | |
|---|---|---|---|---|---|---|---|---|---|---|---|---|---|---|---|---|
| | 1 | 2 | 1 | 2 | 1 | 2 | 1 | 2 | 1 | 2 | 1 | 2 | 1 | 2 | 1 | 2 |
| **Reference Tests** | | | | | | | | | | | | | | | | |
| 1. Instrument Comprehension | — | — | — | — | — | — | — | — | — | — | — | — | — | — | — | — |
| 2. Reaction Time | .60 | .65 | — | — | — | — | — | — | .54 | .49 | — | — | — | — | — | — |
| 3. Rate of Movement | .43 | .42 | — | — | — | — | — | — | .34 | .31 | — | — | — | — | — | — |
| 4. Pattern Comprehension | — | — | .66 | .60 | — | — | .52 | .61 | — | — | — | — | — | — | — | — |
| 5. Mechanical Principles | — | — | .53 | .40 | — | — | .65 | .64 | — | — | — | — | — | — | — | — |
| 6. General Mechanics | — | — | — | — | — | — | — | — | — | — | — | — | — | — | — | — |
| 7. Speed of Identification | — | — | .44 | .38 | .44 | .46 | — | — | — | — | — | — | — | — | — | — |
| 8. Visual Pursuit | — | — | — | — | .38 | .46 | — | — | — | — | — | — | — | — | — | — |
| **Criterion Task** | | | | | | | | | | | | | | | | |
| 9. Complex Coord. Trials 1-5 | — | — | .35 | .41 | — | — | .26 | .29 | .35 | .36 | .38 | .32 | .42 | .40 | .22 | .24 |
| 10. Complex Coord. Trials 12-16 | — | — | — | .27 | — | — | — | — | — | .32 | .47 | .44 | .46 | .44 | .41 | .39 |
| 11. Complex Coord. Trials 49-53 | .42 | .38 | — | — | — | — | — | — | — | — | .38 | .48 | .47 | .45 | .52 | .47 |
| 12. Complex Coord. Trials 60-64 | .43 | .37 | — | — | — | — | — | — | — | — | .34 | .44 | .40 | .45 | .58 | .54 |
| | E | L | E | L | E | L | E | L | E | L | E | L | E | L | E | L |
| **Experimental Tasks** | | | | | | | | | | | | | | | | |
| 13. Rotary Pursuit | .28 | .47 | — | — | — | — | — | — | — | — | — | .28 | .55 | .26 | — | — |
| 14. Plane Control | — | .49 | — | — | — | — | .28 | — | — | — | .33 | .27 | .31 | .38 | — | — |
| 15. Kinesthetic Control | — | — | — | — | — | .34 | .28 | — | — | — | .35 | .40 | — | — | — | — |
| 16. Uni-dimensional Matching | — | .25 | — | — | — | — | — | — | — | — | — | .61 | .45 | .19 | — | — |
| 17. Two-Hand Matching | — | — | — | — | — | — | — | — | — | .28 | .70 | .61 | — | — | — | — |
| 18. Discrimination Reaction Time | .28 | .46 | — | — | — | — | — | — | .46 | .38 | .40 | .28 | — | — | — | — |

*Factor I—Speed of Arm Movement; Factor II—Visualization; Factor III—Perceptual Speed; Factor IV—Mechanical Experience; Factor V—Spatial Relations; Factor VI—Response Orientation; Factor VII—Psychomotor Coordination; Factor VIII—Complex Coordination Test Specific.

for the remaining six tasks (variables 13—18). These tasks were each practiced over repeated trials. In analysis two, scores from the last five minutes of practice were substituted for these same six tasks. The factors extracted in each analysis are summarized in Table 5.2. To facilitate comparisons, all loadings under .25 have been omitted from the table.

Actually, the table combines two separate rotated matrices, one of which is listed under column 1 and the other under column 2. This was possible since the same factors were identified independently in both analyses. The factors are Speed of Arm Movement, Visualization, Perceptual Speed, Mechanical Experience, Spatial Relations, Response Orientation, Psychomotor Coordination, and the factor common only to the stages of practice on the criterion task.

The cross-sectional comparison of the two analyses generally confirm the previous longitudinal practice studies for certain of these tests previously included. An exception is the Rotary Pursuit Test, but this may be due to differences in practice schedule or to the appearance of a Response Orientation in this analysis. However, the inclusion of several measures of advanced proficiency in the same analysis did not result in the identification of new factors; that is, no new factors were found which were confined only to the advanced measures. The question was one of degree of involvement of particular factors already identified. The correlations among advanced measures on different tasks were accounted for entirely by familiar common factors found in other analyses. For example, the correlation between the Complex Coordination and Plane Control tasks is higher when scores later in practice are used. The reason is that each task measures a Speed of Arm Movement factor late in training but not in the early stages of proficiency. The Psychomotor Coordination and Response Orientation factors are common to both tests at early as well as late stages of proficiency.

It should also be noted that there was no decrease in the communalities for these tasks when the late stage scores were substituted for early proficiency scores. In fact, for several tasks the communalities were considerably higher in the late stage analysis. (Thus, for Plane Control, the per cent of common variance increased from 41% to 58% and for Unidimensional Matching the increase was from 45% to 66%.) These results indicated that there is no necessary decrease in predictability of performances from independent measures as practice continues. It is merely the particular combination of common factors that changes. Moreover, it can be seen that the kinds of abilities contributing variance in advanced levels in the psychomotor tasks are defined by other psychomotor measures, even though aptitudes measured by certain printed tests contribute much of the variance at early proficiency levels.

The inclusion of several practice stages for the Complex Coordination Test within each analysis was to allow the appearance of the factor specific to practice on this task. This was not possible with the other tests as only one score was included in each analysis. It can be seen that this "within-task" factor was just as pronounced in analysis two, as in analysis one, and that the importance of this factor increases with practice. Apparently, the inclusion of late stage scores from other tests in analysis two did not help break down this "within-task" variance or help define it.

At this point it was felt that the analyses may not have included the most appropriate reference variables. One might speculate, for instance, that, early in training, performance is a function of individual differences in a number of separate abilities, but that high levels of proficiency are more a function of integrating or patterning these component abilities. Moreover, individual differences in integrating these already well-learned responses may be quite independent of relative standing in the individual component abilities. In other words, individuals may exhibit different facility in integrating their abilities to cope with the new task. As a first, perhaps naive, approach to this hypothesis, tests were considered which had been found to define certain integration abilities in the literature (Guilford & Lacey, 1947). While such integration factors had been identified, they had never been related to the problem of learning. By including a range of independent measures of "so-called" integration abilities along with practiced tasks, it was hoped that the hypothesis that ($a$) loadings of the practice task on the integration factor would increase as a function of practice, and ($b$) this factor may account for at least some of the variance now included in the "within-task" factors could be tested.

Two studies, still unpublished, were carried out, one repeating the use of the Complex Coordination Test and the other using the Two-Hand Coordination Test. The integration tests used were Signal Interpretation, Planning a Course, and Following Directions (from the Air Force) and Coordinate Movements and Complex Movements (from the Navy). Reference tests of Mechanical Experience Reaction Time, Numerical Operations, Control Precision, Verbal Knowledge, Spatial Orientation, Speed of Arm Movement, and Visualization were also included. In each study an integration factor was identified as distinct from those factors. However, in neither case did any stage of performance of the practice tasks lead to this. In the case of the Two-Hand Coordination Task two "within-task" factors were again found, one going up and one coming down with practice. The main source of common variance with other tasks was the Control Precision (or Psychomotor Coordination I) factor, but this decreased with practice during the 20 four-minute trials from loadings of .42 to the .20's. It is possible that the decreasing "within-task" factor might have been identified as Multiple-Limb Coordination had suitable tests of this been included. It should be noted that the correlation between the first trial and the twentieth and last trial on the task itself was only .32, a drop from .79 for the correlation between the first two trials. In other words, early two-hand coordination performance does not predict advanced two-hand coordination performance very well.

In the case of the Complex Coordination Task, previous results were confirmed, but there was no involvement of an integration factor at any stage of practice. In retrospect it appears that the choice of these "integration" tests was not a good one and not very close to the operations that have been called integration. All of these tests emphasize the remembering and application of a number of rules; failure to apply any one rule, typically, involves failure of an item. The critical feature is combining the rules in some way. To test the hypothesis about the integration of component abilities will require more ingenious measures than have been heretofore devised.

There are, of course, other hypotheses to be explored. For example, the importance of kinesthetic abilities has never been investigated. In fact, there are no readily available measures in this area. It is possible, however, that part of the specific variance in motor tasks represents a shift to a dependence on kinesthetic rather than visual cues.

## STUDIES IN TRAINING SETTINGS

### Abilities Related to Progress in Radio-Telegrapher Training

A study (Fleishman & Fruchter, 1960) was carried out on radio code learning which bears directly on this problem of isolating common variance at advanced proficiency levels. While the task of learning Morse Code is, of course, not at all a psychomotor task, this particular study represents an extension of the laboratory studies of skill learning to an actual job training situation. The objective here was to investigate the possibility that the pattern of abilities contributing to proficiency in learning Morse Code may change as practice continues and proficiency increases.

A battery of 14 auditory and printed aptitude tests (Fleishman, Roberts, & Friedman, 1958) was administered to 310 airmen entering radio operator training. During the training, students were given daily "code-checks" as part of the systematic evaluation of progress. These "code-checks" indicated the student's level of proficiency, in terms of the number of code groups per minute he can receive. In the present study, it was possible to determine the number of days it took each student to reach four criterion proficiency levels. Thus, the four criterion measures used were the number of days needed (*a*) to learn to receive four groups per minute; (*b*) to advance from four to six groups per minute; (*c*) to advance from six to 10 groups per minute; and (*d*) to advance from 10 to 14 groups per minute.

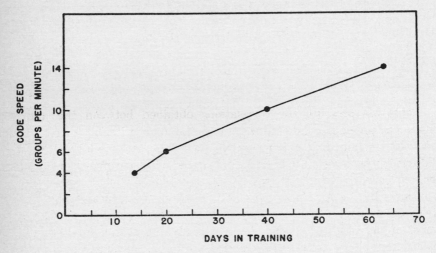

FIGURE 5.4   Learning Curve for Radio-Telegraphers in Training
(From Fleishman & Fruchter, 1960)

The mean number of days it took the group to advance to each successive level of proficiency are as follows: 14.53 days ($\sigma$=4.57) to attain a speed of four groups per minute, 4.38 days ($\sigma$=4.07) to go from four to six groups per minute, 19.24 days ($\sigma$=8.48) to go from six to 10 groups per minute, and 25.49 days ($\sigma$=10.53) to go from 10 to 14 groups per minute. Figure 5.4 shows the learning curve plot of these data. It can be seen that the curve based on these four points is quite smooth and resembles many other learning functions. More points would be needed to demonstrate the appearance of a plateau (which Bryan and Harter [1899] originally demonstrated), but the absence of a plateau in our data is consistent with more recent evidence (Keller & Jerome, 1946; Reed & Zinszer, 1943; Taylor, 1943) that plateaus in code learning are exceptional.

The intercorrelations among these practice stages are presented in Table 5.3. It can be seen that these correlations are not high; in other words, individuals who reach a code speed of four groups per minute most quickly are not necessarily the same individuals who progress from four to six groups, etc., most quickly.

Table 5.3

Intercorrelations of Number of Days Required to Advance
Between the Four Proficiency Levels in Radio-Telegrapher Training
(From Fleishman & Fruchter, 1960)

| Group per minute | 4 to 6 | 6 to 10 | 10 to 14 |
|---|---|---|---|
| To 4 gpm | .28 | .29 | .26 |
| 4 to 6 gpm | | .41 | .36 |
| 6 to 10 gpm | | | .35 |
| 10 to 14 gpm | | | |

Table 5.4 presents the correlations obtained between the ability measures previously administered and the four criterion scores subsequently attained. It is immediately clear from this table that the validities of these tests for predicting speed of code learning drops markedly from early to late stages of training. The Aptitude Index, used routinely by the Air Force to assign individuals to such training, drops from .47 to .32, .15, and .20 through the subsequent stages. Clearly, most of the validity for such tests in predicting overall final standing is attributable to successful prediction during initial phases of training.

To clarify some of these relationships a factor analysis was performed. From the intercorrelations among the ability tests, five factors were identified. These were labeled Visualization, Verbal Ability, Auditory Rhythm Discrimination, Speed of Closure, and Auditory Perceptual Speed. The last three may require more extended definition here.

*Auditory Rhythm Discrimination.* This factor was general to auditory tests, where the critical feature was perception of rhythm patterns rather than speed. Best definers were tests called Hidden Tunes, Dot Perception, and Rhythm Discrimination.

*Speed of Closure.* This factor is defined as the ability to unify or organize an apparently disparate field into meaningful units. The best definers were the printed tests called Mutilated Words and Four Letter Words.

*Auditory Perceptual Speed.* The factor was best defined by auditory tests in which the critical feature was sheer speed of recognition of the stimuli presented. The best measures of this were the Copying Behind, Army Radio Code, and Dot Perception Tests.

Next, the correlations of the four criterion measures (number of days needed to learn four, to advance from four to six, to advance from six to 10, to advance from 10 to 14 groups per minute) with the reference tests were used to project these measures on the factors defined by these tests. The loadings of the four criterion measures on these five factors were examined. The clearest trend was the progressive decrease in the communalities from early to late stages of training. This, of course, was obvious from the correlations. The communality, which was .48 in the

Table 5.4

Correlations* between the Ability Tests and the Number of Days Required to Progress between the Four Criterion Levels in Radio-Telegrapher Training
(From Fleishman & Fruchter, 1960)

| Test Variable | To 4 gpm | 4 to 6 gpm | 6 to 10 gpm | 10 to 14 gpm |
|---|---|---|---|---|
| **Auditory Tests** | | | | |
| Dot Perception ................ | .54 | .23 | .23 | .21 |
| Copying Behind ............... | .40 | .31 | .22 | .26 |
| Army Radio Code Test ........ | .40 | .25 | .12 | .11 |
| Hidden Tunes ................. | .27 | .12 | .13 | .11 |
| Rhythm Discrimination ........ | .18 | .15 | .11 | .15 |
| **Printed Tests** | | | | |
| Mutilated Words .............. | .20 | .26 | .16 | .24 |
| Four Letter Words ............ | .25 | .23 | .09 | .09 |
| Designs ...................... | .29 | .08 | −.01 | −.01 |
| Pattern Comprehension ........ | .23 | .01 | −.06 | .02 |
| Concealed Figures ............ | .24 | .05 | −.10 | .06 |
| Gestalt Completion ........... | .07 | .03 | −.12 | −.16 |
| Marking Accuracy ............. | .12 | .08 | .06 | .03 |
| Word Knowledge .............. | .33 | .18 | .10 | .18 |
| Background for Current Affairs . | .25 | .09 | .01 | .05 |

*Since the correlations are almost uniformly negative with the criteria (number of days to learn), the signs have been reflected. Thus, a positive correlation indicates a high score on the test is related to "rapid progress."

initial stage, dropped to .28 in the second stage, .22 in the third learning period, and .19 for the final stage. In other words, later in learning there is less variance in common with aptitude test scores than in earlier learning periods.

The second indication of this was a shift in the particular factors contributing to performance at different stages of learning. During the early stage of training the factors of Auditory Rhythm Discrimination and Auditory Perceptual Speed were the only factors with loadings above .30. Thus, auditory abilities seem most related to individual differences in speed of learning in the initial learning period. Inspection of the loadings for the second learning period indicated that while the estimated loadings were generally low, the highest of them was on the Speed-of-Closure factor. Auditory Perceptual Speed dropped from .48 to .28, and Auditory Rhythm Discrimination dropped from .37 to .18. (The increase in the Speed-of-Closure factor was attributable to the fact that the Mutilated Words and Four Letter Words tests were the only two tests with either an increase or no change in their correlation from Stage 1 to Stage 2.) There were no loadings above .30 during the last two stages of training.

The multiple correlation coefficients between 14 aptitude test scores and each of the four "stages of learning" criterion scores were also computed. The results of this analysis also indicated that the initial learning period was the most predictable, with the size of the multiple Rs dropping off from the later learning periods. It is possible that the decreasing predictability of performance is due to some loss in criterion reliability at later training stages. There is no direct evidence on this. However, data collected in early training are sufficiently reliable to allow the high validities obtained. It would take a drastic drop in criterion reliability at later stages to account fully for the validity decreases obtained at advanced levels. Moreover, evidence from other studies of learning data (e.g., Reynolds, 1952; Adams, 1954) indicates that consistency of performance during learning is actually higher during later stages. It is also clear that the between-subject variability is sufficiently large during late stages of training, and restriction of range is not a problem. In fact, the standard deviation increased from 4.5 to 10.5; thus, there is more overall variance but less predictable variance.

The results obtained in this study of operational training performance, on an auditory-perceptual task, are consistent with earlier findings (Fleishman, 1956a; Fleishman, 1956b; Fleishman, 1957a; Fleishman, 1957b; Fleishman & Hempel, 1954a; Fleishman & Hempel, 1954b; Fleishman & Hempel, 1955) in laboratory studies of perceptual-motor tasks. In each study it has been found (*a*) that the pattern of abilities contributing to performance on complex tasks changes progressively with practice, and (*b*) there is an increase in a factor specific only to the stages of practice on each of the tasks. This provides the alternative hypothesis that individual differences in performance become increasingly a function of habits and skills acquired during the training. Although the criterion of proficiency in code learning is more objective and less ambiguous than is likely to be the case in many other types of training, this study also suggests that this type of analysis may be usefully applied to other training situations.

## An Analysis of Pilot Flying Proficiency in Terms of Ability Components

This study, in its original conception, was not thought to be a part of this series. However, as shall be shown, it really does bear on the problem of the usefulness of the previously listed ability categories in describing performances in training situation. As is generally known, one of the major accomplishments of the postwar Air Force Program was

FIGURE 5.5

Some items from a check list for one maneuver included in the analysis
(From Fleishman & Ornstein, 1960)

Power-on Stall

Gyros Caged ............................................................... ————

Looks ...................................................................... ————

Two Clearing Turns ....................................................... ————

Direction (±5°) ........................................................... ————

Torque ..................................................................... ————

ENTRY

Pitch Proper .............................................................. ————

RECOVERY

Direction (±5°) ........................................................... ————

Recovery at Stall .......................................................... ————

Stick & Throttle Together ................................................. ————

Throttle to Sea-Level Stop ................................................ ————

Aileron Usage ............................................................. ————

Torque Correction ......................................................... ————

Pitch Control Proper ...................................................... ————

M.P. Reduced to 25″ ...................................................... ————

the development of more objective flying performance measures for use in pilot training. (See Smith, Flexman, & Houston, 1952.) One such instrument allowed for separate evaluation of each of a variety of maneuvers performed by the student in the air. For each maneuver, the instructor checked whether or not the student had performed within predetermined tolerances on a series of successive items. Figure 5.5 gives an example of some of these items for one maneuver.

A maneuver score represented simply the sum of the items checked. In the study to be described (Fleishman & Ornstein, 1960), performance data on 24 different maneuvers were collected for 63 pilot trainees and the intercorrelations among these performances were obtained. Actually, each maneuver score used was an average of four performances on that maneuver from four different flights. In any case, it was felt that a factor analysis of these maneuver intercorrelations might throw some light on the sources of common variance in this complex task. While the N is not large, this type of performance data is difficult to obtain and there was evidence that this sample was closely representative of the larger population of the trainees.

A factor analysis was performed, seven factors extracted, and a blind rotation to simple structure made. Attempts at factor interpretations were made by a psychologist who was also a skilled pilot and thoroughly familiar with the maneuvers. In a sense he "flew" the factors, or at least he "emphathized" the operations of the pilot and aircraft while performing the maneuvers. In going about the interpretations it was at first thought the factors might be interpretable in terms of common subtask operations or requirements. Alternative possibilities included common control movements or control-display relationships. The fact that most maneuvers were factorially complex did not make interpretations any easier. Initially, the pilot-psychologist looked for such evidence of commonality as "do the maneuvers on this factor all involve application of power?" or "do they all involve lining up ground reference points?"

The important point is that there was no explicit objective or attempt, initially, to define these factors in terms of the basic psychomotor ability constructs. However, after repeated failure to "make sense" out of the blind rotations, these best fitted the data. In other words, the ability model developed from experimental-correlational analyses of laboratory tasks seemed most adequate for describing the common requirements of these aircraft maneuvers. The factors identified seemed best described as Control Precision, Multilimb Coordination, Spatial Orientation, Response Orientation, Rate Control, and a factor called "Kinesthetic Discrimination." As an example, the factor eventually named Control Precision contained maneuvers emphasizing a sensitive touch on the rudder controls or on hand-arm control movements (e.g., landing characteristic stall, 90° climbing turn, take off, rudder-control stall). Another factor which was named Spatial Orientation emphasized judgments about one's location in space (forced landings, traffic pattern, rectangular pattern). Highest loadings on another factor were from the maneuvers "coordination exercise" and "climbing turn from level" and other maneuvers placing a premium on simultaneous movements of several limbs. The factor that was labeled "Kinesthetic Discrimination" contained the maneuvers emphasizing "stalls" and slow movements of the aircraft. Pilots describe the control characteristics of these maneuvers as "muddy" or "soft." Perhaps this is the "flying by the seat of one's pants" factor. In general, many of the maneuvers appeared on more than one factor.

More than 13 years ago Neal Miller summarized the wartime research on pilot training and proficiency measurement (Miller, 1947). At that time, Miller stated, "It may be that attempts to make a more penetrating analysis of flying skill will not be profitable until knowledge of simpler psychomotor skills, in situations which are easier to control, has been increased and a clearer idea is developed by the general structure of human perceptual, motor, and intellectual abilities." This prediction is especially interesting in view of the present results. Information about the general structure of perceptual-motor abilities was not available in 1947. Much of the basic research has been done within the last eight years. While there are obvious limitations in the conclusions, the investigators would have been at a loss to interpret the obtained factors meaningfully without the ability concepts developed from the basic laboratory research. Thus, this study provides additional evidence of the usefulness of this ability framework in describing complex operational skills. Similar analyses of the interrelationships among component performance measures of other complex jobs may provide one way of defining the ability requirements underlying proficiency in those jobs.

## Prediction of Complex Tracking Performance

The last three studies to be described were carried out under contract by Psychological Research Associates of Arlington, Virginia. The first study was supported by the Air Force and the extension of this work was supported by the Office of Naval Research (Parker & Fleishman, 1959a). The basic idea of this study was to extend the laboratory research on changing factor structure to a more complex task than had been possible before. Furthermore, practice was to be given over a prolonged period of time. Thirdly, the task was to resemble an operational job, except that it would be possible to control the practice schedule and it would be possible to measure performance in various task components. The study represented a fairly ambitious endeavor. The criterion task developed, with the assistance of Henry Birmingham of the Naval Research Lab, simulated some of the characteristics of a radar intercept mission. The subject's display consisted of a target dot presented on a cathode oscilloscope. The target course was generated by setting the equation of a swinging pendulum into an analogue computer. The subject used an airplane type control stick and rudder pedals to keep the dot centered. The dynamics of the task were such that coordination in three dimensions was required. The task was to "chase" the target. In other words, if the target was to the right on the scope, a right stick movement was indicated to "fly" the plane toward the target. The controls were acceleration controls. In other words, the amount of stick (or rudder) displacement is directly proportional to the acceleration of the dot's movement. When one adds to this certain time lag constants, it can be seen that this is a fairly difficult task. Pretesting of the device was done to adjust its difficulty so that most subjects would begin to level off in 17 hours of distributed practice, and so that different subjects would reach this level at different times. Three units of this device, each including its own analogue computer and scoring console, were set up in a facility sublet from the University of Maryland.

Another major effort was the assembly of a comprehensive battery of psychomotor and printed reference tests. Hypotheses were set up concerning the factors that might be important at some stage of practice on this complex task. Based on factor loadings in previous studies, at least three tests were included to sample each factor. In all, 51 tests were involved. Practically an entire psychomotor lab was crated up and shipped from Lackland Air Force Base to College Park, Maryland. At least two models of each of 24 different psychomotor devices were included and a maintenance man was sent up to check everything out. Each of 203 ROTC students were administered the complete reference battery. Total testing time was 11 hours. In addition, each subject practiced on the tracking device during 17 hourly sessions distributed over a month and a half period.

It is impossible here to go into all the part scores (e.g., integrated absolute error, azimuth error, pitch error, sideslip error, and time on target) and time segments sampled on the tracking task at different stages of practice. For the purposes of this chapter, it can be said that a factor analysis of the correlations among the reference tests alone was carried out and then certain segments of practice on the criterion task were projected onto these factors. Assistance was received in this factor analysis phase by Benjamin Fruchter of the University of Texas. From the correlations themselves, it was immedi-

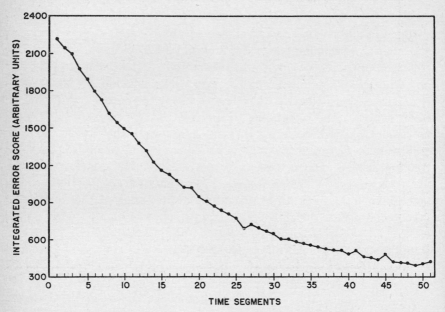

FIGURE 5.6   Performance Curve Based on Integrated Absolute Error Measure in Tracking (From Parker & Fleishman, 1959a)

ately apparent that the results with this task did not conform in any simple way to previous tasks. The reference tests correlated among themselves in the predicted way and yielded stable factors. The 15 factors identified in the reference tests were Spatial Orientation, Control Precision, Speed of Arm Movement, Manual Dexterity, Reaction Time, Verbal Comprehension, Response Orientation, Arm-Hand Steadiness, Perceptual Speed, Visualization, Integration, Pursuit Confusion, Mechanical Experience, Finger Dexterity, and Multilimb Coordination. (Many of these are described earlier in this chapter.) However, the amount of common variance with the criterion task was surprisingly low in the light of the comprehensiveness of this battery.

Figure 5.6 shows the learning curve for the integrated error score. Figure 5.7 shows the overall percentage of variance in tracking performance accounted for at each stage of learning. This figure indicates that all of the identified ability factors when taken together account for no more than 25% of the variance in tracking performance at any stage.

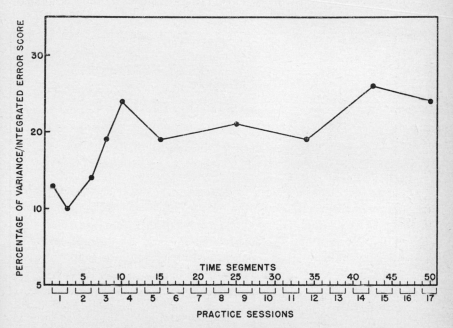

FIGURE 5.7 Percentage of Variance in Tracking Performance Accounted for by All Identified Factors (From Parker & Fleishman, 1959a)

Most of this common variance was due to two factors: Spatial Orientation and Multilimb Coordination. As Figure 5.8 shows, the Spatial factor drops out as practice continues. The Multilimb Coordination factor showed a systematic increase in importance before leveling out in the middle of the training program. At terminal proficiency even this factor accounted for only 8% of the total variance. Thus, it is found there is some shift in the relative importance of these abilities with practice, but the overriding result is that those abilities do not account for the major portion of the variance in tracking performance.

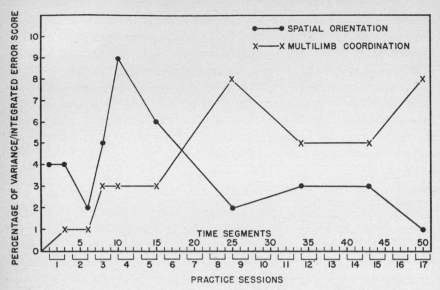

FIGURE 5.8  Changes Occurring in the Importance of Two Ability Factors with Increased Practice in Tracking (From Parker & Fleishman, 1959a)

The case for external measures does not seem as bad, however, when one compares them with the intra-task correlations. Early performance on the task itself did not predict performance during the final hour. Here is a task in which the highly reliable first stage score correlates zero with a highly reliable final score. Even after four hours of practice, the correlation is only .30 with final proficiency. There are six reference tests which correlate at this level with final proficiency. If one is forced to choose between an intra-task measure, even after several hours of practice, and a combination of independent test measures, it is clear that the best prediction of final performance comes from the external measures.

Now to consider the major question raised by this study: why did these 15 clearly defined factors fail to show a greater relation to tracking performance? A partial answer may be that the test battery, despite its comprehensiveness did not include certain relevant ability classes. Adams and others have recently classified the component responses in tracking behavior into observing, predicting, and motor responses. Within this framework it may be that the biggest gap in the test battery was in the area of prediction responses. Prediction responses involve the prediction of the regularities inherent in the input signal and of the effect of control movements upon the error signal.

Simple tracking tests involving prediction responses were included in the reference battery, e.g., the Single Dimension Pursuit and Rate Control tests, but the expected Rate Control factor did not appear. It is also possible that the kind of prediction required in this criterion task, involving prediction of acceleration and higher order target characteristics, is a different order of ability than has been investigated previously. It is suggested that, in complex tracking, abilities in the prediction area become increasingly important whereas observing and motor factors play a less important role in attaining high proficiency levels.

## Predicting Retention of a Complex Tracking Skill

Many of the same subjects, originally tested as much as two years previously in the study just described above, were retested in a followup retention study in progress at the time of this writing. It is clear that retention is remarkable over this period. Where some new subjects cannot even keep the target on the scope even after several sessions, most of the original subjects, even after two years in which they have not seen the task, can walk in, sit down at the device, and begin tracking at a very high level of mastery. Data on retention of tracking skill, after periods of no practice, are rare and have important training implications in their own right. It will be possible to show degree of retention after 1, 3, 5, 9, 14, and 24 months of no practice.

Data analysis is being carried out to evaluate how well the original ability measures, administered to these subjects, predict retention after periods of no practice. From the low correlations obtained in the initial learning study, there is little place for optimism. It is possible that performance after periods of no practice is more predictable than performance at the end of initial learning. If this turns out to be the case, this may tell something about the specific variance built up during practice. This study also included a program of retraining under two schedules (massed vs. distributed). Aside from evaluating the value of the retraining in this type of skill, it is hoped that extra data on changes in ability structure during retraining will be obtained.

## Use of Information about Ability Components in Training Design

A recent report (Parker & Fleishman, 1959b) describes an attempt to make use of analytical information about ability requirements in designing a skill training program. Essentially, this study investigated the possibility that knowledge of the ability pattern underlying proficiency at different stages of learning enables the preparation of an instructional program for increasing training efficiency. The task used was the complex tracking task described above. Three groups were compared. The first group was the original group, which received no formal training beyond a brief explanation of the device. A second group received "common sense" training using standard pedagogical techniques developed with the assistance of cognizant Navy personnel. The third group, the experimental group, was treated in identical fashion as the "common sense" group, but in addition was provided guidance at certain points in training based on the earlier analysis of task components. Thus, knowledge that a certain ability becomes important at a given point in the training schedule was used to emphasize that ability at an earlier time. The question was whether there would be more rapid learning in this group and whether terminal proficiency would be higher.

Two types of analytical information were used. The first was based on the factor analysis previously described (see Figure 5.8). Thus, instructions stressing the spatial aspects of the task were inserted prior to and during the third practice session; information stressing the coordination requirements was given prior to and during the fifth session. Since the contribution of these abilities turned out to be small, this was supplemented by a second type of information. This is the knowledge of the contribution of the different task components (azimuth, elevation, sideslip error) to terminal task proficiency. Table 5.5 shows the correlation between these components at different stages of practice with terminal integrated error score. The indication is that the sideslip component becomes increasingly predictive of overall error. (This is consistent with the factor information about Multilimb Coor-

Table 5.5

Correlations of Component Scores at Various
Stages of Practice with Terminal Integrated Error Score
(From Parker & Fleishman, 1959b)

| | | | | Time Segment | | | | | |
|---|---|---|---|---|---|---|---|---|---|
| | 1 | 3 | 6 | 8 | 10 | 15 | 25 | 34 | 43 |
| Azimuth Error Score | .02 | −.07 | .03 | .11 | .19 | .27 | .28 | .34 | .49 |
| Elevation Error Score | .08 | .10 | .12 | .17 | .26 | .34 | .36 | .42 | .52 |
| Sideslip Error Score | .12 | .04 | −.04 | .00 | .13 | .30 | .34 | .51 | .65 |

dination.) Hence, during the ninth and eleventh sessions, the importance of this component was re-emphasized.

Figure 5.9 presents the curves for the three groups for the time-on-target score, with the indication that the experimental group is superior. In terms of the integrated error measure of performance during the last three sessions, the experimental group showed a 39% increase

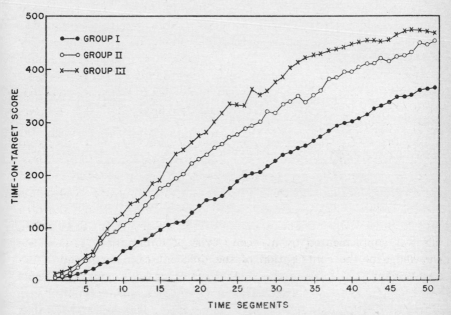

FIGURE 5.9  Comparison of Time-on-Target Measure for Groups I, II, and III
(Each Ss score is based on six one-minute trials of which 54 seconds are scored.
Maximum score per trial is 90 in terms of clock reading.)
(From Parker & Fleishman, 1959b)

over the "common sense" group. It has been suggested by Levine (in DuBois & Manning, 1957, p. 61) that techniques resulting in even a 10% improvement in training efficiency within the military context would allow a substantial saving in the military budget. This study does not attempt to partial out the relative effects of one source of information (ability factors) versus the other (component subtasks). Nor does it throw light on the sequencing of supplementary guidance. And there are some methodological difficulties. However, the evidence is encouraging and should be followed up.

## SOME FINAL COMMENTS

The design of training programs for complex skills ordinarily involves a combination of "expert judgment" and known principles of learning. The emphasis is generally on "common sense" procedures. Recent writers (e.g., Webb in DuBois & Manning, 1957; Gagné & Bolles, 1959) have stressed the opinion that the laws of learning, developed in the laboratory, have for the most part not been applicable to operational training problems. There are many reasons for this, not the least of which is the lack of understanding of the learning process itself, especially in cases of more complex performances. There is at present, for example, a lack of knowledge of the manner in which principles of learning are related to particular characteristics of the tasks learned. This, of course, is related to the question of how well it is possible to generalize the usefulness of learning principles from one task to another. Whether the kind of taxonomy developed through the approach described here will be useful in this regard remains to be seen.

Essentially, what these studies try to do is make use of the fact of individual differences in order to probe into the properties of the task beyond a mere physical description of it. Experimental psychologists by and large have not been concerned with definitions of task variables. This may cause many of the difficulties in generalizing experimental results from one task to another. There is a common tendency to overgeneralize from the results of experiments in one limited area to behavior in another. This gets us into the area of transfer of training. Glib statements about "identical elements" of tasks have not been of much help in predicting transfer, even when these are defined as specific "stimulus-response" connections. The phenomena of stimulus and response generalization have led to the substitution of the concept of "similarity" for the concept of "identity," but this still leaves us with a need to define "similarity" along some set of dimensions. Guilford (1958) has pointed out in this connection, that the lack of transfer demonstrated between memory tasks, may be "explained" by the fact that memory is not a unitary ability. Many transfer studies are carried out in areas consisting of a large number of narrow abilities. The high degree of specificity found in tasks in the studies described here may be the most important finding of these studies. This may certainly place limits on transfer between such tasks.

There is, of course, the question that some of the unaccounted for variance is "motivational" or "personality" variance. There is an increasing interest in the interaction of personality and learning variables. Studies are planned to investigate this possibility.

The fact that there is, thus far, a large specific component contributing to individual differences in learning should not make one lose sight of the common variance already identified. The prediction implications are clear, and as is indicated here, there are encouraging signs that these may be exploited in the structuring of training.

## REFERENCES

Adams, J. A. The prediction of performance at advanced stages of training on a complex psychomotor task. *USAF Hum. Resour. Res. Cent. Bull.*, 1954, No. 53-49.

Brown, J. S. & Jenkins, W. O. An analysis of human motor abilities related to the design of equipment and a suggested program of research. In P. M. Fitts (Ed.), *Psychological research on equipment design.* Washington: U. S. Government Printing Office, 1947. AAF Aviat. Psychol. Res. Rep. No. 19.

Bryan, W. L. & Harter, N. Studies on the telegraphic language; the acquisition of a hierarchy of habits. *Psychol. Rev.*, 1899, *6*, 345-375.

Cronbach, L. J. The two disciplines of scientific psychology. *Amer. Psychologist,* 1957, *12*, 671-684.

Ferguson, G. A. On learning and human ability. *Canad. J. Psychol.*, 1954, *8*, 95-112.

Ferguson, G. A. On transfer and the abilities of man. *Canad. J. Psychol.*, 1956, *10*, 121-131.

Fleishman, E. A. Testing for psychomotor abilities by means of apparatus tests. *Psychol. Bull.*, 1953, *50*, 241-262.

Fleishman, E. A. Dimensional analysis of psychomotor abilities. *J. exp. Psychol.*, 1954, *48*, 437-454. (a)

Fleishman, E. A. *Evaluations of psychomotor tests for pilot selection: The direction control and compensatory balance tests.* USAF Personnel Train. Res. Cent. Tech. Rep., 1954. AFPTRC-TR-54-131. (b)

Fleishman, E. A. Predicting advanced levels of proficiency in psychomotor skill. In G. Finch & F. Cameron (Eds.), *Symposium on Air Force human engineering, personnel, and training research.* Washington: National Academy of Sciences—National Research Council, Pub. 455, 1956. (a)

Fleishman, E. A. Psychomotor selection tests: Research and application in the U.S. Air Force. *Personnel Psychol.*, 1956, *9*, 440-467. (b)

Fleishman, E. A. A comparative study of aptitude patterns in unskilled and skilled psychomotor performances. *J. appl. Psychol.*, 1957, *41*, 263-272. (a)

Fleishman, E. A. Factor structure in relation to task difficulty in psychomotor performance. *Educ. psychol. Measmt*, 1957, *17*, 522-532. (b)

Fleishman, E. A. Analysis of positioning movements and static reactions. *J. exp. Psychol.*, 1958, *55*, 13-24. (a)

Fleishman, E. A. Dimensional analysis of movement reactions. *J. exp. Psychol.*, 1958, *55*, 430-453. (b)

Fleishman, E. A. Abilities at different stages of practice in rotary pursuit performance. *J. exp. Psychol.*, 1960, *60*, 162-171.

Fleishman, E. A. & Fruchter, B. Factor structure and predictibility of successive stages of learning Morse Code. *J. appl. Psychol.*, 1960, *44*, 97-101.

Fleishman, E. A. & Hempel, W. E. A factor analysis of dexterity tests. *Personnel Psychol.*, 1954, *7*, 15-32. (a)

Fleishman, E. A. & Hempel, W. E. Changes in factor structure of a complex psychomotor test as a function of practice. *Psychometrika*, 1954, *19*, 239-252. (b)

Fleishman, E. A. & Hempel, W. E. The relation between abilities and improvement with practice in a visual discrimination reaction task. *J. exp. Psychol.*, 1955, *49*, 301-310.

Fleishman, E. A. & Hempel, W. E. Factorial analysis of complex psychomotor performance and related skills. *J. appl. Psychol.*, 1956, *40*, 96-104.

Fleishman, E. A. & Ornstein, G. N. An analysis of pilot flying performance in terms of component abilities. *J. appl. Psychol.*, 1960, *44*, 147-155.

Fleishman, E. A., Roberts, M. M. & Friedman, M. P. A factor analysis of aptitude and proficiency measures in radio-telegraphy. *J. appl. Psychol.*, 1958, *42*, 129-135.

Gagné, R. M. & Bolles, R. C. Review of factors in learning efficiency. In E. Galanter (Ed.), *Automatic teaching: the state of the art.* New York: Wiley, 1959.

Greene, E. B. An analysis of random and systematic changes with practice. *Psychometrika*, 1943, *8*, 37-52.

Guilford, J. P. Psychological measurement. In J. P. Seward & G. H. Seward (Eds.), *Current issues in psychology.* New York: Holt, 1958.

Guilford, J. P. & Lacey, J. I. *Printed classification tests.* Washington: U. S. Government Printing Office, 1947. AAF Aviat. Psychol. Prog. Res. Rep. No. 5.

Hempel, W. E. & Fleishman, E. A. Factor analysis of physical proficiency and manipulative skill. *J. appl. Psychol.*, 1955, *39*, 12-16.

Keller, F. S. & Jerome, E. A. *Progress in receiving International Morse Code.* Washington, D. C.: U. S. Dept. Commerce, 1946. OSRD Report No. 5366, 1945, Publ. Bd., No. 12152.

Levine, A. S. In P. H. DuBois & W. H. Manning (Eds.), *Methods of research in technical training.* St. Louis: Washington University, 1957. ONR Technical Report No. 3.

Melton, A. W. (Ed.) *Apparatus tests.* Washington: U. S. Government Printing Office, 1947. AAF Aviat. Psychol. Prog. Res. Rep. No. 4.

Miller, N. E. (Ed.) *Psychological research on pilot training.* Washington: U. S. Government Printing Office, 1947. AAF Aviat. Psychol. Res. Rep. No. 8.

Parker, J. F., Jr. & Fleishman, E. A. *Prediction of advanced levels of proficiency in a complex tracking task.* Arlington: Psychological Research Associates, 1959. WADC TR 59-255. (a)

Parker, J. F., Jr. & Fleishman, E. A. *Use of analytical information concerning task requirements to increase the effectiveness of skill training.* Arlington: Psychological Research Associates, 1959. (b)

Reed, H. B. & Zinszer, H. A. The occurrence of plateaus in telegraphy. *J. exp. Psychol.*, 1943, *33*, 130-135.

Reynolds, B. The effect of learning on the predictibility of psychomotor performance. *J. exp. Psychol.*, 1952, *44*, 189-198.

Smith, J. F., Flexman, R. E., & Houston, R. C. *Development of an objective method of recording flight performance.* USAF Hum. Resour. Res. Cent. Tech. Rep., 1952, No. 52-15.

Taylor, D. W. Learning telegraphic code. *Psychol. Bull.*, 1943, *40*, 461-487.

Webb, W. B. In P. H. DuBois & W. H. Manning (Eds.), *Methods of research in technical training.* A report of a conference held at the Naval Air Station, Memphis, Tennessee. St. Louis: Washington University, 1957. Pp. 80-82.

# Chapter 6 | Factors in Complex Skill Training[1]

Paul M. Fitts, University of Michigan

Skilled performance exhibits the three following characteristics: (a) spatial-temporal patterning, (b) continuous interaction of response processes with input and feedback processes, and (c) learning. This is a broad definition indeed, one which encompasses a large part of all human behavior. It includes so-called "motor" skills, but is consistent with the broader meaning of skill employed by Bartlett (1958) in his book on *Thinking*, by Broadbent (1958) in his book on *Perception and Communication*, and by Woodworth (1958) in his work on the *Dynamics of Behavior*.

The last half-century has seen the emergence, due to modern technology, of many new human tasks which have demanded new kinds of complex skills. Driving automobiles and operating other forms of machinery are common examples. With the further development of technology some of these tasks are now becoming less important than they were a few years ago. However, the total number of human activities requiring complex skills has probably not decreased appreciably, especially when we enumerate such varied activities as those involved in athletic pursuits, walking and running, reading and writing, automobile driving, and industrial tasks.

The point is that specific tasks change rapidly as a result of technological change. For example, at the present time the importance of perceptual skills appears to be increasing while the importance of primarily motor skills may be decreasing. There has also been a trend in effect for some time for an increasing amount of skilled work to be done while

[1]Many of the ideas expressed in this chapter are taken from sections of a book on *Skilled Performance* by P. M. Fitts, H. P. Bahrick, M. E. Noble, and G. E. Briggs, which is to be published by Wiley.

the individual is seated. As will be emphasized later, skills performed with the body at rest are in one respect simpler than skills that are executed while the body is in motion. The kinds of skills that appear to be increasing in importance are ones in which the individual must keep track of many separate sources of information (stimuli), collate these separate inputs, and sort out effects produced by his own earlier actions from the effects produced by outside agents.

Such considerations lead to the conclusion that the study of skilled performance and skill training will be of continuing importance. Not only is skill important in its own right, but a comprehensive theory of skill and skill learning should provide a basis for understanding many other forms of behavior in which individuals must deal with sequences of events and must organize their own behavior into an effective sequence of actions under time stress.

## TASK TAXONOMY

The importance of an adequate task taxonomy for skilled tasks is widely recognized in all areas of psychological theorizing today. A taxonomy should identify important correlates of learning rate, performance level, and individual differences. It should be equally applicable to laboratory tasks and to the tasks encountered in industry and in military service. Task taxonomy will therefore receive major emphasis in the present paper. Fleishman has already dealt, in a previous chapter, with several questions of task analysis and classification. The present chapter will extend this analysis, drawing first on results from experimental studies of various task characteristics, and second on results from surveys of the experiences of instructors regarding factors that make the learning of complex skills difficult.

The definition of skill offered at the beginning of this chapter emphasizes the continuous interplay of input, output, and feedback processes. One should therefore seek a taxonomy for *processes* and *activities*, rather than for static elements. In a strict sense it is misleading to assume discrete beginnings and endings of such processes, even though this is often done as a matter of convenience. Keeping this reservation in mind the analysis of skill processes can begin with a consideration of the conditions existing prior to the initiation of some behavior sequence of interest. Here the interest is in the extent to which an individual is prepared or "set" for action, and the relationship of external to self-initiated activity.

## Skill Constancies

The gross features of a skilled activity can be specified in terms of (*a*) the degree of gross body involvement and (*b*) the extent of external pacing of the activity. These two factors specify the nature of the constancies or uniformities that are present in highly skilled patterns of behavior.

In the simplest instance, the body is at rest prior to the beginning of a response sequence, and the individual initiates a behavior pattern which is carried out in relation to a relatively fixed or stable set of environmental objects. Driving a golf ball, picking up a pencil, or threading a needle are simple examples of behavior initiated from such a condition of rest or preparation. The constancies that develop in such behavior patterns are readily apparent and fairly easily measured.

In the next more complex instances, the behavior sequence is initiated either while the body is in motion (with external objects fixed), or while external objects are in motion (with the body fixed or "set"). Examples are the activities of a basketball forward (when shooting while in motion) or of a batter in baseball (when swinging at a thrown ball). Here the uniformities in the individual's behavior patterns are often difficult to observe except in terms of the success or failure of the total sequence (e.g., hitting the ball), since a complex and changing set of relationships is now being dealt with. The sensory neuromotor activity is also more complex than is true when the body is initially at rest.

Finally, at the most complex level of skill constancy, both the individual and external objects undergo change immediately prior to the time when the particular sequence that is of interest begins. A man who is trying to keep his balance on the deck of a pitching ship and at the same time is training his eyes (or perhaps a gun) on an aircraft that is flying overhead is engaged in such a complex task. A football quarterback who throws a running pass is another example. It obviously would be very difficult to record the complete temporal-spatial patterns of motion involved in such activities, and even more difficult to extract the constancies involved in successive sequences, i.e., to identify anything uniform in the behavior. Only the end result appears to be constant and only by considering means-end relationships is the nature of the constancies revealed.

This admittedly gross classification of tasks requiring skill is mentioned chiefly as a way of putting the rest of this chapter in proper perspective. The remaining discussion deals chiefly with skills that men perform from a seated position and with their bodies in a prepared or set position, at least with respect to their immediate environment such as the vehicle in which they are riding. Emphasis is also upon skills that are performed under time stress, where both speed and accuracy of response are sought.

## Task Characteristics Derived from Feedback Concepts

The more detailed taxonomic system which follows, and much of the subsequent discussion, is based upon an analytic approach which considers an individual man, engaged in some form of skilled performance,

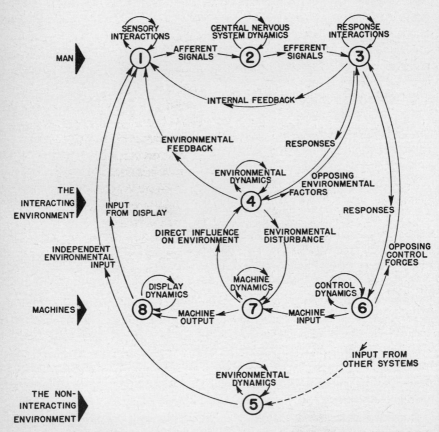

FIGURE 6.1.   Illustration of Some of the Dynamic Feed-Back Loops Involved in Skilled Performance. The nodes in the diagram represent the following dynamic processes: (1) receptor, (2) central nervous system, (3) effector, (4) and (5) social environmental, (6) control, (7) machine, and (8) display.

as a closed-loop system. In such a system the feedback loops are equally as important as the inputs. Figure 6.1 is such a schematic representation of the major dynamic interactions or feedback loops involved in skilled performance. Three major loops are shown.

First there is an internal loop (1-2-3-1) whereby a man's responses provide proprioceptive and kinesthetic stimulation that can influence his subsequent responses. Second there is an external loop (1-2-3-4-1) whereby a man's responses influence his social world and other aspects of his environment, and subsequently result in new stimulation or feedback from other people. Third there is the loop (1-2-3-6-7-8-1) whereby man-machine interactions occur. Each node in Figure 6.1, those representing man's receptors, central nervous system, and effectors, and also external systems, has its own peculiar dynamics. The most important of these are found within the central nervous system. Some major characteristics of perceptual-motor tasks can now be enumerated by reference to this diagram.

*Stimulus and Response Sequences.* First, the sequence of stimulus or response events such as those impinging on Node 1 in Figure 6.1 will be considered. Regardless of their specific form, stimulus and/or response sequences can be specified quantitatively by four characteristics —their degree of coherence, continuity, frequency, and complexity.

A sequence is coherent to the degree that there is a specifiable dependence between successive events or values. Thus spoken English, walking movements, and the succession of notes in a classical musical composition are all highly coherent. Degree of coherence can be quantified in several ways, such as by an autocorrelation function or by a coefficient of redundancy. Examples of tasks that require the learning of relatively coherent movement patterns are rotary pursuit, skating, swimming, and handwriting. (At this point a statement of clarification is necessary. A taxonomic system is proposed which can be used to specify, in terms of purely formal properties, similarities and differences in activities that superficially might appear to have little in common, such as playing music and flying an aircraft. Identification of the bases for measures of the coherence of sequences opens up many research possibilities.)

A second characteristic of any type of sequence is its continuity. Task continuity is a function of the duration of sequences of changing events, and the occurrence of pauses between sequences. Stimulus and response sequences can thus be classified as (*a*) continuous and (*b*) discrete. Steering a car is a continuous task; hitting a baseball is a discrete task. From the standpoint of the subject these distinctions probably lie on a continuum. When discrete events follow each other with sufficient rapidity the task may be called a serial one. Typing is a good example of a serial task.

The frequencies of the changes involved in any type of task can also be specified. In the case of continuous sequences, frequency may be specified in terms of the periodic components which the sequence contains (or its power spectrum). In the case of a serial task, frequency may be specified in terms of the spacing of discrete cycles of activity (or the probability densities of events).

Finally, the complexity of a stimulus or a response sequence can be specified in terms of the numbers of different frequencies, time intervals, amplitudes, signals, or other kinds of variations which occur in a cycle of specified duration. Information measures are sometimes applicable. Needless to say, if the properties of a sequence keep changing in an unpredictable fashion, its formal properties cannot be specified precisely.

Referring to the earlier distinction between self-initiated and externally-initiated sequences, it is clear that the specification of a sequence in terms of its coherence, continuity, frequency, and complexity can apply to either type of activity. In one case it is the external, pacing sequence which usually is specified; in the other, it is self-initiated response sequence which is described.

*Stimulus-Response Coding and Code Transformations.* Thus far nothing has been specified about the particular size, color, pitch, or other characteristics of the stimulus, or about the force, amplitude, or other characteristics of the response movements that constitute a sequence or an activity. Tasks can be specified further by the stimulus and response codes employed, and particularly by the transformations required between stimuli and responses, or between responses and knowledge of response effects. Inputs may be via visual, auditory, tactual or other senses; responses may be vocal or manual; and both vocal and manual responses may take many forms. Thus it is often necessary to specify precisely how stimulus events are mapped into response events.

*Nature and Amount of Input and External Feedback Information.* It is often important to specify the kind and quantity of information, both input and feedback, available in a task. Of special interest, for example, are the many forms of knowledge of results.

*Nature of Internal (Proprioceptive) Feedback.* It is convenient to distinguish between internal and external feedback. Internal feedback is much more difficult to measure or to control than is external feed-back, and consequently less is known about its effects.

*Dynamics of Physical Systems.* In many of the tasks performed in industry and in military service an important factor is the dynamic characteristics of the physical systems such as submarines, automobiles, or other machines that are operated by a man. The lags and oscillations characteristic of such systems determine part of what a man must learn in controlling them.

*Overall Task Complexity.* Finally it is necessary to specify the complexity of the total task as well as the complexity of particular stimulus-response sequences. This can be done in the same way that the complexity of a single stimulus or response sequence is specified. Overall task complexity thus refers to the number of separate sources of input or feedback information, the number of external systems with separate dynamics, etc., which together constitute the total task. The number of separate actions that must be taken serially as well as concurrently determine complexity. Examples of relatively complex tasks include flying an aircraft, directing several aircraft from a ground-based radar station, and monitoring a panel of many instruments. Few attempts have been made to measure the complexity of different tasks quantitatively, so that one can say how much more complex one is than the other; however, this will obviously be a desirable improvement in task taxonomy.

### Summary of Task Taxonomy

This necessarily short overview of task taxonomy will doubtless be insufficient to provide a clear picture of the task characteristics which determine the rate of learning or the ease or difficulty of performance. However, it is hoped that one conclusion is apparent: it is possible to specify many of the important characteristics of on-going patterns of activity, and to define these characteristics in terms of measures that are operationally independent of the criterion (behavior) measures by means of which the progress of learning and achievement or the "difficulty" of a task is customarily specified. In other words, it is possible to avoid circular definitions of factors in task difficulty and thus to open the door to research on the relation of task characteristics to learning and performance. Task taxonomy has many implications for training and training research, as well as for other research areas such as engineering psychology and individual differences. Before considering some of these implications, however, attention should be turned to an important source of data about the nature of skilled activities and about training problems—the experiences of persons who spend their lives instructing others in skills.

## INSTRUCTORS' OPINIONS REGARDING THE PROBLEMS OF SKILL TRAINING

In the earlier sections of this chapter and in the chapter by Fleishman, two somewhat contrasting approaches to the analysis of skill have been outlined. In the typical individual-difference approach outlined in Chapter 5 many relatively short tests may be given to large numbers of subjects and the interrelations among the dependent variables (scores), and sometimes measures of longer learning changes in a particular task are then studied by factor-analytic techniques. In the typical experimental approach many studies are often conducted, with one or perhaps two or three independent characteristics of a skill task systematically varied in each study, and the effects on performance and learning analyzed. These two approaches differ in important respects and therefore should supplement each other in revealing important dimensions of tasks and dimensions of individual differences.

But there is a third approach to an understanding of the nature of skill and of skill training problems, the use of survey techniques which tap the experiences of the men and women who devote their working lives to the training of young people in various skills. The rationale for studies which take as their data the experiences of instructors is perhaps obvious. Such studies certainly need no special justification. Nevertheless, two points should be made. First, instructors are intensely interested in certain aspects of task taxonomy—they are forced continually to think about factors in skill learning, to try to understand the problems of the learner at various stages of training, and to program their instruction in relation to the nature of the skill task and the nature of the learner. Second, instructors have ample opportunity to study the progress of learners and to try out (albeit perhaps in an unsystematic way) different techniques of instruction. It therefore seems reasonable that much can be learned from the systematic collection and analysis of their experiences.

The results of two studies of instructors' opinions in which the author has been involved in the past should now be considered. The first was an analysis of stenographic reports of the statements made by pilot instructors in the cases of 1000 aviation cadets who were eliminated from Air Force pilot training in 1942 (summarized briefly in Guilford &

Lacey, 1947, p. 9). The second was an unpublished study made by Dr. Alfred Smode and the author in 1957, in which tape-recorded interviews were conducted with 40 coaches and physical education instructors at Ohio State University. The two studies were concerned with quite different skills, and the data collection procedures were also quite different. One concerned the learning of how to fly an aircraft, the other the learning of such sports as swimming, diving, tennis, football, baseball, basketball, fencing, and soccer. The latter activities, it should be mentioned, all involve skills in which the total body is in motion rather than seated (as in the case of the pilot). It is these wide differences in the types of activities which make a comparison of the results of these two studies interesting. In fact, one thing the researchers hoped to do in the 1957 study was to examine skilled activities that were quite different from those required of pilots and the tracking tasks so often studied in the laboratory.

In comparing the results of these two studies it becomes apparent at once that instructors in a wide variety of activities are concerned with very similar problems of skill learning. The apprentice pilot finds himself in a relatively novel environment—but so does the novice swimmer and the diver. New sequences of responses must be planned and executed, new coordinations must be learned, new perceptual habits acquired, new strategies developed. A detailed comparison of the results of these two studies is not here attempted. Instead the major classes of learning problems, with which the results are in close agreement, are pointed out. Respondents in both studies gave greatest emphasis to the following four aspects of skill tasks.

*Cognitive Aspects of Skill Learning.* Most instructors believe that an important aspect of skill learning is the development of an understanding of the nature of the task. This factor is most important early in training. Acting on this belief, they resort to many different procedures in order to help the learner gain such an understanding. The use of demonstrations by experts, movies, lectures, watching oneself in a mirror, and directed attention, are examples. All of the 40 athletic instructors mentioned using such techniques. The important point is that to some extent skills can be intellectualized by learners who previously have acquired adequate verbal concepts. At more advanced levels of skill, cognitive aspects involve strategy, judgment, decision making, and planning.

*Perceptual Aspects of Skill Learning.* Most instructors emphasize the importance of perceptual factors in skill learning. The student must learn what to look for, how to identify important cues, how to make critical discriminations. Much emphasis often is given to training in the use of proprioceptive cues, the discrimination of forces and pressures. Breadth of perception or division of attention also is mentioned frequently.

*Coordination.* Practically all instructors refer to the development of coordination. For the pilot this often means integration of hand and foot movements. For the swimmer it means integration of breathing, stroking and kicking. For the golfer it means integration of body, shoulder, arm, and wrist action. Timing of successive movement patterns, timing of body movements in relation to the movements of external objects, and the development of rhythm are also emphasized.

*Tension—Relaxation.* Although a variety of comments are used in describing the personality and temperamental characteristics of students—ranging from anxiety on the one hand to lack of motivation on the other—by far the most frequent comment of instructors about this aspect of student behavior concerns the degree of tenseness-relaxation which can be observed in their movements. Beginners exhibit overall tension in many muscle groups and appear to be doing an excessive amount of work; as they become more proficient they seem to relax, movements seem to require less effort, and they appear "to have all the time they need for the task at hand." These comments, it should be noted, describe an important change in behavior, but a change that may well be a result of the development of skill, rather than a prerequisite.

On the basis of an examination of the data from these two surveys plus data from the experimental study of skill, it is possible to formulate several broad propositions that have to do with the learning of complex skills. Three such propositions, which concern (a) the probable phases in skill learning, (b) the importance of learning sub-routines, and (c) the extent of improvement possible in skilled performance, will be considered next. The propositions are in the nature of broad generalizations. Emphasis is on complex skills, because the propositions are more readily observed in the learning of complex tasks rather than simple ones.

## PHASES IN COMPLEX SKILL LEARNING

It is proposed that the learning of a complex skill progresses through three phases which can be identified for convenience under the headings *cognition, fixation,* and *automation.* It must be emphasized, however, that these phases clearly overlap and that the progression from one to the other is a continuous rather than a discontinuous process. In fact, improvement in most skills appears to go on continuously without noticeable plateaus or discontinuities.

## Cognitive Phase

Evidence from many sources indicates that cognitive processes are heavily involved early in the learning of most complex skills. Thus tests of intellectual abilities and tests of specialized knowledge have been found to predict individual rates of learning during early phases of skill acquisition. Students and instructors attempt to analyze tasks and to verbalize about what is being learned. What to expect and what to do is emphasized, procedures are described, and information is provided about errors, which often are frequent.

One of the most significant series of experiments demonstrating the importance of "intellectualization" in the early stages of skill learning was carried out by A. C. Williams and his associates at the University of Illinois Aviation Psychology Laboratory some ten years ago (Williams & Flexman, 1949; Flexman, Matheny, & Brown, 1950). These studies were concerned primarily with comparisons of the use vs. non-use of a ground trainer in the period of pilot training prior to the first solo flight. The most significant results, however, were obtained from the application of sound principles of learning to the flight situation. As listed by the authors these principles included (a) motivation, (b) knowledge of results, (c) anticipatory set, (d) judicious use of both part and whole learning, (e) performance of the task while receiving verbal instructions, (f) overlearning, (g) judicious use of spaced practice, and (h) intellectual knowledge of maneuvers. Unfortunately the research program was not continued for a sufficiently long period to determine the independent effects of these different principles, nor of the value of training equipment per se versus the importance of the instructional program per se. The net results were dramatic, however, in one respect. In a separate preliminary study with only six students, time to solo was found to be less than three hours. For the main experiment, with 42 students in two groups, the mean number of hours to solo was slightly less than four hours (3.82 hours). This is strikingly shorter than the accepted time of about eight hours to solo, and can be compared to a mean time of 5.28 hours for 48 students in a previous experiment where less use was made of the special procedures. For purposes of the present discussion it is important to note the extensive use made by these psychologists of procedures designed to promote an understanding of flight problems and procedures, i.e., the use of knowledge of results, the use of procedure for establishing appropriate sets or expectancies, "talking through" maneuvers, and emphasis on "intellectualization."

## Fixation Phase

It is proposed that the primarily cognitive phase of skill learning is usually followed by a phase in which correct patterns of behavior are fixated by continued practice, and the probability of inappropriate response patterns or errors is reduced nearly to zero. Whereas the cognitive phase may last for hours or days, the fixation phase, if the task is truly complex, may last for weeks or months. This is the stage in which most laboratory experiments are terminated if, in fact, they are ever extended this far. In the case of the aircraft pilot this phase would extend roughly from before initial solo through the time at which a private license is granted and perhaps to the first hundred hours or so of flying. In the case of a typist it would extend from the point at which the student has learned the position of the different keys and how the fingers are used in striking them to the point where he has perhaps graduated from his first typing course, and reduced his errors to less than 1 per cent, and has acquired a fair degree of typing speed.

## Autonomous Phase

For want of a better word the most advanced level of skill will be called the stage of *automation* of the activity, using a term that was applied by such early psychologists as William James and Münsterberg. This stage is characterized by (*a*) gradually increasing speed of performance in tasks where it is important to improve time or accuracy scores far beyond the point where errors, as ordinarily defined, can be detected, and (*b*) gradually increasing resistance to stress and to interference from other activities that may be performed concurrently.

Recent neurological evidence indicates that there is less and less involvement of cortical associative areas as learning continues in the case of simple conditioned response learning, thus supporting the idea that the stage of autonomous behavior is based on a shift from reliance on visual to reliance on proprioceptive feedback, a shift of control to lower brain centers, and similar changes. However, the present discussion will be confined to the results of a few relevant behavioral studies.

Bahrick and his associates (Bahrick, Noble, & Fitts, 1954; Bahrick & Shelly, 1958) have studied the effects of task variables, such as coherence, and also the effect of extent of practice, on the degree of interference between two activities that are carried on concurrently. In the first study, Ss pressed one of five keys as moving patterns of lights passed behind a crossline. Some Ss were given a random pattern of lights, and others used a cyclical one. When a mental arithmetic task was added early in practice both groups had about equivalent scores on both tasks. Late in practice on the perceptual-motor task, however, mental arithmetic scores were significantly better for the group working with the repetitive or coherent version of the perceptual-motor task.

In a later study a visual and an auditory task were performed together. The visual task consisted of pressing one of four keys in response to one of four stimulus lights. Four light sequences were used, differing in degree of redundancy from 0% to 100%, and 25 practice sessions were given. Again, as predicted, as degree of redundancy increased there was a corresponding decrease in interference between the two tasks, the range in decrement varying from about 40% to as little as 10%.

Additional strong evidence for the presence of a stage in which skills become autonomous comes from the studies of the effects of stress on skilled performance. (See Chapter 7 by Deese.) However, it is worth noting here that a study by R. E. Murphy (1959) and the work of Garvey and Taylor (1959) and others indicates that the magnitude of the effects of variations in task design (e.g., between good and bad designs as indicated by tests under standard conditions) is greatly enhanced by the introduction of stress. It can be assumed that a "good" design of controls, displays, etc., is one that requires the operator to use a highly stereotyped or overlearned response pattern. Thus, the results indicate that highly overlearned, or culturally determined, patterns of behavior are more resistant to stress than are less well learned patterns.

## The Learning of Subroutines

A second general proposition regarding complex skill learning is that such learning can be viewed as the acquisition of skill in a number of semi-independent routines or sequences (subroutines) which may go on successively or concurrently (i.e., in series or in parallel). In view of the original definition of skill, which emphasizes the continuous nature of skilled performance, the idea of viewing a complex skill as an activity involving several semi-independent subroutines seems more appropriate than views which treat of specific S-R elements.

The term subroutine is borrowed from computer programming terminology, and can be defined as a sequence of operations that are called up on the basis of a single cue, once the subroutine itself has been established. Locomotor sequences, that take the individual from one place to another, are examples of important subroutines. Swimming is an excellent example of a task involving several subroutines. Instructors commonly ask their students to practice kicking as one routine, stroking as another, and breathing as still a third. It is also common to practice two of these in combination before trying to per-

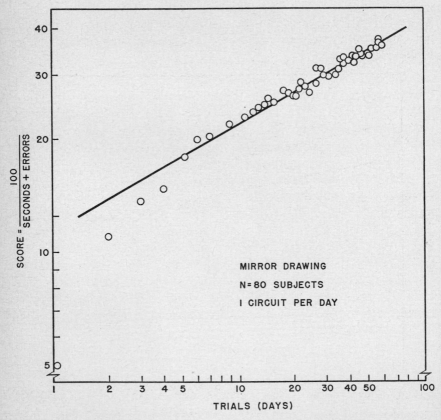

FIGURE 6.2. Improvement in Skill in a Mirror Drawing Task Over 59 Days (after Snoddy, 1926)

form all three at once. So-called "division of attention" tasks also usually involve several subroutines.

## The Absence of Plateaus and Asymptotes

The third general observation about the learning of complex skills, borrowing from Keller's (1958) remarks about the "phantom plateau," may be called the "phantom asymptote." The idea is very simple and as far as the present writer has been able to discover was first proposed by Snoddy (1926). Snoddy pointed out that if increments of performance are measured on a logarithmic scale, then proportional (log.) decrements in the time required to perform an activity result from equal (log.) increments in trials. His general learning equation was

$$log\ C = log\ B + n\ log\ x$$

where $C$ is a score based chiefly on the reciprocal of time of performance and $x$ is the number of trials. One set of data published by Snoddy is shown in Figure 6.2.

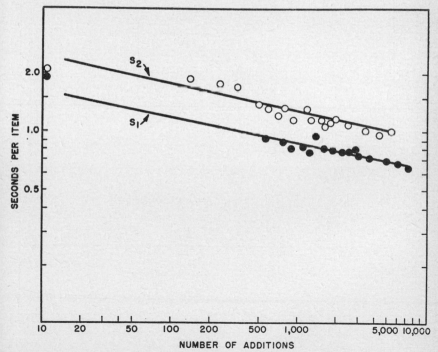

FIGURE 6.3.   Improvement in Speed of Addition with Extended Practice (after Blackburn, 1936)

More recently Crossman (1959) has surveyed the evidence for continued slow improvement in performance with continued practice, basing his review primarily on the work of DeJong and Seymour as well as some of his own work. Some typical results are shown in Figures 6.3 and 6.4.

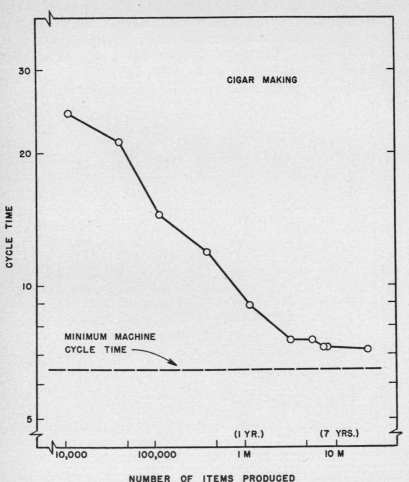

FIGURE 6.4.   Increase in Speed of Performance of a Factory Task (cigar making) with Continued Practice (after Crossman, 1959)

The early trials in some of these studies depart from the linear fit of later data points and show more rapid early learning. However, this might be expected on the basis of the high importance of cognitive factors, and the occurrence of errors in early trials. Late trials on some tasks also often show a lack of further improvement which can be attributed to machine limitations.

Figure 6.5 shows some data from a study by Fitts and Seegar (1953) on choice reaction time. These data, for two versions of an eight-alternative task, show continued learning for 26 sessions covering over two months.

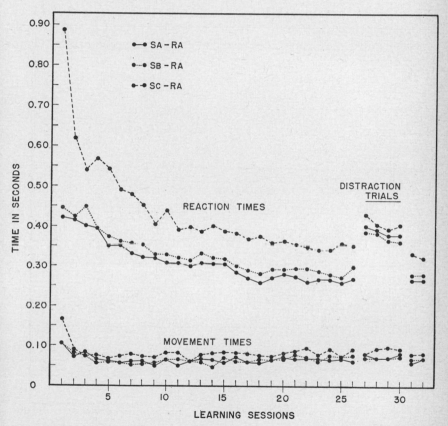

FIGURE 6.5.   Increase in Reaction Time in Three Eight-Choice Tasks with Continued One-Hour Practice Sessions (after Fitts & Seegar, 1953)

Another pertinent set of data are those from the perceptual-motor task (the Purdue Pegboard) used by Snyder and Pronko (1952) in their replication of Stratton's classical experiment on the effects of inversion of the retinal image. As far as the author has been able to determine these results are the only data available on the effects of retinal reversal on a task requiring a high degree of skill in a visually controlled task. The results are shown in Figure 6.6. During 28 days of wearing reversing lenses the subject never reached the level of speed which he had achieved during pretests, but on the second trial after

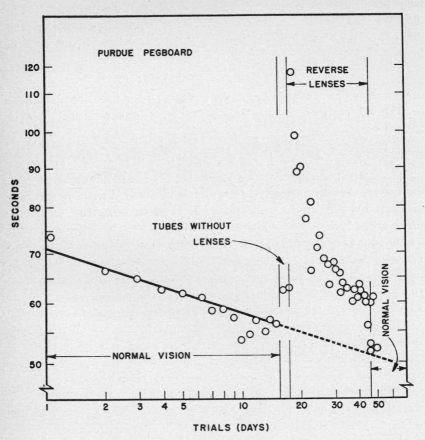

FIGURE 6.6. Performance of a speeded eye-hand coordination task (Purdue Pegboard) before, during, and following the wearing of lenses that reversed the visual field (after Snyder & Pronko, 1952)

removal of the reversing lenses his performance was better than it had ever been, lying almost on the straight-line extrapolation of the data for the original 16 days of pretraining.

In most of these studies of extended training, an increase in skill is evidenced primarily by a decrease in time. Errors are infrequent.

Learning at this stage is seldom investigated by psychologists interested in human learning and yet it is a stage highly important in real life.

One other fact that is obviously true in real life tasks should also be mentioned at this point. It is that the highest achievements in music, in athletic events, and in similar activities often are not attained until five, ten, or often more than ten years of intensive practice. The understanding of such skills poses a great challenge to the learning theorist.

## IMPLICATIONS FOR TRAINING

Several of the points discussed in this chapter have special implications for training in skills. Three of these will now be singled out for consideration.

### Overpractice

The importance of continuing practice far beyond the point in time where some (often arbitrary) criterion is reached cannot be overemphasized. In some types of work, such as most industrial tasks, the individual practices his skill on a daily basis. But in other activities, such as many military tasks, this is not the case. Many military tasks must be practiced under simulated conditions. Realistic conditions of practice (such as firing a real missile, for example) are prohibitively expensive. In such circumstances the amount of practice given to individuals often is the minimum required to reach a criterion. Perhaps only some arbitrary number of hours of practice are given. Individuals who have not had a great deal of practice beyond the stage of initial satisfactory performance probably do not experience the beneficial increase in resistance to stress, fatigue, and interference that comes from extended overlearning.

Overpractice is even more important in tasks which are so designed that individuals are unable to use habit patterns that have been established by life-long experience. When a new task does not conform to a strong population stereotype even very extensive overtraining may not provide the desired level of performance under stressful conditions.

### Training in Subroutines

It is desirable to program training in complex tasks so that extensive practice can be given in separate subroutines. In particular, where invariant subroutines can be identified, considerable gain is to be expected from overlearning these "elements" of the total task. It is also desirable to provide additional training on the total complex task, of course, particularly if there are any interactions between the subroutines. But often it is not feasible to provide facilities for extensive practice on the total task. In such instances the use of "part-task" training is clearly indicated, providing this training can include complete subroutines. According to the general theory developed earlier, overpractice in one or more subroutines should make it much easier for the subject to learn additional new aspects of a complex task. Thus a pilot who has had hundreds of hours of training in a particular aircraft should be able to learn an additional new task (such as a gunnery task) much more readily than a pilot who has only recently mastered the aircraft itself.

## Elimination of Artificial Limits to Performance

In a great many tasks subjects cease to show improvement, not because they are incapable of further learning, but because some condition of the task restricts the opportunity for improvement. Keller (1958) points out that the plateau in code learning reported by Bryan and Harter was due to the fact that tests were made on a telegraph line over which only slow rates of transmission were used. Performance began to improve as soon as the subject was moved to a main line where transmission rates were higher. Lack of feedback of performance is a frequent factor that limits improvement. Crossman (1959) emphasizes the importance of pressure for increased speed as a requirement for long-term improvement. In some instances the apparent lack of continued improvement is a function of the use of a criterion score which in itself is incapable of measuring further changes in performance.

### REFERENCES

Bahrick, H. P., Noble, M. E., & Fitts, P. M. Extra-task performance as a measure of learning a primary task. *J. exp. Psychol.*, 1954, *48*, 298-302.

Bahrick, H. P. & Shelly, C. Time sharing as an index of automatization. *J. exp. Psychol.*, 1958, *56*, 288-293.

Bartlett, F. C. *Thinking*. London, England: Allen & Unwin, 1958.

Blackburn, J. M. *Acquisition of skill—an analysis of learning curves*. London, England. I.H.R.B. Report, No. 73, 1936.

Broadbent, D. E. *Perception and communication*. New York: Pergamon Press, 1958.

Crossman, E. R. F. W. A theory of acquisition of speed-skill. *Ergonomics,* 1959, *2,* 153-166.

DeJong, J. R. The effects of increasing skill on cycle-time. *Ergonomics,* 1957, *1,* 51-60.

Fitts, P. M., Bahrick, H. P., Noble, M. E., & Briggs, G. E. *Skilled performance.* New York: Wiley, 1961. (In press)

Fitts, P. M. & Seegar, C. M. S-R compatibility: Spatial characteristics of stimulus and response codes. *J. exp. Psychol.,* 1953, *46,* 199-210.

Flexman, R. E., Matheny, W. G., & Brown, E. L. Evaluation of the school link and special methods of instruction. *Univer. of Illinois Bull.,* Vol. 47, No. 80, July 1950.

Garvey, W. D. & Taylor, F. V. The use of "artificial signals" to enhance monitoring performance. In P. M. Fitts (Ed.), *Human engineering concepts and theory.* Ann Arbor: University of Michigan Press, 1959. Pp. 16.1.1 to 16.1.14.

Guilford, J. P. & Lacey, J. I. *Printed classification tests.* Washington, D. C.: U.S. Government Printing Office, 1947.

Keller, F. S. The phantom plateau. *J. exp. Anal. Behavior,* 1958, *1,* 1-13.

Murphy, R. E. Effects of threat of shock, distraction and task design on performance. *J. exp. Psychol.,* 1959, *58,* 134-141.

Snoddy, G. S. Learning and stability. *Applied Psychol.,* 1926, *10,* 1-36.

Snyder, F. W. & Pronko, N. H. *Vision with spatial inversion.* Wichita, Kansas: University of Wichita Press, 1952.

Williams, A. C. & Flexman, R. E. Evaluation of the school link as an aid in primary flight instruction. *Univer. of Illinois Bull.,* Vol. 46, No. 71, June 1949.

Woodworth, R. S. *Dynamics of behavior.* New York: Holt, 1958.

Chapter 7 | Skilled Performance and
Conditions of Stress

James Deese, The Johns Hopkins University

In 1952 Lazarus, Deese and Osler presented an analysis of psychological stress for which the point of departure was the definition of stress as an intervening variable. Stress was assigned properties which were designed to schematize stimulus-response relationships under certain stimulus conditions as well as response-response correlations under those conditions. The general point of view presented by these authors was not very far from the discussion of emotion presented earlier by Brown and Farber (1951). It was clear from these as well as from a number of other theoretical and semitheoretical papers which appeared at about the same time that many different investigators were finding it fruitful to regard stress and emotion as intervening variables with emotional and motivational properties.

Lazarus, Deese and Osler (1952) were concerned with the arousal of a state in the individual (a state aroused by a limited class of stimulus conditions, though this is by no means made clear in the paper) and the effects of such arousal upon skilled performance. Obviously, the concern with psychological stress is much broader than the concern with skilled performance, and so the paper dealt with a most limited aspect of the problem of stress. This chapter is confined to a similarly limited aspect of the problem of stress, and, in this sense at least, may be regarded as one successor to the paper by Lazarus, Deese and Osler. In a word, the present chapter will concern itself with those properties of stress that are relevant to the performance of skilled behavior, and hence indirectly to the training of skilled acts.

## RESPONSE-RESPONSE PREDICTION AND
## SKILLED BEHAVIOR UNDER STRESS

Two classes of independent variables were used in the program of research planned by Lazarus, Deese and Osler. These were (*a*) individual differences assessed by psychometric variables and (*b*) variations in the external conditions thought to arouse the stress state. The implication was that the stress state itself could be varied in either of two ways: (*a*) by selecting individuals in whom the potential state of arousal was reliably higher than in other individuals, and (*b*) by selecting the conditions which aroused the state in a representative group of individuals. In the earliest experiments (Deese & Lazarus, 1952) the psychometric variables were group Rorschach scores and global ratings of manifest affectivity. The external conditions of arousal were threat of failure and electric shock.

Lazarus, Deese and Osler had also supposed that they would uncover an interaction between personality variables and stimuli that were stressful. While there were theoretical reasons for expecting such an interaction, it was also expected because of the ambiguous and contradictory evidence that had come from the experimental literature on stress. These authors had reviewed that literature and found little evidence for stable general principles.

About the same time, Taylor, Spence and their co-workers (see Taylor, 1956) began to apply a similar technique of analysis to another intervening variable. This variable was assigned the properties of drive as that condition is described in general Hullian theory. This intervening variable was assessed by individual differences in a psychometric variable, and hence drive, in the experimental program that grew up around this idea, was manipulated by selecting individuals at different levels on the psychometric variable.

The intervening variable, anxiety, advanced by Taylor and Spence was a much more elegant and sophisticated one than that described by Lazarus, Deese and Osler, based as it was upon a general theory of behavior. It also led to a different emphasis. The psychometric variable employed was a particular inventory made of items selected from the MMPI. In the experimental studies employing this inventory, the principal source of independent variation was not in the external conditions of testing, but in task materials. (This was because the theory predicted an interaction between the inventory scores and sources of intratask interference.) However, despite the fact that stress was not of primary concern to workers with this inventory and its associated theory, some experiments have been performed with the stimulus conditions of the sort that are generally characterized as stressful (Taylor, 1958; Besch, 1959).

Other groups of investigators have also dealt with the problem of individual differences in emotional and emotionally motivating conditions and skilled performance. These investigators have usually worked from the point of view of a particular psychometric device (for example, Sarason & Mandler, 1952; Eyesenck, 1956) or from the standpoint of a particular assumed process (Child & Waterhouse, 1953).

Thus, various investigators have gathered a good deal of evidence on the interaction between stable characteristics of personality and skilled behavior under stress arousing conditions. While the literature that has resulted from the work of these investigators is generally thought to be relevant to the central problem of this paper, it does not seem worthwhile to attempt to review the vast amount of empirical evidence concerning the correlations between conditions of personality, stress and skilled performance. Suffice it to say that a very large number of investigators have found correlations between personality measures and skilled behavior and that these correlations vary as a function of the conditions of stress. The fact is, however, that *the obtained correlations are almost without exception small*, and in some cases, contradictory evidence concerning both their direction and magnitude is available.

There is, perhaps, more complete knowledge concerning the various scales derived from the MMPI than for other kinds of predictors. A group of highly correlated scales, the Winne Inventory (Winne, 1951), the Manifest Anxiety Scale (see Taylor, 1956) and the Psychasthenia Scale from the MMPI itself all predict, to very moderate extents, the performance during learning of a variety of tasks. The correlations are uniformly low[1] with, perhaps, the Psychasthenia Scale winning out as the best over-all predictor (Lazarus & Deese, 1953). It is not an exaggeration to say that the correlations obtained thus far are so small as to be virtually useless in the prediction of scores on the

---

[1]The actual magnitudes of the correlations are usually difficult to estimate because of the tradition in studies in this area of using the extremes from the distribution of personality measurements. Little is known about the range of talent on many of the skill measurements used, so interpretation of obtained correlations is hazardous.

skills that have been studied. The uselessness of the correlations thus far obtained is emphasized by the fact that much of the variance in common between the personality measurements and the skill measurements can be taken out by general measures of ability (intelligence). Thus, despite the appealing idea that some variance in skills ought to be associated with objective personality dimensions, the evidence thus far is weak. Furthermore, the evidence on the relations between personality variables and *changes* in performance under stress is even more disappointing.

A word needs to be said about the nature of the correlations that have been thus far obtained before passing from the topic of prediction to new ways of examining the problem of stress. First of all, despite the fact that a large number of different personality scales have been employed, relatively little has been learned because these scales are for the most part very highly correlated. Even investigators who have used scales not derived from the MMPI have failed in the attempt to escape personality tests which correlate highly with the Psychasthenia Scale. Thus, it could be argued, not a very wide range of personality measurements have been tapped in the studies of the correlation of personality and skilled performance.[2]

Partly because of the unsatisfactory predictions obtained from existing scales and partly for other reasons, L. M. Horowitz (1957), in a master's dissertation at Johns Hopkins, attempted to devise a purely empirical personality scale specifically aimed at the prediction of simple skilled performance during learning. Items were collected on the basis of certain face validity criteria. These items were subjected to item analyses against three tasks designed to have low intercorrelations (and thus reflect relatively independent abilities). The skilled tasks were the Minnesota Rate of Manipulation (turning, four trials), the learning of lists of 12 low similarity adjectives (six trials) and mirror tracing (five trials). The largest task intercorrelation was .176.

The personality items were culled from existing items or were invented. An attempt was made to eliminate all complaint items, partic-

[2]It should be said that McCandless and Castaneda (1956) report very satisfactory prediction from the Children's Manifest Anxiety Scale. Likewise, Brown and Holtzman (1955) have been able to produce very sturdy correlations between a study *attitudes* inventory and grades, even after intelligence measures have been partialled out. At various times biographical information has turned out to be useful.

ularly psychosomatic complaint items. Sample items are: "I think I could study successfully even in a noisy room full of people." "I have had periods of days, weeks, or months when I couldn't take care of things because I couldn't get going." "I worry a good deal about pleasing people I work for."

A thorough analysis of the personality items was made, including two separate validation and cross validation studies. The net outcome was very disappointing. The predictive scales that came out of the study had just about the same level of correlation with performance of the skills employed as had been found in previous studies with MMPI derived inventories and the Mandler-Sarason inventory. The final blow was the discovery that the best overall predictive scale that resulted from so much sifting down correlated very highly with MMPI Psychasthenia.

All sorts of more or less mechanical reasons can be given for the lack of predictive efficiency in going from personality inventories to skilled behavior. One very important condition deserves to be mentioned since it is worth further study. This is what De Soto and Kuethe (1960) have characterized as "triangular scatter." A "triangular scatter" occurs when there is some correlation between the mean value for one variate and the variance of scores in that measure for successive values of the other variate. One important way in which such a correlation can arise is when one variate sets an upper bound on the value the other can assume. As an example, De Soto and Kuethe point out that an employee's visual acuity can set an upper bound to his degree of success on a certain job, but this limit does not prevent him from falling below that limit.

Such an effect may be important to the question of the relation between personality inventories and skilled performance, since De Soto and Kuethe have evidence which suggests that scores on the Manifest-Anxiety Scale (or any other similar scale) are determined in part by an upper bound of capability for expressing anxiety. If these authors are correct, low MAS scores may occur when an individual has low anxiety and perhaps higher capability for expressing it. On the other hand, low MAS scores may also occur when an individual has high anxiety but only a very low capability for expressing it. The net effect would be to expect that individuals low in MAS would be more variable in any trait that is correlated with true level of anxiety (such as skilled performance). This question needs to be explored before abandoning the attempt to make sense out of the welter of data on the prediction of skilled acts from personality scores.

The question of psychometric predictability is important, of course, to the question of trying to predict differential effects of stress during training and later performance. To date, however, the evidence of successful prediction from the kind of variables that have been discussed here is very poor. Thus, despite the assumption that much of the variance in performance of skilled acts is associated with personality and motivational factors, the results have been disappointing.[3]

Considering the disappointing nature of the data on the prediction of skilled performance from personality measures, it would seem useful at this point to turn to an analysis of questions which must be solved if meaningful questions are to be asked about psychometric predictability of performance under stress. Therefore, attention is turned once again to the concept of stress.

## THE CONCEPT OF STRESS

The problem faced in this paper will best be dealt with by abandoning attempts to specify. stress as a condition of the individual—as an intervening variable. Rather, the concept of stress is considered as it undoubtedly arose outside of the confines of the psychological laboratory, namely the conception of stress as a collection or class of stimulus events. Stimuli are defined by their common response producing properties (thus the visible wave lengths are those that produce a visual response). Thus, one needs to look at the common properties of those situations which are called stressful.

This emphasis upon the stimulus conditions does not mean that there are no stable states of the individual that are relevant—the reliability of measures of individual differences in personality testifies to the fact that there are—but for the present problem, the performance of skilled behavior under stress, more will be accomplished by a consideration of the stimulus control over behavior rather than a consideration of the stable intra-individual relationships. To be sure, it will not be safe to long ignore the possibility of interactions between

---

[3]The need-achievement measure can also be included in these attempts that have been disappointing. *N-ach* has not been discussed because relatively little of the work on projective devices in general and *n-ach* in particular has been directed specifically towards the problem of skill. One example to the contrary is Lowell's (1952) experiment.

stimulus conditions and states of the individual, but in this particular case, the first problem is to establish the nature of the stimulus conditions and something of their average effects upon behavior.

The properties of stressful stimuli are defined by a set of correlated responses. It will be useful to characterize as stressful those conditions which elicit reports of discomfort or which elicit correlates of discomfort. Such a notion should make it easier to understand the varieties of social and psychological situations in which the term stress has been used (Janis, 1951; Janis, 1958; Basowitz, Persky, & Grinker, 1955; Williams, 1954). Such a notion is not so vague and indefinite as it first appears; it is known that such reports are reliable and can be systematically described by a variety of analytic techniques.

In order to suggest something of the range of stimulus conditions that are stress, the words available in the Semantic Differential Atlas (Jenkins, Russell, & Suci, 1958) have been combed through. It is well known that the Semantic Differential does not so much give the referential meaning of terms as it does certain components of their connotative meaning. Stress, of course, is a variety of connotative meaning of external stimulus conditions.

Fortunately, the word *discomfort* occurs in the Jenkins, Russell and Suci atlas. Listed in Table 7.1 are all of the words from this atlas that are 4.00 units or less in distance in semantic space from the word discomfort. Since there are only 380 words altogether in the Semantic Atlas, and relatively few of these are terms referring to external stimulus conditions, the list in Table 7.1 does not begin to sample stressful stimuli. It does suggest, however, the variety of conditions associated with discomfort. The closeness of such words as bitter, cold, discordant, glaring, intermittent, tense, rancid, putrid, etc., to discomfort reveals the systematic structure of the stimulus conditions for discomfort.

The relevant words in Table 7.1 have in common a description of stimuli responsible for a state of arousal accompanied by feelings of discomfort. This state is one which the individual usually seeks to avoid. This follows from the correlation between things people regard as uncomfortable and the tendency to avoid such things. The tendency to be aroused to discomfort will (*a*) vary between individuals and classes of individuals, (*b*) vary between stimuli, and (*c*) interact with individuals and stimuli. The possibility of a stimulus-individual interaction is a real one, if for no more empirical reason than the suspicion that the stressful properties of certain conditions are acquired

TABLE 7.1

All Words from the Semantic Differential Atlas (Jenkins, Russell, & Suci, 1958)
Having Distances of 4.00 or Less from the Word *Discomfort*.

| Word | Distance | Word | Distance |
|------|----------|------|----------|
| Anger | 4.0 | Hungry | 3.4 |
| Bad | 3.2 | Hurt | 3.0 |
| Bitter | 3.0 | Intermittent | 3.9 |
| Broken | 3.1 | Late | 3.9 |
| Coarse | 3.4 | Pain | 2.8 |
| Cold | 3.4 | Putrid | 2.9 |
| Crooked | 3.2 | Rancid | 3.0 |
| Crude | 2.6 | Severe | 3.3 |
| Discordant | 2.6 | Sin | 3.7 |
| Divorce | 3.3 | Socialism | 3.6 |
| Fear | 2.7 | Sour | 3.3 |
| Feverish | 3.3 | Starving | 3.5 |
| Fraud | 3.8 | Stench | 2.5 |
| Frightful | 3.9 | Stiff | 3.8 |
| Glaring | 3.5 | Tense | 3.5 |
| Hate | 3.2 | Trouble | 2.4 |
| Heartless | 3.0 | Ugly | 3.0 |

and that individual histories will differ in this respect. The possibility
of such interaction complicates the problem, but it cannot be safely
ignored.

It has sometimes been assumed that at least some of the variation
between individuals in responsivity to stressful stimuli could be described by certain physiological concomitants of arousal. For example,
Lewinsohn (1956) has argued that there are distinct classes of physiological responders to stress, responders who are predominantly para-
sympathetic, responders who are predominantly sympathetic and those
who are predominantly muscular in reactivity. Different levels of responding in indices for these classes are related to MMPI scores (Lewinsohn, 1956), and, as will be pointed out, there is some reason for
supposing that the identification of such types of physiological reactivity to stress would be of some use in predicting the effects of
stress upon particular skills. However, it is not likely that predictions
derived from the consideration of physiological variables would be any
better than those derived from personality inventories. However much

individuals may differ in *patterns* of arousal, practically all individuals show at least some reactivity in all indices as the result of stress.

## A NEW METHOD OF ANALYSIS

The emphasis just given to the stimulus definition of stress is by way of preparation for the presentation of a somewhat different approach to the analysis of the effects of stress upon skilled behavior. Much of what has been said thus far has concerned the stability of individual reactions to stress. This, however, is not the context in which concern over the question of stress and skilled behavior arose. Indeed, from the standpoint of the problem of the relationship between stress and skilled behavior, the assumption of *stable patterns* of reactivity to stress need not arise.

The usual assumptions that have been made about the relationship between the external stimulating conditions of stress and skilled performance may be stated as follows:

1. The most common assumption made by the layman concerning stress is that the conditions responsible for discomfort have in common a deleterious influence upon the performance of skilled acts. It is known, of course, that this assumption cannot be generally correct. The fact is, however, that much of the experimental work on stress and skilled performance has made the assumption of deterioration under stress something to be taken for granted. Indeed, a good deal of the earlier work on stress and skill could be characterized as a search for "sensitive" measures, i.e., measures that showed deterioration under stress.[4] This preoccupation has led to a neglect of some of the important effects of stress.

2. A more sophisticated assumption says that there is a specific task component part of a great number of skills and that either positive or negative effects of stress can be predicted from the presence or absence of this component. This is the kind of assumption that provides the basis for the work of Spence, Taylor and others on the influence of anxiety drive upon performance during acquisition. Specifically these investigators have assumed an interaction between drive level and intratask interference and, by extension, an interaction between these and stress.

---

[4]Some investigators have pointed out that the search for stress-sensitive tests is a fruitful enterprise. This is very true; however, it provides a limited point of view from which to understand the effects of stress upon skilled performance.

3. A more general assumption would be to assert that the effects of stress upon skilled performance are specific to particular components of the performance under consideration. This is the general viewpoint taken in this chapter. There are a variety of ways in which such an assumption could be correct. It could be correct if one assumed no generality across tasks. That is to say, it would be true if skilled behavior consisted of a large number of uncorrelated elements or dimensions. Such a situation would be very discouraging. The fact is, of course, that such extreme specificity is not the case. What is more, some general components seem to contribute to the performance of perceptual motor skills as well as to more general kinds of skills (Fleishman, 1956). Thus, it is safe to assume some generality of components of ability across a wide variety of tasks. The problem is then to determine how important each task component may be in reaction under stress. Consideration of this problem can lead to a "synthesis" of the influence of stress upon the performance of a particular task. This means that a study of the effects of stress upon task components rather than the tasks themselves is what is required. While this assumption—that stress may affect different components of skilled acts in different ways—cannot be dignified by the term theory, nevertheless it does lead to some interesting hypotheses. Before discussing some of the consequences of this notion, however, a brief discussion of the rationale of the notion itself may be useful.

One may arrive at the present view by considering the effects of stressful stimuli to be twofold. For one thing stressful stimuli arouse specific responses which may be either compatible with the components of a certain skill (and thus facilitate performance of that skill) or they may arouse responses which are incompatible and thus inhibit or interfere with the performance of the skill. It is this property of stressful stimuli that is most important to the present analysis. In addition, however, it can be assumed that stressful stimuli arouse tendencies to eliminate the stressful stimuli. The empirical grounds for this assertion are well enough known so that it is not necessary to review them here. This assumption does describe a motive state, and a word needs to be said about the motive, since something quite different from the traditional view is involved. Consider the possibility that the *escape or avoidance motive does not interact in any significant way with any of the components of the skill as such.* This view, of course, is in contrast with the views of the sort presented in the anxiety drive theory (Spence, 1958) or by those found in the more general theories relating motive states to need-achievement scores, etc. In these theories the aversive motive state directly influences performance.

The notion presented here implies that the motivational state aroused by the discomfort associated with stressful stimuli determines only the choice behavior of the individual with respect to the task he is performing. That is to say, an individual can choose to work faster, work slower, abandon the task altogether or to ignore stoically his discomfort. While one would suppose that an individual's choice of behavior would be influenced by his estimate of the likely outcome of the task (and hence of his own level of performance on the task), such an influence should have little or nothing to do with the specific components of the task. All other things equal, an individual should be just as ready to abandon one task as another under conditions of stress. Thus, an individual's choice about how to go about working at a task under stress should have nothing to do with whether the task is highly saturated with psychomotor coordination, or whether it demands the use of spatial relations, but should only be the result of the events likely to influence choice.[5] If this notion is correct, then what is indicated is study of the influence of the motivational component of reactions to stress independently of any particular skill.

This separation of the influence of discomfort and the influence of the avoidance motive upon performance through choice behavior has been implied in some earlier work (see, for example, Conrad, 1950), but not much attention has been paid to it. There are, of course, many implications of this separation, but the major one for present purposes is that it permits concentrating directly upon the effects of discomfort arousal upon performance. Thus, it is implied that the major effects of stress upon performance of a particular task operate through the stimulus conditions of the moment. This emphasis upon stimulus conditions leads to the characterization of the present approach as dynamogenic.

---

[5]The problem of experimentally separating out the effects of motivation from the arousal conditions of stress itself is a difficult one. Because the present chapter is limited in space as well as scope it will not be attempted here. One extremely interesting experiment by Pronko and Leith (1956) suggests some techniques, however. In essence Pronko and Leith provide grounds for asserting that the stress arousal for three different groups of Ss is the same, while the preparation Ss make for coping is different—hence different effects upon performance.

At this point it is necessary to draw upon the analysis presented by Meyer (1953) of the mutual influence of simultaneously occurring responses. Meyer describes the interaction of such responses as being the result of the convergence of impulse patterns in the motor system. The details of Meyer's application of the principle of spatial summation to motor facilitation need not concern us, because, with some isolated exceptions, the somatic distribution of motor activity in stress is not important.[6] The important point of Meyer's analysis, however, is the general notion of the simultaneous interaction of different response systems. In order to make use of the general notion of motor interaction in stress, the assumption is needed that the concomitants of the presence of discomforting stimuli include generalized motor activity. Such motor activity is usually characterized as tension. Tension describes an increase in the background activity of the entire somatic system (and probably the autonomic system as well).

The proposition that identifies stress with conditions of somatic arousal is well supported by a wide variety of evidence. Lacey and Lacey (1958), Lewinsohn (1956) and Schnore (1959) all present evidence of the consistency of patterns of bodily arousal in different stressful stimulus conditions. In addition, Schnore (1959) points out an additional fact that has sometimes been neglected. It is that despite stable idiosyncratic patterns of reaction, an individual placed in an arousing situation will show an increase in most physiological functions (including and especially generalized muscle tension). Thus, even though the *relative* magnitude of various physiological indices of tension may be characteristically different for different individuals, some increase on each measure is the general rule for nearly all individuals.

The major problem in the application of the notion of motor arousal to the influence of stressful stimuli upon skilled behavior is in the definition of such stimuli. It might be possible to consider that all such stimuli (all stimuli which arouse discomfort) also produce motor arousal, but this is a large though not an unreasonable assumption.[7] The following is a list of the characteristics of the output of the motor system which are both relevant to skills (motor skills) and the result of the applica-

[6]Localized stimulus effects, such as those found in the standard cold pressor test, may be exceptions.

[7]Motor arousal, of course, is not a property limited to discomforting stimuli (see, for example, Malmo, 1959), but all other arousing events fall outside of the scope of this chapter.

tion of the notion of generalized motor facilitation as a concomitant of stressful stimuli.

1. Increase in tremor rate, amplitude and variability.
2. Increase in the peak force applied by particular muscle groups when activated.
3. Shorter latency of movement (ballistic movement).
4. Increased variability of precision of movement (particularly ballistic movement).
5. Increased magnitude of variability in corrective movements.

Evidence for these assertions comes from a wide variety of sources, most of which have been reviewed by Meyer (1953). Taking these effects together with the hypothesis that generalized tension is the concomitant of stress, some specific predictions can be made about skilled performance under stress. Before doing this, however, one must deal with the difficult problem of the measurement of the effects of stress under conditions of repeated stimulation. This brings up the problem of adaptation to stressful stimuli.

It is commonly assumed that there is some kind of adaptation to conditions of stress, but the details of the process of adaptation have never been made explicit. It is known, of course, that there is physiological adaptation. The question of adaptation in connection with skilled performance, its relation to physiological adaptation and other conditions, however, has received little or no attention. Partly for limitations of space and partly for the sake of simplicity, this problem will be dealt with only briefly in the present account.

There is evidence that some adaptation of the effects of stress upon skill does occur. Deese and Lazarus (1952) were able to produce experimental evidence that leads to an inference of adaptation, and their analysis of the patterns of performance on the USAAF Psychomotor Skill Battery led them to suppose that stress and adaptation to it occurred during the psychomotor testing sessions. The fact that adaptation does occur makes it necessary to take into account testing order if any attempt is made to extract a "stress" factor in any battery of tests.

It is probable that some stressful stimuli are easier to adapt to than others, but there exists neither a good account of the stimulus properties that would be expected to lead to differential adaptation nor evidence that any differential adaptation does occur. Thus, adaptation under stressful stimuli provides problems for analysis. Therefore, at this stage, little more can be done than assert that there is evidence of adaptation to the influences of stress upon skilled performance.

In turning to the basic problem of the prediction of the effects of stress upon perceptual motor skills we may take as a point of departure Fleishman's (1954; Chapter 5) analysis of the dimensions in psychomotor abilities. Fleishman's data and his analysis can be used to illustrate the general approach to the problem suggested here. The account presented here can only be regarded as an example, since the analysis is not independent of the particular tests used and cannot, therefore, be generalized to tests and skills at large. The method of analysis, however, can be generalized, and it is the method that is emphasized here.

Fleishman identifies ten relatively independent factors in the battery of tests he used. These are (*a*) wrist-finger speed, (*b*) finger dexterity, (*c*) rate of movement, (*d*) manual dexterity, (*e*) arm-hand steadiness, (*f*) reaction time, (*g*) aiming, (*h*) psychomotor coordination, (*i*) postural discrimination and (*j*) spatial relations. He presents a table of the loadings on the factors for the 40 tests he employed in his battery. These factor loadings will be used, in conjunction with the assumptions about the effects of stress on the motor components of behavior, to make some rough predictions about the effects of stress upon the skills represented by the test scores.

How this is done may be illustrated by some examples. Consider the four tests which have the highest loading on Factor I (wrist-finger speed, or speed of ballistic movement). According to the assumptions made above about stress and motor arousal, ballistic movements should have a shorter latency under the dynamogenic influence of stress. Therefore, the speed of ballistic movement should be greater. Thus, stress would result in a facilitation of a pure Factor I test. These four tests with high loadings on Factor I, however, also have loadings on other factors. It is quite possible that these other factors would lead to a prediction of deterioration under stress. Therefore, before a prediction may be made with respect to a test having significant loadings for more than one factor, it is necessary to take into account the other factors. In Fleishman's data, the first two of the four tests having a high loading on Factor I are two tapping tests. Both have loadings of .74 on Factor I, and neither have appreciable loadings on any other factor. One would therefore predict facilitation under stress for these two tests.

The third and fourth highest loadings on Factor I are on the pursuit aiming tests. These have loadings of .50 and .48 respectively on Factor I. Both of these have higher loadings on Factor IV (.63 and .68). Factor IV is called by Fleishman, "aiming." This factor, according to the assumptions about arousal should show deterioration under stress. This is because of the assumed increases in tremor amplitude and variability. Therefore, without more elaborate techniques than are being suggested here, no determinate prediction may be made for these two tests. This is because these tests have loadings on both facilitative and deteriorating factors.

As an exercise in the kind of prediction being suggested, Table 7.2 presents all of the names of the tests studied by Fleishman, together with the predictions about the effects of stress upon these tests. These predictions are based upon the assumptions listed earlier and the factor loadings presented by Fleishman. Fortunately, the tests do not have loadings on very many factors, so a surprising number of determinate predictions may be made.

TABLE 7.2

The Predicted Effects of Stress upon the Tests Used by Fleishman (1954)
Characterized as Facilitation, Deterioration or Indeterminate

|  | Test | Prediction |
|---|---|---|
| 1. | Steadiness—Precision | Deterioration |
| 2. | Steadiness—Aiming CM103E | Deterioration |
| 3. | Track-Tracing | Deterioration |
| 4. | Two-Plate Tapping CM202A | Facilitation |
| 5. | Key-Tapping | Facilitation |
| 6. | Ten Target Aiming—Errors | Indeterminate |
| 7. | Ten Target Aiming—Corrects | Facilitation |
| 8. | Rotary Aiming | Facilitation |
| 9. | Visual Reaction Time | Facilitation |
| 10. | Auditory Reaction Time | Facilitation |
| 11. | Minn. Rate of Manipulation (Placing) | Deterioration (?) |
| 12. | Minn. Rate of Manipulation (Turning) | Deterioration |
| 13. | Purdue Pegboard R. H. | Deterioration |
| 14. | Purdue Pegboard L. H. | Deterioration |
| 15. | Purdue Pegboard Both Hands | Deterioration |
| 16. | Purdue Pegboard Assembly | Deterioration |
| 17. | O'Conner Finger Dexterity | Deterioration |
| 18. | Santa Ana Dexterity CM116A | Deterioration |
| 19. | Hand Precision Aiming—Errors | Facilitation (?) |
| 20. | Hand Precision Aiming—Corrects | Deterioration (?) |
| 21. | Discrimination Reaction Time CP-611D2 | Facilitation (?) |
| 22. | Complex Coordination CM701E | Deterioration |

TABLE 7.2 (Continued)

| | Test | Prediction |
|---|---|---|
| 23. | Rudder Control CM120C | Deterioration |
| 24. | Rotary Pursuit CM803B | Deterioration |
| 25. | Dynamic Balance | Deterioration |
| 26. | Postural Discrimination—Vertical | Indeterminate |
| 27. | Postural Discrimination—Angular | Indeterminate |
| 28. | Punch Board | Deterioration |
| 29. | Pin Stick | Indeterminate |
| 30. | Medium Tapping | Facilitation |
| 31. | Large Tapping | Facilitation |
| 32. | Aiming | Indeterminate |
| 33. | Pursuit Aiming I | Indeterminate |
| 34. | Pursuit Aiming II | Indeterminate |
| 35. | Tracing | Indeterminate |
| 36. | Square Marking | Indeterminate |
| 37. | Steadiness | Deterioration |
| 38. | Printed Discrimination RT | Facilitation (?) |
| 39. | Log-Book Accuracy | Indeterminate |
| 40. | Marking Accuracy | Deterioration |

The particular predictions presented in Table 7.2 are, in themselves, not too important. The tasks are significant only in the psychometric sense, and they probably do not represent even a very exhaustive sample of the kinds of skills which are psychometrically useful for perceptual motor behavior. Furthermore, the assumptions about arousal listed above may be in need of some modification. Most certainly the list of assumptions could be expanded.

The principle rather than the actual predictions themselves, however, is the important point. Once this kind of approach to the stress problem is adopted, the wrong kind of oversimplification disappears. The principle provides a scheme for organizing the effects of stress, but it does not restrict inquiry to a single dimension of behavior or to a single direction that these effects may take.

## USES OF THE SKILL-STRESS ANALYSIS

One may well ask whether the approach presented here has anything more to offer than merely being an interesting exercise. It is suggested that it does. Indeed, it may eventually help to solve a number of more or less practical problems. By way of example, consider a recent experimental study of stress performed at Hopkins by R. E. Murphy (1959). Murphy investigated the interesting hypothesis that the difference in performance produced by two different designs of a task would be enhanced under conditions of stress. Thus, if the human engineer finds that design A produces better performance than design B, the hypothesis says that the advantage of A over B should be increased by stress. This is an important notion, since it suggests that the relatively small differences between task designs found under more or less ideal laboratory conditions would be increased to, perhaps, very large effects when the performance is under field conditions. It would be very important to know if this notion is generally correct. Murphy showed that the hypothesis held for a particular task, and he argued from his findings with this task that it would hold generally.

It is unwise, however, to accept so important and sweeping a conclusion without additional support. Moreover, the generality of Murphy's principle cannot be established merely by repeating experiments like Murphy's but using a wide variety of tasks. Rather, an essential link is needed between the conditions of stress and the analysis of tasks. It seems possible that the point of view presented here provides the start towards that link. Furthermore, it provides at least the hope of a rational account of the expected changes in task design results as one goes from the laboratory to the field.

The problem presented by Murphy's hypothesis illustrates the need for the kind of analysis suggested here. In order to predict the relative effectiveness of one or another task design upon behavior under conditions of stress, it is necessary to know, if only in a very qualitative way, the effects of stress upon particular task components as well as the extent to which the task components enter into the different designs.

There are limitations, very serious in the present example, to the techniques suggested here. Perhaps the most serious is the necessity of assuming no interaction between the pattern of task components in a particular skill and conditions of stress. This assumption may turn out to be false for certain kinds of tasks, but as a first approximation an assumption of no interaction should not be too misleading.

## STRESS AND TRAINING

The problem of stress and training presents a suitable area for the application of the kind of analysis suggested here. Any such application, it is well to remember, must take into account the fact that the distribution of skill components (the factor loadings) will change with practice at a task (Fleishman & Hempel, 1954; Chapter 5). One thing is clear from the existing data; no simple idea about the effects of stress during training is adequate. Deese and Lazarus (1952) put forward the hypothesis, supported by some experimental evidence, that the effects of stress would be deleterious early in practice but not so later in practice. Aside from the fact that any such effect would be probably more easily described as the result of adaptation than anything else, there is no real evidence for accepting a general hypothesis of this sort. The point of the present account is that the effect of stress will depend upon the components involved in the skill being performed, and since the relevant components change as a function of practice, it is impossible to say generally what effects will happen early in training compared with late in training, or, indeed, whether or not there will be any differences between early and late practice. Knowing, however, how the components do change (and taking into account adaptation) it should be possible to predict the relative effects of stress upon early and late practice.

From time to time it has been suggested that the appropriate way to look at the problem of stress in training is by means of the transfer paradigm. Such an approach appears to be very reasonable, particularly if one accepts the identification of the concept of stress with stimulus conditions. The essential step in the analysis of stress from the point of view of transfer is in the identification of stimulus and response components. If either the case of stress present during training but not during later performance or the case of stress absent during training but present during later performance is considered, the principle is the same. The response components are the same[8] but the stimulus components change because stress is either absent or present. Classical transfer theory leads to the prediction of a decrement due to altered stimulus conditions. This stimulus generalization can be called decrement. Thus, if stress is absent during either training or performance but present for one of them, learning theory suggests the operation of stimulus generalization decrement and hence poorer performance.

Despite the general usefulness of the concept of stimulus generalization decrement, it will probably not be fruitful to try to make use of this

---

[8]This statement may not be strictly true. Both the factor analytic work and some recent experimental and theoretical work in learning suggests the possibility that the response components of a given task actually do change during learning. Thus, it may not be possible to speak in strict accuracy of the "same" responses being performed during and after training.

notion in understanding the problem of stress and training. The prediction of decrement will probably not hold with any degree of cross-task generality. This is partly because of the loose stimulus character of stress. While any stressful stimulus has a stable component that gives rise to the condition of stress, the specific components of such stimuli vary widely in their composition. Thus, the question of stimulus patterning must enter any predictions about the effects of stress made from the point of view of the transfer paradigm. Therefore, it appears that the occasionally stated view that stress should be deliberately introduced during training if it is to be expected during performance is not so sound as it first appears.

Another difficulty with the application of the transfer paradigm to the problem of stress and training is more important and also more complicated. Furthermore, the extent to which the difficulty is significant depends upon some assumptions about the nature of transfer in motor skills, assumptions that are not universally agreed upon. It can be stated, however, that any stimulus generalization decrement of the sort that could be involved in stressful stimuli and skills may be primarily influential over what can be called the cognitive control of psychomotor skills. If this is so, stimulus generalization decrement would be mainly influential over the verbal and stimulus pre-differentiation aspects of particular tasks. Little is known about such influences, particularly with the kind of complicated skills to which predictions must eventually be addressed.

Thus far nothing has been said about the verbal components of psychomotor skills or about verbal skills in themselves. This has been largely because there is so little to build upon here (see Chapter 6 by Fitts). Meyer (1953) dealt with verbal behavior within the framework of the notion of topographical motor recruitment, largely in order to describe the large literature on muscle tension and verbal behavior. It has been difficult, however, to find any genuine stable patterns in this literature, nor does the application of the notion of topographical recruitment seem to be very useful, particularly in view of what is known about the localization of verbal skills.

Perhaps the most fundamental weakness of the present understanding of the effects of stress upon verbal skills, particularly during learning, is that not enough dimensions of such skills have yet been explored to know what kinds of effects to look for. Many investigators have looked at particular aspects of such skills, aspects that were either chosen arbitrarily or chosen because they were relevant to some special theory. Some information is available, of course, from the existing experimental literature. It is known, for example, from Bourne's (1955) experiment that non-associative facilitation of verbal reproductive memory can occur as the result of induced muscular tension, but it is by no means clear to what extent such an effect would depend upon the particular distribution of response probabilities among the available members of a verbal set.

One assumption that has received some attention is that induced tension will affect response stereotypy (Kuethe & Eriksen, 1957), but it is not known how such an effect is influenced by the restrictions on rate of emission of verbal items. Thus, in the absence of both information about the analytic components of laboratory verbal skills and reasonable hypotheses about how induced tension could affect such tasks, it is not a fruitful enterprise to try to relate stress to verbal skills. Indeed, induced tension at best only provides some of the correlates of the stimulus conditions of stress.

In the absence of experimental data, therefore, any attempt to relate verbal behavior to conditions of stress will be almost entirely hypothetical in character. Previous research has suggested that such variables as rate of emission in free situations (verbal output) (Kanfer, 1958a; Kanfer, 1958b), rate of emission in a controlled situation (color naming) (Katchmer, Ross, & Andrews, 1958), response stereotypy (Kuethe & Eriksen, 1957) are sensitive to the introduction of stressful stimuli. There is, however, no satisfactory way of organizing the effects to be expected. The theory of anxiety as a drive put forward by Spence and Taylor has something to say about the effects of stress upon verbal behavior, but only a single aspect of verbal behavior (intratask interference) is covered, and it is clear that the theory as it stands at present is not adequate to handle all of the data generated by the theory (Besch, 1959).

Thus, the application of the present technique of analysis should be, for the time being, limited largely to motor skills. Eventually it should be possible to describe those aspects of verbal performance (particularly during training) subject to particular influences of stress and then use the characteristics of those aspects to predict the influence of stress upon particular tasks that include verbal skills.

In summary, the present analysis does not suggest anything unique about the training situation. The components of skill do change as a function of practice, and hence the specific predictions about the effects of stress upon a particular skill must change. Thus, the training situation would demand nothing more than the reapplication at successive levels of skill of the kind of analysis of the factor structure of tasks suggested earlier. If the notion of stimulus generalization decrement turns out to be significant for a particular set of tasks, the question of whether or not original training was done under conditions of stress like those to be expected in actual performance may be important. It is likely, however, that other sources of differences between the training and performance situation will be so much more important as to swamp any effects due to generalization decrement.

Finally, a word needs to be said about the autonomic concomitants of stress and arousal. These do occur, and a variety of theorists have given them crucial roles in the influence of stress upon behavior. Little attention has been paid, however, to the question of skills and autonomic arousal. It has always been assumed that any effects autonomic arousal had upon performance were indirect ones achieved through changes in the motivational state. It may be, however, that there are more direct influences. The present author has suggested elsewhere (Deese, 1958) that autonomic arousal may be responsible for direct interference with the performance of certain skilled acts. The hypothesis is that such interference was the result of distraction. If this hypothesis is correct, certain kinds of effects are to be expected. Those skills which involved a high level of vigilance should suffer by the distracting stimuli arising from autonomic arousal,[9] whereas those skills which involve repetitive performance of simple movements should not.

Such guesses do little more, however, than emphasize the need for an analytic approach to the problem of stress and skilled performance. It is necessary to know the details of the effects of stressful stimuli upon behavior generally (the sort of details that come from the studies of autonomic and skeletal activity as well as the studies of mood changes under stress), and it is necessary to know the components of particular skills to be performed under stress. The contribution of specific research on stress and skills should be directed towards the correlation between the general patterns of arousal under stress and the relevancy of particular components of skill. The fundamental difficulty with much of the experimental work thus far on stress and skilled behavior is a deficiency in analysis and synthesis. This chapter has had the purpose of

---

[9]Such an effect should happen, of course, only to the extent that the task is influenced by distraction (noises, flashing lights, etc.) generally.

suggesting the usefulness of factor analysis of tasks in trying to understand the variable influence of stress upon skilled behavior.

## REFERENCES

Basowitz, H. H., Persky, S. K., & Grinker, R. *Anxiety and stress.* New York: McGraw-Hill, 1955.

Besch, Norma F. Paired associate learning as a function of anxiety level and shock. *J. Pers.*, 1959, *27*, 116-124.

Bourne, L. E., Jr. An evaluation of the effect of induced tension on performance. *J. exp. Psychol.*, 1955, *49*, 418-422.

Brown, J. S. & Farber, I. E. Emotions conceptualized as intervening variables—with suggestions toward a theory of frustration. *Psychol. Bull.*, 1951, *48*, 465-495.

Brown, W. F. & Holtzman, W. F. A study-attitudes questionnaire for predicting academic success. *J. educ. Psychol.*, 1955, *46*, 75-84.

Child, I. L. & Waterhouse, I. K. Frustration and the quality of performance: II. A theoretical statement. *Psychol. Rev.*, 1953, *60*, 127-139.

Conrad, R. Speed and load stress in a sensory-motor skill. *Appl. psychol. res. Unit* (Cambridge), 1950, APU 134/50.

Deese, J. *Psychology of learning.* (2nd ed.) New York: McGraw-Hill, 1958.

Deese, J. & Lazarus, R. S. *The effects of stress upon psychomotor performance.* USAF Hum. Resour. Res. Cent. Res. Bull., 1952, No. 52-19.

DeSoto, C. B. & Kuethe, J. L. On the relation between two variables. *Educ. psychol. Measmt.*, 1960, *20*, 743-749.

Eyesenck, H. H. Reminiscence, drive and personality theory. *J. abnorm. soc. Psychol.*, 1956, *53*, 328-333.

Fleishman, E. A. Dimensional analysis of psychomotor abilities. *J. exp. Psychol.*, 1954, *48*, 437-454.

Fleishman, E. A. Psychomotor selection tests: Research and applications in the U.S. Air Force. *Personnel Psychol.*, 1956, *9*, 448-467.

Fleishman, E. A. & Hempel, W. E. Changes in factor structure of a complex psychomotor test as a function of practice. *Psychometrika*, 1954, *19*, 239-252.

Horowitz, L. M. An investigation of the relationship between motivational-anxiety-indicator questionnaires and performance in an experimental situation. M.A. dissertation, The Johns Hopkins Univ., 1957.

Janis, I. L. *Air war and emotional stress.* New York: McGraw-Hill, 1951.

Janis, I. L. *Psychological stress.* New York: Wiley, 1958.

Jenkins, J. J., Russell, W. R., & Suci, G. *Semantic atlas.* Univ. of Minn., 1958.

Kanfer, F. H. Effect of a warning signal preceding a noxious stimulus on verbal rate and heart rate. *J. abnorm. soc. Psychol.,* 1958, *55,* 73-80. (a)

Kanfer, F. H. Supplementary report: Stability of a verbal rate change in experimental anxiety. *J. exp. Psychol.,* 1958, *56,* 182. (b)

Katchmer, L. T., Ross, S., & Andrews, T. G. Effects of stress and anxiety on performance of a complex verbal-coding task. *J. exp. Psychol.,* 1958, *55,* 559-564.

Kuethe, J. L. & Eriksen, C. W. Personality, anxiety and muscle tension as determinants of response stereotypy. *J. abnorm. soc. Psychol.,* 1957, *54,* 400-404.

Lacey, J. I. & Lacey, B. C. Verification and extension of the principles of autonomic response stereotypy. *Amer. J. Psychol.,* 1958, *71,* 50-63.

Lazarus, R. S. & Deese, J. *The relationship between personality measures and skilled behavior under two types of stress.* Manuscript, 1953.

Lazarus, R. S., Deese, J., & Osler, Sonia F. The effects of psychological stress upon performance. *Psychol. Bull.,* 1952, *49,* 295-317.

Lewinsohn, P. M. Some individual differences in physiological reactivity to stress. *J. comp. physiol. Psychol.,* 1956, *49,* 271-277.

Lowell, E. L. The effect of need for achievement on learning and speed of performance. *J. Psychol.,* 1952, *33,* 31-40.

Malmo, R. B. Activation, a neurophysiological dimension. *Psychol. Rev.,* 1950, *66,* 367-386.

McCandless, B. R. & Castaneda, A. Anxiety in children, school achievement and intelligence. *Child Developm.,* 1956, *27,* 379-382.

Meyer, D. R. On the interaction of simultaneous responses. *Psychol. Bull.,* 1953, *50,* 204-220.

Meyer, D. R. & Noble, M. E. Summation of manifest anxiety and muscular tension. *J. exp. Psychol.,* 1958, *55,* 599-602.

Murphy, R. E. Effects of threat of shock, distraction and task design on performance. *J. exp. Psychol.,* 1959, *58,* 134-141.

Pronko, N. H. & Leith, W. R. Behavior under stress: A study of its disintegration. *Psychol. Rep.,* 1956, *2,* 205-222.

Sarason, S. B. & Mandler, G. Some correlates of test anxiety. *J. abnorm. soc. Psychol.,* 1952, *47,* 810-817.

Schnore, M. M. Individual patterns of physiological activity as a function of task differences and degree of arousal. *J. exp. Psychol.,* 1958, *58,* 117-128.

Spence, K. W. A theory of emotionally based drive (D) and its relation to performance in simple learning situations. *Amer. Psychologist,* 1958, *15,* 131-141.

Taylor, Janet A. Drive theory and manifest anxiety. *Psychol. Bull.*, 1956, *53*, 303-320.

Taylor, Janet A. The effects of anxiety level and psychological stress on verbal learning. *J. abnorm. soc. Psychol.*, 1958, *57*, 55-60.

Williams, R. H. (Ed.) *Human factors in military research.* O.R.O., Chevy Chase, Maryland: The Johns Hopkins Univ., 1954.

Winne, J. F. A scale of neuroticism: An adaptation of the Minnesota Multiphasic Personality Inventory. *J. clin. Psychol.*, 1951, *7*, 117-122.

Chapter 8 | Simulators

Robert M. Gagné, Princeton University

Over a period of many years, simulators have been used with ever-increasing frequency in the armed forces for purposes of establishment and maintenance of proficiency in individuals and teams who are engaged in military operations. If one adopts a broad definition of simulators, it can be seen that they have a long military history. Targets for rifle firing were long ago made in a shape which "simulated" the contour of a man. Artillery crews of many previous ages have practiced their team functions with "simulated" guns made of wood, when real cannon were in short supply. Nor has military ingenuity stopped short with such simple techniques. The large-scale tactical exercise can also be considered an example of a highly successful simulation technique, in which many individual targets, weapons, and weapon effects are simulated for the purpose of providing personnel with the conditions under which they may gain in proficiency and put into practice what they have previously learned in a more abstract form. In recent times, the word *simulator* has more commonly been associated with a single set of equipment which can by itself represent to its operator a very large portion of the situation required in the use of a weapon system. Perhaps the best known example of this type is the aircraft simulator (Mahler & Bennett, 1950; Dinsmore & DuBois, 1953; Flexman, Townsend, & Ornstein, 1954). Seated in a covered cockpit, the operator of such a device carries out nearly all of the activities required in a real airplane. He makes preflight checks, starts the engines, goes through a typical take-off procedure, flies a prescribed mission, contends on the way with various weather and emergency conditions, and carries out the activities involved in landing. During all this time, he observes instruments and operates controls which simulate those of the real airplane with a high degree of precision; even the movement of the cockpit and the noise of the engines may be simulated in a highly realistic manner.

Even more recent has been the development of what is sometimes called the *system simulator*, in connection with modern highly complex weapon systems that employ an entire team of "operators" rather than a single one. One example of such a system simulator is an air traffic control simulator, which undertakes to represent the set of operations involving interactions between radar controllers and pilots in landing aircraft in traffic (Matheny, 1955). Another example is the combat information center (CIC) simulator designed to represent the combat information center of a ship, and to provide practice in the team activities required in the operations of receiving, plotting, reporting, and interpreting information on ship locations and movements. As weapon systems have become ever more complex, with the involvement of even greater numbers and varieties of military personnel, the system simulator has evolved far beyond the stage of being a collection of equipment sets in one particular location. Nowadays system simulation may be a matter of many types of equipment operated by many types of individuals or teams, within a communication network extending over a broad geographical area. Some idea of the scope of system simulation may be grasped by consideration of a simulator developed for the purpose of representing the operation of detecting hostile aircraft by radar, and reporting their character, course, speed, and other relevant facts (Chapman & Kennedy, 1956). This basic air defense operation involves many kinds of activities and a variety of trained men. Simulation is also applied to the central integration of such information, and the making of decisions based upon it, in an even more elaborate kind of "combat information center" as is described by Carter in Chapter 14.

Simulators do not always assume the form of hard equipment. Important tasks of navigation and intelligence interpretation, for example, are sometimes represented by simulated maps or simulated aerial photographs. The simulation of decision-making processes in the conduct of military operations may invlove the use of representative war plans, operations orders, coded messages, and other printed materials.

It is easy to realize, then, that there are a great many kinds of simulators. They are used to represent a variety of weapon systems ranging from the simplest individual weapons like a gun through the relatively complex yet individually-operated system such as a fighter aircraft, to the highly complex and spatially disparate team operations of an air defense system. Simulators also differ in their scope of coverage, in other words, in the degree to which they approach representation of an entire operation, regardless of the complexity of that operation. A simulator may represent only a small critical part of the total set of activities involved in flying an aircraft, as for example, a simulator for seat ejection (Rhoades, 1950). In contrast, the entire set of activities required to fly the plane on a mission may be simulated, as has been indicated.

## What is Meant by Simulation?

If all of these variations exist in what are called simulators, it is of interest to ask, what do these various equipment systems have in common? Why should all these varieties of things be called simulators?

First of all, as has already been implied, a simulator attempts to *represent* a real situation in which operations are carried out. (By "operations" is meant a set of events in which a man or men interact with machines or with their environment to bring about a particular result.) Big or small, complex or simple, the simulator is believed by its designer, and hopefully, by its users, to provide exact representation of certain parts of the real "operational situation." In this respect a simulator is often distinguished from a *trainer*. While a simulator is often used for training, there are trainers which do not represent any specific real situation, and which are not designed to do so. An example is the C-11 Trainer for jet aircraft (Woolman, 1955) which is intended to provide general training for jet pilots, but which does not replace any specific aircraft simulator.

Secondly, in representing a real operational situation, a simulator provides its users with certain *controls* over that situation. A target simulator, for example, may be controlled in its distance from the rifleman, or, if it is a moving target, in the rate and direction of its movement. A bombing simulator makes provision for control of the terrain over which it "moves," as well as the rate of movement over this terrain (Brown & Ghiselli, 1951). An air defense system simulator provides its users with control over the number and nature of target indicators on its radar scopes (Chapman & Kennedy, 1956; see Chapter 14 by Carter). It might be argued, in fact, that this characteristic constitutes the major difference between a simulator and the operational situation itself. The latter is usually, by definition, uncontrolled and subject to unpredictable variations; whereas the simulator provides for control (and often, *planned* variation) of these same aspects of the real situation.

Thirdly, the simulator is deliberately designed to *omit* certain parts of the real operational situation. For example, a simulator for sonar operation does not necessarily include the entire submarine compartment in which it is used in real operations, but may consist simply of the receiving set placed on a convenient table and arranged to receive prerecorded underwater signals. An aircraft crew training simulator located on the ground does not include the actual conditions of flight that would obtain if the crew were actually in a moving aircraft. In all simulators, a greater or smaller portion of the operational situation is purposely omitted. There are a number of reasons for this, some of which are implied by the previous discussion:

1. Whenever it is desired to provide control over an aspect of the real situation, then inevitably the unpredictability of this aspect of the situation is omitted. Sometimes this leads to the criticism that the simulator is "unrealistic," and of course, to the extent that natural unpredictability is left out, this is quite true. Nevertheless, as will be seen later, the control of the situation may be essential to the purposes for which the simulator is used.

2. Other aspects of the real situation may be omitted in a simulator because they are not considered important in fulfilling the simulator's purpose. In an automobile driving simulator, for example, no one would consider it important to represent the activity of driving up to a filling station and asking for five gallons of gas. Similarly, the activity of closing the door of an aircraft may not be included in an aircraft simulator. It is to be noted that it is not the importance of the activity itself that is considered in determining such omissions; certainly the closing of a door in an aircraft is an important matter. But it is not considered an important aspect of the *training purpose* of the simulator since it can most readily be trained otherwise. Omissions of this sort get close to the heart of the problem of designing simulators since they pose the question of what parts of the operational situation can reasonably be left out, assuming a particular set of purposes for the simulator. It is necessary, therefore, to return to this question later in considering more fully the purposes of simulation.

3. Still other parts of the operational situation are omitted in a simulator because they are too dangerous, too expensive to represent, or because they raise related problems of practical feasibility. A missile simulator may, for example, leave out the step of actual firing of the missile although all the activities leading up to this point may be faithfully

simulated. An aircraft simulator may represent an engine on fire by a flashing red light rather than by an actual fire.

In general, then, a simulator is designed to represent a real operational situation. Additionally, it provides for certain systematic controls over this situation. And in doing this, it necessarily omits portions or aspects of the real situation, particularly those of natural variability and unpredictability.

## THE PURPOSES OF SIMULATION

As has already been mentioned, the purposes of simulation are of the utmost importance, not only in determining the ways in which simulators are used, but also in establishing the criteria for their design. It is almost always an unfortunate occurrence when a simulator is designed and built without careful attention to its purposes. What usually happens in such cases is that the simulator is not used in any effective manner since the need does not exist for simulating the particular aspects of the operational situation which have been represented. The machine or system is built, so far as hardware is concerned, but it cannot fulfill the needed purposes. The wrong parts of the situation have been represented and the wrong ones omitted. What, then, are the purposes for which simulators are needed? What functions do they serve?

*Training.* First and perhaps most obviously, a simulator can be used for training. Motor skills like aircraft landing (Payne, Dougherty, Hasler, Skeen, Brown, & Williams, 1954), helicopter flying (Dorny, Campbell, & Channell, 1953) or the operation of large guns (Goldstein, Rittenhouse, & Woods, 1952; Horrocks, Krug, & Bowlus, 1952) can be effectively trained by means of simulators, as can procedural tasks like cockpit operations for the aircraft pilot or flight engineer, the operation of missile control consoles, and many others. In addition, many types of decision-making tasks can be represented and trained with use of simulators, ranging from the trouble shooting of complex electronic equipment (Briggs, 1956; Briggs & DuVall, 1957) to the critical and far-reaching decisions which occur in war games simulation. In all these instances, of course, it frequently becomes difficult to distinguish the simulator per se from the training device. The term simulator is ordinarily used when the training has a *specific* purpose (as training pilots for the B-47 aircraft), whereas a training device has a *general* training purpose (as an aircraft landing trainer for student pilots).

This specificity of simulators usually means that they are best intended for a training function which will take place relatively late in the training cycle. Initial training by its very nature is much more general than is late training. The electronic technician, for example, must first learn how to read meters and measure resistances, before he undertakes to learn how to find malfunctions in a specific radar set. For this reason, one of the most common uses of simulators, as opposed to training devices, is that of skill consolidation and maintenance, rather than initial skill learning. Again, the widely employed simulators for pilot training, both in military and commercial usage, are the best known examples of this function. Pilots gain their skills initially in trainers and training aircraft; they maintain these skills by practicing in simulators.

*Assessment of Proficiency.* A second and related purpose of simulators is the assessment of proficiency (Holt, 1949; Townsend & Bamford, 1954; Danneskiold, 1955). A bombing simulator may be used to measure the proficiency of student bombardiers in releasing bombs so as to hit the simulated target (Voiers, 1954). Similarly, a gunnery simulator is used to check the accuracy of firing of student gunners (Goldstein & Ellis, 1956). The kind and amount of simulation of the real situation required for assessing proficiency is not always the same as that required for training, although the overlap is high. For example, a simulator intended for the training purpose of maintaining skill in landing an aircraft would most likely attempt to represent typical landing sequences. If the purpose of such a simulator were that of measuring proficiency, however, it would be more likely to represent unusual or extremely difficult landing situations, in order to obtain an indication of the limits of the skill being measured. Of course, these two purposes are often combined in a single simulator. But it is important that they be explicitly recognized and distinguished when a simulator is designed.

*Development of Operational Doctrine.* A third purpose of simulation, which has gained well-deserved prominence in recent years, is for the analysis of operations, leading to the development of operational doctrine. In the days when weapon systems were as simple as the rifleman with rifle, the field telephone and its operator, or even the tank and its crew, the doctrine of how a weapon was to be used was developed during planned field exercises with the weapon. For many relatively simple military systems, this is still the method employed. But how shall doctrine be developed for weapons that are too expensive to fire, like missiles? What shall be done in air defense when the conduct of an actual "field exercise" utilizing real aircraft to represent the enemy would disrupt entire communities and expose many people to mortal danger? How can one even conceive of a "field exercise" for a rocket-launched satellite? In a number of instances, a successful solution has been achieved by using simulation.

In these highly complex weapon systems, simulation has made it possible to put the entire system, hardware and people, into an operational state (Chapman & Kennedy, 1956; Kopstein & Morgan, 1957; Peterson & Jones, 1958). This in turn has meant that the operation of each system can be analyzed to determine how it really works, what factors influence how it works, and even what the limitations of its effectiveness are. From such analyses have come the descriptions of how the system is to be employed, called operational doctrine. The operational doctrine for a rifle is relatively predictable, and can be obtained by studying directly the use of the rifle by men in the field. Operational doctrine for a number of modern weapon systems is highly unpredictable, and can often be developed only by employing simulation of the system for the purpose of making a careful analysis of its workings and capabilities.

## What Is Simulated?

Having in mind these three distinct but often related purposes of simulators, training, assessment of proficiency, and the analysis of operations, the question of what it is that is being simulated can now be considered. It has been seen earlier that simulation represents the operational situation. What is it that is being represented?

This is an extremely important question, the answer to which can have a profound effect on the design as well as the use of simulators. Representing reality is in itself an expensive undertaking, and the greater the proportion of the real situation represented in a simulator, the closer will such expense approach that of duplicating the entire operation. When the feature of control over these operations is added, the cost of simulation usually multiplies. Consequently, the question of what aspects of the operational situation can be omitted in a simulator is usually a very crucial one.

Should an expensive instrument be used in its entirety in a simulator, or can one use simply the dial of this instrument? Should one simulate rough air in an aircraft simulator, or is this a feature which can safely be omitted? Can one adequately represent terrain in a bombing simulator by means of a photograph, or must one use an exact three-dimensional scale model? These are the kinds of questions which often determine the practical feasibility of a simulator, from both the standpoints of technology and cost. To answer them, a precise conception of what is simulated is essential.

It is clear that what is simulated is not the equipment itself. If this were so, every effort at simulation would end up with an exact duplication of the entire situation, or else in dissatisfaction arising from the fact that such duplication had not been achieved. And many specific examples attest to the fact that the components of simulators are not required to be exact copies of operational equipment. In aircraft simulators, engine noise may be represented, but not the engines themselves. A target simulator may be shaped like a man, but only in two dimensions. A simulated tank may look like a tank, but be made of rubber rather than steel. A radar simulator may use an operating oscilloscope, but not an antenna.

What are simulated are *operations* or *tasks* (which mean parts of operations), that is, interactions between man and machine or between man and his environment. Likewise, what are omitted, for various good reasons, are *tasks*. Basic discussions of these points are contained in reports by Wolfle (1945) and by Miller (1953). If one is to make proper decisions about the design of a simulator, the tasks must first be described in terms which are fully understandable and specific. One cannot make proper decisions about what to leave out on the basis of statements which describe the equipment alone, such as "The operator is seated in front of a radar scope." One must know what the operator does in interacting with the radar scope. Suppose, for example, his job were to push a button as soon as a circular pattern on the scope grew to a predetermined size. If this were the entire task, it is entirely conceivable that it might be simulated without a real radar scope at all. Alternatively, suppose his job is to turn on, adjust, and calibrate the radar scope. Here the task virtually requires the use of an entire and complete radar scope of a particular type. In any case, such a decision can only be made when the interactions of man and machine are known. Knowing what the machine is by itself is not sufficient.

Descriptions of tasks are of course quite specific to the system under consideration and to the equipment it employs. It is possible, though, to classify such operations in terms of the general types of human activities which comprise them. In these terms, simulators have been designed to represent tasks within all of the following categories (Gagné & Bolles, 1959; see Chapter 2 by Miller):

1. *Procedures.* In this category fall simulators designed primarily to represent cockpit procedures for pilots and flight engineers; consoles for

the control of missile firing; procedures for adjusting and calibrating electronic equipment.

2. *Motor skills.*   A simulator may primarily represent a motor skill, as is the case with a gunnery simulator.

3. *Identifications.*   Simulators may represent such activities as the identification of targets, of terrain features, or of emergency signals.

4. *Conceptual tasks.*   Activities requiring concept-using and reasoning may be represented in simulators for equipment trouble shooting, in the direction of aircraft tactics, in navigation, in aerial photo-interpretation.

5. *Team functions.*   Some complex simulators emphasize the representation of the communication of information among members of a crew or team.

As has been pointed out, regardless of the complexity or scope of the operational situation being simulated, a simulator may represent more or less of this situation. Not only is the cost of simulation affected, but the success of a simulator is often critically determined by the extent to which simulation is carried. Thus the question of degree of simulation is often raised, and is of crucial importance in determining good design.

One meaning of the phrase "degree of simulation" is "proportion of the total situation represented." The amount of the total operational situation which is simulated depends, as has been indicated, on a number of factors including the degree of control over the situation which may be desired. The proportion of the real situation that is represented cannot be measured exactly, of course, but it is often sufficient to make rough judgments about it. For example, an automobile driving simulator which included a view of moving terrain representing highway driving would obviously have a higher "degree of simulation" than one which did not have such a view. It may be noted that in this meaning, "degree" of simulation refers to the inclusion or exclusion of *tasks* and not to the question of resemblance between characteristics of the equipment in the simulator and the actual situation.

Suppose there is the problem of determining what degree of simulation should be used in a control stick for an aircraft simulator. The first question to be asked is, "What tasks is the simulator designed to represent?" If its purpose is to train cockpit *procedures*, it seems obvious that the stick pressure will have no particular bearing on the transfer of training to be expected to these tasks in the real airplane. However, if its purpose is the training of *motor skills* required in controlling the aircraft, it appears just as obvious that the matter of stick pressure is an important one. Thus the first question about degree of simulation which must be answered has reference to the kinds of tasks to be included or excluded. If one decides to exclude certain tasks, then the problem of physical resemblance between actual and simulated equipment can in many instances be answered negatively in terms of its being irrelevant to the simulator's purpose.

Having determined task relevance, there is still a second meaning to the phrase "degree of simulation." This is the question of what aspects of the stimulus situation will be reacted to as *equivalent* by the operator of the simulator. There is often an important matter of concern in simulator design that the situation appear real to the operator. For example, the radar picture in a bombing simulator, it is thought, should look like the radar picture in the real situation. Sometimes the engineering psychologist is able to make a prediction on the basis of psychophysical data (Handbook Staff, Tufts University, 1959). But the ultimate answer to the question of situational equivalence must be sought in empirical evidence of transfer of training. In general, studies have demonstrated that fairly radical departures from physical similarity can nevertheless produce high degrees of transfer from a simulated to an actual task. For example, when the task is one of identification of components, representation by means of photographs or drawings is known to provide high amounts of transfer (Gagné & Foster, 1949). Or, when the task is one of concept utilization, it seems entirely reasonable that, among other examples, words like "one, two, three, four" are equivalent to numerals like "1, 2, 3, 4." The realization that simulation of tasks is a matter of stimulus equivalence has led to the proposal that "degree of simulation" be conceived as "psychological simulation" (Wolfle, 1945; Miller, 1953), defined in terms of amount of transfer of training from the simulator to the real situation.

Apart from the matter of insuring that tasks, but not components, are "real," there exists the further possibility of *deliberate alteration* of certain aspects of the task to be learned for purposes of training. A device which adopts this course of action had perhaps better be called a training device (rather than a simulator), and as such lies beyond the scope of this chapter. (See Chapter 9 by Lumsdaine.) It may be noted that the research question posed by such a possibility is not, "How far can one depart from the real situation without lowering transfer too greatly?", but one which is potentially of much greater significance from both a practical and theoretical point of view. This is the question

"Can systematic changes in stimulus factors enhance learning and transfer?" For training purposes, possibilities of enhanced transfer exist in such ways as deliberately (*a*) increasing or decreasing the precision of the training task; (*b*) encouraging or discouraging the number of errors in training; and (*c*) varying the sequence of part-practice to whole-task practice, among others. There is as yet inadequate evidence on these matters (Smode, Beam, & Dunlap, 1959). Obviously, each of them involves a deliberate departure from "simulation." As topics for research in the area of training device design, they are lively and promising questions.

## SIMULATORS IN THEIR TRAINING FUNCTION

As has been pointed out previously, the important question to be answered in making decisions about the design of simulators for training is what shall be represented and what left out. If the operational situation has been adequately described in terms of tasks, such decisions are not particularly difficult. If tasks have not been described, sensible decisions are impossible.

Which of the operations does one wish to train by using a simulator? A procedural operation, a motor performance, a set of identifications, concept-using, team communication functions, or some combination of these? For example, if cockpit procedures are to be trained, these procedures must be faithfully represented by the use of the instruments, signals, and controls with which the individual interacts. But it may be quite unnecessary to represent the characteristics which are reacted to in controlling the aircraft in flight, or the field of view reacted to in landing. Similarly, decisions about what aspects of "radar operation" should be represented in a simulator for training radar operators should be based on a description of precisely what these operations are. If the radar operator must tune and adjust the set, then all the kinds of interactions he makes with a radar set must be represented; if instead he is concerned only with identifying certain wave forms, the simulator could be designed to represent only these.

The optimal function of a simulator in late stages of training and in skill maintenance, as opposed to the stage of initial learning, has some important implications for design. For many types of human activities, a simulator may be not only highly expensive for application to initial stages of learning, but also quite inefficient. It is easy to see that a procedure, for example, may be learned initially to a considerable degree of proficiency by the use of such materials as check lists and pictorial charts. Similarly, identifications of objects, terrain features, and signals may readily be acquired to a relatively high level by practice with pictorial representations (McClelland, Abbott, & Stobie, 1954). Basic concepts and rules must of necessity be learned initially through verbal and pictorial means. Team functions, too, can often be acquired to a considerable degree by learning situations of extremely low degrees of equipment simulation, as when an army gun crew practices on a wooden "gun." Only in the case of motor skills are human activities encountered which appear to require highly accurate simulation from the beginning of learning. The weight of evidence suggests the great importance of exact task simulation from the very beginning of motor learning. Presumably, this is because many of the controlling stimuli in motor skills come from the individual's own muscles, and can therefore only be provided by requiring the movements which are to become habitual. With this important exception, however, it can readily be recognized that simulation has its greatest usefulness for the late stages of learning and for proficiency maintenance.

If advanced learning, the consolidation of skill, and the maintenance of proficiency are the training purposes best served by simulators, what implications does this have for the representation of operational tasks? What varieties of tasks should be represented in a simulator? Lacking evidence to the contrary, it would seem that the best principle would be to make the tasks of the simulator as representative of the real situation as possible, in terms of their variety. This means including a range of tasks that reflect both easy and difficult situations, as well as those of medium difficulty. Designers of simulators are sometimes tempted to emphasize the inclusion of highly difficult tasks. But the importance of such striving for the last measure of proficiency must be weighed against the advantage of "natural" variety and unpredictable difficulty of tasks as they occur in the real situation. Task variety helps to insure that practice is in fact "realistic." Furthermore, the training purpose of a simulator, for best results, must be carefully distinguished from the proficiency assessment purpose, to be discussed next. Simulator tasks which exceed the capability of the trainee may well provide information on the limits of his skill, but by that very fact they cannot be said to *train*.

Simulators can be of tremendous value to a training program (Muckler, Nygaard, O'Kelly, & Williams, 1956). The initially acquired verbal knowledge, identifications, sequences and concepts can be "polished," strengthened, and practiced in use in a simulated situation. It appears as though, when properly used for training, simulators are able to capture, and consolidate into practical skills, knowledge which would otherwise be forgotten before it could be used in an actual operational situation. It is the particular success of simulators that they are able to build useful performances out of the raw material of initially acquired knowledge. Teachers of technical subjects are all too familiar with the student who "knows the book," or who "understands the theory," but who may exhibit a poor performance when asked to "apply his knowledge." When direct job experience and on-the-job learning can be provided immediately, the change in such a student's performance may be considerable. And for many kinds of operations, *simulated* job experience can have an effect which is equally beneficial. For this is exactly what the simulator is designed to do, as its name implies: to provide practice in representative aspects of the real situation.

To be entirely successful, training conducted with simulators should follow carefully prepared plans which are integrated with a total training program. An excellent discussion of the principles of aircraft simulator utilization is contained in the *Flight Simulator Utilization Handbook* (Human Factors Operations Research Laboratories, 1953).

## SIMULATORS IN PERFORMANCE ASSESSMENT

Often combined with the training function of simulators is that of assessing performance (Gagné, 1954). This is perfectly natural since progress in the learning of skills is usually measured by taking samples of performance as practice is continued, in order to determine whether proficiency has been maintained. However, the two functions are not identical, and the kinds of situational controls which may be most effective for learning are frequently different from those controls required for assessing performance.

The most troublesome requirement in the use of a simulator for performance measurement is that of *reliability* of measures. The human individual is a variable organism, and practically all attempts to measure his performances run up against the occurrence of variability from one measurement occasion to the next. The only good way there is to achieve dependable measures of human performance is to use repeated observations. In measuring how good the performance of a pilot is, for example, one does not trust the observation of performance in one check-ride; two, three, or even four observations are obtained. When the pilot's landing performance is assessed, observations during only one landing are not used, but he is required to make several landings. Similar considerations are applied to all kinds of performances of military personnel, from clerks to commanders. A single observation is certainly unreliable, and the more frequently the observations are repeated, the greater confidence there is in the dependability of performance assessment.

These basic facts about reliability have important implications with respect to the use of simulators for performance assessment. Just as assessment is unreliable in real situations unless observations are repeated, assessment by means of simulators under such circumstances is not better. Simulators themselves may give the impression of being less affected by accidental variations in the environment; but this does not insure that the individual will not exhibit variability from one occasion to the next.

So far as design is concerned, assuming the purpose of performance assessment, a simulator needs to make provision for repeated measurements. For this reason the tasks presented by the simulator need to be repeated more than once apiece, and preferably several times. This does not mean that each task must be exactly duplicated, but it does mean that repeated tasks of the same type must be designed to measure the same kind of performance. This requirement is similar to that which exists in any achievement test, where reliability of measurement is attained by using several items of similar content to measure any particular aspect of performance. However, it may be noted that *repetition* of tasks for performance assessment is opposed in purpose to the provision of *variety* in tasks for learning. Thus these two functions of a simulator are to some extent contradictory, so far as design characteristics are concerned. If a simulator is wholly designed for use in performance assessment, it is not likely to be optimally designed for training, and vice versa.

The measurement of performance can be profitably carried out with a simulator for all kinds of human activities, whether they are procedures, identifications, motor skills, conceptual tasks, or team functions. (See, for example, the descriptions of several complex simulated situations in Chapter 11 by Frederiksen, and in Chapter 14 by Carter.) Oftentimes the greatest difficulty in the use of simulators for this purpose arises from the infeasibility of providing repeated measures within reasonable time limits. This is likely to be the case, for example, in a simulator such as that for electronic equipment trouble shooting (Demaree, 1955). The complexity of problems to be solved in such situations may be so great that each single task requires a number of hours to perform, and repeating them may well occupy a period of several days. No clear-cut solution to this difficulty in performance measurement has yet been invented. Regardless of this, simulators frequently provide the most convenient, realistic, and objective method available for the assessment of performance. This is particularly true when team functions are required, as well as when the real operational situation is inaccessible or dangerous. Except by simulation, how can the performance of a space-vehicle crew be assessed?

Is the assessment of performance obtained from a simulated situation a "valid" measure? In one sense, this is an illegitimate question. A simulator is not designed, as is an aptitude test, for the purpose of *predicting* performance in a real operational situation. Rather it is designed, as has been said, to *represent* the real situation. The degree to which it does this can certainly be measured in a direct manner, as has been said, in terms of the amount of transfer of training. Provided such measures are available, it seems extremely doubtful that a correlation coefficient expressing the relation between the performance of individuals in a simulator and some other measure of real performance can contribute any information which is not already known. To the extent that the simulator is "real," the performance is "real," and one cannot define something which is "more real."

This is not to suggest that studies of correlation between performance measures obtained on a simulator and performance measures or ratings obtained in another situation have no value; occasionally they do. One may be interested, for example, in determining the degree to which the introduction of control over the environment in a simulator affects performance, as compared with that in a less highly controlled situation containing a greater amount of variation and unpredictability. But the latter type of measure is difficult to obtain reliably for the very reason that it possesses unpredictability. Even if one does manage to obtain such a measure, there are usually no reasonable grounds on which one can consider it "the criterion" to be "predicted" by a performance score measured in a simulator situation. Ordinarily, it is found that both such measures of performance are obtained under "simulated" conditions —in fact, the environmental control demanded by the obtaining of a performance measure makes the measurement situation inevitably one of simulation (Rulon, Langmuir, Schweiker, Demaree, Crowder, & Lawrey, 1954). Thus a correlation between such scores simply tells us how closely related are performances on two different simulators. But it does not permit one of these to be characterized as a "better simulator" than the other.

## SIMULATION AS A TECHNIQUE FOR
## DEVELOPING OPERATIONAL DOCTRINE

When a new weapon system is introduced into military service, there are many aspects of its operations which are unknown. These must be tried out, usually in a planned fashion, by putting the equipment together with people in a field test situation. As the complexity of systems increases, more and more do such field tests have to take on the characteristics of elaborate simulator situations. One cannot, for example, really try out a manned space vehicle "in the field," for to do so would be to lose control over the vehicle. For this reason, a large installation must be constructed which has all the essential characteristics of a simulator. It is designed to represent the real operational situation; it has provision for exercising control over this situation, so that observations of system operation can be made; and it omits certain aspects of the real situation for the purposes of control and the avoidance of danger to people.

System simulation of this type has been notably successful in the case of an air defense system in which a team of people at a radar installation must monitor, record, interpret, report, and make decisions about returns from aircraft entering an entire sector scanned by the radar equipment (Chapman, Kennedy, Newell, & Biel, 1959). How can such a system operate most effectively in detecting and reporting aircraft, and distinguishing between friend and foe? Obviously, the analysis of its operation must depend upon simulation in which the radar returns are designed to represent all varieties of situations with which the system is expected to contend. The representation in this case was accomplished by introducing a set of systematically varied signals into the radar receivers, so that they appeared as "traffic" to be detected, identified, reported, and interpreted by the air defense team. The team was thereby enabled to carry out any number of simulated missions with real equipment, typical organizational assignments, and usual means of communication.

System simulation of this sort can be designed for purposes of training both individuals and crews, if this is desired. Likewise, the purpose of performance assessment, particularly of the unit as a team, can readily be served. An additional important function, emphasized by this study of air defense system simulation, is that of system analysis, leading to the development of operating doctrine. This was done by introducing systematic variation in the simulated radar returns, particularly in the direction of progressive increase in the "load" of traffic to be handled. Ultimately, the point at which the total system failed to function because of "overloading" could thus be determined. But even more importantly, it was possible to identify the habitual procedures of team interaction and communication which were needlessly setting limits to system effectiveness all along the way. By means of group critiques held after each simulated exercise, the team was able to discover and to put into effect procedures which made possible increasing effectiveness of operation. Thus optimal operating doctrine was developed by the team itself; in other words, there was a kind of "group learning" which led to progressively increasing operating efficiency. (See Chapter 13 by Carter.)

As systems become more complex, as operations cover greater distances including those beyond the earth's surface, and as equipment becomes increasingly subject to indirect control by man, the use of total system simulators can be expected to grow in importance as well as in frequency. The potentialities of this kind of simulation have probably not even begun to be realized. There is a growing body of knowledge about "system analysis" which is only beginning to be documented at the present time. The indications are that simulation of total systems will come to be used more and more extensively not only for training and performance assessment, but for determining doctrines of operation which can insure highest effectiveness for weapon systems.

## IMPLICATIONS FOR EDUCATION

What do the three functions of simulators, training, performance assessment, and system analysis, have to do with education? Of course, the educative process is also concerned with the learning process, with the assessment of performance, and it also has a body of pedagogical procedure which could be called operational doctrine. But are these nominal similarities a matter of mere analogy? Are not there some crucial differences between the aims of education and the aims of military operations which set these two activities quite apart, and make it useless to seek common principles applicable from the one to the other?

To answer these questions, it is necessary first to note still another resemblance between military training and civilian education. This is the fact that, in both cases, two major stages can be distinguished—a stage of initial learning and a stage of final consolidation and maintenance of skills. In civilian education, one thinks of the establishment of basic skills (like the three R's) as taking place, roughly, in the elementary and secondary schools, while the colleges and professional schools are devoted to the refinement of knowledge as well as to the application of knowledge to specialized professional activities. (The latter may often be acquired "on the job," rather than in college itself.)

As has been shown previously, simulation has its greatest and most obvious usefulness in application to the second stage of the process of acquiring skill. This is just as true if one considers civilian education rather than military training. It does not appear that simulators, of whatever type, can be of particular value in connection with the learning of reading, spelling, writing, arithmetic, or even to the learning of basic concepts of history, science, or language. The primary reason, however, does not lie in any inherent difference between these traditional civilian activities and military ones. The reason is simply that simulators are not designed to be applicable to initially acquired knowledge and skill. For this purpose, one could well examine the usefulness of training devices of a variety of types, and this in fact can be done with considerable profit. (See Chapter 9 by Lumsdaine.) One must look elsewhere in the educational process if suitable employment for the simulator is to be found.

## Technical Training

As has been pointed out, one of the most important developments in the simulator field over the past decade or so has been the extension of their use from a rather narrow range of occupations like that of the pilot and radar observer, into a much broader area of technical operations. Besides aircraft simulators, there are now simulators that apply to such occupations as those of the aircraft controller, the control tower operator, the missile guidance operator, as well as to a great variety of technicians who check, adjust, and maintain complex equipment (Briggs, 1956; French, 1956). When used for these purposes, simulators can save time on the job which previously had to be devoted to apprenticeship training. Furthermore, when properly designed and used, they usually insure greater performance capability in people who are assigned to a job for the first time. And their usefulness in maintaining high degrees of skill despite accidental variations in job experience is well known.

The most direct applicability of simulators is therefore to the training of civilian technicians. There appears to have been an unfortunate de-emphasis of the need our society has for such technicians, accompanied by an equally deplorable downgrading of the socially perceived status of "blue-collar" technicians. Many thoughtful people believe that the present shortage of civilian technicians in our society has the aspects of a current national crisis, which is having no small part to play in the relatively slow pace of our technological development.

If it is true that military systems have grown more complex, it is equally true that civilian systems have done the same. This is apparent not only in our automobiles, washing machines, and other forms of consumer products, but perhaps even more so in the greatly increased mechanization and automation of industrial operations. Automobile owners long for the "old fashioned," by which is meant the thoroughly competent, garage mechanic. The decreasing skill of the appliance repairman is apparent to the housewife whose memory of household operations extends back to thirty years ago. As for industrial operations, the occasional displacement of unskilled labor resulting from automation should not blind anyone to the fact that greater and greater numbers of more highly skilled technicians are needed to keep our modern factories going. Clearly, then, the training of technicians constitutes a most important part of present-day requirements for the civilian educational system.

Simulators could have an extremely useful role in the training of civilian technicians, just as they have in the training of military technicians. It is emphasized again that the use of simulators is frequently what makes the difference between a really competent technician, and one who has acquired only "book-knowledge" or "theory." The practice of essential motor skills, of procedures, of decisions that put "knowledge" into practical action can be most effectively carried out in a situation which represents the real situation, that is, in a simulator. Of course, when the operational situation is relatively simple and little danger is involved, dependence can still be placed on "on-the-job" training. But as industrial operations become more complex and perhaps more dangerous (as with the introduction of radiation hazards), it is to be hoped that simulators will be used increasingly for training in the consolidation and application of technical skills.

## Performance Assessment

A similarly cogent argument can be made for the use of simulators in the assessment of technical skills. Should a "trained" technician be accepted as competent because he has passed a written test, or because he has demonstrated an acceptable performance of his job in a simulator which represents the real situation? The possibilities of usage of simulators for this purpose of performance measurement are as great in civilian occupations as they are in military ones.

Consider, for example, the complex performance of automobile driving. There would seem to be considerable room for doubt that present methods of assessing driving competence are adequate. Usually the assessment is based partly on a written test of knowledge about laws and procedures, and partly on a performance test which samples only the basic maneuvers for driving. A properly designed simulator, however, would represent the variety of situations likely to be met in driving a car in traffic and along the highway, and would require the making of typical decisions in these situations. If used in this way, it is to be expected that a more comprehensive assessment of driving skill could be obtained than is the case with present methods. Similar cases could be made out for the use of simulators for measuring proficiency in a number of other technical performances.

## System Analysis and the Development of Operating Procedures

The use of simulators for the analysis of "system operations" is a possibility which has fired the imagination of a number of individuals and organizations. For civilian education, one thinks of the potential applicability of simulation techniques to various kinds of professional activities, such as those involved in banking, marketing, the management of industrial operations, and the conduct of business generally. Again, it should be emphasized that such usage is consistent with the idea of employing simulators in connection with the consolidation and application of skills rather than with their initial acquisition. Colleges, insofar as their purposes pertain to the teaching of fundamental knowledge, cannot use simulators to any great advantage. Professional schools, which are concerned with teaching professional skills and decision making, may well find simulators of great usefulness for the analyses of professional activities and the development of effective operational doctrine.

The basic idea of simulation as a part of professional education is not entirely new. The mock court, for example, has been used for many years in law schools to provide practice in the procedures and decisions made by the lawyer in a real court. But the idea of employing simulation for purposes of "system analysis" and the consequent development of operational doctrine is comparatively recent in origin. It is conceivable that simulation of an economic environment in a business game can lead not only to practice of skills by individual businessmen (Mc-

Donald & Ricciardi, 1958; see Chapter 14 by Carter), but also to an analysis of what effective business operations are really like. A "business system" may, for example, be studied in terms of how its members interact with each other and the effects such interactions have upon the economy, or upon the individual firms which make up the economy. Or, such a system may be analyzed in terms of the operations that are effective in preventing depressions, over-production, or other business crises. Analyses of this sort can lead to the development of sound operational doctrine which could then become a part of professional education for business.

It is not a great leap to speculate about the use of simulators for system analysis in other kinds of professional schools, and in other types of professional activities. For example, why would it not be of value to use "conference simulators" to analyze and identify operational doctrine for holding conferences? Similar questions could be asked about industrial production, or staff meetings, or distribution systems, or the settlement of labor disputes. Obviously, one is moving here into the area of a methodology for the social sciences. Perhaps our society will be able to solve some of its pressing problems and make social advances of continuing significance if men can learn to use simulation techniques for the analysis of such truly complex social situations. And as a single example of particular relevance to education, the simulated classroom which permits such analysis of effective procedures (as contrasted with simple "practice teaching") should not be overlooked.

## REFERENCES

Briggs, L. J. *A troubleshooting trainer for the E-4 Fire Control System.* Air Force Personnel and Training Research Center, July 1956. Development Report AFPTRC-TN-56-94.

Briggs, L. J. & DuVall, W. E. *Design of two fire control systems maintenance training devices.* Air Force Personnel and Training Research Center, September 1957. Technical Report AFPTRC-TR-57-7.

Brown, C. W. & Ghiselli, E. E. *An evaluation of the effectiveness of utilization of the A-6 Ground Trainer.* USAF, Human Resources Research Center, 1951. Res. Bull. 51-14.

Chapman, P. L. & Kennedy, J. L. The background and implications of the Systems Research Laboratory Studies. In G. French & F. Cameron (Eds.), *Symposium on Air Force human engineering, personnel, and training re-*

*search.* Washington, D. C.: National Academy of Sciences—National Research Council, 1956. (Publication 455)

Chapman, R. L., Kennedy, J. L., Newell, A., & Biel, W. C. The System Research Laboratory's air defense experiments. *Mgmt. Sci.*, 1959, *5*, 250-269.

Danneskiold, R. D. *Objective scoring procedure for operational flight trainer performance.* USN, Special Devices Center, February 1955. Technical Report 999-2-4.

Demaree, R. G. Performance testing of electronics maintenance personnel. In *Symposium on Electronics Maintenance.* Washington, D. C.: Advisory Board on Personnel and Training Research, Office of the Assistant Secretary of Defense, Research and Development, August 1955.

Dinsmore, R. A. & DuBois, P. H. *A preliminary study of learning in the B-50D Flight Simulator.* USAF, Human Resources Research Laboratories, September 1953. Memo. Report D-15.

Dorny, L. R., Campbell, J. W., & Channel, R. C. *Study of helicopter flight and tactics training.* U. S. Navy Special Devices Center, August 1953. Technical Report 971-0-1.

Flexman, R. E., Townsend, J. C., & Ornstein, G. M. *Evaluation of a contact flight simulator when used in an Air Force primary pilot training program: Part 1. Over-all effectiveness.* USAF, Air Force Personnel and Training Research Center, September 1954. Technical Report 54-38.

French, R. S. Evaluation of a K-System trouble-shooting trainer. In G. Finch and F. Cameron (Eds.), *Symposium on Air Force human engineering, personnel and training research.* Washington, D. C.: National Academy of Sciences—National Research Council, 1956. (Publication 455)

Gagné, R. M. Training devices and simulators: Some research issues. *Amer. Psychologist,* 1954, *9*, 95-107.

Gagné, R. M. & Bolles, R. C. A review of factors in learning efficiency. In E. Galanter (Ed.), *Automatic teaching: The state of the art.* New York: Wiley, 1959.

Gagné, R. M. & Foster, Harriet. Transfer to a motor skill from practice on a pictured representation. *J. exp. Psychol.,* 1949, *39*, 342-355.

Goldstein, M. & Ellis, D. S. *Pedestal sight gunnery skills: A review of research.* Air Force Personnel and Training Research Center, February 1956. Research Report AFPTRC-TN-56-31.

Goldstein, M., Rittenhouse, C. H., & Woods, J. P. *Studies of performance on the E-26 Flexible Gunnery Trainer.* Air Force Personnel and Training Research Center, May 1952. Research Bulletin 52-17.

Handbook Staff, Tufts College, Institute for Applied Experimental Psychology. *Handbook of human engineering data for design engineers.* U. S. Navy Special Devices Center, December 1949. Technical Report SDC 199-1-1.

Holt, D. *An investigation of the proficiency of ground controlled approach final controllers.* USAF, Human Resources Research Laboratories, Report 2, April 1949.

Horrocks, J. E., Krug, R. G., & Bowlus, D. R. *Training for anti-aircraft artillery gunnery.* U. S. Navy Special Devices Center, August 1952. Technical Report 495-01-1.

Human Factors Operations Research Laboratories, *Flight simulator utilization handbook.* Washington, D. C.: Human Factors Operations Research Laboratories, August 1953. HFORL Report No. 42.

Kopstein, F. F. & Morgan, R. L. *Human factors considerations in the design proposals for a ballistic missile unit proficiency system.* Wright Air Development Center, December 1957. WADC Technical Note 57-352.

Mahler, W. R. & Bennett, G. K. *Psychological studies of advanced naval air training: Evaluation of operational flight trainers.* U. S. Navy, Special Devices Center, September 1950. Technical Report 99-1-1.

Matheny, B. J. *Two simulators for training pilots and controllers in air traffic control procedures.* U. S. Navy, Special Devices Center, June 1955. Technical Report 71-16-15.

McClelland, W. A., Abbott, P. S., & Stobie, W. H. *Teaching radar scope interpretation with motion pictures: 1. Radar navigation.* USAF, Air Force Personnel and Training Research Center, July 1954. Technical Report 54-25.

McDonald, J. & Ricciardi, F. The business decision game. *Fortune,* 1958, 57, 140-143.

Miller, R. B. *Handbook on training and training equipment design.* Wright Air Development Center, June 1953. Technical Report 53-136.

Muckler, F. A., Nygaard, J. E., O'Kelly, L. I., & Williams, A. C., Jr. *Psychological variables in the design of flight simulators for training.* Wright Air Development Center, January 1956. Technical Report 56-369.

Payne, T. A., Dougherty, D. J., Hasler, S. J., Skeen, J. R., Brown, E. L., & Williams, A. C., Jr. *Improving landing performance using a contact landing trainer.* U. S. Navy, Special Devices Center, March 1954. Technical Report 71-16-11.

Peterson, R. O. & Jones, E. M. *Human factors support in the design and use of the Redstone Fire Unit Proficiency Analyser.* U. S. Navy Training Devices Center, March 1958. Technical Report 69-2.

Rhoades, R. S. *Effectiveness of ejection seat training with special reference to SDC Device No. 6EQ-2.* U. S. Navy Special Devices Center, November 1950. Technical Report 383-5-1.

Rulon, P. J., Langmuir, C. R., Schweiker, R. F., Demaree, R. G., Crowder, N. A., & Lawrey, W. L. *Proficiency of Q-24 radar mechanics: II. The Performance Trouble-Shooting Test.* Air Force Personnel and Training Research Center, November 1954. Research Bulletin AFPTRC-TR-54-51.

Smode, A. F., Beam, J. C., & Dunlap, J. W. *Motor habit interference: A resume of the literature and the development of principles for its minimization in training.* Stamford, Connecticut: Dunlap and Associates, prepared for ONR, January 1959.

Townsend, J. C. & Bamford, H. E. *Evaluation of attitude instrument flying proficiency based on performance in a flight simulator.* Air Force Personnel and Training Research Center, Project 400K-7710, September 1954.

Voiers, W. D. *A comparison of the components of simulated radar bombing error in terms of reliability and sensitivity of practice.* Air Force Personnel and Training Research Center, December 1954. Technical Report 54-74.

Wolfle, D. *The use and design of synthetic trainers for military training.* Office of Scientific Research and Development, July 1945. Report 5246.

Woolman, M. *Some effects of synthetic trainers in a B-47 training program.* U. S. Air Force Air Training Command, February 1955. MCAFB-TA&D, 54-18.

Chapter 9

# Experimental Research on Instructional Devices and Materials[1]

A. A. Lumsdaine, University of California,
Los Angeles[2]

This chapter deals primarily with instructional materials and devices as objects of experimental research that is designed to improve the prediction and control of their effects in attaining specific instructional outcomes. It does not deal, except incidentally, with attempts to provide expert judgments or prescriptive guidelines for the design or use of instructional media solely on the basis of educated guesses or rational analyses by educators or psychologists. Thus, for example, it does not treat such compendia of principles or procedures as those illustrated in the series of handbooks and guides provided by R. B. Miller (1953; 1954; 1956) nor such attempts at practical guidance for training-device design as have been put forth elsewhere by the writer (Lumsdaine, 1960a; Lumsdaine, 1960b). The omitting of these prescriptive efforts from primary consideration here is in no way meant to deprecate the useful service that they can provide. Rather, the omission reflects an orientation which places emphasis here on research con-

[1]This chapter is based on literature available up to the beginning of 1961. A more detailed treatment of some of the experimental methods and results discussed in the present chapter will be included in the *Handbook of Research in Teaching*, edited by N. L. Gage under sponsorship of the American Educational Research Association (1962, in press). Part of the preparation of this paper was accomplished in conjunction with research projects sponsored at the University of California, Los Angeles, by the U. S. Office of Education, Educational Media Branch, and at the American Institute for Research by the Air Force Office of Scientific Research, the Office of Naval Research, and the Educational Media Branch of the U. S. Office of Education.

[2]The author also serves as Research Advisor for Educational Media to the American Institute for Research.

sidered as empirical inquiry that obtains new behavioral data in order to contribute to a technology of instruction grounded in experimental findings.

The present chapter also will not describe the development or evaluation of "experimental" prototype training devices in which psychologists working in applied research and development programs have tried to exemplify principles of effective training (e.g., Briggs, 1956; Briggs, 1958; French, 1956a; French, 1956b) except insofar as they are primarily related to experiments on specific characteristics of devices or materials. Descriptions of a number of training devices of this type have been provided elsewhere (e.g., Lumsdaine, 1960a; Lumsdaine, 1960b; Lumsdaine, 1960c).

## INSTRUCTIONAL DEVICES AND MATERIALS

### Some Definitions and Distinctions

The word "instructional" embraces many of the functions of what may be connoted by the terms "training" and "education." "Instruction" will refer to any specifiable means of controlling or manipulating a sequence of events to produce measurable modifications of student behavior through learning. Instructional devices and materials, or "instructional media," refer to a class of instructional resources (e.g., films), or to a group or subset of such a class. An instructional "instrument" generally refers to a particular member of this class or a particular instance—e.g., a particular film.

*Instructional Media.* The "audio-visual" media of instruction comprise a very important and widely used class of such instructional resources. Other tools of learning include various instruments used primarily to permit the student to make relevant responses (e.g., workbooks, self-scoring test forms, and other manipulanda) which can aid in the learning process. Teaching machines or "auto-instructional" devices are an important special class, partly overlapping with audio-visual instruments, which not only serve an information-presenting function but also afford a means for the student to make relevant responses in relation to the material presented. They have the further characteristic that they imply an individually-determined rate of presentation and response, while providing conditions under which the student proceeds with learning, for an appreciable period of time at least, without the active intervention of a teacher. Some of the other forms of visual and audio-visual "aids," by contrast, are tools placed in the hands of the teacher for use as adjuncts to other teacher activities, rather than being expected to provide instruction in themselves.

*Reproducible Instructional Sequences.* The instructional media considered in this chapter generally present to students some form of sequenced presentation, regulated by the inherent structure of the instructional instruments, by well-defined procedures and constraints in the way they are used, or by the characteristics of the mechanical arrangements which are used to present them. They thus tend to generate *reproducible* instructional events, which occur rather predictably in terms of sequence and/or pacing. The materials dealt with include motion picture films, tape recordings, sound film strips, and auto-instructional programs for presentation by a teaching machine or some related device. For the present purpose, they do not for the most part include, as such, charts, diagrams, models, nor isolated photographs or drawings, except when these represent elements in a predictable pattern of instruction which is governed by the constraints of a well-defined procedural sequence. Most of the studies thus excluded represent merely demonstrational tests of specific devices showing that some form of their use did or did not contribute to training, and provide little in the way of potentially generalizable findings.

## CHARACTERISTICS OF EXPERIMENTAL RESEARCH ON INSTRUCTIONAL MEDIA

### Major Types of Experimental Research

Within the field of experimental research aimed at determining the effects of instructional instruments or media, two broad classes have been characterized by Hovland, Lumsdaine, and Sheffield (1949)— "evaluative" experiments, and scientific experiments involving controlled manipulation of specific factors. Both of these two classes of experiments are concerned with the measurement of the effects of instructional media, and they share many of the same requirements for valid experimental design. However, the two classes differ fundamentally in terms of purpose. The latter seeks to test hypotheses for the sake of building a usable science of instructional effects, that is, it seeks to develop a tested body of propositions or theory. These can be used as a later basis for predicting the effects of subsequent instructional instruments, or for making decisions among alternative methods of presentation in designing subsequent instruments. For reasons indicated below, the present chapter is concerned almost entirely with experiments of this type. By contrast, the results of evaluative experiments which merely assess the effects of a particular existing instrument, or compare its effects with those of "conventional instruction," apply only to that particular instrument and thus have only a specific, immediate utility rather than leading to conclusions of general significance.

*Controlled Variation of Specific Factors.* Experiments that can contribute to a usable science of instructional media must seek to reveal the influence of specific factors in the design or use of the media, rather than being confined to overall assessment. These factors should define reproducible characteristics of the instructional stimulus and response features that can potentially be implemented in future instructional materials and devices. In this way experimental data are obtained which can lead to generalizations on which to base future design decisions more wisely. The precision and applicability of experimental findings are likely to be augmented to the extent that the specific factors chosen for manipulation are defined in terms of theoretically oriented variables, and not solely in terms of gross physically descriptive characteristics of instructional media. As pointed out by Hovland, Lumsdaine and Sheffield (1949, p. 8), definition in terms of theoretical variables seems likely to afford a potentially better base for determining the dimension along which the results may be generalizable, and is also likely to identify variables which have a consistently potent influence on the outcomes of instruction.

Emphasis on manipulation of single, defined factors in experimentation is not meant to minimize the importance of interactions or cumulative effects of several variables acting in concert. But such interaction effects can be established only through analytic experiments on which each specific factor is independently co-varied, not through overall comparisons of an aggregate of factors.

*Evaluative Experiments.* Experiments with a technological purpose, on the other hand, have the more immediate practical objective of seeking to assess or improve the particular instrument which is the object of experimental study. The experimental question posed here is: What does a particular instrument (e.g., film) teach? The answer may be sought either through formal, quantitative experiments designed to reveal statistically significant effects of an instrument on the learning of a group of individuals, or may consist of small-scale, informal, exploratory experimentation carried out with a few subjects as a basis for obtaining suggestions concerning desirable revisions in the content or mode of presentation of a particular instructional instrument.

*Limited Generality of Evaluative Data.* Experimental measurement of the effects of a single instrument apply only to that particular instrument, and generalizations of the results of such an evaluative experiment to other instruments of the media it represents have, at most, the status of untested hypotheses. Similar limitations apply when a comparison is made between the attainments effected by a particular instrument and those obtained by some alternative form of instruction often characterized as "conventional" or "currently used" instruction. The restrictions on interpretation of such a comparison arise from the lack of specificity of the instruction with which the instrument in question is compared. Similar restrictions apply in general to the overall comparison of alternative "media."

Many studies of these types have been conducted and reported. Military and civilian studies documenting that films can teach various subjects were reviewed at length by Hoban and van Ormer (1950), in addition to analytic studies of specific factors. These writers also summarized numerous studies presenting evidence that a particular film was shown or failed to be shown superior to some alternative instruction. More recently, Allen (1960) has similarly provided extensive citations of similar results not only for films, but also for the results of numerous instances of the use of instructional television and other forms of audio-visual presentation. Because of their limited generalizability, no attempt will be made here to cite most of the purely evaluative studies of films, television, or other media.

*Diagnostic Evaluation.* Aside from overall assessment in terms of some total score, an important class of evaluative experiments includes those which are conducted for what may be called "diagnostic" purposes, in which specific effects of the instrument on *a number of specific points* related to its objectives are separately measured. Here one pays attention not primarily to a total score but to the amount of information learned on each specific test question or point. The most important use of such diagnostic evaluative experiments is when they are carried out on a preliminary version of an instrument. The results can then be used in modifying or redesigning the instrument so as to correct or strengthen its weak points. Such evaluative studies should ideally be carried out early in the stage of production and repeated after each major stage of revision so that, by successive correction and re-evaluation, achievement of the desired instructional goals can be more and more closely approximated.

## Research and Development on Various Media

*Instructional Films and Related Media.* To date, the most extensive experimental research on the effects of instructional media has been conducted with instructional films. Sound films are particularly amenable to research in that they present a sequenced, paced presentation package, complete with visual material and accompanying dialogue or narration. Experimental research on silent and sound films spans a period of over four decades, from around 1918 to the present time. Most of the earlier studies were directed toward evaluation of the effects of particular films as indicative of the educational capabilities of motion pictures; analytic experiments on specific factors did not start to appear in any volume until the period beginning with the studies conducted in the Information and Education Branch of the War Department and subsequently reported by Hovland, Lumsdaine and Sheffield (1949). Another sizable program of research was conducted at Yale University from 1946 to 1949 and was subsequently reported by May and Lumsdaine (1958). The most extensive single program of experimentation on instructional films to date was conducted under sponsorship of the Office of Naval Research at Pennsylvania State University, under the direction of C. R. Carpenter, over an eight-year period from 1947 to 1955. A fourth major program of research was conducted through an in-service and contract program of the U. S. Air Force under the direction of A. A. Lumsdaine from 1950 to 1953. This program was continued, less intensively, in the context of research on other forms of training aids and devices, from 1954 to 1957. Many of the experimental studies discussed in this chapter derive from these four programs of research.

*Television.* Although a considerable number of experimental evaluation studies of closed- and open-circuit television programs have appeared, few analytic experiments on specific factors in instructional presentation by TV have been reported. Several such studies are in progress currently under projects supported by the U. S. Office of Education under Title VII of the National Defense Education Act, but, as of the time of writing, little has been published on results of such studies. One of the few reports to appear thus far (Gropper & Lumsdaine, 1960) reports experiments which employ methods of eliciting active student response during TV instruction as a way to increase the effectiveness of instruction.

Differences between films produced by direct filming, as compared with kinescope or video-tape recordings from a televised instructional presentation, lie more in the philosophy and practice of production than in any inherent differences characteristic of the media. Aside from minor differences in grain or resolution, the televised lesson, kinescope recording, or video-tape recording differs primarily from the sound motion picture, at the present time, in terms of screen size and the potentiality for using color. In many instances only an expert can detect the difference between prefilmed or live television presentations and monochrome films photographed directly. The instructional properties of film and of recorded television presentations are considered here to be substantially identical, both consisting, in fact, of a series of moving or sequenced pictures accompanied by recorded sound. Certainly, research on factors that make for effective presentation of the audio-visually presented information on a film should, in most particulars, be applicable to similar presentation via a TV screen.

*Auto-Instructional Media.* The development of teaching machines and programs for individual self instruction requiring the active, individual participation of the student has proceeded at a very rapid rate during the past few years. Basically, teaching machines present sequences of programmed instruction to the individual student, requiring frequent overt responses and providing him with prompt feedback in the form of correction or confirmation for each response that he makes. The literature describing development activities and a certain amount of research on auto-instructional techniques extends back to the mid-twenties following the development of Pressey's first teaching machine around 1924. The relatively small stream of papers stemming from Pressey's initial work (1926; 1927) which appeared in the next 25 or 30 years has expanded enormously following Skinner's basic paper (1954). Virtually all of this literature up to mid-1960 is either reproduced in full or abstracted in the recent book of readings edited by Lumsdaine and Glaser (1960). The rather complete control of learner behavior, and the feedback to the programmer provided by the continuous record of student response yielded by auto-instructional programs, should afford the most promising vehicle yet developed for the analytic experimental study of variables affecting human learning and for the incorporation of research findings into improved instruments for practical instruction. However, relatively few analytic experiments in the context of self-instructional learning programs have as yet been published. Those that have been are summarized here along with experiments in the context of research on other media that throw light on similar problems in the sequencing and content of instructional materials and their relation to student response during learning.

*Descriptive Categories for Research on Instructional Media.* Reviews of research on instructional materials have commonly been organized in terms of media categories—films, filmstrips, recordings and the like. This organization is less well calculated to reveal meaningful communalities than an organization in terms of the stimulus features and response provisions of instructional sequences, regardless of the mechanics of how a given sequence of verbally and visually presented information happens to be physically mediated. Accordingly, rather than using such categorizations as film research, television research, research on self-instructional devices, and similar rubrics as primary categories, this chapter will in general deal with stimulus and response features of instructional sequences, regardless of which "media" were employed in the experiments.

## STUDENT RESPONSE AS A FACTOR IN INSTRUCTION

*Provision for Fostering Explicit Student Response*

Experimental studies of the role of active student response, recitation, "participation" exercises and the like derive in part from early studies by Witasek (1907) and Gates (1917). The advantage of active recitation over mere reading found by both investigators forms a point of departure for a number of subsequent studies in which the role of active response by the student has been studied, and represents one of the historical antecedents for current concern with self-instructional media that stress active student response.

*The Effectiveness of Overt-Response Procedures.* The potential advantages of using active-response procedures in employing instructional media has been studied in a number of experiments performed in the context of military training research. The earliest and most widely cited of these experiments was performed during World War II and was reported by Hovland, Lumsdaine and Sheffield (1949). A film was used to teach the military phonetic alphabet, Able for A, Baker for B, and so forth. Two forms of the film were compared in order to study the effect of using active review, or so-called "audience participation." The difference between the two forms was solely in the review sequences which followed the initial presentation of the letter-word equivalents. The control film used a standard, "passive" form of review, in which letters were presented along with their phonetic equivalents. In the active review, the letters only were presented, and the audience members were instructed to try to call out the correct equivalents for each letter in turn. The fact that the correct equivalents had been recently presented provided the basis for their being emitted during the review. Feedback via further "prompts," confirmation, and/ or correction were provided by the fact that the whole group had to call out each response aloud. Results of the experiment showed consistent superiority of the active over the passive group at various criteria of recall-promptness in oral tests given at the end of the training. This superiority was verified in later replication of the experiment, circa 1949. (See Lumsdaine & Gladstone, 1958.) Further analysis of the Hovland, Lumsdaine and Sheffield data showed the interesting result that the difference in favor of the active-response and feedback procedure appeared to be least when least needed and most when most needed—that is, mean differences were greatest for less motivated, slower students in learning the more difficult portions of the material, and least for brighter, highly motivated students in learning the easier portions of the material.

A number of additional experiments on the role of active student response in film instruction have been done in the past decade which extend our knowledge of factors important in the use of frequent active-recitation or practice sequences. Some of these studies have been reviewed by Allen (1957; 1960) and by Cook (1960), though full reports of many of them have not been available outside of government reports with limited circulation. Basic reports on a number of hitherto unpublished studies will be found in a volume edited by Lumsdaine (1961). The usefulness of procedures to provide for active student response has been shown in the case of televised instruction in recent studies by Gropper and Lumsdaine (1960). A 25-minute television lesson in junior high school science was prepared by a qualified science teacher in accordance with a detailed statement of lesson objectives. The same set of lesson objectives was used as the basis for an experimental television presentation covering substantially the same material. This presentation differed from the standard or control lesson in that it provided numerous occasions for students to make active, explicit responses as the lesson proceeded; also, the sequencing of the lesson was organized to maximize the likelihood that correct response could be made at each point. The experimental lesson was shown to be significantly more effective.

*Time as a Variable.* One of the aspects of the above-cited experiments that is deserving of comment is the expenditure of instructional time. There are two kinds of questions which can be asked about the contribution of a specific factor to learning: first, does it help, and second, is it a more effective way to spend instructional time than some alternative way of using the time? The latter generally involves either showing that a given criterion can be attained in less time by one means than by some alternative means, or that the first means produces a higher level of achievement in a constant period of time than does the alternative. In the experiments by Hovland, Lumsdaine and Sheffield, and by Gropper and Lumsdaine, time was controlled in the latter fashion, since both active and passive review procedures took the same amount of time. Time allocation for active-response procedures in other experiments has not always been similarly controlled. For example, in a 1946 experiment at Yale University (Lumsdaine, May, & Hadsell, 1958), the use of pupil-participation questions, with the correct answer given after pupils had responded, added significantly to the amount of substantive information learned from a film on the heart and circulation of the blood. These questions were added to the basic film rather than replacing sections of it, and added some four and one-half minutes to the film-showing time. However, it was noted that showing the film *twice*, which took about 17 minutes, did not yield appreciably higher scores than the single showing with active-response exercises, which took less time (13 minutes). A similar situation with respect to time is encountered in a later experiment by Michael and Maccoby (1953; 1961); substantial gains were obtained from addition of student participation questions which, however, added about three minutes to the basic instructional time of about 14 minutes for the subject matter (defense against atomic attack). The primary purpose of the Michael and Maccoby experiment and of several other later experiments was, however, not primarily to show that active student response is effective but, as described below, to investigate more specific factors which, with a fixed amount of time for recitation activity, bear on its effectiveness.

Some recent small-scale experiments in a different context, in which the time factor also enters, are reported by Evans, Glaser and Homme (1959). In these experiments, conventional textbooks were compared with "programmed" texts that sequenced the material in small steps and required active student response at each step. Here an awkward question for interpretation is again posed by the fact that the somewhat higher mean scores achieved with the programmed materials resulted from an increased amount of time spent in study.

A few experiments have been conducted in which students were required to attempt to carry out active-practice exercises *during* the showing of a filmed demonstration. Roshal (1949) used this procedure for some of his experimental subjects while they viewed a film on how to tie knots, used in an experiment of which other aspects are described in more detail subsequently. The practice procedure did not show a significant increase in proficiency as compared with groups that did not practice actively during the film. The lack of effectiveness in this case was attributed by Roshal to insufficient time for effective practice, with the further deleterious influence that students' attention was divided between trying to watch the demonstration and trying to practice tying the knot. Results of a later experiment by Jaspen (1950) lend some support to this explanation. In Jaspen's experiment, using procedural films to teach the assembly of the breech-block of an anti-aircraft gun, it was concluded that provision for active practice by the students during the film was effective with a slow-paced version of the film but not with a faster-paced film.

*Direct Practice Effects vs. Side Effects of Active-Response Procedures.* One of the objectives of the above-cited experiment by Michael and Maccoby was to assess the direct effects of practice vs. possible motivational effects that would show up in better attention and hence better learning on material not specifically practiced. Indirect evidence from the original experiment by Hovland, Lumsdaine and Sheffield suggested that both kinds of effects would operate, in that the superiority of active over passive review groups was less when added external motivation was provided (by announcing that a test would be given after the lesson) than when the test was not announced. Michael and Maccoby gave practice through use of active-response questions on only *half* of the material covered in the film. They found marked gains on the material practiced, but no appreciable gains on the other half of the material. This pointed to practice as the key factor. The effect was believed by the investigators not to be limited to wholly "rote" learning, however, since in a second experiment (Maccoby, Michael, & Levine, 1961) the practice effects held even though test-question wording differed considerably from that of the practice questions. A later replication of the first experiment (Levine, 1953; Maccoby, Michael, & Levine, 1961) used less interesting subject matter and found gains both on practiced and nonpracticed material for groups that did not have the extraneous incentive of being told they would be tested. However, the latter gains, attributed to motivational or incentive effects, were smaller than the direct practice effects.

## Some Factors Influencing the Effects of Student Response

*Form of Response.* Two recent experiments have compared constructed and multiple-choice responding. The first of these was reported by Coulson and Silberman (1959), who also introduced a form of experimental variation in the number of steps included in a program (described by Holland, 1959; 1960) and in the use of branching to vary program content depending on the subject's performance. Constructed-response frames in the teaching program required the subject to fill in blanks in the sentences presented by each frame. For multiple-choice responding, the subject chose one out of the two to five alternatives supplied for each blank. In either case, the correct answer to each item was revealed to the subject after he had responded. Multiple-choice responding took significantly less time (44 minutes on the average) than constructed response (54 minutes). No significant overall differences were obtained using either multiple-choice or constructed-response criterion tests. However, with a criterion test requiring constructed responses, test scores for the constructed-response programs were superior under the non-branching condition.

In a second experiment on response mode, reported by Fry (1960), paired-associate materials (16 English-to-Spanish words and phrases) were used rather than continuous-discourse materials. There were three conditions, differing in the way time was controlled, and two criterion tests. Scores on multiple-choice criterion tests (either immediate or delayed) approached perfect for all groups and hence showed no significant differences. The results with constructed-answer criterion tests showed the following significant results for both immediate and delayed tests: (*a*) under the first condition, working to a criterion of two correct responses at their own rate, students using constructed responses in training did better on the test than those using multiple-choice responses, but took considerably more time (14 minutes versus 8 minutes) to finish the program. These results have the same ambiguity as those of Coulson and Silberman. However (*b*), when time was controlled by letting students work at their own rate but giving them equal working time (Condition 2), or by arbitrarily keeping time per frame constant

(Condition 3), use of constructed answers in training also produced significantly better results than multiple-choice responding.

*Overt and Covert Responding.* In ordinary reading, listening to a lecture or watching a film, responses are implicit rather than being explicitly evoked by specific questions or gaps which the student is expressly directed to fill in. Explicit responding on cue need not, however, be overt (e.g., written or oral) but can be performed covertly or mentally. The term "covert response" is used here to designate response acts which, unlike the implicit responding to a text or lecture, are *deliberately made* as explicit answers to a question or other express invitation for response, but which are not performed overtly. Such responses may serve as effective symbolic practice, but afford a less clear basis for differential feedback from an instructional program than can be occasioned by overt responses.

A second factor studied by Michael and Maccoby (1953; 1961) was to compare overt versus covert responding to the same set of questions. Time allowed for these two kinds of responses did not differ. They obtained no reliable difference between the effects of the two kinds of responses, even though the experimental conditions were sufficiently sensitive to detect fairly small differential effects. This finding was also replicated in some later studies by these investigators.

Cook and Spitzer (1960) have also found for some instructional situations that "covert" or "mental" responses were apparently about as effective as overt responses. Goldbeck (1960) also concluded that merely reading brief passages in which key words were underlined was not significantly less effective than having students make the active, explicit response of filling in blanks mentally or in writing. However, a recent study by Holland (1960) suggests that whether or not an effective contribution for overt responding is found may depend on the relevance of the responses and how well they are cued. A small-scale experiment reported by Evans, Glaser and Homme (1959) compared overt and covert responding to a self-instructional program in music fundamentals. No significant difference in later test scores was found (though any differences would have had to be quite gross to be detected as reliable with the small $N$'s used). In this experiment time was not controlled, and one of the results cited (though it was also reported as not significant statistically) was that the covert-response group took less time to finish the program. This not only again raises the question of time control from a formal control standpoint, but suggests the importance of deciding under what circumstances more learning in more time, if obtained, is to be regarded as preferable to faster but less complete learning.

In a further experiment by Evans (1960), programs were designed to teach the construction of short deductive proofs involving rules similar to those used in symbolic logic. Several experimental versions of this two- to three-hour program were developed in order to investigate several programming variables, including overt (written) versus covert (mental) responding. Experimental variations in mode of responding significantly affected learning time; subjects not required to make an overt response to each item completed the learning program in about 65 per cent of the time required for composed or multiple-choice responding. Criterion performance in terms of error scores was not significantly affected by differences between overt and covert responding. However, subjects who did not respond overtly to learning programs took significantly more time on performance tests which immediately followed the program than did subjects who made their responses overtly. These differences, however, disappeared in a retention test after one week.

One of the most interesting of several other experiments which have studied covert response was performed by McGuire (1955b; 1961a), who used two rates of presentation. Subjects were given six practice trials in naming mechanical parts that were displayed and named in six presentation trials. The latter lasted two seconds per trial for each part in the fast condition, and four seconds each in the slow condition. Time for the *practice* trials was constant for all subjects. Overt-responding subjects wrote the names of the parts; covert-responding subjects merely named them mentally. The interesting finding was that, despite the lack of any significant difference for the two forms of responding at the slower rate, *covert* responding was significantly better at the faster rate. One interpretation of these results is that if instruction has not adequately prepared the learner to respond correctly, forced overt responding may lead to distracting anxiety, to the practicing of errors, or both.

*Feedback, Reinforcement and Knowledge of Results.* Despite the voluminous literature on the effects of reinforcement and variations in its scheduling on learning by infra-human species, relatively few experiments have studied reinforcement factors systematically as they operate in practical instruction. Where this has been done, the role of reinforcement in the sense of a variable presumed to strengthen directly the effects of immediately preceding practice (in a Skinnerian, Hullian or Thorndikean sense) has seldom been disentangled from other functions of response feedback to the learner. Among these other functions are indirect or cognitively mediated consequences of "knowledge of results."

In the previously cited experiment reported by Michael and Maccoby (1953; 1961), half of the groups who were required to give active, explicit responses—overt or covert—were, after a slight pause allowed for responding, told the correct answer to the question to which they had just been asked to respond. This information was termed "feedback" or "KCR" (knowledge of the correct response). The other half of the actively responding groups were not given KCR. Instructional time, item-by-item and overall, was identical for the two sets of groups. The results showed slight though significant gains for the active-response procedure without KCR but more marked gains (as expected) when KCR was provided.

The results thus contributed toward isolation of several components involved in earlier experiments in which similar feedback was invariably confounded with active response. However, the precise function or functions of the KCR procedure still were not fully clarified since, as the authors (Michael & Maccoby, 1953) point out, the procedure not only had potentially reinforcing properties (confirmation of initially correct responses) but also provided an opportunity for correction of errors and, in effect, *for an additional implicit-practice trial* in which covert practice of the correct response doubtless occurred. This ambiguity is also present in current use of a correct-answer panel, revealed after the student's response to each frame, in teaching machine programs where the student serves as his own comparator.

Some suggestive evidence on the importance of the latter mechanism is found in the results of Hirsch (1952), who compared several forms of "knowledge of results" to questions posed to students as a participation procedure used with films. Hirsch concluded that there was less effect when students were simply told right or wrong than when the correct answer was also presented. The best results were found when this correct answer was presented in the context of repeating the question—a condition which would be most conducive to the "added practice trial" function, and which stresses information-feedback rather than only the reinforcement-reward aspect of a KCR procedure. The results were far from clear cut, however, due to the small size of the gains and large amount of variability.

A perhaps clearer comparison of the effects of different kinds of feedback that were provided by Hirsch's experiment is provided in a study reported by Irion and Briggs (1957). They used a 20-alternative multiple-choice teaching machine called the "Subject Matter Trainer" for both paired-associate and serial learning, and employed various modes of training for each task for a fixed period of 20 minutes per task. They allowed several repetitions of the material, depending on each student's rate of working. In both tasks, giving complete knowledge of results (showing the correct answer after each attempt) was significantly better than partial knowledge of results (a mere right-wrong indication).

## GUIDANCE OR CUEING OF OVERT AND IMPLICIT RESPONSES

### *The Use of Prompting to Foster Correct Responding*

A basic principle underlying the design of most teaching machine programs, as well as other instruction that employs a fixed-sequence program, is that of building up mastery through small, easy steps, so that the learner is kept performing correctly from the very outset of training. Techniques by which this can be done in the learning of verbal material have been elaborated by Skinner (1958) and other writers (cf. Lumsdaine & Glaser, 1960). Basically, they consist of giving the learner a great deal of help initially through prompting cues, which are later gradually reduced or "vanished" to free the learner from needing to depend on them. To date there is more experimental evidence on the value of prompting as such than on the value of vanishing.

*Prompting Just Prior to Overt Response.* An early experiment on the use of semantic prompts in verbal learning was that of Pan (1926), who found that semantic hints indirectly suggesting the response term facilitated paired-associate learning with arbitrarily paired terms. For less artificial tasks, one of the clearest pieces of evidence on the value of partial prompting (response guidance to control errors in practice) comes from a study by Kimble and Wulff (1953; 1961). They used a combination of film strips and workbooks to teach the reading of slide rule scales. Students were given a practice schedule that alternated short segments of audio-visual exposition and demonstration with practice exercises in workbooks in which slide rule scales were reproduced. All groups were given the same exposition and the same amount of practice. The main experimental variable was the use of various forms of prompts. For example, when asked to locate a particular scale value, the prompted group was provided with a constraint cue which limited the possible responses, though without specifying exactly the correct answer. The no-guidance group was allowed to make more errors, by withholding such prompts. (In all cases the students had already been told how to do a similar exercise.) The results showed a clear margin of superiority for the subjects in the prompted group. They did better, on a later test, not only on the items used in practice but also in transferring to other similar items. The margin of superiority was greatest where the prompts had been chosen to help the student avoid certain types of errors which preliminary work had shown were the ones most commonly made.

*Optimal Lengths of Demonstration and Practice Segments.* A study reported by Maccoby and Sheffield (1958; 1961) was designed to test concepts relating to the optimal lengths of demonstration and practice for learning sequential tasks. A filmed demonstration of the assembly of a 30-part ignition distributor was divided into four segments. Each segment had been empirically determined to be a "small step" of such difficulty that approximately 75% of subjects could correctly perform it immediately upon seeing it demonstrated. Three training procedures were used. These differed solely with length of the filmed demonstration used by the learners before practice was attempted. They were: (*a*) short segment practice, in which the learner viewed a demonstration of one step in length and then practiced this short segment before going on to the next segment; (*b*) larger segment practice, in which the units of demonstration and interpolated practice were two steps in length; and (*c*) whole practice, the demonstration of a complete task being followed by attempted practice of a complete task. Each procedure was repeated three times, and each required the same amount of demonstration time. Results were expressed in terms of mean "performance rate" (number of correct assembly responses per unit of time). They showed that use of short segments of demonstration and practice produces high performance during training, but may be accompanied by some decrement in performance in a test situation in which the whole task must be accomplished without demonstrational support.

*Other Experiments on "Size-of-Step."* Step size was varied in the Maccoby-Sheffield study in terms of the length of demonstration before each segment of practice. In this case the longer demonstrational segments provide temporally more remote, or less immediate, cueing for executing the steps of the procedure; and the instructional "steps" preceding student practice are thus larger both in length and difficulty. *Amount* of instructional material is constant. In verbal learning, the "difficulty of steps" has been varied experimentally by decreasing the *number* of steps and thus the amount of instructional material. In a study using verbal material, Evans, Glaser and Homme (1959) varied the number of steps required to get through programmed lessons on number theory and music fundamentals. Data for a small number of cases indicated that with smaller steps less time *per step* (though more total time) was required, and fewer errors occurred in the course of the learning.

Another comparison of long, numerous-step programs versus shorter programs with fewer (and thus harder) steps in connected-discourse verbal subject matter has been reported in the previously cited study by Coulson and Silberman (1959). They also varied "step size" by deleting certain steps from the program to yield fewer steps but with larger gaps separating them. Smaller and more numerous steps gave better learning scores, but these results, like those of Evans, Glaser and Homme (1959), are difficult to interpret because (*a*) the small-step program involved more practice on varied examples and (*b*) it took considerably more time.

*Prompting as Compared with "Confirmation."* Several experiments on paired-associates training have shown superiority for more complete prompting of responses as compared with non-prompting. Some of these experiments also bear on the question of reinforcement and knowledge of results. Cook and Kendler (1956) used letters as stimulus terms and nonsense drawings as the required responses in comparing training procedures which they termed "prompting" and "confirmation." Their procedure on prompting trials was to show the correct response pattern after exposing the stimulus letter but *before* the students were asked to respond to it. A comparison condition replaced the prompting trials with what the authors called "confirmation" trials. In these the subject was told to respond before being prompted by exposure of the correct response figure; then, after he had been allowed time to respond, the response pattern was exposed. The "confirmation" procedure thus provides either verification or correction of the response that the student has given. With both procedures, an unprompted and unconfirmed test trail was given by the experimenters after every three training trials. The condition using prompting trials was clearly superior both in the original experiment and in later varied replications reported by Cook (1958) and by Cook and Spitzer (1960).

Results favoring straight prompting over confirmation-correction were also found in the previously cited experiment by Irion and Briggs (1957). Several methods of feedback following the student's response in each trial were compared to a condition in which direct prompting prior to response was given on all trials. The results showed the prompting condition to be significantly superior to limited (right-wrong) feed-back following the response, for both paired-associate and serial learn-ing, and superior to all of the feedback conditions for the paired associates.

A complicating factor in the support given by these experiments to the use of maximum prompting is that the time intervals used did not preclude anticipatory responding before the prompting cue was given. This objection is somewhat weakened, however, by the results of a study by Kopstein and Roshal (1955; 1961). In the learning of paired associates (giving Russian names for common objects) they compared simultaneous presentation of S and R terms versus "staggered" pres-entation in which the response term joined the stimulus term after an interval of about two seconds. Overt responses to these presentations were not required; acquisition was measured by interspersed test trials following each third presentation of the paired terms. The results clear-ly favored the simultaneous presentation, especially during the early stages of acquisition. The interpretation in favor of immediate cueing to head off incorrect anticipatory responses is not unambiguous but is certainly suggestive.

*Partial Prompting and "Vanishing."* Skinner's principle of "vanish-ing" and contiguity learning theories such as that of Guthrie (1935) would suggest that a mixture of prompted trials (to get the correct re-sponse elicited) and unprompted trials (to give practice in the un-prompted test situation) would be the best condition for learning. This condition was in fact actually present in the prompting condition used in Cook and Kendler's 1956 experiments because of the frequent test trials. Clarification of the conclusions derived from the experimental results of Cook and collaborators is provided in an experiment by An-gell and Lumsdaine (1960). Their experiment was concerned with the use of a partial degree of prompting as compared with complete prompt-ing. The basic comparison was between two groups, one of which re-ceived the prompting *on all trials* in learning a set of paired associates, and one of which practiced responding without prompting on every fourth trial. The paired-associate learning materials used and intra-trial stimulus-response time intervals were substantially the same as those employed by Cook (1958). The results indicated that learning was more efficient under the experimental condition of incomplete prompting (prompting on three-fourths of the trials) than under condi-tions of complete prompting (prompting on every trial).

One of the few attempts to study a transition from more prompting early in training to less in later stages was made in a follow-up to the previously cited experiment by Irion and Briggs (1957). They used a prompting condition followed, for different groups, by each of several unprompted conditions. They attributed the lack of significant differences to the fact that a quite high level had already been attained by the end of the initial prompted period of practice. Further, they did not include a condition in which the prompted mode of practice was used throughout. Clear evidence on the theoretically very important question of transition or "vanishing" in verbal learning is thus not provided from this study. Somewhat clearer evidence is provided by the data for a fourth condition employed in the above cited experiment by Maccoby and Sheffield (1958; 1961). In this "transition" condition the learner practiced after each short segment of demonstration on the first trial, after longer segments on the next trial, and finally after seeing the entire demonstration as a whole. The data indicated (though not altogether conclusively) that this transition method was superior, as compared to the other three methods of alternating demonstration and practice, for maximizing transfer from training conditions to conditions of criterion performance without demonstrational support.

## Other Stimulus Factors in Learning Manual Skills

*Task Representation from the Learner's Point of View.* The importance of depicting a to-be-imitated performance so that the learner observes the task from the same aspect which he will face when he comes to perform the task is commonly held to be preferable to the situation in which the demonstrator faces the learner so that the task performance is reversed left-to-right as the learner views the demonstration. Experimental data verifying this reasonable but frequently ignored assumption were obtained in a Navy experiment performed by Roshal (1949) at Pennsylvania State University using a film on how to tie knots. Two camera angles were used, termed the "zero-degree" camera angle and the "180-degree" camera angle. With the "zero-degree" or "subjective" angle, the camera is placed in about the position from which a student would be viewing the knot if he were tying it himself. With the "180-degree" angle, the demonstration is shown from the angle from which the student would be looking if he were watching an instructor show him how to tie the knot, with the instructor facing the student. The "zero-degree" angle was found to produce reliably better results than the "180-degree" angle in terms of knot-tying proficiency gained from the films. Although the reasons for the superiority of the "zero-degree" angle have not been fully explored, it may be noted that the "zero-degree" angle tries to present to the learner exactly the same cues as those to which he will have to respond when he is actually tying the knot.

*"Perceptual Blueprinting."* In discussions of theory bearing on the learning of organizable sequences, Sheffield and collaborators describe the formation of "perceptual blueprints" as a means of providing cues for the learning of lengthy sequential tasks. (See Sheffield, 1957; Sheffield, Margolius, & Hoehn, 1961.) The essential concept was illustrated in an experimental technique called the "implosion" method, devised for use in review portions of filmed demonstrations of assembly tasks. This method consists of a display of the parts followed by a rapid succession of "stills" of each part added into its appropriate place in the assembly, so that the parts appear to "jump into place" in sequence. This technique was evaluated experimentally using a filmed demonstration of a complex assembly. It was found that the "implosion" device, which required only a very short amount of additional time, made a significant contribution in the teaching of the lengthy mechanical task. The sizable gains from using the "implosion" method seem particularly striking in view of the already highly organized nature of the demonstration that was used; an even greater effect would be anticipated with an inferior, less-organized demonstration.

*Slow-Motion Photography.* Another factor which may affect the adequacy of implicit perceptual responses for guiding later practice is the adequacy of the original perception. A special case is in the learning of motor coordination skills where the skilled act may occur too swiftly to permit the formation of a stable perceptual pattern. Here, the use of slow-motion photography would seem likely to be especially useful; however, hardly any experiments have been completed on this stimulus factor which represents one of the few really unique capabilities of motion pictures. The limited evidence on comparative effectiveness of slow-motion and normal-speed photographic depiction comes mainly from a study by McGuire (1955a; 1961b), who compared the two kinds of depiction in films used experimentally as demonstration aids to learning pursuit-rotor performance. The overall differences obtained were in the direction of favoring use of slow motion but were not large enough to be very significant statistically.

*Moving-Pictures Versus Still-Pictures for Demonstrating a Skilled Art.* The principal evidence here comes from the experiment by Roshal (1949), who compared a moving-picture demonstration of how to tie three knots with a parallel presentation using the same narration accompanied by a series of still pictures that showed the various key stages in the tying of the knots. The movie version was significantly better in teaching the subjects (Navy basic trainees) how to tie the knots. It would appear likely that the advantage of actual motion depiction would depend importantly on the kind of task and on the frequency of transition and rapidity of change of the successive stills. Further data on this question are very much in order, particularly in view of their direct implications for instructional equipment requirements involving large differences in cost.

## OTHER STUDIES OF STIMULUS FACTORS IN INSTRUCTIONAL MEDIA

### Cue Factors in Instructional Films

*Multiple Cues Provided by Animation Techniques.* In a study of animation techniques by Lumsdaine and Sulzer (1951), Air Force basic trainees were tested to assess their ability to read micrometer settings after seeing one of several films on micrometer reading. The films seen by the experimental groups employed simple animation devices, such as pop-on labels, moving arrows, etc., superimposed over the pictorial material so as to visualize symbols and direct attention to critical cues. Control films were identical in narration and in other respects, except that the animation devices in the key sequences in the film were omitted. As predicted, the animated films were superior. Little or no experimental study has been made of the specific characteristics of more complex sorts of animation such as the figure animation used in animated cartoons.

*Pictorial and Auditory "Embellishments."* The producers of the original version of the phonetic-alphabet film studied by Hovland, Lumsdaine and Sheffield (1949) evidently believed that the musical accompaniment and the humorous cartoons and comments employed in the film would make it a better teaching device than unadorned presentation of the material. (See Hovland, Lumsdaine, & Sheffield, 1949, p. 229; May & Lumsdaine, 1958, pp. 58-59.) Results reported by Lumsdaine and Gladstone (1958) showed, however, that the "fancy" presentation using the pictorial and auditory embellishments was not only not more effective but was significantly less effective than a "plain" version in which the letters and equivalent phonetic names were merely presented starkly on a plain background with neither pictorial nor auditory "fancying up." It may be asked why music and humorous effects should have detrimental effects. The hypothesis that immediately suggests itself is that though they may indeed serve as attention-getters, their net effect is to draw attention away from rather than toward the essentials of the learning task. The possible positive effects of the embellishments would then, to be worthwhile, have to more than offset this distracting influence. Under certain conditions this could easily happen; if attention to what is being presented (insuring "exposure" to the learning materials) is the most critical requirement, the presence of the entertaining material might well make the difference between exposure (watching) and non-exposure (e.g., turning off the TV set).

Even for well-motivated learners, pictorial aids somewhat like those used in the film might be advantageous as mnemonic aids if differently employed. Studies of simple association-formation by Lumsdaine (see May & Lumsdaine, 1958, Ch. 10) and by Kopstein and Roshal (1954; 1961) have shown that in learning paired associates, pictures are more effective than words as stimulus terms (though in Lumsdaine's study they were found to be less effective as response terms). This superiority of pictorial cues probably did not operate in the "fancy," pictorialized version of the film studied by Lumsdaine and Gladstone because each picture was used only once. In order to serve an effective mnemonic function, the pictures with the stimulus letters would have to be used on one or more subsequent trials after their initial presentation in association with the phonetic response words, permitting them to serve as partial cues for elicitation of the proper responses.

*Color.* No really definitive studies have been made on specific ways in which color cues may contribute to learning from instructional media. The principal experiments (May & Lumsdaine, 1958; VanderMeer, 1952) have compared black and white versus color prints of the same instructional films. These studies failed to show significant differences in learning favoring the color films (though some of VanderMeer's data suggest slightly superior retention in the case of some of the color films he used). Despite these negative findings a case for the use of color could be made where color cues are essential for a discrimination that is to be learned—for example, in learning to identify code flags, minerals, flowers, etc. Color differentiation can also be clearly advantageous when multiple-color codes keep otherwise confusing visual elements separable, as in complex electrical circuit diagrams. But the experimental evidence suggests that any general value of color for increasing learning merely through increased strikingness or attractiveness has probably been overrated.

*Other Visual-Display Factors.* In a widely cited study by Swanson (1954), several different devices were used as visual aids supplementing lectures to familiarize Air Force mechanics with complex sub-systems of the B-47 medium bomber. All lectures were similar, but the visual aids, though depicting the same equipment, differed markedly. These consisted of mock-ups, two-dimensional symbolic diagrams, and realistic pictorial charts. Absence of any significant mean differences among the post-instruction test scores led to the conclusion that, as lecture supplements, complex and expensive training aids may be no more effective than less complex and expensive aids for the instruction of skilled technicians. But data on the same test obtained later for a control group that heard the lecture with *no* visual aids also failed to show that any of the aids made any significant contribution. A later experiment by Swanson, Lumsdaine and Aukes (1956) was conducted as a follow-up of the above experiment, but used inexperienced airmen as subjects. Two groups each received identical tape recorded lectures but different visual supplementary aids, mock-up and symbolic diagram. A third (control) group heard the lectures with no visual aids. Effects were assessed by three final achievement tests. On a parts-recognition test the mock-up group achieved superiority, on a test of functional inter-connections the diagram group achieved superiority, and on the third test of verbal knowledge there were, as before, no significant differences among the three groups. The conclusion was that the effectiveness of each training aid depends on specific instructional objectives that would determine which aid, if any, would be more effective. Unfortunately, no group was tested with realistic photographs in place of the expensive mock-ups, but it seems likely that the photographic depictions would have served as well as a basis for parts identification.

A positive contribution for visual aids accompanying a recorded lecture was shown by an experiment by Aukes and Simon (1957) for inexperienced trainees in learning system data flow. Aukes and Simon were concerned in part with the possible distracting role of *irrelevant* cues furnished by material extraneous to the point under consideration. Air Force personnel, unskilled in aircraft maintenance, were divided into equivalent groups and given instruction by a tape-recorded lecture on the B-47 rudder power control system. A standard equipment display used as a visual aid to a lecture was found to be significantly less effective than an "add-a-part" display in which only those portions relevant to each major point of the lecture was present during discussion of that point.

*Live Versus Filmed Instruction.* A study by Shettel, Faison, Roshal and Lumsdaine (1956) was concerned with the practical question of whether filmed recordings of lectures could serve as substitutes for, or supplements to, the more expensive and cumbersome mobile training devices then in common use in the Air Force in training mechanics. In each of three replications, live lectures on B-47 maintenance were compared with closely parallel filmed lectures on a verbal test immediately after training and a delayed test given six to eight weeks later. On the immediate test, two of the live-lecture groups scored higher than the corresponding filmed-lecture groups, but the differences, though reliable, were small. On the delayed test, scores were much lower, and no reliable differences were found between any of the live- and filmed-lecture groups. However, for one of the replications, the film was re-shown, as a demonstration experiment, just prior to the delayed test. The fact that this predictably produced a reliable improvement in the scores on that test emphasizes the logistic advantage that, unlike the live lectures, the filmed ones could feasibly be kept available for periodic review, and could be scheduled immediately prior to the time their content was needed in operations, thus avoiding large decrements due to forgetting over the period between instruction and application on the job.

*Visual and Auditory Channels.* One would expect that the relative efficiency of visual and auditory modalities would involve a number of variables. In certain cases where the visual channel is crowded, it is no surprise to find, as in a pilot study reported by Hoehn and Lumsdaine (1958), that audio task instructions can be much more efficient than printed ones. But in the more complex situation of class instruction on complex subject matter, it is unlikely that either modality would be consistently superior. Any stable advantage would almost certainly be a contingent one depending on the nature of the task and learning situation. Thus the inconsistent results obtained by Nelson and Moll (1950) in comparing presentation by audio and visual elements of several existing films are not surprising. Needed are studies that test specific, hypothesized advantages for one or the other modality as a function of other instructional variables.

## Some Verbal Factors in Instruction

*"Readability" of Printed and Recorded Instructional Material.* Despite the rather extensive attention attracted by so-called readability formulae propounded by Flesch (1946; 1949), Dale and Chall (1948) and others, relatively little effort appears to have been devoted to studying experimentally the utility of rules advanced for simplification of language in increasing the effectiveness of learning from instructional media. Most of the comparisons made (e.g., Park, 1945; Chall & Dial, 1948) have compared existing prose passages selected in terms of external criteria as exemplifying differences in level of difficulty, rather than manipulating material by application of the "rules" and then experimentally comparing the comprehension of a resulting simplified version with a more difficult version. An interesting exception is the study by Gladstone (1958) who, rather than dealing with printed presentation, constructed alternative forms of the narration for a 20-minute instructional film by invoking rules for style simplification. The two commentaries had the same factual content. The difficulty level for the easier commentary was at the fourth grade level according to the Flesch formula, and at the sixth to seventh grade level according to the Dale-Chall formula; for the harder commentary, the corresponding levels were ninth-tenth and tenth-twelfth grade. The results of an experimental comparison substantiated in general the expectation, also confirmed by Allen (1952), that more factual material would be learned from the simplified commentary. However, much further experimentation would be needed to determine what aspects of the simplification procedures used were the effective ones.

*Verbalization in Demonstrating Procedures.* McGuire (1955a; 1961b), using a demonstrational film designed to teach pursuit-rotor skill, found not only that groups shown a demonstration scored significantly higher than a no-film (control) group, but also that film plus descriptive narration produced reliably better results than the filmed demonstration alone. An experiment by Thompson reported by May (1946; 1958) studied verbalization as an aid to the learning of an assembly task; the results showed that guided verbalization of steps by the learner facilitated performance if the verbalization was relevant, but hindered performance if the verbalization was irrelevant.

The importance of relevance of verbal labels is also shown in studies that have investigated the utility of teaching nomenclature. Wulff (1955) found that, in terms of selection time, prior familiarization with the parts of the assembly (the same task as that used in a subsequently discussed study reported by Wulff, Sheffield and Kraeling [1954; Wulff & Kraeling, 1961]), was significantly poorer when the parts were not named than was prior familiarization with the parts and their names. This finding may be compared with the results of Jaspen (1950), who found no significant improvement in performance on an assembly task from requiring the audience to learn technical nomenclature of the parts. A more analytic experiment by Saltz and Newman (1956; 1960) was based on conceptualizing instructions as a serial list of cues. Saltz and Newman studied the utility of this conceptualization for assembly instructions by an experiment to test the hypothesis that if the symbols used in the instructions are to aid performance they must not only be connected to the appropriate referents (component-name learning), but must also be connected *to each other* in the order that corresponds to the assembly sequence (order-of-name learning). The criterion task was to indicate the order in which the components of a pressure regulator fit into the main shell of the regulator. A 3 x 3 factorial design was used in which three degrees of component-name learning (none, some, much) and, similarly, three degrees of order-of-name learning were co-varied independently. Results indicated that: (*a*) if there was any previous component-name learning, greater amounts of order-of-name learning resulted in increasingly better assembly performance; (*b*) if there was any previous order-of-name learning, greater amounts of component-name learning resulted in increasingly better assembly performance; (*c*) if there was no previous component-name learning, order-of-name learning had no effect on assembly performance; but (*d*) if there was no order-of-name learning, small amounts of component-name learning facilitated assembly, whereas large amounts of component-name learning produced decrements in assembly performance.

It may be concluded that nomenclature can be effectively used by utilizing its cue properties, but that special attention must be given to seeing that a way is provided so these cues can operate effectively. For example, in facilitating assembly, sequential ordering of the verbal cues appears necessary in order for the cues to function effectively in guiding sequential performance. This can either be assured by an explicit training procedure, as in the Saltz and Newman experiment, or by selecting areas that already possess an inherent order as in the previously mentioned study of Thompson (reported by May, 1946; 1958) in which numbering the parts in the order they had to be used in the assembly considerably facilitated performance.

*Other Studies of Verbal Factors.* Several studies have investigated "rate" of verbalization and other factors in style of verbal commentary accompanying demonstration films. Jaspen (1950) and Zuckerman (1949) varied the rate of verbalization in commentary accompanying assembly and knot-tying demonstration films, respectively, and concluded that a "medium" (90-130 w.p.m.) rate of verbalization was preferable. Unfortunately, rate is to some extent almost necessarily confounded with content and redundancy when the commentary-rate variation is in the context of a fixed-pace demonstration, and it is thus not altogether clear what the effective variable is in such experiments. In any case the specific rate that would be optimal would be expected to depend on the informational requirements of the task. Zuckerman also compared various modes of narration differing in voice and mood and concluded that imperative instructions were superior to passive-voice descriptions of the steps in the task being demonstrated.

## FACTORS IN THE CONTENT AND ORGANIZATION OF INSTRUCTION

### Preparatory Procedures

*Tests or Instructions as Motivational and Attention-Directing Procedures.* The value of using a pre-test to identify points in a film which are to be learned has been studied by several investigators. For example, in the 1951 animation study by Lumsdaine and Sulzer, giving a brief pre-film test of five sample micrometer settings significantly increased the amount learned about micrometer reading. Several experiments reported by May and Lumsdaine (1958) have also shown that the amount learned from certain aspects of a film can be increased substantially by procedures designed to direct the attention of students to these aspects before an instructional presentation. This was done by oral or written instructions, by giving a pre-film test, and by pointing out the "hardest" questions on a post-film test before giving a second showing of a film. However, the increase in amount learned from the material covered by the pre-test tended to be offset by losses in the material not covered. Giving a relevant pre-film test thus can have a selective attention-directing function, stressing certain aspects of content differentially. On the other hand, merely announcing that a test (of some sort) will be given following instruction can serve a general motivating function which, in the 1949 phonetic alphabet study by Hovland, Lumsdaine and Sheffield, had a significant effect in increasing learning. The procedure of announcing a test did not work, however, when Michael and Maccoby (1953; 1961) tried to use it for a similar purpose; here, making the announcement had no significant effect probably because, unlike the Army subjects of Hovland, Lumsdaine and Sheffield, their students were already about maximally motivated.

Another study which showed increased learning by use of pre-film tests was that by Stein (1952). However, using full-length pre-film tests, Stein obtained significant gains only when the pre-film test procedure incorporated "knowledge of results" that, in effect, provided for additional instruction. Though this was naturally effective, Stein's main results thus seem more nearly akin to those on active practice or repetition than to attention-focusing phenomena. In the experiment by Lumsdaine and Sulzer, on the other hand, the effect of the short pre-film test, with no knowledge of results, appears to be one of focusing attention, similar to the effects produced in the May and Lumsdaine experiments. A similar effect for a pre-test preceding a film designed to teach reading of meters and gauges was found in an unpublished study by Peterman and Bouscaren (1954).

Effects of interpolated tests between two sections of film instruction for set-producing or motivational purposes have been investigated by Kimble (1955). His experimental groups were given a test (without provision for correcting errors, or any specific knowledge of results) on reading of slide rule scales. This test was given following preliminary film instruction on the subject and prior to a follow-up film that gave instruction both on scale reading and on the use of the slide rule for multiplying and dividing. Kimble found that the results of the interpolated test were specific, as compared with control groups who had no interpolated test: the experimental groups showed greater gains on the kind of content covered by the test (scale reading) but no appreciable effect on the content not covered (arithmetical operations).

*Familiarization.* A number of studies have been conducted on the value of various forms of so-called familiarization training. Most of these (e.g., Weiss & Fine, 1955; Stein, 1952) merely show that additional time devoted to some form of familiarization produces beneficial results, without showing that using it is more effective than alternative ways in which the time could have been spent. One exception, which also deals with specific cue factors involved in familiarization procedures, is a study by Wulff and Kraeling (1954; see also Wulff & Kraeling, 1961). This experiment involved the notion that generally it is not necessary for the learner to attend to *all* of the features of a task to be learned, but rather that he should learn to attend to certain key features important in performing it. Using the assembly of an automobile ignition distributor as a training task, two training procedures with familiarization were compared with each other and were also compared with training without familiarization. One kind of familiarization involved training subjects to attend to cues that were critical in differentiating the mechanical parts, prior to any assembly training; the other familiarization procedure, which took less time, involved pointing to the same important features of each part *during* assembly training just before the assembly of each part was shown. The most interesting finding was that the group that was given familiarization prior to assembly training performed less well, with respect to selection errors at least, than the group that used the other familiarization procedure (which took less time). The results support the hypothesis that not only will a procedure which directs the learner's attention to important cues facilitate training in the manipulation of complex task elements in which only some features are important, but also that such familiarization is more effective if given in the context of, and just prior to, training in the utilization of each task element than if given as a completely separate, prior procedure.

## Repetition and Review

*Amount of Repetition in Instructional Films.* Instructional films seem generally to be designed with insufficient repetition (and/or too fast a "pace" or "rate of development") for most students to approach mastery on specific knowledge or skills if used without supplementation. Jaspen (1950), for example, found that a "succinct" treatment, chosen as representative of the pace and level of repetition (or lack thereof) commonly employed in many "nuts and bolts" films, was far from adequate to teach an assembly task, for which reasonably successful teaching required a film several times as long as the "succinct" one. The common finding that students achieve far from perfect scores on criterion tests after seeing an instructional film has led several experimenters to study the effects of repeat showings of a film *in toto*, and a few experiments have been conducted on varied amounts or arrangements of repetition within an instructional film. The latter are related, of course, to the previously mentioned studies of size-of-step (e.g., Coulson & Silberman, 1959) for auto-instructional programs, in which a greater number of steps provided (among other things) more repetition.

Typical findings on repetition of films are, predictably, that two showings teach more than does just one (e.g., Kurtz, Walter, & Brenner, 1950). As we would predict from the negative acceleration typical of learning curves, there is, of course, a law of diminishing returns; thus, additional showings may or may not show significant further gains. In a study by McTavish (1949, p. 7) it was found that little or no further gain was produced after one repeat: ". . . the contribution made by repetition of showings fell off rapidly after the first repetition . . . only the increment attributable to the first repetition is statistically significant." McTavish's study and a later study by Sulzer, Lumsdaine and Kopstein (1952) thus both indicate the predictable existence of a "saturation point," one in the case of repetition of entire films and the other study in the case of repeated demonstration within a film. The important thing, however, is not the mere existence of a "saturation point"; rather, the question is what determines where this point will occur. The obvious fact that there is no fixed, low value for the number of repetitions that can be usefully employed is illustrated in comparing McTavish's works with those of Sulzer, Lumsdaine and Kopstein, who studied the effect of number of examples in films on micrometer reading. Different amounts of repetition, ranging from three examples (the number included in a standard "training film") up to ten examples, were employed by using a combination of films and filmstrips. In this study, six or seven examples were much better than three; ten examples were somewhat better than six or seven. Gains from using added examples were, understandably, greater for more difficult aspects of the subject (as shown by post-film test data for the harder-to-read kinds of settings), and, perhaps less predictably, the value of adding more examples was greater for the more intelligent students than for the less intelligent. Evidently the former did not need as much repetition to reach a minimum level of performance, but they were better able to profit from a reasonable amount of further repetition, especially on the difficult material.

One way of trying to introduce greater amounts of repetition within a given time constraint is through a speeded-speech technique used in several experiments reported by Fairbanks, Guttman and Miron (1957). It was hypothesized that time saved by compressing audio instruction by an electronic-chopping technique could be utilized for introducing helpful added redundancy. However, this attempt to squeeze in more learning through two full repetitions of instruction in a given time period was unsuccessful; scores for students who had one uncompressed presentation did not differ significantly from those who had two successive 50% time-compressed presentations. Attempts to use the time saved by compression to introduce selective repetition of key points did result in better learning of those particular points, but at the expense of other points that were not repeated, and no evidence was found for a net, overall gain.

*Type of Repetition.* The question of the relative merits of varied repetition and identical reiteration was investigated in an unpublished study by Kanner and McClure (1956), using films on micrometer reading somewhat similar to those used in the study by Sulzer, Lumsdaine and Kopstein (1952). They compared the use of the same four examples, each seen twice, with the use of eight different examples. In the first of two experiments they performed, they failed to find a statistically reliable difference between the two treatments immediately after training, but they did find a reliable, though small, difference in favor of the varied repetition treatment for the more able subjects when they were tested a week after training. In the second experiment, no statistically reliable differences of any kind were found.

Results of an experiment by Rimland (1955), on the other hand, showed a consistent advantage, over several replications, for two identical repetitions over two different presentations (of about equal separate effectiveness) in teaching a perceptual-motor skill (knot-tying) by filmed demonstration. However, since a *specific* skill was being taught here, this finding is not necessarily incompatible with an hypothesis of greater effectiveness for varied examples in tasks (such as micrometer reading) which require generalization from examples which are used to teach a conceptual or procedural pattern.

*Distribution of Review.* A study by Miller and Levine (1952) investigated two different ways of employing review sequences. This study was concerned with relative advantages of spacing the review sequences through a film following each major topic, versus "massing" the review at the end of the film. The film used in this experiment dealt with Ohm's Law. In the massed review condition, the entire film was shown and then all of it was reviewed. In the spaced review condition, each of the four sections of the film was reviewed immediately after it was shown, and then that aspect of the subject was not further dealt with explicitly. The comparisons showed the massed-review procedure to be superior to the spaced review. An explanation of these results is that the condition of spaced review may be described as a "massed-practice" situation (since review of each topic immediately followed its presentation), while the condition of massed review may be regarded as a "spaced practice" condition in which the second "practice" (review) was deferred to the end of the film and thus was farther separated from the first presentation of each topic. In a later replication with a film on defense against atomic attack, the massed review condition was again found to be superior, at the .05 confidence level, to the spaced review condition.

## Structure and Organization of Instructional Sequences

*Fatigue and Distribution of Effort.* Faison, Rose and Podell (1955) showed that the effectiveness of a single 25-minute film during a single showing could be increased by rest breaks to increase audience attentiveness. The results of this experiment, which utilized infra-red photography as an audience-observation technique, indicated that the insertion of three very short (30-second) rest pauses in a 20-minute film led to reliable increases in an index of audience attentiveness. The underlying relation between duration of the film showing and audience attentiveness was exhibited in a progressive gradual decline in attentiveness for the "straight-through" showing, as contrasted with the abrupt rise in attentiveness following each of the rest pauses under the experimental condition. The introduction of the rest breaks led in turn to reliably greater learning as measured by a post-film test than was found for a continuous showing of the same film.

*Repetitive Versus Continuous Demonstration and Practice.* In two studies by Margolius, Sheffield and Maccoby (1956; 1961) a procedure in which each of several sub-assemblies was demonstrated and practiced *twice,* before moving on to the next sub-assembly, was compared with a treatment in which a sub-assembly was practiced once before demonstration but with the entire demonstration and practice sequence repeated twice. The first of these treatments was referred to as "repetitive"; the second was called "continuous." Two different mechanical assembly tasks were used. The results obtained with the first task favored the repetitive treatment. However, with the second task, no significant difference between the treatments was noted. In interpreting this result, the experimenters point out that the potential advantages of the repetitive procedure stems from its tendency to reduce interserial interference. Since the second task appeared to be already intrinsically well organized, there may have been too little room for improvement in acquisition by procedures designed to minimize intraserial interference between elements of the different subtasks. It may be concluded that the repetitive procedure is potentially advantageous, but that the extent of its contribution to acquisition is likely to be a function of the intrinsic organizational characteristics of the task being demonstrated, being minimal with an intrinsically well-organized task.

A further purpose of the Margolius, Maccoby and Sheffield study was to test the hypothesis that in learning a lengthy, mechanical assembly task by joint use of demonstration and overt practice, the optimum timing of overt practice is at the completion of each "natural unit" of a total assembly task. A "natural unit" was defined as a portion of a task sequence which has its own distinctive context cues, such as a separate sub-assembly. Two methods for selecting demonstration-practice segments were compared: (*a*) use of overt practice at the end of such "natural units" and (*b*) use of an equal number of overt practice periods at the end of arbitrarily defined segments of the task which matched the natural units in their temporal length. Results for the film that was used showed no effects of the difference in treatment. The explanation which the experimenters again offer is that if a task is inherently well organized, as this one appeared to be, there may be little to gain from additional procedures designed to enhance the organization.

*Structuring by Use of Sub-Titles and Outlines.* In the previously described study by Miller and Levine (1952) on spaced versus massed distribution of review, a second question investigated was how the effectiveness of the film might be affected by use of frequent subtitles designed to identify, set off and structure the various topics and sub-topics (electrical current, voltage, resistance and Ohm's Law) taken up successively in the film. Two degrees of structuring, employing (*a*) major sub-titles only, and (*b*) "complete" sub-titling of each sub-topic, were compared with (*c*) a control film with no sub-titles in which each sequence of material followed the next without a break. No significant differences were found among these three treatments; though, as previously noted, significant differences were found between different distributions of review. This may have been due to the fact that the material in the Ohm's Law film was already well structured in terms of its logical organization. In a later study by Northrop (1952), significant differences were reported favoring film versions in which structuring organizational outlines were employed in experimental films, as compared with control films lacking these aids to organization.

*Sequencing of Instructional Materials to Facilitate Discrimination.* Several studies have been conducted in the context of military training which have an important bearing on the sequencing of material, particularly paired-associate materials, and may also have implications for the sequencing of connected discourse material in auto-instructional programs or other instructional instruments. A good example is the paper by Wulff and Stolurow (1957) dealing with "class descriptive" cues that differentiate sub-groups of materials which a trainee must learn to identify. The example used in this study was the standard code system by which aircraft rivets are coded, by color markings, etc., in terms of four properties: length, diameter, head shape, and material. Two forms of organization were used: "class organization" displays showed all the items in relation to one class of differentiating cues, e.g., rivet-head silhouettes or rivet-head markings that indicated diameter; "item organization" displays gave the same information, but with all features about a given item presented one at a time, e.g., a single rivet with each of the four coded characteristics depicted. The latter method made it theoretically unlikely that the learner could utilize class cues effectively during learning, and thus it was predicted that class organization would be more effective. The results supported the theoretical analysis; that is, the method of presentation which fostered utilization of class cues proved reliably superior to the other method.

A second study on sequencing of materials, by Detambel and Stolurow (1956), was concerned with a problem-solving situation in which the trainee was supposed to discover (*a*) which of the components of each display was relevant to the decisions he had to make, and (*b*) which variation in the relevant component indicated that a particular decision was required. Two different training sequences were used. For *synchronous* sequences the trial-to-trial relationships were such that a relevant and an irrelevant component either *both maintained* their value or *both changed* value. In *asynchronous* sequences, by contrast, a relevant stimulus component changed and the irrelevant one did not (or vice versa). Minimum synchrony between relevant and irrelevant components produced significantly larger proportions of solvers than did maximum synchrony, but only at the lower ability levels. Under the *maximum* synchrony sequence, the percentage of solvers increased regularly with increased ability; however, with *minimum* synchrony the percentage of solvers was about equal regardless of ability. The authors concluded that "to the maximum extent possible the displays should be sequenced so that from display to display, when a relevant component changes, the irrelevant component does not change and similarly, when the relevant component does not change, the irrelevant one(s) changes."

A third study bearing on the sequencing of material in teaching that requires discriminative learning is that of Rothkopf (1958) who performed several experiments to determine the role of stimulus presentation sequence in the acquisition of paired-associated habits. The experimental task employed Morse code signals as stimulus terms, and their appropriate alphabetic or numeric equivalents as response terms. The results indicated that the maximal separation of similar stimuli in the practice order produced the most efficient learning. These results contrast with those of an earlier study by Gagné (1950), who found that the *successive* presentation of similar stimuli was the most effective practice sequence in a paired-associate task which employed nonsense figures as stimulus terms and nonsense syllables as response terms. The reversal of the Gagné findings by Rothkopf's results indicates the complexity of factors governing sequencing and other programming, which are likely to operate differently as a function of such factors as (*a*) the susceptibility of Gagné's stimulus materials (but not Rothkopf's) for utilization of mediating descriptive responses, and (*b*) the amount of response-term learning required, and the resulting relative frequency of substitution errors (high for Rothkopf's conditions, low for Gagné's) versus non-substitution errors.

Emeson and Wulff (1957; see also Wulff and Emeson, 1961) report several small experiments conducted to explore the rationale that with difficult learning tasks one must be not only concerned with insuring active practice but must take care to set up training conditions that will foster appropriate or useful practice. These investigators used relatively difficult paired-associate learning tasks requiring students to learn the names of eight electrical circuits. A difficult aspect of the task was that the eight circuits consisted of four pairs of which the members of each pair were almost identical and thus highly confusable. In an initial experiment, unstructured self study was compared with formalized paired-associate learning procedures. Both self study and this formalized paired-associate training were relatively inefficient, but learning was considerably more rapid under conditions of unstructured self study than from the organized paired-associate method. These results, like those of Newman (1957), emphasized the necessity of analyzing a learning task and insuring that appropriate practice and cueing is provided in a formalized set of learning materials, if an attempt to develop and apply science to teaching is to surpass the performance attained by individuals' own modes of learning. In one of several later experiments reported by Wulff and Emeson, two paired-associate procedures were compared which differed only in that for one experimental group the stimulus materials were arranged *in a fixed order* to provide associative support through position cues used during early stages of training. The students using these materials performed better at later stages of practice in which the standard paired-associate arrangement was used (with scrambled order) than did the students who had used the scrambled-order arrangement throughout the entire period of practice.

## FUTURE RESEARCH AND DEVELOPMENT

The experimental work reported in this chapter clearly represents only a beginning in the effort that is needed to develop a solidly anchored technology of instructional media. Through such work, educational psychologists can better identify the variables and functional relationships which most potently influence the modification of behavior through instruction, and thus can play a crucial role in improving the effectiveness and economy of training and education.

The reproducibility of instructional media or materials, as distinguished from "methods," carries with it important implications for the amount of research and development resources which it is economically feasible and justifiable to devote to perfecting them. This applies to the range and complexity of the displays used, the level of the instructional personnel employed in preparing instructional instruments, and the resources that can be expended for development, tryout and revision. A given instructional instrument may be used for only a few minutes of any one student's time, but the cost of perfecting it can be pro-rated in terms of a denominator representing thousands of students for whom the perfected instrument can be used. The property of reproducibility also facilitates manipulation of the properties of instruction which can be defined and specified. Moreover, dealing with the properties of concrete products gives us much greater control of the application of research findings than is true for research findings that pertain to an abstraction such as an instructional "method." As products, instructional instruments can be made subject to specifications in a way that hardly applies to methods, and thus can afford an inherent basis for predictability.

These considerations may be usefully related to the question of implementing research findings. Travers, in Chapter 17 of this volume, has presented a penetrating and quite disconcerting analysis of reasons why the results of research (and the products of invention) may fail to find their way into educational or training practice. It is possible that the results of research or innovation are only likely to result in thorough-going translation into improved practice when they become embodied in concrete devices, materials or other usable products. To a lesser extent, research findings may affect practice when they generate *specifications* for such tangible products, devices or materials, particularly if the application of these specifications has been embodied in illustrative prototypes that have been shown to be useful. It seems likely that research on instruction will much more seldom be applied when its sole product is principles, conclusions, or scientific "laws." One should not expect the conclusions and principles derived from basic research to find their way into educational and training practice unless researchers make the translation themselves or develop a systematic technology through which such translation may be effected (cf. Melton, 1959). It seems likely that the most direct way to accomplish this is through incorporating what is found through research into tangible products in the form of usable devices and materials which can be bought and put to use, and which by their successful use in practice can engender a demand for themselves. Conversely, the decisions encountered in the design of concrete devices and materials can often represent the most useful point of departure from which needs for basic research can be identified in terms that will lead to findings which can eventually be fed back into practice.

The utility of informal tryout as a developmental basis for specific product improvement is likely to be particularly great in the case of small-step programming of self-instructional materials. If a film, or TV lesson, or lecture is seen by subsequent tests to have partly failed, it is difficult to determine at what point the student went off or what specific aspect of the presentation was responsible for his failure to comprehend. The same is true with learning from textbooks. In the small-step auto-instructional program, however, the student's responses provide a potential basis for point-by-point revision of the program.

The potentialities for fruitful basic research also seem particularly great in the case of auto-instructional media, both because of the close control of the learning situation which teaching machines can provide, and because of the directness with which inductive generalizations about the operation of specific factors can be translated into controllable development practices.

It is essential not only that researchers increase the incisiveness with which variables are defined and experimental problems are posed, but also that crucial methodological advances be made. These include, at a minimum, a rationale for coping with the dilemma of instructional time and payoff, and a basis for improving the null-hypothesis paradigm of experimentation, including agreement on standards for setting the sensitivity of experiments. Meanwhile, it is important to insure that research effort results in studies which are, by and large, technically as good as the current state of the art will permit. This in no way precludes the exercise of ingenuity in trying out new approaches, but it does suggest the need for better communication among research workers, and better research training as a prerequisite to scientific experimentation on instructional media.

## REFERENCES

References marked with an asterisk (*) are reprinted in A. A. Lumsdaine and R. Glaser, *Teaching machines and programmed learning.* In this bibliography, certain of these citations will be referred to as L & G.

Allen, W. H. Readability of instructional film commentary. *J. appl. Psychol.,* 1952, *36,* 164-168.

Allen, W. H. Research on film use: Student participation. *Audio-visual communica. Rov.,* 1957, *5,* 423-450.

Allen, W. H. Audio-visual communication. In C. W. Harris (Ed.), *Encyclopedia of educational research.* (3rd ed.) New York: Macmillan, 1960.

Angell, D. & Lumsdaine, A. A. *Prompted plus unprompted trials versus prompted trials alone in paired-associate learning.* Pittsburgh: American Institute for Research, 1960.

Aukes, L. E. & Simon, G. B. *The relative effectiveness of an Air Force training device used intact versus with isolated parts.* Air Force Personnel and Training Research Center, June 1957. Research Report AFPTRC-TN-57-77. ASTIA Doc. No. 131429.

Briggs, L. J. *A troubleshooting trainer for the E-4 Fire Control System.* Air Force Personnel and Training Research Center, July 1956. Development Report AFPTRC-TN-56-94. ASTIA Document No. 098870.

*Briggs, L. J. Two self-instructional devices. *Psychol. Rep.,* 1958, *4,* 671-676. In L & G, pp. 299-304.

Chall, Jeanne S. & Dial, H. E. Predicting listener understanding and interest in newscasts. *Educ. res. Bull.,* 1948, *27,* 141-153, 168.

*Cook, J. O. Supplementary report: Processes underlying learning a single paired-associate item. *J. exp. Psychol.,* 1958, *56,* 455. In L & G, pp. 601-602.

Cook, J. O. Research in audio-visual communication. In J. Ball & F. C. Byrnes (Eds.), *Research, principles, and practices in visual communication.* East Lansing, Michigan: Michigan State University, National Project in Agricultural Communications, 1960. Pp. 91-106.

Cook, J. O. & Kendler, T. S. A theoretical model to explain some paired-associate learning data. In G. Finch & F. Cameron (Eds.), *Symposium on Air Force human engineering, personnel, and training research.* Washington, D.C.: National Academy of Sciences—National Research Council, 1956.

*Cook, J. O. & Spitzer, M. E. Supplementary report: Prompting versus confirmation in paired-associate learning. *J. exp. Psychol.,* 1960, *59,* 275-276. In L & G, pp. 604-607.

*Coulson, J. E. & Silberman, H. F. *Results of an initial experiment in automated teaching.* Santa Monica, California: System Development Corporation, July 1959. In L & G, pp. 452-468.

Dale, E. & Chall, Jeanne S. A formula for predicting readability: Instructions. *Educ. res. Bull.,* 1948, *27,* 37-54.

Detambel, M. H. & Stolurow, L. M. Stimulus sequence and concept learning. *J. exp. Psychol.,* 1956, *51,* 34-40.

Emeson, D. L. & Wulff, J. J. *The relationship between "What is learned" and "How it's taught."* Maintenance Laboratory, Air Force Personnel and Training Research Center, December 1957. Technical Memorandum ML-TM-57-32. (See Wulff & Emeson, 1961)

Evans, J. L. *An investigation of "teaching machine" variables using learning programs in symbolic logic.* Pittsburgh: University of Pittsburgh, December 1960. Cooperative Research Project 691 (9417).

*Evans, J. L., Glaser, R., & Homme, L. E. A preliminary investigation of variation in the properties of verbal learning sequences of the "teaching machine" type. Paper read at Eastern Psychol. Ass., Atlantic City, New Jersey, April 1959. In L & G, pp. 446-451.

Fairbanks, G., Guttman, N., & Miron, M. S. Auditory comprehension in relation to listening rate and selective verbal redundancy. *J. speech & hearing Disorders,* 1957, *22,* 23-32.

Faison, E. J., Rose, N., & Podell, J. E. *A technique for measuring observable audience reactions to training films.* USAF Training Aids Research Laboratory, Unpublished laboratory note, December 1955. TARL-LN-55-45.

Flesch, R. *The art of plain talk.* New York: Harper, 1946.

Flesch, R. *The art of readable writing.* New York: Harper, 1949.

French, R. S. Evaluation of a K-System Troubleshooting Trainer. In G. Finch & F. Cameron (Eds.), *Symposium on Air Force human engineering, personnel, and training research.* Washington, D.C.: National Academy of Sciences—National Research Council, 1956. Publication 455. Pp. 160-165. (a)

French, R. S. *The K-System MAC-1 Troubleshooting Trainer: I. Development, design and use.* Air Force Personnel and Training Research Center, October 1956. Development rep. AFPTRC-TN-56-119. ASTIA Doc. No. 098893. (b)

Fry, E. B. A study of teaching machine response modes. In A. A. Lumsdaine & R. Glaser (Eds.), *Teaching machines and programmed learning: A source book.* Washington, D.C.: National Education Association, 1960. Pp. 469-474.

Gage, N. L. (Ed.) *Handbook of research on teaching.* Washington, D.C.; American Educational Research Association, 1962. (In press)

Gagné, R. M. The effect of sequence of presentation of similar items on the learning of paired associates. *J. exp. Psychol.,* 1950, *40,* 61-73.

Gates, A. I. Recitation as a factor in memorizing. *Archives of Psychol.,* 1917, *7,* No. 40.

Gladstone, A. The readability of the commentary. In M. A. May & A. A. Lumsdaine (Eds.), *Learning from films.* New Haven: Yale University Press, 1958.

Goldbeck, R. A. *The effect of response mode and learning material difficulty on automated instruction.* Pittsburgh: American Institute for Research, 1960. Technical Report No. 1. AIR-328-60-IR-124.

Gropper, G. L. & Lumsdaine, A. A. *Experiments on active student response to televised instruction: An interim report.* Pittsburgh: American Institute for Research, April 1960.

Guthrie, E. R. *The psychology of learning.* New York: Harper, 1935. (Rev. ed., 1952.)

Hirsch, R. S. *The effects of knowledge of test results on learning of meaningful material.* (Instructional Film Research Program, Pennsylvania State University) Port Washington, New York: USN Training Device Center, Office of Naval Research, September 1952. Technical Report No. SDC 269-7-30.

Hoban, C. F., Jr. & van Ormer, E. B. *Instructional film research, 1918-1950.* (Instructional Film Research Program, Pennsylvania State University) Port Washington, New York: USN Training Device Center, Office of Naval Research, 1950. Technical Report No. SDC 269-7-19.

Hoehn, A. J. & Lumsdaine, A. A. *Design and use of job aids for communicating technical information.* Air Force Personnel and Training Research Center, January 1958. Technical Report AFPTRC-TR-58-7. ASTIA Doc. No. AD 152109.

Holland, J. G. A teaching machine program in psychology. In E. H. Galanter (Ed.), *Automatic teaching: The state of the art.* New York: Wiley, 1959.

*Holland, J. G. Teaching machines: An application of principles from the laboratory. In *Proceedings of the Educational Testing Service Invitational Conference,* October 1959, on "The impact of testing on the educational process." Princeton, N.J.: Educational Testing Service, 1960. In L & G, pp. 215-228.

Hovland, C. I., Lumsdaine, A. A., & Sheffield, F. D. *Experiments on mass communication.* Princeton: Princeton University Press, 1949.

Irion, A. L. & Briggs, L. J. *Learning task and mode of operation variables in use of the Subject-Matter Trainer.* Air Force Personnel and Training Research Center, October 1957. Technical Report AFPTRC-TR-57-8. ASTIA Doc. No. AD 134252.

Jaspen, N. *Effects on training of experimental film variables; Study II: Verbalization, "How-it-works," nomenclature, audience participation, and succint treatment.* (Instructional Film Research Program, Pennsylvania State University) Port Washington, New York: USN Training Device Center, Office of Naval Research, March 1950. Technical Report No. SDC 269-7-11.

Kanner, J. H. & McClure, A. H. *Varied versus identical repetition in filmed instruction on micrometer reading.* USAF Training Aids Research Laboratory, Unpublished Laboratory Note, April 1956. TARL-LN-56-11.

Kimble, G. A. *The value of an interpolated test in increasing the effectiveness of a training film.* USAF Training Aids Research Laboratory, Unpublished Laboratory Note, December 1955. TARL-LN-55-10.

Kimble, G. A. & Wulff, J. J. *The effect of "response guidance" on the value of audience participation in film instruction.* Washington, D.C.: USAF Human Factors Operations Research Laboratories, 1953. HFORL Report No. 34, also HFORL Memo Report No. 36.

Kimble, G. A. & Wulff, J. J. "Response guidance" as a factor in the value of audience participation in training film instruction. In A. A. Lumsdaine (Ed.), *Student response in programmed instruction: A symposium.* Washington, D.C.: National Academy of Sciences—National Research Council, 1961.

Kopstein, F. F. & Roshal, S. M. Learning foreign vocabulary from pictures versus words. *Amer. Psychologist,* 1954, *9,* 407-408. (Abstract)

Kopstein, F. F. & Roshal, S. M. Method of presenting word pairs as a factor in foreign vocabulary learning. *Amer. Psychologist,* 1955, *10,* 354. (Abstract)

Kopstein, F. F. & Roshal, S. M. Verbal learning efficiency as influenced by the manipulation of representational response processes. In A. A. Lumsdaine (Ed.), *Student response in programmed instruction: A symposium*. Washington, D.C.: National Academy of Sciences—National Research Council, 1961.

Kurtz, A. K., Walter, J. S., & Brenner, H. R. *The effects of inserted questions and statements on film learning (rapid mass learning)*. (Instructional Film Research Program, Pennsylvania State University) Port Washington, New York: USN Training Device Center, Office of Naval Research, September 1950. Technical Report No. SDC 269-7-16.

Levine, S. The role of motivation in the effects of "active review" on learning from a factual film. *Amer. Psychologist*, 1953, *8*, 388-389. (Abstract)

*Lumsdaine, A. A. Teaching machines and self-instructional materials. *Audiovisual comunica. Rev.*, 1959, *7*, 163-172. Reprinted in L & G, pp. 5-22, as Teaching machines; An introductory overview.

Lumsdaine, A. A. Design of training aids and devices. In J. D. Folley, Jr. (Ed.), *Human factors methods for system design*. Pittsburgh: American Institute for Research, 1960. (a)

Lumsdaine, A. A. *Graphic aids, models and mockups, as tools for individual and classroom instruction*. Washington, D.C.: National Academy of Sciences—National Research Council Symposium on Educational and Training Media, 1960. (b)

Lumsdaine, A. A. Use of self-instructional devices. In J. D. Folley, Jr. (Ed.), *Human factors methods for system design*. Pittsburgh: American Institute for Research, 1960. Pp. 291-326. (c)

Lumsdaine, A. A. (Ed.) *Student response in programmed instruction: A symposium*. Washington, D.C.: National Academy of Sciences—National Research Council, 1961.

Lumsdaine, A. A. & Gladstone, A. Overt practice and audio-visual embellishments. In M. A. May & A. A. Lumsdaine (Eds.), *Learning from films*. New Haven: Yale University Press, 1958. Pp. 58-71.

Lumsdaine, A. A. & Glaser, R. (Eds.) *Teaching machines and programmed learning: A source book*. Washington, D.C.: National Education Association, 1960.

Lumsdaine, A. A., May, M. A., & Hadsell, R. S. Questions spliced into a film for motivation and pupil participation. In M. A. May & A. A. Lumsdaine (Eds.), *Learning from films*. New Haven: Yale University Press, 1958. Pp. 72-83.

Lumsdaine, A. A. & Sulzer, R. L. *The influence of simple animation techniques on the value of a training film.* Washington, D.C.: USAF Human Factors Research Laboratory, 1951. HRRL Report No. 24.

Maccoby, N. & Sheffield, F. D. Theory and experimental research on the teaching of complex sequential procedures by alternate demonstration and practice. In G. Finch & F. Cameron (Eds.), *Symposium on Air Force human engineering, personnel, and training research.* Washington, D.C.: National Academy of Sciences—National Research Council, 1958. Publication 516.

Maccoby, N. & Sheffield, F. D. Combining practice with filmed demonstration in teaching complex response sequences. Summary and interpretation. In A. A. Lumsdaine (Ed.), *Student response in programmed instruction: A symposium.* Washington, D.C.: National Academy of Sciences—National Research Council, 1961.

Maccoby, N., Michael, D. N., & Levine, S. Further studies of student participation procedures in film instruction. In A. A. Lumsdaine (Ed.), *Student response in programmed instruction: A symposium.* Washington, D.C.: National Academy of Sciences—National Research Council, 1961.

Margolius, G., Sheffield, F. D., & Maccoby, N. Optimum methods of combining practice with filmed demonstration in teaching complex response sequences. I. Serial learning of a mechanical assembly task. (Originally, Methods of combining practice with filmed demonstration in teaching complex response sequences) *Amer. Psychologist,* 1956, *11,* 444. (Abstract)

Margolius, G., Sheffield, F. D., & Maccoby, N. Repetitive versus consecutive demonstration and practice in the learning of a serial mechanical-assembly task. In A. A. Lumsdaine (Ed.), *Student response in programmed instruction: A symposium.* Washington, D.C.: National Academy of Sciences—National Research Council, 1961.

May, M. A. The psychology of learning from demonstration films. *J. educ. Psychol.,* 1946, *37,* 1-12.

May, M. A. Verbal responses to demonstrational films. In M. A. May & A. A. Lumsdaine (Eds.), *Learning from films.* New Haven: Yale University Press, 1958.

May, M. A. & Lumsdaine, A. A. (Eds.) *Learning from films.* New Haven: Yale University Press, 1958.

McGuire, W. J. *Factors influencing the effectiveness of demonstrational film for teaching a motor skill: II. Slow motion, added narration and distributed showings.* USAF Training Aids Research Laboratory, Unpublished Laboratory Note, December 1955. TARL-LN-55-50. (Mimeo.) (a)

McGuire, W. J. *The relative efficacy of overt and covert trainee participation with different speed of instruction.* USAF Training Aids Research Laboratory, Unpublished Laboratory Note, December 1955. TARL-LN-55-46. (b)

McGuire, W. J. Audience participation and audio-visual instruction. In A. A. Lumsdaine (Ed.), *Student response in programmed instruction: A symposium.* Washington, D.C.: National Academy of Sciences—National Research Council, 1961. (a)

McGuire, W. J. Some factors influencing the effectiveness of demonstrational films. In A. A. Lumsdaine (Ed.), *Student response in programmed instruction: A symposium.* Washington, D.C.: National Academy of Sciences—National Research Council, 1961. (b)

McTavish, C. L. *Effect of repetitive film showings on learning.* (Instructional Film Research Program, Pennsylvania State University) Port Washington, New York: USN Training Device Center, Office of Naval Research, November 1949. Technical Report No. SDC 269-7-12.

Melton, A. W. The science of learning and the technology of educational methods. *Harvard educ. Rev.*, 1959, *29*, 96-106.

Michael, D. N. & Maccoby, N. Factors influencing verbal learning from films under conditions of audience participation. *J. exp. Psychol.*, 1953, *46*, 411-418.

Michael, D. N. & Maccoby, N. Factors influencing the effects of student participation on verbal learning from films. In A. A. Lumsdaine (Ed.), *Student response in programmed instruction: A symposium.* Washington, D.C.: National Academy of Sciences—National Research Council, 1961.

Miller, J. & Levine, S. *A study of the effects of different types of review and of "structuring" sub-titles on the amount learned from a training film.* Washington, D.C.: USAF Human Factors Research Laboratory, March 1952. HRRL Memo Report No. 17.

Miller, R. B. *Handbook on training and training equipment design.* Wright Air Development Center, Wright-Patterson Air Force Base, 1953. WADC TR 53-136.

Miller, R. B. *Psychological considerations for the design of training equipment.* Wright Air Development Center, Wright-Patterson Air Force Base, December 1954. WADC TR 54-563.

Miller, R. B. *A suggested guide to functional characteristics of training and training equipment.* Maintenance Laboratory, Air Force Personnel and Training Research Center, May 1956. ML-TM-56-14.

Nelson, H. E. & Moll, K. R. *Comparison of the audio and video elements of instructional films.* (Instructional Film Research Program, Pennsylvania

State University) Port Washington, New York: USN Training Device Center, Office of Naval Research, November 1950. Technical Report No. SDC 269-7-18.

Newman, S. E. Student versus instructor design of study method. *J. educ. Psychol.*, 1957, *48*, No. 6.

Northrop, D. S. *Effects on learning of the prominence of organizational outlines in instructional films.* (Instructional Film Research Program, Pennsylvania State University) Port Washington, New York: USN Training Device Center, Office of Naval Research, October 1952. Technical Report No. SDC 269-7-33.

Pan, S. The influence of context upon learning and recall. *J. exp. Psychol.*, 1926, *9*, 468-491.

Park, J. Vocabulary and comprehension difficulties of sound motion pictures. *School Rev.*, 1945, *53*, 154-161.

Peterman, J. N. & Bouscaren, N. *A study of introductory and summarizing sequences in training film instruction.* USAF Training Aids Research Laboratory, Unpublished Staff Research Memorandum, 1954.

*Pressey, S. L. A simple apparatus which gives tests and scores—and teaches. *School & Society*, 1926, *23*, 373-376. In L & G, pp. 35-41.

*Pressey, S. L. A machine for automatic teaching of drill material. *School & Society*, 1927, *25*, 549-552. In L & G, pp. 42-46.

Rimland, B. *Effectiveness of several methods of repetition of films.* (Instructional Film Research Program, Pennsylvania State University) Port Washington, New York: USN Training Device Center, Office of Naval Research, May 1955. Technical Report No. SDC 269-7-45.

Roshal, S. M. *Effects of learner representation in film-mediated perceptual-motor learning.* (Instructional Film Research Program, Pennsylvania State University) Port Washington, New York: USN Training Device Center, Office of Naval Research, 1949. Technical Report No. SDC 269-7-5.

Rothkopf, E. Z. Signal similarity and optimal signal arrangement of lesson and drill orders in alphabetical Morse code training. In G. Finch & F. Cameron (Eds.), *Symposium on Air Force human engineering, personnel and training research.* Washington, D.C.: National Academy of Sciences—National Research Council, 1958. Publication 516.

Saltz, E. & Newman, S. E. *Relationship between language variables and decision making in an assembly task.* USAF Training Aids Research Laboratory, Unpublished Laboratory Note, 1956. TARL-LN-56-22.

Saltz, E. & Newman, S. E. The effect of prior learning of symbols on performance in reasoning. *Amer. J. Psychol.*, 1960, *73*, 91-99.

Sheffield, F. D. *Perceptual mediation in the learning of organizable sequences: Theory and experiment.* Maintenance Laboratory, Air Force Personnel and Training Research Center, September 1957. Technical Memorandum ML-TM-57-14.

Sheffield, F. D., Margolius, G., & Hoehn, A. J. Experiments on perceptual mediation in the learning of organizable sequences. In A. A. Lumsdaine (Ed.), *Student response in programmed instruction: A symposium.* Washington, D.C.: National Academy of Sciences—National Research Council, 1961.

Shettel, H. H., Faison, E. J., Roshal, S. M., & Lumsdaine, A. A. An experimental comparison of "live" and filmed lectures employing mobile training devices. *Audio-visual communica. Rev.*, 1956, *4*, 216-222.

*Skinner, B. F. The science of learning and the art of teaching. *Harvard educ. Rev.*, 1954, *24*, 86-97. In L & G, pp. 99-113.

*Skinner, B. F. Teaching machines. *Science*, 1958, *128*, 969-977. In L & G, pp. 137-158.

Stein, J. J. *The effect of a pre-film test on learning from an educational sound motion picture.* (Instructional Film Research Program, Pennsylvania State University) Port Washington, New York: USN Training Device Center, Office of Naval Research, November 1952. Technical Report No. SDC 269-7-35.

Sulzer, R. L., Lumsdaine, A. A., & Kopstein, F. F. *The value of using multiple examples in training film instruction.* Washington, D.C.: USAF Human Resources Research Laboratory, May 1952. HRRL Report No. 25.

Swanson, R. A. *The relative effectiveness of training aids designed for use in mobile training detachments.* Air Force Personnel Training Research Center, March 1954. Research Review AFPTRC-TR-54-1.

Swanson, R. A., Lumsdaine, A. A., & Aukes, L. E. Two studies in evaluation of maintenance training devices. In G. Finch & F. Càmeron (Eds.), *Symposium on Air Force human engineering, personnel, and training research.* Washington, D.C.: National Academy of Sciences—National Research Council, 1956.

VanderMeer, A. W. *Relative effectiveness of color and black and white in instructional films.* (Instructional Film Research Program, Pennsylvania State University) Port Washington, New York: USN Training Device Center, Office of Naval Research, 1952. Technical Report No. SDC 269-7-28.

Weiss, W. & Fine, B. J. *Stimulus familiarization as a factor in ideational learning.* USAF Training Aids Research Laboratory, Unpublished Laboratory Note, 1955. TARL-LN-55-48.

Witasek, S. Uber Lesen und Rezitieren in ihren Beziehungen zum Gedachtnis. *Z. Psychol.*, 1907, *44*, 161-185, 246-282.

Wulff, J. J. *The teaching effectiveness of a filmed mechanical assembly demonstration with supplementary nomenclature training.* USAF Training Aids Research Laboratory, Unpublished Laboratory Note, 1955. TARL-LN-55-8.

Wulff, J. J. & Emeson, D. L. The relationship between "What is learned" and "How it's taught." In A. A. Lumsdaine (Ed.), *Student response in programmed instruction: A symposium.* Washington, D.C.: National Academy of Sciences—National Research Council, 1961.

Wulff, J. J., Sheffield, F. D., & Kraeling, D. *"Familiarization" procedures used as adjuncts to assembly task training with a demonstration film.* USAF Training Aids Research Laboratory, Unpublished Staff Research Memorandum, 1954.

Wulff, J. J. & Kraeling, D. Familiarization procedures used as adjuncts to assembly-task training with a demonstration film. In A. A. Lumsdaine (Ed.), *Student response in programmed instruction: A symposium.* Washington, D.C.: National Academy of Sciences—National Research Council, 1961.

Wulff, J. J. & Stolurow, L. M. The role of class descriptive cues in paired-associates learning. *J. exp. Psychol.*, 1957, *53*, 199-206.

Zuckerman, J. V. *Commentary variations: Level of verbalization, personal reference, and phase relations in instructional films on perceptual motor tasks.* (Instructional Film Research Program, Pennsylvania State University) Port Washington, New York: USN Training Device Center, Office of Naval Research, 1949. Technical Report No. SDC 269-7-4.

Chapter **10**    *The Training of*
*Electronics Maintenance Technicians*

*Glenn L. Bryan, Office of Naval Research*[1]

The development of complicated electronic systems has mushroomed. They now cover an amazing variety of applications. They have enabled modern man to supplement and extend his capabilities in truly remarkable ways; and the end is not in sight. In a thriving world economy, serving exploding populations, there are mounting pressures for bigger and better electronic systems—but there is another side to the picture. Along with the many blessings associated with the new technology, there has developed a great need for numerous highly trained personnel.

This chapter is concerned with the many problems and issues involved in the training of men to install, care for, and repair the marvelous new equipments. It presents an overview of electronics maintenance training and presents some relevant research findings. Most of this research has been accomplished under military sponsorship. This reflects the critical importance of electronic equipments for present-day armed forces and the disastrous consequences of system failure. Many military systems involve vast electronic networks and the effectiveness of these systems is limited by the competence of the technicians assigned to keep the equipments in working order. In the final section of the chapter, it is pointed out that the research findings concerning electronics trouble shooting are generalizable to non-electronic training, such as the training of medical diagnosticians.

## SCHOOL TRAINING

In the interests of efficiency, formal school training is usually employed as a means of introducing the trainee to electronics. One of the first

[1]This chapter was prepared while the author was the director of the Electronics Personnel Research Group, University of Southern California. This group is supported through contracts with the Office of Naval Research.

questions to confront planners involves the content of beginning courses. There are now many, many different types of electronic equipment. All of the various types have numerous features in common, but they also have features specific to each single type. This raises the very basic training issue as to whether a man should be trained to maintain all the manifold varieties of equipment, or just equipments of a given kind. If specialization is decided upon, some method must be used to determine the best clustering of equipments for the specialists to learn.

Of course, in the actual case the generalist vs. specialist decision depends upon numerous practical considerations. For example, in the Navy such factors as limited shipboard space and the need for the individual ship to be largely self-sufficient preclude too narrow specialization. On the other hand, in the Army and Air Force, a higher degree of specialization is said to reduce training time and to take advantage of the average talents that are available.

But, from a theoretical standpoint, the decision hinges on the amount and kind of transfer from one type of electronics training to another. It would appear that the evaluation of the transfer effects of learning about one particular type of equipment prior to learning about a specified second type of equipment would be a matter for straightforward empirical experimentation. However, there is little evidence that such studies have been conducted. This may be a reflection of the fact that training researchers have not been able to obtain support for more definitive transfer experiments. Instead, training researchers have dealt with the issue in more general ways. Their investigations indicate that there is a considerable amount of material that is, or should be, generalizable over a broad range of electronic equipments. They agree that it is appropriate and efficient to organize the training schools in such a manner that a "core curriculum" containing elements common to several maintenance jobs is included in the training course of various specialists. This curriculum could serve as a basis for cross-training whenever such training became necessary or desirable.

Somewhat less agreement is found concerning the actual composition of the core curriculum. It is probably true, as concluded by Miller and Folley (1956), that there is no unique set of knowledge, concepts, and skills that is the core of all electronics specialties, but rather, even core content must be tailored to the particular specialties under consideration. In spite of this, there are several general areas that may be agreed upon as common electronics training needs. The more important of these are mentioned below.

*Technical Vocabulary.* The neophyte is confronted with an overwhelming number of new terms. One of his early tasks is to learn the meanings of these terms and the concepts underlying them. His subsequent success in receiving instruction, either written or oral, is partially dependent upon his mastery of this technical vocabulary. This probably accounts for the fact that maintenance proficiency, particularly in trouble shooting, is frequently found to be correlated with GCT (The Military General Classification Test), verbal comprehension, and job knowledge tests.

*Graphic Aids.* Various types of diagrams are furnished to the technician as training material while he is a student, and as job-aids after he has completed his formal training. These include such things as block diagrams, schematic diagrams, and wiring diagrams. It may also include diagnostigrams, trouble locators, and other specialized materials which will be discussed in connection with trouble shooting later in the chapter. In any case, it is necessary that the trainee develop good familiarity with the symbols and their hardware counterparts. Efforts to minimize the requirement for this sort of learning, and recognition of the fact that some technicians do have trouble in this area, are seen in the development of the POMSEE booklets[2] and various Trouble Locators (Berkshire, 1954; Warren, Schuster, & French, 1957). All of these seek to help technicians bridge the gap between the wavy lines on the schematic, the words in the book, and the physical components packed into the equipment.

*Test Equipment.* The maintenance technician requires a certain amount of knowledge about test equipments and how to use them. Although not all test equipment is of general usefulness, since there is an increasing tendency to develop special test equipments for special electronic equipments, there are a few old standbys. These can be taught as a part of the core training. Also, in the area of test equipment, a question is encountered of the type that plagues one throughout the study of electronics personnel training: "Is it necessary to go into the reasons *why* the test equipment works, or should one just try to develop good

---

[2]These are Navy publications put out by the Bureau of Ships which, in part, provide a set of instructions for use by ships' technicians in doing required preventive maintenance and in determining whether equipment is operating at prescribed standards. (The initials stand for Performance, Operational and Maintenance Standards of Electronic Equipment.) A brief resume of the POMSEE program appears in the September 1953 issue of the *BuShips Journal.*

cookbook procedures and teach these?" There is no clear-cut experimental evidence to resolve this question. However, there is ample evidence that a great deal of test equipment is being misused or neglected because technicians do not understand it. (This is not to suggest that this is the *only* reason why test equipment is misused or neglected.)

*Tools and Their Uses.* Most electronic equipments contain mechanical, electrical, and hydraulic components. Training must take this fact into account. Therefore, a trainee must learn a number of different tools, learn to recognize them on sight, and learn to use them properly. Some new equipments are constructed so that the use of the soldering iron is not as essential as it once was, but there is still a need for the trainee to develop skill in the use of soldering tools, wire strippers, and so forth. Unfortunately, this phase of maintenance training is often taken for granted (Wilson, Ruch, & Wolbers, 1950). A recent study by Williams and Whitmore (1959) demonstrated that Army technicians at all experience levels failed to use good soldering techniques. It may well be that more time should be devoted to hand tools early in training. And, of course, if the job requires skillful use of tools, considerable practice is necessary to develop high skill levels.

*Safety Practices.* Since many equipments produce electrical energy great enough to harm personnel, it is necessary to teach trainees how to protect themselves from these hazards and how to render assistance to a fellow worker if necessary. The same applies to hazards due to working at heights and around rotating machinery. It is desirable to incorporate this type of information in the early phases of a man's training.

*Basic Electricity and Electronics.* There are strong differences of opinion regarding just how much "theory" should be taught the technician. But, it is generally conceded that the man must be taught enough to permit him to understand the functions of the various circuit elements, to appreciate the general relationships among circuit parameters, and to work out the various data-, power-, and signal-flow paths through circuits. At present, there seems to be agreement in the military services that only as much of this type of information as is absolutely essential to the understanding of other training topics, or to performing on the job should be included in the core curriculum. One interesting study (Edgerton, 1956) sought to determine whether theory (the "why") should be taught before or after the "how to do it" phase of training. It was found that the order of training did make a difference, and that the decision to teach theory before or after is dependent upon the particular training goals employed. Rulon and Schweiker (1956) have emphasized the desirability of teaching theory along with the "how to do it" so as to promote recall in the work situation. Undoubtedly, this approach has merit. Unfortunately, the thorny problem of defining "theory" has not been resolved.

To review, everyone agrees that there is a core of information and skills involved in a wide variety of electronics tasks and assignments, but research studies are in less than complete agreement as to exactly what constitutes the core material. In one sense, a core training program can be very efficient, in that it can eliminate unnecessary duplication of training effort. On the other hand, if a needless topic is included in a core program, an extremely large number of man-hours are wasted.

## The Continuation Of School Training

Once the trainee has completed the core training program, he is ready to receive instruction on those aspects of his prospective job that distinguish it from other electronic specialties. Obviously, the curriculum content for this phase of his training will be dependent upon the particularities of the job for which he is being trained. It is difficult to obtain adequate descriptions of existing jobs to serve as bases for the development and refinement of maintenance training courses. It is even more difficult to develop courses of training before the job exists. And yet, in this era of mushrooming electronic development, it is both desirable and necessary to train maintenance personnel during the same period of time that the equipment itself is being developed. This creates a need for accurate prediction of the maintenance requirements of new equipments early in the equipment development cycle. Miller, Folley and Smith (1953a) have shown that sufficiently accurate predictions can be made to serve as the basis for the development of training curricula for new equipments.

*School Training Methods.* Regardless of the *content* of the school curriculum, there is an interesting research area associated with training *methods* themselves. Certain features of electronics might lead one to expect that the procedures for teaching electronics maintenance might be radically different from those employed to teach other subject matter. For example, since electrons are invisible and since there are many dynamic aspects to circuit theory, one might expect that the trainee would have trouble conceptualizing what was going on in complicated circuits; and indeed they do.

The problem of determining the best method for teaching the electronics maintenance man has received considerable attention. One Air Force study suggested that the trainee should be taught from effect to cause by means of backtracks to parallel the work situation, to learn theory from the simpler circuits in the systems, and to learn "within-tolerance" conditions from practice with many "out-of-tolerance" indications. To some extent most modern instruction courses seek to follow these suggestions. However, as yet, no training technique has come along to revolutionize electronics training. A great deal of it is still accomplished by conventional classroom and laboratory methods.

Considerable effort has been expended in the development of various types of training aids for school use. However, few of them have become generally integrated into electronics maintenance training. Perhaps one of the main reasons for this cool reception to training aids is that they frequently cost more money than stretched training budgets can stand. Also, some aids appear to require more training time than they are judged to be worth; and it has often turned out that the use of such devices has not yielded clear improvement over the results from existing techniques. To cite some examples: the Air Force tested the training effectiveness of synthetic trouble-shooting materials (USAF Training Analysis and Development Directorate, 1954) and concluded that they did not fulfill the Air Force training needs. Murnin, Vander-Meer, and Vris (1954) compared a training aid which required the trainee to interconnect circuit components by means of actual wires, versus a diagram upon which the trainee drew pencil lines to represent interconnections. They found that there was no advantage to the three-dimensional materials. Finally, a study by Swanson (1954) indicated that five different types of demonstration materials, ranging from elaborate working models to simple placards, were equally effective as training aids even though they differed greatly in terms of their costs and complexity.

*The Importance of Spaced Learning.* There are a number of studies which indicate that maintenance students have trouble assimilating, integrating, and remembering material which they are taught in school. There seem to be two good reasons why this should be the case. First of all, the nature of the material to be learned is such that it requires considerable integration before it becomes useful to the learner. Material of this type frequently requires repetition and opportunity for practice before it is mastered. Secondly, tight training schedules intended to minimize the portion of a man's enlistment spent in training schools are not designed to permit the student to acquire extensive practice and to overlearn needed habits.

*The Importance of Laboratory Instruction.* The nature of the material to be learned by the trainee requires that he have adequate opportunity to practice with the type of equipment that he will eventually be called upon to maintain. Ideally, this would take place in the training school laboratory, using equipments set aside for training purposes and under the direction of competent training personnel. But many schools find that they can do little more than give the student a nodding acquaintance with the equipment. As a result, some of the essential training is projected into the field.

## ON-THE-JOB TRAINING

*"Breaking In."* When the newly trained technician is sent to his field assignment, he is still in need of certain types of training. There is evidence to indicate that he has certain technical needs associated with his transition from the school environment to the job environment. For the most part, these are usually satisfied in an informal way. The trainee is counted upon to pick up what he needs, to compensate for his own deficiencies. Baldwin, Mager, Vineberg and Whipple (1957) found that this sort of thing happens to Army electronics mechanics. These mechanics were tested to assess the effects of field experience on their technical knowledge and skills. It was found that the mechanics showed general improvement in their maintenance skills as a function of experience during their first six months in the field. After that, they showed no tendency to improve further in the skills tested, except in trouble-shooting ability which continued to develop with field experience. Presumably, the reason for continued improvement was related to the fact that the field situation provided opportunities to work with the gear in ways that were not possible in the training school situation. The study reported by Briggs and Besnard (1955) emphasized the training advantage of "reinforced practice" for electronic system technicians.

*Methods of Field Training.* There are a number of methods by which field training can occur. One of these is self-training. Although a great deal of this takes place, it is fair to state that it is risky for the military services to assume that it is sufficient to satisfy the training needs. Shipboard observations (Grings, Bryan, Svenson, & LaPorte, 1953a) and the testimony of various shipboard electronics personnel suggest that this may not be a very important source of technical electronics training with the Navy. And, there is little reason to believe that the situation is better in the other services.

Even under circumstances where group training is feasible, it is generally reported (Grings, Bryan, Svenson, & LaPorte, 1953b; Vineberg, 1955) that the most effective form of training for the newly assigned school graduate is individual tutoring and guidance. Unfortunately, in many cases experienced men with adequate instructional skills are not available. The fact that individual training is so desirable, but so hard to obtain in the practical situation, either in school or in the field, has lent impetus to the development of "teaching machines" for post-school electronics training.

*Closing the Information Loop.* Of course, it is useful to feed information back from the field to the schools. In some way or another, there is always a "formal" provision for this to occur. In spite of this, it is not unusual for training courses to get far out of line from the actual jobs. Lucier, Fischl and Courtney (1958) have suggested procedures intended to guarantee better and more timely feedback of personnel information with the Navy. Wilson, Mackie and Buckner (1954) have demonstrated the necessity for using performance tests in addition to paper-and-pencil tests and ratings for checking on the output of the training schools. Generally speaking, the lack of external criterion information against which to evaluate school curricula and teaching methods imposes a severe limitation upon systematic improvement in formal school training via feedback from field requirements.

## MAJOR JOB RESPONSIBILITIES

### Routine Care of Equipment

A considerable part of the maintenance effort is directed to routine care of equipment. While there is marked improvement in some modern pieces of gear in terms of the amount of care they require, most electronics equipments must be attended to regularly, and properly, if they are to work successfully. To those who are unfamiliar with electronics, teaching technicians to do this would not seem to constitute much of a training burden. However, such is not the case. Even routines which are written in the most painstaking way must be practiced before the man becomes proficient in them.

For example, the Navy Bureau of Ships developed the POMSEE program for use by virtually untrained men. Even though all of the steps were carefully spelled out and profusely illustrated, it was necessary for the technician actually to go through the activities following the printed instructions several times before he reached the point where he could do them in a reasonable time with a reasonable expenditure of effort. In connection with one research effort (Bryan, Bond, & La-Porte, 1957), technicians who had received regular school training, but had not done the POMSEE on a particular type of equipment, were required to do so on their own ships under the watchful eye of a research worker. It took over two days for them to complete the prescribed procedures the first time, and less than half a day thereafter. Obviously, the effectiveness of technicians on the job could be improved by actually leading them through all the steps in their maintenance routines on the equipments for which they are responsible. In addition, it is necessary to train the technician *when* to administer routine care to the equipment as well as *how* to do so. It is the ironic fact that too much checking can shorten the life of the equipment.

A portion of the training should be directed to the use of handbooks and other materials. Analyses of this type of material have repeatedly shown that these materials are hard for the technician to use in the field. There are many reasons for this, but it is clear that much improvement in the situation could be realized by making changes in the materials themselves. Nonetheless, at any given time, the maintenance man has only certain materials available to him, and cannot wait until new ones are written. His job effectiveness is impaired unless he is given sufficient training and practice in the use of the available printed materials. Similar comments apply to the record-keeping requirements of his job.

Probably one of the most important aspects of routine maintenance is the checkout of equipments and systems to be sure they are peaked up and working properly. From a training standpoint, this calls attention to the fact that the trainee must be taught a clear conception of how equipment works. And he must be provided with suitable standards against which to evaluate the performance of each equipment. There are many problems involved in providing useful standards of this sort. Although strides have been made in the direction of obtaining better and more realistic standards in recent years, there is still room for improvement. Training-wise, it is important for the trainee to be convinced that the standards are potentially useful to him, and then to learn exactly how to use them.

Those who like to solve personnel problems by adding more hardware to existing systems look forward to the day when equipment will be self-monitoring and will automatically check itself out. The notion here is that the system will continuously, or at frequent intervals, report its status to a human operator. This concept is not dramatically new. Such devices as "Power On" lights and fuse alarms have been installed for many years. However, the newer systems, particularly those containing large-scale digital computers, have incorporated highly sophisticated applications of this self-monitoring concept. In many cases, this has been extended to monitoring the system during extensive checkout routines which expose it to situations and patterns at the limit of the system's capability. Some of these routines, for example, the marginal checking routines used in certain large digital computer systems, are intended to detect, and hence prevent, incipient failures. The development of such automatic checking equipment has a definite impact on training. However, it does not eliminate the need for trained maintenance men. Rather, self-checking digital systems actually introduce some new training requirements. Some maintenance technicians must now develop competence in computer coding, must learn about the details of information processing within the systems, and must learn to interpret the various patterns of indications such as lights, print-outs, etc. that are available (Bryan, Rigney, Bond, LaPorte, Hoffman, & McAllister, 1959).

Thus far in this chapter, attention has been focussed upon that period in the maintenance man's career when he has completed formal school training and has been sent out to a unit. It has been pointed out that he typically lacks many of the practical skills that the job requires of him. Furthermore, he is likely to grow rusty with respect to many of the things that he learned in school because he has little opportunity to review them on the job. Although lip service is paid to on-the-job training, it appears that a special, carefully planned transition should be considered as a means of supplementing school training in preparing the technician for his job.

## Trouble Shooting

By far the most important, and most difficult to teach, responsibility of the maintenance technician is trouble shooting. In its most general meaning, the term refers to any technique employed to correct malfunctions. The process begins when a problem is recognized and, even though the goal is clear, the route to the goal is not immediately known; it ends when the trouble is corrected. If this broad definition is used, a great deal of activity takes place under the name of trouble shooting which is little more than routine following of directions.

Where this is the case, the training problem is, theoretically, simplified to training the individual how to read, understand, and follow prescribed routines. Trouble Locators (Berkshire, 1954; Warren, Schuster, & French, 1957) are examples of materials designed to guide the trouble shooter's efforts in the field in a very specific way. Diagnostigrams and backtracks (Rulon & Schweiker, 1956) were also developed to assist the trouble shooter to organize and define the problem information and to help him accomplish the trouble-shooting task. Preliminary tryouts of these indicated that they have good potential, but it has yet to be shown that the widespread adoption of such job aids would result in radical changes in future training requirements.

A more challenging type of trouble shooting is that in which the technician is confronted with a defective system, where he has no cookbook to follow, or perhaps he has already followed the cookbook without remedying the trouble. Obviously, this type of situation occurs in the field, and someone must be trained to cope with such situations. Because of critical requirements for good trouble shooters in the military services, a great deal of work has gone into the study of trouble-shooting processes and the development of various devices and other materials intended to promote the learning of trouble shooting. In an effort to be orderly, a somewhat arbitrary breakdown of the typical trouble-shooting process is presented in the following section, along with selected studies illustrative of the type of research findings that have been reported.

## A FORMAL ANALYSIS OF TROUBLE SHOOTING

This section is devoted to a formal analysis of trouble shooting. As such, it does not represent trouble shooting as it occurs in actual practice; but it points out the heterogeneous nature of trouble shooting and may also serve to direct training attention at the various aspects of the task. In addition, it may also provide a framework for the development of automatic trouble-shooting routines to be programmed into systems containing computers.

*Symptom Recognition.* The first stage in trouble shooting occurs when the technician becomes aware that the system is not functioning as it should; there are signs that something is wrong. In some cases, this is obvious. In others, it is not. Certainly, a logical first step in the training of trouble shooters would be to give them intensive practice in determining whether the equipment was functioning properly, or whether something was wrong.

*Symptom Elaboration.* An extremely important, but often over-looked phase in the trouble-shooting process is the exploration of the initial stimulus situation to ascertain the complete stimulus (symptom) pattern being generated by the equipment. Not infrequently, thoroughness at this point will result in the discovery of a displaced switch or faulty tuning which will completely eliminate the symptoms of a malfunction. Unfortunately, there is a tendency for technicians to attempt to solve the trouble-shooting problem before they have defined it. Perhaps, this is an indication that they regard their task as a search rather than the solving of a problem. In any event, analyses of some 1500 freely elicited trouble-shooting protocols (Bryan, Bond, LaPorte, & Hoffman, 1956) substantiated the fact that experienced Navy technicians frequently failed to structure their trouble-shooting problems sufficiently during their early stages. Undoubtedly, it would be useful to design training courses to give each trainee considerable practice in symptom elaboration before allowing him to engage in the next stage in the trouble-shooting process.

*Formulation of Hypotheses.* In the ideal case, the next step is the formulation of all of the hypotheses which could account for the pattern of symptoms being observed. In actual practice this seldom happens. Moore, Saltz and Hoehn (1955) required a group of airmen to list "all possible causes that they could think of that might be responsible for the symptoms" as a part of a preplanning technique. Results comparing the effectiveness of the preplanners vs. controls led them to recommend this type of activity as a means for improving trouble-shooting effectiveness.

*Selection of Hypothesis.* At this point, one of the hypotheses must be selected for testing. Perhaps this is the point where so-called "probability trouble shooting" is most valid; here it would dictate the selection of the most likely hypothesis which was in line with past experience with that particular piece of equipment or equipments of that sort. The selection of the hypothesis should also take into account the difficulties associated with tampering with certain portions of the circuitry and the like. Under some circumstances, a trouble shooter might elect to test the second most attractive hypothesis instead of the most attractive, on the grounds that the first one would involve difficulties that should be avoided if at all possible. It should be noted that this view is somewhat different from the usual view of probability trouble shooting which tends to encourage premature and unsystematic component replacement.

*Formulation of a Testing Plan.* At this point the technician should formulate a more or less concrete plan for testing the hypothesis. It is probably best if the plan extends beyond the selection of the first test to be made. In any event, the plan should include definite criteria for abandoning the hypothesis under test. Technicians without a plan tend to proceed in unsystematic ways and to persist in courses of action that are not productive. These conclusions are substantiated in the preplanning study referred to above.

*Acquisition of Circuit-Status Information.* Now, the technician is required to implement the trouble-shooting plan that he has made. Typically, this will require him to obtain test equipment readings. This is the point in the process where checking procedures like the "half-split" method (Miller, Folley, & Smith, 1953b) may be useful. As indicated earlier, there is evidence that today's technicians do not use test equipment to its best advantage. Failure to use the test equipment provided, or using it improperly, is extremely handicapping, since the test equipment readings are the "stuff" that the technician must process to achieve a solution to the trouble-shooting problem.

*Interpretation of Discrete Readings.* As each reading is obtained, it has to be interpreted. At least in the early stages of a trouble-shooting problem it is likely that the technician does not try to do more than classify the readings he gets into broad qualitative categories (such as normal, high, low, absent, etc.). Problems which permit clear-cut classifications are much easier to solve than those which produce many borderline readings. In all likelihood, concentrated efforts to train men how to interpret the readings they obtain would be of considerable value. The development of "go/no-go" indicators assumes that it is possible to pre-establish the boundary between "normal" and "abnormal" and thus to eliminate this troublesome phase in the trouble-shooting process.

*Organization of Information.* There is a great deal of overlap between this stage of trouble shooting and the preceding one. However, malfunctioning components are seldom located by considering measurements singly, but rather by patterns of readings. The trouble shooter must construct these patterns (which is to say that he must organize the readings) for himself. The fact that this type of activity is a necessary part of trouble shooting is dramatized in those equipments which include a great many "go/no-go" indicators. Although all of the information necessary to the solution of a problem may be displayed in the form of console lights, the problem may be far from solved.

Gagné (1959) has called attention to the relationship between certain aspects of the trouble-shooting sequence and conventional concept formation studies. It may well be that this is one point at which studies of concept formation and studies of trouble shooting could benefit by mutual exchange. For it is at this phase of the trouble-shooting sequence that the individual is confronted with undifferentiated elements of information which can be combined in different ways. Formation and application of concepts such as continuity, simultaneity, rise time, gating, and so forth are necessary to take the trouble shooter farther down the road.

*Selection of an Alternative Hypothesis.* If the initial hypothesis has to be rejected, it is likely to be rejected on the basis of a pattern of information developing which is at odds with the hypothesis under test. In going back to select another hypothesis, the trouble shooter should not take the one that seemed to be the second best bet at the start of the problem. He now has obtained additional information about the circuit and should be in a far better position to choose a hypothesis consistent with the total information available. Trouble-shooting protocols show that technicians are indecisive about rejecting hypotheses. It would undoubtedly be a good idea to provide trouble-shooting trainees with specific practice which required them to recognize the fact that their initial hypothesis had been discredited and should be replaced by another. A flexible device such as that employed by Dale (1957) would appear to be useful for this purpose.

*Confirmation of Hypothesis.* This idealized sequence is concluded when the technician makes some crucial adjustment or component replacement that eliminates the source of the difficulty. This is a crucial point in the sequence from the standpoint of training since this is the principal place where reinforcement occurs. Crowder (1954) found that a group of 126 Q-24 radar mechanics failed to make a sufficient confirmatory check before replacing a subunit in 397 out of 600 problem trials where such a check was possible and necessary. In actuality, it is not unusual for a technician to complete the repair of an item of equipment and to restore it to normal operating condition without knowing exactly what has caused the difficulty. From a theoretical point of view, the confirmation of the correct hypothesis is important to learning. Obviously, "solving" a trouble-shooting problem without knowing what has been done to achieve the solution has very little training value.

## Trouble-Shooting Training Research

In view of the fact that substantial efforts have been made in the trouble-shooting research area, it would be reasonable to expect that a great deal of training research had been accomplished. However, a careful review of the literature indicates that the bulk of the trouble-shooting research has not been directed at training, but to the analysis of trouble-shooting protocols and the development of proficiency tests. In many cases, the same study will deal with training diagnosis and proficiency measurement. Under these circumstances, training research is apt to come out a poor second. There are a number of good reasons why training research in the area of trouble shooting is extremely difficult to conduct.

The most difficult problem that confronts the experimenter who wishes to conduct a trouble-shooting training experiment is the fact that it is hard to get an agreed-upon measure of trouble-shooting competence to serve as a criterion measure. Another reason that training studies in this area are not very popular is that the training process is highly time-consuming. It is indeed optimistic to expect that a few days of training will revolutionize a man's habits of thought. If this could be done at all, one would expect to have to devote a great deal of time to the task. But experimental subjects are hard to come by; it is difficult to get access to them for weeks at a time. In consequence, many of the training "research" studies are little more than tryouts using a novel training procedure, curriculum, or aid. While there is nothing wrong with such tryouts, they are certainly not detailed training research. Finally, many trouble-shooting training studies are limited because only a small number of equipments are available for training purposes. It is difficult to design an adequate training study when the entire project must be carried out using only one or two pieces of equipment.

*Trouble-Shooting Training on Actual Equipment.* The customary way to train a man to troubleshoot is to give him supervised practice on the actual electronic equipment. This is usually accomplished by inserting known faults into the gear and then requiring the trainee to find them. Although some proficiency tests have employed live equipment (Evans & Smith, 1953), it has not been a popular technique for controlled experiments. There are many reasons for this. Among them are the following: very little usable equipment is available for training purposes, there may be dangers to trainee and equipment, and trained instructors are in short supply. Briggs, Besnard and Walker (1955) and Rigney and Bryan (1954) have enumerated others.

*Trouble-Shooting Training on Synthetic Equipment.* As a result, most of the training research has dealt with symbolic representations of equipments, ranging from simulators, through mock-ups, to diagrams. Standlee, Popham and Fattu (1956) listed 110 studies dealing with trouble shooting; a preponderance of them employed some substitute for the actual equipment. Several of them were concerned with comparing trouble-shooting protocols made while working with the actual equipment with protocols generated while working on its synthetic counterpart. In all cases, the experimental results appear to justify the use of the more controllable media. (See Chapter 8 by Gagné and Chapter 9 by Lumsdaine.)

One technique for training men to become trouble shooters employs "right-wrong" feedback. Typically, the trainee is presented with a stimulus situation, usually a question, and a small number of alternative responses. He selects a response and is informed, in one way or another, whether or not he has selected the correct one. Usually he is allowed to continue selecting alternatives until he has located the correct one. Of course, the notion of providing prompt feedback to the learner is not a new idea. It has a long history and has been applied to all sorts of subject matter. It has proved to be quite effective in the trouble-shooting training situation. Almost all of the trouble-shooting training devices incorporate some type of feedback along with other techniques for promoting learning. Some rely, more or less exclusively, on simple right-wrong feedback; the Green Light Rater (Twyford, O'Hara, & Goldman, 1958) and the Punchboard Tutor (Cantor & Brown, 1956) are examples of this type of device. In both cases the trainees respond to a multiple-choice question and are informed of the correctness of the alternative that they have chosen.

"Right-wrong" feedback has also been employed to teach procedures and sequences. The Subject-Matter Trainer (Besnard, Briggs, Mursch, & Walker, 1955) may be used in this manner. The trainee is asked a question which he answers by pressing a button beside one of 20 displayed responses. If the response he selects is correct, a green light is lighted adjacent to the selected alternative. Otherwise, a red light comes on. By arranging the questions in an appropriate order, it is possible to require the student to indicate "what to do first," "what next," and so on.

Devices such as Crowder's Scrambled Books (Crowder, 1959) and the TUTOR[3] add two additional feedback dimensions: flexibility, the trainee determines the next step in the learning process by his own response; and verbal material which is added to supplement the "right-wrong" feedback. In using these devices the trainee selects an alternative response to a multiple-choice question, and then turns to a designated page (or frame) number. At that point he is told whether his choice was correct or incorrect. He is also given remedial information, general principles, or whatever the person writing the program feels would be helpful, and is then asked another question.

A rather different type of trouble-shooting trainer confronts the trainee with a problem, i.e., the symptoms of a malfunction, makes available a pool of information about the status of the circuitry, and provides him with a way to check whether or not he located the defective part. Actual operational electronic equipment, the Tab-Test (Glaser, Damrin, & Gardner, 1952), the MASTS (Grings, Rigney, Bond, & Summers, 1953), the Trainer-Tester (USN Bureau of Naval Personnel, 1954), the AUTOMASTS (Bryan, Bond, LaPorte, & Summers, 1954), the K-System MAC-1 Trainer (French, 1956), the E-4 Troubleshooting Trainer Simulator (Briggs, 1956) and the Trouble-Shooting Board (Glaser & Phillips, 1954) are all representative of this type of trainer. The underlying training philosophy depends mainly upon the benefits of practice and review of the trouble-shooting protocols by the instructor.

Two other devices seek to train trouble shooting at a very general level in the hope that analytical skills transfer to specific trouble-shooting situations. One of these, the Generalized Electronics Trouble Shooting Trainer (Warren, Atkins, Ford, & Wolbers, 1955) deals with flow diagrams. The trainee is taught efficient ways to analyze these diagrams using a set of instructional materials and the G-E-T-S Trainer. The other, the Logical Analysis Device, is based upon a laboratory instrument described by John and Miller (1957). It provides practice in solving problems involving logical relationships. For the most part, it has been investigated in terms of its potential as a

---

[3]Essentially this device is a mechanized version of the Scrambled Books, in which individual motion picture frames are projected. As added features it maintains a record of responses and is able to present movie sequences.

selection test, but it has been suggested that it would also have value as a means for training trouble shooters. Experimental validation of the transfer effects afforded by these two devices has not yet been accomplished. However, the work of Miller and Slebodnick (1958) indicates that trouble-shooting strategy can be taught as a set of principles and practiced with abstract material so as to generalize to specific situations.

Many of the training approaches just described are "wholistic" in that they attempt to teach trouble shooting *in toto*. In most of these cases, it is felt that each trainee will learn trouble shooting by doing trouble shooting in a relatively unstructured framework. Advocates of this viewpoint emphasize the importance of requiring the trainee to structure the trouble-shooting problem for himself. For example, as Grings put it (Grings, et al., 1953):

> It is important to emphasize that the technician has to structure the problem for himself. He starts with a certain number of 'givens' in the situation: output symptoms, front panel indications, operator reports, supplementary reference material, and his own experience. Between this start and the end of the problem lies a solution route which *he determines*. It may have numerous byways, or it may proceed by the shortest possible path from start to successful solution of the problem. The point to reiterate is that this path is a result of the interaction between the situation and the individual. No two technicians solve the same problem in exactly the same way. There are no fixed alleys in the 'maze' they traverse. Each individual selects his own test points in the circuits and is faced by his own choice points, each of which is a resultant of some of his behavior up to that time.

The benefits of this "learn by trouble shooting" approach to troubleshooting training appear to derive from sheer experience and the use of such supplementary techniques as post-mortem review. In any event, trouble-shooting effectiveness does improve as a function of unguided practice. This has been demonstrated formally many times (e.g., Bryan, Bond, & LaPorte, 1955).

On the other hand, a recent example of guided practice is contained in an experiment which compared the training effectiveness of several different ways of teaching trouble shooting (Bryan & Schuster, 1959). This study was conducted at the Navy Electronics Training School at Treasure Island, California. One hundred sixty-two students served as subjects and devoted the entire 19th week of their training course to the experiment. The first day of each experimental week was spent in intensive study of the DAS-3 Loran (an operational navigational aid which combines a superheterodyne receiver and fairly complicated pulse type networks). During the following three days the subjects were divided into a number of groups, each of which received a different type of trouble-shooting training. On the last day of the experimental week the subjects were given a criterion test to measure their trouble-shooting proficiency. In addition, a number of trainees also were individually tested four weeks later on an independent sample of trouble-shooting problems administered by school instructors using different radar equipment.

One purpose of the experiment was to measure improvement in trouble-shooting proficiency attributable to sheer practice. The results obtained clearly indicated that such improvement did occur. However, those trainees who were given guidance during the three-day learning period improved even more. Presenting the student with written after-the-fact explanations of the guidance principles also proved beneficial. The psychologically interesting feature of the experiment and the exciting possibilities for useful application hinge upon the fact that guidance was given without prior rationalization. This statement can be clarified by a brief look at one of the guidance techniques. These groups employed a laboratory device named the Optimal Sequence Trainer which is shown in Figure 10.1.

The trainee was required to go through the following sequence during his trouble-shooting practice. He had to examine the symptom

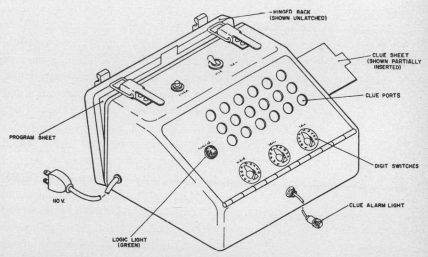

FIGURE 10.1. Exterior View of the Optimal Sequence Trainer (OST)

material given to him in order to decide what check to make to initiate the trouble-shooting sequence. There were about one thousand possible alternatives open to him, ranging from simple knob twisting to more complicated test equipment readings. When he had nominated a check, the trainee would set a three digit code number representing his intended action into the Optimal Sequence Trainer by means of the digit switches on its front panel. If his selection exactly duplicated that of a "ghost expert" the green logic light on the face of the OST would come on. If he failed to duplicate the expert's choice, no light would light and the trainee would have to refer back to the problem materials and decide upon another check. If the green light did come on, provision was made for the technician to obtain the results of the approved check. The experimental procedures were set up to deny him information under any other circumstances.

The Optimal Sequence Trainer also had a prompting feature to indicate which check should have been made if the trainee was unable to discover the expert's choice within a period of seven minutes. Problems were changed in the machine by changing the program sheet and the clue sheet. The effect of all of this was that the trainee had to "second guess" the expert at each step in the trouble-shooting sequence without any advance information regarding the expert's principles of trouble shooting. During the early portions of the three-day practice session many of the men trained in this manner felt as if they were trying to follow footprints in the snow while blindfolded. Toward the end of the three-day period they began to act as if they had learned to "think like" the expert.

The fact that the experimental results indicated that men could be trained to think like a trouble-shooting expert by being required to follow in his footsteps was deemed particularly desirable. This desirability stems from the fact that it is not uncommon for an expert trouble shooter to behave inconsistently with respect to his own pious pronouncements of general trouble-shooting principles. Careful analyses of an expert's trouble-shooting protocols strongly suggest that trouble-shooting problems are highly situational and are not ordinarily solved by the routine application of general principles. A particularly gratifying result of the experiment was that the men who had received guidance, "learned to think like the expert," not only excelled in the criterion test given at the end of the experimental week but also in the equipment performance test independently administered four weeks later.

## IMPLICATIONS

The foregoing has been an effort to touch upon the important areas of maintenance training. It is desirable at this point to stop and point out what appear to be the important implications of the maintenance training research. First of all, it seems that the decisions concerning course content can be made on the basis of the transferability of knowledges and skills. In specific cases this poses serious problems because the training researcher is often unable to attract support to finance specific systematic transfer studies. Hence, he is often forced to work at a more general level than he feels comfortable.

Secondly, there appears to be a definite need for supervised on-the-job training to assist the man recently assigned a technical maintenance responsibility. This is required since the new man must adapt his school learning to his specific job situation. Furthermore, in many cases, he needs to be trained in those supplementary aspects of his new job which are so specific to it that they could not have been included in a general training course. Failure on the part of many organizations to provide aggressive on-the-job follow-up training frequently allows newly-learned skills and knowledges to become rusty while the neophyte technician becomes disillusioned while serving in some menial capacity. Research-wise, the problems in this area seem to center upon the invention and evaluation of on-the-job training techniques.

Thirdly, it appears that the most intriguing research area in the electronics training domain involves the trouble-shooting processes. With the advent of increasingly complicated systems, it is urgent that someone be trained to understand each system and its objectives. These men must be able to perform such activities as system monitoring, system alignment, system management, system diagnosis, and system repair. Psychologists are aware of the fact that more research is needed to produce fuller understanding of the processes involved in tasks such as monitoring, diagnosis, and so forth. In addition, once such understandings are obtained it will still be necessary to develop effective means for training men so that they may be able to perform these necessary systems functions.

Unfortunately, the production of training research results often appears to be an end in itself. Even though current training research literature contains a great deal of useful information, it has not been implemented by those responsible for the conduct of training. The usual reasons given for this are: (*a*) new ideas are usually resisted, (*b*) training personnel frequently resent the invasion by the training researcher, and (c) there may be poor communication between training researchers and those who actually conduct the training. It seems, however, that immediate and important gains could be made in the training of trouble shooters and other maintenance personnel by applying the research information at hand.

Much of that learned in the study of trouble shooting is directly applicable to other areas. While many examples might be given, perhaps an obvious one will suffice. The training of medical diagnosticians is a chronic problem for medical schools. An analysis of the task of making a medical diagnosis indicates that it has much in common with electronics trouble shooting. For one thing, the neophyte physician must learn to manage his diagnostic resources. He must conduct the diagnosis in such a manner that he arrives at a correct diagnosis without unnecessarily requiring expensive and time-consuming lab tests. Just as the electronics trouble shooter, the doctor must decide what information to obtain, interpret each item of information in its own right, and organize the obtained information into a pattern consistent with the syndrome of a known malady. The parallels between this course of action and the steps detailed in the idealized trouble-shooting sequence presented earlier in this chapter are obvious. Without a doubt, the techniques and devices developed to train electronics trouble shooters would also prove useful in training physicians-to-be.

The implications of trouble-shooting research are not limited to applications and extensions. It is also a rich source of basic information relevant to such topics as transfer, concept formation, problem solving, decision making, thinking, and learning. Gagné (1959) has pointed out the pertinence of trouble-shooting studies to these more conventional psychological topics. Unfortunately, the fact that so many of these studies have not appeared in professional journals has caused them to be overlooked. For example, Duncan (1959) in an otherwise excellent review of the problem-solving literature chose to disregard all such studies. It would indeed be unfortunate if the vast fund of information produced under military sponsorship continued to escape the attention of the academically-oriented researcher. It is not absolutely necessary that this be the case. Contrary to notions sometimes expressed, the reports produced and distributed directly by sponsoring agencies are not impossible to acquire. They are usually available upon request. It is not particularly difficult to obtain a good idea of what is being done in the way of military-sponsored trouble-shooting research. Many are abstracted in the *Psychological Abstracts*. They are all abstracted in the *Armed Forces Technical Information Bulletin* of the Armed Forces Technical Information Agency, which is available to civilian contractors. Furthermore, Fattu (1956), Standlee, et al. (1956), and Stiles and Demaree (1958) have all produced extensive annotated bibliographies of trouble-shooting studies.

In all likelihood, this important body of information will eventually be integrated into the growing theoretical structure of the science of human behavior. Perhaps it will offer some basis for structuring subject-matter areas that are currently ill-defined and poorly integrated. One thing is certain: any behavioral theory that fails to account for the varied and important activities of the human trouble shooter will be inadequate.

## REFERENCES

Baldwin, R. D., Mager, R. F., Vineberg, R., & Whipple, J. E. *The AAFCS M-33 Mechanic Proficiency Test: I. Comparison of mechanics with and without field experience. II. Development and cross-validation.* Washington, D. C.: The George Washington University, Human Resources Research Office, May 1957. Technical Report 38.

Berkshire, J. R. *Field evaluation of a trouble-shooting aid.* Lackland AFB, USAF Personnel Training Research Center, June 1954. Technical Report AFPTRC-TR-54-24.

Besnard, G. G., Briggs, L. J., Mursch, G. A., & Walker, E. S. *Development of the Subject-Matter Trainer.* Lowry AFB, Armament Systems Personnel Research Laboratory, March 1955. Technical Memorandum ASPRL-TM-55-7.

Briggs, L. J. *A troubleshooting trainer for the E-4 Fire Control System.* Lowry AFB, Maintenance Laboratory, May 1956. Technical Memorandum ML-TM-56-16.

Briggs, L. J. & Besnard, G. G. *The benefits from increased practice in training electronic system mechanics.* Lowry AFB, Armament Systems Personnel Research Laboratory, October 1955. Technical Memorandum ASPRL-TM-55-12.

Briggs, L. J., Besnard, G. G., & Walker, E. S. *An E-4 Fire Control System performance test: I. Functional description.* Lowry AFB, Armament Systems Personnel Research Laboratory, March 1955. Technical Memorandum ASPRL-TM-55-8.

Bryan, G. L., Bond, N. A., Jr., & LaPorte, H. R., Jr. *An experimental battery for measurement of the proficiency of electronics technicians.* University of

Southern California, Electronics Personnel Research Group, March 1955. Technical Report 12.

Bryan, G. L., Bond, N. A., Jr., & LaPorte, H. R., Jr. *An analysis of problems related to scheduled maintenance of electronic equipment aboard naval ships.* Los Angeles: University of Southern California, Electronics Personnel Research Group, June 1957. Technical Report 22.

Bryan, G. L., Bond, N. A., Jr., LaPorte, H. R., Jr., & Hoffman, L. S. *Electronics trouble shooting: A behavioral analysis.* Los Angeles: University of Southern California, Electronics Personnel Research Group, March 1956. Technical Report 13.

Bryan, G. L., Bond, N. A., Jr., LaPorte, H. R., Jr., & Summers, S. A. *The Automasts: An automatically-recording test of electronics trouble shooting.* Los Angeles: University of Southern California, Electronics Personnel Research Group, August 1954. Technical Report 11.

Bryan, G. L., Rigney, J. W., Bond, N. A., Jr., LaPorte, H. R., Jr., Hoffman, L. S., & McAllister, Beverly N. *The role of humans in complex computer systems: Maintenance.* Los Angeles: University of Southern California, Electronics Personnel Research Group, January 1959. Technical Report 26.

Bryan, G. L. & Schuster, D. H. *An experimental comparison of trouble shooting training techniques.* Los Angeles: University of Southern California, Electronics Personnel Research Group, November 1959. Technical Report 30.

Cantor, J. H. & Brown, J. S. *An evaluation of the Trainer-Tester and Punchboard Tutor as electronic trouble-shooting training aids.* Nashville, Tennessee: George Peabody College for Teachers, October 1956. Technical Report NAVTRADEVCEN 1257-2-1.

Crowder, N. A. *Proficiency of Q-24 radar mechanics: V. Level of trouble shooting performance observed.* Lackland AFB, Texas: USAF Personnel Training Research Center, December 1954. Technical Report AFPTRC-TR-54-102.

Crowder, N. A. Automatic tutoring by means of intrinsic programming. In E. Galanter (Ed.), *Automatic teaching: The state of the art.* New York: Wiley, 1959. Pp. 109-116.

Dale, H. C. A. *An apparatus for investigating certain aspects of fault-finding.* Cambridge, England: Medical Research Council, Applied Psychological Research Unit, 1957.

Duncan, C. P. Recent research on human problem solving. *Psychol. Bull.,* 1959, *56,* 397-429.

Edgerton, H. A. *Should theory precede or follow a "How to do it" phase of training?* New York: Richardson, Bellows, Henry & Co., December 1956.

Evans, R. N. & Smith, L. J. *A study of performance measures of trouble shooting ability on electronic equipment.* Urbana, Illinois: University of Illinois, College of Education, October 1953.

Fattu, N. A. *A catalog of trouble shooting tests.* Bloomington, Indiana: Indiana University, Institute of Educational Research, December 1956. Research Report 1.

French, R. S. *The K-System MAC-1 Troubleshooting Trainer: I. Functional description.* Lowry AFB, Colorado: Armament Systems Personnel Research Laboratory, April 1956. Technical Memorandum ASPRL-TM-56-8.

Gagné, R. M. Problem solving and thinking. *Annu. Rev. Psychol.,* 1959, *10,* 147-172.

Glaser, R., Damrin, Dora E., & Gardner, F. M. *The tab item: A technique for the measurement of proficiency in diagnostic problem-solving tasks.* Urbana, Illinois: University of Illinois, College of Education, June 1952.

Glaser, R. & Phillips, J. C. *An analysis of tests of proficiency for guided missile personnel: II. The Trouble-Shooting Board.* Washington, D. C.: USN Bureau of Naval Personnel, August 1954. Technical Bulletin 55-16.

Grings, W. W., Bryan, G. L., Svenson, D. W., & LaPorte, H. R., Jr. *Shipboard observation of electronics personnel: Implications for the training of electronics personnel.* Los Angeles: University of Southern California, Electronics Personnel Research Group, February 1953. Technical Report 3. (a)

Grings, W. W., Bryan, G. L., Svenson, D. W., & LaPorte, H. R., Jr. *Shipboard observation of electronics personnel: Shipboard activities of electronics technicians.* Los Angeles: University of Southern California, Electronics Personnel Research Group, March 1953. Technical Report 4. (b)

Grings, W. W., Rigney, J. W., Bond, N. A., Jr., & Summers, S. A. *A methodological study of electronics trouble shooting skill: I. Rationale for and description of the Multiple-Alternative Symbolic Trouble Shooting Test.* Los Angeles: University of Southern California, Electronics Personnel Research Group, August 1953. Technical Report 9.

John, E. R. & Miller, J. G. The acquisition and application of information in the problem-solving process: An electronically operated logical test. *Behav. Sci.,* 1957, *2,* 291-300.

Lucier, O., Fischl, M. A., & Courtney, D. *Application of a systems concept to personnel research.* Philadelphia: Courtney, August 1958. Report 22, Project J.

Miller, R. B. & Folley, J. D., Jr. *Development of core training for F-86D electronics maintenance positions: IV. Principles and techniques.* Lowry AFB, Maintenance Laboratory, June 1956. Technical Memorandum ML-TM-56-4.

Miller, R. B., Folley, J. D., Jr., & Smith, P. R. *The validity of maintenance job analysis from the prototype of an electronic equipment: Part II. K-1 Bombing-Navigational System.* Pittsburgh: American Institute for Research, February 1953. (a)

Miller, R. B., Folley, J. D., Jr., & Smith, P. R. *Systematic trouble shooting and the half-split technique.* Lackland AFB, Human Resources Research Center, July 1953. Technical Report 53-21. (b)

Miller, R. B. & Slebodnick, E. B. *Research for experimental investigations of transferable skills in electronic maintenance.* Lackland AFB, USAF Personnel Training Research Center, January 1958. Technical Report AFPTRC-TR-2.

Moore, J. V., Saltz, E., & Hoehn, A. J. *Improving equipment maintenance by means of a preplanning technique.* Lackland AFB, USAF Personnel Training Research Center, September 1955. Technical Note AFPTRC-TN-55-26.

Murnin, J. A., VanderMeer, A. W., & Vris, T. *Comparison of training media: Trainee manipulations and observation of functioning electrical systems versus trainee drawing of schematic electrical systems.* State College, Pennsylvania: Pennsylvania State University, June 1954. Technical Report SPECDEVCEN 269-7-101.

Rigney, J. W. & Bryan, G. L. Special problems in the construction of electronics trouble shooting tests. Paper read at Amer. Psychol. Ass., New York, September 1954.

Rulon, P. J. & Schweiker, R. F. *The training of flight-simulator maintenance personnel: A proposed course that emphasizes trouble shooting.* Lowry AFB, Maintenance Laboratory, July 1956. Technical Memorandum ML-TM-56-17.

Standlee, L. S., Popham, W. J., & Fattu, N. A. *A review of trouble shooting research.* Bloomington: Indiana University Institute of Educational Research, December 1956. Research Report 3.

Stiles, Helen J. & Demaree, R. G. *Maintenance personnel and training research: A bibliography.* Fort Bliss, USA Air Defense Human Research Unit, March 1958. Staff Memorandum.

Swanson, R. A. *The relative effectiveness of training aids designed for use in mobile training detachments.* Lackland AFB, USAF Personnel Training Research Center, March 1954. Technical Report AFPTRC-TR-54-1.

Twyford, L. C., O'Hara, J. G., & Goldman, A. *Green Light Rater.* Port Washington, New York: U.S. Naval Training Device Center, December 1958. Technical Report NAVTRADEVCEN 20-OS-3-1.

USAF Training Analysis and Development Directorate. *An evaluation of Trainer-Testers (Superheterodyne receiver)*. Gulfport, Mississippi: DCS/O Headquarters Technical Training Air Force, 1954.

USN Bureau of Naval Personnel. *Introducing electronics testing*. Washington, D. C.: U. S. Government Printing Office, 1954. Nav Pers 92043A.

Vineberg, R. A performance test for the AAFCS M-33 radar mechanic and observations on trouble-shooting behavior. In P. M. Fitts (Ed.), *Symposium on electronics maintenance, 3-5 August 1955*. Washington, D. C.: Office of the Assistant Secretary of Defense, Advisory Panel on Personnel and Training Research, 1955. Pp. 87-101.

Warren, N. D., Atkins, D. W., Ford, J. S., & Wolbers, H. L. *Development of a training program for teaching basic principles of trouble shooting*. Lowry AFB, Armament Systems Personnel Research Laboratory, October 1955. Technical Memorandum ASPRL-TM-55-19.

Warren, N. D., Schuster, D. H., & French, R. S. *The Trouble-Locator: A trouble-shooting aid for a complex electronic system*. Lowry AFB, Maintenance Laboratory, November 1957. Technical Memorandum ML-TM-57-22.

Williams, W. L., Jr. & Whitmore, P. G., Jr. *The development and use of a performance test as a basis for comparing technicians with and without field experience: The NIKE AJAX IFC maintenance technician*. Washington, D. C.: The George Washington University, Human Resources Research Office, January 1959. Technical Report 52.

Wilson, C. L., Mackie, R. R., & Buckner, D. N. *Research on the development of shipboard performance measures: IV. A comparison between rated and tested ability to do certain job tasks*. Los Angeles: Management and Marketing Research Corporation, February 1954.

Wilson, C. L., Ruch, F. L., & Wolbers, H. L. *The use of performance tests in the measurement of shipboard performance of electrician's mates*. Los Angeles: Psychological Research Center, May 1950. Report 4.

Chapter *11*  |  *Proficiency Tests*
*For Training Evaluation*

*Norman Frederiksen, Educational Testing Service*

In recent years there seems to have been a rapidly growing awareness of the need for training evaluation and for developing proficiency measures for use in evaluation which better reflect the sought-for outcomes of instruction. An important reason for this interest in evaluation is undoubtedly the increased feeling of urgency about education which characterizes the post-sputnik era. Educators are suddenly being called upon to question the lecture and discussion methods that have been traditional and to devise improved methods of instruction. With the advent of television teaching, the language laboratory, and the teaching machine, the professional educator is confronted with the need to evaluate outcomes of various kinds of educational treatment in order to choose those which produce the best results. And in order to perform such experiments, the need for suitable criterion measures becomes pressing. The home-made tests and course grades which used to be thought satisfactory are now seen to be inadequate. Criterion measures which more accurately reflect the objectives of instruction and which permit judgments to be made separately about various aspects of the teaching program are needed.

Factor studies have shown that "intelligence" is not a unitary thing but is composed of a number of relatively independent factors. One would expect that the domain of educational achievement would be even more heterogeneous; but factor studies of the intercorrelations of college grades and aptitude tests have shown quite clearly a single "grades" factor (French, 1951). Course grades have high loadings on this factor, while aptitude tests have no significant loadings. (The existence of this grades factor may be one reason why attempts to make differential predictions of success in school and college have not been highly successful.) While the grades factor can probably be accounted for in part on the basis of variations in interest, personality, motivation, or even by "halo," another possible explanation is that methods of measuring achievement have not adequately reflected the variety in educational objectives. The objectives of instruction are quite varied, including changes not only in knowledge and understanding but also in attitudes, social skills, appreciations, and manipulative abilities. The typical achievement tests do not adequately reflect these diverse purposes. With the exercise of resourcefulness and imagination, it should be possible to produce achievement measures which more adequately assess educational outcomes other than those concerned primarily with knowledge and understanding.

### Specifying Objectives of Instruction

It should be obvious that one cannot hope to provide appropriate methods for evaluating instructional outcomes unless he has a clear idea of what those outcomes should be. Yet evaluations of instructional programs are sometimes made in which criterion measures are chosen because of their easy availability rather than through a careful study of what the students are supposed to be able to do as a consequence of the training.

Not that statements of objectives do not exist. Most public schools can find in their files detailed statements of objectives for every course. Military training programs are almost certain to have carefully drawn-up specifications of training objectives. A difficulty often encountered, however, is that the objectives are stated in such vague terms that they provide little help to the person who wishes to translate training objectives into proficiency tests. The statement that "a prime objective is preparation for intelligent citizenship in a democracy" may sound good in a college catalogue, but it gives neither the teacher nor the person charged with responsibility for evaluating instruction much guidance as to how to proceed.

When beginning a training evaluation study, it will often be necessary to reformulate objectives before going on to the problem of proficiency measures. Occasionally one must start from scratch in deciding what outcomes of instruction are desired. Or it may be necessary only to make sure that the objectives are translated into statements which clearly have something to do with observable behavior. The final report of the Cooperative Study of Evaluation in General Education provides an interesting account of how such problems were solved by the committees who worked on problems of evaluation in various areas of general education (Dressel & Mayhew, 1954).

A distinction is sometimes made between *immediate* and *ultimate* objectives (Lindquist, 1951). Ultimate objectives involve important modifications of behavior in later life; sometimes they cannot be realized for many years after the completion of the instruction. Participation in the political life of a democratic society might be an ultimate objective of a high school course in American history. As it stands, such an objective could be evaluated only many years later by observing the political activity of the individual; practically, even that would not succeed because by then the effects of the course would have been so diluted by other influences that they could not be detected—even if the students could be found.

In practice, therefore, it may be necessary to deal with more immediate objectives. These immediate objectives should be stated in terms of observable behaviors which are closely and logically related to the ultimate objective. Thus, in the previous example, the immediate objectives chosen might have to do with showing interest in contemporary political affairs by reading newspapers and news magazines, listening to political speeches and discussions, participating in local or school political activities, or knowing (through the students' own spontaneous efforts) something about political events and personalities.

If the results of a training evaluation study are to come to anything, it is essential that they be acceptable to the instructional staff. Too often the evaluation staff works independently of the school staff, and if the results are not too flattering to the enterprise, the teachers may dismiss the whole thing by saying in effect that nobody in his right mind would expect the students to do well on those tests anyhow. Training evaluation studies are of no use if they are not used. If instructors and evaluators work closely together in formulating objectives in behavioral terms and reach agreement as to the types of criterion measures to be employed, it is much more likely that the instructors will take the results to heart and try next time to do something which will be more successful in producing the desired change in behavior. It is also much more likely that the test-maker will build useful evaluation instruments.

For purposes of training evaluation, then, it is of crucial importance that the objectives of instruction be known. They must be known both to the instructional staff and to the evaluation staff, and they must be known in time to be used by both—by the instructional staff in teaching and by the evaluation staff in the preparation of criterion measures. If necessary, statements of ultimate criteria must be restated in terms of more immediate objectives and in terms of observable behavior of individuals.

## TYPES OF TRAINING EVALUATION MEASURES

Many methods of measurement have been used in training evaluation, and there are many ways in which they could be classified. In this section one possible classification will be presented, in which seven methods of obtaining measures for use in evaluating the outcomes of instruction are distinguished:

1. Solicit Opinions
2. Administer Attitude Scales
3. Measure Knowledge
4. Elicit Related Behavior
5. Elicit "What I Would Do" Behavior
6. Elicit Lifelike Behavior
7. Observe Real-Life Behavior

All of these methods are of course not necessarily feasible for any one particular situation. This section will describe each of these methods and discuss some of the advantages and disadvantages of each.

## *Solicit Opinions*

One method of evaluating instruction is to ask the students' opinions. The students may be queried informally, or elaborate questionnaires may be prepared and administered to the students. It is common on some campuses for students to publish the results of polls which purport to evaluate college courses. At the University of Washington student opinion surveys are conducted by the institution and are used as a partial basis for evaluation of faculty members (Guthrie, 1954). At a recent conference on appraisal of teaching in universities, a large part of the discussion was devoted to the use of student opinion as an evaluation technique (Appraisal of Teaching in Large Universities, 1959).

There is no doubt that highly reliable judgments about teaching can be obtained from students. Remmers reports that with as few as 20 students reporting, reliabilities as high as .90 can be obtained with his Purdue Rating Scale for Instruction (Remmers, 1927). This is a graphic rating scale for each of ten characteristics of college teachers. With a new instrument, the Forced-Choice Rating Scale for Instruction, reliabilities of .96 were obtained (Remmers, 1959). It is of course possible that such high reliabilities are in part the result of discussion and agreement among the students prior to administration of the rating instrument.

There are a number of fairly obvious faults with the method of soliciting students' opinions as a device for training evaluation. Students are likely to be gentlemen; they seem inclined to say reasonably favorable things about a course, perhaps because they do not wish to offend the instructor. Even when objective evidence shows no improvement beyond that gained by an untrained control group, preponderantly favorable opinions may be found. Permitting opinions to be expressed anonymously no doubt increases somewhat the candor with which replies are made; but one cannot count on complete frankness even when questionnaires are unsigned. Another difficulty, of course, is that the student may not be a good judge of an instructional program, except from a fairly superficial point of view. The student can perhaps be counted on to judge such factors as his interest in a course, but not the importance of the skills which are taught or how well they are taught.

The method, in general, would be most useful in cases where interest is confined to learning the opinions of the students. These opinions, while not necessarily related closely to the success of the instruction in other respects, are not unimportant. The continued existence of a program of instruction is bound to depend to some extent on the existence of satisfied customers. The climate of opinion, therefore, may be a very useful thing to study; but it should not be confused with information as to how successfully the course objectives are being achieved. As a way of evaluating success in achieving training objectives, the method has little to commend it except the ease with which it can be done.

In addition to student opinion, the opinion of experts may be solicited. This is the procedure typically followed in public school evaluations, for example, or when a supervisor sits in the back of the classroom to observe a teacher at work. The process may vary from casual to elaborate. The expert may be armed with a detailed check list on which he can tick off items such as appearance, voice, absence of mannerisms, poise, competency in subject area, and attentiveness of the class (Johnson, 1955)—items representing current doctrine as to what constitutes good teaching. These evaluations may be very useful to an instructor who wishes to correct faults in his presentation. However, it is not uncommon to find instructors who consistently violate such rules but who are still thought to be highly successful teachers. However useful for certain purposes, evaluation by expert opinion still misses the pay-off question: to what extent has the behavior of the students been modified in the desired direction as a consequence of the instruction?

## Administer Attitude Scales

Among the objectives listed for an instructional program, change of attitude in some specified direction is likely to be mentioned. The music teacher hopes that his students will learn to enjoy good music; the English teacher tries to create in his students a preference for good literature; and the science teacher wants his students to understand and respect the work of scientists.

The most obvious approach to finding out to what extent the desired attitudes have been adopted by the student is to ask him. In its simplest form, then, attitude measurement is just a way of getting opinions of students, with all the drawbacks mentioned previously. The method of self-report may, however, involve more sophisticated approaches than a simple questionnaire. These approaches make use of various types of attitude scales. An attitude scale differs from a questionnaire in that all of the items on the form are relevant to a single factor and contribute to a single score, rather than dealing with a variety of topics.

Thurstone was one of the pioneers in the measurement of attitude (Thurstone & Chave, 1929). A Thurstone attitude scale consists of a number of sentences expressing points of view toward some object or issue, ranging from favorable to unfavorable. In taking the test one merely indicates his agreement or disagreement with each proposition. The scale values of the items having been determined by previous research, the examinee's attitude is reflected by the scale values of the statements he agrees with.

The second widely used type of attitude scale is the Likert scale (Likert, 1932). Each item in such a scale is a statement which is favorable or unfavorable to the factor or issue in question. The examinee indicates the extent of his agreement with each statement by checking *strongly agree, agree, undecided, disagree, strongly disagree*. These answers are assigned numerical values ranging from one to five, taking into account whether the item is favorable or unfavorable; the sum of the values corresponding to the answers chosen is the score. The adding of these numbers to make a score is justified by use of item analysis procedures in constructing the scale to insure internal consistency of the items.

An important weakness of many attitude scales, especially those of the Likert type, is that they are susceptible to bias due to response set. For example, a set to choose the socially desirable response may appreciably influence attitude test scores (Edwards, 1953). One method that has been used in an attempt to overcome the tendency to give the socially desirable answer to attitude items is the forced-choice technique (Edwards, 1954). In this method one first gets ratings of the social desirability of the questionnaire items and then pairs items which are equal in mean social desirability ratings. The student is required to choose the member of each pair which is most true of him; and since he cannot choose on the basis of desirability he presumably must resort to use of relevant attitudes in making the judgment. The method assumes, however, that everyone has about the same views as to what is socially desirable. The method obviously would not be appropriate for a person whose notion of what is socially desirable differs from what is typical. A recent study (Messick, 1960) shows that in fact there may be a rather large number of "schools of thought" among students as to what is socially desirable.

Why would an instructor include attitude change as a desired objective of a course? An attitude is really merely a psychological construct which is useful in thinking about certain consistencies in behavior. The instructor is not interested in attitude merely as a psychological condition of the individual; he is interested in behavior change in the area defined by the attitude. He is interested in changes in music listening or performing activities, or in number and type of books read, or in the advanced courses chosen. The term attitude is introduced merely as a substitute for a long list of specific, spontaneous behaviors of a wide variety which are relevant to a course objective; it is a generalization about an area of behavior. Use of a paper-pencil attitude scale to measure these behavior tendencies is an appealing idea because of its relative ease and economy. In fact, however, we rarely have any evidence that the score on the attitude scale is correlated with the behaviors to any marked degree. In studies in which attitude scores have been compared with behavioral data, occasionally strikingly high correlations have been observed (Thurstone & Chave, 1929); but there are also reported many instances where the relationship between attitude score and behavior was essentially zero (Corey, 1937). It is unquestionably risky to assume without evidence that attitude test scores would predict behavior in test situations, particularly in areas where the respondents have some incentive to respond in the "right" direction. Perhaps one should consider the possibility of behavioral measures before he resorts to the use of attitude scales.

## Measure Knowledge

The most commonly used method of assessing achievement is undoubtedly to measure knowledge of facts, rules, and principles pertaining to the domain being treated. Tests to measure knowledge may be composed of true-false, multiple-choice, matching, or fill-in items, may require the writing of essays, or may involve many other item types. Such tests are relatively easy to construct; some of them may be scored by machine, and they are easily administered to large groups of people.

If the training objective is to produce knowledge, then the measurement of knowledge is obviously an appropriate method of assessing the results of training. Too often, however, the real objectives have to do with behaviors other than the ability to recite or recognize facts and principles. Unfortunately, it has become almost traditional to use tests of knowledge as achievement tests. The assumption that ability to perform a task is closely related to knowledge of related facts and principles may be sound for some situations but certainly not for all. Items in a gunner's mates school achievement test which required knowledge of such things as muzzle velocity were certainly not closely related to ability to disassemble and assemble equipment, analyze casualties, and replace worn and broken parts. To the extent that the desired objectives of training have to do with performance, it seems preferable to use measures of that performance as the basis for evaluation. Incidentally, the prevalence of knowledge tests for measuring educational achievement may help to account for the "grades" factor and for the failure of aptitude test batteries to make differential predictions of success.

## Elicit Related Behavior

It is becoming apparent, perhaps, that in order to evaluate training it is desirable to observe behavior of the type the students are being trained to perform. But for many reasons it is difficult to elicit or evaluate behavior which closely approximates the ultimate criterion, and we may resort to observation of behavior which is thought to be logically related to the criterion behavior.

Examples of this method may be found in the evaluation of writing. The ultimate criterion of a successfully taught course in English composition should be the ability to write English prose that meets the instructor's standards of unity, coherence, clarity, freedom from errors in mechanics, and so on. One would therefore suppose that all that would be necessary is to give a theme-writing assignment to students and grade the resulting papers. But the grading of themes is notoriously unreliable. So we may resort to having the student perform exercises which are logically related to the ultimate criterion but are more controlled and easier to evaluate. We may give editing or rewriting exercises, such as the interlinear test of the College Board (English Composition Test, 1949), and count the number of errors found and corrected by the student. We may present items composed of several short sentences which are to be rewritten as one sentence, or items composed of disarranged sentences which are to be rearranged to form a paragraph.

In a science area, one of the course objectives might be to teach students to interpret data. The evaluation method which would seem to approximate the ultimate criterion most closely would be to present data and ask for interpretations. The free responses which would result present problems of evaluation similar to those of English themes. A method of eliciting behavior which is logically related to the ultimate criterion is to present the data along with various possible conclusions, and for each conclusion to require the student to indicate, using a standard set of alternatives, to what extent the conclusion is justified by the data.

The method of eliciting related behavior is comparatively easy to use, particularly when objective test formats can be employed. Items may be relatively easy to produce. But since the relationship of the related behavior to the ultimate criterion must be inferred on the basis of logical relationships, the validity of the criterion cannot be taken for granted.

## Elicit "What I Would Do" Behavior

This technique involves the presentation of brief descriptions of problem situations, and the task of the examinee is to state what he would do to solve the problem if he were in the situation. Responses may be free or multiple-choice. Items are relatively easy to construct and the test is easy to administer and, if multiple-choice, easy to score.

Some of the National Teacher Examinations contain items of the "What I would do" type. Here is an example of this type of item (National Teacher Examinations Bulletin of Information for Candidates, 1960):

> "A student begins working on his homework during a class discussion. It would be best for the teacher to:
>
> A. Call the student aside after class and explain that when he does homework in class he sets a bad example for the rest of the students.

B. Make a general announcement to the effect that homework is not to be done during the class activities.

C. Say nothing because students carrying heavy schedules need some class time for preparing homework.

D. Ignore the situation because some students benefit more from individual study than from class discussions.

E. Ask the student his opinion on an issue concerning the topic under discussion."

An objection which applies to the multiple-choice version of such a test is that the candidate does not have to invent the solution but only evaluate those presented to him. In an area such as school teaching, the real-life problems certainly do not present themselves in multiple-choice form. As a method for judging how well training has prepared a student to be a school teacher the method therefore has obvious limitations—which incidentally apply to many other multiple-choice items. The student's test-taking behavior may not represent what he would do in the situation so much as it represents an attempt to choose the "correct" answer desired by the examiner. The situations are usually so briefly described that it is difficult to present really difficult or challenging problems without running into the difficulty of not giving sufficient information to enable the candidate to choose an answer wisely. It has been stated that there is only one reasonable answer to such "situational" items: "It depends." Furthermore, items of this type fail to get at the *style* of behavior which may be displayed in the real-life solution to a problem.

## Elicit Lifelike Behavior

This category includes tests which approach the realism of the life situation. The tests may be situational tests requiring elaborate equipment such as a flight simulator, or they may require nothing more elaborate than paper and pencil (Weislogel & Schwartz, 1955). Tests in this category have in common the characteristic that in the test situation the examinee is behaving as though he were in a real-life situation which calls for behavior of the sort he is being trained to perform, rather than saying what he *would* do or displaying characteristics which are logically related in some way to the training objective.

In a real-life situation one must wait for opportunities for the behavior to appear, and these opportunities will vary considerably from one person to another. In the simulation, opportunities are provided for the behavior to occur equally for all candidates. One might wait a long time for real-life situations to occur which are suitable for evaluating the outcomes of a life-saving course; but they can be provided quite easily in the swimming pool by having someone simulate a drowning man. The face validity of tests of this sort is high, provided a good job of simulation is done.

With this technique it may also be possible to measure objectives stated in terms of attitudes, but to do so in terms of behavior rather than by self-report methods. The test provides opportunities for the behavior to occur, and it is only necessary to count the instances when it does occur. The studies of honesty performed by Hartshorne and May (1928) are familiar examples of this approach.

A distinction needs to be made between tests in which examinees know the attributes to be scored and tests in which they do not know fully the purpose of the test. This distinction is especially important in the measurement of attitude and other characteristics not requiring skill. To measure attitude, opportunities are provided for the attitude to reveal itself. If the examinee knows that his performance is to be scored in terms of politeness, for example, it would be easy for him to use many *please's* and *thank you's* to roll up a high score. This limitation would perhaps make it difficult to use the technique as a routine end-of-course examination, but it does not present a serious obstacle to its occasional use in training evaluation.

## Observe Real-Life Behavior

This category involves the "ultimate" criterion of the success of any training—the extent to which it affects real-life behavior. This is the ideal criterion, the validity of which cannot be questioned. But when subjected to close examination the process of making observations of real-life behavior and the conditions under which the observations have to be made are not so attractive.

A basic requirement of a good psychometric instrument is that test conditions be standardized. In real life this condition is necessarily violated; consequently, variations in observed behavior may be attributed to variations in opportunity or variations in the subject's willingness to attempt difficult tasks rather than to differences in ability. The poor speller may actually misspell fewer words in real life than the good speller, simply because the poor speller does not attempt the hard words. Occurrences of the criterion behavior may be so rare that no opportunities to observe it arise. Sometimes the criterion behavior is so remote in time that it is not feasible to observe it, or by the time it happens the effects of training have been hopelessly diluted by the effects of many other learning experiences, as in evaluating the objective of producing intelligent participation in a democratic society. Sometimes the criterion behavior is of such a private nature as to be inaccessible to the examiner. Observation of real-life criterion behavior is likely to be costly in time and effort; it may be extremely difficult to analyze the relevant aspects of behavior out of the complex matrix of behaviors. While behavior in real life does represent the ultimate criterion, the psychometric problems of measurement it presents are likely to be insurmountable.

It is because of these difficulties that in practice the technique most often used in evaluating real-life behavior is the rating technique. Having nothing that can legitimately be counted or measured, one must resort to subjective judgments. Enough is known about the rating technique to conclude that as a method of training evaluation it does not successfully overcome the difficulties entailed in observing real-life behavior.

Having completed this brief survey of types of evaluation measures, what general conclusions can be drawn? All the types are undoubtedly useful to some degree and under appropriate conditions. The objective, presumably, is to get as close as is feasible to the ultimate criterion; but as has just been seen, when one gets too close to the real-life situation, control of the conditions for adequate observation is lost. Observation of real-life behavior is ordinarily not a suitable technique for measurement. The type of measure that is recommended for first consideration in a training evaluation study is the type which most closely approximates the real-life situation, that which, in this chapter, has been called eliciting lifelike behavior. If it is not feasible to wait for the behavior to happen in real life, then lifelike occasions can be provided for the behavior to occur in a test situation.

### ELICITING LIFELIKE BEHAVIOR—SOME EXAMPLES

In this section a number of examples will be cited of tests designed primarily for evaluation purposes which involve providing realistic opportunities for the criterion behavior to appear. Most of these tests were developed by staff members of Educational Testing Service (ETS) working in cooperation with instructors from various training programs. The examples were chosen to show the variety of training evaluation problems which can be attacked by tests of the sort which elicit lifelike behavior.

*The Medical History Test.* A number of medical schools have been concerned that modern medical education may tend to produce physicians who are less concerned with patients as real, live human beings who have personal, family, and economic problems, than as mere medical cases—lumps under a blanket with interesting charts. At one school an experiment in medical education has been in progress for several years, aimed at changing the attitudes of the student physician in the direction of making him more aware of the patient as a person. ETS was asked to help evaluate some of the outcomes of this experiment.

One of the first steps was to translate some of the statements about attitude into statements about observable behavior. How can one tell, by observing the work of the physician, what his attitudes are with regard to these human values? One of the answers to this question was that the physician would ask appropriate questions of the patient in order to get pertinent information about family, financial, and personal problems. Another was that he would take account of such information in planning for the management of the case.

Observation of real-life behavior was not feasible as a method for the usual kinds of reasons: it was not feasible to wait several years for the student physicians to get to the point where they were responsible for patients; if such waiting had occurred, there would have been so many intervening experiences that the effects of the training would have been considerably diluted; the real-life situations would have differed so greatly from physician to physician that there would have been tremendous variation in opportunity. The objective of the test constructors was to try to measure change behaviorally rather than by inferential methods or by means of self report; so the attempt was made to think of methods of simulating real-life problems in such a way as to elicit lifelike behavior of the sort that was of interest.

A test called the "Medical History Test" was developed cooperatively by members of the ETS staff and faculty members of the medical school. The test was administered by means of a tape recording which contained information about three cases. The student was required to use the information in ways which were quite realistic and which revealed aspects of behavior thought to be relevant to the experimental training.

The test was built around the outline of a typical case work-up, which includes the following parts: (*a*) Present Illness, (*b*) Past History, (*c*) Family History, (*d*) Social History, (*e*) Systems Review, (*f*) Physical Examination, (*g*) Laboratory Examination. Information from the case work-up was recorded on tape by a physician in a manner such as might be used in presenting a case for discussion at a staff conference. After the students heard the statement of the Present Illness, which was a fairly complete account of why the patient was seeking medical assistance, the tape was interrupted, and the students were given ten minutes to write ten questions that they would want to ask the patient at this point.

When the tape resumed, the students heard the doctor describe the Past History, Family History, Social History, and Systems Review of the patient. Again the tape was stopped, and this time the students were instructed to write down, from their notes or their memory, all items of information which they thought were significant from the standpoint of diagnosis and management of the case.

The rest of the recording presented the results of the Physical Examination and Laboratory Examination. At this point the complete case work-up had been presented. Students were instructed to write a differential diagnostic statement and an outline of a plan for the management of the case. A total of three cases was presented. The cases chosen were those which were thought to be particularly relevant to the objectives of the experimental teaching.

The attitude score was obtained merely by counting the number of statements written by each student which seemed to indicate concern for the patient as a social human being with problems. These statements came mostly from the list of significant items of information and from the management plan. The list of questions to ask the patient was found not to contribute much to the score because at such an early stage in the case workup most of the questions were purely medical. Scoring rules were formulated to guide the scorer in deciding whether or not a given statement should be scored. Here are some examples of items of information from one case which would contribute to the attitude score:

Does not have many friends and prefers to spend free time by himself
Bowls once a week
Earns $96 per week
Considered changing jobs because of pressure
Has been a spree drinker for eight years
Wife has threatened to leave home because of his drinking
Wife crippled for last five years by arthritis
A cousin assists in her care when patient is at work.

In addition to the attitude score, a medical skill score was also obtained by evaluating the statements of a more purely medical nature. The skill score was made a part of the third-year comprehensive examination. The attitude score was judged to be reasonably satisfactory. Estimates of its reliability were .74 and .75 for two successive years; these estimates were obtained by a method which tends to yield underestimates. The skill score was found to be less reliable than the attitude score.

The Medical History Test constitutes one attempt to measure an outcome of instruction by providing opportunities for the pertinent behavior to be carried out in a reasonably lifelike situation. This test is of the type where student knowledge of all the measurement purposes would invalidate the test. Such a test, from the standpoint of measuring attitude, might be unsatisfactory for operational use. It should be pointed out, too, that use of such a test in the context of a medical school comprehensive examination predisposes the student to think in terms of those aspects of the medical school curriculum which outweigh the relatively little done towards the objectives of the experimental program.

*The In-Basket Test.* A number of years ago the Human Resources Research Institute became interested in the evaluation of training at the Air University. Under contract with HRRI, Educational Testing Service undertook a project concerned with studying outcomes of instruction in one of the courses called the Field Officer Course (Frederiksen, Saunders, & Wand, 1957). The tests which were developed at that time are prototypes of a number of in-basket tests used in various research studies at ETS.

One of these studies is concerned with school administration (Hemphill, Griffiths, Frederiksen, et al., 1961). It involves the development of a rather elaborate situational test as a means for studying administrative behavior. It is planned to use this situational test in studying the outcomes of various kinds of educational treatments used in teaching school administration. This study is being done, with support from the U. S. Office of Education, by staff members from Teachers College, Columbia University, and Educational Testing Service. The situational test is administered to examinees in groups of 20. It requires five days of testing time.

Beginning Monday morning, the examinees are introduced to a school of which each is to be the new principal. The school is a fictionized school, Whitman School, located in the city of Jefferson in the hypothetical state of Lafayette. Each subject is temporarily given a new name, Marion Smith. The subjects are instructed that they are not to play a role, that they are not to pretend to be someone else. Each is to bring to the new job his own background of experience, his own knowledge and personality; and during the test he is to perform the duties of the new principal of Whitman School.

The participants spend the first day and a half in learning about Whitman School and the community in which it is located. First, a film strip with commentary is presented; this gives the participants a view of Jefferson such as they might get in driving about the city with a guide who knows a lot about Jefferson and its school system. Then the principals are given an opportunity to study the Jefferson School-Community Survey—a survey recently completed by the School of Education at Lafayette State University.

Then the group views a sound color film which takes the subjects inside Whitman School, where they see the staff and faculty at work. The subjects are next given personnel folders for the teachers and staff, a floor plan of the school, a staff roster for the school system, and a special sociological study of the Whitman School faculty. All this material is available for reference throughout the week.

On Tuesday morning the indoctrination regarding the new school is completed with additional material for study. Printed materials include a Staff Handbook, the School Board Handbook, excerpts from the Lafayette school law, copies of the most recent school census, a class sizes list, a school calendar of events for the year, and a report of achievement test scores. The examinees also listen to tape recordings of a school board meeting and of conversations involving teachers and parents.

At the end of the day and a half of orientation, the subjects have as much information about the school as would be expected of a new principal in an actual situation. It is now reasonable to expect the subjects to take action on problems arising in the administration of the school. When presented with a problem, they cannot claim that the only reasonable answer is "It depends."

The balance of the week is devoted to work sessions in which each Marion Smith performs the duties of the principal of Whitman School. All the participants are presented with exactly the same problems under the same conditions. Most of the problems are presented in written form, but some are presented by way of kinescopes and tape recordings. Each new "principal" is given memo pads, letterheads, paper, pencils, pens, paper clips, rubber bands—the usual desk facilities. His instructions are merely to be the principal of Whitman School. He is not to say what he *would* do—he is to *do* it. He actually writes memos, calls meetings, prepares agenda, makes notes in preparation for interviews, and the like.

The primary method of presenting problems in our study is the so-called in-basket test. This test consists of facsimiles of the letters, memoranda, and other contents of the in-basket such as is found on every principal's desk. Four such tests are presented, each requiring a half-day session. The examinee is not necessarily expected to complete an in-basket; part of the task is to decide which of its contents are more important and should receive prior attention.

About 35 problems are included in each in-basket. They were chosen in the light of a theoretical formulation intended to reflect the job of an elementary school principal. Here are some examples of the problems found in one of the in-baskets you would see if you were Marion Smith:

1. A note from your secretary, Ruth Platz, indicating that a Mr. Davies called to say he will come in tomorrow to inspect the heating plant.

2. A letter from a parent requesting that her child be transferred to another school.

3. A memo from the superintendent's office announcing that safety films will be shown and bicycle inspections will be conducted by the police department.

4. A memo from an assistant superintendent requesting you to participate in a radio series in commemoration of American Education Week.

5. A note from one of the teachers requesting a special ruling on sick leave.

6. A form for you to sign from one of your teachers giving approval for a class trip to a museum.

7. A note from a teacher requesting help in arranging for a conference with a parent who apparently doesn't want a conference.

8. A report of test scores from a teacher for children in her class.

In addition to the desk work involved in the four in-baskets, the subjects are required to perform such tasks as participating in committee work, observing teachers (by way of kinescopes) and then filling out probationary teacher report forms and making notes in preparation for interviews with the probationary teachers, and reacting to conference situations presented by means of tape recordings.

This is a brief description of a rather elaborate situational test. Each participant leaves a record of the behavior which he carries out in response to realistically presented problems. The participants have reported that the situation is realistic, that they build up images of the people involved which are so vivid that they form likes and dislikes much as they would in a real school. The advantage, of course, of the simulated school over a real school is that the situation is highly standardized. Each participant receives the same opportunities to learn the background and each is presented with exactly the same problems under identical conditions. Therefore, differences in behavior can be attributed to the participants. In real schools, differences in administrative behavior can be attributed in part to differences among the schools; in the situational test, the differences must be attributed to the subjects themselves.

Each participant leaves an envelope full of memos, letters, notes to himself, reminders to make phone calls, instructions to his secretary, appointment calendars, and the like. How can this material be scored? The first step towards developing a scoring procedure was to examine in-basket responses from the point of view of observing how the respondents differ. As a result of such examination by a number of observers a large pack of cards was collected, each card containing a statement of some kind of difference observed in the way the principals behaved. The cards contained phrases like "overly critical of the work of others," "compulsive," "seeks temporary solutions," "postpones decisions," "neat," "credulous—accepts statement without checking," "makes unwarranted assumptions," "authoritarian attitude," "suspicious of motives of others," etc. A second source of ideas for scoring categories came from theories of administration.

Eventually these modes of behavior were collapsed to make about 68 scoring categories. Examples of categories in the present scoring manual are "socially insensitive," "discusses with subordinates," "concluding decision," "leading action," "initiates structure," "communicates by writing," "courteous to subordinates." A manual gives appropriate definitions and detailed rules for scoring. Scoring is done by recording a zero or a one under each category heading for each problem. With about 35 problems per in-basket, a total of 140 problems are scored for each of the 68 categories. Not all the categories proved to have satisfactory reliability, but 40, with reliabilities ranging from about .55 to .97, were chosen for use in further analysis. It is hoped that use of this instrument and others like it will be useful in studying outcomes of training for work in school administration.

*The Russell Sage Social Relations Test.* Several years ago the Russell Sage Foundation supported a study of elementary school objectives (Kearney, 1953). A primary purpose of the study was to focus attention on the measurement needs in the area of evaluation of elementary education. The report of the investigators specified many objectives other than the conventional academic ones, including some involving social skills, such as skill in cooperative group planning and action.

The Russell Sage Social Relations Test, developed by Dora Damrin (1959), was a direct outcome of the project. It represents an attempt to build a test which could be used to evaluate schools with respect to their success in teaching "social relations." More specifically, the test is intended to measure the performance of a class with respect to "(1) skill in cooperative group planning procedures and (2) skill in techniques of cooperative group action." The test is of the type which provides standardized occasions for eliciting behavior relevant to the educational objectives.

The approach is straightforward. To measure skill in group planning and acting, the class is given problems which require them to plan and act in a cooperative way. For each problem, 36 interlocking construction blocks of various colors and shapes are distributed to the children. They are also given a model made of similar blocks which they are to reproduce exactly with their 36 blocks. The three problems involve models of a house, a footbridge, and a dog.

The first part of the test has to do with the planning phase. The examiner tells the children what their task is and that they may help each other, discuss things freely, and work cooperatively. They may have all the time they wish for planning, but they are allowed only 15 minutes for constructing the model. When the plan is completed and all the children have it in mind, the construction job is carried out and is timed by the examiner. The second and third models, which are more difficult, are built in a similar way.

During the time the children are in the process of planning, an observer keeps a record of their behavior, using standardized observation sheets. The data so collected are later translated into numerical scores which reflect the skill of the group in various aspects of cooperative group planning. A similar set of observations is made for the action phase of each problem. Scoring has to do with such characteristics as amount of participation, communication, autonomy of the group, organizational techniques, quality of the final plan, and time required to complete the model. Notice that the Social Relations Test yields scores for the group as a whole. Such a test may be useful for training evaluation studies, even though scores for individual participants are not provided.

*The Physical Science Study Committee Physics Test.* A group of physicists, under the leadership of Professor Zacharias at MIT, have become concerned that the teaching of high school physics has typically become a matter of teaching substantive knowledge of physics to the exclusion of teaching the skills employed by the physicist in investigating the universe about him. The Physical Science Study Committee (PSSC) has been engaged in the development of a secondary school course in physics which gets away from the authoritarian presentation of facts and principles to be memorized and tries instead to give the student something of the experience of the physicist who devises ways of making observations which will give him better understanding of phenomena in nature. Through this emphasis on method the student begins to acquire some of the skills of observation and interpretation through graphic and mathematical means which characterize the work of the physicist. Some of the objectives of the PSSC physics course may be stated as follows (Ferris, 1960): (*a*) ability to apply knowledge to unfamiliar situations, (*b*) ability to analyze problem situations mathematically, (*c*) ability to use graphical presentations of data, and (*d*) ability to make relevant observations.

The development of achievement tests did not in this case wait for the time when tests had to be administered. Instead, test specialists worked with the members of the PSSC in developing tests aimed at the course objectives. They were particularly concerned that the test require the student to demonstrate skills of the sort implied by the objectives listed above rather than mere knowledge of facts and principles. One approach was to present in the examination a situation which the students had not observed before, and to require them to use the data from this new situation in answering the test items.

In the PSSC course the students study wave motion, using a ripple tank as laboratory equipment. Wave motions produced both by a point source and by a plane wave generator are studied. The students learn that light displays many phenomena which can be explained in terms of the behavior of waves as observed in the ripple tank—reflection, refraction, interference, etc. In the examination, a ripple tank situation which is new to the student is presented. A wave generator which is not only vibrating but is also in motion is the new situation. The student is required to make relevant observations, deal with them graphically and mathematically, and infer from them phenomena such as the Doppler effect and the sound barrier (which have not been dealt with previously in the course). Here are some sample items:

Questions 1-6 relate to the following information and diagram.

The diagram below consists of a portion of a wave pattern generated in a ripple tank. The pattern is that caused by the vibration of a point-source generator (S) *which is not only vibrating but is also moving with constant speed in the direction indicated.* The speed of the generator is half as great as the speed of propagation of the waves. The speed of the waves relative to the tank is independent of the motion of the point-source generator.

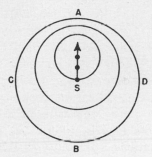

1. The frequency of the waves is
   (A) greater at point A than at point B
   (B) greater at point B than at point A
   (C) independent of the direction of propagation
   (D) determined only by the rate of vibration of the generator
   (E) none of the above

2. In the direction of motion of S, the velocity of the waves *relative to the source* is how many times the velocity of the waves *relative to the tank?*
   (A) ¼                        (D) 2
   (B) ½                        (E) 4
   (C) 1

3. The apparent frequency of the waves passing B is how many times the frequency of vibration of the source?
   (A) ½                        (D) ³⁄₂
   (B) ⅔                        (E) 2
   (C) 1

4. Which one of the following graphs best represents the frequency of waves observed at any fixed point in the ripple tank as a function of the observed wave length?

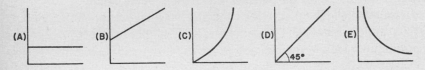

5. Based on the above observations in the ripple tank and a knowledge of the wave nature of light, one might correctly predict that a distant star moving toward earth with a speed of the order of magnitude of 10% of the speed of light should appear to be

   (A) considerably closer than it is at the instant of observation
   (B) moving somewhat faster than it actually is
   (C) slightly bluer in color than it actually is
   (D) somewhat smaller than it actually is
   (E) varying in intensity between a minimum and maximum value

6. If the velocity of the wave generator in the ripple tank were to approach in magnitude the speed of wave propagation, a point would be reached at which

   (A) interference would cause the wave pattern to disappear
   (B) the frequency of propagation relative to the source would become zero
   (C) a pattern of nodal lines would be formed behind the generator
   (D) a complete standing wave pattern would be formed
   (E) successive superposition would cause reinforcement of waves in front of the generator

This test is included as an example to show that in order to use the method we have called eliciting lifelike behavior it is not always necessary to use elaborately staged situational tests. Here in the format of a multiple-choice test are test items which appear to require the student to demonstrate his ability to apply skills to new problem situations. The mutiple-choice test has been criticized earlier on the grounds that the correct answer is suggested to the examinee and therefore he does not have to think of it himself. This criticism holds for some of the items above, but not all of them. In some cases the choices represent an end-product of a chain of reasoning without suggestion of the nature of the chain; this would ordinarily be true when the choices are expressed symbolically as in items 2 and 3. In spite of the fact that the multiple-choice format is used, these items illustrate an approach to achievement testing which succeeds in getting at skills rather than merely knowledge in standard situations which represent the real-life situation for which students are being trained.

In summary: There has been an increasing need for improved materials and methods for training evaluation, perhaps because of the many innovations in educational procedures that are being introduced. In order to evaluate a training program, it is obviously necessary to have a clear idea of the desired outcomes of the training in terms of observable behavior.

Training evaluation requires some method of measuring the desired outcomes. These methods may involve soliciting opinions of students or experts, using attitude scales, measuring knowledge of facts and principles, eliciting for observation behavior which is logically related to the desired outcome, eliciting behavior in the "What would you do?" situation, eliciting lifelike behavior in situations which simulate real life, and observing real-life behavior. Any of these methods may be used for certain purposes. The real-life behavior is closest to the ultimate objectives of instruction, but observing behavior in real life is rarely a good technique for evaluation because of lack of control of the test situation. The method of eliciting lifelike behavior in situations which simulate real life is recommended for first consideration as a measurement technique.

## REFERENCES

*Appraisal of Teaching in Large Universities.* Ann Arbor: University of Michigan, 1959.

Corey, S. M. Professed attitudes and actual behavior. *J. educ. Psychol.*, 1937, *28*, 271-280.

Damrin, Dora E. The Russell Sage Social Relations Test: A technique for measuring group problem solving skills in elementary school children. *J. exp. Educ.*, 1959, *28*, No. 1.

Dressel, P. L. & Mayhew, L. B. *General education: Explorations in evaluation.* Washington, D. C.: American Council on Education, 1954.

Edwards, A. L. The relationship between the judged desirability of a trait and the probability that the trait will be endorsed. *J. appl. Psychol.*, 1953, *37*, 90-93.

Edwards, A. L. *Manual for the Edwards Personal Preference Schedule.* New York: Psychological Corporation, 1954.

English Composition Test. In *A description of the College Board Achievement Tests*. New York: College Entrance Examination Board, 1959. Pp. 13-41.

Ferris, F. L. Testing for physics achievement. *Amer. J. Physics*, 1960, *28*, 269-278.

Frederiksen, N., Saunders, D. R., & Wand, Barbara. The in-basket test. *Psychol. Monogr.*, 1957, *71*, No. 9 (Whole No. 438).

French, J. W. The description of aptitude and achievement tests in terms of rotated factors. *Psychometr. Monogr.* Chicago: University of Chicago Press, 1951, No. 5.

Guthrie, E. R. *The evaluation of teaching: A progress report*. Seattle: University of Washington, 1954.

Hartshorne, H. & May, M. A. *Studies in deceit*. New York: Macmillan, 1928.

Hemphill, J., Griffiths, D., Frederiksen, N., et al. *Dimensions of administrative performance*. Princeton, N. J.: Educational Testing Service, May 1961. Report to the U.S. Office of Education.

Johnson, G. B. An evaluation instrument for the analysis of teacher effectiveness. *J. exp. Educ.*, 1955, *23*, 331-344.

Kearney, N. C. *Elementary school objectives*. New York: Russell Sage Foundation, 1953.

Likert, R. A technique for the measurement of attitudes. *Arch. Psychol., New York*, 1932, *22*, No. 140.

Lindquist, E. F. Preliminary considerations in objective test construction. In E. F. Lindquist (Ed.), *Educational measurement*. Washington, D. C.: American Council on Education, 1951. Pp. 119-158.

Messick, S. Dimensions of social desirability. *J. consult. Psychol.*, 1960, *24*, 279-287.

*National Teacher Examinations Bulletin of Information for Candidates*. Princeton, N. J.: Educational Testing Service, 1960.

Remmers, H. H. The college professor as the student sees him. *Purdue University studies in higher education*, 1927, No. 11.

Remmers, H. H. On students' perceptions of teachers' effectiveness. In *The appraisal of teaching in large universities*. Ann Arbor: University of Michigan, 1959. Pp. 17-23.

Thurstone, L. L. & Chave, E. J. *The measurement of attitude*. Chicago: University of Chicago Press, 1929.

Weislogel, R. L. & Schwartz, P. A. Some practical and theoretical problems in situational testing. *Educ. psychol. Measmt.*, 1955, *15*, 39-46.

Chapter *12*     *On-the-Job and Operational Criteria*

*Clark L. Wilson,*
*Batten, Barton, Durstine & Osborn, Inc.*

At first glance, one working in this field of training research would expect that the measurement of actual performance on the job would have received a great deal of research attention over the years. After all, one would reason, there is no way of knowing how to train people unless you can measure, first of all, how they perform when they are finally assigned to a job.

Unfortunately, this has not been the case. Historically, except for ratings and other gross measures, relatively little attention has been paid to the real problem of measuring how well a man can perform the actual task for which he is trained. Applied psychologists, educators and training specialists have produced great numbers of reports on training assessment, but the vast majority use school graduation or classroom measuring instruments. To all intents and purposes one finds only isolated attempts to measure performance on the job by other than rating methods when that performance was intended to serve as a measure of the effectiveness of the training that preceded it. Put another way, the amount of such measurement research in proportion to the amount of training is discouragingly small.

With this rather peculiar history it is desirable to place the whole problem of on-the-job performance measurement in its proper current perspective. The first consideration is the practical research climate. In the past 50 years most of the research talent and effort available for practical personnel research has been directed toward selection studies. Compared to the magnitude of research on selection, training has been relatively, though not entirely, neglected.

Further in this vein, the selection research that has been done has been aimed at predictor development with inadequate attention to criteria. Here, also, the bulk of criterion development has been based on ratings as a technique. Jones (1950) reviewed 2100 selection study reports published prior to 1948 and found that only 427 even mentioned a quantitative validity coefficient. But only eight studies (.04% of the total) gave any statistical information, such as the reliability of the criterion. Thus the area of selection research has been developing without any real, or surely not adequate, attention to measurement of the final criteria. Considering both training and selection, the latter being the predominant area of the two, it appears that researchers in both areas have been equally neglectful. The need for better criterion development has not been felt sufficiently strongly to spur action.

A second practical consideration is the fact that most persons interested in training research have been employed in training or school situations. As a natural consequence they use end-of-course measurement as criteria. The use of on-the-job measurements has rarely been adopted. It must be said that these school criteria are often, no doubt, highly valuable and serviceable. Some situations exist, surely, in which they are fully sufficient. There are others in which on-the-job-measurements are just not feasible, as later sections of this chapter will discuss. The main point, here, however, is that there has been little strong interest in actual on-the-job performance measures among many of the people who could profit most by them.

There have been other reasons for the lag in the development of these devices. For one thing, practical performance tests often require measuring one person at a time while written tests and rating scales can handle groups, thus the expense is high. Also the graduates of a single school are often scattered into many companies on stations in wide-spread geographical areas. If the school research man wants to follow his graduates, his costs and problems, including sampling difficulties, mount out of proportion.

Under the circumstances, one is faced with the question of whether or not any more precise measuring devices are really required. If training research people have been getting along over the years with end-of-course and classroom measurements and on-the-job ratings, then "is there a need for anything more?" To set these aspects into perspective the functional and theoretical considerations that form the basis of the need for better measuring approaches must be discussed.

The basic role of an effective measurement of a man's on-the-job performance is to feed information back to the person who is responsible for his training either at school or on the job. In other words, in the training research context, the only reason for measuring the level of performance of a man on the job is to provide criterion information to those who are responsible for his training. These responsible people may be working with him in a combined training-supervisory capacity, or they may be responsible for a school through which the individual passed before he was assigned to the job.

If one conceptualizes the use of performance measurements in this fashion, as an integral part of the learning process, then from learning theory (McGeoch & Irion, 1952) certain specifications for those measurements follow. In addition to the basic measurement requirements of reliability and validity, the requirements derived from learning theory include at least the following:

1. The measures must be quite specific. In order to be effective they must identify specific aspects or elements of the job so that both trainer and trainee may take action to improve performance by improving these elements.

2. For maximum utility the measures must be available to trainer and trainee soon after the test performance.

3. Performance should be measured often, for by doing so the amount of reinforcement provided is increased with a consequent increase in the speed of learning toward the level of perfection.

The discussions in this chapter will be concentrated largely on those requirements that would properly be categorized under the first requirement above—specificity of measurement. For the most part, the other two requirements cited pertain to the administrative use of performance measurements rather than to the characteristics of the measurements themselves. However, with respect to the above requirement for immediate availability, it should be noted that on-the-job performance measures are probably the optimal information feedback agency to trainees in on-the-job situations. When on-the-job measures are fed back to school situations, there is a time delay and their value is largely limited to the general shaping of the training course and the uses of the trainer.

## Types of Measures

In the measurement of performance on the job a variety of measures are available and in use. They range across the spectrum from the measurement of a person's performance in the context of his regular job by some objective means to the use of generalized ratings. More specifically, this chapter will deal with three classes or general groups of measures: (*a*) Operational Performance Measures; (*b*) Work Samples; and (*c*) Ratings. Essentially, these three classes of measures represent degrees of departure from the real working world.

Under *Operational Performance Measures* methods are discussed for measuring a trainee's performance in the context of his regular job. Five sub-groups of measures are in this category: (*a*) tangible product measures; (*b*) measures of specific behavior elements; (*c*) gross performance measures; (*d*) inferred performance (promotion, performance or morale of subordinates); and finally (*e*) malperformance such as accidents, labor turnover, etc. Under the heading of *Work Samples* will be discussed those measures that are based on tests designed as replicas or segments of the regular job. *Ratings* represent the widest departure from the actual on-the-job situation. They have been used extensively in selection studies but their use in training studies is seriously limited because of the apparent inability of observers using current rating methods to render sufficiently specific evaluations.

## OPERATIONAL PERFORMANCE MEASURES

This section deals with those measures of job performance which are observable and measurable in the regular job context without any special structuring of the job for measurement purposes. The measures that are described here, to be sure, cannot be said to be completely free from overlap with the measures in other broad groups in the chapter. However, they are the most important measures because they are available "in nature" and, as such, reflect the real world. At the same time, they are often good measures in the sense that they can be both highly specific and reliable.

### Tangible Product Measures

This category concerns the measurement of characteristics of the product that the trainee or worker actually turns out. In the case of lathe operators, for example, one can measure the size, fit, finish, taper, etc. against a standard measuring gauge. One is inclined to think first of industrial-type production situations but there are many others. They range all the way from the hand labor production outputs such as bricklaying, basket weaving, hand carpentry, etc. through the range of the aesthetic type of product such as a painting or a work of music.

Progressively more difficult measuring problems are encountered as one progresses from the objectively measurable product which can be evaluated on the basis of size, fit, etc. to the more subjective end of the continuum. Clear across this range there are some objective measures but they tend to decrease in adequacy as the aesthetic end is approached. By the same token, even with the most cut and dried kind of product, there is often some subjective kind of judgment that has to be made in its evaluation. Bricklaying should end in a pleasing perspective over and above its structural assessments.

To make the point more meaningful, however, we can cite a study of Navy Machinery Repairmen (Mackie & High, 1959). In this case 33 measures were available on the test product, a "Valve Stem and Hex Fitting." While this was used as a test product, it was also assigned to trainees by supervising officers as a regular production item. All of the product measures were related to actual production requirements. Sixteen of these 33 measures were objective measures which could be made with the use of a pair of calipers, a rule or other measuring device. Seventeen were measures of fit, finish, and alignment which had to be subjective judgments. The range of inter-observer agreement for the more objective items using measuring devices was from .70 to .98 in this situation. The range of the subjective measures was .71 to .99. In this study the judges were experienced petty officers making measurements and subjective ratings on well-defined characteristics. Thus, adequate measures of characteristics can be had, even though they are subjective. The world of work offers an almost infinite number of possibilities of such measurements.

It can be expected that many situations will occur in real life where reliabilities will drop well below those indicated in this particular situation. The important point is, however, that judges can agree with each other in making subjective judgments about definitely functional aspects of performance. The lore of psychological research, if not the literature, is replete with cautions concerning the use of product measures which depend on subjective judgments. For example, one psychologist[1] became interested in the reliability with which whisky tasters could make their judgments. By appropriate test-retest designs, he found that experienced tasters did not agree with their own judgments when presented a batch the second time without knowledge of their previous ratings. Nor did they agree with each other. Another psychologist[1] was involved in quality control studies based on the decisions of visual inspections of small glass end pieces for optical systems. Inspectors were required to reject glasses with ex-

---

[1]Personal Communication

cessive scratches as determined by judgment. By resubmitting batches of both previously accepted and rejected glasses, he found that inspectors would still reject a near equal proportion of the two groups. The proportions rejected were not significantly different from their initial rates. However, there are many situations where product characteristics measurements of this kind can be used as feedback into a training program and as a criterion to the great benefit of that program. The research man must evaluate his measures for reliability and meaningfulness.

There is one additional very important caution in using product characteristics measures. The machinery or other equipment that is used in turning out the product may be highly variable in *its* performance. The differences from one machine to another may be such as to contribute more variability to the final product than does the difference in performance of the operator. For example, if one is to require the production of a fitting on a lathe or other machine tool, it is important that he know the extent of the differences between lathes available to the various persons being tested. This kind of "error variance" has also been noted in studies on electronic equipment.

In summary, product measures as criteria for either training or selection programs can be among the most satisfactory measures when they are available and reliable. If these measures can logically be shown to reflect the variability in trainee performance independent of machine performance and with reliable judgments from observers, then they should be used. The utilization of these where presently available in industry and the military would provide a basis for a great deal of improvement in the level of training efficiency. There appears to be a tendency for supervisors and instructors to make overall judgments of products rather than systematic detailed measurements of characteristics.

## *Measures of Specific Behavior Elements*

This section discusses methods by which jobs or tasks are broken down into individual, quite specific activities. The performance of each of these activities is then observed while the job is being performed. In an informal way the real world is full of experiences in which specific elements of an activity are observed and evaluated. For example, in learning a golf swing or even in playing golf one constantly reminds himself, by habit, "head down, arms stiff, backswing high, full follow-through, etc., etc." So, in an everyday way one tends to observe the specific elements of his own or other people's performances. In the more structured measurement situation in the world of work some attention has been paid to this approach to evaluation of job performance. Knauft (1948) has done considerable work with check list ratings to develop criteria of job performance in several industrial situations. For the most part he was concerned with developing criteria for the validation of predictors. He used "total scores" as developed by giving unit weight to the correct performance of each specific behavior and found his measures to be adequately reliable as general job performance measures and criteria.

Several illustrative studies have been conducted under military auspices (Wilson, Ruch, & Wolbers, 1949; Vaughn & Rulon, 1950; Hill, Buckley, & Older, 1952; Houston, Smith, & Flexman, 1954; Simon, 1954; Wilson, Mackie, & Buckner, 1954a; Wilson, Mackie, & Buckner, 1954b). These studies have all been somewhat in the training context but have also had the purpose of developing insights into general job performance measurement. The work of Houston, Smith and Flexman is most specifically in the training context and bears further discussion. In their work they classify the items in their proficiency measures into two types: *scale items* were those where the pilot's performance could be read from instruments such as altimeters or air speed indicators and then compared with assigned values; and *categorical items* in which a judgment had to be made by an instructor that the student was "correct-incorrect" or "high-normal-low," etc.

By analysis and the collection of normative data they were able to set up standards and determine what in effect were "difficulty levels" for each item. By this means they could set standards which were quite specific and could establish the level of training of the student. Intermediate goals could be set for attainment which would depend upon the amount of training or experience the student had had. In this way the instructor knew what to expect from this student and it was possible for the school administration to vary the standards depending upon their needs for either protection or relaxation on specific elements. By calculating levels of acceptable or non-acceptable performance, the errors of a specific trainee could be spotted or errors common to many students could be identified and training techniques altered to fit the situation. They noted that instruction techniques tended to change with time so that certain common errors would tend to diminish and emphases would be shifted.

Measures based upon this general type of check list of specific behaviors tend to be very serviceable. Basically, the check lists are intended to be guides to the observer and as long as he is in a position to make the observation, the individual elements of performance can be observed quite objectively. In fact, though the methodological research has not been intensive, there has been quite a history of the use of check lists as training aids in helping to teach people to perform specific jobs. In the military there are many instances where check lists are posted on ships and other military installations for the aid of personnel in performing certain tasks. For example, on Navy ships one often sees two, three, four or five item check lists on metal plates made fast to bulkheads that inform the individual how to shut certain doors or hatches and under what circumstances they should be shut. There are many variations of this basic idea up to the more complex check lists used by supervisory pilots or others in riding "check flights" with airplane pilots.

Simon (1954) offers a simple but basic classification of the sources of errors in these kinds of instruments. The other writers mentioned above also discuss them in varying detail. Simon emphasizes three main error sources: (*a*) *Sampling Errors*. It is especially important to have an adequate representation of the specific behaviors of a job if one is attempting to develop a good measure of total job performance. (*b*) *Observer Variation*. Quite adequate reliabilities have been obtained in most all of the studies mentioned above when using a specific behavior element measurement device. However, it is plain to see that if the check list is not properly constructed and if the observer is allowed too much leeway in making judgments, there can be a serious error source in the variability of the observer from trial to trial. (*c*) *Time Sampling*. This is the examinee side of the coin with respect to (*b*) above in that the behavior of the trainee may vary from time to time and this variability of performance will create error in the measurement system.

It is probable that this check list approach to the measurement of specific behavior elements is most serviceable in jobs where the trainee is the operator of a piece of equipment which does not turn out a product. Where there is no product and no direct consequence such as sales volume or speed of overall performance to be observed, the check list approach is almost the only measurement possibility.

## Gross Performance Measures

This sub-group includes those measures of the behavior of a trainee or the consequences of those behaviors where no specific product or specific behavior is available to be measured, for example, such aspects as speed, quantity, quality or accuracy of performance, etc. In measuring such gross performances in the real world one is invariably faced with a wide range of uncontrollable or unmeasurable variables, the one being tantamount to the other. These tend to obscure the performance of the individual to the point of making it nearly impossible to measure with confidence and validity. A few examples will readily indicate the problem.

In assessing the performance of salesmen, the differences in territories and the large number of other variables that are related to those territories often produce so much variance that the measurable performance of the individual is swamped completely. Then, there is the ever present problem of accounting for the difference in motivation between salesmen. So often, the performance of a man is variable as a result of the fluctuation in motivation. This makes on-the-job performance a poor measure since his motivation to perform in the school or training situation may be quite different, either higher or lower, from that on the real job.

In World War II, and since, there has been a great deal of attention paid to miss distance, or circular error, as a criterion for assessing the performance of crews in bombing and depth-charge attack (Grings, 1952). Invariably, it is found that these gross measures are too filled with uncontrollable variables to permit their use and, hence, their reliabilities are too low for either training or selection criteria.

There is another serious defect in most of these gross kinds of measures in that they fail on the basic requirement of providing specific information to be fed back into training efforts. So many influences contribute to the number of sales a man can make, the number of service calls he can perform in a given period of time, the extent of error he makes in marksmanship, etc. that the measure of total performance becomes a gross mix of specifics. The identification and quantification of those specifics within that mix are lost with a consequent loss of value in the training situation.

An example of a study which runs contrary to this generalization in which gross performance measures tended to be more specific and valuable is one that was based on the records of 61 file clerks (Gaylord,

Russell, Johnson, & Severin, 1951). These investigators employed records on six different performance criteria. The reliabilities were good in that all were over .84 and all but one above .94. The variables measured along with their intercorrelations and reliabilities are shown in Table 12.1.

Table 12.1

Reliabilities and Intercorrelations of Six Performance
Measures on File Clerks (Gaylord et al., 1951)

|  | Reli-ability | Intercorrelations 1 | 2 | 3 | 4 | 5 |
|---|---|---|---|---|---|---|
| 1. Filing Information | .97 | | | | | |
| 2. Filing Folders | .97 | .55 | | | | |
| 3. Loaning Folders | .97 | .58 | .46 | | | |
| 4. Locating Information | .97 | .58 | .48 | .93 | | |
| 5. Filing Medical Cards | .84 | .54 | .03 | .31 | .35 | |
| 6. Transferring Records | .94 | .15 | .21 | −.16 | −.16 | .02 |

In this study, Gaylord et al. apparently achieved a degree of specificity of measurement as is indicated by both the verbal labels they put on each of the criteria and the generally low-to-moderate intercorrelations. While not comparable with the specific behavior elements already discussed, these measures appear to be sufficiently accurate and specific to permit coaching or training to take place for the improvement of the performance of the file clerks.

Further notice should be made of the fact that the inter-relationship between six measures of this sort is, in some cases, extremely low and in all cases less than the reliabilities would permit. This is a characteristic of job performance measurements which permeates the literature rather completely. Two reliable and meaningful measures may turn out to be almost independent. This is good in that it indicates the measures are desirably specific but it makes for a problem in trying to develop an overall criterion measure. More discussion will be devoted to this at a later point in the chapter.

The general approach most often taken in an attempt to get around the difficulties and inadequacies of gross performance measures in the practical situation is essentially that of examining the more extreme cases in some detail. By having a close look at the extremely good or extremely poor performers, one can often modify training courses on the basis of judgment. In working with sales figures one frequently finds that certain individuals will stand out of the group as particularly good or particularly poor performers. When the research man learns that there is no reliability to his more objective measures but still there is a demand for improved training or selection, he is then forced to take what is essentially a clinical approach toward the analysis of these "obvious deviates." For example, suppose a new insurance agency were created as one of a hundred. Further imagine that with all important environmental variables controlled or compensated, the new agency climbed in sales to the median position out of the whole hundred. This record is outstanding and a study of the manager's methods is justified by the company to aid in shaping a training program for other agencies. One often finds cases such as this that can be judged significantly different from the norm in performance. He is then forced to have a closer look at these individual cases and to deduce what, if anything, can be gleaned of value for training programs. To be sure, one may not be able to quantify such observations satisfactorily or obtain adequate reliability or specificity. On the other hand, the importance of the problem is often such that any kind of systematic assessment may be of great value.

In summary, this group of gross performance measures is the kind that is most often encountered in industry and the kind that is most often available for study. Unfortunately, it is the source of serious uneasiness to the training researcher while, at the same time, it possesses the greatest face validity and appeal to industry management. Top management is likely to think in terms of sales dollars or gross performance just as a military command tends to think first of hits on target. The historical unsuitability of this kind of criterion is one of the great disappointments to those who would study either training or selection. But, the sheer grossness of these measures makes them of relatively little use in the shaping of a specific training program. It is possible, where reliability can be established, that there may be some value in these measures for making the gross "Yes-No" decision whether a training program should be used or not. But if the question is one of the design of the specifics of the training program, these measures can almost unqualifiedly be said to be seriously inadequate.

## Inferred Positive Performance

Measures of performance in this group are one step further removed from the type discussed in the preceding section. They involve indirect gross measures and include such metrics as promotion from one job level to another, measures of turnover, grievances, and the morale of subordinates. Here the direct behavior or the immediate consequences of the trainee are not being observed but, rather, the cumulative indirect consequences are being measured.

Most of the comments made in the preceding section about the inadequacies of measuring performance characteristics for the feedback of specific training information apply to this indirect set of measures. However, there have been some interesting uses of these types of measures and many of them continue. For example, the writer found he could use job level attained as a criterion for the validation of aptitude tests. Two tests in combination predicted the criterion at the level of .35.[2] However, such a measure of promotion would have little value as a training criterion.

Employee morale is used much more often than promotion as a training criterion. Many industrial psychologists have become involved in the measurement of employee attitudes and the consequent design of programs to improve the morale deficiencies uncovered. There is a fine line between persuasion and training in this context, and this must be kept in mind. However, morale measurements are being used almost every day as criteria to design training programs for supervisors. Typically, interviews are conducted with employees by mail or face-to-face by a research person. Often this is an individual outside the company particularly chosen to encourage frankness of reply on the part of the employee. The results of such interviews are analyzed by departments and/or shifts, where possible, without disclosing the identity of the respondents when small numbers are being interviewed. As a result of this kind of analysis it is possible to indentify the morale of working sub-groups who answer to a single supervisor. Even further, individual supervisors are often the subjects of questions in these interviews. In such cases employee attitudes towards the supervisor are quite directly sought. As a consequence of such studies, supervisory programs are designed to improve management skills and bring about more effective coordination and cooperation in the working situation. Once again, it is important to distinguish between attitude or performance changes that are a consequence of persuasion, propaganda and the like, and those which are a function or a consequence of training of either the individual worker or the supervisor.

A recent study has carried the general class of indirect measures a little further (Turner, 1960). In this study, 11 objective measures

---

[2]Unpublished report.

were constructed from information regularly supplied at two manufacturing plants. The measures and their reliabilities are shown in Table 12.2.

Table 12.2

Reliabilities of Criterion Measures (Turner, 1960)

| Criterion Measure | Plant 1 Reliability | Plant 2 Reliability |
|---|---|---|
| Grievances | .28 | .30 |
| Turnover | .37 | .28 |
| Absences | .74 | .60 |
| Suggestions | .14 | .45 |
| Hospital Passes | .86 | .57 |
| Disciplines | .32 | .39 |
| Absentee Flexibility | .36 | .74 |
| Scrap | .88 | .76 |
| Expense Tools | .79 | .87 |
| Expense Processing Supplies | .88 | .79 |
| Efficiency | .86 | .68 |

Turner conducted a factor analysis of these measures and found a broad factor which he called "Employee Relations" with high loadings on Disciplines, Absences, Grievances, Turnover and Expense Tools in both plants. His second factor was loaded almost solely on Scrap and he obtained a third factor which varied somewhat between the two plants but which had high loadings on Turnover and Efficiency in both. As far as this study goes the factors would appear too general to be of use in shaping training programs but of sufficient consistancy to point up the need for training in general areas. Future studies along this line could well be more revealing since Turner's communalities are considerably less than his reliabilities would permit in some instances.

In summary, this particular sub-group of inferred positive measures is dominated by the employee morale kind of measure. There is, quite possibly, material benefit to be gained from the exploration of this general class of measures; however, it may be expected that they will often lack the directness and specificity necessary for the design of specific programs. Of course, the employee morale interview questionnaire can be quite specific and may tend to overcome some of these difficulties.

*Malperformance Measures*

This sub-group considers such things as accidents, product rejects, labor turnover, tardiness and absences from work. In many instances these measures will be the negative ends of the scales already discussed in the preceding sub-groups. However, they do occupy an important and distinct place in the scheme of training and selection even though some of them may be different sides of the coins already examined. For example, one can measure defects and distortions such as pits and gashes found in a piece of metal stock after it has been turned on a lathe and milled. Such a measure is very likely to fit in with the positive measures of fits, finishes and balances already discussed in the first sub-group on tangible product measures.

Accidents, both personal and vehicle, have received a great deal of research attention by those interested in driver selection. This field, of course, is especially important because of the very great economic and human waste that results from accidents. Some progress has been made in the prediction of accidents. The writer, in some unpublished reports, found that it was possible to attain validity coefficients in the range of .25 to .35 between a battery of pencil and paper tests largely measuring perceptual speed and the number of "At Fault" accidents experienced by drivers of trucks delivering milk. A committee of supervisors judged which accidents were "At Fault" or "Not At Fault" for which the driver was responsible from those caused by conditions beyond his control. For selection purposes, validity coefficients at this level permit one to establish high cutting points on the test score range and effect a demonstrable reduction in accident experience. For selection purposes, it was profitable to establish a high cutting point on the test score range and effect a demonstrable reduction in accident experience. However, no analysis was made of the possible *trainable* factors in the accident criterion. Instead, Personnel Department officials, of their own accord, began to use the test scores from this battery of tests as training aids, in a very broad sense. If a man scored high on the tests he was told that he had the basic aptitudes to drive without accidents and, therefore, should have no "At Fault" accidents on his record as it accumulated after hiring. On the other hand, if the driver scored low on the test score range he was told that he had to be unusually careful in order to avoid accidents because his test score would indicate that he was shy some of the basic aptitudes. As a result of this combined selection and "training" effort the company has shown a reduction in accident rates as compared with the milk industry as a whole.

In working with accidents as a criterion measure in either training or selection studies, one needs to be careful in the statistical techniques he uses. It is quite possible to obtain apparent results when, in fact, chance alone is operating (Blum & Mintz, 1951; Webb & Jones, 1952; Teel & DuBois, 1954). To a great extent the statistical problem results from the fact that so few people have accidents and reliabilities are low. This same phenomenon may be present in other malperformance measures so that caution should be observed in such instances.

In summary, malperformance measures, like some of the other more gross measures so far described, are of material importance to training research people. On the other hand, though the accidents, rejects, and other evidences of malperformance are of tremendous human and economic importance to industry, very little effort has been put toward identifying the trainable characteristics within these criteria in sufficient detail to permit specificity of feedback into the training situation. Rather, training efforts to overcome these deficiencies have largely been aimed at developing attitudes which would serve as the basis for employees wanting to avoid high, and therefore, poor, scores on these measures. There is great material profit from both a research and performance point of view to be gained in more detailed study of some of the specific trainable characteristics that go toward predisposing a person to have accidents or to otherwise fail in performance of his job.

## Work Samples

This class of measures, as its name implies, is based on tasks, jobsegments, evolutions or any portion of the total work load that makes up a job and which might be judged to be important. Tests based on these samples may either be conducted in the context of the job using the regular machinery, equipment and space, or they may be based on simulators or test situations specially constructed to duplicate the task.

In the history of applied psychology, work samples have an early place. Munsterberg (1913, Ch. 8) devised a work sample test for streetcar operators. Actually, his test did not duplicate the job in detail; rather, it made use of symbolic representation. Rolling toward the operator, who was in a cubicle, was a belt on which were painted squares and symbols of various kinds to indicate obstacles to which the operator had to react by the manipulations of a control handle. Work sample tests over the years have been used primarily in personnel selection. As in the case of Munsterberg, attempts were made to devise tests to identify the aptitudes possessed by applicants, and therefore serve as predictors of job success. To a certain extent, also, they served as training devices in many instances. Viteles (1932) gives an extensive history of the development of these devices up to 1932. As time went by, the fashion in selection tests changed from the work sample type of measure to today's aptitude tests. At the same time, the measurement of skills on the job was accomplished more and more by rating devices. As a consequence of these trends, the use of work sample tests tended to diminish. Today, with better perception of training methods and the need for more intensive and specific measures of job performance, a revival of interest in this kind of measuring device may well be indicated.

The categorization of types of work sample tests is difficult because of the great number of possibilities. Before attempting to discuss the various classes of measurement that fall in this general group, it is desirable to look at some of the more important ways in which these tests can vary:

1. *The reproducibility of the task.* Many tasks are readily reproducible, but there are also many instances where it is literally impossible to reproduce a realistic job situation. In the advertising business, for example, it would be highly desirable to know how to measure the effectiveness with which an advertising agency account representative handles himself in dealing with a client. There are many situations of this nature, especially in service-type occupations such as the field of sales and general management. This is also true in the handling of complex mechanical and electrical systems. For example, piloting airplanes requires certain kinds of skills which cannot be reproduced adequately. Few work samples ever can reproduce the real operational task exactly. The fact that measurement is taking place inevitably demands some environmental changes or controls. (See Chapter 8 by Gagné.)

2. *The equipment to be used.* This will depend largely upon the task, of course. In some instances the trainee must operate a piece of equipment in place; in others he must use tools and machinery to produce a product. In yet other situations he uses only a test instrument to check the condition of the system he is monitoring and, of course, in some cases no equipment at all is involved.

3. *The degree of intellectual involvement.* Some tasks require only that the operator monitor while others require him to perform quite complex reasoning functions. In the monitoring kind of task he may only follow a pointer, keep the automobile aimed in the right direction, adjust

temperatures or pressures by turning a valve, or manipulate the elevator handles to stop the car where the light is red. On the other hand, more professional level occupations would require the application of more complex brain power. (See Chapter 11 by Frederiksen.)

4. The *measurement techniques employed*. In most instances, the choice of technique is dictated by the kind of task. For example, in a task involving the operation of equipment, the method of measurement is usually to use an observer with a check list of specific behavior elements in hand. (See above.) Proficiency checks on airplane crews are also instances that fall into this category. Where products are turned out the method of measurement can be the same as that referred to under the general heading of "Tangible Product Measures" previously discussed in this chapter. Where checking and testing instruments on circuits or other systems are involved, it is often possible to prepare a record sheet on which the trainee records the readings obtained or makes simple check marks to indicate "yes-no" observations.

These four aspects represent the main variables on which work sample tests will differ from each other. Because of the many degrees of position on these various continua, the combinations of conditions on them which dictate the design of the test are quite large. To give some examples of the kinds of thing that can be done with work sample tests, Table 12.3 presents a brief description of each of a series of tests used in a study of submarine electrician's mates (Wilson & Mackie, 1952).

This table points up several aspects or features encountered in the use of work sample tests. Some of these are problems and others are advantages:

1. *Test Reliability*. Individual test reliabilities range from .52 to .93. On a comparison set of tests for another job, Enginemen, the range was from .67 to .84. From these results it can be concluded that these individual work sample tests can be made sufficiently reliable to measure performance on individual tasks. It seems likely that the reliabilities below .70 could be increased by lengthening the tests involved. However, the principle holds that individual task tests can be made reliable and sufficiently so for the specificity of measure needed in training program improvement.

2. *Restriction in Test Design*. Observation of the list of tests in Table 12.3 will show that the megger was used in two tests and the fuse testing equipment was also used in two tests. Thus, one wonders about

Table 12.3

Work Sample Tests Used in a Study of Submarine Electrician's Mates (Wilson & Mackie, 1952)

| Test | Directions | Measurement | No. Items | Time (min.) | N | Reliability | r with Pay Grade |
|---|---|---|---|---|---|---|---|
| *Control Cubicle* The actual control cubicle aboard a submarine was utilized in this test. Controls used in specified operations were to be pointed out but not manipulated by the men taking the test. | Show the exact operations you would go through to add generator No. 1 to the line while generator No. 3 is cut in. Generator No. 1 is running. Point out, in order, each knob and switch you would use. Tell what you are doing and what readings you are setting. Do not manipulate the controls. | One point for each step on the check list which was correctly carried out. Maximum possible raw score was 19. | 19 | 10 | 111 | .70 | .36 |
| *Use of a Megger: Ringing Out DC Motors* A megger was used to find open circuits and grounds in series-wound and compound-wound DC motors. Casualties had been built into the motors. | Using a megger, ring out the two DC motors in front of you. Locate any grounds or opens which may exist in either motor. Indicate the condition of the field and armature circuits. | One point for each field and armature circuit condition correctly determined, except in one case where a partially correct determination received half credit. Maximum possible raw score was 7. | 7 | 10 | 317 | .58 | .25 |
| *Use of a Megger: Ground Reading Test* A standard Navy lighting distribution box has grounds and resistances inserted into some of its subcircuits. | Measure the insulation to ground reading on all lighting branches coming out of this distribution box. Record the readings of each circuit lead in the space provided. | One point for each correct reading. Maximum possible raw score was 21. | 21 | 10 | 312 | ND* | .41 |

*ND—Not Determined

Table 12.3 (con't)

| Test | Directions | Measurement | No. Items | Time (min.) | N | Reli- ability | r with Pay Grade |
|------|-----------|-------------|-----------|-------------|---|----------------|------------------|
| *Circuit and Fuse Testing:* <br> *A. Circuits* <br><br> A standard Navy 12 circuit fuse panel was modified so that some of the circuits were not energized and some of the fuses were blown. In this Part A of the test, only the circuits were to be tested. Wiggins Testers or test lamps were used. | Using the voltage tester, check each of the 12 circuits on the test board and indicate on your answer sheet whether or not each of the circuits is energized. | One point for each correct answer. Maximum possible raw score was 12. | 12 | 5 | 317 | .93 | .40 |
| *Circuit and Fuse Testing:* <br> *B. Fuses* <br><br> The same standard fuse panel used in the preceding test was used here. In this Part B, the condition of the fuses in each energized circuit was to be determined. The same test sheet was also used. | If you have found a circuit to be energized (Part A), test both of the fuses in that circuit and indicate whether or not each fuse is good. | Final score was the proportion of correct answers to the total number of answers given. Maximum possible raw score (proportional) was 1.0. | 24 | 5 | 317 | .84 | .20 |
| *Repairing Sound Powered Telephones* <br><br> Open circuits and shorts were inserted at various points in each of two sets of regulation sound powered telephones. All casualties could be found without special test equipment. | Find out what parts in each of these two telephone sets have casualties and place a check mark in the appropriate place on the answer sheet. Then choose from the list of repair methods the one you would use to correct each casualty. | One point for each casualty found, and one point for each correct repair method chosen. Maximum possible raw score was 8. | 8 | 15 | 315 | .52 | .13 |

Table 12.3 (con't)

| Test | Directions | Measurement | No. Items | Time (min.) | N | Reliability | r with Pay Grade |
|---|---|---|---|---|---|---|---|
| *Storage Batteries* | A small battery was filled with a noncorrosive electrolyte, the specific gravity of which was so adjusted as to indicate that the battery needed charging. The test sheet contained questions to be answered concerning the condition of the battery and the kind of equipment used in testing it. | One point for each question answered correctly. Maximum raw score was 8. | 8 | 5 | 176 | .57 | .43 |
| *Use of Common Hand Tools* | Common hand tools were arranged on a board and numbered. Tasks requiring the use of tools were listed on the test sheet. | In the blank appearing after each question, place the number of the tool on the tool board that you would use in doing the specified task. If the task calls for more than one tool, list the number of every tool which you would use. | Two points for each correct answer. If more than one tool was called for, fractional scores were given for each tool correctly named. If a tool other than one specified was named and was considered reasonably adequate for the task in question, partial credit was given. | 20 | 15 | 318 | .63 | .49 |

Table 12.3 (con't)

| Test | Directions | Measurement | No. Items | Time (min.) | N | Reliability | r with Pay Grade |
|---|---|---|---|---|---|---|---|
| *Job Knowledge* This was a written test consisting of 40 multiple-choice questions about the practical and theoretical aspects of the Electrician's Mate's job. | In this test booklet you will find incomplete statements followed by five alternative endings. You are to select the alternative ending which correctly, or most correctly, completes each statement. | One point for each correct answer. Maximum possible raw score was 40. | 40 | 30 | 313 | .86 | .50 |
| *Safety Precautions* A booklet of photographs taken aboard a submarine was assembled which showed crew members engaged in various activities. In some of the pictures basic safety precautions were being violated. | In this test booklet you will find pictures of men performing tasks aboard submarines. You are to indicate on the answer sheet what safety precautions, if any, are being violated. | One point for each picture correctly analyzed. If more than one violation appeared in a picture, the point was divided by the number of violations, and fractional scores were given for each violation indicated. Maximum possible raw score was 15. | 15 | 10 | 308 | .77 | .27 |

the reach, or adequacy of sampling, of work sample tests. The tests in this instance were chosen because of the judged importance of the tasks on the part of officers and chief petty officers. However, there were some tasks that were not tested because it was impossible to reproduce adequately the actual task condition. An example of this would be the use of the control cubicle. Of the tests listed, the Control Cubicle had to be conducted while the equipment was inoperative. It would have been desirable to conduct extensive testing at various conditions of this control cubicle but the equipment was not available for this purpose.

This brings up the question of the adequacy with which one can sample from a total number of tasks that make up the universe of a particular job. One is frequently faced with operating facts of life that require the measurement of what is measurable rather than everything that is important. This restriction, however, may be a more serious obstacle to those working on selection problems than those in the field of training. To put together a composite criterion for use in the validation of predictor tests, it is necessary to have a proper representation of all the skills and aptitudes required in the job. To be sure, these must be weighted in terms of some kind of importance to the job in the final make-up of a sound criterion. However, in the case of training, one can benefit from the adequate measurement of an individual task because this bit of information, by itself, is the exact kind of specificity that is needed for purposes of feeding information back into the training situation either for trainer or trainee. It would be desirable, of course, to be able to measure all important tasks in a total job situation, but when it is not possible to measure some, then benefit can be had from those that are measurable with reliability. One danger, of course, is the emphasizing of important tasks just because they are measurable.

3. *Symbolic Knowledge Tests.* In the series of tests shown in Table 12.3 the "Use of Common Hand Tools" test was considered by officers and chief petty officers to be a very important phase of the Electrician's Mate's knowledge and skills. As a result, a whole series of tasks were set before the subject in written form and he chose the tools from the tool board that he would use to perform each of these tasks. Strictly speaking, this can hardly be called a work sample test in that the trainee is performing no more of a task than identifying some tools that are actually in front of him. It is probable that many experienced measurement psychologists would agree that this same knowledge would be measured as well with written tests using drawings of tools or simply tool names. No issue is taken with this point. The test was included in this

battery because of the importance given to the skill or knowledge by those who were used as judges and to lend some face validity to the task. In fact, in the Enginemen test series, which is not considered in detail in this chapter, there was a much greater tendency to go toward this general kind of test. To a great extent, this was dictated by the fact that the Engineman's job was mainly to operate diesel engines, and there was little opportunity to reproduce the tasks involved.

Concerning the question of specificity of measurement, Table 12.4 is presented to show the intercorrelations between the tests described in Table 12.3. It will be noted that the highest intercorrelation, .47, is

Table 12.4

Intercorrelations of Performance Tests
for Electrician's Mates

| | Test | Reli- ability | 1 | 2 | 3 | 4a | 4b | 5 | 6 | 7 | 8 |
|---|---|---|---|---|---|---|---|---|---|---|---|
| 1. | Control Cubicle .......... | .70 | | | | | | | | | |
| 2. | Use of a Megger: Ringing Out DC Motors .. | .58 | .16 | | | | | | | | |
| 3. | Use of a Megger: Ground Reading Test .... | * | .42 | .32 | | | | | | | |
| 4a. | Circuit and Fuse Testing: A. Circuits ...... | .93 | .02 | .22 | .13 | | | | | | |
| 4b. | Circuit and Fuse Testing: B. Fuses ....... | .84 | .23 | .23 | .22 | .47 | | | | | |
| 5. | Repairing Sound Powered Telephones ..... | .52 | .20 | .09 | .08 | .01 | −.03 | | | | |
| 6. | Storage Batteries ........ | .57 | ** | −.02 | .10 | .22 | −.05 | .05 | | | |
| 7. | Use of Common Hand Tools .............. | .63 | .27 | .31 | .24 | .28 | .27 | .08 | .15 | | |
| 8. | Written Job Knowledge*** ........... | .86 | .44 | .27 | .40 | .39 | .27 | .09 | .34 | .44 | |
| 9. | Safety Precautions*** ... | .77 | .27 | .00 | .08 | .18 | .13 | .07 | .20 | −.04 | .28 |

\* No reliability computed because distribution of scores would have required test-retest which was not feasible.

\*\* Insufficient number of cases.

\*\*\* Not a part of the performance battery. Both were knowledge tests.

between the two "Circuit and Fuse Testing" sub-tests. The next highest, .42, is between the two "Megger" tests. Aside from these, observation of the table will show that most of the intercorrelations tend to range below .30. It can be deduced from this that the intercorrelations of the individual work sample tests are well below the level permitted by their reliabilities which are also shown in the table. A comparable conclusion can be drawn from the experience with the Enginemen who were studied in the same investigation. These low intercorrelations between work samples point up an important general observation concerning criterion development. As was noted earlier in Table 12.1, objective measures will often show little relationship with each other. Beyond this, objective measures will seldom show any strong relationship with subjective measures such as ratings even though both are reliable. For the selection problem this presents considerable difficulty since a battery of tests must predict some optimum combination of criterion measures in a total performance assessment. Determining the weights to assign to each criterion measure for that optimum combination is a task of the first magnitude. In the training research situation, however, these low relationships are, in a sense, fortunate because it means the measures tend toward a specificity that makes for better feedback into training curriculum design.

In summary, work sample tests can be very valuable aids in the measurement of job performance whether for purposes of establishing a criterion for the validation of selection devices or for purposes of improving a training program. In fact, the latter use is one of their best. This type of test, when reliability can be obtained and when the sample fairly represents the real task, performs the duty of giving specific information in a manner that can be matched only by the measurement of tangible product characteristics or by the measurement of specific behavior elements.

## RATINGS

This final group of evaluation methods is the one most often used in selection research. However, though the history of rating studies is long, woefully little progress has been made in bringing rating methods to the point where they are of real major value as criteria in the field of training research today. To distinguish the term "ratings" from the other classes of measurements in the context of this chapter, it can be defined as "cumulative impressions or evaluations made by an observer and recorded at a time later than the observation." Particularly, this is to distinguish "ratings" from the evaluations made by an observer in the measurement of specific behavior elements discussed previously.

The most serious problem with the use of ratings in training research results from the relative inability of researchers, to date, to obtain the degree of specificity necessary. Ratings have surely been used over 50 years in personnel psychology as criteria for selection studies. From the beginning, the concept of "halo" has been identifiable as the central problem. High intercorrelations of rating scales despite great and extensive efforts to define rating variables in mutually exclusive manners, have rendered ratings disappointing to anyone doing research in the field of selection and have almost eliminated their value in training studies.

Many studies have been conducted to try to find better ways of rating performance. In the Department of the Army, the Adjutant General's Office, Personnel Research Branch (U.S. Army, 1951, et seq.) conducted an extensive series of studies on rating methodology, systematically examining many aspects of the problem. Taylor (1958, p. 3) whose background includes service with the Adjutant General's Office sums up the problems of ratings in this manner:

> The inadequacies of performance evaluation are not a function of the forms on which the data are collected. These are nothing more than vehicles which formally convey a communication. If the communication is faulty, inadequate or distorted, it is not possible for the vehicle to correct the faults of the material it carries.

> We, then, would lay the blame for the inadequacy of performance evaluation at the feet of those who evaluate rather than, as so often has been the case, on the forms by which these evaluations are conveyed. As implied above sound evaluation must be based, in the first instance, upon systematic observation of job performance. Two aspects of observation are involved. First, there must be opportunity for such observations, and secondly, there must be a measure of observational skill. In many cases, both of these elements are seriously deficient. The opportunity to observe a subordinate in his performance of his job-duties varies widely with the nature of the task and its level. Frequently, at the first level of supervision, the span of control is so great and the nonsupervisory responsibilities so extensive that the superior is able to attend to the performance of individual subordinates only under rare, dramatic, or even catastrophic circumstances. Even when a number of people supervised is nominal, five to ten, the supervisor's other responsibilities frequently demand so much of his time and energy that he has little left to devote to watching his people function unless something has gone wrong. There are many jobs, both military and civilian, whose nature is such that it practically precludes the workers' ever being directly observed by their superior in the performance of their work. Truck drivers and industrial salesmen, traveling auditors and couriers, are but a few examples that come immediately to mind. Further, it seems almost axiomatic that the higher the rank or position of the personnel involved, the less frequent is the contact between them and the greater the physical separation.

Wilson, Mackie and Buckner (1954a; 1954b) conducted a series of studies using Navy submarine personnel to investigate the relationship between ratings and actual performance as measured by work sample tests. The results support Taylor's implied lack of validity for supervisors' ratings and inferentially substantiate his thesis concerning their lack of opportunity to observe. In these studies, to obtain the supervisors' evaluations, each rater was given a check list booklet containing a description of specific tasks required in a man's performance aboard ship. Job sample or knowledge tests were prepared to measure the same abilities directly. In the ratings each supervisor was asked:

Indicate whether the man can do the job:

*Unsupervised*—without supervision or any technical help whatever. Can do the whole job by himself.

*Occasionally supervised*—needs only an occasional check to see that everything is going okay.

*Continuously supervised*—needs to be told what to do and helped practically throughout the job. Men who cannot do the job at all should also be checked in this role.

In addition to checking each man in one of the above categories, we would also like to know whether or not you have personally observed each man doing the task in question *recently enough so that you can be absolutely sure* that you have checked him correctly. *If you have recently seen him do it,* place a check in the space provided.

With this kind of check list scaling device the rated group was dichotomized leaving those who could perform the most tasks "unsupervised" in the *plus* category with the other two groups in a *minus* category. In addition, another separate analysis was carried out studying individuals who were "actually observed" in performing the various tasks.

In the first of these analyses a correlation was obtained between total check list scores and total scores of the on-the-job tests. That is, the rated ability of a man as measured by the number of tasks his supervisors thought he could do "unsupervised" was correlated with the number of job sample tests he could pass. Again, the check list contained items which matched exactly the job sample tests. (Some of the job sample tests were recognition tests using pictures and some were identification tests using actual tools and other equipments.) Table 12.5 shows the intercorrelation between these check list total scores and scores on the actual performance tests. At best, even with the aid of the heterogeneity contributed by using the samples made up of all pay

Table 12.5

Correlations Between Check List Total Scores
and Performance Test Scores by Navy Pay Grades

| | Engine-men (EN) | N* | Electrician's Mates (EM) | N* |
|---|---|---|---|---|
| Strikers (nonrated men) ............... | .18 | 196 | .20 | 127 |
| Third Class Petty Officers .............. | .07 | 120 | .53 | 137 |
| Strikers and Third Class ............... | .27 | 316 | .37 | 264 |
| All pay grades (Strikers through CPO's) | .44 | 518 | .58 | 397 |

*N=number of ratings
CPO=Chief Petty Officer

grades, Strikers through Chief Petty Officer's, the relationship between the scores on the rating check list and the scores on the work sample test battery reached to the level of .58 for the Electrician's Mate group and .44 for the Enginemen.

In the second analysis a similar correlation was computed but in this case it was based on only those tasks which raters had "actually observed." These ratings were correlated with the scores on the corresponding job sample tests. In this instance, in other words, only those items rated or tested were scored in which the raters said they had "personally observed each man doing the task in question recently enough so that you can be absolutely sure that you have checked him correctly."

Table 12.6 shows the results of this study comparing "total" with "observed" scores for strikers and third class petty officers only. The analysis was confined to these two groups in order to obtain a closer look at the relationship between a man's performance when measured by his supervisor's assessment based on what the supervisor said was actual observation and when measured by his performance on a sample test designed to measure the same elements of performance. It was considered most important in the light of the results from Table 12.5 that

Table 12.6

Mean Correlations Between
Check List Observed and Total Scores
and Performance Test Scores

(Strikers and Third Class)

| | Within Pay Grade | | | | Across Pay Grade | | | |
|---|---|---|---|---|---|---|---|---|
| | EN | N* | EM | N* | EN | N* | EM | N* |
| Observed Scores ............. | .01 | 233 | .21 | 225 | .08 | 233 | .25 | 225 |
| Total Scores ............... | .14 | 316 | .37 | 264 | .27 | 316 | .37 | 264 |

*N=number of ratings

the heterogeneity contributed by the presence of all pay grades be restricted. This latter set of results is comparable to the information contained in Table 12.5. Results are also shown "Within Pay Grade" and "Across Pay Grade." In the former the effect of Pay Grade is partialled out whereas in the latter Pay Grade is allowed to function and contribute heterogeneity.

Here we come face to face with one of the most important problems in the use of ratings as evaluative procedures. Even when the raters indicate that "they are absolutely sure" that they have checked a man correctly as indicated by the "observed score" relationships, we find no improvement in the relationship between rated and tested performance over the ratings performed without this assurance of observation. This is the problem that Taylor has noted. In short, the problem of the rater making observations, whether it be opportunity or skill in rating, is one of the central and critical points in the whole rating approach to evaluation. Until this can be solved it will be exceedingly difficult to obtain the specificity of variance needed in rating scores to make them of creditable value as criteria for training research studies.

In contrast, however, while the ratings obtained by most any format and system are inadequate for training research, they do show value for selection studies. For example, in a study similar to the one just discussed (Wilson, et al., 1954b), the total scores obtained by a check list approach correlated .40 for Electrician's Mates and .42 for Enginemen with a battery of aptitude tests administered, while the subjects were still in submarine school, two years before rating time. Thus, though ratings lack the specificity necessary for training studies, they do provide predictable variance for selection studies. The investigations quoted here (Wilson, et al., 1954a; Wilson, et al., 1954b) as well as other studies throughout the literature demonstrate quite clearly that assessments obtained from ratings are relatively independent of those obtained from practical performance test measures, written job knowledge measures or other metholds of assessment. On the other hand, ratings can often be shown to be sufficiently reliable to indicate that something is being consistently measured. By the same token, as indicated here, assessments made by ratings are predictable by other objective measurements such as aptitude tests. It is therefore concluded that variance measured by ratings can be valuable for use as selection criteria but lacking in specificity to the point where they cannot contribute much as training research criteria.

It is not the purpose of this chapter to provide a detailed discussion of ratings in general. Rather, the aim is to discuss ratings in the context of training research. The literature in the field of rating studies is extensive and goes back many years in the field of applied psychology. In the field of training research ratings appear to offer little of value in a critical study of training methods. On the other hand, it is conceivable that some training programs are aimed at such gross effects that a rating criterion could serve the purpose of measuring the performance differences between people who have had training and those who have had none. If finer discrimination than this is required it is probable that the criterion will have to come from some method of measurement other than ratings as they are defined in this chapter, i.e., "cumulative impressions recorded at a time later than the observation of the performance is made."

## REFERENCES

Blum, M. L. & Mintz, A. Correlation versus curve fitting in research on accident proneness: Reply to Maritz, *Psychol. Bull.*, 1951, *48*, 413-418.

Gaylord, R. H., Russell, Eva, Johnson, C. & Severin, D. The relation of ratings to production records: An empirical study. *Personnel Psychol.*, 1951, *4*, 363-371.

Grings, W. W. The evaluation of experimentally controlled criteria. *Psychol. Bull.*, 1952, *49*, 333-338.

Hill, J. H., Buckley, E. P., & Older, H. J. *Post training performance of aviation machinists mates*. Washington, D. C.: IR in Human Relations, May 1952. Institute Rep. No. 5.

Houston, R. C., Smith, J. F., & Flexman, R. E. *Performance of student pilots flying the T-6 aircraft in primary pilot training*. 1954. AFPTRC-TR-54-109.

Jones, Margaret H. The adequacy of employee selection reports. *J. app. Psychol.*, 1950, *34*, 222-223.

Knauft, E. B. Construction and use of weighted check-list rating scales for two industrial situations. *J. appl. Psychol.*, 1948, *32*, 63-70.

Mackie, R. R. & High, W. S. *Research on the development of shipboard performance measures. Supervisory ratings and practical performance tests as complimentary criteria of shipboard performance.* Los Angeles: Human Factors Research, Inc., June 1959. ONR Tech. Rep. No. 9.

McGeoch, J. A. & Irion, A. L. *The psychology of human learning.* (2nd ed.) New York: Longman, 1952.

Munsterberg, H. *Psychology and industrial efficiency*. New York: Houghton Mifflin, 1913.

Simon, G. B. *Evaluation and combination of criterion measures by factor analysis: A study of B-25 by airplane and engine mechanics*. 1954. USAF Pers. Train. Res. Cent. Res. Bull. No. 54-23.

Taylor, E. W. *The influence of rating scale construction upon the characteristics of ratings rendered*. Cleveland: Personnel Research and Development Corporation, October 1958.

Teel, K. S. & Du Bois, P. H. Psychological research on accidents: Some methodological considerations. *J. appl. Psychol.*, 1954, *38*, 397-400.

Turner, W. W. Dimensions of foreman performance: A factor analysis of criterion measures. *J. appl. Psychol.*, 1960, *44*, 216-223.

U. S. Army. A study of officer-rating methodology. Personnel Research Section, Personnel Research and Procedures Branch, The Adjutant General's Office, Department of the Army. (A series of reports partially listed below.)

PRS Report 900—Part I. *The over-all design of the study*. 30 July 1951.

PRS Report 901—Part II. *Ratings made by identified and anonymous raters*. 17 April 1952. (a)

PRS Report 902—Part III. *Order of rating and validity of rating*. 17 April 1952. (b)

PRS Report 904—Part V. *Validity and reliability of ratings by single raters and multiple raters*. 17 April 1952. (c)

PRS Report 905—Part VI. *Independence of criterion measures from predictor variables*. 17 April 1952. (d)

PRS Report 906—Part VII. *Validities of four types of five-step rating scales*. 17 April 1952. (e)

PRS Report 907—Part VIII. *Validity of two types of rating techniques: Forced choice items and rating scales*. 17 April 1952. (f)

PRS Report 908—Part IX. *Validity of ratings by hard and easy raters*. 17 April 1952. (g)

PRS Report 909—Part X. *Effect of selected rater characteristics on validity of ratings*. 17 April 1952. (h)

U. S. Army. Studies of Officer Efficiency Report, WD AGO Form 67-1, In Operation. Personnel Research Section, Personnel Research and Procedures Branch, The Adjutant General's Office, Department of the Army. (Successive Reports)

PRS Report 936—Part IV. *Factors affecting consistency of successive reports.* 3 April 1952. (i)

PRS Report 971. *A comparison of the validity of officer ratings rendered by hard and easy raters.* 22 August 1952. (j)

U. S. Army. Technical Research Report. Personnel Research Branch, Adjutant General's Office, Department of the Army.

PRB 1084. *Field test of officer efficiency report.* June 1954. (a)

PRB 1085. *Reaction of general officers to officer efficiency reporting methods.* June 1954. (b)

PRB Technical Research Note 50. *Prediction of combat effectiveness of officer candidate school graduates.* November 1955.

Vaughn, K. W. & Rulon, P. J. *A study of the voluntary flight safety behaviors of naval aviators.* Washington, D. C.: Division of Aviation Medicine, USN, NRC Committee, October 1950. Aviation Psychology Report No. 9.

Viteles, M. S. *Industrial psychology.* New York: Norton, 1932.

Webb, W. B. & Jones, E. R. *Pilot accidents in the United States Air Force.* St. Louis: Washington Univ., August 1952. HRRL Rep. No. 30.

Wilson, C. L. & Mackie, R. R. *Research on the development of shipboard performance measures. Part I: The use of practical performance tests in the measurement of shipboard performance of enlisted naval personnel.* Los Angeles: Management and Marketing Research Corporation, 1952.

Wilson, C. L., Mackie, R. R., & Buckner, D. N. *Research on the development of shipboard performance measures. Part III: The use of performance check lists in the measurement of shipboard performance of enlisted naval personnel.* Los Angeles: Management and Marketing Research Corporation, February 1954. (a)

Wilson, C. L., Mackie, R. R., & Buckner, D. N. *Research on the development of shipboard performance measures. Part IV: A comparison between rated and tested ability to do certain job tasks.* Los Angeles: Management and Marketing Research Corporation, 1954. (b)

Wilson, C. L., Ruch, F. L., & Wolbers, H. L. *The use of performance tests in the measurement of shipboard performance of electrician's mates.* Los Angeles: Psychological Research Center, 1949.

# Chapter 13

# Experimental Study of
# Team Training and Team Functioning

Murray Glanzer,
Walter Reed Army Institute of Research

The main purpose of this chapter is to search out those problems in team training that are open to experimental examination. The analysis of such problems will be more profitable than stating, at length, principles that can be little more than hypotheses at this stage in the study of team functioning. In order to accomplish this purpose, this chapter will go over some attempts that have been made to see how teams behave in the field and some attempts to study special aspects of teams in the laboratory.

The term "team" is used for a wide variety of groups—from a group of basketball players, who are in close and constant interaction for relatively short periods of time, to a group of research workers, whose interactions are limited and occur over long periods of time. The discussion below will refer to a restricted family of military teams, since they are the teams on which there is the most information and since they are teams that frequently give rise to explicit training problems.

Although it is possible to discount any well-founded general principles in the area of team training, there are a number of hypotheses that arise from work on individual training. They receive support from the large role played by individual proficiency in team performance. They also receive support from the close analogy that can be made between team and individual performance. Skilled activity by an individual means that the individual's responses meet certain requirements of timing, coordination, and sensitivity to environmental changes. Skilled activity by a team means meeting the same requirements. The general principles that apply to the training of individuals could, therefore, also apply to the training of teams. These general principles are the following:

*Immediate Feedback or Reinforcement.* Feedback on the accuracy of every response should be as fast as possible.

*Simulation.* The training situation should be as similar as possible to the criterion situation. There are, however, many exceptions to this principle. It sometimes must be modified according to the special characteristics of the situation. For example, it is not necessary to have every piece of costly equipment that is used in the criterion situation. Indeed, simplified models of the situation may often be preferable during early stages of the training, in order to make these stages easier for the trainee. (See Chapter 8 by Gagné.)

*Representativeness.* Ordinarily, the individual or team is required to work in a range of situations and on a variety of problems. This range and variety should be approximated in the training.

*Statement and Incorporation of Requirements.* This is closely related to the principles of simulation and representativeness. All the criteria that have to be met for adequate performance should be made explicit and incorporated into the training situation. For example, very often it is desired that the trained individual should be able to transfer his skills over to other types of equipment and to related problem situations. If that is the case, then the training should prepare him for this requirement.

*Principles of Learning.* There are a number of generalizations supported by experimental studies of learning which may apply to a given training situation. The principle of immediacy of feedback mentioned above is one of these, but has been separated as perhaps the most important and the one with the fewest exceptions. There are a number of others whose relevance to training situations should be considered. They concern variables such as the distribution or massing of practice tasks, and the use of previously learned behavior sequences, i.e., meaningfulness.

Even when these principles can be applied to team training, their application is not obvious or simple. Their application is, in a sense, an engineering job, requiring a considerable knowledge of just how the team functions. Just as the engineer takes the principles of physics and applies them to a set of materials, so does the training expert take these principles, translate them, and fit them to a collection of interacting individuals.

In order to see what these translation problems are, as well as for the main purpose of clarifying the experimental problems in team training, a long-term program of research on team training will be described.

The research, carried out under the sponsorship of the Office of Naval Research, addressed itself to four questions:

What does a team look like when it is functioning and how can it be described or measured?

What are the specific training problems of the team?

What information in the experimental and social psychological work on group structure and efficiency is relevant to the questions above?

What is the most useful way to picture the critical aspects of the team's activity and to reduce these aspects to laboratory proportions?

In order to answer these questions, the following steps were carried out:[1] (*a*) Several types of Navy teams were studied in the field and their activities were recorded in detail. (*b*) Various techniques for summarizing the interactions of these teams were adapted or were developed and the summaries obtained by applying these techniques were examined for systematic characteristics. (*c*) A survey was made of training procedures used with these teams. (*d*) A large-scale collection of data was made, covering the errors made by these teams during the course of training. These data were analyzed to determine the causes of inefficiency in team performance and training. (*e*) Training aids and performance measures for teams were constructed on the basis of the error data.

At the same time that teams and their training were being examined, an extensive survey was made of the literature, to discover relevant analytic and experimental work. Two areas were examined in detail—work on the measurement of group structure stemming from sociometry, and work, stemming from group network studies, on the effects of structure in small group performance.

## THE DESCRIPTION OF TEAMS

*Procedure*

The first question was—what does a team look like? In order to answer this question, detailed observations were made on a variety of Navy teams (Glaser, Glanzer, & Morten, 1955). The attempt was made to record as much of the activity of the team as possible, and then to reduce the data to a set of meaningful descriptive statistics. For this purpose, extensive observations were made on four types of Navy teams: (*a*) A gunnery team (more precisely, the anti-aircraft gunnery team)

[1]The work outlined here was done in collaboration with Robert Glaser at the American Institute for Research under Contract Nonr 2551 (00).

which is concerned with acquiring, tracking and firing at air targets. The entire team, manning stations in the gun director, target plotting room, ammunition handling rooms and gun mounts, consists of approximately 35 men.[2] For purposes of analysis, a single functioning unit was taken, consisting of all the gunnery personnel involved in the firing of a single gun. (*b*) A combat information center team which is concerned with identifying, tracking and recommending action with respect to both air and surface targets. In the case of air targets, it controls intercepting aircraft. The team has approximately 15 men. (*c*)

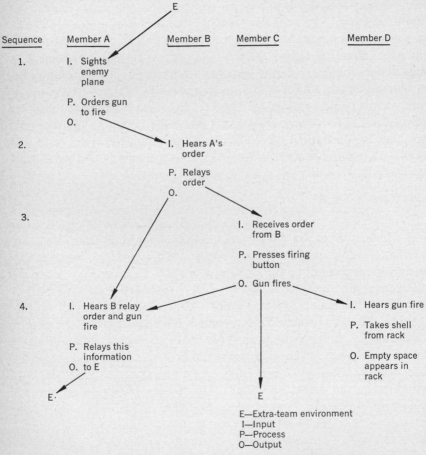

FIGURE 13.1.   Section of Flow Diagram Describing Team Activity

---

[2]The team size varies, depending on the size of the ship and the specific problem.

A ship control team which directs the movements of the ship. It usually includes the captain of the ship and consists of approximately 15 men. (*d*) A flight deck team which controls the launching and landing of aircraft on a carrier. It consists of approximately 25 men.

The data were based on direct observation of the teams during the course of fleet exercises and later were checked by detailed interviews with the team members. A detailed job analysis was made of the team's functioning. This analysis included a description of each act carried out by the team and the exact sequence of the acts. Every act of the team members was broken down into three elements: *input*, the signals or stimuli that elicit the behavior; *process*, the response; and *output*, the signals or stimuli resulting from the process. Thus, if a member of a combat information center (CIC) team saw a target, determined its range and bearing and shouted out the results of his computations, the act was described as follows: *input*: scope observation; *process*: determines range and bearing; *output*: shouts range and bearing. This act can then be linked to the next act performed by the team, since the output of one member usually became the input of another member. It was possible, therefore, to set up a flow diagram for the team. An example of part of such a flow diagram may be seen in Figure 13.1.

## Some New Problems

This descriptive work was guided by a number of preconceptions derived primarily from the sociological and social psychological literature. Many of these ideas were, as will be pointed out below, incorrect. A number of unexpected problems were, moreover, discovered.

*Unclarity of Team Boundaries.* Little difficulty was expected in determining the team's boundaries, i.e., who belonged and who did not belong to the unit. For the teams studied, however, the demarcation of boundaries was never clear. In the case of certain teams, such as an airplane crew, the equipment and the task fairly well isolate the team. In other cases this is not so or is only superficially so. For example, in a football team, the coach would not ordinarily be considered an integral member of the team. A moment's consideration, however, will show that by any criteria of participation or interaction, he has a central role in the team's activity. There were many such borderline members in the Navy teams that were studied. There was also the problem of individuals functioning in two teams. Fairly distinct teams, e.g., CIC and gunnery, turned out to overlap, with members in common. Each team not only had unclear outside boundaries, but could also be considered to consist of a number of distinct subsidiary teams. For example, the gunnery team consisted of a gun mount team, a director team, a plotting room team, two handling room teams, etc.

In general, then, in the actual functioning situation, a team is an arbitrary unit that must be analyzed out of a complex organization. It is not a simple given unit. This point has relevance for training, because quite often the unit taken for training is a small part of the entire team. The unit is often chosen for administrative convenience and not for its appropriateness with respect to the criterion situation. This procedure, which violates the principles of simulation and representativeness, may leave a major part of the necessary training incomplete.

*Instability of Team Structure and Composition.* Another characteristic that went against preconceptions concerning teams was the marked change in composition and structure that some teams underwent with a change in the problems they faced. For example, the type of activity that characterized a CIC team during a surface plot problem was so different from its activity during an air plot problem that for purposes of analysis it could be treated as two different teams.

## Team Statistics

After the data had been assembled, various types of measures were imposed to simplify the data. There were some indications from the psychological literature as to how this might be done. Attempts were made along a number of different lines, all of them, however, aimed at summarizing the network of interactions or communications that took place between team members.

*Interaction.* Collapsing the flow diagram into a matrix of interactions or a sociogram is one possible simplification of the data. For example, the four acts in Figure 13.1 can be summarized by the matrix in Table 13.1. The activity of the team during the entire course of a problem may be summarized in similar fashion. Once the entire activity of the team is thus summarized, a number of mathematical or geometric manipulations can be carried out in order to determine the centrality of a position or the degree of hierarchical arrangement of the group. When these are done, however, the picture developed of the team is quite misleading. Collapsing the flow diagram into an interaction matrix requires the assumption that the probability of an interaction is stationary with respect to time. This is never true of the structured teams like the CIC and gunnery teams above. In these teams a member responds to another member only at a given point in the sequence of team actions. The se-

quence is almost completely fixed. The only major element of a probabilistic character in efficient team functioning is the entry of stimuli
from the environment. Thus, to say that nine out of ten responses made
by member X were to member Y tells only part of the story. The full
story is an almost completely deterministic one, not a probabilistic one.
X makes the nine responses only at certain points in the sequence of
team activities.

Table 13.1

Matrix Summarizing Interactions in Figure 13.1

RECEIVER

|  |  | A | B | C | D | E |
|---|---|---|---|---|---|---|
|  | A | – | 1 | 0 | 0 | 1 |
|  | B | 1 | – | 1 | 0 | 0 |
| SENDER | C | 1 | 0 | – | 1 | 1 |
|  | D | 0 | 0 | 0 | – | 0 |
|  | E | 1 | 0 | 0 | 0 | – |

Moreover, the fact that an individual has a high probability of interaction or a high rate of interaction with other members did not mean
that he was important, nor did a low rate mean that he was unimportant. There were supervisors who were difficult to incorporate into the
team's action pattern because they only responded when an error was
made. By simple computing of interaction rate, they were indistinguishable from the least important supernumerary in the team.

*Centralization.* A great deal of centralization in the team's communications was expected. The expectation was based upon work in the
psychological literature, for example, the Bavelas-Leavitt network
studies (Bavelas, 1948; Bavelas, 1950; Leavitt, 1951). It was soon found
that the Navy teams, although obviously highly centralized, with a
very clear rank and responsibility assigned to each team member, were
not centralized in the communication or interaction sense. That is, the
team's leader and key supervisor very frequently made no overt re-

sponses and had few communications addressed to him during the course of the team's activity. This led to a distinction between two types of centralization, (*a*) centralization of power or responsibility, and (*b*) centralization of communication. These two types of centralization do not necessarily go with each other. This point was picked up in the later network studies (Trow, 1957). There are often key members of a team who remain passive observers until a major departure from correct procedure occurs. At that time, they intervene in the team's activity. An interesting question is this: Why is it that communication and power centralization so often correspond? It seems that these two types of centralization correspond when all parts of the team cannot be easily observed by the supervisor. Thus, in teams in which the supervisor cannot see some of the team members because of the arrangement of personnel or equipment, there is a greater tendency to centralize communications on the major supervisor.

Psychologists, nowadays, usually recommend decentralized or "democratic," as opposed to "autocratic," supervision in small groups. This recommendation always concerns the form of the communications in the group. It may be helpful with small groups, but only when the group is an "open," i.e., visible, system that does not require special communications in order to inform the leader or supervisor concerning individual performance. Centralization of communication in such a system may be inefficient because it detracts from the basic supervisory function.

*Overloading.* A number of interesting findings came out of the various attempts at purely descriptive work with the Navy teams. Cases were sought in which there would be problems of overloading of the communication channels, or heavy requirements with respect to coordination. Neither of these difficulties seemed to be prominent. In the vast majority of cases (70-80%), an individual had only a single communication to attend to at one time. Fewer than 10% of the communications involved more than two simultaneous messages, and in most cases these were not independent messages, but were redundant.

*Coordination.* With respect to coordination requirements, it was found, contrary to expectation, that even in busy teams there were only two team members, on the average, working at the same time. Even these were frequently carrying out independent or unrelated actions, so that there was no great need to coordinate their activity, in the sense of making sure that two or more specific actions were completed at a given time. (This type of requirement occurs for teams like football teams, in which several members have to move to specified positions at a given time.) This type of coordination might be called simultaneous co-ordination. The teams, of course, did show what might be called successive coordination, that is, close matching and timing of successive responses.

*Extra-Team Input.* Another finding of interest concerns the role of extra-team input. It was expected that a good part of the team's activity would be a function of stimuli from outside, i.e., either from the general environment or other teams carrying out related work. This was not the case. Between 75% and 90% of the input that team members dealt with was generated by their own group.

In general, the teams examined (and they covered a fair proportion of the types of groups functioning in the Navy) consisted of people working more or less in tandem, with one team member's action followed by another's, usually in response to a signal given by the preceding team member. The chain of responses was highly determined, rather than stochastic in nature. Many of the difficulties expected, such as overloading and coordination problems, seemed less important than the proficiency of the individual.

In summary, the direct examination of the teams that appeared at first to be clear and stable units revealed rather protean entities that had hazy boundaries and that changed, sometimes markedly, in both form and function. The initial attempt to deal with them as simple units with simple, measurable characteristics did not seem profitable. It seemed more profitable to focus attention on the individuals and their responses within the team. This direction was further indicated by the fact that the structural, wholistic problems expected in the team seemed relatively minor.

*Implications for Training.* If team performance can be viewed almost entirely as a chain of individual performances, why is team training necessary? There are certainly reasons to minimize it as much as possible, since it presents two major difficulties in a training program:

1. It is wasteful of time. As can be seen from the fact that most of the teams consisted of individuals working one or two at a time in tandem, the major part of the team is doing little or nothing during the team exercise. Indeed, later interviews with instructors showed that a major problem was the maintenance of alertness and motivation just because of the prolonged waiting that the team members had to undergo during team exercises.

2. It is inefficient for the isolation of individual errors. The observer is faced with a chain of responses. Some of these are difficult to observe

because the team may be so arranged that some members are not visible from all stations. Although an error will eventually be spotted, it may have worked its way a considerable distance through the system before it is caught. This results in three problems: (*a*) it is not always possible to determine who initiated the error; (*b*) even when the originator of an error can be traced, there is considerable delay in giving feedback; (*c*) errors result in increase of wasted time.

Since the training of a team as a unit has these difficulties, why is an extended period of team training felt to be necessary? Why not take the time that is usually given to team training and devote it to further individual training? Theoretically, team training could be dispensed with, if certain requirements could be met. If the trainer were able to specify the inputs used by the subjects in making their responses, then each team member could be trained separately and then put together with other similarly-trained individuals to form a smoothly-running team. The provision that the inputs be specified is, however, a considerable one. The cues that are present in the team situation are not easy to isolate. In particular, two special types of cues, surely used by team members, are hard to reproduce: (*a*) Cues from special aspects of other team members' activities, e.g., sounds of other members. The formal cues, such as commands, obvious to the outside observer are not necessarily the ones that are most useful to the team member. (*b*) Cues from the entire chain of preceding actions. The team member may make use of a number of preparatory cues that are difficult to reproduce in individual situations.

In summary, it was found that the team is a complex organization of interlocking responses whose proficiency could, theoretically, be reduced to the proficiency of the individuals composing it. The success of such a reduction, however, would depend on much more information about teams than is currently available.

## The Specific Difficulties of Team Training

The second question listed in the introduction was—what are the team's training problems? The first step in answering this question was the overall examination of training procedures in the Navy (Glanzer & Glaser, 1955). To decide to reduce team proficiency to a matter of individual proficiency is certainly premature, simply on the basis of the observation of teams. This direction toward individual analysis was, however, encouraged by the data developed in the course of examining the training of these teams.

Some of the information about problems in team training will not be considered in detail here; it was essentially administrative and was not concerned with any basic principles of training. For example, in the course of examining training programs at military installations, a number of difficulties was found such as incomplete groups being sent for training, and inappropriate selection of personnel, e.g., individuals who lacked prerequisite training being entered in the schools. A more general problem relates to the breakdown of communication between the field and the training school. There were cases in which training was given for tasks not required aboard ship. Sometimes this was a result of an equipment lag that prevented the appropriate use of information from the field. The continued use of obsolete equipment at the training schools made it impossible to use appropriate training situations. These administrative problems will not be considered further, except that it should be noted that very often the team training program is hampered by such difficulties more than it is by an incorrect approach to the training. In many instances it was found that the training staff was fully aware of the most appropriate procedures, but could not use them because of administrative difficulties such as those mentioned above.

The relative *absence of satisfactory proficiency measures* for team performance was one point of interest raised by the overall examination of training procedures. Training programs, both individual and team, often are least satisfactory in the matter of proficiency measurement. Measures of the outcome of training are important for two reasons. They indicate the degree to which the trainee is proficient in the task and they indicate whether the training procedures are adequate. These reasons have been recognized in the very rapid growth of measurement techniques applied to the outcome of individual training. (See Chapter 11 by Frederiksen & Chapter 12 by Wilson.) One factor that makes it difficult to construct team proficiency measures is that testing a team requires a considerable period of time. For this reason, even when team proficiency measures are used, they are restricted to a few problems. This is essentially a restriction to tests that have a few items and entails low reliability. There is one technique frequently used to compensate for the one-item character of team tests. This is multiple scoring of individuals within the team. Since each team member usually carries out several acts, it is possible to derive a score or rating based on several acts for each individual. This is an important supportive technique in measuring the team's efficiency. Although this procedure can be misleading if it is taken alone, since it is possible to have the majority of the individual members of a team do well and yet have the team function poorly as a unit, its use directs attention again to the performance of the individual team members. Thus, on practical grounds, focussing on individual performance recommends itself again.

After the overall examination of training procedures was completed, the next major effort was to collect information on the *specific difficulties* facing teams during the course of training, with special attention to individual performance. In order to obtain such data, a phase of Navy training called "underway training" was given special study (Glanzer & Glaser, 1957). During this phase, the teams on a ship are given their final training prior to the ship's going on full-scale operational exercises. Groups of trained observers are assigned to the ship by the training command. The observers evaluate the performance of the various teams on a ship and make recommendations to the teams and to the ship's commander. The teams observed during this period may contain anything from a complete crew of veteran members to a majority of novices. The highly trained observers were given additional training in the use of a special set of recording forms that required the following information: (a) positions in the team, (b) errors committed, and (c) corrective action. The forms supplemented the forms ordinarily used by the observers in their work with the teams.

Data were collected over a five-month period on a total of 506 exercises involving teams from 72 different ships. The teams on which data were collected were CIC, ship control and gunnery. The errors were analyzed with respect to frequency of occurrence, team positions, and types of activity involved. Analysis was also made of the relationship between positions making errors and the positions in the teams correcting the errors and of the correspondence of corrective procedures with what the experienced observers considered to be the best procedure. The general results pertinent to the discussion in this chapter are the following: (a) Contrary to expectation, error rates were somewhat higher for the high-ranking team members than for lower ranks. This difference may be a function of the observers' focussing their attention on the higher ranking personnel. (b) Only a small proportion of the errors were corrected within the team. The majority went unnoticed or had to be corrected by the observer in order to keep the exercise going. (Table 13.2 illustrates the data obtained. The intersection of the vertical and horizontal portions indicates what team position made an error and what position corrected it.) (c) The responsibility for correction in most cases was not clear. Analysis of the correspondence between actual correction procedures and what the observer thought should have been done indicated this. In most cases, furthermore, the expert observer was not able to assign the responsibility for the monitoring and correction of a given error. The absence of definition of responsibility for correction could account for a major part of the lack of corrective action.

There were two main recommendations that followed from the analysis of the data: (*a*) Since the top-level team members contribute a large number of errors and also have difficulty in making necessary corrections, it is desirable at this stage of training to have additional participants to share the supervisory load of the top-level personnel. This participation should be maximal during the early stages of training and gradually decreased as the team's supervisors become more experienced in handling the situation. (*b*) Since it is often not clear who is responsible for correcting an error, it is necessary to examine these errors and specify the responsibility more precisely. The team members should, at the very least, be made aware of the fact that their efficiency

Table 13.2

Correction Structure for Ship Control

| Personnel Making Error | No one | Captain* | Executive Officer | Navigator, Asst. | Officer of the Deck | OOD, Asst. | Signal Officer | Comn. Officer | TOTAL |
|---|---|---|---|---|---|---|---|---|---|
| Chief Petty Officer | 1 | 1 | | | | | | | 2 |
| Helmsman | 2 | | | | | | | | 2 |
| Junior Officer of the Watch | 4 | | | | | | | | 4 |
| Lee Helmsman | 3 | | | 1 | | | | | 4 |
| Navigator | 12 | | | | | | | | 12 |
| Navigator, Assistant | 4 | | | | | | | | 4 |
| Officer of the Deck | 24 | 6 | 1 | | | | | | 31 |
| Officer of the Deck, Assistant | 2 | | | | | | | | 2 |
| Quartermaster of the Watch | 11 | | | | | | | | 11 |
| Signal Officer | 2 | 1 | 1 | | | | | | 4 |
| Status Board Keeper | 4 | | | | | | | | 4 |
| Communication Officer | 2 | | | | | | | | 2 |
| Talkers | 25 | 2 | | | | 2 | 1 | 1 | 2 | 33 |
| Total | 96 | 10 | 2 | 1 | 2 | 1 | 1 | 2 | 115 |

Personnel Correcting Error

*Captain or Officer in Tactical Command

with respect to the correction of errors is low and requires improvement. Correction efficiency has a key role in both the training and the functioning of a team. A team that cannot correct its own errors can, of course, not train itself. It is also difficult for outside experts, who are essentially additional supervisors, to train it. For each team member who is unable to monitor and correct errors, an additional outside training expert must be assigned to the team. One of the complaints that was frequently voiced by training personnel during the general survey of training procedures was that they were given teams that consisted entirely of novices (Glanzer & Glaser, 1955). They stressed the difficulties that they had with these teams, and requested that experienced supervisory personnel accompany each team sent for training. The full meaning of this request became apparent with the number of uncorrected errors later found in team training exercises (Glanzer & Glaser, 1957).

The answer to the question, "What are the difficulties found in team training?" was two-fold—errors by individual team members, rather than through any higher order coordination of personnel, and inefficiency in correcting these errors. Although more complex factors might play a role, they are much less prominent than these two. These considerations led to a somewhat different picture of the basic problems in team training from the one that was held at the outset. This new picture will be considered in detail after an examination of the contribution of some of the experimental work in team training.

## CONTRIBUTIONS OF THE LITERATURE

What information in experimental and social psychological work is relevant to the description of team functioning and the analysis of training problems? In order to discover possible contributions from the literature on group behavior, an extensive survey was carried out. The survey included the following areas:

*Studies and Discussions of the Dimensions of Groups.* Numerous attempts have been made to set forth a comprehensive set of variables or dimensions to describe groups. Many of these have been a part of studies directed at establishing particular relations between variables (Deutsch, 1949). Some of the attempts were primarily directed at establishing a basic set of dimensions either on the basis of factor analysis (Cattell, Saunders, & Stice, 1953) or on a priori grounds (Hemphill & Westie, 1950). The dimensions include a wide variety, from easily-measured factors such as size, stability, and interaction rate, to indirectly-measured factors such as flexibility, hedonic tone and homogeneity of emotional maturity. The dimensions of the first type were used in the initial work on the description of the Navy teams (Glaser, 1958; Glaser et al., 1955).

*Analyses of Group Structure by Means of Sociometry, Matrix Algebra, Graph Theory, and the Logic of Relations.*[3] The emphasis on the easily and objectively measurable characteristics of team behavior led to the concern with more precise analysis of group interaction and relations. The techniques available for such analysis have been surveyed and published in a separate report (Glanzer & Glaser, 1959). Although they are a fruitful source of hypotheses and suggestion concerning problems of organization of teams, they are not directly relevant to the problems found in training teams.

*Studies of the Relation of Attitudes, Perception, and Motivation to Group Performance.* This type of study has had great popularity in applied psychological work.[4] The implicit assumption in much of the work seems to be that if a relation between attitude, percept, or motivational measure, and performance can be established, then the attitude, percept or motivation causes the proficiency. It is further assumed that an independent operation, e.g., group discussions, will change the attitudes and therefore change the group's proficiency. In the case of task-oriented teams, it could, however, be argued that the direction of causality goes primarily in the opposite direction, that is, the group's proficiency determines its morale.

*Studies of the Use of Special Techniques for the Improvement of Group Performance.* There has been a great deal of work on the use of discussion techniques in changing attitudes (Hare, 1953; Lewin, 1958) and performance (Coch & French, 1948). There also has been work on discussion and presentation techniques in giving feedback concerning performance (Irwin, Milaukas, & Levy, 1956; Levy, 1954; Torrance, 1953; Chapter 14 by Carter). Here two traditions meet, with some advantage—the psychological tradition of studies of discussion techniques and the military tradition of de-briefing and the critique after an exercise. Although it is desirable that post-exercise discussions

[3](Clark, 1953; Katz, 1947), (Luce & Perry, 1949), (Harary & Norman, 1953) and (Copilowish, 1948).

[4]Chapman & Campbell, 1957; DeGaugh & Knoell, 1954; Fiedler, 1954; Fiedler, Hartmann, & Rudin, 1952; Goodacre, 1951; Goodacre, 1953; Greer, Galanter, & Nordlie, 1954; Havron, Lybrand, & Cohen, 1954; Katz & Hyman, 1947; Knoell, 1956.

concerning team performance be made as effective as possible, a question should be raised about putting too heavy a reliance on it as the main type of feedback to the team. As a feedback mechanism the post-exercise discussion or critique has a very undesirable characteristic, namely, a large time gap between the response and the feedback.

*Studies of the Relation of Individual Proficiency to Group Performance.* In the preceding sections of this chapter, it was mentioned that a high level of proficiency of a few team members could greatly accelerate the training of the team. The general question of how the skills and performance of the team members interact or combine has been studied in a variety of laboratory settings (Borgatta, Couch & Bales, 1954; Rohde, 1954). In the case of actual teams, it has been pointed out that certain positions, if filled by a high-proficiency member, can compensate for the errors of other team members, while other positions do not have this compensatory function (Voiers, 1956). This leads back to the area of team organization. The study of the effects of individual proficiency also leads over into the general area of cross-training and leadership (Halpin, 1954; Kahn & Katz, 1953; Spector & Suttell, 1956; Suttell & Spector, 1955; Wilson, High & Comrey, 1955).

*Studies of Communication Networks.* These are discussed briefly below and in a separate report (Glanzer & Glaser, 1961). Much of the work mentioned above is not immediately relevant to the study of team training. A reason for this is that the model group that motivates most of the work is that of the unstructured group (that is, the group without any clear pattern of assigned roles) carrying out a relatively unstructured task, e.g., group discussion, socializing, etc. Teams, however, have definite goals and the members have definite functions assigned to them. Even when actual teams are used, the variables are more often derived from work with unstructured groups than from the specific characteristics of the team. Nevertheless, the work referred to in the sections above was examined in detail and used as a basis for hypotheses and measures of group functioning.

*Some Specific Studies.* Several of the studies which have very direct relevance to the special problems of team functioning will be summarized here in some detail. These studies may be considered to develop from the group network studies initiated by Bavelas (1948; 1950) and Leavitt (1951). In the network studies, the experimenter determines the communication channels that are open between a group of subjects who have to solve a common problem requiring cooperative work. For example, the subjects may have to discover which card, out of the set of five each subject holds, is held by all subjects. The experimenter, by allowing only certain subjects to communicate with each other, is considered to manipulate the group structure, e.g., he may make it more or less centralized. Some of the networks used in these studies are presented in Figure 13.2. A line between two positions indicates an open channel.

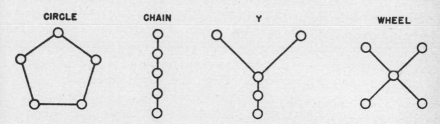

CIRCLE     CHAIN     Y     WHEEL

FIGURE 13.2.  Communication Networks Used in the Network Studies

Though at first it seemed that this approach opened up the entire area of group structure and functioning to direct experimental examination, it soon became apparent that this was not so. It also became apparent that the experimental situation was a highly artificial one, lacking some of the crucial characteristics of real life groups and, in particular, of teams. For example, in the group networks, the members know nothing about the activities of any individuals except the ones with whom they have immediate contact. There are very few groups or teams that have this characteristic. The network studies, moreover, tend to focus on the best way to organize the team, rather than the best way to train it.

In recognition of the limited generality of these original network situations, two other groups of investigators, who had the model of actual teams before them, redefined the problem of the effects of group structure on performance. Their redefinitions tended to make their experimental work more closely relevant to the problems found in military teams. Their starting point was the Air Force team.

Lanzetta and Roby[5] redefined group structure to refer to specialization and interrelation of jobs in a team. In doing this, they kept close to the

[5]Lanzetta and Roby, 1956a; Lanzetta & Roby, 1956b; Lanzetta & Roby, 1957; Roby, 1957; Roby & Lanzetta, 1956a; Roby & Lanzetta, 1956b; Roby & Lanzetta, 1957; Roby & Lanzetta, 1958.

problem of how the team might best be organized. They carried out a series of studies in which teams modelled after bomber crews solve simple problems based on the tasks involved in flying an airplane. They vary the amount of dependence of the team members upon each other for information. Their basic interest is the same as that of Bavelas—how does the work organization, particularly as determined by communication channels, affect the efficiency of the group? They have introduced, however, a more sophisticated use of group structure. In their groups, each man can communicate with every other team member. He can, however, get the particular type of information he needs at a particular moment only from certain team members. This makes the functioning of these experimental teams correspond more closely to actual teams. In their work, Lanzetta and Roby recognize the fact that the chain of responses made by team members is deterministic, not probabilistic. Moreover, the communication restrictions arise out of the task as they do in the real groups, not out of an arbitrary blocking of the channels.

In the experimental situation used by these investigators, three subjects were seated in booths with an intercom system. Each booth contained a set of switches which the subject had to manipulate on the basis of information input he received, and a set of operating instructions. The experimenter could arrange the problems so that the input a subject needed to carry out his task went directly to his own booth, or so that the relevant input went to another booth. In the latter case, the subject had to request the information from the other

Table 13.3

Input-Output Relations in the Task Used by Lanzetta and Roby

| Control | Relevant Information Input | | | | | |
| --- | --- | --- | --- | --- | --- | --- |
| | Compass heading | Air temperature | Generator voltage | Fuel pressure | Air speed | Rate of climb |
| Power setting | X | X | | | | |
| Steering mechanism | X | | | X | | |
| Landing gear | | | X | X | | |
| Control switch | | | X | | | X |
| Selector knob | | | | | X | X |
| Reset lever | | X | | | X | |

Note: An "X" in a given row and column indicates that the instrument reading at the column heading is relevant to a decision for the controls in the row.

booth. The problem was completed when all of the subjects had made the appropriate switch settings. For example, there may be two switches in each booth, and, in order to move them appropriately, two items of information are necessary. Thus, the power setting switch and the steering mechanism switch may be in one booth. In order to work the power setting switch, the subject in that booth may need compass heading and air temperature readings. These readings may be presented directly on the control panel in the booth, or one or both of them may be presented to another booth. If the information is presented to another booth, then the subject has to obtain it from that booth before he can set his switch. A matrix describing a typical relation between input reading and output is given in Table 13.3.

Using this experimental arrangement, Lanzetta and Roby carried out a series of experiments in which the following variables were manipulated and their effect on team efficiency evaluated: (*a*) dependence on others for information—the amount of information that subjects have to get from other booths; (*b*) dispersion of information—the number of different booths that the subject has to talk with to obtain his outside information; (*c*) task load—the rate of presentation of the input material; (*d*) load balancing—the distribution of the number of instrument displays and control switches for which the subjects were responsible. These variables were, in general, effective in determining the efficiency of the groups.

Although the work of Lanzetta and Roby is ingenious, and contributes much to the understanding of the effects of team structure, it lacks two important things. One of these is a theoretical system for their findings. Because of this lack, most of their experimental work is concerned with common sense hypotheses. There is little surprising in the fact that a man who has to check with several people before he can make a response is slower than a man who has to check with only one. Another lack, from the particular point of view of this paper, is that in focussing primarily on the structural problem, they neglect the problems of training. The indications from the Navy teams studied are that it is the training that holds the major difficulties. The results of the Lanzetta-Roby studies touch on the training problem only tangentially.

The training problem is attacked more directly in a program of research carried out by Rosenberg and Hall (Hall, 1957; Rosenberg, 1959; Rosenberg, 1960a; Rosenberg, 1960b; Rosenberg & Hall, 1958). These investigators also start out with both a concern for structure and a concern for actual groups. They, too, start with the air crew as their model. However, they define structure in a completely different way from Bavelas, or Lanzetta and Roby. Furthermore, in attempting to set up experimental situations appropriate to their definition, they move far away from the type of group that appears in the studies of other investigators.

Rosenberg and Hall point to the composition of information feedback to the individual as the key characteristic of structure. They define structure, therefore, in terms of information feedback and study the effect, upon performance, of feedback situations in which the individual receives information only about his own preceding response, only about someone else's response, or about some mixture of information from his own and others' responses. The contribution of this type of study to the understanding of team functioning is obvious. When the team works, it produces a complex of responses. It is not very easy for either the outside observer or the team members themselves to see just who did what. Under such conditions, confounded feedback necessarily occurs. Confounding of feedback is aggravated when the team gets feedback primarily on its overall efficiency. Then the individual receives confounded feedback with respect to his own response, which may have been good, bad or indifferent.

Two feedback schemes used by Rosenberg and Hall are outlined in Figure 13.3. $S^d$ is the cue for the response, $R$ is the response and $S^f$

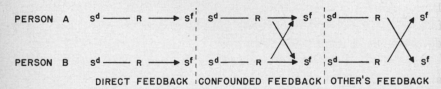

FIGURE 13.3. Feedback Paradigms Used by Rosenberg and Hall

is the feedback. In direct feedback, the individual receives information only on his own response. In confounded feedback, the individual's feedback is a function of his own and someone else's response. With this basic paradigm, Rosenberg and Hall ran a series of experiments in which the composition of feedback was varied. One of the tasks they used required that a knob be turned a certain distance, e.g., eight turns. The subjects received feedback as to whether the knob had been turned the correct amount. The subject and his partner were seated at separate desks, each with its own knob. In direct feedback, each subject in the pair had to turn the knob four turns in order for his feedback to read "correct." Rosenberg and Hall (Hall, 1957; Rosenberg & Hall, 1958) used a wide variety of feedback conditions and evaluated their effect on individual and team accuracy and the development of special roles. As might be expected, confounded feedback resulted in the development of complementary behavior (one subject became a "six-turner," the other, a "two-turner"). The complementary behavior was effective enough to keep the team accuracy equal to that under the direct feedback condition.

The specific results of the Rosenberg and Hall studies are of less interest than the general approach. For the first time, a central part of the team training process is examined experimentally. The examination is based on the assumption that team performance can be reduced to a sum of individual performances, with some special factors introduced by the team environment. This assumption receives support from the examination of actual teams, described earlier (Glanzer & Glaser, 1957; Glanzer, Glaser, & Klaus, 1956). There it was pointed out that the training problem consisted wholly of individual errors and the getting of feedback to the individuals. The approach of Rosenberg and Hall is also of special interest because it moves the team training problem into the area of learning theory. Some of the power that can be generated by this move has been indicated in some recent work by Burke and his associates.[6] Klaus and Glaser (1961) are also carrying forward a program of research on the role of learning variables in the development of team performance.

In summary, much of the previous work on groups has been directed at the problems of motivation and organization. Some of the more recent work, however, has directed attention to the mechanics of training the individual within the team setting. In both the work on training and in the work on team organization, there has been a growing appreciation of the special characteristics of the actual team as opposed to the laboratory discussion group. Two series of investigations that grew directly out of work with actual teams have been summarized briefly here and their implications considered.

---

[6]This work was reported by Cletus Burke and his associates in a paper titled *Applications of a Linear Model to Two-Person Interactions,* given at the Midwestern Psychological Association meetings, 1959.

## BASIC EXPERIMENTAL PROBLEMS

What is the most useful way to picture the critical aspects of the team's activity and to reduce these aspects to laboratory proportions? There are two aspects of team behavior that have received attention. One is its organization—the other, its training. For various reasons, organization has received considerably more experimental attention than training. One reason is that organization seems to furnish neater experimental problems, e.g., which is more effective, centralized or decentralized structure? Examination of teams in training results, however, in the following findings: (*a*) The individual error is the major source of difficulty. Wholistic, emergent phenomena, e.g., disorganization, can always be traced to a few discrete responses made by individual members. The cure for this difficulty is not necessarily more individual training, since the team environment presents special problems of transfer for even the well-trained individual. (*b*) Slowness of feedback to individuals concerning their response is a prime obstacle to efficient team training.

From these findings arise two problems in training which have been relatively neglected in experimental work with teams: (*a*) the problem of monitoring or supervision—how to make sure that responses are evaluated as to their adequacy; and (*b*) the problem of feedback or reinforcement—the effect of various techniques for informing the team member about his responses.

The problem of monitoring is integrally related to the feedback problem. There has been no work done on it. This is particularly surprising, because the monitoring problem contains questions that have great practical significance, interesting general or theoretical implications, and simple experimental form. The low level of correction efficiency noted in Navy teams undergoing training indicates the practical significance of the problem of monitoring and supervision. The effectiveness of reinforcement, or feedback, depends on the adequacy of these functions.

The second problem concerns the special characteristics of feedback introduced in the team setting, such as confounding and delay. There has been some experimental work in this area (Rosenberg & Hall, 1958). The relation of this work to the more popular investigation of the effects of organization or structure is obvious, since the work grew out of a tradition of experimental work on team structure. Indeed, the structure of the team often determines the type of feedback that members receive.

Understanding of the problem of monitoring is central to the proper use of, and assignment of, work to supervisors. It is important first to consider the essential nature of the job of a monitor or supervisor. He observes a sequence of the actions by the team members and checks departures from correct procedure. This is essentially the vigilance task that has received extensive study recently. The characteristics that make a vigilance task difficult also made supervisory performance inefficient, for example, unpredictability of the stimuli in the sequence. The team's behavior, from this viewpoint, is an informational display, sequential in nature, that requires the supervisor to respond to given signals (errors).

The type of experimental work that follows from this viewpoint is clear. Here are some of the experimental questions that now become relevant: (*a*) How much information can an individual monitor on a single channel? This is the translation of the question—How well can a single supervisor monitor a single worker? (*b*) What effects are introduced by the requirement that an individual monitor several independent channels? This is the question of how many men one supervisor can monitor, i.e., the extent of supervisory span. (*c*) What effects are introduced by introducing dependency between the monitored channels? These questions can be answered in simple vigilance experiments in which the inputs are completely controlled by the experimenter. In this way, decisions concerning the function of the supervisor that are ordinarily made on an arbitrary basis can be put on a rational and experimental basis. It then would be possible to measure the uncertainty in a team's performance and compute the amount of information it transmits per second, in order to decide whether the supervisor has too much, or too little, to do.

The concern with errors and feedback leads to a different type of analysis of the structure of the team than that used by previous investigators. There are of course other aspects of the supervisor's job that are not touched by this analysis. The supervisor has, for example, some degree of control over the structure of the information that reaches him. He has some degree of control over the task and its arrangement. A crucial aspect of the supervisor's job may be his efficiency in structuring or restructuring the team so that the informational load placed on him is optimal. This type of analysis is directed at those aspects of structure that cause reduction in errors and facilitate feedback from responses.

The simplest way to set up a team is in series, i.e., a response by member A is followed by a response by B; B's response is followed by C's, etc. The reliability of the team is then a product of the reliability of the individual members. For example, if there are ten men working in series in the team, each of whom is accurate or reliable .95 of the time, the probability of a correct response completed by the team is $.95^{10}$ or approximately .599. One way to combat unreliability is to organize the team in parallel. In the simplest case, each step is carried out by two men and the team's activity continues only if both men agree in their response, i.e., responses by $A_1$ and $A_2$ are followed by responses by $B_1$ and $B_2$, etc. By this system of checking, if each member has .95 accuracy, then the accuracy of a pair of men carrying out the same response is raised to .9975 and the accuracy of the entire team, consisting of ten pairs of members, is $.9975^{10}$ or .975. Complete duplication of the team, such as that considered above, would not, of course, be carried out, because it is costly in personnel. Duplication, however, is used to some degree in all teams. It is done in the following ways: (a) Duplication at critical positions. Positions that have high probability of errors are set up in parallel. An example of this is the duplication of scope watchers in CIC teams. (b) Assignment of supervisors. The supervisor may be considered to be a substitute for a parallel team. His job is to check on a number of individual responses and to make sure that each is correct before it continues on in the system. The supervisor, however, may not have very high reliability at any point, since he ordinarily has to distribute his attention over several responses. Thus, his effective reliability may be only that of .50 at any given point in the response chain. (c) The assignment of cross-checking functions to team members. Instead of assigning specialized supervisors, in many highly-trained teams, the team members have to carry out supervisory or monitoring functions for others' responses, in addition to carrying out their own immediate responses.

All of these points are closely related to the view of the supervisor as carrying out an information processing or vigilance task. For example, the monitoring of co-workers becomes again the multichannel problem. The individual has to monitor the inputs relevant to his own job and that of the responses of his co-workers. The experimental implications of this view have been indicated above.

There are, however, further implications of the analysis of team structure with respect to feedback. The team in which all members are at a low level of proficiency is one that overloads the specialized supervisor and also one that cannot have co-worker cross-checking. The error rate in this team would be high, its feedback on responses would be inefficient and its learning rate would be expected to be low. On the other hand, the training of one untrained individual who is surrounded by trained team members should be relatively fast, since he can have the advantages of immediate, unconfounded feedback at all times during training. A variant of the untrained-man-surrounded-by-trained-men procedure is the apprentice system frequently used in Navy teams. These considerations lead to the following experimental questions: (*a*) What are the effects of partial reinforcement (stemming from incomplete monitoring) on the learning and long-term performance of team members? (*b*) What is the distribution of functions (i.e., individual responses and co-worker monitoring) that optimizes the learning rate for a team?

In the preceding sections, this chapter has outlined work done in the past with teams and has presented a prospectus of future, needed work. (Some of these implications and others are considered by Klaus and Glaser [1960] in a discussion of a program of research on team training.) The prospectus was based on detailed examination of actual teams. On the basis of this examination, the importance of the following was underlined: (*a*) the information processing and feedback aspects of team behavior, and (*b*) the supervisory and monitoring functions in the team. These factors were emphasized both because they have a crucial role in the performance and training of teams and because they are amenable to precise experimental operations.

## REFERENCES

Bavelas, A. A mathematical model for group structures. *Appl. Anthrop.*, 1948, 7, 16-30.

Bavelas, A. Communication patterns in task oriented groups. *J. acoust. Soc. Amer.*, 1950, 22, 725-730.

Borgatta, E. F., Couch, A. S., & Bales, R. F. Some findings relevant to the great man theory of leadership. *Amer. sociol. Rev.*, 1954, 19, 755-759.

Cattell, R. B., Saunders, D. R., & Stice, G. F. The dimensions of syntality in small groups. *Hum. Relat.*, 1953, 6, 331-356.

Chapman, L. J. & Campbell, D. T. An attempt to predict the performance of three-man teams from attitude measures. *J. soc. Psychol.*, 1957, *46*, 277-286.

Clark, R. A. Analyzing the group structure of combat rifle squads. *Amer. Psychol.*, 1953, *8*, 333.

Coch, L. & French, J. R. P. Overcoming resistance to change. *Hum. Relat.*, 1948, *1*, 512-532.

Copilowish, I. M. Matrix development of the calculus of relations. *J. symbol. Logic*, 1948, *13*, 193-203.

DeGaugh, R. A. & Knoell, Dorothy M. *Attitudes relevant to bomber crew performance in combat.* Lackland AFB, Air Force Personnel and Training Research Center, 1954.

Deutsch, M. An experimental study of the effects of cooperation and competition upon group process. *Hum. Relat.*, 1949, *2*, 199-231.

Fiedler, F. E. Assumed similarity measures as predictors of team effectiveness. *J. abnorm. soc. Psychol.*, 1954, *49*, 381-388.

Fiedler, F. E., Hartmann, W., & Rudin, S. A. *The relationship of interpersonal perception to effectiveness in basketball teams.* University of Illinois, College of Education, Technical Report No. 3, 1952.

Glanzer, M. & Glaser, R. *A review of team training problems.* Pittsburgh: American Institute for Research, 1955. ONR Technical Report.

Glanzer, M. & Glaser, R. *Performance characteristics of three types of Navy team.* Pittsburgh: American Institute for Research, 1957. ONR Technical Report.

Glanzer, M. & Glaser, R. Techniques for the study of group structure and behavior: I. Analysis of structure. *Psychol. Bull.*, 1959, *56*, 317-332.

Glanzer, M. & Glaser, R. Techniques for the study of group structure and behavior: II. Empirical studies of the effects of structure in small groups. *Psychol. Bull.*, 1961, *58*, 1-27.

Glanzer, M., Glaser, R., & Klaus, D. J. *The team performance record: An aid for team analysis and team training.* Pittsburgh: American Institute for Research, 1956. ONR Technical Report.

Glaser, R. Descriptive variables for the study of task-oriented groups. In R. A. Patton (Ed.), *Current trends in the description and analysis of behavior.* Pittsburgh: University of Pittsburgh Press, 1958. Pp. 1-21.

Glaser, R., Glanzer, M., & Morten, A. W., Jr. *A study of some dimensions of team performance.* Pittsburgh: American Institute for Research, 1955. ONR Technical Report.

Goodacre, D. M. The use of a sociometric test as a predictor of combat unit effectiveness. *Sociometry*, 1951, *14*, 148-152.

Goodacre, D. M. Group characteristics of good and poor performing combat units. *Sociometry*, 1953, *16*, 168-178.

Greer, F. L., Galanter, E. H., & Nordlie, P. G. Interpersonal knowledge and individual and group effectiveness. *J. abnorm. soc. Psychol.*, 1954, *49*, 411-414.

Hall, R. L. Group performance under feedback that confounds responses of group members. *Sociometry*, 1957, *20*, 297-305.

Halpin, A. W. The leadership behavior and combat performance of airplane commanders. *J. abnorm. soc. Psychol.*, 1954, *49*, 19-22.

Harary, F. & Norman, R. Z. *Graph theory as a mathematical model in social science.* Ann Arbor: University of Michigan, 1953.

Hare, A. P. Small group discussions with participatory and supervisory leadership. *J. abnorm. soc. Psychol.*, 1953, *48*, 273-275.

Havron, M. D., Lybrand, W. A., & Cohen, E. *The assessment and prediction of rifle squad effectiveness.* Washington, D. C.: Personnel Research Branch, The Adjutant General's Office, 1954.

Hemphill, J. K., Rush, C. H., Bakan, D., & Perloff, Evelyn. *Studies in aircrew composition. I: Measurement of cross-training in B-29 aircrews.* HRRL Memo Report No. 23, 1952.

Hemphill, J. K. & Westie, C. M. The measurement of group dimensions. *J. Psychol.*, 1950, *29*, 325-342.

Irwin, I. A., Milaukas, E. W., & Levy, B. I. *A procedure for evaluating instructor technique during critiques of crew performance.* Randolph AFB, Crew Research Laboratory, Air Force Personnel and Training Research Center, Air Research and Development Command, 1956.

Kahn, R. L. & Katz, D. Leadership practices in relation to productivity and morale. In D. Cartwright & A. F. Zander (Eds.), *Group dynamics: Research and theory.* Evanston, Illinois: Row, Peterson, 1953.

Katz, D. & Hyman, H. Industrial morale and public opinion methods. *Int. J. opin. attit. Res.*, 1947, *1*, 13-30.

Katz, L. On the matric analysis of sociometric data. *Sociometry*, 1947, *10*, 233-241.

Klaus, D. J. & Glaser, R. *Increasing team proficiency through training.* Pittsburgh: American Institute for Research, 1960. ONR Technical Report.

Knoell, Dorothy M. *Relationship between attitudes of bomber crews in training and their attitudes and performance in combat.* Lackland AFB, Air Force Personnel and Training Research Center, 1956.

Lanzetta, J. T. & Roby, T. B. Effects of work-group structure and certain task variables on group performance. *J. abnorm. soc. Psychol.*, 1956, *53*, 307-314. (a)

Lanzetta, J. T. & Roby, T. B. Group performance as a function of work distribution patterns and task load. *Sociometry*, 1956, *19*, 95-104. (b)

Lanzetta, J. T. & Roby, T. B. Group learning and communication as a function of task and structure "demands." *J. abnorm. soc. Psychol.*, 1957, *55*, 121-131.

Leavitt, H. J. Some effects of certain communication patterns on group performance. *J. abnorm. soc. Psychol.*, 1951, *46*, 38-50.

Levy, B. I. *A preliminary study of informal crew conferences as a crew training adjunct.* Lackland AFB, Air Force Personnel and Training Research Center, 1954.

Lewin, K. Group decision and social change. In Maccoby, Newcomb & Hartley (Eds.), *Readings in social psychology.* (3rd ed.) New York: Holt, 1958. Pp. 197-211.

Luce, R. D. & Perry, A. D. A method of matrix analysis of group structure. *Psychometrika*, 1949, *14*, 95-116.

Roby, T. B. On the measurement and description of groups. *Behavioral Sci.*, 1957, *2*, 119-127.

Roby, T. B. & Lanzetta, J. T. *An investigation of task performance as a function of certain aspects of work-group structure.* Lackland AFB, Air Force Personnel Training Research Center, June 1956. Research Report TN-56-74. (a)

Roby, T. B. & Lanzetta, J. T. Work group structure, communication, and group performance. *Sociometry*, 1956, *19*, 105-113. (b)

Roby, T. B. & Lanzetta, J. T. Conflicting principles in man-machine system design. *J. appl. Psychol.*, 1957, *41*, 170-178.

Roby, T. B. & Lanzetta, J. T. Considerations in the analysis of group tasks. *Psychol. Bull.*, 1958, *55*, 88-101.

Rohde, K. J. An evaluation of the extent to which the task ability of the man in charge of a group is determinative of that group's success in performing the task. Paper read at Midwest. Psychol. Ass., New York, 1954.

Rosenberg, S. The maintenance of a learned response in controlled interpersonal conditions. *Sociometry*, 1959, *22*, 124-138.

Rosenberg, S. Cooperative behavior in dyads as a function of reinforcement parameters. *J. abnorm. soc. Psychol.*, 1960. (a)

Rosenberg, S. A laboratory approach to interpersonal aspects of team performance. *Ergonomics*, 1960. (b)

Rosenberg, S. & Hall, R. L. The effects of different social feedback conditions upon performance in dyadic teams. *J. abnorm. soc. Psychol.*, 1958, *57*, 271-277.

Spector, P. & Suttell, Barbara J. *Research on the specific leader behavior patterns most effective in influencing group performance.* Washington, D. C.: American Institute for Research, 1956.

Suttell, Barbara J. & Haefner, D. P. *Descriptions of 12 typical Navy teams aboard destroyer-type ships.* Washington, D. C.: American Institute for Research, 1955.

Suttell, Barbara J. & Spector, P. *Research on the specific leader behavior patterns most effective in influencing group performance.* Washington, D. C.: American Institute for Research, 1955.

Torrance, E. P. Methods of conducting critiques of group problem-solving performance. *J. appl. Psychol.*, 1953, *37*, 394-398.

Trow, D. B. Autonomy and job satisfaction in task-oriented groups. *J. abnorm. soc. Psychol.*, 1957, *54*, 204-209.

Voiers, W. D. *Bombing accuracy as a function of the ground school proficiency structure of the B-29 bomb team.* Lackland AFB, Air Force Personnel and Training Research Center, 1956.

Wilson, R. C., High, W. S., & Comrey, A. L. An iterative analysis of supervisory and group dimensions. *J. appl. Psychol.*, 1955, *39*, 85-91.

Chapter 14

# Exercising the Executive Decision-Making Function In Large Systems

*Launor F. Carter, System Development Corporation*

Psychologists, businessmen, and military strategists have written millions of words on problems of decision making but only very little on methods of training individuals for decision making. Usually discussions of decision making consider such problems as the relative superiority of individual or group decision processes, ethical considerations in decision making, problems of communication in transmitting decisions, etc. In a recent review by Wasserman and Silander (1959) an effort was made to develop a comprehensive bibliography on decision making; of the 431 titles abstracted only one contained the word "training." Similarly Lichtenberg and Deutsch (1954) have published a review of research on the staff process in decision making, and again no major reference is made to decision-making training.

One of the reasons it is so difficult to train the individual for decision making is because of the idiosyncratic nature of so many decision situations. It is of little help to counsel the executive to be objective, unemotional, broad, foresightful, and good, unless these fine qualities can be placed concretely in the context of the kinds of decisions the executive must make. Decisions are usually made within the environment or surround of some kind of a system situation. Consider the problem of making decisions within the system context. One must always ask how any decision will affect others, how the decision can be carried out, how it will be communicated, how it will affect production or distribution or sales, how it will affect competing organizations, etc. In other words most decisions are made within a context of many competing pressures whose influence is unclear and whose interactional components are not well understood. If this were not the case, there would really be no problem requiring *human* decision making. In their exciting work, Newell, Shaw and Simon (1958) consider the kinds of decision-making situations which correspond to decision-making problems in complex organizations if such situations could be reduced to clearly defined, deterministic, logically specified decision problems. As has been emphasized, for the executive most system-oriented decision situations are not of this nature.

The immense complexity of modern systems and the way in which fairly small changes can pose difficult decision problems as they interact with the remainder of a system has been nicely illustrated by Forrester (1958). Forrester postulated a production-distribution system making a single product and having a product distribution chain from factory to factory warehouse, to distributors, to retailers. By making certain reasonable assumptions regarding the lags in inventory replacement, ordering time, delivery time, etc., he was able to show that small changes of 10% in retail sales could, within four or five months, cause fluctuations in increased demand for factory production by as much as 40%. If, on the basis of this demand information, management decided to increase plant capacity, serious overcapacity could easily result, with associated losses.

Similar examples could be drawn from many fields, but they would all emphasize that decisions in one part of a system reverberate through the rest of the system—for better or worse, depending on the nature and timeliness of the decision. Many military situations are particularly subject to extremely complex decision-making and information-processing problems. Because of this, some of the most advanced decision-making exercising techniques have been developed in the military context. Of particular interest is the System Training Program developed for the USAF Air Defense Command. Originally this simulation training was developed for training individual crews at the lowest echelons in techniques of data processing and decision making. But as the program became established, it became apparent that the actions of individual crews were more effective when the higher command headquarters were involved. The introduction of the battle staff as an integral part of the rest of the system being trained became well accepted and has expanded to such an extent that military decision makers at the very highest level now practice their decision-making functions within a system training context. In the next section the details of a typical exercise are presented. Then there follows a discussion of business games. Finally, some more general consideration will be given to general problems of decision-making training.

## EXERCISING THE DECISION-MAKING PROCESS IN A LARGE SYSTEM: AN EXAMPLE

A specific example will be given of the way in which system exercising for decision making has been applied in a very large system. System training exercises can be run at many different levels of complexity; they can vary from single site-centered exercises involving only one crew, all the way to very large exercises, large both in the geographic sense and in the sense of involving very many people and many echelons of command. For several years the System Development Corporation and the Air Defense Command have been conducting exercises of complete defense forces. A force exercise involves all of the radar sites, divisions, and control centers within an air defense force. For instance, on the West Coast the participating sites and divisions stretch from the Canadian border to the Mexican border and go back into Arizona, Utah, and Montana. All of the defense net in this area is frequently exercised in the detection of aircraft coming in, the correlation of these aircraft with flight plans, and the passing of the resulting information up to the division control centers and to the force control center so that appropriate action can be taken at all the different levels where decisions need to be made.

Recently the System Development Corporation and North American Air Defense Command (NORAD) have been conducting a series of planned nation-wide exercises; actually these are more than nation-wide exercises since they involve all of the North American continent and the sea barriers, as well as the simulation of many other agencies. In principle, however, these exercises are no different than those that have been conducted at division or force level. The NORAD exercises are large and complex and basically are designed to exercise all those aspects of the aircraft control and warning net that have come into existence throughout the North American continent. The NORAD exercises and the many other exercises that have and will be run by the various forces, and by NORAD itself, are part of the routine, yet are vitally necessary training that must be engaged in by every large, complex military information-processing system. Military agencies must spend time and energy so that the actual flow of data, the presenting of information to the proper sources, and the making of decisions on the basis of this data can all be practiced—practiced so that if there were an actual emergency, the commanders, and of course the data processing system itself, would have been exercised and trained so that appropriate and proper action could be taken at the time it is needed.

An exercise conducted sometime ago shall be described here to give an example of the decision-making situations which can be presented through simulation techniques. This NORAD exercise, called "Desk Top," presented an extremely large effort which was accomplished only through the very intimate association of the many officers involved at NORAD and at many lower echelons of command. It involved the co-operation of these officers with the System Development Corporation, which is engaged in planning such exercises jointly with the military and in producing all of the necessary simulation materials to make such exercises possible.

The following list will indicate something of the extensiveness of the NORAD defense system and the units involved in Exercise "Desk Top":

1. NORAD Headquarters
2. NORAD Region Headquarters
3. NORAD Division Headquarters
4. U.S. Radar Stations
5. U.S. Army Air Defense Command Regions
6. U.S. Army Air Defense Command Defenses
7. Airborne Early Warning Aircraft on Both Coasts
8. Picket Vessels on Both Coasts
9. Canadian Air Defense Command Headquarters at St. Hubert
10. Four Canadian Air Divisions
11. Pinetree System of Canadian Radar Stations
12. Mid-Canada Line Radar Stations
13. DEW Line Stations
14. Alaskan Headquarters and Radar Stations
15. 64th Air Division Headquarters and Radar Stations
16. Barrier Forces
17. Other Agencies—Iceland, Office of Civil and Defense Mobilization, Federal Aviation Agency, American Telephone and Telegraph Units, Strategic Air Command

This is obviously a complex system which is subject to many factors which affect its efficiency. To illustrate the operation of this system, imagine the introduction of two enemy raids into the system. These aircraft now have to be detected, plotted, and identified. If they are identified as hostiles, a complex series of events occur which include the following system activities:

1. Fighters are scrambled or missiles assigned.

2. The tracks and other data are told to adjacent radar stations, to division headquarters, and to Army air defense units.

3. Divisions and regions forward tell this information to adjacent headquarters and to NORAD Headquarters where the information is displayed.

4. Various states of warning are established and disseminated throughout the command and also to Strategic Air Command Headquarters.

5. Weapons and personnel are brought up as fast as possible.

6. The combat staffs at each headquarters prepare to meet the attack which develops.

7. Other staff members are engaged in activities pertinent to their functions. These include such functions as:

   a) Communications and Electronics
   b) Intelligence
   c) Logistic Support
   d) Personnel
   e) Medical
   f) Public Information
   g) Disaster Control
   h) Liaison
   i) Weather

All become involved in integrated activities to support the combat facilities. Intelligence officers must gather and evaluate information concerning approaches, types of invaders, tactics, etc., so that these can be used by their units and other units to meet the attack most effectively. The communications officers must call in special communications circuits, the logistics officers may have to provide additional armament at an alternate landing base because the primary base may well be closed by bad weather, etc. It is easy to understand that there are many opportunities for the system to become inadequate in one or more areas and to this degree have its effectiveness reduced. To emphasize this point, suppose the effects of battle damage caused by bombing an area. The effects of this may call for decisions concerning the desirability of continuing to defend this area, the redeployment of weapons to other areas, medical care, prediction of fall-out effects, and civil defense actions. Staff officers at all levels become involved in coping with these effects, and because of communications damage, important decisions may be made without sufficient information. Concurrently, the Joint Chiefs of Staff are informed, and they, as well as the President, Congress, and other agencies take various actions.

The task then was to provide a simulated air picture and the other elements required to allow the system to function in the way which would be required under similar actual conditions. A further task was to establish methods of observing and recording the behavior which took place and to provide feedback so that system learning would occur.

As an additional requirement, the exercise had to be conducted in such a way that adequate real air defense was maintained while the exercise was in progress.

Something of the number and distribution of units involved has been presented. In the exercise described, General Partridge (the NORAD Commander) and his entire staff, as well as the commanders and their staffs at each headquarters, participated. The total number of officers and men operationally engaged in the exercise was at least 15,000.

In designing a training exercise for such a complex system, both the military and the civilians involved in the design and production of the exercise must have a very intimate understanding of several things: first, the civilians are responsible for the production of simulated materials, and these civilians must understand and be intimately familiar with the military system for which they are planning simulation materials. On the other hand, the military must clearly understand and know how to use the simulation material which has been prepared. To achieve this purpose, it is wise to involve military people along with the civilian experts in the design of each system training exercise. In the case of this particular exercise a NORAD military committee, headed by a brigadier general, was formed, and a corresponding committee was formed by the System Development Corporation, headed by one of their senior training specialists. These two committees worked very closely together for a period of about six months to develop the training plan and materials and to thoroughly brief and indoctrinate all of the people who were to employ the simulation concepts and materials for the exercise.

One of the tasks facing the two committees was to verbalize the concepts of the exercise and then to provide guidelines for translating these concepts into action. It was agreed that the unique features of the System Training Program would be combined with additional techniques to provide an exercise which would have the following characteristics:

1. It would reflect the then current estimates of attack patterns.
2. It would incorporate, to the maximum degree possible, realistic features which would be expected in the event of actual attack such as battle damage, electronic countermeasures, weapons status and performance, interaction with higher and adjacent organizations, SAC flights, etc.
3. The intent of the exercise would be to provide a realistic training experience at all echelons.
4. Another major purpose would be to examine and evaluate, under closely controlled circumstances, the performance and effectiveness of major

system activities such as: communications, tactics, staff decisions, applicability of regulations, interactions among the system components, dissemination of alerts, etc.

5. The emphasis was to be upon staff activities at all levels, and the exercise would include simultaneous participation of all units being exercised.

To translate these concepts into action, a variety of methods was employed. A brief description of the methods used by the major units will give an understanding of the simulation techniques. The U. S. radar stations and the SAGE facilities had actual synthetic radar presentations on their scopes, and these displays were provided either by means of films or magnetic tapes. The airborne warning aircraft, picket vessels, and other units obtained radar surveillance information either from maps, scripts, or both. Army Air Defense Command radar information was also provided by means of scripts produced from maps. Given the radar scope data, all units then processed this as if it were actual radar information. The aircraft control and warning squadrons plotted, identified, took tactical action, and forward and lateral told information as if it were an actual air situation. The airborne warning aircraft and picket vessels used the normal air-to-ground or ship-to-shore communications. In all possible respects information was processed through normal channels as though it were real.

It would be well to emphasize a distinction which is implied by the previous paragraph but may not be sufficiently clear. This distinction is that at many locations the personnel involved had simulated material supplied to them which was of such a nature that for all intents and purposes they were playing the war as though it were real. That is to say, there were actual scope presentations which looked like aircraft coming in, there were flight plans, there were intelligence inputs, etc. On the other hand, there were agencies at some locations which did not have material which closely simulated the actual physical inputs that they would have in a real emergency situation; rather, they had material which allowed them to simulate the behavior which that particular agency would probably take in the case of an emergency.

For example, the DEW Line, the Alaska stations, etc., passed data forward through transmission lines in a fashion that was very similar to what it would be in a case of emergency. The Air Defense Command's aircraft control and warning squadrons, the radar sites, had actual film in their problem reproducers and blips on the scopes—blips would appear and move, there would be flight plans or there would not be such flight information in the case of invaders, there would be electronic countermeasures presentation on the scopes. The radar sites would have to handle all of this information as they normally would, and as the squadron processed the information, they would have to tell it to higher echelons and to various other defense installations that needed to receive the information. Thus, the normal planned communication and data transmission systems were exercised.

On the other hand, there were agencies that were not involved in the exercise themselves, but rather someone in a "backroom" at one of the exercising command headquarters who simulated the behavior of the particular unit involved. For example, the Joint Chiefs of Staff were not actually involved in this particular exercise; yet if there were a real emergency, the NORAD Headquarters would have to contact the Joint Chiefs for relaying information to them and receiving instructions from them. Since the Joint Chiefs were not actually in the exercise, it was necessary to have someone simulating the action and transmitting the information which the Joint Chiefs might be expected to take in the case of the real thing. In the particular exercise being described, the Joint Chiefs of Staff were played by an Air Force major general. Due to his long experience and previous assignment at high headquarters, it was felt he could do a reasonably good simulation job. The actions he would take depend to some extent on the way in which the situation developed and the amount of information which was passed to him from the NORAD Headquarters. On the other hand he also had various scripts prepared for him so that he knew what should be happening, and thus if he felt that a particular decision needed to be made, he could make intelligent comments or queries to participating headquarters. Thus, scripted materials were prepared for those people simulating the various agencies. Parenthetically, it should be said that in later exercises the Joint Chiefs themselves participated, with very gratifying results.

Before describing further the actual conduct of the exercise, mention should be made of the several types of materials which were prepared for the conduct of Exercise "Desk Top." There were prepared a large number of films so that the actual blips would be seen on radar scopes; likewise, there were magnetic tapes prepared to give digital information inputs for the SAGE direction centers. To provide the materials for realistic simulation of an integrated air picture for each radar station, it was necessary to produce 268 films plus 134 electronic countermeasure films, in addition to the tapes used at the SAGE direction centers. In all a total of 37,000 feet of film and over 50,000 different maps were required in addition to numerous other special scripts and aids. There were threat warning scripts; these scripts allow the monitors to know the nature of a developing attack and to anticipate the various actions that should be taken by the battle staffs. In this way those observing the exercise could get an appreciation of what was going on and how effectively the exercise was being conducted. There were also sabotage scripts; for instance, one might suppose that if there were an actual war, various telephone communications or water supplies might be sabotaged. A limited number of such scripts were prepared, and at the appropriate time the exercising unit would be informed that its telephone lines had all been sabotaged. Then responsible officers would need to take whatever action was appropriate in view of the sabotage which had taken place.

As an example of a slightly different type of simulation material, a number of battle damage scripts were prepared. These scripts indicated what the damage would be for each specific hostile bomber in case it were to get through and bomb its particular target. For example, one would know that there was a hostile bomber planned for, let us say, Omaha. If that bomber is intercepted before it arrives at Omaha, then the battle damage script is never used. On the other hand if the hostile is not intercepted before it gets to Omaha, then it is presumed to have dropped its bomb, and commanders would need to know what damage took place. The battle damage script specified the damage in detail, and the military command would be informed that this particular damage had taken place whenever a hostile got through. Thus, the battle staffs were forced to take action which would be appropriate to the continued performance of the air defense mission.

One of the major purposes of conducting the exercise described is to find out the manner in which the system works and difficulties that keep the system from working more effectively. It is not believed that it is possible to obtain a real, absolute measure of the effectiveness of the system from simulated exercises, but important facts regarding the flow of information, where information gets slowed down, lost, or misinterpreted can be obtained. Also, information can be supplied so that commanders can practice making decisions and taking the actions which would be necessary in the face of an emergency. Naturally the results or outcome of these exercises cannot be discussed since the details are highly classified; however, the following listing will give an idea of some of the analyses that have been performed.

Types of analyses performed:

1. Summary of friendly and invader aircraft and action taken

2. Summary of SAC alert and bomb times
3. Times of notification of NORAD agencies of the existence of invader aircraft in the system
4. Nuclear detonation report summary
5. Summary of the efficiency of early warning processing
6. Alert latencies for NORAD agencies
7. Anti-aircraft action summary
8. Summary of fighter resources available by time periods
9. Weapons commitment
10. Engineered circuit summary
11. The loss of invader and unknown tracks displayed at successive command levels
12. Time latencies in displaying track information at Air Defense Command levels
13. Number of interceptors committed as reflected at successive command levels
14. Real-life circuit outages which would result with the size bomb and ground zero simulated in the exercise; accurate report of time required and method which would be used to restore service under actual conditions.

This extended description of a training exercise will give an appreciation of the extent to which simulation can be used for decision-making training. The military exercise described above is unique in its size and complexity, but other parts of the military service conduct exercises based on a similar philosophy. Of course, the military situation is somewhat special in the sense that, hopefully, military commanders will never be placed in the position of making these decisions in real life. In contrast to most situations, operational military decision making is of the greatest importance but can seldom be exercised in earnest. The next section now turns to business games as a somewhat different context for decision-making training.

## BUSINESS GAMES

Recently there has been a greatly increased interest in business games. In 1959 the Institute of Management Sciences met in Paris, and it is reported that the sessions of greatest interest, to Europeans as well as Americans, were those on business gaming. Recently a national symposium (Proceedings of the National Symposium on Management Games, 1959) was held on this subject, and a large number of games were described. Not only are these games being used in training at universities and management training centers (Bellman, Clark, Malcolm, Craft, &

Ricciardi, 1957), but business consultants are developing them for training purposes within a particular company (Andlinger, 1958) and for use at business conventions (Supermarket Executive Conference, 1958).

The complexity and size of business games vary greatly depending on the purposes for which they are designed and on the computer resources available. One class of games has been labeled "total enterprise games," which refers to the fact that a large portion of all the functions of a particular enterprise are programmed into the game. There are also specialized games in which a particular activity is simulated in considerable detail, say warehousing or sales-production interaction. In some cases games have been developed to represent a whole industry, as for example, the petroleum industry in all its facets: exploration, extraction, refining, distribution, sales, and finance. Apparently most major petroleum companies have similar problems, and such a game might be useful to many organizations. There are also proprietary games developed by particular companies to enable executives to try out different actions depending on the assumptions underlying the operations they have programmed for their game. Among companies which seem to have such games are Boeing, Pillsbury, General Electric, and Standard Oil of New Jersey. These proprietary games are also used for training middle management in management philosophy. A number of universities have constructed business games, with the better known being developed at U.C.L.A., Carnegie Institute of Technology, and the University of Washington. These vary considerably in complexity and use computers varying in size from IBM's 650 to 709 computers.

In typical games the designer makes assumptions regarding the influence on the business enterprise of such factors as price of the products, costs and capabilities of production, advertising and selling costs and results, research and development costs and results, investment costs and effects of plant and equipment, and dividend rates. Many of these functions are invariantly defined while others have randomness built into their effect. For instance, research and development usually produce product improvement as a function of the amount of money invested, but with the effectiveness of the outcome modified by random factors.

The players are usually formed into groups of four or five without any organizational structure being defined. Often teams compete against each other, each team representing a business attempting to maximize its goals in a competitive market. At the beginning of play each team is given identical consolidated reports of profit and loss, statement of financial condition, plant capacity, etc. Players are allowed to spend funds for plant expansion, research and development, advertising, market research, and similar items. The outcome of such expenditures is usually not known to the players, but has been programmed into the enterprise model used in playing the game. Play is in non-real time with a few hours or a day's play representing a calendar quarter or six months' real time. At the end of each time period a computer calculates the results of a period's operations and appropriate reports are furnished each team. On the basis of these reports and the players' records of their actions, they proceed to plan and execute their operations for the next time period and so on until five to ten years' operations have been completed. At the end of a play a critique of the play and the decisions made is conducted, with discussion of factors which might have improved the players' performance. The length and intensity of these post-play periods seem to vary greatly. The above description of business games for the purposes of this chapter is necessarily general; detailed description of several games will be found in the Proceedings of the National Symposium on Management Games (1959).

## Some Problems in Decision-Making Training

Exercises such as large military training programs or business games result in system improvement, not only because of improvements in the performance of individual participants, but because of the development of team skills. In addition, it is possible to modify the system itself as the result of experience gained during the exercise.

In the following paragraphs a discussion of many of the factors involved in devising these exercises will be presented. To a very large extent these comments are based on general experience, but the System Development Corporation has been gathering considerable data on this subject (Alexander, Ford, Jensen, Jordan, & Rogers, 1959) and anticipates the publication of much of it in the near future.

### Degree of Realism Required

In some kinds of exercises it is of great importance that the system being trained be simulated with an extremely high degree of realism while in others only gross approximation is needed. (See Chapter 8 by Gagné.) If the focus of the exercise is on general principles and these principles are thought to apply in many situations, then no great degree of exactness in simulation is required. If the players come from a heterogeneous background or if they are not going to work together as a team in real life, then exact replication of a real situation is relatively unimportant. On the other hand, if a company is examining its own operation with its own management, then exact attention to realism may be very important to assure that incorrect relations and conclusions are not drawn.

In the System Training Program for the air defense system, very great care has been taken to assure that all aspects of simulation correspond to reality. The reason for this is that military decision makers are seldom able to practice in real-life situations; thus when they practice in a simulated environment, it is important they practice the exact procedures which would be followed if they were to take emergency action in a real wartime period.

Another factor arguing for realism in simulation is the problem of motivation. There are two problems here. First is the problem of motivating the players to exercise with enthusiasm. If they believe that the exercise represents real-life situations which will have pay-off in their organizations, much of the problem of motivation will have been overcome. The enthusiasm with which players engage in business games is good evidence of their intrinsic motivational character. It is reported that players become so engrossed in the play that they lose track of time and become so emotionally involved that intense arguments and fist fights have occurred.

Another aspect of motivation which has occurred in military exercises, particularly at lower echelons, is the tendency to "fight the equipment." As personnel errors are made, it is easy, and a first reaction, to blame the difficulty on equipment failures rather than on personnel or organizational difficulties. Thus, in military exercises the greatest realism is required to assure that difficulties will not be readily dismissed as inadequacies in simulation. As one progresses to higher levels in the organization and as the actions to be taken become more clearly of a decision-making and information-processing nature, there is a tendency to accept simulation more readily and the problem of producing simulation materials becomes easier from the standpoint of the exact duplication of physical stimuli.

## Simulation Materials

There is tremendous variability in the complexity and realism of simulation materials. In business games the designers can easily make up an initial profit and loss statement without requiring that it correspond exactly to any particular real statement. At the other extreme, the films produced to place video targets on radar scopes are produced only as the outcome of a long series of complicated calculations on digital computers and subsequent conversion into analogue display for filming. No general rules can be stated about the complexity of simulation materials except that they are usually more expensive and time consuming than is anticipated.

When exercising real systems with simulated materials, it is usually necessary to expend much effort on the simulation materials. On the other hand, when preparing exercises for generalized systems, such as in enterprise business games, the simulation materials themselves are relatively easy to prepare, but the mathematical model of the enterprise is much more important. The designers must specify with great exactness how the different variables in the model interact and how they affect the outcome. If this departs too much from reality, the players may either reject the exercise or draw wrong conclusions regarding functional interactions which determine the nature of business operations.

## *Learning from the Experience: Feedback, Discussion, Decision Making*

Probably the greatest weakness of all exercise systems is the failure to adequately maximize learning after the exercise proper has been concluded. It is much too easy to play a game or participate in a military exercise and at the end return to regular duties or otherwise leave the situation. The exercise period is the time to discover problem areas and inadequacies; the post-exercise period is the time to consider how to correct them. Of course, there are simple skills which can be taught during an exercise, but real system problems of organization and modification are best accomplished after the exercise has defined and illustrated these problems.

Objective recording of the players' actions and a detailed record of the operation of the system is essential. While exercises are being conducted, observers need to record behaviors which are critical to success. The classes of material to be recorded must be identified before the exercise starts, special forms need to be prepared, and observers trained. In some business games and military exercises, many of the actions taken can be recorded by computers and stored for later display. In addition to pre-programmed records, there should be an observer who watches broad, global aspects of the exercise and who can concentrate on the way in which critical problem areas are handled.

The way in which the collected performance record is fed back to participants varies considerably. In some cases the observers join the participants to transmit their observations and, depending on their status, to lead the discussion. In other situations the collected information is given the participants, and they are expected to use it as fits their needs. Each method, and variations on it, is appropriate depending on the homogeneity of the participants, the status of the observers, the ability of the participants to engage in profitable discussion without guidance, etc.

In Air Defense Command exercises, the attempt is made to have the total crew engage in a debriefing immediately after the exercise. Often a crew will consist of several officers and a number of enlisted men. A permissive discussion in this situation is somewhat contrary to military practice, and yet the system is so complex that no one person can have identified all of the problems or followed all of the actions taken. Similarly solutions to many of the problems involve questions of interaction between a number of different people—people frequently only connected together through communication links. In this situation it seems that much problem solving can occur through fairly extended discussion and consideration in the total crew context. In these discussions some officers are able to lead excellent problem-solving sessions, but other officers have difficulty. This difficulty often does not arise out of problems of officer-enlisted relations, but rather from the normal problems so many people have in fruitfully leading discussion groups. In coping with this inadequacy, courses have been conducted for discussion group leaders and several manuals have been published on discussion group leadership (Katcher & Hunter, 1957).

Even when there has been reliable and extensive observation of system performance and where problems have been isolated and discussed and sound solutions conceived, a serious problem remains. Often the solution arrived at with such cost seems not to be put into effect. There are many reasons for this. It is hardly necessary to mention the general resistance to change—even change for the better. There is a considerable literature on resistance to change (Lippitt, Watson, & Westley, 1958), and it is illustrated in military exercises. There are additional problems in large systems where behaviors are usually governed by various standard operating procedures or by directive. To get these changed often requires extensive coordination and may not be within the authority of the group experiencing the problem. Likewise, in a large system certain difficulties may best be solved by equipment changes or by communications modifications. Even though the problem is identified and solutions determined, it may be impractical to effect a solution. Another problem occurs where there are several crews or shifts. A particular problem may be solved by one shift, but no appropriate mechanism may exist for passing on the solution to the next shift. In the air defense exercises much emphasis is placed on the entering of all problems in a log book with the details of any solution being written up. Operations officers are required to review these logs periodically and see that problems or solutions are not lost through system inertia.

In spite of efforts such as described above, it is probable that the post-exercise learning period could be greatly improved. Not only can observational techniques be refined, but techniques of group problem solving need to be better understood and practiced. When one considers the relative sophistication of typical exercise materials and techniques, it seems probable that the greatest potential for improving the decision-making process lies in the post-exercise part of the experience.

## How Much Is Learned in Simulation Exercises?

Is decision-making skill learned in these military exercises and business games? All of the usual problems of measuring improvement in performance apply to this training and most of these problems are yet to be completely solved. In assessing what and how much is learned, the following points can be made:

1. Decision making is a loosely defined skill. People talk about decision making in situations which vary from the immediate small play-to-play decisions in games such as blackjack to the very large decisions made in industrial enterprises, decisions such as must have been involved when General Motors decided to introduce a compact car in 1960 or in the military situation where a commander must decide whether or not an emergency war situation exists. It is possible to relate various abilities or training programs to decision-making improvement in small, well-defined situations, but almost impossible in really important, relatively non-recurrent type decision situations.

2. In certain of the military exercises, it is possible to measure with considerable accuracy the improvement resulting from system training. Several years ago the System Development Corporation conducted a before-after type measurement of the improvement resulting from the introduction of system training in one of the air divisions. Performance was measured before the introduction of training and again after several months' training experience. At one site a very intensive series of objective and observational measures were obtained.

The detailed results of this work are now being prepared for publication. It was found that very significant improvement took place in many functions such as detection, cross-tell, identification, etc. But just which activities might be included as decision-making activities is not clear. The personnel at these sites improved in performance in important areas such as deciding whether or not a particular plane was friendly, or in deciding to pass control to an adjacent sector. But these are hardly "major" decisions. It would be much harder to objectify the decisions of commanders concerned with more global aspects of defense.

3. In business management games there are real possibilities of developing experimental situations where decision-making training can be evaluated. So far there seem to be only impressionistic reports (Proceedings of the National Symposium on Management Games, 1959) regarding the value of the gaming situation in training for decision making. Business men and students alike feel that they learn something important from these experiences. It would be quite possible to define criteria such as business profits, share of the market, production capability, etc., as goals to be achieved by players in business games. By manipulating such things as formal classroom training, course content, game results, feedback, etc., it would be possible to determine what effect such training had on the criteria and thus to determine factors contributing to effective decision making. Of course, the generality of such results would be limited by the degree of transfer from the game to the real-life situation.

4. It is possible to assert dogmatically, without experimental evidence, that in some cases military exercises lead to improved system performance. An example can be drawn from a system training exercise in which a division command control post was put out of action by simulated bombing. Under this situation an alternate control post located 50 or 60 miles away was supposed to take command. When the alternate took over, it was discovered that its communication lines went through the same area as would be bombed out when the prime control post was lost. Naturally this situation was corrected in short order, but it illustrates the point that in complex systems the best logical design often is not sufficiently sophisticated to foresee all possible difficulties. In another exercise one commander was constrained from launching his forces early enough because a decision could not be reached at a higher headquarters. Because of this experience, the whole question of launch authority came under renewed scrutiny. In situations such as the above, it is obvious that the exercises lead to system improvements

and to marked changes in the commanders' ability to make and execute decisions.

In many training situations—military exercises, classroom instruction, symposia, business games—it is extremely difficult to say just what is learned. At times there are dramatic examples which give assurance that such training is useful, but careful research is needed to understand what is going on and to improve the details of presentation to maximize learning.

Decision making can be considered from several different dimensions. One continuum deals with the size of the decision—there are small decisions of relatively little importance and large world-shaking decisions at the other extreme. Another dimension is related to the amount of general judgment, or, in contrast, technical knowledge, required in the decision; at times a decision can be readily made if the technical facts are available, while at other times matters of general experience, "feel," or "practical experience" seem to be predominant. Another variable in considering decision-making is the extent to which the outcome is readily apparent. In some situations a decision can be made and feedback is immediate—you decide to finesse and make it—while at other times the outcome of the decision remains in doubt for years—was massive retaliation really a good policy? Since there are so many facets of decision making, it is impossible to specify an overall formula for decision-making training. Yet, some general points can be made about training for decision making:

1. First, many decision-making situations require facts and technical knowledge. It seems apparent that technical training and familiarity with the evaluation of factual material are necessary for sound decision making.

2. The outcome of many decisions involves much more than the physical or fiscal aspects that appear on the surface. Problems of human interaction, acceptance, motivation, etc., may become the overriding factor in good decision making. Although this topic has not been discussed here, there is a large literature (Browne & Cohn, 1958; Hare, Borgatta, & Bales, 1955; Maier, Solem, & Maier, 1957) which should be consulted.

3. As social, business, and military systems become larger and more complex, the outcome of decisions becomes unclear. How variables interact and influence far-flung parts of an organization are only dimly understood.

In these situations it is possible to use simulation to great advantage. The examples discussed in this paper illustrate the way in which decision makers can realistically practice the decisions they may have to make in the real world, and there is good reason to believe their decision making is improved as a result of exercise through simulation.

## REFERENCES

Alexander, L. T., Ford, J. D., Jr., Jensen, B. T., Jordan, N., & Rogers, M. S. *Problems encountered in developing and maintaining a field system training program, SP-107.* Papers read at the 1959 Human Factors Society meeting. Santa Monica: System Development Corporation, 1959.

Andlinger, G. R. Business games—play one! *Harvard bus. Rev.,* 1958, *36,* 115-126.

Bellman, R., Clark, C. E., Malcolm, D. G., Craft, C. J., & Ricciardi, F. M. On the construction of a multi-state, multi-person business game. *Operations Res.,* 1957, *5,* 469-503.

Browne, C. G. & Cohn, T. S. *The study of leadership.* Danville, Illinois: Interstate Printers, 1958.

Forrester, J. W. Industrial dynamics: A major breakthrough for decision-makers. *Harvard bus. Rev.,* 1958, *36,* 37-67.

Hare, A. P., Borgatta, E. F., & Bales, R. F. *Small groups: Studies in social interaction.* New York: Knopf, 1955.

Katcher, A. & Hunter, M. *How to lead a debriefing—A guide for senior directors, TM-132.* Santa Monica: System Development Corporation, November 1957.

Lichtenberg, P. & Deutsch, M. *A descriptive review of research on the staff process of decision making.* Lackland AFB, 1954. AFPTRC Research Bulletin, TR-54-129.

Lippitt, R., Watson, J., & Westley, B. *The dynamics of planned change.* New York: Harcourt Brace, 1958.

Maier, N. R. F., Solem, A. R., & Maier, A. A. *Supervisory and executive development.* New York: Wiley, 1957.

Newell, A., Shaw, J. C., & Simon, H. A. Elements of a theory of human problem solving. *Psychol. Rev.,* 1958, *65,* 151-166.

*Proceedings of the National Symposium on Management Games.* Lawrence: University of Kansas, Center for Research in Business, 1959.

Supermarket Executive Conference. Electronic brain referees war maneuvers! *Meat and food merchandising,* March 1958.

Wasserman, P. & Silander, F. S. *Decision making: An annotated bibliography.* Ithaca, New York: Cornell University, 1959.

Chapter *15*

### Recent Developments in Training Problems, and Training and Training Research Methodology[1]

*Alfred F. Smode, Dunlap and Associates, Inc.*

This chapter is a compilation of recent innovations in general methods of training and training research. The term "recent training innovation" as used here, refers to training methods, materials and procedures that have emerged during the last decade. These developments have opened or may open new areas for research in training, thereby offering possible ways of increasing knowledge and technique in training. The term includes both new approaches, tools, procedures and techniques and also novel or unique ways of employing older techniques and methods. All aspects of the management of the learning experience are included. The purpose of the chapter is to provide research workers in the field of training with a survey of new ideas, techniques and procedures; it includes an indication of the problems leading to the new development. Some of the research implications of these innovations will be pointed out throughout the chapter, but the reader will undoubtedly see additional possibilities for their utilization. Primary sources of information are indicated for the use of those readers who wish to follow up such additional ideas.

The innovations discussed here come from many different sources and from many areas in the behavioral sciences. The items have been culled from published reports and from material that has not yet reached the publication stage. Many of the most recent innovations have been identified during discussions with numerous leading scientists in the field of training. Any given innovation may or may not have been developed and employed specifically in training research. In instances where an innovation has been developed in a non-training

[1]This work was supported in part by the Office of Naval Research, Personnel and Training Branch, Washington, D. C., under Contract Nonr 2490(00).

context, its inclusion in this chapter is based on the judgment that it possesses potential methodological value for the training field.

The discovery of ways for improving training comes about in two basic ways. One way is by means of invention or induction. This relates to aspects of creativity and the discovery of new ideas. Another way is through experimentation and field tests to evaluate the soundness of ideas and techniques. Experimentation, in turn, may be essentially empirical, or it may be based on a rational-deductive approach. Specifically, new ways for training come into being in the following ways:

1. An individual conceives an idea for solving some training problem and develops it to the point where it can be introduced into a training program. Such ideas often are adaptations of innovations which have appeared in other areas, in relation to other problems.

2. Innovations may arise not only as inventions, but as a result of systematic analysis and evaluation of existing procedures and materials. Improvement may come about as a result of systematic manipulation of training variables.

3. A specific theory or broad training concept may lead to hypotheses and deductions for improvements in training.

It should be emphasized that only rarely are novel ideas subjected to careful tests or validation studies. Usually they are either adopted or rejected without any real knowledge of their true value for training.

Two criteria have been employed in selecting innovations for inclusion in this chapter. First, regardless of its original use or intent, the innovation must be judged to show promise for training. Second, devices and techniques are not cited simply because they are new, novel, or exciting, but rather because it is judged that they make possible new areas for research.

## Training, Evaluation and Research Methodology

It is difficult to discuss training research without involving innovations in training per se, for the two are closely related. Often the development of a new training procedure or device makes possible new areas for research. It is axiomatic that personnel charged with the conduct of training are interested in using improved training methods. It is not always obvious, however, when training has been improved. Much of the training methodology now in use has not been formally validated, that is, no systematic studies have been conducted to determine how well it is accomplishing what it is supposed to accomplish. The setting up of conditions for the tryout and validation of a training method is a laborious and time-consuming task, generally requiring an "opportunity" which permits this sort of activity. As often as not, if one can generalize from the limited number of formal tests that have been made, procedures and devices used in training often look good (have high face validity) but, in fact, may not facilitate learning any more than alternative but less novel procedures. Their net effect may be to increase the elegance with which a problem is approached but they may contribute very little, if any, to the attainment of performance efficiency.

Where an innovation for training has been developed, it is necessary to know what effect it is supposed to have in the training sequence before any evaluation of the outcomes can be attempted. In some instances, a training innovation can be evaluated by conventional methods; in other instances, a new research technique may be required in order to evaluate it. The content and procedures of training have changed at a faster pace than has its research methodology. The current emergence of wholly new and complex training problems further complicates the training picture in that innovations in research methodology often need to be developed in order to handle these increasingly complex problems. Training research is involved in the testing of procedures and materials to be used in improving training. It should be pointed out that research may not always generate new ideas, but research can be relied upon to *test* new ideas. The methodological issues revolve around the question of how to evaluate these new ideas.

In summary, it is clear that there is a close relation between innovations in training and in training research. A new idea for training may be evaluated by conventional research methods or may require an innovation in research before it can be evaluated. A research innovation may also be used to evaluate conventional training procedures and, indeed, may solve an old training problem (such as assessing learning and performance effects in task acquisition). Furthermore, a research innovation may have implications for training procedures. For example, an improved criterion measure is a direct contribution to research, but this criterion can sometimes be utilized as an innovation for the training sequence, e.g., a unique way of providing knowledge of results to the trainee. In view of these considerations, the present approach will cite innovations in training, indicate where these appear to have implications for research, as well as point out innovations in specific methods for research in training.

## The Framework for Discussion

A wide array of innovations in method have been identified and selected for this chapter. In order to arrange and discuss them effectively, the innovations have been grouped in terms of where they would be of use in an inclusive learning-training program. Specifically, the conceptual framework corresponds to the major ingredients or components of concern in the complete training activity cycle, that is, (*a*) the analysis of the task, (*b*) the means of providing and controlling the learning experience, (*c*) the means of measurement and evaluation of performance, and (*d*) the means of providing information feedback both immediate (for task performance) and system-wide (for group critique and improvement).

Within the constraints imposed above, the innovations are subsumed under four major headings in the following conceptual framework:

1. *New ways of Determining the Requirements for Training*. This relates to new ways of describing human behavioral requirements in the planning of training programs:

   A. Procedures for the analysis of task requirements
      (1) Task structure
      (2) Taxonomy for the specification of tasks

2. *New Ways of Providing Learning Experiences*. This relates to new or novel situations employed in studying the behavior that is being trained. It is concerned with new or novel tasks:

   A. Types of problems or tasks
      (1) Team training and small group research
      (2) Decision making and problem solving

   B. Complex devices that provide opportunities for system training
      (1) Perceptual and perceptual motor control tasks
      (2) Devices used in decision making and management tasks
      (3) Teaching machines and other devices used for training in intellectual skills

   C. Ways of establishing and/or controlling the working environment
      (1) Simulation of space flight
      (2) Stress
      (3) Confinement, isolation and sensory deprivation

3. *New Ways of Measuring the Progress and Outcomes of Training*. This is concerned with ways of measuring behavior and analyzing the nature and progress of learning:

A. Ways of observing free activity behavior
   (1) Observation techniques
   (2) Group observation

B. Scoring and recording devices
   (1) Recording devices for mass communication
   (2) Scoring devices

C. Motor skill scoring
   (1) Types of frequency measures
   (2) Analysis of performance in continuous tasks

D. Ways of analyzing data from learning studies
   (1) Correlational technique
   (2) New applications of factor analysis to learning
   (3) New ways for specifying learning curves

4. *New Ways of Providing Knowledge of Results.* This relates to new ways of manipulating procedural variables in task performance:

A. Information feedback as a factor in learning
B. Motivational aspects
C. Knowledge of results and reinforcement

Each of these major headings deserves special consideration and forms the basis for a major section in the remainder of this chapter. In addition, a final section is devoted to a summary and evaluation of the classes of innovations cited.

## New Ways of Determining the Requirements for Training

Many responsible people in training establishments still hold the view that training is intended to teach a man how to learn his job, the implications being that a man learns his job while on the job. This philosophy has hampered serious attempts at determining the efficiency and validity of the training effort or its constituent contents and techniques in producing job-related skills, and has perpetuated the practice of letting textbooks and textbook exercises shape the content of training. In the absence of job performance criteria, the distribution curve in test outcomes, modified by supply and demand in the manpower pipeline, dictates by arbitrary cut-off points who passes and fails. At the conclusion of training, especially of technical personnel, trainees are sent off as apprentices to "learn their job on the job."

The new point of view is moving away from deriving training content through the matching job titles with textbook and subject matter titles. It is moving toward answering the question: How and what do we teach in order to enable a man to perform his job-tasks competently within the beginning period of job assignment? A corollary question is: How do we teach this capability economically?

In order to answer questions posed by this new philosophy, it becomes essential to scrutinize on-the-job performance requirements in detail with a sophistication heretofore unnecessary. Because there are many details even in what may seem "simple" jobs, concepts and methods are necessary for organizing the searching out, sampling and cataloging of these details. In order that the description of job performance requirements will serve not only as a criterion for the trainee and for training, the analysis should ideally be codified in terms that point to alternatives in training technique, where such alternatives are appropriate to training design decisions.

Finally, in this viewpoint, training is designed for a job or set of job-tasks just as a machine is designed to perform an explicit, objective set of performance functions. A job knowledge is synthesized from a set of relatable behaviors into concepts which readily permit association and generalization; job-knowledges are not arbitrarily selected from a chapter in a book because the title of an operation matches the title of the chapter. The trainee graduates not because of what he knows, but because of what he can do. The practical realization of this viewpoint rests on techniques for preparing job-task descriptions of performance requirements, and in couching these descriptions so as best to serve for training design decisions.

## Procedures for the Analysis of Task Requirements

Task analysis is a systematic method for determining the behavioral requirements in task performance. In simplest terms, task requirements can be stated by tracing through a cycle of task events and specifying the stimuli present and available and the responses required on the available response supports. Temporal relationships are part of this description, as are disturbances and environmental conditions. The functional unit of description is display and displayed information, response support and response, and feedback about response adequacy. The term "Equipment Task Analysis" (Miller, 1953a; Miller, 1956a; Miller & Folley, 1951) has been given to this procedure. It was formulated in concept and format and applied by Miller (under Air Force sponsorship) to machine systems while they were still under prototype development in order to anticipate training and other personnel requirements by one or more years. Miller has expanded on his early work by insisting that the task description should include analysis of perceptual, short-term recall, long-term recall, decision making and motor processes implied by the initial equipment task analysis. (See Chapter 2 by Miller.) This effort will lead to a perception of the patterns of behavioral process potentially significant to training design (Miller, 1953a). In studies of troubleshooting (Miller, 1953a; Miller, Folley, & Smith, 1953), the interaction between the way a task is performed and its difficulty was recognized in problem-solving situations. The task analyst therefore should be given responsibility for studying the required operations in order to optimize the behavioral processes required to produce the task results. It is at this point that task analysis and the development of training plans and programs necessarily overlap.

Attempts are being made in the Air Force to apply task analysis techniques of varying degrees of sophistication to the preparation of personnel requirements structures for weapon systems under development. These attempts include job structures, manning tables, tables of organization, training and instruction handbooks, and comprise the Qualitative Personnel Requirements Information (QPRI) program. The work at the American Institute for Research has extended the analysis and prediction of personnel requirements into the field of team operations (Glanzer & Glaser, 1955; Glanzer, Glaser, & Klaus, 1956). The HumRRO study, called Project UPSTREAM, is anticipating training requirements for future air defense guided missile systems (Human Resources Research Office, 1959). A related study (Project FORECAST) is attempting to expand on general methods for forecasting the content, learning difficulty, and the optimum organization of training programs for classes of weapon systems.

Systematic procedures for the development of job knowledge, and the organization of knowledge content for efficient learning and generalization to job-tasks has been proposed by Miller in a series of studies at the American Institute for Research (Miller, 1955; Miller & Van Cott, 1955). Applications, in part, have been made for specific maintenance tasks and, in a recent Navy contract, trouble shooting on a missile system was completely reduced to a cross-indexed set of check procedures which incorporated efficient strategies for narrowing a fault to the malfunctioning component.

Dunlap and Associates and the American Institute for Research have developed and applied methods for laying out decision-making sequence charts in the form of logical trees with binary (yes-no) branches. Also, Dunlap and Associates (supported by the U. S. Naval Training Device Center) is currently developing an approach for simplifying the methods of systems analysis so that they may be applied (with minimum mathematics) to the determination of requirements for training devices in systems under development.

## Task Structure

A beginning has been made in relating task descriptions to training design alternatives. In a Wright Air Development Center report, Miller (1956a) has suggested a fairly general task structure and related it to part-task training. He has proposed the following categories: identification, nomenclature and locations of work objects; detection of indications calling for task response; identification of task cues and cue patterns; "self-instructed" procedures; decision making and problem solving; automated response and tracking behaviors. These categories are exclusive only in degree. A procedure is proposed for partitioning a total task-complex into trainable segments, for sequencing these segments, and for assigning appropriate training device characteristics to these respective task factors. This overall procedure still awaits a formal tryout.

## Taxonomy for the Specification of Tasks

At present there exists no unified or generally accepted scheme for the classification of tasks. No general agreement can be found for the important task dimensions in a training effort. Generalized attempts such as differentiating tasks in terms of verbal or motor learning, insightful vs. conditioned response learning, or schemes such as the definitions of occupational titles have proved too gross for effective usage in the specification of training requirements. Despite the lack of an acceptable task taxonomy, some interesting progress is being made in this area.

Miller and his colleagues (Miller, 1953a; Miller & Folley, 1951) have indicated the values that would derive from a comprehensive taxonomy: It would permit fairly precise estimates of the applicability of findings in research documents to a given task situation, and answer questions as to the tasks to which findings from specific laboratory tasks such as motor skill, card sorting and coin tossing experiments can be applied. The taxonomy would provide a set of standard categories for the description of task and training requirements, and these in turn would be mated to design structure in training. Miller and Folley (1951) have proposed a classification scheme of electronics maintenance tasks, suggesting that some of the task structure categories might be treated as an initial attempt at a task taxonomy. Cotterman (1959a) has suggested a classification scheme for identifying task variables which interact with the learning process. The concern is for factors involved in actual task performance, i.e., performance in the end stage of training. He has offered a tentative set of task categories and proposed that the inductive procedure be followed for establishing a categorical structure. In other words, psychologists would pool their judgments in formulating the taxonomy. The Wright Air Development Division is supporting research along the lines proposed by Cotterman (1959a; 1959b). One study at the University of Illinois is setting up a task classification in which the criterion for task grouping requires that the effects of a specifiable group of basic variations in learning conditions be invariant with respect to the grouped tasks. Another study by Psychological Research Associates, Inc., is attempting to develop a guide for the selection of training media. An attempt has been made to group tasks in accordance with the relative effectiveness of the various training media.

Fleishman (1956a; 1956b) has taken an experimental approach to task classification through the study of ability requirements in tasks. By factor analyzing performances on a variety of human learning studies in the laboratory, he finds that task factors change as the individual passes through successive stages of learning complex tasks. These findings point out clearly that a useful task classification scheme should take into account the relative stage of learning to be described, or for which training is to be prescribed. (See Chapter 5 by Fleishman.)

## New Ways of Providing Learning Experience

This section reviews novel training situations; it is concerned with novel tasks, innovations in task situations which make possible particular kinds of training, and research which heretofore could have been accomplished only modestly or not at all.

### New Types of Problems or Tasks

*Team Training and Small Group Research*

There is good agreement that improvements in group performance accrue as a result of emphasis on team training. While the importance of team training is widely recognized, the currently available informa-

tion about teams is meager. It is only recently that systematic effort
has been devoted to problems of team performance. Some of the deficiencies in this type of training are due to the lack of clearly stated
criteria for good teams, the lack of useful principles for training procedures, and the lack of adequate measuring devices for team behavior
as distinct from individual behavior (Glaser & Glanzer, 1958).

What has been needed is a proper taxonomy and analysis of team
functions. The assembly of adequate information on team performance
has been hampered partly by the complexities involved in team problems. The specification of learning conditions requires technical developments above those required for the individual, the additional problems involving such aspects as monitoring and supervision, information
processing, and feedback on team performance. Some of the training
difficulties involve the determination of errors, both individual and interactive, and the inefficiencies in error correction. This is not to say
that great qualitative differences exist between team training and individual training, for team performance is highly dependent on the sum
of individual performances. As more information becomes available,
it is conceivable that the complexities identified with team training may
be reduced considerably. Glanzer, in Chapter 13 of this volume, writes
that, theoretically, team proficiency can be substantially reduced to the
proficiency of the individuals composing the team if certain requirements are met, for example, the specification of the inputs used by individuals in making their responses. Such a reduction, however, requires considerably more information about teams than is currently
available (e.g., Klaus & Glaser, 1960).

Much of the previous work on groups has been directed at the problems of organization and group dynamics. Studies have been made of
social process variables usually in informal groups where the individuals
collectively determine group goals and the manner of achieving them.
Less emphasis has been given to the study of the skills required for effective group performance. The study of task variables in the small
group setting has received attention. Glaser (1958) has summarized
the work of Bales; Christie, Luce and Macy; and Forgays and Roby
on the procedures for describing group functioning in terms of a set of
general categories of behavior. These are identified for particular kinds
of groups and problem-solving tasks and recorded in terms of frequency
and pattern of occurrence. Similar attempts can be seen in the work of
McGrath (1958) in the investigation and analysis of task characteris-

tics of military groups and in March and Simon's (1958) attempt at formalizing organizational behavior.

Significant effort has been devoted to team organization in the study of communication networks in group behavior. This research is concerned with the manipulation of group structure which is accomplished by specifying the communication channels available to the group in task solution. The early work is identified with the Bavelas model (1948; 1950) for group structures. Basically, the interest is in the effect of group organization on performance determined by communication channels. This work has generated a number of laboratory studies on networks. Glanzer and Glaser (1959; 1961) discuss the work of Bavelas, Leavitt, Shaw and his associates, and the results stemming from the Group Networks Laboratory at M.I.T.

Roby and Lanzetta (Lanzetta & Roby, 1957; Roby & Lanzetta, 1958) have extended the study of optimum group organization by utilizing models of real teams (Air Force bomber crews) employing more realistic communication channels. Rosenberg and Hall (Hall, 1957; Rosenberg & Hall, 1958) have similarly concerned themselves with the structure of real crews (Air Force). However, instead of communication channels, they have defined structure in terms of the composition of information feedback to the individual. Their research indicates that team output is heavily dependent upon the sum of the individual performances. This assumption that team performance is essentially the sum of individual performance is supported by work conducted at the American Institute for Research by Glanzer, Glaser and Klaus with actual Navy Teams (Glanzer, Glaser, & Klaus, 1955; Glanzer & Glaser, 1957). They found that team training difficulties were attributable to individual errors and to inefficiency in correcting errors due to problems in information feedback. (See Chapter 13 by Glanzer.)

These varieties of studies concerned with the identification of team structure and operation shed some light on the definition of procedures conducive to increasing team efficiency.

One general type of team problem or task can be characterized as having a large number of possible answers and no rational (mathematical) solution other than the use of linear programming. The transportation problem and the assignment problem are examples. Within the framework of small group training and also problem solving, Fitts, at the University of Michigan,[2] (sponsored by the Air Force Office

---

[2]Personal communication from Paul Fitts, University of Michigan.

of Scientific Research) has employed such a task to determine what heuristic procedures people use in problem solving. A typical task is the assignment of units of supply from sources to destinations with the objective of minimizing the total distance over which all units are moved. Random and optimum solutions are obtained on an IBM 704 computer, and performance is scored relative to these reference points. The task is adaptable to the study of both individual and team training.

The Laboratory of Aviation Psychology, Ohio State University, has completed an eight-year program of research studying a variety of topics relating to the role of human controllers in air traffic control (Fitts, Schipper, Kidd, Shelly, & Kraft, 1958; Schipper, Kraft, Smode, & Fitts, 1957). The classes of system variables investigated included load or input variables, information or display variables, and procedural or organizational variables. A simulator (Hixon, Harter, Warren, & Cowan, 1954) was developed for generating up to 30 independent targets (representing aircraft) and displaying these targets on a number of different plan position (PPI) and altitude displays. This ATC simulator has been used by teams of up to three controllers plus approximately 20 pilots. Team research projects have investigated questions of training, optimum division of work load, and organizational structure (group communications). One of the innovations of this equipment is that it permits the use of meaningful and reliable system output measures, such as average time required for each aircraft to traverse the radius of the area of control, the fuel consumption of each aircraft and the number of conflicts (violations of safety rules).

Other team training approaches that appear useful in research are the case method in human relations (Berrien & Bash, 1957) and group discussions, particularly the leaderless group discussion techniques (Ansbacher, 1951; Bass, 1954). These techniques are not new, having been employed in other contexts (human relations and situational testing respectively). However, they make possible ways of providing training opportunity for the development of behaviors that are difficult to formalize and assess, such as group problem solving and leadership development. The beginnings for a systematization of knowledge on team training are indicated in the above, as well as in the efforts of various organizations to set up and implement team training programs. Representative of these efforts is the work of the System Development Corporation (SDC). Their training program is cited here as a significant example of how team training can be accomplished.

The System Training Program provides team training exercises in an Air Defense System context (Alexander, 1959; Chapman & Kennedy, 1956; Goodwin, 1957). These training exercises are synthetic inputs which substitute for the system's normal information inputs. The synthetic inputs are programmed so as to permit accurate recording of the system response, thus providing the means of performance information feedback to the system. Teams or groups are installed and the task specified. The task environment is so structured that the teams are able to vary their own way of solving problems (i.e., non-rigid task specifications). In solving the operational problems presented, it has been observed that the team tends to restructure itself in terms of its performance optimum. This training forces teams to suffer the consequences of poor performance, thus providing indications of behavior that may occur in actual damage situations. Crew responses are recorded and correlated with the known stimulus inputs. Since no real opportunity exists for communication of the kind needed to solve problems as they are encountered in the operational cycle of the system, debriefings (group discussions) are held following each exercise. These problem-solving sessions enable team members to contrast their results with system goals. Umpires provide non-specific feedback (i.e., general feedback to the team as a whole). The decisions reached by the group are operationally tested in subsequent exercises and re-evaluated.

This type of training provides the capacity to exercise the system and to evaluate proficiency as a means of finding better ways of coping with mission problems. This increases the capability of the system to handle new and more complex situations. The aim of the program is to identify the most useful procedures for achieving success and to identify the task situations that are optimum for training. (See Chapter 14 by Carter.)

## Decision Making and Problem Solving

*Games.* Gaming represents a promising innovation for training research in problem solving and decision making, for it enables the manipulation of decision rules and strategies for individuals or teams in a structured task environment. It also provides a medium for the study of organization processes in problem solution and the effects of group structure on team performance. The value of the game as a research tool resides in the ease with which it can be structured to represent the essence of a given operational situation. Manipulation of variables can be systematically achieved by the changing of information patterns, duration of play, decision rules, group interaction rules relating to organization and leadership, communications, competition and conflict, etc. One of the attributes of the game is time compression, which is the capability of simulating in some detail (via careful programming) those realistic problem situations which in real life involve lengthy and sequential time periods but which can be solved within the confines of the short time required to complete the playing of the game. For instance, a management game that simulates several companies in a competitive commercial situation may involve only a few hours or days of play but may represent a series of events that covers a consecutive ten-year period of real-time operations.

An additional feature of gaming is that it represents a new way for providing learning experiences. It appears exceedingly useful for training in certain problem-solving and decision-making situations and in business or military planning. Heretofore, training in the solution of actual problems involving decision making and executive planning has been difficult to achieve due to the inability to simulate relevant task conditions. Games provide the opportunity for training in "automating" the human ability to process multiple variable information (training the individual to think and decide under relatively high speed). It directs him to observe interactions among complex variables, thus teaching the individual cause and effect of pattern relations. Games also permit the experimenter to test the limits of different procedures (chance taking vs. conservative behavior) and to run "tests-to-break-down" things which may be inadvisable to do in the real world.

Another important outcome of game playing is that it makes possible a situation where participants may learn to work effectively together as a team, thus providing a means of training in group interaction for the attainment of specific goals. It also provides each member of a team with many opportunities to observe the behavior of other members of the team so that each comes to learn the strong and weak points of others, their personality characteristics, etc. Learning in a gaming situation appears to be facilitated through the utilization of a post-game evaluative critique in which immediate knowledge of achievement information is fed back to participants. An advantage of the game is that the learner can go back to decision points in the game to try out alternative strategies, thus allowing for the further testing of solutions. Lastly, and of no small significance, is the fact that games are interesting, often fascinating, teaching devices which produce a high level of personal involvement in the participant. The intrinsically satisfying aspects of this technique are generally conducive to rapid and effective learning.

It should be emphasized, however, that the training benefits of a game are directly dependent upon a number of considerations. To begin with, the selection of players for any given game is crucial. Greater value accrues when the participants are confronted with problems having transfer to their daily work activities, than when people are engaged in a game situation that is relatively unknown or meaningless with regard to their vocational pursuits. Their only incentive may be to win a small amount of money for performance. A game is only an approximation of reality. For instance, a management game does not involve areas in which crucial decisions must be made, such as technological advance, environmental and governmental influences, catastrophe, mergers and coalitions, labor-management problems, product substitution by customers, etc. Also, the game does not serve as a complete substitute for basic knowledge and experience in the situations it depicts. However, the possibilities for improving many of the general skills and capacities required in real-life team tasks seem evident.

*Management Games.* In the economic context, a sizable number of business games have been developed for purposes of training and research. (See Chapter 14 by Carter.) The heightened interest in management gaming is reflected in publications such as the Proceedings of the National Symposium on Management Games (1959), and in organizations such as the TIMS group on management games,[3] which is made up of individuals with a common interest in management gaming. The varieties of management games run the gamut from simple non-computer type games involving only a few variables for manipulation to highly complex games involving many people and electronic computing equipment. Within this framework two classes of management games can be identified. These may be termed as (*a*) total enterprise games, and (*b*) specialized functions or specific industry games.

Total enterprise games relate to problems of general management involving the competitive business world in general, and provide practice in top management decision making. These games are usually complex and interactive, and often require the use of electronic computers to simulate the dynamics of the market. The many games of this type differ among themselves chiefly in the number of types of decisions required

[3]This TIMS group refers to The Institute of Management Sciences, College on Management Games, Merrill M. Flood, University of Michigan, Chairman.

in the course of play. Representative of this class of game are the following: The American Management Association business game, which is a multi-stage, multi-person business game for executive training and research (Bellman, Clark, Malcolm, Craft, & Ricciardi, 1957; Ricciardi, 1957); the McKinsey Business Management Game, which is a non-computer, non-competitive game dealing with capital goods companies (Andlinger, 1958); the International Business Machines computerized executive training game, the Carnegie Institute of Technology computerized game for teaching game playing, the University of California (UCLA) executive game for research on team behavior in business situations, and the Pillsbury Company management training game (Proceedings of the National Symposium on Management Games, 1959).

Specialized functions or specific industry games deal with particular areas of business and have been used for research and pedagogical purposes. These games are usually not interactive, the participants competing only for best score. Representative games here include: The Case Institute of Technology non-computer interactive game, developed for purposes of research on team behavior in the business setting; the University of Oklahoma game, developed for research in a single industry; and a variety of relatively simple games that present a single function in a business setting, such as the General Electric Company "Dispatch Game," a non-computer, non-competitive game simulating production control dispatching, "Smart," a computer game dealing with personnel allotments in a systems management context, and "Inventrol," a non-computer, competitive game concerned with procurement and inventory control (Proceedings of the National Symposium on Management Games, 1959).

*Military Games.* Military officers have long recognized the war gaming technique as a potential analytical tool for testing military concepts and plans and as a highly useful means for personnel training. War games may range from the use of simple techniques, such as maneuver boards, to the use of highly complex electronic devices involving computers, and from highly schematic to very realistic field or sea exercises. Although war games have been played for centuries,[4] it is the advent of high speed computers that has extended the utility of gaming. Examples of the new generation of war games include the Navy Electronic Warfare simulator (Naval Aviation News, 1959;

---

[4] For example, the German and the Japanese Army Commands have employed chess-like games for training in strategy (Kriegspiel, Go).

Robertson, 1957), the Operations Research Office (ORO, The Johns Hopkins University) games, such as SAM (effectiveness of alternative multibattery air defense systems against aerial attack), ZIGSPIEL (post-attack mobilization model), and logistic simulation (Harrison & Walker, 1957). War gaming of a classified nature is currently under way at RAND, CORG, and PROJECT MICHIGAN.

Military games of the sort cited above relate to training involving tactical or strategic problem solving in a simulated war environment. Games with this training objective represent only a small part of the value of gaming technique in the military environment. A wide variety of jobs in the military setting can be identified in which games can be used effectively for training. Edwards (1957) holds that gaming techniques are particularly suitable for training in procedural tasks and for decision tasks in which the skills and knowledges needed for the task may or may not be known. Different game characteristics are required, depending on the class of task. A significant contribution to gaming research has been the former Air Force Personnel and Training Research Center program of research on the nature of decision making and the teaching of generalizable decision-making skills (Edwards, 1957). This program has recognized that the one constant factor in the variety of decision-making tasks is the set of skills people use to make decisions, and has identified certain human skills which are believed to be common to all decision-making tasks. At least some of these skills can be most effectively taught by the use of gaming technique.

Illustrative of attempts at using gaming technique for both research and training purposes is a simple operational game derived from radar air traffic control (Kinkade & Kidd, 1959). The game was designed to investigate information processing and decision making in the air traffic control context. The performance of single individuals and two-man teams with and without intercommunication was compared.

*Malfunction Location (Tasks and Problems).* A serious problem in maintenance training today is providing individuals having relatively limited technical training and educational background with a practical understanding of the functioning of complex electronic systems so that malfunctions can be quickly located and remedied. These complexities have stimulated the development of techniques for training and for analyzing and evaluating the performance of individuals engaged in electronic equipment maintenance. These techniques include new ways for training in maintenance and new methods for studying equipment maintenance behavior. Trouble shooting consists of making a series of checks or tests that localize a fault usually to a replaceable component. The essential decision-making element consists of determining what checks need to be made in converging on a solution. The selection of successive checks that maximize the information obtained per check in localizing the trouble is subject to logical rules, hence logical criteria. The actual making of the check itself may be thought of as a procedure independent of the logical processes of selecting successive test points. This is the underlying foundation of most "simulations" of the trouble-shooting requirement, whether the simulation is with diagrams and paper and pencil or with equipment which permits the making of artificial checks and tests. The rationale behind training with this kind of simulation is that the decision-making element is separated from the ancillary procedures which in the real situation separates decisions from outcomes and from other decisions by so much time and intervening activity that the trainee has little opportunity to learn decision-making strategy as such. The acts of decision making are weakened in training value by time and intervening activities irrelevant to the logical problem. By eliminating this irrelevance during phases of training and bringing these decisions, their consequences and logical implications, closer together in time, the trainee can better learn and practice strategy rules.

Several basic techniques for accomplishing trouble-shooting training have been utilized. One way has been to employ "right-wrong" feedback, in which the trainee is informed whether or not his response (selected from among several) is correct for a given stimulus situation. Another way has been to set up malfunction symptoms in an equipment and to provide the trainee with checking procedures and information about status of circuitry, etc., so that he may locate the fault in the equipment. A third way has emphasized generalized trouble-shooting training based on the belief that analytical skills will transfer to specific trouble-shooting situations. A continuing development is that of formalizing procedures (strategy rules) for efficient trouble shooting. The principle is that of choosing a sequence of checks which maximize the average information obtained from each successive check. The teaching of such strategies may eliminate the need for maintenance personnel to know electronics principles, requiring only that they be able to read flow diagrams and make test readings (Miller, et al., 1953). Evidence indicates that strategy in fault location taught in principle and utilizing abstract material has transfer value to specific situations

(Miller & Slebodnick, 1958). (Such techniques are discussed in some detail by Bryan in Chapter 10.)

Within this framework for maintenance training, a variety of synthetic equipment has been developed, employing a great many variables in assessing performance. Essentially, the evaluation has been in terms of the number of correct solutions to problems or locations of malfunctions, and the relative efficiency of the procedures used. Performance measures have included the number of problems solved, number of checks made, number of replacements, performance time, quality of checks, use of references, use of test equipment, use of information available from symptoms and/or checks, and errors. The varieties of trouble-shooting tests are subsumed here under the following gross groupings: (*a*) pencil and paper tests, (*b*) performance tests, (c) automatic recording of checks (ARC) tests, and (*d*) simulator tests. This scheme follows closely that developed by Fattu and his associates (Fattu, 1956; Standlee, Popham, & Fattu, 1956).

Paper and pencil tests are a commonly used form of trouble-shooting test and represent a useful way of measuring knowledge. They are, however, not well suited to measuring the structure of a complete solution in a trouble-shooting task. Their format is not flexible enough to elicit adequate samples of performance, but they appear to be useful in measuring individual steps in the trouble-shooting process. Representative tests of this sort are described in the reports listed as references. [5]

Performance tests attempt to reproduce the relevant and critical task aspects. Their advantages are that they structure and control both the task and the situations in which they occur, emphasize accurate appraisal of technical skills, and provide a high degree of realism and a closer relation to job-like measurement. Their disadvantages include equipment costs, testing costs and excessive time requirements which as a consequence, permit only limited sampling of tasks per individual. [6]

Automatic recording of checks (ARC) tests attempt to translate some of the features of actual equipment trouble shooting into paper and pencil form. The feature of this type of test is that the information

[5]Demaree, Crowder, Morrison, & Majesty, 1954; Fattu, Bern, Stunkard, & Standlee, 1956; French, 1956b; Glaser, Hahn, & Phillips, 1954; Grings, Rigney, Bond, & Summers, 1953b; Saupe, 1955.

[6]Besnard & Briggs, 1956; Demaree, Crowder, & Morrison, 1955; Rulon, Langmuir, Schweiker, Demaree, Crowder, & Sawrey, 1954; Saupe, 1955; Siegel, Jensen, & Danzig, 1955; Vineberg, 1955.

to be gained from check procedures is concealed until a cover is removed by the performer (i.e., a tab torn off, a capsule removed, covering material erased, paper perforated, etc.). This technique provides an automatic recording of the number of checks made and also immediate feedback of performance information to the individual. ARC tests have greater realism than paper and pencil instruments but less realism than simulation tests, since verbal description must replace physical simulation throughout. There are, however, similarities between this type of test and the equipment type of test. In both instances the trainee uses the same reference materials, and the same intellectual aspects of checkpoint selection are present. However, the ARC item restricts the number of units that can be replaced and the number of checks made. Most of the possible relevant checks are included so that the effect of this restriction is to limit the possible errors that can be made. Thus realism suffers in the ARC item. Both types of tests are somewhat similar in the diagnostic skills required. Representative ARC tests are described in the references listed below.[7]

Simulator trouble-shooting tests are simplified representations of real equipment. The advantages of trouble-shooting instruments of this sort are the degree of realism achieved and the simplicity of their functioning. In most cases a variety of malfunctions can be inserted into the device with relative ease. They also provide for automatic recording of behavior, and, in many instances, scoring methods have been devised that summarize the information in the behavior record. Aside from the testing or assessment value of this class of device, it also possesses great training potential. The scope is broad enough to provide practice for the range of trouble-shooting skills required in the operational situation, and it appears that they provide more efficient trouble-shooting training than any form of teaching available, with perhaps the exception of individual tutoring. Representative of this type of test are the references listed below.[8]

---

[7]Cantor & Brown, 1956; Demaree, et al., 1954; Glaser & Phillips, 1954; Glaser, Damrin, & Gardner, 1954.

[8]Briggs, 1956; Briggs, Besnard, & Walker, 1955; Bryan, Bond, LaPorte, & Summers, 1954; Bryan, Bond, LaPorte, & Hoffman, 1956; French, 1956a; Grings, Rigney, Bond, & Summers, 1953a; Rulon & Schweiker, 1956; Warren, Atkins, Ford, & Wolbers, 1955.

COMPLEX DEVICES THAT PROVIDE OPPORTUNITIES FOR SYSTEM TRAINING

People often are asked to function as components in a dynamic man-machine system. Training for such system tasks requires the use of devices which simulate machine dynamics. The dynamic devices for training research cited in this category include both real-time computers for solving the dynamics of a task situation and actual equipments from complex systems. One major difference between these devices and management or war gaming devices is that the latter usually may operate in fast time (i.e., events happen much more rapidly than in real life) whereas the former usually must operate in real time.

The increasing complexity of current and future systems, with attendant work space problems, reduced error tolerances, unique environmental conditions and qualitatively superior performance requirements, has made necessary an increased reliance on simulation techniques in training. In certain instances, simulation may be the *only* way to train for and to evaluate aspects of future systems. Simulators are adjustable to a variety of task conditions and, as such, are able to duplicate the whole range of task conditions predicted for the operational situation. The precision in control that dynamic simulation offers permits great variation in task conditions which, in turn, enables a greater freedom in manipulating the learning process. Also, the critical training conditions can be duplicated while bypassing the routine and easy. This emphasizes both the saving of time and the attendance to central features of the task. An important and crucial aspect of dynamic simulation is that it makes possible, with a high degree of fidelity, the representation of stressful and unique environmental conditions that are found or may occur in the operational context (for example, space flight). Simulation techniques are also useful in performance evaluation. They make possible a variety of proficiency measures that heretofore have been difficult or impossible to obtain. System performance limits can be assessed, high system loadings and overloading (breakdown point) can be determined, and measures of integrated team performance can be obtained. (See Chapter 8 by Gagné.)

Devices of this sort have additional training features, for they afford the trainee the opportunity to try out novel ways of reacting and to learn about aspects of the task that are obscure without this flexibility. The trainee is provided with the opportunity for making serious errors and experiencing the consequences and for practicing emergency procedures. With specific reference to ballistic missiles systems, they provide a systems exercising capability. The mark of success in systems of this sort is that they need never be operationally utilized (i.e., the philosophy of a deterrent force). Except for occasional confidence firing, the operational weapon system may never proceed through the full course of the combat cycle, yet, at any moment, the system must be ready to operate at peak efficiency. The innovations to follow will be discussed in terms of the type of task situation to which they relate. They are subsumed under tasks involving: (*a*) perceptual and perceptual-motor control, (*b*) decision making and management, and (*c*) intellectual skills.

## Perceptual and Perceptual-Motor Control Tasks

*Human Centrifuge.* Centrifuges are capable of simulating most of the range of g-forces predicted for manned space vehicles (with the exception of sustained zero-g), enabling the collection of much performance data on the ground before man actually travels into space. A variety of stressful situations can be investigated, including sound and vibration effects, the influence of tumbling, behavior in artificial atmospheres under conditions of confinement and reduced sensory input as well as monotonous and unchanging sensory stimulation, prolonged artificial centrifugal gravity, and short-term lack of gravitational stimuli to the homestatic system of man. One of the features of devices of this sort is the ability to simulate performance conditions involving the variable of acceleration. Linear and angular accelerations can reduce the efficiency of motor performance and may completely incapacitate an operator. Also, the simulation of vehicle motions provides a variety of cues, obtainable no other way, that have utility for the training sequence. These events heretofore have not been experienced by man.

One of the most sophisicated devices of this sort is the Navy's human centrifuge at Johnsville, Pa.[9] Research investigations with this device have been concerned with pilot tolerance studies, pilot control studies utilizing centrifuge closed loop control, and control functions in the X-15 research vehicle. Research efforts include the study of problems of re-entry from orbit to determine the capabilities and limitations of human control of a vehicle under high sustained accelerations, and also the investigation of the optimum utilization of a pilot during boost into orbit. Of importance here are the definition of minimum

---

[9]Aviation Medical Acceleration Laboratory, U. S. Naval Air Development Center, Johnsville, Pennsylvania (in conjunction with the U. S. National Advisory Committee for Aeronautics).

and desirable stability and damping characteristics for the vehicle, comparison of pilot performance under both direct and command-type control systems, information presentation requirements, and emergency techniques (Brown & Collins, 1958; Woodling & Clark, 1959). Another representative device for investigating perceptual motor control is the U. S. Air Force-owned centrifuge located at Convair Astronautics Division, San Diego, California. This omni-environmental test facility (centrifuge and a space chamber) can simulate, during the flight cycle (launching, orbiting, and re-entry), acceleration, oscillation, tumbling, vibration, noise, heat, and hypobaria, as well as confinement and isolation.

*Complex Simulation Equipment.* The dynamic devices represented here are examples of a class of equipment that realistically simulate a variety of system parameters. As such, they are highly useful for training and the evaluation and measurement of continuous tasks where performance involves a continuously changing response to a continuously changing stimulus, and where responses are in terms of continuous operator adjustments to error changes.

Fitts and his former associates at Ohio State University (under support from Air Force Personnel and Training Research Center) carried out an operational analysis of a specific Air Force system, the F-86D Aircraft plus an airborne E-4 fire control system (Harter & Fitts, 1956). The system was represented approximately by use of a commercial analog computer. A series of tracking training experiments was carried out on issues of the fidelity of simulation such as the inclusion of realistic "visual noise" on the target position display and the effects of training with different stick forces. This Ohio State group has also developed a portable simplified electronic tracking apparatus (SETA) (Gain & Fitts, 1959). It contains three computer units, a built-in problem generator, timer, compensatory display and scoring meter (integrated absolute value of error). The apparatus can be used together with external controls, displays, problem-generators or recorders and two or more can be gauged to provide a two- or three-dimensional task.

Another example of this type of activity is the Dunlap and Associates, Inc., program of research (under support of the U. S. Naval Training Device Center) on the study of trainable aspects of tracking performance and the functional characteristics of devices for this kind of training. They have dynamically simulated tracking tasks for submarine control and have constructed a general tracking trainer which may be useful in training an operator to control any vehicle wherein he does not see the real world but rather some analogs displayed visually (Kelley, Bowen, Ely, & Channell, 1958).

Dynamic real-time simulators tend to become quite complex and expensive especially when high-speed computers are employed to represent dynamic features. An innovation of promise for wide-scale research is evidenced in attempts to eliminate much of the complexity and expense of this type of simulation while still retaining the essential features. Fitts, under support from the Air Force Office of Scientific Research (previously cited in the section on team training), has developed a relatively simple and versatile dynamic system simulator. Counters are used to provide numerical displays which can represent an almost endless variety of system variables. The experimenter or the subjects who work in the simulated system can affect the rate of change of individual counters, thus simulating the movement of vehicles, change in external conditions, etc. The simulator has been used to represent a logistics system. The task may be set up for individual solution, or groups of subjects may collaborate in task problem solving.

Within the area of skill development in driver training, a variety of devices and techniques have been developed to achieve optimum integration of the operator with the vehicle. Representative of this concern are the studies carried out by McFarland (1958), who developed an instrumented system to provide graphic records of driver actions which are analyzable in terms of frequency, rate, extent and duration of specific responses. Learner,[10] at the General Motors Technical Center, has utilized a high-speed digital computer for obtaining measures of driver performance such as frequency and amplitude components of response, the degree of anticipatory responses, and how responses change over time as a function of training. He has also developed a driving simulator which permits the operator to observe road geometry ahead of the vehicle.

*Perceptual Training.* In many types of motor skills, the learning of perceptual relations is of great significance to task mastery. Skill learning to a large extent is determined by the complexity of the stimulus situation to which the learner must react rather than the demands made on his motor capacities. This has been demonstrated in a variety of studies on stimulus generalization and predifferentiation (Smode, Beam, & Dunlap, 1959). An important class of innovations relates to the

---

[10]Personal communication from David Learner, General Motors Technical Center.

understanding of the perceptual side of skill training specifically to the extent to which we can determine the important perceptual cues in training. It appears that learning can be facilitated by emphasizing training on selected cue families abstracted from the operational stimulus context (Miller, 1953b). Critical sources of information are abstracted from the total stimulus complex. These necessary and sufficient cues for task performance are presented as the stimulus inputs to the trainee.

A variety of devices have demonstrated this concept. Representative of this is the program of Williams and his co-workers (Bell, 1951; Brown, Matheny, & Flexman, 1950; Payne, Dougherty, Hasler, Skeen, Brown, & Williams, 1954), who have trained student pilots to make simulated aircraft landings based on perceptual relations in landing. They devised a method of projecting the image of a runway that changed in perspective as a function of aircraft position in relation to it. This projection was tied in with a Link trainer to simulate the actual perspective cues associated with landing an aircraft.

## Devices Used in Decision Making and Management Tasks

A variety of existing problem-solving and decision-making devices have utility for training and research. One such class of equipment involves gaming technique which employs realistic dynamic devices for simulating decision-making environments. Representative examples in management gaming are the complex, interactive total enterprise games which involve electronic computers. Their counterparts in the military environment are the computerized war games.

Complex trouble-shooting simulator tests represent another class of problem-solving devices. Examples here include the Malfunction and Circuitry trainers (MAC) (French, Crowder, & Tucker, 1956; French, 1956a; French & Martin, 1957), the Multiple Alternative Symbolic Trouble-Shooting tests (MASTS and AUTOMASTS) (Bryan, et al., 1954; Grings, et al., 1953a; Grings, et al., 1953b), AIR Force equipment simulators and subject matter trainers (Besnard, Briggs, & Walker, 1955; Briggs, 1956; Rulon & Schweiker, 1956) and the Generalized Electronic Trouble-Shooting Trainer (GETS) (Warren, et al., 1955).

Attempts are underway to develop general problem-solving devices for research in decision making. Representative of this general class is the PSI apparatus developed by John and his associates and employed in a program of research by Rapoport at the University of Michigan, Mental Health Research Institute (Gyr, 1959; John, 1956; Rapoport,

1958). In brief, the device is a board containing nine bulbs arranged in a circle with a tenth bulb in the center. Control buttons affect certain lights in terms of three specified relations (activate, activate in conjunction with another button, inhibit). The task is to discover a sequence of moves that will obtain an end objective (lighting the center bulb). The apparatus provides a logical problem-solving task that places several demands on the performer. Initial moves provide information that is necessary for reaching a solution (such as which control operations affect which displays); subsequent moves can be used to test hypotheses based on logical reasoning. Problems may vary greatly in level of difficulty. Besides individual application, the apparatus has been used extensively in studies of group problem solving, and has been adapted for use as a selection device by the Psychological Corporation.

The Ohio State University has devoted effort to the design and construction of a general purpose decision-making simulator.[11] This device, concerned with information processing and control (IPAC), is utilized in a program of research to obtain basic data on group behavior in problem-solving decision-making task situations.

*Teaching Machines and Other Devices Used for*
*Training in Intellectual Skills*

Automated teaching involves the use of a machine or other device which provides a display of the material to be acquired, a means for responding to the material and a means of presenting feedback of the results of performance, based on the device's capability for response assessment. This way of instruction permits a high level of control in the manipulation of learning variables and in the management of the learning process. Devices of this sort enable the preparation and presentation of text materials in discrete program steps or units, require active participation of the learner during all stages in the learning process, make possible the ordering of programmed material into progressive conceptual units to take the learner to high levels of proficiency in a given subject, provide immediate and relevant feedback of performance information to the trainee, and allow learning to progress at an optimal rate for each individual. These instruments, adaptable to a wide range of intelligence, also have unique capabilities for response assessment and may be regarded as self-motivating, providing a high degree of intrinsic job satisfaction to the user.

[11]Personal communication from George Briggs, Laboratory of Aviation Psychology, Ohio State University.

Devices employed in automated teaching range from simple instructional materials and paper and pencil tasks through small electromechanical devices to digital computation machines. The important features are that all or some of the tutoring functions are provided by automated sequences of instruction that are prepared in advance of use and are capable of effective instruction when presented to the learner. Examples of classes of automated teaching devices are presented in the subsequent sections. These selected devices clearly exemplify the major differences of opinion on the crucial factors involved in optimizing the learning process. Nevertheless, all these pioneering researches are aimed at optimizing the effectiveness of automated teaching. It should be apparent that the problems of teaching effectiveness are identified most closely with problems associated with programming, rather than with the particular type of "hardware" employed in automated teaching devices.

Systematic research on automated teaching can be traced to the early work of Pressey, which began in the 1920's and has continued to the present decade. His early work resulted in several devices for the automatic testing of intelligence and information. In his later work, Pressey (1950) developed a punchboard device for the immediate self-scoring of objective examinations. Punchboards of this type (Angell, 1949; Peterson, 1930; Pressey, 1950), Tab tests (Glaser, et al., 1954), and programmed textbooks (Crowder, 1958; Glaser, Homme, & Evans, 1960) are essentially non-mechanical automated teaching devices. They are not truly teaching machines, for they do not have the machine capability for adequate control of feedback information and program progression.

The current status of teaching machines is in good part due to the work of Skinner. Based upon the critique of earlier self-scoring devices and experiences with his early machines, Skinner (1958) has specified several important features that he views as minimal requirements for effective teaching machines. An important requirement is that the learner must compose his response rather than select it from a set of alternatives such as found in a multiple-choice device. One reason for this is that recall rather than recognition is desired; another reason is that effective multiple-choice material must contain plausible wrong responses which are out of place in the process of shaping behavior because they strengthen non-desired responses. Another requirement is that the trainee must be taken through a sequence of steps carefully designed to minimize the probability of incorrect responses. Each step must be small enough that it can always be taken, yet, in so doing, the trainee moves ever closer to the desired behavior. This refers to Skinner's belief in providing stimulus support to insure that the trainee does not make many errors during initial learning. The purpose of giving many stimulus cues is to insure that the desired response will be made. Once the correct response is made, it can be reinforced and, slowly over time, the superfluous stimuli can be removed. Work is also underway at the University of California at Los Angeles to construct an improved version of the Skinner machine. It has provisions for displaying a graphic record of progress to the learner so that he can compete with his antecedent performance in the course of learning geometric concepts (Coulson, Jensen, & Silberman, 1959). Several machines have been constructed having the required characteristics previously set forth (Edwards, 1957; Skinner, 1958), and a series of experiments are being conducted with school children aimed at developing associative discriminative skills and concepts of form, class, numbers, spatial arrangements, etc. (Corrigan, 1959). Lately, a variety of portable teaching machines have been put on the market. One machine being commercially considered is the Solartron Electronic Group's "thinking" electronic teacher (Solartron Electronic Group, 1959). The device is stated to be able to take punch card operators from initial stages of training to a degree of skilled performance. As proficiency is attained, the lessons set by the machine become progressively more difficult.

While a great deal of effort has gone into machines using "single track" programs of the kind just discussed, other significant work has been devoted to intrinsic or multiple-choice programming. This programming is intrinsic in that alternative programs of instruction are so built into the material that the learner automatically selects the appropriate program as a consequence of his immediately preceding behavior. The technique does not depend on elaborate programming mechanisms or even the learner's self-evaluation of his response. Within this framework, Crowder (1958) has developed an automatic tutoring device which is a simple teaching instrument in book form called a "scrambled book." The material a student sees next is dependent upon the response he makes to a multiple-choice question. If one can presume the student's answer is determined by his level of knowledge at the time of choice, then it appears that the scrambled book is geared to the individual since it adapts the program of material to the student's present state of knowledge. Practical application of intrinsic programming has been devoted to teaching electronic trouble shooting (Besnard, et al.,

1955) also to trigonometry, number theory and the card game of bridge. This technique has value for training research, for it appears that as much is learned by making mistakes as by obtaining correct answers.

The System Development Corporation (Coulson, et al., 1959) has embarked on a program of research devoted to the study of suitable subject matter for teaching machines, effective display of items and provision for knowledge of results, and the motivational aspects arising in the use of this type of device. A prime goal is to compare relative advantages of "single-track programs, branching programs and differential treatment based upon diagnostic testing." Future efforts may conceivably expand the field of automated teaching by utilizing machines in decision-making skills and adapting automated techniques to group learning. A comprehensive source book of work in the field of teaching machines and programmed learning is now available (Lumsdaine & Glaser, 1960).

## New Ways of Establishing and/or Controlling the Working Environment

It is generally agreed that in the near future man will be expected to function in situations increasingly hostile to his well-being, involving increases in the variety and magnitude of stresses caused by environmental factors. The study of human behavior under these conditions becomes increasingly and proportionately important. Unique ways for permitting and improving training and adaptation are required to permit the individual to experience in the practice environment the event predicted for the operational situation. The innovation for research here is the duplication of the task environment and the systematic introduction and control of the stress events in order to determine the types and extent of training required to handle the situation. The stressor agents may involve excessive loads on the operator, invoked by personal danger or hazard, the occurrence of problems requiring unusual and complex decision making, or emergency situations which give rise to additional task demands and which may involve the element of danger. The stressor agents may also involve "underloading" the operator, that is, stimulation below the level required for adequate and intact functioning such as may occur in situations characterized as deprived in sensory inputs in an isolated environment.

### The Simulation of Space Flight

The commitment of complex advanced systems for space travel presents training problems for which solutions cannot be readily found within our present knowledge. No single simulator has been devised to investigate man's performance in unusual and hostile environments. Essentially there is a variety of task and measurement situations. However, progress is being made in the realistic simulation of all the special conditions of true space journey. At the Aero Medical Laboratory (Wright Air Development Center) research aircraft fly Keplerian trajectories. Also, near frictionless surfaces have been developed and used to study some of the problems of men working under zero-g conditions. A person who is seated on a frictionless seat, for example, may be required to do maintenance. Similarly, a water immersion zero-g simulator has been developed by National Aeronautics and Space Administration, Langley Air Force Base.

A prime example of additional work in this area is the on-going development of human centrifuges and space chambers and acceleration and motion simulators which currently can simulate most aspects of space flight, the notable exceptions being zero gravity and ionizing radiation. Another example can be seen in proposals for ideal space flight simulators, such as the suggestion of a rocket-assisted balloon-borne capsule (Beson, 1959). Such envisaged equipment could produce the conditions peculiar to space flight, including launch shock, flight control, re-entry, recovery, and psychological stress.

*Stress*

The increasing complexity of new weapons systems has imposed an increase in task-induced stresses on the operator. These pressures are brought to bear on the operator due to excessive demands arising in the task situation. It is conceivable that future task characteristics will require the operator to perform a large number of different functions involving a complex of skillful responses as well as simple discrete responses. (See Chapter 7 by Deese.) The requirements for the detection and interpretation of signals will become more precise and the rate of performance will become more variable, involving intermittent periods of responding and controlling as well as monitoring. The sequences of response will be based in part on the out-of-tolerance conditions of automated equipment which may be basically unpredictable.

A program of research at the USAF School of Aviation Medicine, Randolph AFB, Texas has used task environments having characteristics mentioned above.[12] They have developed a simulator for use in a re-

---

[12]Personal communication from Bryce Hartman, USAF School of Aviation Medicine.

search program on the experimental analyses of factors contributing to the functional disruption of operator effectiveness arising from operational stresses. The simulator has the capability of creating a variety of task-induced time pressure and load pressure stresses. Both objective behavioral and psychophysiological measurement techniques are employed. A number of other laboratories (such as those at the Aero Medical Laboratory [Wright Air Development Center] and the Georgia Division of Lockheed Aircraft) are working on similar problems.

A program of research on task-induced stress has begun at the Mental Health Research Institute, University of Michigan, for the systematic investigation of information overload in task performance. The military services have accepted the importance of inducing stress in the training situation as a means of facilitating performance in the operational context. A well-known example is the Air Force pilot training in emergency procedures. The Army is employing stress training (HumRRO, task FIGHTER) (Human Resources Research Office, 1959), the assumption being that training under selected stressful situations will better prepare the soldier for combat. The use of drugs for inducing stress (Lanzetta, Wendt, Langham, & Haefner, 1956) also appears promising for research on task behavior under conditions of high stress and emergency. Effective use of this technique, however, waits on refinements in drug technology.

## Confinement, Isolation and Sensory Deprivation

A good deal of effort has been devoted to problems associated with training under conditions of excess, such as cold, heat and hunger. It is reasonable to assume that training value exists in the converse of the above, that is, in situations imposing a lack of stimulation. It is generally believed that a constant and adequate level of sensory stimulation is required for the maintenance of normal intelligent adaptive behavior. What happens to performance when the sensory inputs to man fall below this "adequate" level? The emergence of tasks involving reduced levels of sensory stimulation and the human problems anticipated in space travel have generated a growing concern for new ways for training in situations characterized as deprived in sensory inputs to the operator.

Although the U. S. Navy has long been interested in the problem of confinement in submarine crews, the systematic experimental approach to the study of sensory deprivation in humans is relatively recent in origin, dating from the work stated by Hebb and his associates at Mc-

Gill University (Bexton, Heron, & Scott, 1954; Heron, 1957; Heron, Doane, & Scott, 1956). Previous to this, the data have come from animal studies and from anecdotal and autobiographical reports from humans. These reports from real life experiences indicate that mental abnormalities such as hallucinations, delusions and disorientation may emerge when the individual is isolated for extended periods of time in a restricted or monotonously repetitive environment (Bombard, 1954; Byrd, 1938; Wheaton, 1959). More recently it has been recognized that the technique of "brainwashing" involves solitary confinement for extended periods of time with deliberate impoverishment of sensory stimulation to the individual (Schein, 1956).

Essentially, the sensory deprivation studies emphasize the features of social isolation and reduced or constrained sensory stimulation. Studies employing reduced sensory stimulation have immersed subjects in tepid water (Lilly, 1956) and confined them in dark soundproofed (tomb-like) cubicles (Vernon, McGill, & Schiffman, 1958). Studies involving non-patterning of stimuli have emphasized the reduction of variability in sensory stimulation. The conditions of confinement have required subjects to wear translucent goggles and ear plugs to occlude visual and auditory stimuli; to wear gauntlets, gloves or cuffs on the hands and arms to reduce tactile stimulation; and to lie still in a supine position to minimize kinesthetic and positional cues (Bexton, et al., 1954; Heron, et al., 1956; Heron, 1957; Solomon, Leiderman, Mendelson, & Wexler, 1957). Studies imposing the structuring of stimuli have mainly been clinical in orientation and have investigated the effects of isolation in polio respirators (Freedman, Grunebaum, & Greenblatt, 1958; Leiderman, Mendelson, Wexler, & Solomon, n.d.; Solomon, Wexler, Mendelson, Leiderman, & Kubzansky, n.d.). All of these studies of humans subjected to various forms of confinement show radical behavioral changes under what appear to be relatively innocuous conditions. These studies have been oriented toward the collection of behavioral data under conditions of confinement and isolation. A single essentially immobile subject is required to do nothing but "wait out" the time of the experimental session. The generalizations obtained here are not wholly applicable to the training environment. In the operational situation, emphasis is placed on behavior under conditions of minimal sensory input of a monotonous unchanging nature rather than upon the deprivation of sensory stimulation per se in a task-less environment (for example, space flight, protracted submarine voyages, automobile driving on superhighways, etc.). The individual will be mobile, may be in the company of other individuals, and presumably will perform a variety of tasks, primarily of a monitoring nature, in a monotonous environment. Nevertheless, the laboratory data are important inputs to a body of training knowledge in this area of sensory underloading. It may be necessary to provide opportunities for training under conditions of reduced stimulation so that the trainee may experience these events and develop tolerances to the ill effects in order for him to perform effectively under these severe conditions.

Research on confinement and isolation has begun in the military context in order to facilitate training in this area, and representative examples are cited below. HumRRO is particularly interested in techniques for resisting an enemy's use of coercive confinement and conversely, confinement to obtain information from the enemy, and methods for improving vigilance and effectiveness in monotonous surroundings. The research (Project ENDORSE) investigates the effects of sustained sensory deprivation and social isolation upon behavior. Of interest are changes in behavior as a function of isolation, and the clarification of the role of isolation in complex learning (Human Resources Research Office, 1959). A program of research conducted by Ruff, Levy and Thaler (Duddy & Dempsey, 1961; Levy, Ruff, & Thaler, 1959; Ruff, 1959; Ruff, Levy, & Thaler, n.d.) at the Aero Medical Laboratory, Wright Patterson AFB, is currently investigating the significant variables in isolation and sensory deprivation as they relate to the selection, training and protection of future space crews. One group of investigations is devoted to the study of prolonged confinement under simulated operational conditions. A second group of experiments is more basic, investigating the stimuli, supplies and structuring that are necessary for effective functioning. These groups of experiments not only involve the quantity, modality and patterning of physical stimuli that impinge on the subject, but also personality, motivation and background variables. Isolation in the Arctic has been also the subject of study by the military (e.g., Eilbert, Glaser, & Hanes, 1957).

## New Ways of Measuring the Progress and Outcomes of Training

Many new problems in measurement have arisen as a result of recent training problems; new measures have been evolved, in part as a result of these specific new problems, in part as a result of work on old problems or on measurement topics per se. New measurement techniques have a variety of implications for improving training. A measure may solve a specific training problem, may be employed as a means of knowledge of results to the trainee, or be useful in guidance. Even in instances where a measure is difficult to obtain and cannot be used routinely in training, it may still have applicability for research designed to improve training. The following section is organized in a way that permits the discussion to range from non-parametric, "free activity" measures to precise quantitative measurement techniques.

## NEW WAYS OF OBSERVING AND RECORDING FREE ACTIVITY BEHAVIOR

The techniques for observation cited here make possible the investigation of training efficiency in novel ways. In some instances, these techniques permit extension of the range of instructor influence where heretofore observation has been difficult. Both individual and group observation techniques are cited.

### Observation Techniques

New ways for observing behavior have been developed that appear promising for improving training, for example, the use of closed-loop television. The use of infrared recording techniques is also worth mentioning, and although at present these are limited, perhaps with refinements may prove valuable in performance evaluation.

Another potentially fruitful approach in observing the progress and outcomes of training is to be found in the application of participant-observation techniques (Festinger & Katz, 1953; Whyte, 1951). This mode of observation involves the participation of a trained observer in the network of social interactions among trainees. Often the observer's objectives may be concealed, but they need not be. Among the special advantages of this method are the location of factors suppressing the latent efficiency of team performances, and the covert extension of evaluation procedures *beyond* the formal training and testing phase.

### Group Observations

The mass of data accumulating on social interaction in the group or team setting appears to offer fine research possibilities for the study of team structure and process. The current varieties of research on communication networks, group composition, the effects of groups upon its members, and problems of leadership style (Gilchrist, 1959) hold out promising leads for the improvement of team training. One of the current difficulties in assessing team performance is lack of adequate measuring techniques. This is due, in part, to difficulty in specifying task characteristics and general categories of behavior for working groups. This shortcoming has generated a variety of research (Glaser, Glanzer, & Morten, 1955; Glaser & Glanzer, 1958; McGrath, 1958; Roby & Lanzetta, 1958).

Two general methods for manipulating the test situation have been employed in team activity. These can be descriptively called the overload method and the subtraction method (Glanzer & Glaser, 1955). In the overload method, successively greater work loads are imposed upon the team. Performance efficiency is related to the amount of load. This technique is useful for determining optimum system loading, system breakdown points, and changes in team organization as a function of system loading. It has been successfully employed in the System Development Corporation program of Air Defense system studies (Alexander, 1959; Goodwin, 1957) and by Fitts in the study of air traffic control (Fitts, et al., 1958). The subtraction method holds the task load constant while manipulating the number of personnel in the team. Thus, the effects of personnel subtraction on team performance can be determined. The measures relate to team efficiency as a function of number of personnel, and the interchangeability of team personnel. These data are useful in setting up cross-training requirements and minimum and optimum personnel requirements in team activity.

A representative attempt to develop team measures is the work of Glaser and Glanzer at the American Institute for Research on the specification of dimensions of team structure and operation for Navy teams (Glanzer, et al., 1956; Glaser, 1958; Glaser, et al., 1955). This research has identified a number of descriptive variables for which measures can be obtained. These dimensions include input magnitude, activity level and complexity, degree of sequential activity, intra-team dependence and supervisory needs, speed and pressure requirements, saturation, and various communications variables.

## New Scoring and Recording Devices

New scoring and recording devices have introduced refinements in proficiency measurement as well as made possible new types of measurement heretofore unobtainable in the assessment of part task and overall performance. Features of devices of this sort include the capability for presenting diagnostic information as well as information useful in the critique of important task situations. In addition, they may serve as a useful adjunct to the teaching process. In some instances, a device may minimize instructor participation; in other instances, it may be of value only to the instructor.

## Recording Devices for Mass Communication

Instructional film has been employed for a number of years as a means of facilitating learning in the training situation primarily as a supplement to standard instructional techniques. At present, a good deal is known about optimizing the training effectiveness of instructional film. This has come about through the experimental study of the variables influencing learning and transfer. An example of systematic efforts in this regard is the instructional film research program in mass communication conducted at the Pennsylvania State University (Carpenter, Eggleton, John, & Cannon, 1950). Although the use of film technique in training is well established, certain unique applications are worthy of note. Lindahl's (1945) work in an industrial training program has shown the value of film for teaching a complex skill (contact disc cutting). New trainees who were taught cutting wheel operations by means of movement analysis films soon worked more efficiently than veteran operators formally untrained who had not been provided this performance information.

Film technique can be used for time compression. This procedure enables rapid playback of an activity that requires a great length of time to unfold and develop, thus emphasizing the dynamic continuity in a process that is not readily apparent in real time. It also represents an excellent means for providing knowledge of results by enabling the learner to see the total task situation develop. On the other hand, time expansion movies (slow motion) can be used as a critique of an operator's performance during important phases of task performance: details can be seen which escape observation at normal speeds of response. This technique has been used extensively in recording sporting events. The Naval Electronics Laboratory was one of the first to employ time compression movies, and they are currently being used in the SAGE system and Project MICHIGAN. Fitts employed this technique consistently in recording data from the program of research on Air Traffic Control (Fitts, et al., 1958; Schipper, et al., 1957).

Closed-loop television in conjunction with efficient recording techniques (such as videotape or kinescope) is another mass communication medium that has value both for training and research. It extends the range of instructor influence by providing close-up demonstration for large groups of observers. Attempts have been made to incorporate the dynamics of the classroom relationship into the TV presentation of surgical techniques (Thomas, 1958). This communication link overcomes somewhat the drawback of the instructor's necessary isolation from the students. Closed-loop television permits research that could not have been accomplished before, especially the evaluation of instructor influence in the teaching environment, and the effectiveness of various teaching procedures (Rock, Duva, & Murray, 1951; *Symposium on television training and training research*, 1952; see Chapter 9 by Lumsdaine).

## Scoring Devices

A variety of new scoring devices has been developed both for mass communication such as the classroom communicator (Carpenter, et al., 1950) and for individual scoring such as decade counters (Smode, 1958), self-scoring punchboards (Angell, 1949; Peterson, 1930; Pressey, 1950), and trouble-shooting devices (Cantor & Brown, 1956; Glaser, et al., 1954). These will be discussed in more detail in the last section of this chapter devoted to devices for providing information feedback.

A new technique for recording eye movements in performance is the Mackworth portable eye motion camera. Basically, the procedure employs film on which a white marker dot represents the fixation point of the eye. Initially, this was done by a television procedure (Mackworth & Mackworth, 1958). Since then much development work has been put into an alternative optical procedure based on a similar apparatus. This new optical equipment permits the recording of eye movements by means of a head-mounted movie camera and a periscope which superimposes the corneal reflection onto the scene picture.[13]

## MOTOR SKILL SCORING

In recent years research activity in the area of motor skills has concentrated on the development of quantitative analytical measures that reflect the nature of the underlying behavior processes. Two basic classes of measures employed in such investigations may be characterized as amplitude measures and frequency measures. These two types of measures are essentially independent. Conventionally, human tracking performance has been measured by means of some score derived from the

---

[13]Personal communication from Norman Mackworth, Dunlap and Associates, Inc.

magnitude or amplitude distribution of error. Scores definable by reference to the amplitude distribution of error include such measures as the standard deviation of the distribution, or root mean square (RMS) value, of the error; the average deviation of the error distribution, or integrated absolute error; and time-on-target scores. In such cases zero error is usually defined with respect to some external reference; it is not the mean or the subject's responses. In some instances, error amplitude and time-on-target scores have been employed in situations where their usage is unjustified, such as in comparing the shapes of learning curves. Some interesting relations have been developed by Fitts and his former associates at Ohio State University concerning the assumptions and usage of these two types of scores (Bahrick, Fitts, & Briggs, 1957; Fitts, Bennett, & Bahrick, 1956).

More recently the frequency characteristics of skilled motor performance have been viewed with growing interest by behavorial scientists. Frequency measures of extent of error indicate the rapidity of error changes independent of the magnitude of the error. Empirical data concerned with the determination of autocorrelation functions and the derivation of scores related to the frequency characteristics of tracking error are becoming more prominent in the literature. Frequency measures make possible new ways for doing training research by providing analytic indicants of behavior during the course of training. For example, frequency measures may be used to yield information on the amount of effort expended in performance. The two performances may be the same in terms of some mean amplitude score, yet the performances may be quite different in that in one case a significantly greater amount of effort was employed to achieve the same end score. Thus, a subject may be compensating for lack of skill by working harder at the job. Frequency measures provide also the ability for determining how the subject is achieving his performance by indicating the method used in problem solution. For instance, in a tracking task, it has been proposed that the subject who is thinking ahead (anticipatory reactions) would tend to make slow, low-frequency response movements, whereas the subject who is attending to immediate stimuli would tend to respond with fast high-frequency movements. At given stages of training, one method may be as good as the other in terms of some performance criterion, but anticipatory methods may be better in terms of ultimate level of proficiency. Frequency measures may also reveal important factors relating to fatigue, alertness, etc.

The measurement innovations, as represented by new frequency and amplitude measures, may aid training research by providing (a) better reliability in scoring, (b) more economical scores, (c) less artifacts in scoring, and (d) standardized scores having real meaning. Training research becomes more valuable to the extent that the outcomes of training can be assessed by standardized measures.

*Types of Frequency Measures*

Several possible approaches exist for analyzing the frequency characteristics of error. The simplest but least precise approach is the inspection of graphic records. The most precise and analytical approach is the power density spectrum, which is conventionally represented as a plot of the mean squared amplitudes against frequency. The technique has been employed over a period of years, predominantly by engineers, to determine the general characteristics of a class of continuous time functions such as music and speech. A discussion of the use of the power density spectrum in auditory research can be found in Licklider (1951). Recently, this technique has been utilized in analyzing the frequency characteristics of a motor task (Sutton, 1957).

The frequency characteristics of an ergodic signal can also be specified by an autocorrelation function which identifies periodicities in a time varying series by indicating the correlation of the series with itself at later times (Fitts, et al., 1956; Licklider, 1951). Autocorrelation offers an alternative approach in which the same information that is contained in the power density spectrum is presented as a continuous function in the time domain. This measure makes possible the estimation of the portion of the response that is periodic and the portion that is random, and also makes possible an analysis of the periodic portion of the subject's response. The autocorrelation function has been defined mathematically (Clark & Warren, 1953; Licklider, 1951), the mathematical relation between the autocorrelation function and the power density spectrum has been defined and the advantages obtained through the use of the autocorrelation technique set forth (Clark & Warren, 1953). Unfortunately, the use of the autocorrelation function in research has been restricted in the past because of the expense of building special purpose electronic equipment. Of the few special purpose correlating machines in existence, probably the most widely known correlator is located at the Massachusetts Institute of Technology. Several years ago, a photometric correlator was developed at the Ohio State Laboratory of Aviation Psychology for use in conjunction with electronic tracking equipment (Clark & Warren, 1953). This correlator makes possible the use of several quantitative analytical frequency measures and allows the direct interpretation of correlation functions without the necessity for further transformation. Another useful frequency measure is the crosscorrelation function. It differs from the autocorrelation function in that the two sets of values being correlated are derived from different time series.

Recent refinements in the direct recording of error signals (voltages) on magnetic tape and the transduction of continuous signals into digitalized data have made it possible to utilize high-speed digital computers in obtaining various frequency measures. This computational procedure will probably be used increasingly as researchers gain access to such general purpose equipment. They are being presently used at such places as the IBM Research Center and the General Motors Technical Center and at the University of Illinois.

## Analysis of Performance in Continuous Tasks

In the following discussion, methodological innovations in motor skill scoring will be cited. Because of their novelty, the primary emphasis is on frequency measures of performance, with some consideration for new ways of utilizing amplitude measures.

Techniques have been developed for improving instrumentation for manual control that have implications for tracking performance evaluation. Well known in this regard is the work of Birmingham and Taylor (1954) on quickened displays. This type of approach enables improvement in tracking by providing a prediction capability in control. This aid in predicting is reflected in lower amplitude scoring as well as in reducing the amount of effort in performance. A recent contribution in this area has been made by Kelley (1958) of Dunlap and Associates, Inc., who has developed a predictor instrument for manual control. It is designed to give the operator of a control system information about the future of the variable he is controlling. A special computing device gives the capability of extrapolating present conditions into the immediate future. The operator is enabled simply to correct potential errors before they actually occur by modifying what is predicted into what is desired.

A technique for equating problems of different difficulty levels has been developed by Dunlap and Associates, Inc., in a study of tracking training concerned with the scoring of performance in a simulated vehicle (Kelley, et al., 1958). Problems were developed, each of which required the operator to stabilize the vehicle (in this case, a submarine) at zero output. Scoring circuits accumulated the integral of the absolute value of error and/or the integral of error squared over the period of each trial. An automatic control system was employed in place of the operator, which developed a control signal based on a linear combination of the output and the derivative functions of output that are used for control. The entire system was then placed on an accelerated time base (one second = 100 seconds of real time). The automatic coefficients were adjusted to give a minimum score for each problem. This recorded score formed the standard against which human performance was compared. For each problem, the subject's score was that which exceeded the score of the automatic system. It should be noted that good human solutions may be smaller than the automatic linear system scores by virtue of non-linearities introduced by the operator. Ideally, the method would utilize minimum non-linear automatic system scores. These would represent the absolute minimum possible. They are, however, extremely difficult to obtain.

A significant contribution to the analytical measurement of motor performance has been made by Fitts and his group in the Laboratory of Aviation Psychology, Ohio State University (Fitts, et al., 1956). Their program of research has been concerned with the development of analytic measures of tracking behavior. In the main, the emphasis has been on tracking error rather than on response or stimulus patterns, since error is concerned with the relations between actual response and the desired response, and skill is generally based upon this relation rather than upon response patterns per se. The error scoring contributions made by this group include refinements in amplitude measures of error and the development and utilization of short cut or approximate frequency measures of error. This laboratory has developed electronic scoring devices which automatically provide RMS error, time-on-target, and transition error scores. The transition or crossing score gives an indication of on-target, off-target relations by scoring the number of times the error signal exceeds a specified plus or minus voltage. This score, when taken at any point other than at zero, is related both to the amplitude and the frequency distributions of error. Fitts and also Grant (at the University of Wisconsin) have been among the first to employ this score as a measure of tracking performance. Approximate scores that are most direct indicants of frequency are scores for zero crossing error, and zero crossings of the derivatives of error.

## New Ways for Analyzing Data from Learning Studies

Several classes of techniques that are refinements in derived statistical scores or new ways for specifying learning curves can be identified that have pertinence for research in training improvement. In the main, these techniques are refinements for attacking the ever-present problems that exist in evaluation and measurement.

### Correlation Technique

One of the problems in measurement is the inability to determine precisely at what level the individual starts in a training sequence, and hence the criterion of final grade may not adequately represent performance. To get around this, past researches have used crude gain score (difference between pre-training and post-training scores) as a measure of improvement. However, crude gain scores appear to be uncorrelated with aptitude measures and other measures of gain. Recently DuBois (DuBois & Manning, 1958; Manning & DuBois, 1958) has described an application of correlational analysis to the measurement of improvement, called residual gain score. In test validation, correlating aptitude measures with final grade may lead to spuriously high validity coefficients (due to test-wiseness, verbal facility, etc.). In contrast, residual gain is independent of and uncorrelated with initial status, hence may remove some of the non-appropriate variance from the criterion. When it is correlated with outside variables, the correlation is with gain defined as independent of initial status, rather than a mixed function, an unknown part of which is initial status. Thus, the residual gain criterion may be more realistic than the criterion of final standing in a training sequence. (For further discussion of this, see Chapter 3 by DuBois.)

### New Application of Factor Analysis to Learning

Within the framework of factor analysis, the work of Wherry[14] and that of Fleishman (1956b; 1958; Chapter 5) has raised questions concerning the nature of the criteria for learning. Analytical data have indicated that behavioral factors important in early stages of learning tend to change or drop out in later stages of learning a complex task, and new factors may enter. Where this progressive change of behavior factors is consistent for a task among trainees, it is desirable not only to identify them but to measure them in order to more precisely diagnose the progress of the trainee. Thus, a measure obtained at a stage of learn-

---

[14]Personal communication from Robert Wherry, Ohio State University.

ing may be more valid and useful than measures of the terminal criterion. This information may be important in the choice of instructional
material (and the form of the knowledge of results to the trainee) especially during transition phases from one qualitative pattern of behavior to another in the development of proficiency. One can expect
some disturbances in gross output by the trainee during such transitions.

A recent alternate approach to the analysis of the learning process is
the technique of simplicial analysis. Where factor analysis is concerned
with the molecular identification of elements, simplicial analysis is concerned with the learning profile and the molar discovery of structure. It
appears that this technique is useful for the identification of the valid
criteria for learning (DuBois, Manning, & Spies, 1959).

## New Ways for Specifying Learning Curves

One of the recurring problems in statistics is the adequate representation of interaction factors in performance. In the struggle to account for
these factors greater concern is being shown for patterning of responses
in the test situation. In the assessment of learning, final performance
measures or the sum of total performance measures are often inadequate. What is needed are measurements of patterns of growth. An innovation of promise here is techniques for specifying curves of learning. An example of this is the interest in trend tests (Grant, 1956).

## NEW WAYS OF PROVIDING KNOWLEDGE OF RESULTS

This final section of the chapter deals with recent views of the old problem of providing knowledge of results and reviews new ways that have
been developed for manipulating this procedural variable in task performance. It has been known for a long time that knowledge of results
facilitates task performance and makes task learning more interesting.
Analysis indicates that these effects are attributable to the major functions that knowledge of results subsumes, which include information
presentation, motivation, and reinforcement. Accordingly, the procedures and devices representing new ways for providing knowledge of results will be grouped in terms of these major functions. The treatment
is more historical in orientation than the previous sections, for the
discussion refers to much of what has gone before. Many of the innovations already cited have additional values attributable to knowledge
of results variables. For example, team training, games, or teaching machines are of themselves interesting and tend to sustain an adequate

level of motivation in the performer. Similarly, better scoring procedures will reflect true achievement levels, hence are more reliable. This may have the effect of maintaining adequate motivation in the trainee.

## INFORMATION FEEDBACK AS A FACTOR IN LEARNING

Knowledge of results has an important use as an indicator of performance goals either qualitatively, as reward or punishment, or quantitatively in an achievement context which tells the performer how the results of his responses conform to some objective reference. In the latter category refinements have been made, such as Miller's (1953b) distinction between learning feedback, which consists of cues or signals telling the trainee what he should have done at a given point in the task, and action feedback, which consists of cues or signals which tell the trainee what to do next in response to the changing demands of the task. Similarly, Annett and Kay distinguish between intrinsic feedback such as proprioceptive stimulation resulting from making motor responses, and augmented feedback such as that provided by the instructor or by a feedback circuit from a machine or training device (Smode, 1958). Generally, it is thought that achievement information feedback (a) increases the rate of improvement early in practice on a new task, (b) increases the level of performance in tasks that are highly overlearned, and (c) increases the frequency of reports that tasks are more interesting and less fatiguing as compared with conditions in which achievement information is withheld. (In addition, these three features, considered together, have led to the inference that knowledge of achievement has a motivating effect on behavior [Smode, 1958].)

A variety of procedures and devices for presenting information feedback that hold promise for training improvement have been recently developed. One of the significant new approaches for controlling operator performance level is the technique of augmented feedback which provides extra performance cues or information to the operator when his performance is within specified accuracy limits. In a study of tracking performance, Smode (1958) employed two levels of information feedback in a uniform one-dimensional tracking test. For the control conditions, information was presented verbally at trial termination; for the augmented conditions, achievement information was presented immediately as accrued, in small incremental steps through an audiovisual mode of presentation. The two schedules of information feedback differed with respect to (a) the amount of achievement information presented, (b) the sensory mode of information presentation, and (*c*) the temporal character of presentation. Augmented feedback was introduced by providing a decade counter which cumulated a time-on-target score during a tracking trial plus an auditory click; both feedback signals occurred at the rate of two per second when on target. Augmented feedback during training significantly elevated performance above that of the control procedure. Analysis of transfer-trial performance levels indicated that augmented feedback also had an effect on learning this task. The feature of importance here is the recognition that the ultimate performance criterion is often too gross for the trainee to appreciate increments of improvement. The real value obtains in discovering relevant (and interesting) sub-goals and relating these periodically to the ultimate goal. It is interesting to note that the decade counter used here is representative of a class of counting and timing devices that is useful in providing precise augmented information feedback. The counter is versatile in that it may be used as a clock for displaying elapsed time, or it may be used as a frequency counter (for displaying discrete steps of time-on-target, or error in predetermined increments).

The System Development Corporation has effectively utilized analytical performance information feedback in their system training program exercises for the Air Defense Command which have been described above. At problem termination, debriefing sessions are held in which umpires provide immediate knowledge of performance to the team in a general non-evaluative manner, directed primarily to the gaining of insight for team improvements in successive problems. These problem-solving sessions make possible the team assessment of current performance in terms of system goals.

An attempt has been made to optimize the efficiency of a training program by utilizing analytical information about ability requirements in task performance. Psychological Research Associates, under ONR support (Parker & Fleishman, 1959; Chapter 5 by Fleishman), have studied the extent to which knowledge of the ability pattern underlying proficiency at different stages in a complex tracking task enables the preparation of an instructional program for increasing training efficiency. An experimental group was provided guidance at certain points in training based on information concerning the perceptual-motor ability pattern underlying proficiency in the task. This information resulted from an earlier factor analysis of task components. To provide a baseline for evaluation, two additional groups were used: one group received no formal training beyond a brief explanation of the device; a second group received "common sense" training using standard pedagogical techniques. The instructions for guiding the experimental group were based on this rationale: knowing that a certain ability becomes important at a given point in the practice schedule, training can be structured to emphasize this ability at an earlier time. By bringing the proper abilities into use earlier, the training program may be condensed, thus lessening training time and perhaps increasing terminal proficiency. The results indicated that this technique resulted in more rapid learning with a higher terminal proficiency for this complex tracking task.

Courtney and Company (Lucier, Fischl, & Courtney, 1958), working with Navy (BuPers) fleet performance records, have concentrated on feeding relevant performance information back into the personnel system. The application of the principle of immediate and relevant feedback of information in the context of the system has resulted in the maintenance of better training information and better personnel allotment.

Classes of devices have been developed for providing the trainee with immediate information relevant to performance. Carpenter and his associates in the Instructional Film Research program at the Pennsylvania University have devised a classroom communicator for the evaluation of instructional and informational programs and for research on the learning process (Carpenter, et al., 1950; DuBois & Manning, 1957). The system comprises 40 individual response stations, a master console, a central answer display panel, and a bank of 40 total score indicators. The system makes possible the immediate display of group performance information as well as immediate feedback of performance information to the trainee. The system also provides for the tabulation of total test score per individual at the termination of the test period. As a research tool, it provides the opportunity for investigating methods of response reinforcement and extinction, as well as for testing the possibilities of social facilitation of learning through group cooperation and competition. The motivational features of the device are excellent since it overtly involves the individual in the learning process. Thelen, at the University of Chicago, has developed a similar device[15]. It provides each individual in the group with two buttons (good, bad, yes, no, etc.) to be used in group discussion. The group results are displayed, thus providing immediate non-verbal feedback of information in that everyone can communicate at the same time on a given issue. Possible modifications include the use of meters in place of lights to tabulate fre-

[15]Personal communication from Herbert Thelen, University of Chicago.

quency of button activation, and the use of recording pens and paper tape synchronized with the recording of the conversation for determining the points at which decisions are made.

Another class of instrument possessing the immediate information feedback capability involves the varieties of self-scoring punchboards. These devices not only test and score but also have a teaching function in that the immediate feedback of knowledge of results has an important instructional effect. Pressey (1950) has developed several machines for the testing of information, the notable example being a punchboard device for the immediate self-scoring of objective examinations which has been modified and used by the Navy as the "Self Rater." Similar devices employing the same principle are Angell's punchboard used in college quizzes (Angell, 1949) and Peterson's Chemo-cards (Peterson, 1930).

Procedures and devices have demonstrated the improvements in performance that accrue as a function of providing immediate feedback of relevant performance information. This technique is notably represented in maintenance instructions by a variety of trouble-shooting trainers which were discussed earlier. Tests such as the Subject Matter Trainer, the Punchboard Tutor, and formboards (Besnard, Briggs, Mursch, & Walker, 1955; Besnard, et al., 1955; Cantor & Brown, 1956; Glaser & Phillips, 1954), permit practice as well as the learning of technical subject matter under conditions of reinforced practice with minimum instructor participation. Similar values accrue from previously mentioned automated teaching techniques, notably programmed textbooks and scrambled books (Crowder, 1958; Glaser, et al., 1960) which, as a consequence of response, guide the trainee along multiple conceptual paths leading to greater task comprehension.

Most trouble-shooting apparatus provides relatively quick feedback of information relevant to performance. However, the class of trouble-shooting device that is most outstanding in this regard are the tests that may be called the automatic recording of checks (Fattu, 1956; Standlee, et al., 1956). These tests, as indicated in the previous section on malfunction location, reveal the consequences of performance immediately after the response has been executed. This is accomplished via punchboards (Cantor & Brown, 1956; Pressey, 1950), tabs (Glaser, et al., 1954), formboards (Glaser & Phillips, 1954), and printed overlays which, when erased, reveal the desired information (Cantor & Brown, 1956). The important feature of the foregoing devices is that they permit the early assessment of the extent and duration of error responses, thus providing insights into the progress of training.

## MOTIVATIONAL ASPECTS

Providing knowledge of results in the task situation usually not only facilitates performance but has the effect of increasing motivation to perform. The increasing frequency with which men are required to monitor machines or to work under conditions that may result in boredom makes the use of procedures that increase motivation of special importance. It has been demonstrated that the feedback of performance information not only has a directive effect on performance noted in the tendency towards error correction, but also an incentive effect which involves a more favorable attitude toward the task. The research on augmented feedback has indicated that this type of feedback is especially effective in increasing motivation (Smode, 1958).

Industrial research has shown that motivation to perform is related to job content and the manipulation of procedural variables in performance. Often, incentives extrinsic to a task cannot be utilized effectively to facilitate performance (a good example is the military job). One way to minimize this problem is to provide tasks which of themselves are interesting, engender pride in accomplishment, etc. This avenue of approach for manipulating human motivation has given rise to the study of variables involved in intrinsic job satisfaction (Katz & Kahn, 1952). Although it is influenced by other factors, it is derived most from the skill level of the task and the variety and interest level in the work content. The implications for training improvement are that motivation to perform is highly related to content as well as methods and procedures in the task.

In passing, it should be noted that many techniques and devices that are best described as "gimmicks" may work primarily because of their motivational value. Training programs can benefit from tricks of the trade developed by experienced "oldsters" who have used them successfully in training. The prime examples are the physical education coaches and instructors who develop top flight athletes with an assist from these trade tricks. It appears useful that procedures be developed for exploiting techniques and devices of this sort. (See Chapter 6 by Fitts.)

## KNOWLEDGE OF RESULTS AND REINFORCEMENT

Motivation and reinforcement are related problems. Usually when motivation to perform is understood, certain behaviors can be reinforced. The nature of what is a reinforcer is defined by what is the motivation, i.e., the specific goal towards which performance of the moment is directed. Learning is facilitated by immediate, constructive positive reinforcement (Gagné & Bolles, 1958). One of the important concepts of reinforcement is that retention of habits under conditions of nonreinforcement is increased when probabilistic reinforcement is used during initial training. Skinner (1953; 1954) and his co-workers have found that, under certain conditions, partial or intermittent reinforcement gives rise to increased performance and greater effort expenditure in humans. It has not been demonstrated, however, that superior learning occurs under these conditions. The approach appears to be an important problem for training research.

## Summary and Evaluation

It would be presumptuous to attempt a rigorous evaluation of the congeries of methodological innovations covered in this report. To begin with, very few validation studies exist in the literature and therefore an evaluation effort must necessarily involve "educated" guesses. Another difficulty in attempting an evaluation is that the rating given to any given innovation will depend on the criterion used by the judge in his evaluation. If, for instance, the judgment emphasized priorities based on the availability of limited funds for solving immediately pressing problems, the assessment would be quite different than if the criterion emphasized long-term research goals which presumably may have little relation to short-term applied research needs. Finally, training problems are changing so rapidly, due to technological developments, that it is difficult to evaluate innovations in terms of the importance of the training areas that might benefit from the innovation.

The point of this is that even very knowledgeable individuals could differ significantly in assessing the contributions in certain areas. Nevertheless, an attempt at assessment will be made. It is in the form of a summary evaluation of the current status of classes of innovations based on the work already conducted in given areas and the observation that some problems or areas appear to be growing in importance for training as indicated by the frequency of reports in the literature. By emphasizing the quantity and completeness of research conducted in a specific area as well as implications for immediate and/or future value, this summary assessment circumvents some of the problems just mentioned. Accordingly, the innovations cited are subsumed under three major assessment categories:

1. Specific methods that are immediately available for wider research and training use.
2. General methods that have already generated considerable research effort.
3. General trends that may have future methodological importance for training.

To minimize personal bias in assessment, 20 leading scientists who attended the conference on training research held at the University of Pittsburgh[16] were individually asked to judge the innovations in terms of their importance for a continuing research effort in training. The summary, which follows, has attempted to reflect the consensus of these raters. The discussion summarizes trends and areas of importance for training, in each of the three major categories, and the innovations are grouped within these larger contexts.

## *Specific Methods Immediately Available for Wider Use in Training and in Research*

Various new techniques as well as refinements of standard methods are currently available for wider use in training situations. Generally, these techniques have been intensively investigated and their use in specific problem areas is fairly well understood. The only additional research effort needed relates to the extension of these techniques to specific new training instances. Innovations in measurement are prominent in this group.

Innovations in this category include the various types of frequency measures and refinements in amplitude scoring for the analysis of performance in continuous tasks; new techniques for analyzing data from learning studies, particularly the refinements in correlational analysis; new applications of factor analysis; and new techniques for discerning patterning of response (trend testing) and specifying curves of learning.

The "free activity" measures for observing and categorizing behavior are also immediately available for application in many new training situations. These include the participant observer techniques, methods for measuring system loading, mass communication tech-

---

[16]This is the conference, described in the Preface, that resulted in the publication of this book.

niques such as television in conjunction with video tape or kinescope, and film used for time compression. Included also are the scoring devices for both group and individual assessment such as the classroom communicator, decade counters, self-scoring punchboards and selected trouble-shooting tests. Mackworth's portable eye motion camera is a good example of new devices immediately useful for recording performance.

It appears that some automated teaching devices such as programmed textbooks and "scrambled books" have already been developed to an extent that warrants their inclusion in this category.

## General Methods That Have Already Generated Considerable Research Efforts

Many new problems and areas of interest have been explored considerably during the last decade. While these innovations are fairly well understood, shortcomings or gaps in knowledge and application still exist which invite further systematic research and development. The areas of interest in this category include: team training and small group research; decision making and problem solving; automated teaching; complex simulation; and confinement, isolation and sensory deprivation.

*Team Training and Small Group Research.* Much of the work on group behavior during the past decade has been directed towards problems of team organization and motivation, with relatively little emphasis on training. Currently, data on means of implementing team training is meager, due in part to the difficulty in applying learning principles pertinent to team functioning. These principles are neither simple nor obvious. To achieve this, more information is required on *how* a team functions. A recent trend favorable to training is the growing appreciation of the need for studying the special characteristics of actual teams as opposed to the study of groups in the laboratory setting. Additional research efforts may now be addressed to such problems as: How does group structure and operation relate to team performance? How does the manner of information transmission among team members affect performance? What are the optimum ways of augmenting information feedback to facilitate performance? What are the optimum training procedures for teams in a system context?

*Decision Making and Problem Solving.* The considerable volume of research on gaming offers a variety of attractive possibilities for training improvement. In general, games which provide a simulated dynamic task environment offer many new possibilities for investigating individual and team performance variables and provide the opportunity for training in both procedures and member coordination in complex decision-making tasks. However, extensive gaps in our knowledge of the use of gaming techniques serve to make the value of this technique of limited utility today. A considerable research effort is required to realize the full potential of gaming. Present games fail to include many of the major variables in performance and usually do not take into account the many adventitious circumstances that occur in real life. Also, the validity of the cause and effect patterns learned in playing these games is constrained by the validity of the mathematical model underlying the game. The training value of games in terms of what they teach or what skills they develop is really not known. Indeed, one of the big arguments for continuing research in this area is that, strictly speaking, no one has proved that games test anything other than the ability to learn to play games effectively.

Malfunction location is another area that has been intensively investigated, and an adequate body of information is currently available for use in specific maintenance training situations. It appears, however, that much of this information has not been put to effective use in training. Additional research efforts should be devoted to applying the available information specifically to training of maintenance personnel, as well as integrating the useful data into the more general psychological areas of learning, concept formation, problem solving and decision making.

*Automated Teaching.* Much interest has developed recently in automated teaching, particularly with regard to teaching machines. Although not currently achieved, many potential values for training may exist in this mode of teaching. These include the ability to structure and evaluate methods of learning as well as to determine optimum programming sequences of learning material. Current machine design can be characterized by operational simplicity. This constrains flexibility by the lack of capacity which limits the number of alternative responses and by the lack of modifiability in that teaching techniques cannot be altered to account for progress in learning. However, research is currently underway to overcome these shortcomings. This should make possible the gradual identification and evaluation of the crucial factors in automated teaching. To this end, the particular type of "hardware" employed is secondary, except that it should have display versatility and flexibility in adapting to the kind of student response most appropriate to the content being learned. Thus, the most important aspect in the effectiveness of teaching machines is the programming. This appears to be the direction for future research since knowledge on effective programming is somewhat skimpy and inadequate. Major problems include recall vs. recognition; error vs. no error responses (and the rate of error responses for those advocating the making of errors in the course of learning); step size (spacing between adjacent items on the program); complexity of the programmed material; order of presentation of the material; self pacing vs. forced pacing of material; and multiple- vs. single-tracked programs. Few large scale evaluations of automated instruction have been undertaken. Previous concern has been primarily oriented towards practical problems of designing and using machines and testing and revising sample programs. (For additional information on this topic, see Chapter 9 by Lumsdaine.)

*Complex Simulation.* The dynamic simulation of anticipated characteristics of space flight is a research area continually increasing in importance. The growing awareness of the problems envisaged for man in space is ever extending the already sizable research efforts in this area. New approaches and refinements in devices and techniques for simulation are needed for investigating the problems likely to be encountered in space. Greater flexibility and versatility in dynamic devices such as centrifuges and multi-degree-of-freedom flight simulators are needed to gather information for training man under the anticipated stresses of space travel. The continuing research requirements include control-display relations and the human transfer function under conditions of linear and angular accelerations, the psychological and physiological capabilities of man in the hostile space environment, and on-going refinements in the criteria of simulation.

Another area of importance for complex simulation is that of perceptual relations in complex performance. A continuing research effort is needed here since much information is still unavailable about perceptual learning with regard to what characteristics to simulate, when and how to introduce noise, and the sequences of exercises leading to efficient as well as effective learning.

*Confinement, Isolation and Sensory Deprivation.* The systematic study of sensory deprivation in humans is of recent origin and lacks accepted or standard methodology. New ways are required for investigating the phenomena that arise under these behavioral conditions.

The majority of the investigations have been conducted in the laboratory setting. While many of the resulting observations have contributed to our knowledge of human behavior, the implications of these results in regard to training requirements are still unclear. Different emphases are required to gain information having utility for the training effort. A greater orientation toward social-psychological aspects of confinement and isolation seems indicated.

Previous studies have observed the effects of confinement and isolation on the single individual. These techniques need to be extended to the study of individuals in groups under confinement. Emphasis need also be placed on determining the minimum sensory inputs required for maintaining contact with reality, and the effects of perceptual deprivation where the operator is denied the full ability to structure his environment. Also, data on minimum alertness requirements in performance are needed. It may be possible to develop training techniques whereby the individual is provided means for self-stimulation that will countereffect, at least in degree, his impoverished stimulus environment. Offshoots of these approaches may provide data having screening value for performance qualifications under the stressful conditions of isolation and confinement. The finding that consistency in thought is difficult to maintain under these conditions may have value for training in propaganda resistance. Problems associated with shelter existence (underground radiation defense) require research effort especially with regard to training masses of people to accept and function in this form of confinement.

## General Trends That May Have Future Methodological Importance for Training

This final category embraces those methodological innovations that have stimulated relatively little research effort to date but which are nevertheless judged to be of increasing importance to training. Since the recognition of their value is of recent origin, many of these problem areas are not fully understood and often are insufficiently formulated for study. Many problems are yet unsolved which invite programmatic training research efforts. The important classes of innovations here include procedures used for the analysis of task requirements, techniques for investigating the microstructure of learning, techniques using analytical knowledge of results, and the concept of information overload.

*Procedures for the Analysis of Task Requirements.* Task analysis techniques have been applied in preparing estimates of personnel requirements for military weapon systems that are still under development. However, the decision structure for these personnel actions have not been formalized to the point that the information essential to such decisions can be specified. As a consequence, masses of job-task information of various kinds are produced and must be sifted unsystematically in reaching personnel decisions. The entire operation is inefficient since, in all likelihood, much information is gathered that need not be gathered, and it is presented in a form that requires a vast amount of human processing leading to results that are difficult to test for their validity in order to make improvements. Much effort is required in putting communicable structure into design alternatives and decisions which make up training and other personnel actions.

An important advance needed for theoretical and applied psychology is a classification of tasks based on transfer of training and other functionally related characteristics. This taxonomy should be based on behaviors that share the same qualitative and quantitative characteristics in learning, transfer of training and performance, rather than on individual differences in abilities. Amassing the empirical data from which to synthesize a task classification system looms as a monumental enterprise. However, the recognition and definition of the problem and the initial inductive and experimental work may be regarded as significant milestones for the psychology of training. Even though one may question the progress in the solution of task taxonomy for the purposes cited, it is significant that the problem has been identified not only as an important missing link between pure research and applications but as a major step in basic research itself.

*Techniques for Investigating the Microstructure of Learning.* The development of more analytical measures of performance represents a continuing need in training improvement. The findings that demonstrate qualitative changes in behavior pattern with succeedingly higher orders of practice have provided a breakthrough for knowledge and control of the learning process. Emphasis is being directed to the qualitative changes in the performance processes that mediate external stimulus and overt response at successive stages of practice (or "experience" to use a broader term). An example of such a change is the gradual dropping out of verbal self-instructions and conceptualizations in the stimulus-response relationship which thereby becomes to some degree "automatized." Other examples of change are in the apprehension of different and more extensive stimulus patterns preceding a given pattern of motor response. Further study may show what kinds of "stimulus bite" are most effective for certain kinds of task, and thus make it possible to program training so as to reduce the acquisition of habit patterns that must be unlearned in order to reach higher levels of performance.

To the extent that the task to be learned requires a succession of these qualitative changes, it is apparent why so many learning experiments have limited applicability to training of complex skills. The attempt to obtain homogeneity of the learning situation precludes the appearance of these qualitative changes and discontinuities. Nor do they show up in the relatively short time during which an experimental subject is run on complex tasks where skill levels are actually reached only after weeks, months, or even years of practice.

*Analytical Knowledge of Results.* It has long been recognized that task performance can be facilitated by the manipulation of procedural variables. The majority of work, however, has been of a qualitative nature, lacking in analytical specification of variables. One of the significant trends in the specification of performance information is the work on augmented feedback. The realization here is that an important value accrues from information feedback when relevant and interesting subgoals can be presented which are directly related to the ultimate goal of performance. Important research areas include the determination of optimum information requirements in a task, the effectiveness of various modes of information presentation, and the temporal relations in information feedback.

*Information Overload.* As systems become more complex, greater pressures are often brought to bear on the operator due to the excessive demands arising in the task situation. These task-induced stresses are importantly determined by the type and frequency of information requirements in performance. Under conditions in which man is required to perform a variety of monitoring, interpreting, translating, overriding and operating functions such as predicted for advanced flight vehicles, information overload has important consequences for training. Research is needed on factors contributing to the functional disruption of operator effectiveness arising from task stresses of this sort. This innovation is still primarily in the form of a new conception of stress; it offers considerable promise for future research, however.

In closing, it should be pointed out once more that the value of any innovation lies in the ingenuity of the person who sees an opportunity to use it in solving some research or training problem. It is hoped that the present compilation may suggest some new applications to the reader.

## REFERENCES

Alexander, L. T. *Report of research conducted during 1958.* Santa Monica, California: System Development Corporation, February 1959. TM-329.

Andlinger, G. R. Business games—play one! *Harvard business Rev.*, 1958, *36* (2), 115-125.

Angell, G. W. The effect of immediate knowledge of quiz results on final examination scores in freshman chemistry. *J. educ. Res.*, 1949, *42*, 391-394.

Annett, J. & Kay, H. Knowledge of results and skilled performance. *Occup. Psychol.*, 1957, *31*, 69-79.

Ansbacher, H. L. The history of the leaderless group discussion technique. *Psychol. Bull.*, 1951, *48*, 383-391.

Bahrick, H., Fitts, P., & Briggs, G. Learning curves—facts or artifacts? *Psychol. Bull.*, 1957, *54*, 256-268.

Bass, B. M. The leaderless group discussion. *Psychol. Bull.*, 1954, *51*, 465-492.

Bavelas, A. A mathematical model for group structures. *Appl. Anthrop.*, 1948, *7*, 16-30.

Bavelas, A. Communication patterns in task-oriented groups. *J. Acoust. Soc. Amer.*, 1950, *22*, 725-730.

Bell, J. M. *A landing display for use with a contact flight simulator.* Port Washington, New York: U. S. Naval Training Device Center, March 1951. SDC TR 71-16-8.

Bellman, R., Clark, C., Malcolm, D. G., Craft, C., & Ricciardi, F. On the construction of a multi-stage, multi-person business game. *Operations Res.*, 1957, *5*, 469-503.

Berrien, F. & Bash, W. *Human relations: Comments and cases.* (2nd ed.) New York: Harper, 1957.

Besnard, G. & Briggs, L. *Comparison of performance upon the E-4 fire control system simulator and upon operational equipment.* Lackland AFB, April 1956. Development Report AFPTRC-TN-56-47.

Besnard, G., Briggs, L. J., Mursch, G. A., & Walker, E. S. *Development of the subject matter trainer.* Lowry AFB, March 1955. Technical Memorandum ASPRL-TM-55-7.

Besnard, G., Briggs, L., & Walker, E. *The improvement subject matter trainer.* Lowry AFB, Armament Systems Personnel Research Laboratory, April 1955.

Beson, E. The balloon-borne capsule as a space flight trainer. Paper presented at the 27th Annual Meeting of the Institute of Aeronautical Sciences, New York, January 26-29, 1959. IAS Report 59-46.

Bexton W., Heron, W., & Scott, T. Effects of decreased variation in the sensory environment. *Canad. J. Psychol.*, 1954, *8*, 70-76.

Birmingham, H. & Taylor, F. *A human engineering approach to the design of man-operated continuous control systems.* Washington: Naval Research Laboratory, April 1954. Report No. 4333.

Bombard, A. *The voyage of the Heretique.* New York: Simon and Schuster, 1954.

Briggs, L. *A trouble-shooting trainer for the E-4 fire control system.* Lackland AFB, July 1956. Development Report AFPTRC-TN-56-94.

Briggs, L., Besnard, G., & Walker, E. *An E-4 fire control system performance test: I. Functional description.* Lowry AFB, March 1955. Technical Memorandum ASPRL-TM-55-8.

Brown, E., Matheny, W., & Flexman, R. *Evaluation of the school link as an aid in teaching ground reference maneuvers.* Port Washington, New York: U. S. Naval Training Device Center, December 1950. Technical Report SDC-71-16-7.

Brown, J. L. & Collins, C. C. Air-to-air tracking during closed-loop centrifuge operation. *J. Aviat. Med.*, 1958, *29*, 794-804.

Bryan, G. L., Bond, N. A., LaPorte, H. R., & Summers, S. A. *The AUTOMASTS: An automatically recorded test of electronics trouble-shooting.* Los Angeles: University of Southern California, August 1954. ONR Technical Report No. 11.

Bryan, G., Bond, N., LaPorte, H., & Hoffman, L. *Electronics trouble-shooting: A behavioral analysis.* Los Angeles: University of Southern California, March 1956. ONR Technical Report No. 13.

Byrd, R. E. *Alone.* New York: G. P. Putnam, 1938.

Cantor, Joan H. & Brown, J. *An evaluation of the trainer-tester and punch-board tutor as electronics trouble-shooting training aids.* Port Washington, New York: U. S. Naval Special Devices Center, October 1956. SPCTR 1257-2-1.

Carpenter, C., Eggleton, R., John, F., & Cannon, J. *The classroom communicator.* Port Washington, New York: U. S. Naval Special Devices Center, October 1950. Technical Report SDC-269-7-14.

Chapman, R. & Kennedy, J. The background and implications of the Systems Research Laboratory studies. In G. Finch & F. Cameron (Eds.), *Symposium* on *Air Force human engineering, personnel and training research.* Washington, D. C.: National Academy of Sciences, National Research Council, Publication 455, 1956. Pp. 65-73.

Clark, J. & Warren, C. *A photometric correlator.* Lackland AFB, Human Resources Research Center, 1953. Research Bulletin No. 53-42.

Corrigan, R. E. Automated teaching methods. *Automated teaching Bull.,* 1959, *1,* 23-30.

Cotterman, T. E. *Task classification: An approach to partially ordering information on human learning.* Wright-Patterson AFB, Wright Air Development Center, January 1959. WADC TN 58-374. (a)

Cotterman, T. E. Problems in describing and categorizing tasks for determining training needs. Paper read at Autumn Meeting of Ohio Psychol. Ass., Dayton, Ohio, October 1959. (b)

Coulson, J., Jensen, B., & Silberman, H. *Research in automated teaching.* Santa Monica, California: System Development Corporation, March 1959. Field Note FN 1522.

Crowder, N. A. *An automatic tutoring book on number systems.* Vol. 1. Timonium, Maryland: Hoover Electronics Company, 1958.

Demaree, R., Crowder, N., & Morrison, E. *Proficiency of Q-24 radar mechanics: Summary of findings.* Lowry AFB, March 1955. ASPRL TM 55-6.

Demaree, R., Crowder, N., Morrison, E., & Majesty, M. *Proficiency of Q-24 radar mechanics: I. Purposes, instruments, and samples of the study.* Lackland AFB, November 1954. Research Bulletin AFPTRC-TR-54-50.

DuBois, P. & Manning, W. (Eds.) *Methods of research in technical air training.* St. Louis: Washington University, May 1957. ONR Technical Report No. 3.

DuBois, P. & Manning, W. *The measurement of learning.* St. Louis: Washington University, May 1958. ONR Technical Report No. 6.

DuBois, P., Manning, W., & Spies, C. (Eds.) *Factor analysis and related techniques in the study of learning.* St. Louis: Washington University, August 1959. ONR Technical Report No. 7.

Duddy, J. & Dempsey, C. *Design strategies for human integration with a complex habitat. I. Crew facilities for the aircraft nuclear propulsion program.* Wright-Patterson AFB, Wright Air Development Center, in press.

Edwards, W. War games for training purposes. Paper read at Second University of Michigan Conference on War Games, Ann Arbor, Michigan, October 3, 1957.

Edwards, W. *Skinner's teaching machines.* Lowry AFB, Maintenance Laboratory, Air Force Personnel and Training Research Center, May 1956. Laboratory Note ML-LN-56-3. In A. A. Lumsdaine & R. Glaser (Eds.), *Teaching machines and programmed learning.* Washington, D. C.: National Education Association, 1960. Pp. 611-614.

Eilbert, L. R., Glaser, R., & Hanes, R. M. *Research on the feasibility of selection of personnel for duty at isolated stations,* Lackland AFB, July, 1957. Technical Report AFPTRC-TR-57-4.

Fattu, N. A. *A catalog of trouble-shooting tests.* Bloomington: Indiana University, December 1956. ONR Research Report No. 1.

Fattu, N., Bern, H., Stunkard, C., & Standlee, L. *Development of a written evaluation of mechanic proficiency for airborne electronic navigation equipment repairmen.* Lowry AFB, Armament Systems Personnel Research Laboratory, April 1956. ASPRL TM-56-11.

Festinger, L. & Katz, D. (Eds.) *Research methods in the behavioral sciences.* New York: Dryden Press, 1953.

Fitts, P., Bennett, W., & Bahrick, H. Application of autocorrelation and cross correlation analysis to the study of tracking behavior. In G. Finch & F. Cameron (Eds.) *Symposium on Air Force human engineering, personnel and training research.* Washington, D. C.: National Academy of Sciences, National Research Council, Publication 455, 1956. Pp. 125-141.

Fitts, P., Schipper, L., Kidd, J., Shelly, M. & Kraft, C. Some concepts and methods for the conduct of system research in a laboratory setting. In G. Finch & F. Cameron (Eds.) *Symposium on Air Force human engineering, personnel and training research.* Washington, D. C.: National Academy of Sciences, National Research Council, Publication 455, 1958. Pp. 174-187.

Fleishman, E. Psychomotor selection tests: Research and application in the United States Air Force. *Personnel Psychol.,* 1956, *9,* 449-467. (a)

Fleishman, E. Predicting advanced levels of proficiency in psychomotor skills. In G. Finch & F. Cameron (Eds.) *Symposium on Air Force human engineering, personnel, and training research.* Washington, D. C.: National Academy of Sciences, National Research Council, Publication 455, 1956. Pp. 142-151. (b)

Fleishman, E. Dimensional analysis of movement reactions. *J. exp. Psychol.,* 1958, *55,* 438-453.

Freedman, S., Grunebaum, H. & Greenblatt, M. *Perceptual and cognitive changes in sensory deprivation.* Cambridge: Harvard Medical School, June 1958.

French, R. S. *The K-system MAC I trouble-shooting trainer. I. Development, design, and use.* Lackland AFB, Air Force Personnel and Training Research Center, October 1956. AFPTRC-TM-56-119. (a)

French, R. S. Evaluation of a K-system trouble-shooter trainer. In G. Finch & F. Cameron (Eds.) *Symposium on Air Force human engineering, personnel and training research.* Washington, D. C.: National Research Council, Publication 455, 1956. Pp. 160-165. (b)

French, R. S., Crowder, N. & Tucker, J. *The K-system MAC I trouble-shooting trainer. II. Effectiveness in an experimental training course.* Lackland AFB, Air Force Personnel and Training Research Center, October 1956. AFPTRC-TM-56-120.

French, R. S. & Martin, L. *A flight line trouble-shooting trainer for a complex electronic system: The MAC II trainer.* Lackland AFB, Air Force Personnel and Training Research Center, July 1957. AFPTRC-TN-57-106.

Gagné, R. & Bolles, R. *A review of factors in learning efficiency.* Princeton: Princeton University, November 1958. AFOSR-TN-924.

Gain, P. & Fitts, P. *A simplified electronic tracking apparatus (SETA).* Wright-Patterson AFB, Wright Air Development Center, August 1959. WADC TR 59-44.

Gilchrist, J. C. Social psychology and group processes. In P. Farnsworth & Q. McNemar (Eds.), *Annual Review of Psychology.* Palo Alto, California: Annual Reviews, Inc., 1959. Pp. 233-264.

Glanzer, M. & Glaser, R. *A review of team training problems.* Pittsburgh: American Institute for Research, September 1955. NR-154-079.

Glanzer, M. & Glaser, R. *Performance characteristics of three types of Navy teams.* Pittsburgh: American Institute for Research, May 1957.

Glanzer, M. & Glaser, R. Techniques for the study of group structure and behavior: I. Analysis of structure. *Psychol. Bull.,* 1959, *56*, 317-332.

Glanzer, M. & Glaser, R. Techniques for the study of group structure and behavior: II. Empirical studies of the effects of structure in small groups. *Psychol. Bull.,* 1961, *58*, 1-27.

Glanzer, M., Glaser, R., & Klaus, D. J. *The team performance record: An aid for team analysis and team training.* Pittsburgh: American Institute for Research, December 1956. NR-154-079.

Glaser, R. Descriptive variables for the study of task-oriented groups. In R. A. Patton (Ed.), *Current trends in the description and analysis of behavior.* Pittsburgh: University of Pittsburgh Press, 1958. Pp. 1-21.

Glaser, R., Damrin, Dora, & Gardner, F. The tab item: A technique for the measurement of proficiency in diagnostic problem solving tasks. *Educ. psychol. Measmt,* 1954, *14*, 283-293.

Glaser, R. & Glanzer, M. *Training and training research.* Pittsburgh: American Institute for Research, August 1958.

Glaser, R., Glanzer, M., & Morten, A. *A study of some dimensions of team performance.* Pittsburgh: American Institute for Research, September 1955. NR-154-079.

Glaser, R., Hahn, J., & Phillips, J. *An analysis of tests of proficiency for guided missile personnel. I. Multiple-choice tests.* Pittsburgh: American Institute for Research, August 1954. Technical Bulletin 55-16.

Glaser, R., Homme, L., & Evans, J. An evaluation of textbooks in terms of learning principles. Paper read at meeting of the American Educational Research Ass., Atlantic City, February 1959. In A. A. Lumsdaine & R. Glaser (Eds.) *Teaching machines and programmed learning: A source book.* Washington, D. C.: National Education Association, 1960.

Glaser, R. & Phillips, J. *An analysis of tests of proficiency for guided missile personnel. II. The trouble-shooting board.* Pittsburgh: American Institute for Research, August 1954. Technical Bulletin 55-16.

Goodwin, W. R. The System Development Corporation and system training. *Amer. Psychologist,* 1957, *12,* 524-527.

Grant, D. A. Analysis-of-variance tests in the analysis and comparison of curves. *Psychol. Bull.,* 1956, *53,* 141-154.

Grings, W., Rigney, J., Bond, N., & Summers, S. *A methodological study of electronics trouble-shooting skill. I. Rationale for and description of the Multiple-Alternative Symbolic Trouble-Shooting Test.* Los Angeles: University of Southern California, August 1953. ONR Technical Report No. 9. (a)

Grings, W., Rigney, J., Bond, N., & Summers, S. *A methodological study of electronics trouble-shooting skill. II. Inter-comparisons of the MASTS test, a job sample test, and ten reference tests administered to fleet electronics technicians.* Los Angeles: University of Southern California, August 1953. ONR Technical Report No. 10. (b)

Gyr, J. W. *An investigation into, and speculations about, the formal nature of a problem solving process.* Ann Arbor: University of Michigan, Mental Health Research Institute, June 1959. Preprint No. 31.

Hall, R. L. Group performance under feedback that confounds responses of group members. *Sociometry,* 1957, *20,* 297-305.

Harrison, J. O. & Walker, S. H. Summary of gaming activities at Operations Research Office. Paper read at Second Conference on War Games, University of Michigan, Ann Arbor, Michigan, October 1957.

Harter, G. & Fitts, P. *The functional simulation of complex systems by means of an analog computer, with the F-86D, E-4 system as a specific example.* Lackland AFB, Air Force Personnel and Training Research Center, December 1956. AFPTRC-TN-56-133.

Heron, W. The pathology of boredom. *Sci. Amer.*, 1957, *196*, 52-56.

Heron, W., Doane, B., & Scott, T. Visual disturbances after prolonged perceptual isolation. *Canad. J. Psychol.*, 1956, *10*, 13-18.

Hixon, W., Harter, G., Warren, C., & Cowan, J. *An electronic radar target simulator for air traffic control studies.* Wright-Patterson AFB, Wright Air Development Center, 1954. WADC TR 54-569.

Human Resources Research Office. *Work program, fiscal year 1959.* Washington, D.C.: The George Washington University.

John, E. R. *Contributions to the study of the problem solving process.* Ann Arbor: Mental Health Research Institute, University of Michigan, 1956. Preprint No. 1.

Katz, D. & Kahn, R. Human organization and worker motivation. *Industr. Productivity*, 1952, 146-171.

Kelley, C., Bowen, H., Ely, J., & Channell, R. *Tracking training II: A case history.* Port Washington, New York: U. S. Naval Training Device Center, March 1958. NAVTRADEVCEN 1908-00-2.

Kelley, C. R. Instrumentation for continuous control. Paper read at Annual Meeting of the Amer. Psychol. Ass., Washington, D.C., September 1958.

Kinkade, R. G. & Kidd, J. S. *The effect of team size and inter-member communication on decision-making performance.* Wright-Patterson AFB, Wright Air Development Center, April 1959. WADC TR 58-474.

Klaus, D. J. & Glaser, R. *Increasing team proficiency through training. I: A program of research.* Pittsburgh: American Institute for Research, 1960.

Lanzetta, J. T. & Roby, T. B. Group learning and communication as a function of task and structure "demands." *J. abnorm. soc. Psychol.*, 1957, *55*, 121-131.

Lanzetta, J. T., Wendt, B. R., Langham, P., & Haefner, D. The effects of an "anxiety reducing" medication on group behavior under threat. *J. abnorm. soc. Psychol.*, 1956, *52*, 103-108.

Leiderman, P., Mendelson, J., Wexler, D., & Solomon, P. *Sensory deprivation: Clinical aspects.* Washington, D.C.: Office of Naval Research, Contract Nonr 1866(29), undated.

Levy, E., Ruff, G., & Thaler V. Studies in human isolation. *J. Amer. Med. Assoc.*, 1959, *169*, 236-239.

Licklider, J. C.  Basic correlates of the auditory stimulus. In S. S. Stevens (Ed.) *Handbook of experimental psychology.* New York: Wiley, 1951. Pp. 985-1039.

Lilly, J. C.  Mental effects of reduction of ordinary levels of physical stimuli on intact, healthy persons. *Psychiat. Res. Rep.*, 1956, *5*, 1-9.

Lindahl, L. G.  Movement analysis as an industrial training method. *J. appl. Psychol.*, 1945, *29*, 420-436.

Lucier, O., Fischl, M., & Courtney, D.  *Application of a systems concept to personnel research.* Washington, D.C.: Office of Naval Research, August 1958. Contract Nonr-2212(00), Project J. Report No. 22.

Lumsdaine, A. A. & Glaser, R.  (Eds.) *Teaching machines and programmed learning: A source book.* Washington, D.C.: Division of Audio-Visual Instruction, National Education Association, 1960.

Mackworth, J. F. & Mackworth, N. H.  Eye fixations recorded on changing visual scenes by the television eye-marker. *J. Opt. Soc. Amer.*, 1958, *48*, 439-445.

Manning, W. & DuBois, P.  Gain in proficiency as a criterion in test validation. *J. appl. Psychol.*, 1958, *42*, 191-194.

March, J. & Simon, H.  *Organizations.* New York: Wiley, 1958.

McFarland, R.  *Human factors in vehicular design and operation with special reference to accidents.* Washington, D.C.: Annual Report to the Commission on Accidental Trauma, Armed Forces Epidemiological Board, for period 1 March 1957 to 28 February 1958.

McGrath, J. E.  *A framework for integration of small group research studies.* Air Force Office of Scientific Research, Air Research and Development Command, Washington, D.C., February 1958. AFOSR-TR-57-87.

Melton, A. W. & Briggs, G. E.  Engineering psychology. In P. Farnsworth & Q. McNemar (Eds.), *Annual Review of Psychology.* Palo Alto: Annual Reviews, Inc., 1960. Pp. 71-98

Miller, R. B.  *A method for man-machine task analysis.* Pittsburgh: American Institute for Research, June 1953. WADC TR 53-137. (a)

Miller, R. B.  *Handbook on training and training equipment design.* Pittsburgh: American Institute for Research, 1953. WADC TR 53-136. (b)

Miller, R. B.  *A theory of concept mediation in learning and performance.* Pittsburgh: American Institute for Research, December 1955. (Prepared for Air Force Personnel and Training Research Center.)

Miller, R. B.  *Task and part-task trainers and training.* Pittsburgh: American Institute for Research, January 1956. WADC TR 56-41. (a)

Miller, R. B. *A suggested guide to position-task description.* Lowry AFB, Armament Systems Personnel Research Laboratory, April 1956. ASPRL-TM-56-6. (b)

Miller, R. B. & Folley, J. D., Jr. *A study of methods for determining skill, knowledge and ability requirements for maintenance of newly developed equipment.* Pittsburgh: American Institute for Research, June 1951. (Prepared for Human Resources Research Center, San Antonio, Texas.)

Miller, R. B., Folley, J. D., Jr., & Smith, P. R. *Systematic trouble-shooting and the half-split technique.* Chanute AFB, Human Resources Research Center, July 1953. HRRC TR 53-21.

Miller, R. B. & Slebodnick, E. B. *Research for experimental investigations of transferable skills in electronic maintenance.* Lackland AFB, Air Force Personnel and Training Research Center, January 1958. AFPTRC TR 58-2.

Miller, R. B. & Van Cott, H. P. *The determination of knowledge content for complex man-machine jobs.* Pittsburgh: American Institute for Research, December 1955. (Prepared for Air Force Personnel and Training Research Center.)

*Naval Aviation News.* Fabulous war game, "Ready." NavAer No. 00-75R-3, January 1959, pp. 16-17.

Parker, J. F., Jr. & Fleishman, E. A. *Use of analytical information concerning task requirements to increase the effectiveness of skill training.* Arlington: Psychological Research Associates, 1959.

Payne, T., Dougherty, D., Hasler, S., Skeen, J., Brown, E., & Williams, A. *Improving landing performance using a contact landing trainer.* Port Washington, New York: U. S. Naval Training Device Center, March 1954. SDC 71-16-11.

Peterson, J. C. A new device for teaching, testing and research in learning. *Trans. Kansas Acad. Sci.,* 1930, *33,* 41-47.

Pressey, S. L. Development and appraisal of devices providing immediate automatic scoring of objective tests and concomitant self-instruction. *J. Psychol.,* 1950, *29,* 417-447.

*Proceedings of the National Symposium on Management Games.* Center for Research in Business, The University of Kansas, Lawrence, Kansas, May 1959.

Rapoport, A. Quantification of performance in a logical task with uncertainty. In *Symposium on Information Theory in Biology.* New York: Pergamon, 1958.

Ricciardi, F. M. Business war games for executives: A new concept in management training. *Management Rev.,* 1957, *46,* (5), 45-56.

Robertson, E. L. War gaming at the Naval War College and the electronic maneuver board system. Paper read at Second Conference on War Games, University of Michigan, Ann Arbor, Michigan, October 1957.

Roby, T. & Lanzetta, J. Considerations in the analysis of group tasks. *Psychol. Bull.*, 1958, *55*, 88-101.

Rock, R. T., Jr., Duva, J., & Murray, J. *The effectiveness of television in instruction in training Naval air reservists*. Port Washington, New York: U. S. Naval Special Devices Center, April 1951. SDC 476-02-52.

Rosenberg, S. & Hall, R. L. The effects of different social feedback conditions upon performance in dyadic teams. *J. abnorm. soc. Psychol.*, 1958, *57*, 271-277.

Ruff, G. E. Isolation. *Astronautics*, 1959, *4*, (2), 22-23, 110.

Ruff, G. E., Levy, E., & Thaler, V. *Some influences on reaction to reduced sensory input*. Unpublished paper, Wright-Patterson AFB, Biophysics Laboratory, Aero Medical Laboratory, Wright Air Development Center.

Rulon, P., Langmuir, C. R., Schweiker, R. F., Demaree, R. G., Crowder, N. A., & Sawrey, W. L. *Proficiency on Q-24 radar mechanics. II. The performance trouble-shooting test*. Lackland AFB, Air Force Personnel and Training Research Center, November 1954. AFPTRC Res. Bull. 54-51.

Rulon, P. & Schweiker, R. *The training of flight-simulator maintenance personnel: A proposed course that emphasizes trouble-shooting*. Lowry AFB, Maintenance Laboratory, July 1956. ML-TM-56-17.

Saupe, J. L. *An analysis of trouble-shooting behavior of radio mechanic trainees*. Lackland AFB, Air Force Personnel and Training Research Center, 1955. AFPTRC 55-47.

Schein, E. H. The Chinese indoctrination program for prisoners of war. *Psychiatry*, 1956, *19*, 149-172.

Schipper L. M., Kraft, C. L., Smode, A. F., & Fitts, P. M. *The use of displays showing identity versus no identity: A study in human engineering aspects of radar air traffic control*. Wright-Patterson AFB, Wright Air Development Center, 1957. WADC TR 57-21.

Siegel, A., Jensen, J., & Danzig, E. *An investigation and test of the trouble-shooting ability of aviation electricians*. Philadelphia: Institute for Research in Human Relations, January 1955. ONR Report No. 1.

Skinner, B. F. *Science and human behavior*. New York: Macmillan, 1953.

Skinner, B. F. The science of learning and the art of teaching. *Harvard educ. Rev.*, 1954, *24*, (2), 86-97.

Skinner, B. F. Teaching machines. *Science*, 1958, *128*, 969-977. Also in A. A. Lumsdaine and R. Glaser (Eds.), *Teaching machines and programmed learning: A source book*. Washington, D.C.: National Education Association, 1960.

Smode, A. F. Learning and performance in a tracking task under two levels of achievement information feedback. *J. exp. Psychol.*, 1958, *56*, 297-304.

Smode, A. F., Beam, J. C., & Dunlap, J. W. *Motor habit interference: A resume of the literature and the development of principles for its minimization in training.* Stamford, Connecticut: Dunlap & Associates, Inc., January 1959.

Solartron Electronic Group, Ltd. SAKI, a machine that learns from experience. *Data Processing*, April-June 1959.

Solomon, P., Leiderman, H., Mendelson, J., & Wexler, D. Sensory deprivation: A review. *Am. J. Psychiat.*, 1957, *114*, 357-367.

Solomon, P., Wexler, D., Mendelson, J., Leiderman, P., & Kubzansky, P. *Modifications of the conscious state in sensory deprivation.* Washington, D.C.: Office of Naval Research, Contract Nonr-1866(29), undated.

Standlee, L., Popham, W., & Fattu, N. *A review of trouble-shooting research.* Bloomington: Indiana University, Institute of Educational Research, December, 1956. ONR Report No. 3.

Sutton, G. The error power spectrum as a technique for assessing the performance of the human operator in a simple task. *Quart. J. exp. Psychol.*, 1957, *9*, 42-51.

*Symposium on television training and training research.* Joint Panel on Training and Training Devices, Department of Defense, Research and Development Board, Washington, D.C., December 1952.

Thomas, K. Simplified medical television: Product of Navy research. *Res. Rev.*, Office of Naval Research, November 1958, pp. 6-11.

Vernon, J., McGill, T., & Schiffman, H. Visual hallucinations during perceptual isolation. *Canad. J. Psychol.*, 1958, *12*, 31-34.

Vineberg, R. A performance test for the AAFCS M-33 radar mechanic and observations on trouble-shooting behavior. In *Symposium on electronics maintenance.* Advisory Panel on Personnel and Training Research, Office of the Assistant Secretary of Defense, Research, and Development. Washington, D.C., August 3-5, 1955.

Warren, N., Atkins, Dorothy W., Ford, J. S., & Wolbers, H. L. *Development of a training program for teaching basic principles of trouble-shooting.* Lowry AFB, Personnel Research Laboratory, October 1955. ASPRL-TM-55-19.

Wheaton, J. L. *Fact and fancy in sensory deprivation studies.* Brooks AFB, USAF School of Aviation Medicine, August 1959. Review No. 5-59.

Whyte, W. F. *Research methods in social relations.* New York: Dryden, 1951.

Woodling, G. & Clark, G. Studies of pilot control during launching and re-entry of space vehicles, utilizing the human centrifuge. Paper read at the 27th annual meeting of the Institute of the Aeronautical Sciences, New York, January 1959.

| Chapter 16 | Identifying Training Needs and Translating Them into Research Requirements |
| --- | --- |

*Theodore R. Vallance and Meredith P. Crawford,
Human Resources Research Office,
The George Washington University*

The main question to which this chapter is addressed is: How can the administrator of training research and development (R&D) know when he is confronted with a problem to which he should apply some of his resources? As such, the chapter is in part an essay on decision making. Also, it is a description of the working of a relatively formal system for making research decisions. Finally, some implications are drawn for the selection of educational research projects. Of necessity then, this chapter differs from the others in that it deals not so much with psychological variables, but mainly with systemic variables. In other words, the interest is not primarily in research content but in the various things that must happen in order to get training research under way.

### SOME DEFINITIONS AND DISTINCTIONS

The term "systemic variables" refers to aspects of the training research process or system, and aspects of the operational system which training research presumably serves. By implication, the concern is with how training systems work to produce improvements in the skill levels of the people being trained to keep some operating system operating, or to effect improvements in the efficiency with which required levels of skill are attained.

Before getting into the subject, it is well to lay out some definitions to serve as guide lines to the discussion. The term "training research" will be used to refer to applied research whose end products have a reasonable chance of being used in developing training processes which will improve training efficiency and on-the-job performance. The reason for asserting that training research is always applied research is that the term "training" clearly implies a teleology within a system of events

*497*

serving some set of values. This being the case, research or any other effort within the system directed toward increasing its efficiency cannot help but be practical or "applied." The adoption of the convention that training research is wholly applied research will facilitate discussion of research and development in the rest of this chapter and will skirt a number of knotty problems which sometimes crop up in efforts to establish and maintain distinctions between basic and applied research.

In order to make clearer use of the term it will be helpful to set up, however briefly it is used, a distinction between basic and applied research. Let "basic research" refer to scientific activity initiated primarily for the purpose of extending or systematizing man's knowledge about the world, with only incidental regard to the applicability of the research findings toward the solution of a particular, practical problem. For example, a scientist may pursue research using nonsense syllables to explore the general validity of the Skaggs-Robinson hypothesis (McGeoch, 1942) as an explanation of retroactive inhibition in verbal learning and to relate the hypothesized variables to other parts of a theoretical system. Let the term "applied research" refer to scientific activities initiated for the purpose of extending technology with a negligible interest in the testing of any particular hypothesis relating to a general theory. An example of applied research in learning would be a series of efforts to test the application of the Skaggs-Robinson hypothesis to a number of conditions in practical training situations.

The term "training development" will be introduced here to apply to efforts to direct already developed technology toward the solution of a stated practical problem. A synonymous term, "psychological engineering," is a suggestive analogue to applications of other scientifically derived technologies and techniques to the solution of various kinds of problems. Carrying the example a little further, a training development effort might draw upon basic and applied research on the conditions of validity for the Skaggs-Robinson hypothesis to develop a set of subject schedules to optimize the use of training time toward a given instructional objective. It is immediately apparent that a great amount of basic and applied research must precede a developmental effort that is successful in effecting a major and lasting improvement in a technology of training. And with the term "technology of training" reference is made to the things which a training institution characteristically does in the course of setting up and managing a training program—determining training objectives, specifying training content, planning lessons and training aids, developing examinations—all of which are done with the guidance of manuals or accumulated institutional lore.

Now for the term "research requirement." This may be the simplest term of all to define, but the most difficult one for which to find clear referents in the world of events. It stands for a decision that has been made to devote a given amount of research effort toward some specified end.

## METHOD AND SCOPE OF THIS CHAPTER

That this chapter is concerned with systemic variables means that it will deal with decisions by research administrators as to what research effort should be directed toward what goals, implying goals within some specifiable system. And the term "system" will be taken to mean, following Malcolm Hoag (1957), a set of interrelated actions about which policy decisions must be made.

Unless limitless resources are assumed to be available, a systems analysis approach to the specification of goals, to the evaluation of goals, and to the evaluation of proposals and projects, will be necessary to assist in the making of administrative research decisions. In this discussion it is assumed that there is a need to allocate limited resources, and, therefore, a requirement to identify values within the system presumed to be aided by research, those values that need research attention, and ways of ordering these values and directing limited research resources toward maximizing the efficiency of the system, given the limitations of the research capability. Thus, the identification of training research needs becomes a problem in systems analysis. The researcher will find it helpful to view himself as a part of an operations research system, whose function is the usual operations research function, namely, of contributing information to "management," in this setting mostly training executives, for use in making decisions. This chapter, then, will be concerned mainly with formal training research requirements, that is, requirements which have been developed through formal procedures and which bear specifiable relationships to the objectives and operating characteristics of the system in which the applications of research might be helpful.

Because most training research is done on behalf of educational, manufacturing, military, or other producing systems, training research tends to be somewhat programmatic: it tends to consist of more than one research effort, and therefore to require or suggest some unity of purpose, function, and form. Therefore, the chapter will not be concerned, except by inference, with training research in relatively informal systems.[1]

This chapter will not attempt to review the various methods of spotting training problems. There are several good methods, such as suggestion systems, surveys of various degrees of formality, conferences, diagnostic testing procedures and others, each with its good and bad features, advantages, and pitfalls. Also, there are already available some good general references on how to discover training needs, such as the U. S. Civil Service Commission's booklet entitled *Assessing and Reporting Training Needs and Progress* (1956). And for the military researcher there is a wealth of good ideas yet to be exploited in the *Report of Working Group on Human Behavior under Conditions of Military Service* (Adams, Buel, Barclay, & McDowell, 1951). The chapter will be concerned, therefore, not so much with how to go about finding training problems as how to go about translating these into the content of training research.

### CONDITIONS NECESSARY FOR THE ESTABLISHMENT OF FORMAL TRAINING RESEARCH AND TRAINING DEVELOPMENT REQUIREMENTS

There are four conditions that are necessary and sufficient for the conduct of training research in a practical operating system. These are:

1. An agency that has and can pose a problem whose solution would result in increased proficiency of human performance on the job, or an increased efficiency of training.

2. An agency that can perform the required research and development activities.

3. An agency that can support with funds, materiel, and non-research manpower the R&D activities.

4. An agency that can act to cause implementation of a successful solution to the problem initially proposed.

Each of these shall now be considered one at a time in a little more detail.

---

[1]An example is a set of experiments (Meyer, 1934; Douglass & Tallmadge, 1934; Vallance, 1947) on the effects of various examination-sets or expectancies on efficiency of learning of test-related subject matter. While clearly training research, the experiments did not arise from a specification of a problem within an operational agency, but rather from some theoretically derived and sometimes provocative hunches on the part of the research workers who, when their work was finished, hoped that it might be put to use by someone.

*A Problem-Posing Agency.* Obviously, some clear statement of a problem is necessary to get research thinking underway. An "agency" may be the supervisor of a production line in a manufacturing plant, a military headquarters, or "management" in virtually any organization. But what is a training problem of the sort that deserves research attention? There appear to be three determinations that must be made very early in developing a formal training research requirement.

First and most obvious, a training problem must be identified. A training problem exists when a responsible agent recognizes that a skill is being performed at a level of proficiency such that an increase in the efficiency of the next larger operating system, of which this skill is a part, can be reliably predicted from an increase in the skill level (or for the training organization, an increase in the efficiency of acquiring the skill). In other words, proficiency is too low, training is too expensive, or takes too long.

The second determination must be that the cost of increasing the skill (or for a school, the rate of the skill's acquisition) through lengthening the training period, or selecting initially more apt or more experienced persons, would exceed the gain to the system from increased human proficiency. In other words, taking the usual or available administrative steps would, for one reason or another, be too expensive in terms of the expected increase in system efficiency.

The third determination is that the use of expert advice on adjustments to the operating system, or to the training program, is judged unlikely to result in suitable increases in performance levels or acquisition rates. If these three determinations can be made, then a need for research may be said to exist.

This, however, is not to say that a formal requirement for research exists, for up to this point, no hierarchical arrangement of problem importance has been made, nor have a number of other considerations been examined, such as cost of research, availability of personnel, time requirements, and others. So far as training research is concerned, the most important functions of the operating agency are to determine the existence of problems whose solutions can most efficiently be derived through research, and to determine the degree of system improvement that will justify implementing the solution. This will typically occur as an outcome of a very close relationship with experienced research people, but the responsibility remains with the operational agency. A parallel process for determining research needs in industrial research is illustrated in the statement of L. T. Work (1953) that when "the market for a class of goods is saturated and there is no way to expand it, then research has a place to insure retaining or bettering a position with respect to the business in the field."

*The R&D Facility.* Essentially, this refers to a laboratory with necessary skills and facilities for planning and conducting research and development activity. This agency may be large or small, simple or complex. It may be a component or a coordinate of the problem-posing agency, or it may be separate and independent. Some cost to the problem-posing agency is assumed, however, in the eventual use of the R&D facilities.

*A Logistical Support Agency.* This agency may be, in many cases, the same as the second one above in that the R&D agency may have within its own capabilities all of the funds, materiel, and other nonresearch manpower with which to carry on the R&D activities. Typically, however, in training research the scientist must rely on things and people outside the structure of his laboratory in order to get his work done. His experiments will sooner or later require human subjects from plant maintenance shops, industrial training courses of various kinds, grade schools, high schools and college. This is especially true in military training research. Obviously, drawing human subjects from operating systems involves a cost that must be clearly recognized by the R&D agency, and clearly evaluated by the agency supplying the personnel. If the scope of the research is large, a high level determination is frequently required before research can be expected to progress very far. Thus, this discussion emphasizes an agency with the necessary authority to provide this type of support to the training research. And obviously, the research must make practical sense to this agency.

*An Implementing Agency.* Again there may be repetition in listing this as a separate type of agency. This is particularly likely in military training research, in which it is frequently found that the agency capable of implementing a successful solution to an operational problem is not only the agency which posed the problem in the first place, but is also the one to provide the extra-R&D logistical and personnel support.

It is preferable to consider the agency of implementation separately in order to emphasize the importance of spelling out both the problem from which the research began and the implementation plan which must follow. Training research is essentially, as noted before, a teleological process in the service of a value system. Those in overall control of the system should assume that some use will probably be made of the product developed through the expenditure of system resources, namely,

R&D money plus the non-R&D support. Furthermore, it should be noted that a preliminary estimate of implementation costs should go into the determination of whether or not a formal research requirement exists; the implementing agency, even though it be only the problem-posing agency exercising another function, is best suited to do this. Ideally, when the problem-posing and the implementing agencies are one and the same, it may even be possible to determine before the research is done, especially if it is of a development sort, how much increase in human proficiency will be required to produce an increase in system efficiency such as to justify both the cost of the research and the cost of implementation.

The considerations discussed above concern problems within a currently operating training system. In the rapidly developing technology of industry and the military establishment, there is the problem of anticipating the training required to get men ready to operate or maintain new equipment by the time it rolls off the production line. In this case, the problem-posing agency may have to be persuaded that training difficulties will be encountered if prior research is not accomplished. The R&D agency will have to assess the new operational problems and then plan empirical studies, using contemporary equipment, fabricated mockups or the like to obtain empirical data on problems that may be assumed to exist in the future. This kind of activity is especially important in the military establishment and in fast changing industrial situations, and represents a challenge to the analytical and forecasting skills of the training researcher.

The specifications just enumerated and elaborated above outline the conditions necessary and sufficient for the establishment of *formal* research requirements within operating systems. An informal research requirement is a decision to undertake research which is not backed up by all of the above specifications. This is not to say that informal requirements do not have value. It is only to say that their value is undetermined until after the research is completed. The research may represent hunches, hobbies, or predilections of researchers or research administrators, and may have any or no degree of relevance to real problems in operating systems. The present contention would be that training research is most efficiently pursued, i.e., operating problems of known significance have maximum probability of being solved, if the above conditions are met.

It is not the intent of the foregoing discussion, however, to assert that all useful training research, even that conducted within a research facility whose overall operations are rather formalized, should be the specific outgrowth of a highly formalized process of need determination and requirement establishment. As the example in the next section will bring out, it is important to provide for a considerable amount of informal or unprogrammed research.

A PRACTICAL EXAMPLE OF A SYSTEM FOR ESTABLISHING FORMAL
REQUIREMENTS FOR TRAINING RESEARCH AND DEVELOPMENT:
THE WORK PROGRAM OF THE ARMY'S HUMAN RESOURCES RESEARCH OFFICE

Having specified some conditions and rules for establishing research requirements, a practical example will be described. The development of the Work Program of HumRRO (1961b) represents a reasonable approximation of the procedure outlined in the section above. The example is selected, not only because of the authors' familiarity with it, but because the HumRRO program is quite fully formalized and represents one end of the formalization continuum in the process of establishing research requirements. Also, it seems to work reasonably well and to have evolved with some increases in efficiency over the years as a procedure for establishing, monitoring, and terminating R&D requirements. In the interest of suggesting some generality to the procedure, it should be noted that HumRRO is not only among the largest training research and development organizations in the United States, but is quite diversified both with respect to geography and problem areas under study. Of course, no claim is made that the method used in HumRRO, or even the model suggested in this chapter, is the best way of establishing research requirements; it is simply the best that the program has been able to devise so far.

A brief overview of the history, mission, and organization of HumRRO will be helpful in setting the background for this example. HumRRO was established in August 1951 as a contract between the department of the Army and The George Washington University. Its mission was "the Administration of the Human Resources Research Program, specifically in the areas of Training and Training Methods Research, Motivation, Morale and Leadership Research, and Psychological Warfare Research . . ." Since 1955, when the effort in psychological warfare was transferred to the Special Operations Research Office of The American University, the work of HumRRO has been concentrated in the field of training research, including man-weapon system analysis, and research in motivation, morale, and leadership.

HumRRO is a fairly complex organization as the organizational chart in Figure 16.1 shows, and its complexities stem from a fairly close integration with the Army, particularly with that Army headquarters most capable of serving as the poser of problems, the supporter of research, and the implementer of research products, the Continental

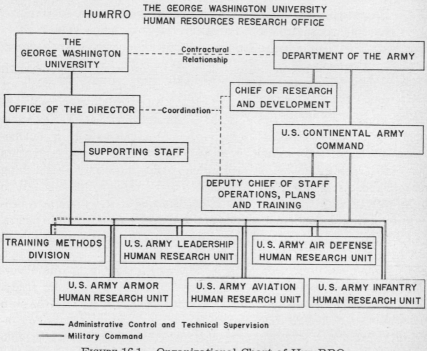

FIGURE 16.1.   Organizational Chart of HumRRO

Army Command (CONARC), located at Fort Monroe, Virginia. It is particularly important to note the coordination lines between the Director's Office and this Headquarters (CONARC), and Office of the Chief of Research and Development. Likewise, there is a special significance to what appear to be dual command lines coming from Headquarters CONARC, to the five Human Research Units, and from the Director's Office to those same Units. The Human Research Units are staffed with military personnel consisting of one or more field grade officers and a dozen or more enlisted men, who are under the command of Headquarters CONARC. The Human Research Units are also staffed with from eight to twenty-one research personnel who are members of the HumRRO staff and under the technical direction and administrative control of the Director's Office. The mission of the two kinds of people in the Human Research Units is the same: the accomplishment of the official HumRRO Work Program. The Training Methods Division, while lacking a permanently assigned military component, also maintains active liaison with the various problem-posers, logistics supporters, and implementers of HumRRO research in Headquarters CONARC, and in the various technical services of the Army (such as the Chemical Corps, Ordnance Corps, Signal Corps, etc.). The connection with The George Washington University provides continuity and reinforces the image of HumRRO as an impartial research agency. The Work Program consists of a set of formally authenticated research requirements which involve about 105 civilian scientists, plus another half dozen or so serving primarily in supervisory roles in the Director's Office.

Organized as it is, HumRRO affords a virtually unlimited opportunity for communication between research people and military personnel. This easy flow of information, plus the sharing of problems of research accomplishment, the close contact with operating problems, and the accessibility to responsible headquarters, makes possible an approximation to the procedure outlined earlier for establishing formal research requirements.

By way of introduction to how the Army's system of developing training research requirements works, a short description of the final form of the HumRRO Work Program will be helpful. The annual Work Program is a document published as of July 1 of each year by the Director of HumRRO on the authority of the Chief of Research and Development, Department of the Army. Funds and priorities are assigned to Tasks by the Chief of Research and Development. The Work Program contains some 35 to 40 Task Statements. A Task Statement is an authenticated training research requirement and is the general guidance document for the work of from one to as many as eight researchers for the fiscal year. An example of a Task Statement from the FY 62 Work Program is given in Figure 16.2. Typically, the Task Statement is worded somewhat generally, and lists a number of more specific Subtasks which constitute the actual research effort at a given time. Subtasks are also authenticated requirements, but they almost always receive their authentication from military headquarters below the Department of the Army level. As can be seen in the example, an effort is made to forecast the various steps in the training research process. (In Figure 16.2 the code for Subtask scheduling is: P—Planning; C—Col-

FIGURE 16.2.   An Example of a Task Statement from the
Annual HumRRO Work Program

TASK STATEMENT

1. Improved Methods for Training Aerial Surveillance Personnel—OBSERVE

2. Principal investigator: Francis H. Thomas, U.S. Army Aviation Human Research Unit

   Location of main effort: Fort Rucker, Alabama

   Sponsor: Headquarters, U.S. Continental Army Command

3. Scope:

   a. *Objective of research.* To develop improved methods for training human aerial observers. The research will (1) determine the requirements to be placed on air observers, under nuclear tactical concepts, (2) determine the critical skills prerequisite to meeting these requirements and develop the means for measuring these skills, and (3) develop and evaluate improved methods for training observers.

   b. *Background.* The first subtask provided information as to the major requirements and critical skills areas for effective aerial observation in future battle area surveillance. Training methods for improving skills in visual search, target recognition, geographical orientation, and target location were developed and evaluated by means of a standardized aerial-observer field test and post-training tests. The basic-skills training program relied heavily on prolonged practice using 35-mm color slides. For maximal effectiveness and standardization, techniques must be developed to motivate the student to continue the considerable amount of necessary practice. This motivation can best be achieved by programmed techniques in simplified automated-teaching procedures. It is believed that training research from Tasks METHOD and TEXTRUCT will be appropriate information sources.

   c. *Method of attack.* The second subtask will incorporate the training techniques developed in OBSERVE I into simple automated teaching procedures. Current procedures will be examined to determine the most applicable procedures for unit-level instruction. Alternate modes will be evaluated in terms of teaching effectiveness, economy, and practicality. The product anticipated from this subtask will be a training "package" for the implementation of the basic-skills program at the unit training level.

4. Estimated professional man years required:

   FY 1962: 3

   FY 1963: 3

5. Coordination:

The Adjutant General's Office, Office of the Chief of Transportation, U.S. Naval Training Device Center, U.S. Army Aviation School, Air Research and Development Command, Army Pictorial Center, U.S. Army Intelligence Center, U.S. Army Combat Surveillance Agency.

6. Summary and forecast:

I. A study of improved methods for training of personnel in visual aerial observation.

FY 1962

| 1 | 2 | 3 | 4 |
|---|---|---|---|
| D | S |  |  |

II. Unit-level aerial observer training package.

| FY 1962 | | | | FY 1963 | | | |
|---|---|---|---|---|---|---|---|
| 1 | 2 | 3 | 4 | 1 | 2 | 3 | 4 |
| P | P | P | CA | CA | D | D | S |

lection of Data; A—Analysis; D—Preparation of Draft Report and Review; S—Submission to Office, Chief of Research and Development. Progress is listed by quarters of the fiscal year.)

This chapter will now consider how the steps and the four agencies required for formal training research and development operate in the process of developing the annual Work Program.

*Posing the Research Problem.* Officially speaking, a problem for training research attention comes from an agency which can be called the "Consumer." It has a training problem and desires to use the results of research. Typically, a Consumer is one of the 30 or so schools within the Army, such as The Armor School at Fort Knox, Kentucky, The Air Defense School at Fort Bliss, Texas, or the Command and General Staff College at Fort Leavenworth, Kansas. Or the Consumer may be a U.S. Army Training Center. Occasionally, formal requests for research come from agencies that do not conduct training, but are cognizant of certain areas in which training problems may develop, such as the Office of Special Weapons Development located at Fort Bliss, Texas. The initial problem statement by the Consumer includes an indication of why training research is necessary, i.e., why the problem cannot be efficiently solved by the Consumer's own resources. The requirement for such an indication is usually a good screen to keep to a minimum requests for educational services that a school should be able to provide for itself. Commanders are reluctant to admit to having obvious weaknesses in their schools.

In actual practice HumRRO researchers participate very actively in the initial formulation of researchable problems at the consumer level. The HumRRO Units are well integrated with the business as well as the social life of their Posts, and have an excellent opportunity to see the Army's training problems from a common perspective with the Army. More often than not, the formal requests for research that come upward in Army channels are based on suggestions initiated by Hum-RRO civilian scientists. In addition, a considerable amount of research activity can and does go on outside the formal system for establishing research requirements. The close working relations with the Consumers are thus used to good advantage through setting up pilot studies with local support to determine more clearly the nature of a problem and its research feasibility.

A request for or inquiry into the possibility or feasibility of training research is routed to the Director of HumRRO through a "Sponsor." A Sponsor is a headquarters superordinate to the Consumer and has authority to alter the mission of the Consumer (or other subordinate commands) as necessary for accomplishing the research should it be undertaken. The Sponsor also has the necessary power to direct the implementation of research results. For about 80 per cent of HumRRO research, the sponsoring headquarters is U.S. Continental Army Command. The balance is sponsored by the Chiefs of several of the technical services—mainly Signal Corps, Ordnance Corps, and Chemical Corps. If the headquarters receiving the request for training research (the potential Sponsor) concurs, the next likely step is an inquiry to HumRRO concerning the feasibility of undertaking the proposed research, and for additional comments on the problem. By the time this happens, the Director's Office has probably already received through HumRRO channels and informally through military channels quite a bit of information on the problem and the forthcoming request.

The foregoing actions can take place at any time during the year, whenever a problem comes to light. In the main, however, they occur in an annual cycle involving all the tasks in a fairly orderly process that culminates in the final Work Program as published on authority of the Chief of Research and Development. As an early step in the development of the regular Work Program, Headquarters CONARC queries its subordinate commands and coordinate headquarters (e.g., Ordnance Corps, Signal Corps, Chemical Corps) about problems which should be considered for HumRRO attention. Replies are usually in by mid-autumn, and are reviewed and screened by a committee representing most of the general and special staff sections at Headquarters CONARC. The Director of HumRRO is represented at the committee's meetings to advise and become informed on likely requirements. Those suggestions that appear significant and relevant to the HumRRO mission and capabilities are forwarded to the Director of HumRRO through the Office of the Chief of Research and Development for consideration in developing the following fiscal year's Work Program.

*Review of Problems by the R&D Agency.* Once a request, or a group of requests, is received in the Director's Office from a potential sponsor, it is reviewed from the standpoints of mission relevance, researchability, likely benefit to the Army, availability of research personnel, and probable research cost—all of these in comparison with other tasks underway. The review is accomplished by members of the Director's staff in collaboration with the Directors of Research of the laboratories where the research is likely to be done. If it is determined that research is probably required, the Director of Research of the appropriate laboratory with the assistance of his military chief drafts a Task Statement. This usually requires a very few weeks, and constitutes, as can be seen from the example, a preliminary estimate of the situation, and a considerably clearer statement of the problem and its component sub-problems. The Task Statement, after review in the Director's Office, is relayed to the Sponsor for further consideration.

Upon approval by the Sponsor, the Task Statement then goes via the Director of HumRRO to the Office of the Chief of Research and Development for final authentication. In OCR&D a committee, known as the Army Human Factors Research Advisory Committee, representing CONARC and all Army General Staff Sections and some special staff sections, may be convened to evaluate the proposed Task Statement in competition with other work underway. By the time this stage is reached it is frequently difficult to distinguish the civilian from the military inputs to the plans as they then exist, so interwoven are the actions of scientists and soldiers in the HumRRO system. After recommendation by the AHFRAC, the Chief of R&D acts formally. Approval incorporates the Task within the Work Program.

*Assurance of Logistical and Personnel Support.* Approval of a Task Statement at the Sponsor level normally signifies not only the Sponsor's agreement with the development and statement of the problem, but a tentative affirmation of intent to provide the necessary research support in the form of troops, materiel, and coordinations as required.

The requirements for research support are spelled out much more explicitly in the various Subtask proposals which follow after more careful study and planning has been completed. When a Sponsor approves a Research Proposal, the commitment is fairly explicit that support will be forthcoming. Support may come from the Post where the Human Research Unit that takes on the project is located, or it may have to be taken wherever it can be found, frequently overseas or in other schools or units in continental United States. Because the final authentication of the requirement as present in the Task Statement takes place within the highest headquarters of the Army, there is rarely any lasting difficulty encountered in obtaining research support. It is easy to see the great advantage in this procedure from the standpoints of precise planning and of savings in time in effecting the details of support at a given Army Post. HumRRO researchers travel under military orders which give them access to the essential personnel and facilities wherever and whenever they work away from home. Care is always taken, however, to give the supporting agency early and full information on the nature of the research and the support requirements in order to minimize disruption of Post routines, and to keep the local commander and his staff officers fully informed of the progress of the work as it goes along.

*Implementing Research Products.* This stage of the research process is usually quite complicated, and fortunately for present purposes need not be stated in detail. The concern with implementation is with the thought that must be given to it at the time research requirements are being established. The thesis is that implementation actions, with all that they imply by way of costs, risks, and gains, must be considered early in the planning cycle for training research, or else the risk of wasted effort runs high. Dr. William H. Martin, when he was the Army's Director of Research and Development, said, "The purpose of this association of the R&D programs and the military plan is to permit each to react on the other for the determination of optimum adjustments of each with the needs and possibilities of the other. This concurrent consideration of the R&D program and of the military planning to fulfill a mission, and their consequent interaction on each other, I consider to be of outstanding importance both to research and development and to operations." (1956)

Within HumRRO the regular processes of planning and review raise the question: What can be done with the results? What can the Army gain in efficiency or effectiveness if HumRRO has the research information? And an important corollary question is: What will be done with the results? It is quite insufficient to proceed toward a problem solution that is sure to encounter strong attitudinal resistance despite the apparent economies that may result from implementation. One early HumRRO task, for example, showed that considerable savings could result from substituting a small caliber gun for a much larger one in early phases of a fire control training course. The report of this research was coolly received because it ran counter to an attitude and a policy at the time which held that full-caliber training was desirable for several reasons (albeit of questionable empirical validity) that were not fully explored before the research got started, and therefore were not represented in the measures taken in the experiment. Had enough sophistication about the training system, especially about the options available for improving on it, been available to the research planners, the project would undoubtedly have been quite different. The point here is that implementation prospects must be fully analyzed and understood in deciding on a heavy research commitment. One of the major advantages in having HumRRO well integrated into the Army is that researchers are able to get a satisfactory outlook on the chances of a research effort leading to something that the Army can use at some time. Long ago the notion was abandoned that good training research will automatically have value to the Army and will be welcomed with open arms. True, results of several projects that were completed in the early days before the elaborate requirements development process was established have been taken over and used. But the number of dead ends and abortions in those days was much higher also.

One aspect of Army use of a training research product that deserves note is the degree to which the product developed and tested in research settings will stand up in use after it is turned over to the Army. Naturally, the attempt is made to run the final tests of a new training program under realistic conditions, that is, conditions which will permit generalization of the procedures to all of the training situations in which it is to be used, and HumRRO has been fairly successful in this regard. But there remains the possibility that that which is finally put into effect will in one training situation or another not be the HumRRO-recommended program, but a superficially similar one which might or might not produce the same skill or skill levels. Stability, or freedom from being modified out of recognition, is a desirable attribute of a foreseeable end product and one that should be considered whenever possible in setting up a training research requirement. Unfortunately, this is hard to determine in advance, and must be accepted as one of the riskier aspects of doing training research which is expected to be immediately useful.

## DISCUSSION

The quick tracing of the processes used in HumRRO to establish training research requirements has suggested a number of ideas and problems that were not taken up in detail. A few will be considered here:

*Relationships Between Requirements for Development and Requirements for Research.* A development requirement typically grows from a rather clear perception of a practical problem and calls for the engineering or fabrication and test of a training procedure or program to solve that problem. Thus, a development requirement tends to be fairly specific and to foresee a rather definite end product. For example, one task was started with the practical objective of developing improved methods for training tank gunners. A specified block of hours in the tank crewman training program was given over to tank gunnery, and the hope was to produce a modified training program that would increase the speed and accuracy of firing tank guns in the same or a shorter training time. As with most development requirements, the ends were readily foreseen to justify a certain outlay of effort.

Experience has shown that a research requirement, on the other hand, arises from an objective only dimly viewed, or from obstacles that crop up unforeseen in the course of doing a development job which may, incidentally, serve to remind one that the earlier view of the developmental goal was not as clear as it was first thought to be. For example, in the tank gunnery problem just mentioned, before the task had gotten very far it became apparent that considerable research had to be done to determine just what were the major causes of target error in tank gunnery, or more specifically, if the human component of target error was large enough to be itself a worthy target for research. The outcomes of a series of studies of gun-laying accuracy and its relation to hit probability showed that any further research effort directed toward improving psychomotor precision in the final stages of aiming would be wasted (Schmitz, 1957). The entire project was reoriented as a result, and is dealing with other aspects of human performance in the tank gunnery problem. The findings that ballistic and mechanical factors accounted for a very large proportion of the dispersions of rounds on the target in the HumRRO test situation became a basis for further efforts by the Ordnance Corps to improve the extra-human components of the tank gun system.

*Maintaining Scientist Motivation in an R&D System That Exists to Solve Practical Problems.* One may wonder if being tied to clearly practical developmental objectives is likely to impose restrictions on research that might be unpalatable to researchers. For two reasons it is believed that this is essentially a pseudo-problem.

First, there is much of fundamental scientific and technological significance that can and must be done in support of development work. It is true that many young scientists come from a Ph.D. curriculum oriented toward basic research, and this means most new entries into the scientific manpower market feel that they cannot find lasting satisfaction in purely developmental jobs or in picking up fundamental research problems as obstacles en route to a practical end. But once on the job, it soon becomes evident that there are truly challenging, not to say formidable, problems of fundamental scientific relevance whose solution would materially facilitate progress toward the developmental goal, or make possible a better end product. Several HumRRO tasks with clear and practical objectives are engaged with a number of basic problems, among them: the effects of extreme and prolonged sensory impoverishment on attitudes and values; the relationships between several measured abilities and the amount of information a person can effectively process; the most efficient methods of establishing units of subject matter content for the programming of teaching machines; the psychophysics of complex sounds in the open air; effects of prolonged exposure to extreme cold weather on various skill complexes; and a good many others.

There is, to be sure, a certain hazard in leading a research sponsor to expect an early research solution to his problem. This risk can be minimized if the sponsor can be induced to recognize at the start that the state of the science is not such that a product to solve the immediate problem can be conjured up in just a little time, that research back-up for a developmental solution will be needed. The capabilities of psychological science should not be oversold. Experience, both pleasant and painful, has indicated that the more fully the sponsor understands and appreciates the technical problems, the gaps in knowledge, the inadequacies of process and methodology, and the naivete of researchers in the operational field, the fewer will be the occasions for defending the research and the happier will be the sponsor with the signs of progress along the way. In other words, research freedom in an immediately pragmatic system can be bought in return for an honest appraisal and candid statement of the research problem.

The second reason why the notion of unpalatable research restrictions may be a pseudo-problem is that there is a very considerable intellectual challenge to the researcher who seeks to optimize his functioning within a practical operating system through the efficient selection, definition, and refinement of problems and the design of efficient experiments. After several years of experience in an applied research organization, the scientists come to perceive the consumer's operating problems and their own particular competences in such a way as to effectively bring to bear the content of their science and its research methodology. Thus the organization becomes an effective mediator of the research goals of its scientists and the operating goals of the sponsors and consumers of applied research.

*The Extent to Which a System Must Be Analyzed Before Deciding to Undertake an R&D Job.* The purpose of R&D within a training process is to improve training efficiency or to produce a more efficient human component for an operating system. Research and development should be undertaken when these appear as the most economical means for producing the desired gains in efficiency. It follows, therefore, that the training or operating system should be analyzed only so far as to satisfy the researcher that a reliable gain in efficiency can be produced, and to satisfy the agent responsible for the training process or the working system that the costs of doing the research and using the results will be less than the cost of not doing the research.

Application of this rule will differ in each case, depending mainly on the preciseness and completeness of the information needed. Sometimes in the total absence of quantitative cost and gain estimates, a decision will be made to go ahead with research simply because of sheer conviction of the importance of getting a problem solved. No one has asked for a dollar value of a possible 10% increase in the staying power of the combat infantryman; yet the Army has put more than half a million research dollars into trying to develop an understanding of the basic psychology of stress and its effects on combat effectiveness, and will probably put in that much more. If the problem is not characterized by urgency or saliency, there will probably be a stronger tendency to look more carefully into costs and gains before making the research investment.

In this connection, Klein and Meckling (1958) have raised an interesting question: Should the operating system be thoroughly analyzed so as to permit the R&D end product to be very clearly established and thereby provide a clear set of intermediate goals? Or should the end product be stated in more general terms, and be itself subject to modification as research goes forward? They argue for the latter procedure, claiming that greater economy and a better end product will be the result of freedom to develop components that do not hew to the restrictions imposed by a fully specified end product. Klein and Meckling argue through an example in the heavy bomber field that translation to the training R&D field is readily made; their paper will repay careful study.

*The Appropriate Position in the Hierarchy of Authority Over Supporting or Implementing Actions for Establishing the Requirement for Training Research.* The administrative cost of formally establishing a research requirement in relation to the importance of the project sets limits on how far the research administrator should carry his formalizing activities. What these limits should be depends mainly on the expected duration of the project, the direct and supporting costs, the importance of getting the solution, and various combinations of values on these scales. The purposes of a formal process for developing requirements are to ensure their validity (is work being done on the really important problems?), their stability (freedom from whimsical termination and consequent loss), and their eventual usability. The purpose of having a research requirement finally authenticated formally is to ensure completion of the project.

In this regard the hypothesis is offered that the position of the desired authenticating agency is a multiplicative function of the total cost, the expected duration of the work, and the reciprocal of the value of the product. In other words, if a project is costly, will take a long time, and its chances of producing a large net gain are low, it had better be sold on high. The position of the authenticating agency should be at least high enough to ensure such utilization as is foreseen for the end product of the research.

*Some Differences Between Requirements for Training Research and Other Kinds of Applied Psychological Research.* It would be presumptuous to try to treat this topic over a wide range of conditions and research areas, but a few observations may at least have some heuristic value.

First, training research is commonly carried on in close relations to some operational setting, e.g., a school course, an on-the-job training program, a production line, and usually lasts for a fair amount of time. Therefore, responsible managers are going to need, and can readily obtain, a good understanding of what is going on. This can clearly have advantages in the form of cooperation and advice, as well as entail some risks of tampering with experimental conditions or of giving offense if unsolicited advice is not properly responded to by the researcher.

Second, administrative complexities in establishing the requirement may be somewhat greater for training research, especially in a military system, because of the clearness with which consequences can be foreseen. A major change in a training course can have repercussions in instructional costs, manpower flow, job descriptions, job structures, and job evaluations, all of which are more visible throughout the organization and perhaps more assessable than the consequences of a change in, say, illumination levels, aptitudes of new employees, or the spacing of rest periods.

Third, the requirements for experimental control in the actual conduct of much training research frequently impose restraints on the responsible managers of a training system. Such situations call for careful preparation, not only to avoid damage to managerial egos, but, and more importantly, to make reasonably sure that the experimental treatment will produce no serious decrement in performance for which someone other than the researcher will be held responsible. One extreme example of this consideration is in a project now being developed in HumRRO to improve and reduce the very great cost of certain critical aspects of training Nike Hercules air defense units. It could be disastrous to the city being defended should the experimental program under test for any reason, and at just the wrong time, produce a significant decrement in the capability of just one Nike battery.

*The Role of the Scientist in Establishing a Training Development Requirement.* In an established training R&D organization, the scientists are interested in the value of the developmental end product as well as in the research leading to it. Even if this were not the case, the scientist would still play a major role in establishing a development requirement through his estimates of the "researchability" of the subordinate problems. The scientist must bring to bear his knowledge of the component problem areas in order to provide some estimate of the probability of success for the enterprise as a whole. One HumRRO task grew out of a need for more efficient utilization of available officer talent in one of the combat arms. The problem posed was "What is the maximum span of control that a division commander can exercise?"

Stated in this form, the question was not a good one for training research. An analysis of combat operations and the organization of combat units showed the problem to be truly formidable however stated, but led to a simplification and breakdown into a set of problems of much smaller scope. Several conferences of scientists and soldiers led to the decision that a set of problems of the form, "What factors influence the number of units an officer can command in a defined combat situation and with a specified level of effectiveness?", could be reasonably expected to yield to a research attack. Thereupon, the formal procedures for setting up a research requirement were instituted, and led to establishing a long range task on the span of control problem.

The HumRRO example of a system for establishing formal requirements for R&D has shown that the scientist should help to identify as well as clarify training problems and propose research on them. It is added here that the scientist should also be encouraged to propose long-range research on variables that are not right now parts of training problems but which might reasonably become so in the future. This is very hard to do and the risks are great. But research that has partially solved training problems before they arise can have tremendous payoffs in both dollars and time.

## A Model for Guidance in Establishing Requirements for Training Research and Development

A great deal has been written and said about procedures for evaluating research and research proposals.[2] Most of the literature deals with research in general rather than with research in specific fields, and therefore does not provide a basis for comparing methods for evaluating products and proposals across disciplines. The evaluation literature pertaining to psychological research is small indeed. The most recent and comprehensive treatment was a 1958 symposium (Vallance, et al., 1958) which dealt with military research requirements. Unfortunately, the papers on this symposium have not been made available in the literature.

The various proposal evaluation schemes typically make use of a ratio of estimated research cost to estimated value of end product, making possible a rough comparison of the value of a number of current options.

[2]Hartshorne, 1953; Hertz, 1947; Kliever & Bancroft, 1953; Malcolm, Roseboom, Clark, & Fazar, 1959; Quinn, 1958; Vallance, Carp, Grether, Hammock, Hill, Kemp, Melton, Tucker, & Weiss, 1958; Wechsler & Brown, 1953.

Few rules have been suggested for determining the absolute value of a research proposal before it should be accepted, and those that have been are admittedly arbitrary (Kliever & Bancroft, 1953). While a fairly sophisticated program review and evaluation technique for the Polaris missile project has been described (Malcolm, et al., 1959), no examples have been found of attempts to apply linear programming or other allocation models to R&D activities, and so to provide a basis for efficient assignment of R&D resources to a given number of problems competing for R&D attention. Perhaps this is an impracticable task itself because of the essentially innovative nature of research and the consequent low predictability of outcome values.

An approach to evaluation of proposals for training research has been suggested by Hammock (1958). He states the absolute estimated value of an R&D project as the difference between the estimated payoff and the estimated cost, and further specifies his terms as follows:

1. *Estimated Value* = (estimated payoff) − (estimated cost)
2. *Payoff* = (payoff per trainee affected) × (number of trainees affected)
3. *Payoff Per Trainee Affected* =
    $\Sigma$ (performance unit gained) × ($ worth of each unit) +
    (training time saved) × (average $ cost per time unit) +
    ($ savings in equipment costs) + (any other $ savings)
4. *Number of Trainees Affected* =
    $\Sigma$ (number affected for each year, 1 to n) +
    $\dfrac{1}{y}$ $\Sigma$ (number affected partially for each year, 1 to n)
5. *Cost* = (costs to sponsor) + (costs to R&D agency)
6. *Cost to Sponsor or R&D Agency* =
    (personnel costs) + (equipment costs) +
    (travel costs) + (other costs)

In expression 4, $\dfrac{1}{y}$ is intended to be an average fraction of partial effects, which are presumably training effects falling variously short of what is required for practical increments in output of the system containing the job, but which can be made up by experience on the job. Hammock recognizes the likely operation of various intangibles, such as probability of success (which enters into nearly every sub-project of a research program), whether the results are available from previous studies, and whether an interested research staff is available or can be procured to do the work. Values presumably could be generated for these terms, but their validity would be suspect, to say the least. To broaden the cost estimate somewhat, an item should be added that deals with the costs of implementing the results of research.

Although the shortcomings of practically all evaluative schemes are readily apparent, the value of formal proposal appraisal cannot be denied. For even if the values assigned to the terms are of unknown validity, a review of a group of R&D options against a common set of terms can at least make possible a fairly standardized clinical judgment. And more importantly, those who propose and those who dispose can think, plan, and communicate in a similar language to the constant improvement of research efficiency and value.

## SOME IMPLICATIONS FOR RESEARCH PLANNING IN PUBLIC EDUCATION

This chapter would not be complete without referring the procedures that have been discussed to research on problems of education outside the Army. What relevance do these procedures have for setting up research problems, for example, in a public school system? Because of limitations of scope and space, the attempt will be made here only to suggest how the steps that have been outlined in the earlier section on conditions necessary for the establishment of formal R&D requirements may look in application to educational research in a public school system. Further suggestions of the relevance of certain HumRRO research procedures to general educational research have been described by Crawford (1959), and in several summaries of HumRRO research (Human Resources Research Office, 1954; 1955; 1956; 1957; 1958; 1960; 1961a).

A source of valid educational problems is essential to applied educational research that is to be useful. Whatever method is used to give expression to educational problems that may become the object of educational research, some kind of group consideration, whether it be a set of informal conferences or formal staff actions, will lead to a better selection and a more clearly formulated problem than individual action alone. Furthermore, the viability of the requirement that emerges will probably be much greater than if supported only by an individual.

The facilities for R&D in public education range from a single researcher pursuing a line of interest or preparing a graduate thesis to some fairly substantial continuing institutions, such as the Research Division of the National Education Association, and the many foundations which support, through grants, a great amount of research. Some school systems maintain their own research divisions, which may bear the same formal relationship to their systems as HumRRO does to the Army. The parallel is not general, however, for much of educational research is funded from outside the educational institutions that may benefit. A proposal has been made (National Academy of Sciences, 1958) for an Organization for Educational Research which would undoubtedly have some significant advantages over the relatively fragmented ways in which much educational research is conducted. A major advantage of a continuing research organization is that it becomes a repository not only of documented research, but also a storehouse of unrecorded information on research problems and methods. Also, a successful organization takes on values as "a place to get things done" and can grow in effectiveness through its reputation among those it serves.

Unless the research is done within and for an operating educational system and derives from formal requirements, the application of research in education is largely dependent on the alertness of educational administrators or their staffs in spotting useful research findings in the general literature. Because most educational research tends to be based on less formal requirements it may be that implementation is a major problem in the overall efficiency of educational research as it is practiced in this country. No one has to go on record as wanting the research or being willing to implement useful outcomes. As a result, research is frequently undertaken with no verified operational problem in mind, and that which is completed often depends on chance events for its utilization.

Again, the importance of considering implementation possibilities early in the planning stage should be emphasized. An early asking of such questions as, "Who can use this research?" and "How can it be translated into action?" goes a long way toward forcing a clear definition of problems, and there is no reason to doubt the value of such questions in any educational research activity. This is not to say that all research should have a clear application to problems of educational operations, for much supporting research is necessarily undertaken with only the hope that some subsequent research step will benefit. The point is, simply, that the more clearly the application of an end product can be foreseen, the better can be the conceptualization, planning, support, and execution of the research program.

# REFERENCES

Adams, S., Buel, J., Barclay, G., & McDowell, P. *Report of working group on human behavior under conditions of military service.* Joint Project of R&D Board and Personnel Policy Board in Office of Secretary of Defense. Washington: 1951.

Crawford, M. P. Research and development in training and education. Paper presented at symposium, The Contributions of Military Research to Education and Training, at Northwestern University, Evanston, Illinois, December 1959.

Douglass, H. R. & Tallmadge, M. How university students prepare for new types of examinations. *Sch. & Soc.*, 1934, *39*, 318-320.

Hammock, J. C. Methodology of establishing military research requirements. Paper read at Amer. Psychol. Ass., Washington, September 1958.

Hartshorne, E. Research cost analysis and project evaluation. In D. B. Hertz & A. H. Rubenstein (Eds.), *Research operations in industry.* New York: Kings Crown Press, 1953, 87-104.

Hertz, D. B. Management's role in planning research. *Chemical Engng,* 1947, *54*, 123-130.

Hoag, M. W. *What is a system?* (Document P-1035). Santa Monica, California: RAND Corporation, 1957.

Human Resources Research Office, The George Washington University.
*What HumRRO is doing.* Research Bulletin 1. Washington: 1954.
*What HumRRO is doing.* Research Bulletin 2. Washington: 1955.
*What HumRRO is doing.* Research Bulletin 3. Washington: 1956.
*What HumRRO is doing.* Research Bulletin 4. Washington: 1957.
*What HumRRO is doing.* Research Bulletin 5. Washington: 1958.
*What HumRRO is doing.* Research Bulletin 7. Washington: 1960.
*What HumRRO is doing.* Research Bulletin 8. Washington: 1961. (a)
*Work program,* fiscal year 1962. Washington: 1961. (b)

Klein, B. & Meckling, W. *Application of operations research to development decisions.* (Document P-1054). Santa Monica, California: RAND Corporation, 1958.

Kliever, W. H. and Bancroft, R. Z. Choosing and evaluating research projects. *Product Engng,* 1953, No. 6, 184-187.

Lazier, W. A. Planning the research project. In *Proceedings of the Sixth Annual National Conference on the Administration of Research (September 8-10, 1952).* Atlanta: Georgia Institute of Technology, 1953. Pp. 59ff.

Malcolm, D. G., Roseboom, J. H., Clark, C. E., & Fazar, W. Application of a technique for research and development program evaluation. *Operations Res.*, 1959, 7, 646-669.

Martin, W. H. Carrying out a military research and development program. *Signal*, 1956, *10*, 38-39.

McGeoch, J. A. *The psychology of human learning*. New York: Longmans, 1942.

Meyer, G. An experimental study of the old and new types of examination: I. The effect of the examination set on memory. *J. educ. Psychol.*, 1934, *25*, 641-661.

National Academy of Sciences, National Research Council. *A proposed organization for research in education*. Report to Advisory Board on Education of a Conference held at Madison, Wisconsin, July 9-11, 1958. Washington: 1958.

Quinn, J. B. The measurement and evaluation of research results. Unpublished doctoral dissertation. Columbia University, 1958.

Schmitz, M. A. *Consistency in laying the main tank gun in a life-fire situation* (U). Washington: Human Resources Research Office, The George Washington University, 1957. Technical Report 39.

United States Civil Service Commission. Assessing and reporting training needs and progress. *Personnel Methods Series No. 3*, 1956.

Vallance, T. R. A comparison of essay and objective examinations as learning experiences. *J. educ. Res.*, 1947, *41*, 279-287.

Vallance, T. R. (Chairman), Carp, A., Grether, W., Hammock, J. C., Hill, C. W., Kemp, E. H., Melton, A. W., Tucker, J. A., & Weiss, R. A. Symposium on methodology for establishing of military research requirements. Symposium at Amer. Psychol. Ass., Washington, 1958.

Wechsler, I. R. & Brown, Paula (Eds.) *Evaluating research and development*. Berkeley: Human Relations Research Group, Institute of Industrial Relations, University of California, 1953.

Work, L. T. The philosophy and economics of an industrial research program. In D. B. Hertz & A. H. Rubenstein (Eds.), *Research operations in industry*. New York: Kings Crown Press, 1953. Pp. 3-23.

Chapter 17 | *A Study of The Relationship of Psychological Research To Educational Practice*

Robert M. W. *Travers, University of Utah*

Over a century has passed since the German philosopher Johann Friedrich Herbart first proposed that educational procedures should be guided by scientific research. Herbart himself was a philosopher whose interest in pedagogy stemmed from his work in philosophy and, as an occupant of a chair of philosophy formerly held by the great Immanuel Kant, was in a much better position to influence educational thought than he was to influence educational practice. His influence on thought was widespread and lasting but his influence on educational practice is much more difficult to discern. One can point to some experimental schools in Germany during the second half of the last century which attempted to put into practice the idea that scientific research should be the key to educational advance. One can also point to a few isolated educators in this country, such as Horace Mann and Francis Parker, who espoused a similar point of view. History has shown little enthusiasm for educational reform based on systematic research of the kind in which the scientist engages. It is the purpose of this chapter to examine some of the history of the relationship of scientific research to educational practice, and to attempt to point out some of the ways in which this relationship might be improved.

Half a century after the death of Herbart, Joseph Mayer Rice set out to reform education through disseminating the rather spectacular results of a program of educational research designed to provide a basis for improving teaching in the classroom. The story of his failure to bring about reform is known to every educational historian, but even the name of Rice is unfamiliar to most graduates of teacher training programs. So the lesson to be learned has been largely lost. Rice's spectacular findings, though widely disseminated, were as effective as a sophomore's essay in producing educational change. He was the first to discover that the results of research do not bring about educational change, however persuasive the results may be. The educational subculture is basically resistant to the efforts of an agent such as the research worker to produce change; perhaps in this respect it is much like other subcultures.

The lesson to be learned from Rice's excursion into the field of educational research and educational reform is important, and his brief career as an educational reformer provides an appropriate introduction to this chapter. Rice was a physician by profession, but after a rather brief practice of medicine during the years 1881-88 became interested in problems of education and left for a two-year visit to Europe where he studied pedagogy and psychology at two great centers of educational thought, namely, Jena and Leipzig. Rice undoubtedly came under the Herbartian influence as well as that of Wundt and in 1890 returned to America fired with a zeal for educational reform. Like most reformers, his immediate impulse was to tell the public in strong terms that the time for reform had come, and this he did in a forceful article picturesquely entitled "Need School Be a Blight to Child-Life" (1891). In this article he compared some schools he had observed in Germany where "education is regulated more or less by scientists" with schools he had seen in America where the pupils were instructed mechanically. Perhaps the readers considered the comparison of German schools with American schools invidious. Public reaction was nil. To bring his case before an even wider public and to expand in detail on the need for educational reform he followed his article with a book entitled *The Public School System of the United States* (1893) in which he summarized the observations he had made on 1200 teachers located in various schools from Boston to Philadelphia in the East to St. Louis and Minneapolis in the Middle West. The book was hardly more successful than the article. Educators paid no attention to the opinions of a layman, who in professional circles rapidly became dubbed as a crackpot. Legend relates that he was met with jeers when he attempted to present his findings to a meeting of the National Education Association.

Like most reformers, Rice was a man dedicated to his cause. If his observations in the classroom were to be brushed aside as the worthless opinions of an amateur, then what he needed was a carefully collected compilation of facts. In terms of the mood of educators in Germany, from which he had so recently returned, this was to be not only the preferred, but also the only sound way of producing educational change. Thus in 1895 he set out to collect information about the skills of school children in arithmetic, spelling, and languages and to relate those skills to the way in which the children had been taught. On the basis of these studies he found that the amount of time devoted to the acquisition of a particular skill such as spelling had little to do with the level of skill acquired. In a majority of the schools the time devoted to spelling could be at least halved without any reduction in the level of skill which would be acquired. The results of his study of spelling appeared in a new article in the *Forum* under the fetching title of "Futility of the Spelling Grind" (1897). Other articles presented data attacking other aspects of current teaching in the schools and finally the entire research enterprise was drawn together in a book entitled *Scientific Management in Education* (1913).

Rice's effort to produce educational reform had absolutely no effect on his contemporaries. The outcry of public indignation which he expected would arise as a result of the publication of his research never even reached the level of a murmur. Professional educators could not have shown less response to his findings and recommendations, for little reference is found to him in the educational literature of the period. Yet 50 years later one finds that most of the reforms towards which he had directed his efforts have been incorporated in education. Progressive education of the mid-30's might well have derived its charter from the writings of Rice in the mid-90's. One also finds 50 years later that it is still not the research scientist who brings reform to education.

The failure of Rice to use research as an instrument of educational reform is a familiar story which has been re-enacted many times during the last half century. While considerable scientific research has been undertaken on problems related to those encountered in education, the impact of these results on teaching practice has been slight. Large research establishments which have developed within the military for conducting research on training problems have often had impact only at the local level. The United States Air Force, which developed the largest of these organizations, was unable to support a sustained scientific effort to improve training practices.

## COMPONENTS OF THE SYSTEM TO BE CHANGED

One approach to the study of the problem is to begin by examining the essential components of the system to be changed and to consider the difficulties of producing changes in these components. What the writer considers to be essential components are represented in a diagrammatic form in Figure 17.1. The left-hand section of this chart shows in a diagrammatic form the general nature of the system to be changed. The two major components are behavior systems and consist of the behavior systems of the student and the behavior systems of the teacher.

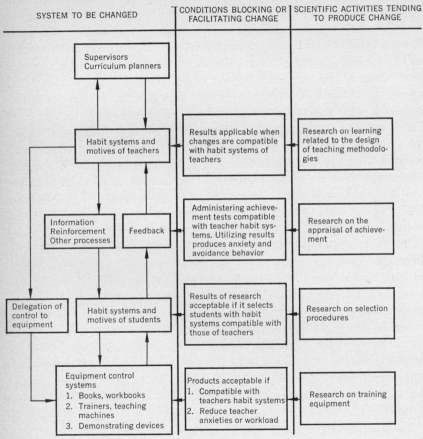

FIGURE 17.1. Representation of the Major Components in the Teaching-Learning Mechanism in Schools

The middle section and the right-hand section of the chart represent forces attempting to produce change and factors which tend to inhibit or facilitate change. Much of training research is designed to find teacher behaviors that will increase the effectiveness with which student behavior undergoes modification. Teacher behavior in a particular program may be modified by one of two procedures. One way is by the selection of new teachers who manifest the desired behavior that is needed for the effective functioning of the system. Another is to attempt to modify the behavior directly. The latter is the usual procedure attempted but one suspects that the results tend to be quite unsatisfactory. Behavior is not generally that easily modified. Teachers do not change their ways of behaving simply by being told that learning would proceed with greater efficiency if they behaved differently. The few studies which have been undertaken in which an attempt was made to modify teacher behavior and in which a record was made of what teachers actually did in the group generally show only small differences before and after the change was instituted. This is hardly surprising. The shrewd marriage counsellor has long given up the practice of telling the partners how they should behave, for he knows full well that even with cooperative parties behavior is not that easily changed. Educational research based on the assumption that teachers will change their behavior if they are told how to make their teaching more efficient is very naively undertaken. Rather must one assume that teacher behavior is likely to be the component in the system least amenable to direct change.

The first point then is that teacher behavior is probably the most difficult component to modify in the entire system. Selection of teachers manifesting the desired habit systems is probably the easiest way of producing change. A part of the difficulty of modifying teacher behavior stems from the fact that a particular teacher is likely to show a marked tendency to emit certain kinds of verbal behaviors rather than others and changing the behavior of the teacher involves changing verbal habits which are likely to be well established and powerfully reinforced. Examples of the problems produced by this are not hard to find. A certain teacher in a high school is a fine scholar in the field of American history, but cannot make presentations or lead discussions at the level of the students. After some years of struggling with this problem, the principal decides that there is little hope of modifying the behavior of this teacher but solves the problem by assigning to him only very bright students. Another example is that of a school in the armed services which has prepared men for electronic maintenance work by giving them a rather thorough grounding in theory of electricity; research workers, after a thorough study of the training problem, point out that such a theoretical approach has little value and that class time should be devoted to other types of training. The instructors objected strongly to the idea and continued to teach theory of electricity. Teachers may be expected to continue to emit the verbal behavior they have emitted in the past even when research demonstrates that other verbal behaviors would be more desirable. Sometimes it can be suspected that most university curricula represent simply a set of topics about which the faculty like to talk; perhaps it cannot be otherwise. If educational and training practices are to be changed, the teacher component is not the component with which to begin.

The second major component of the system is the behavior of the student which the whole system exists to modify. Success of the system is assessed in terms of the extent to which the behavior of the pupil is modified so that it meets certain specifications. In a training situation these specifications should be set by the requirements of the job, but in practice they are set by the judgments of the instructors. This means that the successful student is one who is capable of acquiring the habit systems which the instructors reinforce. This requires a certain consistency between the behavior of the student and the behavior of the instructor. Inconsistency in this respect is one of the greatest sources of inefficiency in training and education. The remedy is usually that of selecting students by means of tests and in such a way that the students selected are the ones which tend to achieve high grades given by the instructors. How far such practices select students who are able to learn in accordance with policy statements about the system and how far such selection procedures merely select students whose habit systems are compatible with those of the instructor is not known. The failure of aptitude tests to predict job performance even though they may predict instructors' grades suggests that the latter is a tenable hypothesis in many educational systems. Certainly, instructors who emit behavior about Ohm's law want to have students eager to learn about Ohm's law and capable of doing so. An instructor in this case who was confronted with a group of students which did not emit behavior (questions and comments) related to Ohm's law would probably manifest frustration. Teachers want students who emit behavior compatible with that which they emit or capable of learning to emit similar behavior.

If modifications of training procedures were limited to the modification of teacher behavior, the outlook for training research would be a very dreary one, for well-established behavior patterns of the adult human show great stability. However, another important process occurs in the educational system; this is that the teacher component of the system delegates control from time to time to the equipment components of the system. Equipment includes such items as textbooks and workbooks, films and other visual aids, teaching machines and practical problem-solving situations.

The system to be changed also includes supervisory control, which varies according to the particular system. That supervisors can exercise some control over the behavior of teachers is evident to anyone who has spent time in schools but such control is unlikely to change the basic habit systems of the teachers involved. A principal might well succeed in extending the time which teachers devote, say, to spelling, but would be unlikely to change the amount of time during which the teachers spend in direct control of the class. Principals can also change the behavior of the teachers in the school through the retention of those who display a particular pattern and the turnover of those who do not. Selection and turnover may go far towards solving the supervisors' problem of producing particular behaviors in teachers, but the problem of the person engaged in educational research is that of how to change the behavior of the principal so that this will result in teacher behaviors consistent with the results of research. Here again, the problem is that of changing behavior, an area in which not too much success has been achieved. Indeed, it appears that, from what at present is known of techniques for changing behavior, the behavioral elements in the teacher and supervisor components are probably the least amenable to modification.

The system includes a feedback component which is usually ill-developed and informal. The feedback component is, of course, the procedure through which information concerning student progress is fed back to the instructor. Examinations as well as informal evaluation procedures constitute this component. Feedback concerning the achievement of the student has two possible kinds of effects on the instructor. It may produce pleasure responses or anxiety responses. If the instructor responses are pleasurable they are likely to reinforce whatever instructor behavior has preceded them. If feedback is anxiety producing it is likely to be rejected and hence uninfluential in changing the learning process. These responses to feedback represent a major weakness in the operation of the feedback mechanism in the system and perhaps account for much of its inertia and resistance to change. Achievement tests introduced by an outside agency often fail to function within the feedback component because they are anxiety producing and hence, while one finds that numerous batteries of achievement tests are widely used throughout the public schools, rarely is much use ever made of the results. Every test consultant is familiar with the school that buys tests, administers them, scores the answer sheets, and locks the results in the school file. This familiar ritual all too often omits the final and anxiety producing step of interpreting the results and perhaps modifying the educational program.

## INFLUENCE OF THE BEHAVIORAL SCIENCES ON EDUCATION

That education has improved over the last 50 years cannot be denied. No longer can an observer see, as Rice pointed out, children spending hours each day being drilled in spelling. Punitive behavior on the part of teachers has probably declined and more of teacher behavior is constructive than it was in the past. Numerous changes are noticed when one compares the data collected by Rice with those of modern observers. A part of this change can be attributed to the fact that today most teachers are college graduates and are intellectually more capable than their predecessors. There has also been an accumulation of practical knowledge which, over the years, has slowly influenced classroom practices. Teachers have found it rather unprofitable to spend several hours a day drilling children in spelling and thus the practice has been slowly eliminated. A slow change for the better has undoubtedly taken place, and, despite present day criticisms to the contrary, the evidence seems fairly clear that progress has been made in the teaching of subject matter. But what part has scientific research played in this progress?

Every psychologist knows that educational psychology was born near the turn of the century as an infant of brilliant promise. The experimental psychology of learning as it emerged through the work of Thorndike was thought by many to herald the new era, prophesied by Herbart, in which a science of behavior was to be the central guiding force in the development of educational practice. When James McKeen Cattell brought the young Thorndike to Teachers College he must surely have had this possibility in mind. Any expectations which Cattell may have had about the potentialities of his protegé must have been far exceeded by actual accomplishments. That Thorndike's influence on education was great is beyond debate, and yet the success of his work did not lead to the establishment of large research units in the teacher training institutions and the school systems of the country. True, one can point to the development of a similar learning laboratory at Chicago through the influence of Judd, a laboratory which made some important contributions to education. Nevertheless, the influence of Thorndike on education must be regarded as the influence of a single great man, rather than as one which firmly established the position of the natural scientist as a leader in educational advance. Indeed, many would say that the period of Thorndike working at Columbia and Judd working at Chicago represents the peak of the impact of educational psychology on school practices and that since that time there has been a slow decline in this impact.

The influence of Thorndike is of interest to assess in terms of the model of the teaching situation which has been previously discussed. If school practices and procedures are studied today, the lasting influence of Thorndike is clearly apparent in many of the materials used, but little of his influence can be discerned in the teaching methodologies which are observed. This, of course, is what one would expect. Teaching materials can be modified without disturbing the pattern of teacher behavior and these modifications will be accepted. The acceptance of principles established by Thorndike for the design of printed materials is clearly seen in every textbook produced for use in school. A reader which did not use a controlled vocabulary, a concept developed by Thorndike, would not be accepted by a publisher today. Almost every book that reaches the schools today shows the profound results of the research and applied activities of Thorndike. Recent efforts to design equipment for classroom use in terms of established psychological principles by such persons as Pressey and Skinner represents a revival of interest in this matter.

Despite the success of both Thorndike and Judd in attacking educational problems through experimental techniques, schools of education made no attempt to establish laboratories which would study experimental psychological problems related to learning. Today laboratories for psychological experimentation just do not exist within schools of education which, likewise, do not employ experimental psychologists. Educational psychologists have survived in schools of education, but without experimental laboratories and usually without research facilities.

Most educational psychologists asked today to define their role within the field of education would probably say that their role was threefold. First, they train specialized personnel such as school psychologists and counselors for the school systems of the country usually through some joint program of courses in education and psychology. Second, they have the function of interpreting to educators at large current scientific developments in psychology and of sifting those that have the best potential applications to problems of education. Third, they have the function of conducting research on problems of education within the framework of thinking provided by psychology. Over the last few decades the first of these functions, the training of school personnel, has become primary, while the research functions have had a role of dwindling importance; at least this is the opinion of a number of educational psychologists. Some would even state this position in even more extreme terms. Indeed, a project has been developed jointly by the Department of Psychology of Northwestern University and the School of Education of that same institution to investigate the schism that has developed between the two areas.

What has been said about the influences of educational psychologists on educational practice does not imply that other psychologists have not influenced educational thought. In referring to educational thought, reference is made here to current literature and other sources of verbal statements about education. Educators represent, like other professional groups, a verbal community in which certain propositions are highly reinforced by other members of that community. Some psychologists have been highly influential in determining the statements which educators make about education. This does not mean, of course, that the statements made about education are necessarily related to what teachers actually do. The statements which the writer of this chapter makes about desirable teaching practices are not too closely related to what he actually does in the classroom. This is probably true of most persons engaged in education.

The influence of psychology other than educational psychology on the verbal behavior of educators comes from two distinct sources. On the one hand there is the psychological influence which finds its source in the Gestalt psychologists and which led to the present day phenomenological approach to psychology. For many educators, this approach to psychology is psychology, and Gestalt psychology is the psychology of learning. It is perhaps odd to reflect that educators have espoused that approach to problems of learning which has least to say about how the teacher can manipulate the learning situation in order to make learning as effective as possible. Traditional Gestalt psychology and modern phenomenological psychology have almost nothing to say about how the teacher should function but rather do they attempt to describe the nature of some of the internal events that accompany learning. Hence, it is hardly surprising that this trend in psychological theorizing has had relatively little influence on classroom procedure. A highly significant fact in this connection is that a proposed yearbook of the Association for Supervision and Curriculum Development which purports to discuss the relation of education to psychology is planned to emphasize throughout concepts derived from phenomenology. For many educators today, perhaps for even a majority, such concepts do not represent *a part* of psychology; they represent psychology. This is seen in the extensive use of concepts derived from phenomenological psychology which are evident in any discussion today of educational problems. This influence is even apparent in many elementary textbooks of educational psychology which have been written largely from a phenomenological viewpoint.

The second line of influence comes from the clinical tradition which finds its roots in the work of Sigmund Freud. Some of Freud's followers became primarily interested in problems of child development and through the work of such persons as Melanie Klein began to make an impression on educational thought. If mental health in adult life were to be achieved then the problems of mental health developed in early childhood must be worked out during school years. While the followers of Freud insisted that this should be done by a trained therapist there were those who believed that the teacher could play a role in the therapeutic process. From this background there emerged the recognition of the need for a professionally sound guidance system, but also the concept that the classroom teacher should function as a therapist. The attractiveness of clinical approaches to psychology to those engaged in teaching or educational administration is easy to understand when one understands the climate of educational thinking that has emerged over the last 20 years. The tendency has been to expand, at least in the printed job descriptions, the role of both the student and the teacher within the school. In such job descriptions, the role of the teacher is to be more and more a diagnostician to whom the student turns when some obstacle to learning is encountered. Since many of the obstacles to learning lie within the personality of the learner, the teacher must also function as a therapist.

Since the teacher has no training as a therapist, the situation could be an embarrassing one. It is here that the enormous attractiveness of much of the Rogerian viewpoint becomes apparent, for implied in this system of therapy is the idea that any person who will function as a sounding board for the individual's troubles can function as a therapist. From the point of view of the teacher, therapy will take place if the teacher conducts his class in a thoroughly permissive way and provides situations in which the student can express his problems and conflicts. The purpose of such expression within a permissive atmosphere is that it supposedly permits some kind of internal reorganization which, in turn, results in responses which are more adaptive than those previously undertaken. It is not fair to Rogerian approaches to take the viewpoint that it permits even the amateur to function as a psychological therapist, but this is the way in which related ideas have often been interpreted. Preoccupation with the concepts of clinical psychology has not helped to promote a scientific approach to educational problems but rather has led to a free acceptance of ideas which resemble more closely folklore than scientific generalizations. The relationship of clinical psychology to education has harmed rather than hindered the development of a thoroughgoing, scientific approach to problems of the classroom.

### RESEARCH AS A TOOL OF PROGRESS AS IT HAS EVOLVED IN THE EDUCATIONAL SUBCULTURE

The immediate response of the frustrated scientist who finds that his research findings are not eagerly seized upon by the educational profession is to dub the educator as a stupid, rigid person who is not interested in educational progress. This is, of course, an emotional reaction to frustration for there is incontrovertible evidence that educators are considerably above the average intellectually; research has never shown them to be particularly rigid, and even a cursory perusal of current educational literature will reveal a zeal for progress which may be even frightening to the outsider who may be much more conservative in the changes which he anticipates. The problem is not just that educators are dull nor that they do not want change, but rather is it that they expect change to come through channels other than those with which the scientist is familiar. In other words, the educational culture over the years has attempted to establish its own machinery through which change is to be brought about and this machinery does not include to any degree the frustrated scientist sitting on the sidelines. The educator, like members of other subcultures, is to some extent a victim of the mores and practices of his own subculture, and it is these which appear to have resulted in barriers which limit the extent to which the results of research from the scientific subculture can be assimilated.

What appears to be one of the major barriers which prevents the educational subculture from assimilating the results of scientific research is the conception of research which has been evolved by educators. Over the last hundred years there has developed on the educational scene a widely held concept of research which has had widespread support from the educational community. This concept of research and its origins must now be considered.

Over the last 100 years, the most important single force shaping the research behaviors of educators has been the National Education Association and its predecessor the National Teachers Association which held its first meeting in 1857. As a result of considerable pressure from the leaders of the Association, a Committee on School Statistics was appointed in 1860 and was followed by later committees which produced reports designed to be guides for the reporting of statistical information by the various states. J. Cayce Morrison (1956) who has reviewed the early development of the National Education Association points out that, at least in the early years of the Association's development, any influence it had on research was through the emphasis on the improvement in the collection of statistical data. Whatever this movement lacked in imagination it made up for in enthusiastic support by the rank and file of the Association, and in 1864 the Association had placed before it a resolution urging the establishment of a national bureau for the compilation of educational statistics. The resolution was adopted and members of the Association interviewed not only members of Congress but also the President himself urging the establishment of such a bureau. In 1867, by act of Congress, a Bureau of Education was established within the Federal Government and this later became the Office of Education which has functioned over the years under many different agencies. This bureau was also to function as a fact-finding agency busily occupied with the matter of collecting data which somehow were going to improve educational programs everywhere. This statistical function has remained one of central importance over the years and one which has found substantial support among educators.

The National Education Association was not only concerned with establishing fact-collection agencies outside of its organization, for the time soon arrived when the decision was made to establish its own fact-finding agency. In 1922 it established a Research Division which was to provide the "facts" which teachers might need. The Research Division of the National Education Association has functioned as a fact-finding agency since its foundation and produces statistical tabulations of the results of findings with great regularity. The reports cover such varied topics as salaries, the supply and demand of teachers, retirement plans and so forth. The material published probably has no influence on classroom practice and is hardly intended to have this effect. Much of it is of use to administrators, possibly supporting the policies of many by indicating that what they do is in line with what other administrators do. This may well give aid and comfort to those who do not deserve such aid and comfort.

Within the framework of research as a fact-finding enterprise there has been little interest in the development of theory. This one can understand, for theory development has hardly been the forte of those whose interests are directed towards life's practical problems. Theory construction has hardly been an identifiable activity within the field of education, though there have been some attempts to reshape theories drawn from the outside. Theories of education based on the philosophies of Jean Jacque Rousseau and John Dewey are illustrations of the ways in which the theoretical developments of persons largely outside of the field of education have had some bearing on educational practice. Such adaptations of theory have had little impact on research practice, and there has been almost no attempt to state such theories in terms which the research worker can use. Most of the vague theorizing for which education is noted has no impact or bearing on research. It cannot have. Theory, to have impact on research, has to have properties which this kind of theorizing lacks. The time will come when there will have to be established standards for theory construction in education. When that time comes educational theories may be useful for guiding research as well as practice.

The direction which the National Education Association gave to research as a fact-finding operation seems to have influenced school systems and universities in the establishment of research agencies. During the last quarter century many school systems have established the position of Director of Research. On the surface this might indicate that school systems which established such positions had become dedicated to the improvement of classroom practice through the scientific study of educational problems, but this is far from the case. The Director of Research in most school systems is usually a person to whom there has been delegated the task of collecting and compiling the statistics that describe the system and that are necessary for carrying out normal administrative functions. The service which he performs is a valuable one and a school system might have great difficulty in carrying on without him. Some agency has to perform this highly important task. The misfortune is that it has to be carried on by a director of research who is likely either to define research in terms of the work he performs, or who recognizes that scientific research is something other than that which he does but that he does not have time to engage in it.

As the present century progressed some bureaus of educational research operated by directors of research slowly broadened their activities to include matters other than records of attendance, surveys of teacher personnel and community needs. A few have at times actually undertaken research similar to that undertaken by the behavioral scientist, but the pressure has been for them to stay with matters of immediate practical importance in administrative decision making. When the bureaus have been staffed with persons capable of undertaking scientific research, the talents of such personnel have often been used to conduct studies which can provide evidence to justify the worth of some practice which has been recently introduced and which must be defended before the public. Hence, one finds that such bureaus of research have often conducted studies comparing one teaching methodology with another. A brief discussion of the role of such studies in advancing education is highly relevant here because their merits and limitations are not widely recognized.

Studies of outcomes of gross differences in educational method bear at least a resemblance to classical scientific designs, but a close examination of what they accomplish reveals that this resemblance is superficial. Indeed, the methodology of such studies has been so deceptively similar to those of classical experimentation that differences have not been recognized to the extent to which they should be. First, the purposes of such educational studies differ fundamentally from the purposes of most scientific research. The major purpose of such studies of teaching practice is to justify a program and hence they tend to be repeated in community after community, wherever the particular teaching method has to be defended from attack. There is almost no attempt to build each study on the work which has previously been undertaken. The writer's evaluation of the last 50 studies which have been undertaken which compare the outcomes of one teaching methodology with another is that they have contributed almost nothing to our knowledge of the factors that influence the learning process in the classroom. Many of them do not even identify what the experimentally controlled variables are and indicate only that the study compares the outcomes of educational practices in the community where the study originates with educational practices elsewhere. Such studies, if they were conducted by scientists, would probably start with a theory of learning in classroom situations which would postulate that certain changes in learning conditions would result in certain changes in performance. Within such a framework, hypotheses can be tested and a body of organized knowledge slowly built. The typical study which compares two teaching methodologies is not pursued along lines which scientists have found to be useful procedures for building an organized body of knowledge. They represent efforts which the scientific community would be unlikely to endorse. They serve a purpose, true, but the purpose is an empirical justification of practice and not that of building an organized body of knowlege.

A second feature of classical scientific methodology, which contrasts it with the type of education research under consideration, is that the scientist tends to deal with phenomena which are selected because they present some special convenience for testing the hypothesis that is to be tested. For this reason the geneticist has developed a vast amount of his scientific knowledge on the basis of studies of the fruit fly, Drosophila, which might otherwise be considered to be a rather uninteresting and unimportant little creature. For a similar reason, Hebb at McGill University has conducted most of his developmental studies on chimpanzees, not because he is primarily interested in chimpanzees as such, but because they provide an opportunity to collect information which can ultimately build a science. The same data cannot be conveniently collected on children. In contrast, in studies which involve gross comparisons of teaching methods, interest is focused on the phenomenon itself. The phenomenon is not chosen because it provides special opportunities for throwing light on some broad problem of education and so that generalizations can be made concerning the value of particular practices for achieving particular goals. Indeed, often it is particularly poorly suited for achieving this kind of goal. Here again, there is a rather clear contrast between the approach of practical men concerned with immediate problems and scientists who are concerned with the broader problems of building an organized body of knowledge.

This does not mean that such studies are devoid of scientific interest for they have made a twofold contribution to the development of educational research. On the one hand they represent an important period of research effort which has contributed immensely to our knowledge concerning profitable ways of pursuing educational research. In addition, they have contributed to our knowledge of many educational problems through a process of serendipity. These contributions have been substantial and outweigh any of the scientific weaknesses which this body of research may show.

A second kind of activity which is commonly sponsored by bureaus of educational research and which is commonly designated as a research activity is curriculum development. Many school systems will parallel a bureau of educational research with a bureau of curriculum research. Here again, one finds a confusion of terms, for curriculum research does not correspond to any of the activities which the behavioral scientist ordinarily refers to as research, but rather is it an exploratory activity designed to discover new materials which will have educational value. It probably cannot be otherwise at this time. Research in the curriculum area ultimately requires development along three lines, namely, (a) a theory of learning which specifies the conditions under which learning takes place most effectively, (b) a body of empirical laws which permits the evaluation of specific educational materials and procedures for achieving specific objectives, and (c) a system of values which determines the direction in which learning is to occur. Curriculum research, if it is to be developed as an organized and systematic effort, is highly dependent upon the behavioral sciences to provide a theory of behavior and upon philosophy to provide a system of ethics. In much curriculum research undertaken today, a theory of behavior is implicit rather than explicit. Curriculum research agencies do not include either behavioral scientists or philosophers and hence do not generally have the staff necessary to undertake systematic curriculum research. Under existing conditions curriculum development agencies are limited in what they can accomplish. They can perform many useful services by advising and suggesting. They can bring together teachers to exchange the experiences they have had with new curricula materials or methods. They can provide teachers with many materials for class use which might otherwise be difficult for the teacher to locate. They can also inject new ideas into classroom practice and thereby keep the educational system alive and prevent it from falling into a rut. Such an agency can also introduce educational changes as they are required by the community. Such services are important, if not vital, to any educational program. The only misfortune is that by designating the agency as a research agency the illusion is created that such an agency conducts scientific research which it is not equipped to do. Other agencies simply are not set up to conduct the research which needs to be done, and which this agency cannot do.

Military training programs present very similar problems. In such organizations curriculum sections conduct what they refer to as curriculum research which should really be called curriculum development. The curriculum sections, staffed by persons with a rather typical educational background, perform a highly useful job but are not able to conduct research which might lead to radical departures in curriculum. The theory of behavior on which they base their work is often primitive if not obsolete. One may be reminded at this point that a major part of the curriculum of the Air University was, at least in recent times, based on a theory of problem solving published by John Dewey (1910), and one which is thoroughly obsolete in terms of what is known at the present time about problem solving. Curriculum sections rarely have access to up-to-date knowledge of learning and neither are they staffed by persons likely to have such knowledge.

### SUBSTITUTES FOR THE METHODOLOGIES OF THE BEHAVIORAL SCIENCES

The problems which have been discussed in this chapter are ones which have been pondered by educators. Educational literature includes many articles which reflect on the fact that the "outside" researcher who comes into a school to conduct a scientific investigation rarely is able to influence the practices of the teachers. One must credit education with both recognizing the problem and with trying to solve it. One proposal is that traditional research approaches to problems of education should be abandoned in favor of a set of techniques collectively discussed under the topic of *"action research."* The latter term was first used by Kurt Lewin, but in a far different sense from that in which it is currently used in educational literature. Lewin used the term to refer to research in a real-life situation in contrast to research within a laboratory, but those who write on action research in education imply more than this. They imply that research must be done not only in actual school situations but by those who must ultimately bring about the changes, namely the teachers. Stephen Corey (1953, Preface, p. VIII) who has spearheaded this movement and achieved fame in educational circles through his book *Action Research to Improve School Practices* states the matter in this way:

> Most of the study of what should be kept in the schools and what should go and what should be added must be done in hundreds of thousands of classrooms and thousands of American communities. The studies must be undertaken by those who may have to change the way they do a thing as a result of the studies. The schools cannot keep up with the life they are supposed to

sustain and improve unless teachers, pupils, supervisors, administrators, and school patrons continuously examine what they are doing. Singly and in groups, they must use their imaginations creatively and constructively to identify the practices that must be changed to meet the needs and demands of modern life, courageously try out those practices that give better promise, and methodically and systematically gather evidence to test their worth . . . This is the process I call action research.

Action research in education undoubtedly acquired impetus through the development of operations research during the war. This type of program of research was focussed on problems of immediate practical importance related to national defense and was able to muster some of the finest scientific minds for the solution of these problems. As one might expect, some of the by-products of this work were scientific developments of the first importance and included many important advances in mathematics. This is a far cry from action research as conceived by the educator. One can hardly compare the efforts of the classroom teacher, poorly equipped in research techniques, attempting to solve classroom problems, with the efforts of highly trained scientists also attempting to solve problems of immediate practical importance but equipped with high speed computers and a wealth of specialized research training.

Just how action research differs from taking a problem-solving approach to the daily problems that arise in connection with education is not clear at all. Countless persons throughout history have attempted to solve the daily problems presented by human behavior in learning situations as well as in other situations but the results have not been startling. No doubt civilization has progressed over the ages but there is a real question whether this can be attributed to the individualized efforts of large numbers of individuals solving their daily problems in some kind of way. Certainly in the area of human relations where such efforts are being continuously made, progress has not been notable. The appeal for everyone to become a research worker is likely to be extremely popular for it offers to all an avenue to prestige monopolized up to this time by a small group of intellectuals. However, popularity of such a movement has nothing to do with the probability that it will achieve success. A few of the unconsidered problems faced by the action research movement in education need to be discussed here in order to provide a fair appraisal of what it can accomplish.

First, one might expect that a method of arriving at knowledge which was important enough to be given a name of its own might have developed a set of methodologies of its own. The action researchers place great emphasis on the development of appropriate group relations as a necessary condition for the development of knowledge about the practical problems with which the group is concerned. This is well illustrated in the widely used book by Corey who devotes the greater part of a chapter to the matter of how to handle sensitive feelings in a group situation where action research is to be undertaken. This in turn supposedly reduces various kinds of blocks which may well interfere with intellectual processes. Much greater emphasis is placed on this aspect of methodology than on such matters as the previous training of the participants. This is not to say that action researchers are making a mistake in emphasizing the importance of suitable human relations in a group problem-solving situation, but those who read about action research often obtain the impression that good human relations represents a sufficient as well as a necessary condition for effective problem solving.

Second, writers on action research do not make clear the kinds of assumptions on which their entire procedure and outlook are based. Implied in the writing is an epistemology considerably different from that which characterizes the current climate of thinking in the behavioral sciences. As far as one can determine from the rather vague statements in the work already cited as well as in other works, such as that by Shumsky (1958), the assumption is made that action research is pursued more or less in the way in which problems are solved according to the account given by Dewey of problem solving (1910). The teacher has some feelings of uneasiness about a situation, and these eventually become verbalized in the form of a problem. Facts are then gathered which lead either to the solution of the problem, or to the reformulation of the problem, or the problem remains unsolved. Implied in this is the notion that if one can gather enough facts then the solution to the problem inevitably follows. This, of course, is entirely in keeping with the research tradition within the educational sphere; the fact-finding process is believed to be one which will ultimately result in the solution of most educational problems. The assumption is made that the facts are there to be discovered much as gold nuggets exist and can be discovered by a looking and observing process. These statements appear to represent a fair statement of the epistemology of the action researchers. It might also be added that the epistemology underlying action research would have been a quite acceptable basis for research until relatively recently. Most professional research workers, but not all, discarded this approach to the acquisition of knowledge because it did not appear to be leading anywhere. Major advances in the behavioral sciences, as in any other scientific area, have come through an understanding of the distinction between observables and unobservables and hence the development of hypothetical constructs. This the action researchers completely ignore. As far as can be determined from their writings, the action researchers are to remain with observable events, that is to say with facts, and it is these that are to provide solutions to their problems. The relatively sophisticated epistemology on which current behavioral science is based appears to offer much more promise of leading to useful knowledge. If the action researcher in the schools is to have much hope of success he will need training in modern concepts of the nature of knowledge and how it is acquired. Since relatively few seem interested in such training, at least if one is to judge from the performance of doctoral candidates, action research seems doomed to pursue a course which had been found to be relatively unprofitable because it is epistemologically naive.

Action research from the point of view of epistemology represents only one of several related activities within the educational field that have been developed for the primary purpose of expanding knowledge of educational phenomena. Another which needs to be mentioned because of its wide impact on educational thinking is the *child study movement* which has had a history of over half a century behind it. A journal devoted to this topic was in existence before the turn of the century. A distinction must be drawn here between the development of "child psychology," as it has developed within the behavioral sciences from G. Stanley Hall up to modern times, and "child study" as it has developed within the field of education. A brief discussion of the child study movement will help bring out the fundamental differences that exist between this approach to the acquisition of knowledge about child behavior and the typical approach of the modern scientist.

The child study movement has had a long history of activity as a pseudo-scientific movement within education. It has had its ups and downs and has had an extraordinary way of attaching itself to some psychological theory of little acceptability to psychologists. One of the early enthusiastic writers in this field was Kirkpatrick (1903) who published a racy little volume entitled *Fundamentals of Child Study* which was such a success that it ran into more than a dozen printings and new editions during the following decade. The book was tied ideationally to the theory of instincts as developed by Lloyd Morgan and presented the theme that an essential feature of child study was the observation of the manifestation of the instincts in the individual child. In contrast to some of the modern advocates of child study, Kirkpatrick did at least recognize that simply looking at children was not enough but that observations had to be made within some theoretical framework.

The movement finds its focus today in the work of the Institute for Child Study located at the University of Maryland. A central feature of the program is the establishment of child-study groups among teachers in schools. These groups generally undergo a three-year program of in-service training. A statement by Prescott, the director of the Institute (1957), indicated that during the previous decade 40,000 or more persons had completed three or more years' work in the child study program in the schools and that some four and five thousand members of the educational profession were being served annually through the resources of the institute. The basic program of such study groups is to study children. According to Prescott, "At the first meeting, after the discussion of purposes, processes, and the code of ethics, the group takes up the kind of children to be studied. . . . Participants are urged to begin promptly to tap the various sources from which information may be obtained. Emphasis is placed upon recording the information objectively, specifically, descriptively, and completely . . ." This same document recommends that three months' work be spent in learning how to gather information objectively. At a later stage the group of teachers gets together and suggests hypotheses concerning the cause of particular aspects of behavior. According to Prescott, "the group may require two meetings to complete their making and testing of multiple hypotheses on the first record they process in this way." By the end of the first year the participants in this group process should, according to Prescott, be aware of three factors that "shape the child's motivation and determine his learning readiness in the classroom." These three factors are given as follows: "(1) The developmental tasks and conscious goals that the child is striving to accomplish. (2) The adjustment problems which the child faces, which occupy his mind and make it difficult for him to accomplish his developmental tasks and to meet the schools expectancies and demands. (3) The child's assets in terms of experience background, personal relationship, interest, aptitudes, and learning capacities."

As the participant in the child-study group proceeds through the second and third year, observation is directed to a wider and wider range of behaviors and scientific reading is engaged in to supplement the work. However, as one understands the child-study movement, the emphasis is on *the observation of behavior* and its interpretation rather than on the kinds of approaches to the study of behavior which would be characteristic of related programs of study within typical academic institutions of higher learning. This position is quite clearly stated by Prescott who emphasizes that "The child-study program is *not* a course of instruction which participants receive. Rather, it is a program of guided experiences that participants undergo and through which they gradually learn to see school situations through the eyes of individual children."

The general objective towards which the child-study movement is directing its efforts is acceptable to almost every person associated with education. Nobody can seriously question the idea that if the teacher could, through observation, establish the laws of behavior related to learning for each child, then a program of learning could be developed which would be the most efficient one for that particular child for reaching particular educational objectives. Conversely, there is widespread agreement that much of the activity of a typical classroom provides a very inefficient set of conditions for learning because the teacher does not understand the learning requirements of individual children. The emphasis placed by the child-study movement on rational rather than blind approaches to learning is thoroughly commendable. Experimental psychologists and educators alike agree that the development of efficient learning conditions for a living organism requires that the agent controlling learning conditions begin by making a careful study of the organism that is to learn and the lawfulness of its behavior. In the case of organisms bred to provide a uniform laboratory stock, such as the familiar laboratory rat, what is known about one set of rats can be appropriately applied to other samples of rats though exceptions do occur quite commonly. Some rats simply will not behave in the same way as do other rats. But in the case of the human, the variation in the learning behavior from one specimen to another is large. Apart from genetic differences between children, differences in characteristics related to learning which are generated by differences in life history force upon the educator the need for arranging somewhat different learning conditions for each human organism. The case for training teachers in the techniques and skills involved in child study is a strong one.

Agreement with the objectives of the child-study movement must not obscure the weaknesses of the procedures that are generally advocated to achieve these objectives. One cannot exaggerate the wide gap that exists between the concepts of behavior used in the training of teachers in child study and the present-day concepts of the behavioral sciences. The child-study movement in its present form cannot be considered as an example of the impact of the science of behavior on the development of education but rather does it represent a direct conflict with the approaches and procedures which have been so effective in producing advances in our knowledge of behavior over the last few decades.

First a contrast can be made between what is generally implied to represent an understanding of child behavior as it is expressed in the child-study movement and as it is expressed in the majority of contemporary writings in the behavioral sciences. The position of the child-study group appears to be well represented by a quotation already given which states that the trainee in child-study techniques gradually learn "to see school situations through the eyes of individual children." Basically this is the notion that the adult can, through training, project himself inside the skin of a child and describe what it is like to be that particular child. The notion that one can jump inside another's skin and look out through his eyes and experience his thinking processes is an idea derived from popular folklore rather than from the work of any group of scientists. The idea as it is presented by Prescott does not represent in any way the highly sophisticated type of phenomenological theory of the kind which Lewin tried to develop though it does mimic his sophistication in the use of his vocabulary, the terms of which are often used in entirely different meanings from the way in which they are used in his writings (for example, the use of the term life space). In contrast, in the behavioral sciences when one refers to understanding a living organism, a child being a specific instance, the scientist means that he has acquired some understanding of the laws of behavior of the organism. To understand a child is to understand some of the laws of behavior which can be used to predict behavior. This does not involve any kind of mental gymnastics such as learning what it is like to perceive the world through the eyes of the child, a feat which may be an impossible one.

A second important distinction between the approach of the child-study group and the approach of the behavioral scientist lies in role and significance of observation. Child-study enthusiasts stress the idea that the place to begin child study is by the collection of all the available facts about a particular child. The position is taken that the facts are there and only have to be found by conducting a search much as one finds sea shells by searching the sea shore. Observing children has merit in that it reveals some of these facts. The position is hardly a tenable one for human beings have been observing other human beings for countless generations without arriving at any startling insights into human nature. One might expect teachers to spend long periods observing and collecting data about particular children without ever arriving at any understanding of the lawfulness of the behavior of those children. The problem faced by the scientist always has been *what to observe*. Mere looking and recording has been found to be a rather useless pursuit which has little likelihood of resulting in insight into the phenomenon observed. Some observations which would have been considered to be trivial 50 years ago are now considered to be of vital importance in understanding personality. For example, a fastidious emphasis on cleanliness on the part of an adolescent might have been passed off as a trivial peculiarity half a century ago, but today a psychologist would consider it to be a behavior of considerable potential significance. *What is to be observed* is the central difficulty in planning a program of observation of child behavior and the fact is that relatively little is still known concerning the characteristics that are crucial to the identification of lawfulnesses in behavior. Doubts concerning the value of child observation as a means of acquiring understanding of child behavior are reinforced by a paper by Cox and Anderson (1944) which demonstrates that the longer the teaching experience of the teacher the less she is likely to handle a classroom problem in a way to reduce the difficulties.

## THE AMERICAN EDUCATIONAL RESEARCH ASSOCIATION: A NEW FOCUS FOR SCIENTIFIC RESEARCH ON EDUCATIONAL PROBLEMS

It would be unfair to leave the impression that the only research activity in education consists either of fact-finding enterprises or pseudo-scientific research methodologies. Individual persons scattered through universities, school systems and state education departments are engaged in educational research, but until recently have had no organization through which they could be seen and identified as a body. Within the last decade the American Educational Research Association has begun to emerge as the focus of such activity, but the trend is a recent one, for the Association originally emerged from an entirely different atmosphere.

The Association developed out of a previously organized body known as the National Association of Directors of Educational Research which was an attempt to promote "research" among practitioners. The latter organization was founded in 1915 and its promoters appear to have derived much of their zeal from the enthusiasm for measurement which had then begun to be felt in the educational field. The new Association formed in 1915 was born just five years after Thorndike had published the first calibrated instrument for measuring an educational product, namely, his handwriting scale. The chief driving force behind the Association was the hope that educational advancement would occur as the newly developed techniques of educational measurement acquired widespread usage. One can well see how these new techniques fitted in well with concepts of educational research which were then in existence. If educational research were to be a fact-finding enterprise delivering the facts needed for educational reform, then the newly developed psychological measuring techniques extended greatly the range of facts that could be collected. With the new techniques fact-finding began to acquire the appearance of a genuinely scientific enterprise. The concept of research of the new Association fitted well the concept of research which the National Education Association had promoted for nearly half a century, and five years after its foundation the new Association became a department of the National Education Association. The membership represented well the kind of research interest which the National Education Association had long promoted both within its own organization and also on the outside. In fairness one may say that the fusion of the two organizations has not been as restrictive as one might have expected it to be.

Early meetings of the American Educational Research Association as well as those of its predecessor were focussed on practical problems. According to Frank Hubbard[1] it was only much later when the organization came to include representatives of universities that the papers became more technical and focussed less directly on the immediate practical problems of operating schools. The influence of the academic scientist has had a slow but growing influence on the organization although its membership is still dominated by persons whose concern is with immediate practical problems of education. The growing influence of the scientist in the affairs of the Association is shown in the fact that at recent meetings invited addresses have been given by such persons as B. F. Skinner and Harry Harlow, but this has been an innovation of the programs of the last few years. Such an influence must remain a minor one for many years to come for the number of scientists in academic positions who are interested in educational problems is neces-

[1]Personal Communication

sarily far less than the number of directors of research and persons in similar positions who are interested in fact-finding activities related to the problems which educators face daily. One may expect the Association in time to play an increasing role in the development of a science of behavior in educational situations, but for the present it serves too many other useful functions needed by its members for this to become the only one. For the few who wish to develop such a specialized science of behavior, the Association is a meeting place and a sounding board, but the group involved is a small one in comparison with the total membership.

The present efforts of the American Educational Research Association to sponsor research in the scientific tradition is also finding a powerful ally in the United States Office of Education that has broken away to some extent from its fact-finding functions and has now become one of the major supporters of scientific research related to problems of education. The joint influence of these two organizations represents the most important point of contact between the behavioral sciences and educational practice at the present time.

## CHARACTERISTICS OF EDUCATIONAL PERSONNEL AND THE RESULTING RESEARCH ORIENTATION

The development of educational research as a fact-finding enterprise has its roots both in the nature of the task which teachers and others in education perform and also in the personality characteristics of those who are attracted to education as a career. The job of both the teacher and the administrator requires persons who like making numerous down-to-earth decisions as a part of their daily routine. Such an activity is hardly likely to attract the theoretically oriented person who wants to become a career research worker. The teacher also has to be enthusiastic about what he is doing and can hardly share the scepticism with which the research worker approaches problems of education. The teacher is interested in studies which will justify what he is doing before his public or which will show that his procedures are more effective than those of the next person. Teachers are, above all, highly dedicated persons, but dedication often brings with it a fear that outside influences may damage rather than improve classroom procedures.

Before discussing the characteristics of educational personnel, a brief consideration must be given to certain factors in their training which makes for high homogeneity and, indirectly, for high cohesiveness in the educational subculture. In particular, the certification of school personnel and the coursework which such certification requires must surely limit the range of interests and talents of those that enter the educational field. The teaching certificate has generally become the basic requirement of nearly all educational positions from that of the classroom teacher to that of the superintendent in the large city. In many states such specialized personnel as school psychologists and school social workers must also have teaching certificates; this generally means that these states are unable to hire either school psychologists or social workers. The requirement of a teaching certificate prevents a school system from employing persons who have not, so to speak, come right out of the educational mold. There are even many teacher training institutions that insist that all professors have teaching certificates valid in the public schools, a practice which is in sharp contrast to that of medical schools which hire numerous non-medical specialists to train their students. Since those who choose to obtain an education leading towards a teaching certificate represent a group with restricted interests and talents, the result is that the educational process ultimately becomes controlled by such a group. An analogous situation in industry would be if a corporation such as the General Electric Company were to be operated and controlled only by persons with an engineering degree. This would bring the progress of the company almost to a standstill for where would be the physicists, chemists, and mathematicians that have produced most of the company's marketable advances. The characteristics, then, of those that are attracted to education as a career and the effect which their characteristics may have on educational development will now be considered.

An excellent international review of the characteristics of teachers has been provided by Vernon (1953). Typically, an undergraduate group of students of education is derived from a middle class and lower middle class culture and the interests of the group are not primarily scientific. From the point of view of providing the schools with teachers who will find satisfaction in their work, the effect of this self-selection process is probably quite excellent. From the point of view of providing the school and the school administrations with personnel actively interested in the application of scientific findings and methodologies to the solution of school problems, the results are deplorable for the highly cohesive and homogeneous subculture that is thus produced is ill adapted to providing for itself machinery through which it can utilize the fruits of scientific inquiry. Scientific ideas and approaches are so foreign and remote from the thinking of much of this subculture that one can hardly expect the work of the scientist to have any real impact on it. Indeed, one might expect there to be not only a lack of impact but perhaps a resistance to any potential impact, for most subcultures resist the injection of new ideas which are foreign, or unusual, or not consistent with those already held.

That students entering schools of education come from an intellectually superior group is beyond dispute. Probably 90 per cent of teachers come from the top 20 per cent of the population in terms of I.Q., but the follow-up study of Terman and Odem (1947) of a group of gifted children suggests that persons of exceptionally high intelligence are rather unlikely to enter the teaching profession. Data collected at the University of Utah by Jex and Merrill[2] over a period of many years indicates that students who enroll in the college of education have somewhat lower entrance scores than those in the liberal arts college. However, the education students obtain a relatively higher grade point ratio in their freshman courses than do the liberal arts students taking the same courses which suggests that they are overachievers. The latter is consistent with data indicating that the American teacher is mainly a product of a lower-middle-class environment and attracts persons with high motivation to improve their position. Thus, those entering education may be perceived as a capable group, with fewer individuals in the highest intelligence brackets than other professional groups, but coming from a social group which is achievement oriented and traditionally conservative in attitudes.

In terms of interests as measured by an instrument such as the Strong Vocational Interest Blank, the teacher's field of interest appears to be determined largely by his academic field of specialization. Female elementary school teachers have interest patterns extremely similar to that of housewives. According to Morey (1949) elementary school teachers in America have interests that are feminine, domestic, and social. Junior high school teachers are more interested in organizing, while secondary school teachers have greater abstract interests and a greater need for independence. Since the scientific background among personnel in education is rather rare, one does not expect them to manifest high scientific interests of the kind which might lead to an interest in scientific advances related to their field. Of particular interest is a study by Jex and Merrill (1958) of a group of science teachers selected for an academic year institute sponsored by the National Science Foundation. This group

[2]Personal Communication

of teachers in the mathematical-scientific area did not show a particular resemblance in interest pattern to physicists, chemists, mathematicians, but rather did they resemble persons in the technical and applied fields. Perhaps this is hardly surprising for the more theoretically oriented persons with scientific training would be expected to take positions in universities and industries where such abilities can be utilized. Thus even the science teachers who might be expected to provide a focal point where scientific advances might impinge on education do not generally have the structure of interests likely to work in this direction. The climate of the educational subculture as it is manifested through the pattern of interests of its members is not that of a scientific community but rather is it one with a strong practical orientation.

Some additional information concerning the intellectual climate of education in relation to its capacity either to seek out or to use the results of scientific research is seen in some of the recent studies of profiles of teacher needs. In one study by Johnson (1959), in which the Edwards Personal Preference Schedule was administered to a number of groups of graduates of a teacher education program, a striking characteristic of all groups was the tendency for scores to be high on the deference scale and low on the scale for autonomy, a finding which also appeared in the Jex data. This finding is also consistent with some data collected by Tudhope (1944) on British teachers on the basis of which he commented that they manifested a "lack of adverturesomeness."

The point to be made is that while those entering the educational profession show a great range of characteristics, the group as a whole though intellectually from the superior range is relatively low in its scientific interests. In addition, the group manifests a high need to work within a structure and a relative lack of a need for independence of thought and action. The population is such that it is unlikely to generate a subculture characterized by a constant flow of new ideas and an enthusiasm for innovations. The relatively low level of scientific interests perhaps reflects more than anything a lack of contact with science and hence a lack of understanding of the role which scientific inquiry might play in the advancement of education. These characteristics do not make the subculture hostile to scientific approaches to problems, but rather one might expect them to result in apathy. One would anticipate that these characteristics would also permeate the higher educational echelons because of the current policy which requires that candidates for the higher positions be the holders of a teaching certificate.

## THE OUTLOOK

Few would disagree with the proposition that important changes will ultimately be brought about in the classroom through the work of the behavioral scientist. How this is to be done is a matter for dispute. The writer believes that the history of the problem suggests that the impact of scientific knowledge on training procedure and educational procedures is likely to be greatest if the following conditions are met:

1. If the behavioral scientists concentrate on the development of training equipment and devices which do not require major changes in the habit structure of teachers, they are likely to meet with the least opposition in producing educational reforms. Since many teachers delegate classroom control to equipment for a sizeable fraction of the day, such developments are unlikely to meet with opposition except from the few who do not delegate control to equipment or materials.

2. If research related to the behavior of teachers is undertaken and if such research suggests that changes in teacher behavior are desirable then systematic work must be undertaken on the problem of changing teacher behavior. It can no longer be assumed that teacher behavior will change because research indicates that it should change.

The hope that the educational community will produce its own scientists from the ranks of teachers and administrators must surely be abandoned. The behavioral scientist must play an increasing role in the training of the educator so that some doctoral candidates will emerge from schools of education who can fill the dual role of educator and behavioral scientist. The rigor of thinking demanded by the behavioral sciences today (with certain notable exceptions) might eventually improve the rigor of thinking in the development of educational theory. Then again, the behavioral scientist must have the opportunity of becoming more aware of the practical problems of the classroom. There is a need to develop miniature theoretical systems related to events in the classroom, and perhaps this type of exploration is more urgently needed than attempts to apply current learning theories to classroom situations for the classroom often appears to be far outside of the boundary conditions of the laws of learning already discovered. The project at Northwestern University, insofar as it increases contacts of behavioral scientists with educators at the training level, is a move in the right direction, but a dozen more such projects are probably needed before the effect will be felt. If such contacts can be well-established in schools of education, then it is conceivable that an occasional future superintendent of schools may perceive the possibility of opening up a position for a well-trained scientist in his school system. This would require considerable conviction on his part because the plan would undoubtedly meet opposition from the school board down. Perhaps, ultimately, the school system might be able to point with pride to its research department which would then be functioning in much the same way as a research department in a large industry. This in turn might establish standards by which other research efforts in other school systems might be judged.

Small scale research efforts in separate school systems are hardly likely to have the impact on education that is really needed. The problems of education are probably such that a large scale programmatic research effort is required to provide the body of knowledge needed to effect educational change and the responsible organization would have to have stability over a period of many years in order for it to come to the point of being productive. The experience provided by the Air Force Personnel and Training Research Center indicates that within a decade such an organization can begin to yield highly significant research findings. The organization would have to be both led and manned by scientists whose status is well-established and most of these would have to come from outside of the educational field. This follows successful research practice in other fields. Engineering problems are typically investigated by teams which include chemists, physicists, mathematicians, and other non-engineering specialists. Such an organization serving the civilian economy might well have a much better opportunity of survival than one serving the military.

The proposal has been made many times that what is needed in education is a group of persons who will function as intermediaries between the academic research worker and the educational practitioner. This can hardly be seen as a solution to the problems under consideration. For nearly half a century the educational psychologist has attempted to serve education in this capacity and with only limited success. The problem is much more than just one of interpreting the results of current research so that they can be made available to the educator in a useable and palatable form. Curriculum specialists also have shared this function but the results of their efforts do not reflect any startling impact of scientific knowledge on educational practice. In the case of most scientific discovery, considerable work must be undertaken before the knowledge thus gained can be applied directly to the solution of practical problems. Practical problems often lie outside of the boundary conditions of the laws discovered in the laboratory.

Perhaps as important as any of this is the need to develop, within education and at a grass roots level, two ideas. One of these is the idea that as yet very little is known about teaching processes and that what is being done is probably very inefficient compared with the methods that will ultimately be evolved. The second idea is that research is a very difficult enterprise to undertake and one that generally requires the cooperation of many highly trained experts. Progress will come through the support of research at this kind of professional level and hence such research must be supported. The achievement of this support for the scientist may take another generation. For the present it can be noted that a substantial beginning has been made in the recently adopted policies of the United States Office of Education and in the interest shown in this matter by professional organizations and groups.

## REFERENCES

Corey, S. M. *Action research to improve school practices.* New York: Teachers College, Columbia University, 1953.

Cox, Grace B. & Anderson, H. A study of teacher's responses to problem situations in school as reported by teachers and students. *Amer. J. Orthopsychiat.*, 1944, *14*, 528-544.

Dewey, J. *How we think.* Boston: Heath, 1910.

Jex, F. B. & Merrill, R. M. *An evaluation of the first academic year institute, University of Utah, 1957-58.* Salt Lake City: University of Utah, Research Monographs in Education, 1958.

Johnson, Lynn E. Personality profiles of teacher graduates. Master's thesis, University of Utah, 1959.

Kirkpatrick, E. A. *Fundamentals of child study.* New York: Macmillan, 1903.

Morey, E. Vocational interests and personality characteristics of women teachers. *Aust. J. Psychol.*, 1949, *42*, 658-666.

Morrison, J. C. The National Educational Association and educational research. *Rev. educ. Res.*, 1956, *26*, 205-209.

Prescott, D. A. *The child in the educative process.* New York: McGraw-Hill, 1957.

Rice, J. M. Need school be a blight to child-life? *Forum,* 1891, *12,* 529-535.

Rice, J. M. *The public school system of the United States.* New York: Century, 1893.

Rice, J. M. Futility of the spelling grind. *Forum,* 1897, 163-172, 410-419.

Rice, J. M. *Scientific management in education.* New York: Hinds, Noble & Eldridge, 1913.

Shumsky, A. *The action research way of learning.* New York: Teachers College, Columbia University, 1958.

Terman, L. M. & Oden, Melita H. *The gifted child grows up.* Stanford: Stanford University Press, 1947.

Tudhope, W. B. Motives for the choice of the teaching profession by training college students. *Brit. J. Psychol.,* 1944, *14,* 129-141.

Vernon, P. E. The psychological traits of teachers. In *Yearbook of education.* Yonkers-on-Hudson, New York: World Book Company, 1953. Pp. 51-75.

|  | A Structure for a |
|---|---|
| Chapter **18** | Coordinated Research and |
|  | Development Laboratory |

*Thomas F. Gilbert,* [1, 2] *The Mathetics Foundation and the University of Alabama*

Everyone seems to agree that "research" is the high road to the solution of that part of the educational crisis that cannot be resolved with money alone. The word "research" has nearly the generality of the verb "to be," and its generality increases with the value the public gives to it. The difficulty of the generality is that it obscures worthy distinctions among various unique talents, all of which are required to bring an idea from abstract conception to field application. The failure to recognize clearly and to coordinate these separable talents may well be the foremost reason that behavior research has not provided a single unequivocal solution to a major behavioral problem in education in 50 years, if indeed it ever has. This fact is most strikingly evident when it is noted that the most "revolutionary" development in the classroom is only a technical refinement of already existing procedures, i.e., television. This is not to say that all research efforts have been failures. Psychometrics, the science of measuring men's aptitudes and achievements, may well be the most advanced and precise form of social science. But the description and prediction of test performance, however noteworthy the purpose it serves, is by no means the procedure directly relevant to the problem of modifying behavior in the classroom. There is not a breath of hope that measuring instruments will make a competent, socially facile artist or mathematician from a newborn infant.

The success of psychometric research is directly related to the fact that the responsible scientists, typically, are closely in touch with their

---

[1] Now at Tor Laboratories, Inc.

[2] The stimuli for this paper were produced largely by Dr. John M. McKee, Director, Division of Mental Hygiene, Alabama State Health Department.

potential consumers. Psychometrics was largely developed in the teachers' colleges or among educational and clinical psychologists. Not so with the experimental analysis of learning and behavior. Those who investigate learning in the laboratory may never enter a public school or institute for the training of the blind after their own school days are over. And those who teach arithmetic or Braille may be exceptional if they have had more contact with the laboratory principles of behavior than is provided by two or three chapters from a text used in a survey course on the subject.

The experimental analysis of behavior has not failed to provide useful tools for educational practice because of inherent inadequacy. On those rare occasions where the research activity of the behaviorists has been allowed to operate freely in the setting of military and industrial problems, dollar and cents results have been obtained. Business and the Army are buying this research and setting up laboratories for the experimental analysis of behavior in ever increasing quantities. And quite aside from the recognized relevance of research in human assessment and social survey, the experimental analysis of behavior remains the science most basic to problems of education in all its forms. Nevertheless, the situation is such that there is no public agency assuming effective responsibility for introducing the problems of the teacher to the behavior laboratory nor providing the teacher with engineered products of that laboratory. Both educator and scientist are working hard enough. Their efforts simply are not coordinated; they are out of touch with one another. This absence of coordination by a public agency of the total research effort in education has led to a state of reciprocal ignorance between laboratory scientists and field workers.

## Consequences of Poor Research Coordination

When distinctions among unique research activities are made, they are usually designated by the terms, "applied" and "basic." Naturally, every investigator would like to believe that his work is both applicable and basic in some sense or another. This terminology does not describe the useful differences in research skills. In the science of behavior, one can argue, these adjectives tend to solidify irrelevant and confusing sociological differences already created in the organization of these research activities. More than one basic laboratory behaviorist stands aloof from the mundane efforts of those who attempt to improve methods of training the mentally retarded or of teaching history. And many an applied educational investigator ignores the ivory-housed theorists, or half-digests as profound truth what was offered as provisional guess. This atmosphere makes it easy for the laboratory behaviorist to forget that, in the long run, the value of his research will be judged by its relevance to activities such as education. Easy, too, for the educational researcher to forget that engineering sciences mold their products from the principles articulated in the laboratory. The fetishistic attachment to the word "basic" too frequently serves to hide the trivial, to obscure functional distinctions in research activity, and to justify non-support to those who consider the word a euphemism for "impractical." Designations such as "applied" indicate to many research people unrealistic restriction of inquiry and a vaguely dishonest commercialism, connotations which discourage much talent from application to pressing social problems.

The generally assumed choice between applied or basic research is an unrealistic one. If the problem is great and if research is a primary tool, nothing less can be done than to discover efficient means for coordinating research efforts in all their forms, both for the sake of economy and for the sake of getting the job done. The implied choice between "basic" and "applied" research, or between team and individual research creates needless dilemmas and uneconomical apportionment of skills to tasks. It leaves the determination of support priority to popular appeal, the need for stopgap procedures, vested interests, and unknown quantities or other irrelevant factors. It tends to increase the insularity existing among the various research interests. This insularity, in turn, creates a situation in which there is practically no one assuming the responsibility for introducing continuity into the total research effort.

On the matter of responsibility for carrying theory to practice, each relevant profession can be defended in its own turn. Fixing the blame for the dilemma is less important, however, than discovering means for coordinating the total research effort while preserving the independence of the individual investigator. The very word, "coordination," too readily implies restraint of inquiry to the laboratory investigator who has been burnt under that banner before. And it too readily implies conferences, committees, and team projects to the field worker who understandably finds it difficult to believe that individual effort is adequate to the task. But science is not created in committee, nor do its principles go into practice directly from the technical journal. Many a hand must intervene. It is the neglect of systematic arrangement of the intermediate activities which is the major reason for the impotence of the research effort. The neglect can be seen when it is observed that most research in learning takes place either in the classroom or the animal laboratory. Principles derived from any artificial scientific laboratory must undergo much development and modification before they are ready for field and classroom tryout. And, as has been said, in behavior research little provision is made for the intervening developmental activity.

Coordination of different behavioral research skills, when it does occur, is usually built around rather specific problems imposed upon the researcher from sources outside his usual activity. While the team project may be useful in handling a specific problem at a given time, it has limitations as a method for the more general organization of research activity. In the first place, when rather immediate and specific problems form the basis for coordinated effort, there is a tendency to exclude from the organization the men whose work will not be relevant to the problem for 20 years. Furthermore, the method discourages time-consuming excursions which, if permitted, might produce consequences of inestimable value. Finally, the team project places limitations on the expression of the separate skills involved, since there is required an almost day-to-day integration of these efforts. Each arm of the team must have fairly specific knowledge of the progress of every other arm, and the rate of progress of one is geared to that of the others.

## Criteria for a System of Coordination

For the "basic" scientist the feedback from useful application is particularly tenuous, especially in the science of behavior. A well-coordinated research effort which effected efficient flow of principles to application would have the additional consequence of providing scientists more immediate information about the value of their work. This, in turn, might increase the behaviorists' awareness of the social problems which so urgently need that awareness. The differential feedback should become even more immediate through a system in which fundamental development of laboratory principles exists to provide a testing ground previous to the possibility of application. For those principles which do not lend themselves to intermediate development are, indeed, incomplete.

An additional consequence of a coordinated research effort would be a greater respect for the potential of the laboratory investigation of behavior. The present unvoiced criterion for the value of behavior research is that it can be put to practice. Such a criterion is much too harsh and no doubt accounts for the fact that many "basic" researchers stand aloof to social usefulness as a basis for judging the value of their work. This unrealism does little to aid the cause of support for such research, and further strengthens the barriers between laboratory and field. Where intermediate development intervenes, the barrier is bridged and the necessity of the more remote becomes clearer to all. Furthermore, direct evidence that "abstruse" principles are on their way to concrete expression may abate some of the impatience that has been the nemesis of uncommitted science.

Neither standard university organization nor team projects provide the coordination necessary to give continuity to the total research and development effort. What is proposed here is an experiment in the organization of research skills which, it is believed, will more nearly approach the optimal conditions for production by field laboratory workers. The method of organization is certainly not new, and has characterized some of the most successful research efforts in the nation. In formal description, at least, it meets most of the criteria implied in this introduction. In brief, these criteria are:

1. Provision for the complete independence of the research scientists, within the limits of their competence and the general field of behavioral science.

2. Provision for the support of every stage of research effort from uncommitted inquiry, through development, design, field testing, training, and follow-through.

3. Provision for the optimal conditions under which workers at various stages of research function are aware of the problems and procedures of workers at other stages.

4. Provision for each variety of research skill to bear equal responsibility for total output of research effort, but the responsibility for any given operation to be borne only by those directly involved.

When the above provisions are made within an organization unity, further conditions should not have to be imposed to insure the continuity of the research effort; it should follow naturally from the interest of the individual researchers in seeing the continuation of their work, as well as from the realization that there exists equal responsibility for valuable production.

## Behavioristic Basis for Research Coordination

An attempt to "unify" the behavioral sciences is not being proposed here. This motivation has been the basis for a number of efforts to give continuity to various behavioral sciences. Thus, sociologists, psychologists, psychiatrists, anthropologists, linguists, mathematicians, and psychoanalysts will form institutes, journals, research programs, and meet together in many other ways. While the educational value of these efforts for the scientists involved will not be denied, one may be skeptical of this arrangement as being directly relevant to the demanding problems of education in the community. Such gatherings have produced much philosophy and many words, but little research useful in schoolroom and clinic.

Rather than seeking common ground for the several disciplines, what is proposed is an organizational recognition of separable research talents which already have one outstanding common ground. That common ground is the goal of discovering means of modifying the behavior of individuals through techniques which are widely applicable and capable of being engineered. The research activities which form the core of the proposed organization are those which have been most specifically concerned with the experimental analysis of learning, from applied educational psychology to laboratory behaviorism.

The particular bias that forms the basis for the research program proposed herein is the experimental analysis of behavior and the general techniques of operant conditioning as developed by B. F. Skinner. A specific behavioristic approach, however, to a coordinated research effort need not prevent the use of relevant procedures which traditionally have not characterized the orientation. The writer would propose the general methods of operant conditioning for two reasons only: they have shown considerable promise for payoff in formal and social education; they are highly specific and communicable, and their results can be put to rigorous test. It should be emphasized that the approach will give form and direction to a research program; it is not proposed for the sake of proving something about the exclusive value of the point of view. A community with a relevant and properly coordinated program of research and development should be ready to abandon any procedures which are not paying off. Specific and demonstrable payoff is the ultimate criterion.

### PROBLEM ORIENTATION AS A BASIS FOR RESEARCH AND DEVELOPMENT COORDINATION

*The Pitfalls of Technique Orientation.* Research relevant to education has been directed almost exclusively by some specific technique or hypothesis. As an example of technique (as opposed to problem) oriented research, the occasions can be cited on which investigators set out to examine the value of a specific tool, and never leave that tool whether or not the problem has been resolved. Thus, an investigation will revolve around the questions of whether non-directive psychotherapy can alleviate neurosis, whether the Rorschach can detect potential delinquency, whether television can teach arithmetic, whether conditioning can produce normality from schizophrenia, or whether the tachistoscope can overcome reading deficiency. While research is always in the business of testing techniques, when the techniques take precedence over the problem, much is lost. The questions of the greatest social interest are: *How* can neurosis be alleviated? *How* can arithmetic be efficiently taught? *How* can a schizophrenic be made normal? *How* can reading deficiencies be overcome? It is maintained that, even where the problem was the original instigator of research, techniques, once evolved, have an overwhelming tendency to take over and perpetuate themselves as the guiding orientation. A researcher seems to say, "I have this technique (Rorschach, conditioning procedure, pill, insulin therapy, etc.); I wonder what I can do with it?" One can hope that research can be so coordinated, the atmosphere so arranged, that the researcher will never forget his original question "How can arithmetic be efficiently taught?" and will be so thoroughly involved in that question that he cannot possibly develop an overriding, vested interest in any technique except insofar as its payoff value can be indicated. Such an investigator will be virtually free from the dogma of a particular method. One whose research career is marked by the history of applying this test or that procedure to 20 different problems is in a fair way of being accused judiciously of having more interest in a gimmick than a problem. That this state of affairs is a frequent one in psychological science, from animal laboratory to clinic and school, is evidenced by the long, exhausting controversies over questions such as "Is the Rorschach valid?" "Does television teach?" and so on indefinitely. Similar controversies about whether one has a clear statement of a problem are rare indeed.

*The Pitfalls of Hypothesis Orientation.* Another prevailing guide to research is devotion to an hypothesis. A researcher may approach the problem of schizophrenia with an ingrown conviction that the disorder is only a result of conditioning, and this orientation may lead him to experimentation which could be quite irrelevant to the problem, particularly if the behavior of schizophrenia is merely symptomatic. And similarly, a research devoted to the problem of reading deficiency may be so shaped by the hypothesis that reading readiness is strictly a matter of maturation that he will miss opportunities for discovering methods of teaching all two-year-olds to read. Naturally, science must forever be trying out hypotheses, but when they take precedence over the problem, the problem frequently gets lost in the bush. Thus, endless controversies may rage around the assertions that conceptualization is produced suddenly by insight or gradually by conditioning, or around the assertions that neurosis is produced in infancy or later in the schools. In the meanwhile, as sides are chosen and the heat of battle grows, the incidence of neurosis increases and the problems of teaching arithmetic may attain the proportions of a national crisis.

Hypothesis orientation has a basic defect that also characterizes technique orientation. In the case of the latter, one well may discover that television teaches as well as the usual classroom methods. If it were the case that the classroom methods represent the worst possible procedures, what will have been gained by the demonstration? What will have been lost is the question of "How best?" An example of the kind of irrelevancy produced by these orientations can be provided by an actual event in behavior research. Many Army officers were of the opinion that the superiority of one outfit over another in the matter of marksmanship was directly traceable to differences in the leadership provided by non-commissioned officers. The leadership hypothesis is a natural and prevalent one in the military. A strong devotee would have approached the problem of discovering means for improving marksmanship training by studying means of increasing the efficiency of leadership. Leadership no doubt has its effect on company marksmanship; the hypothesis devotee may indeed discover means of providing better leadership which, in turn, will have an effect upon marksmanship scores. The Army is, however, an organization in and upon which the demands for "payoff" are ever prevalent. One military research group (HumRRO) directed itself toward the problem of marksmanship by setting aside the prevailing theories and allowing the task to direct its analysis. Its first job was to discover *what* the problem was. It was conceivable that there was no problem at all. Perhaps rifle firing training was near its maximal efficiency. An openminded research effort will not only reject the tendency to become a devotee of one particular construction of the problem, it will even question whether a problem exists. HumRRO eventually discovered how to increase the accuracy of marksmanship to such an extent that HumRRO trained companies, even with inferior non-commissioned officers, can outshoot other companies with the best non-coms. This does not deny that leadership is irrelevant. It does demonstrate that a plausible hypothesis indicated the study of variables (leadership) which were of minor importance to the task. When devotion to an hypothesis becomes greater than devotion to a problem, such may be the expected result. Hypotheses are trial guesses at answers, and devotion to them tends to change them into dogmatic truths.

*How Problem Orientation May Be Insured.* One of the primary conditions for maintaining problem orientation is simply the existence of circumstances in which the problems are constantly at hand, with the added condition that the researchers all bear equal responsibility for their resolution. Given this situation, where payoff is construed as the criterion for all research, where the demands for payoff do not stand in the way of the many failures necessary for success, where the responsibility for the total research effort is distributed among all involved, where each worker is left free to follow his essential talents, and where more immediate and pertinent "feedback" is available to everyone, the problems creating the research effort cannot easily be obscured. Attachment to a particular technique or hypothesis can grow rapidly where the worker has no real feedback from the effects of his work and little opportunity to observe the specific day-to-day struggles of those field workers for whom his work presumably has relevance. Where one works in the context of an appropriate coordinated research effort and is left free to follow where he will, against the background of the problems, the defensive and dogmatic attachment will die of its own inappropriateness. The "publish or perish" criterion for research value will be replaced by a "be relevant or be ignored" criterion. Both behaviorism and psychoanalysis agree that nothing can be so effective in getting rid of a behavior as the ignoring of it.

## THE ORGANIZATIONAL STRUCTURE OF A COORDINATED RESEARCH AND DEVELOPMENT LABORATORY

The fact that the operational structure outlined below resembles that of some industrial laboratories is neither coincidental nor a result of uncritical mimicry. A somewhat similar concept of research functions has prevailed. In classifying these separable and interdependent research functions, attention has been given to differences in purposes and procedure rather than to differences in subject matter. These various research skills can be exemplified by observing the course of the development of a scientific product, whether it be the transistor or a new method of teaching arithmetic. Examples will be provided that will serve as ostensive definitions of each component of the laboratory organization.

## Exploratory (Theoretical) Research

This label is meant to designate the focal, not exclusive, function of the investigators involved. The word "exploratory" is used in place of the word "basic" because the latter suggests a value interpretation rather than a true function. Everyone likes his work to be considered "basic" in some sense; and in that sense, whose work is more "basic" than the applied researcher or the school teacher? There is a value in so-called basic research simply because history has demonstrated that social payoff has come from the research of those who are re-examining the traditional methods and concepts of science. Their behavior is necessarily exploratory since they are not attempting to apply or develop existing procedures or knowledge. The very fact of questioning existing scientific methods leaves them without traditional thoroughfares. They must explore to accomplish their task. This re-examination is no more or less "practical" than so-called applied research. It is impractical only when its production fails to get developed into engineered procedures—it runs the danger of being "impractical," or at least of being ignored for a long time, simply because it often occurs in isolation from developmental activities.

One of the difficulties which "basic," or exploratory, research must face is that questioning the established science seems to imply that traditional procedures are "wrong." When the life work of many intelligent people has been geared to these procedures, and when they have been producing valuable goods, it is neither complimentary nor sensible to believe that one could have been "wrong." This conception is nurtured by the commonly held view that the history of science and philosophy is the history of error: that Kant proved Hume wrong, that Einstein proved Newton wrong. In the latter part of the nineteenth century and the early twentieth century, the Newtonians often constructed their radical physical theories as having just this implication. The tendency, in science, to resist change is documented in any history of the subject. And there is little wonder. It is quite likely that this attitude is a fundamental expression of the conception that truth is absolute, that one is either right or he is wrong. If, on the other hand, the view is taken that science is an ever increasing *approximation* to the truth, resistance to change and suspicion of exploratory research may not be so plentifully nurtured.

Newton was "right" within considerable limits, and Kant did not reject Hume as a foolhardy theorist, but, accepting most of Hume's analysis, he attempted to prescribe its limitations and account for its "truths" by further construction.

The points being made are that exploratory science is just as practical and applied as any other research endeavor, that it only seems not to be when its products are not put to use, that it does not threaten the integrity of existing procedures, and that it is just as necessary a part of any practically oriented research program as engineering and development. Isolation of exploratory operations engenders, in the "basic" scientists, the attitude that "practical" research is trivial and erroneous, and leads the "applied" researchers to look upon "basic" science as irrelevant and obscure. Worse still, the isolation often has the effect of leading to a state where both attitudes are partly justified. While this situation is largely disappearing in the physical sciences, it is certainly characteristic of behavioral science.

No matter how abstruse and irrelevant the exploratory science operation may seem in an educational research and development center, it can be justified on the following grounds, even setting aside the value of its own scientific success. It is inexpensive; serious and continuous exploratory work occurs in a small ratio to engineering and developmental activities. The Bell Telephone Laboratories, combined with Western Electric, account for less than one per cent of the total Bell System budget. Secondly, such a laboratory can more than pay for itself by serving as a channel to significant developments in science that have occurred elsewhere. For example, the American Telephone and Telegraph Company anticipates considerable savings in training costs and time as a result of the development of programmed self-instructional methods. These methods, which were being created among "basic" university scientists, were introduced to the Company by a Bell Laboratory operant conditioner running a pigeon behavior laboratory. If his presence accounts for AT&T developing an improved training program five years earlier than it might have otherwise, and if less than ten per cent of the anticipated savings are realized, the researcher will have justified his budget for over 100 years. If scientists working in a Midwestern university create the basis for developing an efficient means for controlling stuttering, the presence of a similar scientist in an educational development program could make the difference in whether the developmental activity began to produce an engineered product now or in ten years. Thirdly, the presence of an exploratory research operation in a developmental setting may be the determining factor in whether or not these scientists work on problems relevant to education. The Nobel Laureates at Bell Labs may not have come to work on the transistor had they not been in a setting which guaranteed their consciousness of the communication industry's problems. Fourthly, the basic research operation may serve as a training device for developmental researchers, where new techniques may be learned, where the current status of the science is kept before all engaged in the programs' activities. And finally: the exploratory scientist may serve as a considerable source of critical survey to those who, so involved in the details of their immediate problems, get little chance to view their problems from the perspective of distance. Working at a more general level, they may see relations between their problems and similar problems outside their specific field of endeavor, thus providing a clue to solutions which might otherwise have been missed.

*The Selection and Activities of Exploratory Scientists.* A well-devised exploratory science operation requires three basic ingredients: first, able men competently trained in the methods of their science; second, up-to-date equipment and technical assistance; third, the freedom from any restrictions on their tendency to explore. How can one maximize the likelihood that these men will explore in the general problem areas to which the research operation is dedicated? The best way is to employ men who have shown an interest, through past behavior, in exploring in these general areas. It is a self-contradictory postulate that exploratory scientists can be directed to explore in a specific direction. Exploring indicates going into the woods where no one has been, and to direct the path these men should follow is tantamount to implying that you know what is in those woods. The employment of exploratory scientists can only be guided by the promise of the scientists' past histories, and the risk must be squarely faced that when men enter the woods, some do not come out again, and some come out at unexpected places. There is a certain amount of self-selection provided by the nature of any organization, however. If it is dedicated to the solution of educational problems, and if responsibility is divided among all, men willing to shoulder that responsibility tend to come forth.

A grave danger does exist in employing all members of a research and development operation from the ranks of self-styled basic researchers, hoping that they will distribute among themselves the "annoying applied science" responsibility. What tends to happen is that less able and aggressive investigators get the "left-over" applied problems, relieving the more capable and aggressive to pursue, unfettered, their talents. The developmental work just does not get done. The actual occurrence of this state of affairs in some research operations has led to further criticism of exploratory science support. Another rather unsuccessful approach has been to employ exploratory investigators on developmental projects with the inducement that they may spend part of their time on "basic" research. While this may work in a few individual cases, it is not to be generally advocated. It tends to construct the developmental and engineering operations as annoying asides which must be suffered. Furthermore, the basic research time frequently becomes relegated to "after-hours" pursuits. Exploratory science, when performed by a competent man, is generally even more than a full-time operation. Developmental science requires as much loving care and competence as "basic" science. In these situations exploratory scientists become unhappy and, worse, begin to feel guilty that their exploration may not be paying for itself. If one wants the benefits of exploratory science, he can get them by supporting the exploratory operation exactly for what it is.

## Fundamental Development

A second research function necessary to give continuity to the effort of carrying knowledge from theory to practice consists of the laboratory investigation of the many variables potentially relevant to principles and procedures discovered in the exploratory investigations. This is another activity hidden by the word "basic" research. Following the development of transistor theory, much experimental work was required to understand the physical characteristics of the many materials and conditions which had some bearing on the construction of a transistor. Such investigation may lead the scientist into productive research in solid state physics of a very fundamental nature. It is not the responsibility of fundamental development to produce a transistor, but to produce the further knowledge necessary.

In order to illustrate the nature of fundamental development and its differences from exploratory research, an example from behavioral research can be cited. O. R. Lindsley (1957), while investigating some characteristics of auditory thresholds in relation to his explorations of psychotic behavior, "accidentally" hit upon a method which showed promise for the study of behavior in sleep. It is interesting to note that this discovery may not have been made had he been preforming a formal, "parametric" experiment on thresholds. True to the requirements of exploratory science, he dropped his threshold studies in favor of pursuing the "sleep" method. He worked out the basic techniques and presented a few illustrative experiments, along with a description of the implications of the methodology for inquiry into other areas. This is a good example of exploratory research. The primary purpose of the laboratory for the exploratory scientist is to provide experience for the investigator rather than formal data for the description of functional relations. The laboratory is a miniature world in which such a scientist can produce a great deal of informal variation (experiment) for the sake of maximizing the chances for discovery. The published experiments are performed after the investigator knows the outcome; they are performed as demonstrations. When the exploratory investigator is finished, most of the work is still to be done. In the case of Lindsley's technique there was required an investigation of the relationship between the data provided by the EEG, more exacting descriptions of the sensitivity of the method to drugs, anaesthesia, sleep deprivation, physical work, and the like; further, more systematic and formal studies were required to examine when and how various complexities of behavior drop out during sleep. In short, a whole new area of research on sleep was opened up by the discovery. Lindsley's technique came to interest some medical researchers investigating anaesthesia. This research provides a good example of fundamental development. The purpose of the research anaesthesiologist is to make more exacting descriptions of the behavioral effects of various anaesthetic agents, differential time constants for different people, recovery times and character, and the like. All such information will be a step toward the development of a simple, inexpensive, easily used method of tracing the course of anaesthesia in and out of the operating room. It must be pointed out that with the completion of much of this research, many things must still be done to make the technique a widely useful engineering article.

A second example is provided by the work of James G. Holland (1957) on observing behavior. Holland, as a result of exploratory study, developed a very precise method for investigating and measuring human observing behavior. His published experiments are illustrative rather than definitive, and serve not only to demonstrate the nature and precision of the method, but also indicate that such behavior is, by and large, subject to the same controlling methods as simpler operants. The exploratory work is largely done, but practically nothing is known about the various variables relevant to this behavior. Since the child learning arithmetic or reading must learn, at the outset, certain kinds of "looking" behavior when regarding a field of numbers, the Holland method has considerable implications for fundamental development of knowledge relating to the training of early habits involved in number and word perception. Systematic investigation of some of these variables may provide not only clues to the improvement of arithmetic and reading teaching, but also may produce laws which have more general value to many other kinds of tasks in which observing behavior is involved. When this work of fundamental development is through, engineered methods of teaching arithmetic must still be developed. Fundamental development is a step along the way which leads from theory to practice. Its products bring knowledge a little closer to field engineering, but much else must follow.

It is not the intent to imply that the talents involved in fundamental development in any way exclude the talents of exploratory science. They are separable functions which one man may or may not be able to perform with efficiency. Some men who are good at one may be good at the other, or they may not. The task of fundamental development seems to require much competent laboratory and other technical skill, compulsive and precise work, and a love for careful quantitative description. Exploratory science, while requiring a degree of these same skills, does not seem to be so highly dependent upon them as fundamental development. Exploratory science appears to require a considerable degree of "creative" ability, the word creativity possibly being nowhere better defined than in the capacity for producing effective exploratory research. Furthermore, as Thurstone has indicated, creative ability is correlated with an erratic, variable temperament which, in some, will not serve as the finest ingredients for good fundamental development. The selection of fundamental development scientists will take these factors into account.

## Specific Development

Once new principles and techniques of science are discovered and their relevant variables described, there remains the task of developing, in model form, the engineered products made possible by this science. After Bell Telephone scientists had created the theory of the transistor and established knowledge about materials relevant to the idea, a transistor still had to be produced. Producing an efficient transistor requires unique skills rather different from those involved in the more "basic" laboratory. Parts must be acquired, investigated, and assembled with an eye toward the field of use as well as toward the knowledge from which the possibility was derived. The production of an actual working transistor serves as both a test for the value of the preceding research, but feeds back problems to the basic laboratory. The development of a specific product is the function of specific development engineers. The transistor which they produce, while it may work quite well according to the lights of theory, is still not ready for use in the living room television set. It is what is familiarly known as a "mock up." Research is a primary tool of specific development, since much experimentation of a laboratory nature must be done to determine how various arrangements operate.

As another example, once the parameters involved in learning number concepts have been specified, the specific development program has still to produce an arithmetic teaching program. If it works within the operations of the self-instructional (so-called "teaching machine") methods most recently described by B. F. Skinner, arithmetic items must be written and continuously tested out on the children for which they are intended. Here again, the laboratory is the place in which the research is carried out. It is too early to go to the classroom, although the specific development laboratory may have some of the features of the classroom. The program is written and revised as it is taught to a small number of selected children whose services are paid for. Rather than using "control-experimental" group research procedures, much more intensive information is gained from a few subjects. By gaining continuous feedback from the children, the specific development people will finally produce a program they think is a practicable one for teaching other children. Their job will be incomplete in many particulars which may not be discovered until the program is actually taken into the classroom. However, had they waited until they had written a program before carrying it to children, and then only to the classroom, they would have lost much valuable detailed information as well as wasted time in proceeding with methods which this information would have discarded earlier.

Whereas the laboratory of more fundamental research represents the natural world in highly stylized and abstract ways, the specific development laboratory may represent this world in more contemporaneous detail; for example, it may be designed as a model classroom or clinic. It must, however, have some access to the more stylized laboratory for the simple reason that specific development must go on regardless of the stage of fundamental development. In producing a program to teach arithmetic, the specific development people will need to make decisions concerning behavior about which there is no reliable research knowledge. Rather crudely fashioned experimentation can provide some practical answers to pressing questions, permitting the program to continue. Naturally, the value of coordinated research is that specific development has easy access to the fundamental laboratory personnel who should be able to supply information if it exists—and further, the specific development program is simultaneously providing problems to the fundamental laboratory.

The selection of specific development personnel will require more careful attention to training in specific subject-matter skills. These people might be expected to be the kind who have more ingenuity in matters of engineering than they have temperament for the careful, compulsive work required of fundamental development. Along the dimensions of "creativity" and "compulsivity" one might expect them to be somewhat more similar to the exploratory scientists. History may bear this out; after all, Galileo, certainly a foremost exploratory scientist, was a fair man in specific development; witness his microscope, telescope, and thermometer. And one of the historical prototypes of restless, erratic, creativity is Thomas A. Edison, a genius in specific development.

*Design and Proving*

Once transistor and arithmetic programs are developed into working realities, they are not yet ready for introduction into the field communication systems or classrooms. The transistor produced by the specific development program is not one which will be most extensively manufactured, installed, or understood by technicians. It may be one which would fail in the arctic cold or tropical heat. Its characteristics may change when it is wet. And many field conditions which specific development people will not be able to anticipate will determine its eventual success. Similarly with the arithmetic program. While it may be shown to teach various children well in the laboratory, it may fail with certain rare exceptions, and in such instances variations must be provided. The optimally efficient and inexpensive machinery for its deliverance must be designed. It may require too much of a change in the physical structure of the classroom to be practical without modification. It will certainly require changes in the work habits of the teacher. Questions will arise about how the program is to be produced for the partially blind, the left-handed, and those who have had some arithmetic training at home. In short, the product must undergo many detailed modifications before it can be a practical instrument in the school or clinic.

In addition to the design of a consumable product, design and proving engineers are charged with demonstrating product effectiveness under very exacting field conditions. It is here, more than anywhere, that the statistical design of experiments becomes relevant—not merely for the sake of demonstrating that the new methods are superior to the "usual" ones, but, more importantly, to test out the efficiency and economic value of several minor variations in the conditions of use. Naturally, this requires skills of criterion development in the design and proving researchers. A further reason for the large group experiments under field conditions is to sell the product by producing convincing evidence of its value. And finally, the field tests provide many problems which cannot be answered by design and group experiments alone, but must feed back to the exploratory and developmental scientists.

The selection of design and proving engineers must take into account that their activities are so close to the field that certain social skills are required in order to assure the success of the job. These people will work closely with teachers, clinicians, and special training instructors, as well as institutional administrators. As a result, the work must be carried out with some sales skill, sensitivity to the social conditions of the field, and a keen awareness of the actual problems of the field worker. However, design and proving is more than a social soiree, but requires special skills in research design, statistical operations and inferences, criterion development, human factors with reference to machinery, and many of the more objective techniques of social psychology. Other skills such as equipment design and electronics may be called for, and the design and proving engineer should at least know when and where these services are needed and can be found.

## Training and Follow-Through

Having provided an efficient method of teaching arithmetic and having seen it successfully engineered and installed in the classroom, the research organization may be tempted to detach itself from the program. Nothing could be more dangerous where the requirement of payoff is the final criterion for the value of such an organization. Imagine that the arithmetic program operates successfully in the test schools chosen for its initiation; if it is passed on to other schools by way of manuals and verbal instructions, misunderstanding of the objectives and directions will inevitably follow. This consequence may be so serious that the public school system which once adopted the program will abandon it as impractical for widespread consumption. If such conditions prevail, the research effort is just as much a failure as if it had not produced a product in the first place. When a workable transistor design is proven and handed to the manufacturer, the research operation does not quit. It must help see that instructors in the technical schools learn how the device operates, and how it is installed and maintained. Furthermore, a system is used whereby continued information can be obtained about field operation over long periods of time. The device may not stand up as well as it did in the laboratory tests simply because of the existence of unanticipated field conditions. Follow-through information will supply new problems to the design and proving people who, in turn, may have to call upon developmental and exploratory scientists.

*The Use of Cadre Groups.* The training and follow-through section would have to be enormous indeed if it took upon itself the training of all potential consumers of research products. This is the proper function of colleges, trade schools, professional training centers, and on-the-job continuation training. A research and development center would pass on its knowledge by providing a training program for certain key people in these schools. These key people can, in turn, perform as a kind of "cadre" around whom modifications in professional training can develop when needed. Many individuals are employed at present to serve, in part, just such a function. These are school psychologists, mental health workers, professors of educational psychology, professors of psychiatry and clinical psychology, teachers of public health nurses, and the like. These cadre groups, in addition to insuring the proper training of the field workers with whom they work, can serve as a channel through which formal follow-through information is continuously fed back to the research staff.

Training and follow-through personnel are an integral part of the research operation, and they will be efficient to the extent that they have expert knowledge of the laboratory products and operations. The selection of such people will have to take into account that they require the sort of professional training that will enable them to have the needed expert knowledge. It is also clear that, to be good teachers, they will be required to use social skills in communicating this knowledge. Furthermore, their prime source of professional training will have to be in the areas in which the laboratory products are to be consumed.

## Parallel Operations in "Social" and "Formal" Education

In planning and carrying out the research and development structure briefly outlined in this chapter, it is proposed that work of such a project cut across the rather artificial boundaries imposed on education by the school wall. These boundaries are not artificial for some purposes, but one can visualize them so for the purposes of research and development. The investigation of human learning will provide knowledge applicable to all manner of specific situations in which this learning goes on: in schoolroom, prison, institutes for the blind and deaf, training homes for the mentally retarded, mental hospitals, and the like. The primary reason for the distinction between so-called formal education and other learning activities is that society has recognized that there are certain skills which nearly all members of the society need, and which can be successfully trained in a formal setting. That such education forms the basis for much social behavior is too much of a truism to be argued, even though the artificial distinction sometimes becomes a barrier to the understanding of the implications of formal education. The community education of parents, the re-education of delinquents, and the teaching of arithmetic, produce highly interlocking social consequences and require a similarly high degree of interaction in producing these consequences.

To avoid these artificial distinctions the research and development operation proposed in this chapter should direct its attention to both schoolroom formalities and the community education which forms so great a part of the purposes of mental hygiene agencies. This parallel operation can be effected in two ways: by the selection of personnel, and by the development of a coordinated training institute which attends to both educational areas. After all, the principles of providing conditions under which human behavior can become modified are not bounded by building walls.

### REFERENCES

Holland, J. G. Technique for behavioral analysis of human observing. *Science,* 1957, *125,* 348-350.

Lindsley, O. R. Operant behavior during sleep: A measure of the depth of sleep. *Science,* 1957, *126,* 1290-1291.

# INDEX

Films, 257, 266, 268, 269, 271
Prompting, 265
ROSS, S., 218
ROTHKOPF, E. Z., 282
ROUSSEAU, J. J., 538
RUCH, F. L., 298, 353
RUDIN, S. A., 393
RUFF, G., 461
RULON, P. J.
Performance measurement, 237, 353
Maintenance training, 299, 305, 447, 448, 453
RUSSELL, E., 356
RUSSELL, W. R., 205
Russell Sage Foundation, 341

SALTZ, E., 273, 306
SAPON, S. M., 88n, 96, 97, 115
SARASON, S. B., 107, 201
SAUNDERS, D. R., 337, 392
SAUPE, J. L., 447
SAWREY, W. L., 447
Scaling, 72-74
Guttman scale, 73
Homogeneous, 73
Nominal scales, 81
Ordinal scales, 78, 81
Scanning, 38-39
SCHEIN, E. H., 460
SCHIFFMAN, H., 460
SCHIPPER, L. M., 440, 463, 464
SCHMITZ, M. A., 513
SCHNORE, M. M., 210
SCHOENFELD, W. N., 14
School administration
*See* Education
SCHUSTER, D. H., 297, 305, 312
SCHWARTZ, P. A., 332
SCHWARZ, R. E., 91
SCHWEIKER, R. F., 237, 299, 305, 447, 448, 453
SCOTT, T., 460
Search, 38-39
SEEGAR, C. M., 193
Semantic differential, 205
Semi Automatic Ground Environment (SAGE), 415, 416, 464
Sensory deprivation, 459-61, 481-82
Sequential behavior, 181-82, 189-91
SEVERIN, D., 356
SEYMOUR, W. D., 192
SHAW, J. C., 409
SHAW, M. E., 439
SHEFFIELD, F. D.
Instructional media
Experimental research, 249, 250, 252
Films
Pictorial embellishments, 268
Practice effects, 257, 263
Pre-sensitization, 273, 274
Prompting, 266
Response mode, 254, 255
Time factor, 256

Perceptual blueprinting, 267
SHELLY, C., 189
SHELLY, M., 440, 463, 464
SHETTEL, H. H., 271
SHUMSKY, A., 544
SIEGEL, A., 447
SILANDER, F. S., 409
SILBERMAN, H. F., 12, 264, 276, 456, 457
SILBERMAN, J. E., 258
SIMON, G. B., 270, 353, 354
SIMON, H. A., 409, 439
Simplicial analysis, 471
Simulation, 449-50, 481, Chapter 8
Aircraft, 235
Air crew training, 453
Analysis of operations, 228-29, 238-39
Bombing, 228
Centrifuge, human, 450-51
Concept learning, 233-34
Civilian education, 42, 240-41, 242
Decision making, 224, 227, Chapter 14
Degree of, 231-32
Distinguished from training device, 225, 227
Education, 239-42
Games, 242-43, 418-20
Gunnery, 228
Large-scale systems, Chapter 14
Materials, 416-17
Materials, 421-22
Meaning of, 225-27
Military defense exercise, 411-18
Motor skills, 233-34
Pilot training, 223-24
Procedures, 233-34
Proficiency measurement, 228, 235-37, 241-42, 332-33, 362
Examples of, 334-45
Reliability, 235-36
Validity, 237
Purposes of, 227-29
Radar operation, 233
Realism, 226, 229-32, 420-21
Social situations, 243
Space flight, 457-58
Stages of learning, 233-34, 239-40
Stages of training, 227-28
Stress, 458-59
System, 224, 238-39, 242-43
Task description, 230-32, 234
Team functioning, 234, 238-39, 380
Technical training, 240-41
Techniques
Large scale system, 415-16
Tracking, 451-52
Training, 227-28, 232-35
Transfer of training, 231-32
Trouble shooting, 227-28, 236, 448, 453
Situational tests, 334-45
*See also* Simulation
Skaggs-Robinson hypothesis, 498
SKEEN, J. R., 227, 453